Life of

Napoleon Bonaparte

By Sir Walter Scott

Volume I

OmniaVeritas

Sir Walter Scott

Life of
Napoleon Bonaparte
Volume I
1827

Published by
Omnia Veritas Ltd

www.omnia-veritas.com

Napoleons Logement Quai Conti

ADVERTISEMENT 19
ADVERTISEMENT TO EDITION 1834. 21

CHAPTER I 23

VIEW OF THE FRENCH REVOLUTION 23

Review of the state of Europe after the Peace of Versailles—England—France—Spain—Prussia—Imprudent Innovations of the Emperor Joseph—Disturbances in his Dominions—Russia—France—Her ancient System of Monarchy—how organized—Causes of its Decay—Decay of the Nobility as a body—The new Nobles—The Country Nobles—The Nobles of the highest Order—The Church—The higher Orders of the Clergy—The lower Orders—The Commons—Their increase in Power and Importance—Their Claims opposed to those of the Privileged Classes. 23

STATE OF EUROPE.. 24
GERMANY 27
FLEMISH DISTURBANCES 30
INTRIGUES OF RUSSIA 33
FRENCH MONARCHY 34
DECAY OF THE NOBILITY 39
THE CLERGY—DUBOIS 46
TIERS ETAT 48

CHAPTER II 51

State of France continued—State of Public Opinion—Men of Letters encouraged by the Great—Disadvantages attending this Patronage—Licentious tendency of the French Literature—Their Irreligious and Infidel Opinions—Free Opinions on Politics permitted to be expressed in an abstract and speculative, but not in a practical Form—Disadvantages arising from the Suppression of Free Discussion—Anglomania—Share of France in the American War—Disposition of the Troops who returned from America. 51

STATE OF PUBLIC OPINION 51

FRENCH LITERATURE AND PHILOSOPHY... 55
INFIDELITY... 58
FEUDAL SYSTEM 62
SUPPRESSION OF FREE DISCUSSION 65
ANGLOMANIA... 67
AMERICAN WAR 68

CHAPTER III 73

Proximate Cause of the Revolution—Deranged State of the Finances—Reforms in the Royal Household—System of Turgot and Necker—Necker's Exposition of the State of the Public Revenue—The Red-Book—Necker displaced—Succeeded by Calonne—General State of the Revenue—Assembly of the Notables—Calonne dismissed—Archbishop of Sens Administrator of the Finances—The King's Contest with the Parliament—Bed of Justice—Resistance of the Parliament and general Disorder in the Kingdom—Vacillating Policy of the Minister—Royal Sitting—Scheme of forming a Cour Plénière—It proves ineffectual—Archbishop of Sens retires, and is succeeded by Necker—He resolves to convoke the States General—Second Assembly of Notables previous to Convocation of the States—Questions as to the Numbers of which the Tiers Etat should consist, and the Mode in which the Estates should deliberate. 73

DERANGEMENT OF THE FINANCES *74*
ECONOMICAL REFORMS *77*
NECKER'S COMPTE RENDU *81*
TIERS ETAT *83*
STATE OF THE REVENUE *85*
BED OF JUSTICE *88*
RIOTS AND INSURRECTIONS *92*
STATES-GENERAL CONVOKED *93*
THE TIERS ETAT *95*

CHAPTER IV 99

Meeting of the States-General—Predominant Influence of the Tiers Etat—Property not represented sufficiently in that Body—General character of the Members—Disposition of the Estate of the Nobles—And of the Clergy—Plan of forming the Three Estates into two Houses—Its advantages—It fails—The Clergy unite with the Tiers Etat, which assumes the title of the National Assembly—They assume the task of Legislation, and declare all former Fiscal Regulations illegal—They assert their determination to continue their Sessions—Royal Sitting—Terminates in the Triumph of the Assembly—Parties in that Body—Mounier—Constitutionalists—Republicans—Jacobins—Orleans. 99

INFLUENCE OF THE TIERS ETAT *99*
VIEWS OF THE NOBLESSE *103*
INFLUENCE OF THE TIERS ETAT *105*
ROYAL SITTING *108*
CONCESSIONS OF THE KING *110*
PARTIES OF THE ASSEMBLY *113*
REPUBLICANS *116*
JACOBINS *118*

TREACHERY OF THE ARMY	120
MURDER OF FOULON AND BERTHIER	124
CONDUCT OF THE KING	125
EMIGRATION	132
THE DAY OF DUPES	133
THE VETO	137

CHAPTER V **139**

Plan of the Democrats to bring the King and Assembly to Paris—Banquet of the Garde du Corps—Riot at Paris—A formidable Mob of Women assemble to march to Versailles—The National Guard refuse to act against the Insurgents, and demand also to be led to Versailles—The Female Mob arrive—Their behaviour to the Assembly—To the King—Alarming Disorders at Night—La Fayette arrives with the National Guard—Mob force the Palace—Murder the Body Guards—The Queen's safety endangered—Fayette's arrival with his Force restores Order—Royal Family obliged to go to reside at Paris—The Procession—This Step agreeable to the Views of the Constitutionalists, Republicans, and Anarchists—Duke of Orleans sent to England. 139

BANQUET AT VERSAILLES	141
INSURRECTION IN PARIS	142
MOB SURROUND THE PALACE	145
MURDER OF THE BODY GUARDS	148
PROCESSION TO PARIS.	150
VIEWS OF THE CONSTITUTIONALISTS.	153
ORLEANS SENT TO ENGLAND.	156

CHAPTER VI **159**

La Fayette resolves to enforce order—A Baker is murdered by the Rabble—One of his Murderers executed—Decree imposing Martial Law—Introduction of the Doctrines of Equality—They are in their exaggerated sense inconsistent with Human Nature and the progress of Society—The Assembly abolish titles of Nobility, Armorial bearings, and phrases of Courtesy—Reasoning on these Innovations—Disorder of Finance—Necker becomes unpopular—Seizure of Church-Lands—Issue of Assignats—Necker leaves France in unpopularity—New Religious Institution—Oath imposed on the Clergy—Resisted by the greater part of the Order—General view of the operations of the Constituent Assembly—Enthusiasm of the People for their new Privileges—Limited Privileges of the Crown—King is obliged to dissemble—His Negotiations with Mirabeau—With Bouillé—Attack on the Palace—Prevented by Fayette—Royalists expelled from the Tuileries—Escape of Louis—He is captured at Varennes—Brought back to Paris—Riot in the Champ de Mars—Louis accepts the Constitution. 159

MARTIAL LAW PROCLAIMED *160*
ABOLITION OF TITLES OF HONOUR *164*
DISORDER OF FINANCES *166*
CONFISCATION OF CHURCH LANDS *168*
TRIAL BY JURY *172*
FEVER OF LEGISLATION *175*
CROWN PRIVILEGES *176*
LOUIS'S NEGOTIATIONS *178*
PROJECTED ATTACK ON VINCENNES *181*
ESCAPE OF THE KING *183*
REVOLT IN THE CHAMP DE MARS *187*
LOUIS ACCEPTS THE CONSTITUTION *189*
CONSTITUTIONAL ASSEMBLY *191*

CHAPTER VII **193**

Legislative Assembly—Its Composition—Constitutionalists—Girondists or Brissotins—Jacobins—Views and Sentiments of Foreign Nations—England—Views of the Tories and Whigs—Anacharsis Clootz—Austria—Prussia—Russia—Sweden—Emigration of the French Princes and Clergy—Increasing Unpopularity of Louis from this Cause—Death of the Emperor Leopold, and its Effects—France declares War—Views and Interests of the different Parties in France at this Period—Decree against Monsieur—Louis interposes his Veto—Decree against the Priests who should refuse the Constitutional Oath—Louis again interposes his Veto—Consequences of these Refusals—Fall of De Lessart—Ministers now chosen from the Brissotins—All Parties favourable to War 193

CONSTITUTIONALISTS *194*
JACOBINS *197*
FORCE OF PARTIES *198*
VIEWS OF ENGLAND *201*
BURKE'S "REFLECTIONS" *204*
FEAST OF FEDERATION *207*
AUSTRIA—PRUSSIA—SWEDEN *210*
DECLARATION OF PILNITZ *213*
LA FAYETTE *216*
VIEWS OF THE PARTIES *217*
CHANGE OF MINISTRY *220*
WAR WITH AUSTRIA *224*

CHAPTER VIII **227**

Defeats of the French on the Frontier—Decay of Constitutionalists—They form the Club of Feuillans, and are dispersed by the Jacobins—The Ministry—

Dumouriez—Breach of confidence betwixt the King and his Ministers—Dissolution of the King's Constitutional Guard—Extravagant measures of the Jacobins—Alarms of the Girondists—Departmental Army proposed—King puts his Veto on the decree, against Dumouriez's representations—Decree against the recusant Priests—King refuses it—Letter of the Ministers to the King—He dismisses Roland, Clavière, and Servan—Dumouriez, Duranton, and Lacoste, appointed in their stead—King ratifies the decree concerning the Departmental Army—Dumouriez resigns, and departs for the Frontiers—New Ministers named from the Constitutionalists—Insurrection of 20th June—Armed Mob intrude into the Assembly—Thence into the Tuileries—La Fayette repairs to Paris—Remonstrates in favour of the King—But is compelled to return to the Frontiers—Marseillois appear in Paris—Duke of Brunswick's manifesto. 227

CLUB OF FEUILLANS 228
KING'S GUARD DISBANDED 231
ALARM OF THE GIRONDISTS 232
DISMISSAL OF ROLAND, ETC 235
THE TWENTIETH OF JUNE 238
MOB FORCE THE TUILERIES 240
LA FAYETTE ARRIVES AT PARIS 244
PETION AND MANUEL SUSPENDED 246
BARBAROUX 249
DUKE OF BRUNSWICK'S MANIFESTO 251

CHAPTER IX 255

The Day of the Tenth of August—Tocsin sounded early in the Morning—Swiss Guards, and relics of the Royal Party, repair to the Tuileries—Mandat assassinated—Dejection of Louis, and energy of the Queen—King's Ministers appear at the Bar of the Assembly, stating the peril of the Royal Family, and requesting a Deputation might be sent to the Palace—Assembly pass to the Order of the Day—Louis and his Family repair to the Assembly—Conflict at the Tuileries—Swiss ordered to repair to the King's Person—and are many of them shot and dispersed on their way to the Assembly—At the close of the Day almost all of them are massacred—Royal Family spend the Night in the Convent of the Feuillans. 255

TENTH OF AUGUST 256
DEJECTION OF LOUIS 259
CONDUCT OF THE MINISTRY 260
CONFLICT AT THE TUILERIES 264
FALL OF THE MONARCHY 266

CHAPTER X 269

La Fayette compelled to Escape from France—Is made Prisoner by the Prussians, with three Companions—Reflections—The Triumvirate, Danton, Robespierre, and Marat—Revolutionary Tribunal appointed—Stupor of the Legislative Assembly—Longwy, Stenay, and Verdun, taken by the Prussians—Mob of Paris enraged—Great Massacre of Prisoners in Paris, commencing on the 2d, and ending 6th September—Apathy of the Assembly during and after these Events—Review of its Causes... 269

LA FAYETTE ESCAPES FROM FRANCE..270
ROBESPIERRE..272
REVOLUTIONARY TRIBUNALS 275
DANTON'S PLAN OF EXTERMINATION 276
COMMUNE OF PARIS...279
MASSACRES OF SEPTEMBER..284
MASSACRE IN THE BICETRE 285
APATHY OF THE ASSEMBLY 288

CHAPTER XI 293

Election of Representatives for the National Convention—Jacobins are very active—Right hand Party—Left hand side—Neutral Members—The Girondists are in possession of the ostensible Power—They denounce the Jacobin Chiefs, but in an irregular and feeble manner—Marat, Robespierre, and Danton, supported by the Commune and Populace of Paris—France declared a Republic—Duke of Brunswick's Campaign—Neglects the French Emigrants—Is tardy in his Operations—Occupies the poorest part of Champagne—His Army becomes sickly—Prospects of a Battle—Dumouriez's Army recruited with Carmagnoles—The Duke resolves to Retreat—Thoughts on the consequences of that measure—The Retreat disastrous—The Emigrants disbanded in a great measure—Reflections on their Fate—The Prince of Condé's Army. 293

NATIONAL CONVENTION...293
FRANCE DECLARED A REPUBLIC 295
DUKE OF BRUNSWICK'S CAMPAIGN...296
EMIGRANT REGIMENTS DISBANDED..300
ATTACK OF SAVOY 303

CHAPTER XII 307

Jacobins determine upon the Execution of Louis—Progress and Reasons of the King's Unpopularity—Girondists taken by surprise, by a proposal for the Abolition of Royalty made by the Jacobins—Proposal carried—Thoughts on the New System of Government—Compared with that of Rome, Greece, America, and other Republican States—Enthusiasm throughout France at the Change—Follies it gave birth to—And Crimes—Monuments of Art destroyed—Madame

Roland interposes to save the Life of the King—Barrère—Girondists move for a Departmental Legion—Carried—Revoked—and Girondists defeated—The Authority of the Community of Paris paramount even over the Convention—Documents of the Iron-Chest—Parallel betwixt Charles I. and Louis XVI.—Motion by Pétion, that the King should be Tried before the Convention. 307

UNPOPULARITY OF LOUIS XVI 308
ABOLITION OF ROYALTY 312
NEW SYSTEM OF GOVERNMENT 314
FRANCE, A REPUBLIC 319
SACRILEGE OF SAINT DENIS 323
MADAME ROLAND 326
DANTON—ROBESPIERRE—MARAT 329
MARAT 330
DUMOURIEZ'S PROPOSAL 334
DOCUMENTS OF THE IRON CHEST 336
CHARLES I AND LOUIS XVI 338
PREPARATIONS FOR THE KING'S TRIAL 341

CHAPTER XIII 345

The Trial of Louis—Indecision of the Girondists, and its Effects—The Royal Family insulted by the Agents of the Community—The King deprived of his Son's society—The King brought to trial before the Convention—His first Examination—Carried back to Prison amidst Insult and Abuse—Tumult in the Assembly—The King deprived of Intercourse with his Family—Malesherbes appointed as Counsel to defend the King—and De Seze—Louis again brought before the Convention—Opening Speech of De Seze—King remanded to the Temple—Stormy Debate—Eloquent Attack of Vergniaud on the Jacobins—Sentence of Death pronounced against the King—General Sympathy for his Fate—Dumouriez arrives in Paris—Vainly tries to avert the King's Fate—Louis XVI. Beheaded on 21st January, 1793—Marie Antoinette on the 16th October thereafter—The Princess Elizabeth in May 1794—The Dauphin perishes, by cruelty, June 8th, 1795—The Princess Royal exchanged for La Fayette, 19th December, 1795. 345

INDECISION OF THE GIRONDISTS 345
ROYAL FAMILY IN THE TEMPLE 347
LOUIS SEPARATED FROM HIS SON 351
LOUIS CHOOSES HIS COUNSEL 354
OPENING SPEECH OF DESEZE 357
DEBATE 358
LOUIS CONDEMNED 362
DUMOURIEZ ARRIVES IN PARIS 363
DEATH OF LOUIS XVI 368

LOUIS'S LAST TESTAMENT 369
DEATH OF THE DAUPHIN 372

CHAPTER XIV 375

Dumouriez—His displeasure at the Treatment of the Flemish Provinces by the Convention—His projects in consequence—Gains the ill-will of his Army—and is forced to fly to the Austrian Camp—Lives many years in retreat, and finally dies in England—Struggles betwixt the Girondists and Jacobins—Robespierre impeaches the Leaders of the Girondists—and is denounced by them—Decree of Accusation against Marat—Commission of Twelve—Marat acquitted—Terror of the Girondists—Jacobins prepare to attack the Palais Royal, but are repulsed—Repair to the Convention, who recall the Commission of Twelve—Louvet and other Girondist Leaders fly from Paris—Convention go forth in procession to expostulate with the People—Forced back to their Hall, and compelled to Decree the Accusation of Thirty of their Body—Girondists finally ruined—and their principal Leaders perish—Close of their History... 375

PROJECTS OF DUMOURIEZ 376
DUMOURIEZ DEFEATED 379
DECREE AGAINST MARAT 381
INSURRECTION AGAINST GIRONDISTS 382
INSURRECTION OF THE 31ST OF MAY 385
FALL OF THE GIRONDISTS 389
FATE OF THE GIRONDIST LEADERS 392
LOUVET—RIOUFFE—BARBAROUX 394

CHAPTER XV 399

Views of Parties in Britain relative to the Revolution—Affiliated Societies—Counterpoised by Aristocratic Associations—Aristocratic Party eager for War with France—The French proclaim the Navigation of the Scheldt—British Ambassador recalled from Paris, and French Envoy no longer accredited in London—France declares War against England—British Army sent to Holland, under the Duke of York—State of the Army—View of the Military Positions of France—in Flanders—on the Rhine—in Piedmont—Savoy—on the Pyrenees—State of the War in La Vendée—Description of the Country—Le Bocage—Le Louroux—Close Union betwixt the Nobles and Peasantry—Both strongly attached to Royalty, and abhorrent of the Revolution—The Priests—The Religion of the Vendéans outraged by the Convention—A general Insurrection takes place in 1793—Military Organization and Habits of the Vendéans—Division in the British Cabinet on the Mode of conducting the War—Pitt—Windham—Reasoning upon the Subject—Vendéans defeated—They defeat, in their turn, the French Troops at Laval—But are ultimately destroyed and dispersed—Unfortunate Expedition to Quiberon—La Charette defeated and executed, and the War of La Vendée finally terminated—Unsuccessful Resistance of Bourdeaux,

Marseilles, and Lyons, to the Convention—Siege of Lyons—Its surrender and dreadful Punishment—Siege of Toulon. 399

STATE OF PARTIES IN BRITAIN 400
BRITISH AMBASSADOR RECALLED 403
WAR WITH ENGLAND 403
MILITARY POSITION OF FRANCE 407
LA VENDEE 409
LA CHARETTE 413
WAR OF LA VENDEE 414
DIVISIONS IN THE BRITISH CABINET 423
WAR OF LA VENDÉE 426
TREATY WITH LA CHARETTE 428
STATE OF THE PROVINCES 431
REVOLT OF LYONS 433

CHAPTER XVI 443

Views of the British Cabinet regarding the French Revolution—Extraordinary Situation of France—Explanation of the Anomaly which it exhibited—System of Terror—Committee of Public Safety—Of Public Security—David the Painter—Law against suspected Persons—Revolutionary Tribunal—Effects of the Emigration of the Princes and Nobles—Causes of the Passiveness of the French People under the Tyranny of the Jacobins—Singular Address of the Committee of Public Safety—General Reflections. 443

REVOLUTIONARY TRIBUNAL 450
AFFILIATED SOCIETIES 453
FEROCITY OF THE POPULACE 456
REVOLUTIONARY ARMY 459

CHAPTER XVII 463

Marat, Danton, Robespierre—Marat poniarded—Danton and Robespierre become Rivals—Commune of Paris—their gross Irreligion—Gobel—Goddess of Reason—Marriage reduced to a Civil Contract—Views of Danton—and of Robespierre—Principal Leaders of the Commune arrested—and Nineteen of them executed—Danton arrested by the Influence of Robespierre—and, along with Camille Desmoulins, Westermann, and La Croix, taken before the Revolutionary Tribunal, condemned, and executed—Decree issued, on the motion of Robespierre, acknowledging a Supreme Being—Cécilée Regnault—Gradual Change in the Public Mind—Robespierre becomes unpopular—Makes every effort to retrieve his power—Stormy Debate in the Convention—Collot D'Herbois, Tallien, &c., expelled from the Jacobin Club at the instigation of Robespierre—Robespierre denounced in the Convention on the 9th Thermidor,

(27th July, 1794,) and, after furious struggles, arrested, along with his brother, Couthon, and Saint Just—Henriot, Commandant of the National Guard, arrested—Terrorists take refuge in the Hôtel de Ville—Attempt their own lives—Robespierre wounds himself—but lives, along with most of the others, long enough to be carried to the Guillotine, and executed—His character—Struggles that followed his Fate—Final Destruction of the Jacobinical System—and return of Tranquillity—Singular colour given to Society in Paris—Ball of the Victims..463

COMMUNE OF PARIS 465
GODDESS OF REASON 467
ROBESPIERRE 470
DANTON ARRESTED 473
DANTON'S TRIAL 475
DANTON EXECUTED 477
FESTIVAL OF THE SUPREME BEING 480
CHANGE IN THE PUBLIC MIND 484
ROBESPIERRE UNPOPULAR 485
ROBESPIERRE DENOUNCED 491
ROBESPIERRE'S DEFENCE 492
THE NINTH THERMIDOR 494
ROBESPIERRE DENOUNCED 495
TERRORISTS AT THE HOTEL DE VILLE 498
CHARACTER OF ROBESPIERRE 502
THE THERMIDORIENS 504
FREEDOM OF THE PRESS 507
JACOBIN CLUB REOPENED 509
TRIAL OF CARRIER 511
JACOBIN CHIEFS BANISHED 515
THE FIRST OF PRAIRIAL 516

CHAPTER XVIII 521

Retrospective View of the External Relations of France—Her great Military Successes—Whence they arose—Effect of the Compulsory Levies—Military Genius and Character of the French—French Generals—New Mode of Training the Troops—Light Troops—Successive Attacks in Column—Attachment of the Soldiers to the Revolution—Also of the Generals—Carnot—Effect of the French principles preached to the Countries invaded by their Arms—Close of the Revolution with the fall of Robespierre—Reflections upon what was to succeed. 521

EXTERNAL RELATIONS 521
MILITARY GENIUS OF THE FRENCH 524
NEW MILITARY SYSTEM 526

RETROSPECT *532*

Advertisement

The extent and purpose of this Work, have, in the course of its progress, gradually but essentially changed from what the Author originally proposed. It was at first intended merely as a brief and popular abstract of the life of the most wonderful man, and the most extraordinary events, of the last thirty years; in short, to emulate the concise yet most interesting history of the great British Admiral, by the Poet-Laureate of Britain.[1] The Author was partly induced to undertake the task, by having formerly drawn up for a periodical work—"The Edinburgh Annual Register"—the history of the two great campaigns of 1814 and 1815; and three volumes were the compass assigned to the proposed work. An introductory volume, giving a general account of the Rise and Progress of the French Revolution, was thought necessary; and the single volume, on a theme of such extent, soon swelled into two.

As the Author composed under an anonymous title, he could neither seek nor expect information from those who had been actively engaged in the changeful scenes which he was attempting to record; nor was his object more ambitious than that of compressing and arranging such information as the ordinary authorities afforded. Circumstances, however, unconnected with the undertaking, induced him to lay aside an *incognito*, any farther attempt to preserve which must have been considered as affectation; and since his having done so, he has been favoured with access to some valuable materials, most of which have now, for the first time, seen the light. For these he refers to the Appendix at the close of the Work, where the reader will find several articles of novelty and interest. Though not at liberty, in every case, to mention the quarter from which his information has been derived, the Author has been careful not to rely upon any which did not come from sufficient authority. He has neither grubbed for anecdotes in the libels and private scandal of the time, nor has he solicited information from individuals who could not be impartial witnesses in the facts to which they gave evidence. Yet the various public documents and private information which he

---
[1] Southey's *Life of Nelson*, 2 vols. fcap. 8vo. 1813.

has received, have much enlarged his stock of materials, and increased the whole work to more than twice the size originally intended.

On the execution of his task, it becomes the Author to be silent. He is aware it must exhibit many faults; but he claims credit for having brought to the undertaking a mind disposed to do his subject as impartial justice as his judgment could supply. He will be found no enemy to the person of Napoleon. The term of hostility is ended when the battle has been won, and the foe exists no longer. His splendid personal qualities—his great military actions and political services to France—will not, it is hoped, be found depreciated in the narrative. Unhappily, the Author's task involved a duty of another kind, the discharge of which is due to France, to Britain, to Europe, and to the world. If the general system of Napoleon has rested upon force or fraud, it is neither the greatness of his talents, nor the success of his undertakings, that ought to stifle the voice or dazzle the eyes of him who adventures to be his historian. The reasons, however, are carefully summed up where the Author has presumed to express a favourable or unfavourable opinion of the distinguished person of whom these volumes treat; so that each reader may judge of their validity for himself.

The name, by an original error of the press, which proceeded too far before it was discovered, has been printed with a *u*,—Buonaparte instead of Bonaparte. Both spellings were indifferently adopted in the family; but Napoleon always used the last,[2] and had an unquestionable right to choose the orthography which he preferred.

Edinburgh, *7th June, 1827.*

---

[2] Barras, in his official account of the affair of the 13th Vendémiaire, (Oct. 5, 1795,) calls him General *Buonaparte*; and in the contract of marriage between Napoleon and Josephine, still existing in the registry of the second arrondissement of Paris, dated March 9, 1796, his signature is so written. No document has ever been produced, in which the word appears as *Bonaparte*, prior to Napoleon's appointment to the command of the Army of Italy.

ADVERTISEMENT TO EDITION OF 1834

Sir Walter Scott left two interleaved copies of his Life of Napoleon, in both of which his executors have found various corrections of the text, and additional notes. They were directed by his testament to take care, that, in case a new edition of the work were called for, the annotations of it might be completed in the fashion here adopted, dates and other marginal elucidations regularly introduced, and the text itself, wherever there appeared any redundancy of statement, abridged. With these instructions, except the last, the Editor has now endeavoured to comply.[3]

"Walter Scott," says Goëthe, "passed his childhood among the stirring scenes of the American War, and was a youth of seventeen or eighteen when the French Revolution broke out. Now well advanced in the fifties, having all along been favourably placed for observation, he proposes to lay before us his views and recollections of the important events through which he has lived. The richest, the easiest, the most celebrated narrator of the century, undertakes to write the history of his own time.

"What expectations the announcement of such a work must have excited in me, will be understood by any one who remembers that I, twenty years older than Scott, conversed with Paoli in the twentieth year of my age, and with Napoleon himself in the sixtieth.

"Through that long series of years, coming more or less into contact with the great doings of the world, I failed not to think seriously on what was passing around me, and, after my own fashion, to connect so many extraordinary mutations into something like arrangement and interdependence.

"What could now be more delightful to me than leisurely and calmly to sit down and listen to the discourse of such a man, while clearly, truly, and with all the skill of a great artist, he recalls to me

---

[3] [Sir Walter Scott's Notes have the letter S affixed to them, all of the others having been collected by the Editor of the 1843 Edition.]

the incidents on which through life I have meditated, and the influence of which is still daily in operation?"—Goëthe's *Posthumous Works*, vol. vi., p. 253.

    Sed non in Cæsare tantum Nomen erat, nec fama ducis; sed nescia virtus Stare loco: solusque pudor non vincere bello. Acer et indomitus; quo spes quoque ira vocasset, Ferre manum, et nunquam temerando parcere ferro: Successus urgere suos: instare favori Numinis: impellens quicquid sibi summa petenti Obstaret: gaudensque viam fecisse ruina.

Lucani, Pharsalia, Lib. I.[4]

---

[4] "But Cæsar's greatness, and his strength, was more Than past renown and antiquated power; 'Twas not the fame of what he once had been, Or tales in old records and annals seen; But 'twas a valour restless, unconfined, Which no success could sate, nor limits bind; 'Twas shame, a soldier's shame, untaught to yield, That blush'd for nothing but an ill-fought field; Fierce in his hopes he was, nor knew to stay Where vengeance or ambition led the way; Still prodigal of war whene'er withstood, Nor spared to stain the guilty sword with blood; Urging advantage, he improved all odds, And made the most of fortune and the gods; Pleased to o'erturn whate'er withheld his prize, And saw the ruin with rejoicing eyes."—Rowe.

CHAPTER I

VIEW OF THE FRENCH REVOLUTION

Review of the state of Europe after the Peace of Versailles—England—France—Spain—Prussia—Imprudent Innovations of the Emperor Joseph—Disturbances in his Dominions—Russia—France—Her ancient System of Monarchy—how organized—Causes of its Decay—Decay of the Nobility as a body—The new Nobles—The Country Nobles—The Nobles of the highest Order—The Church—The higher Orders of the Clergy—The lower Orders—The Commons—Their increase in Power and Importance—Their Claims opposed to those of the Privileged Classes.

When we look back on past events, however important, it is difficult to recall the precise sensations with which we viewed them in their progress, and to recollect the fears, hopes, doubts, and difficulties, for which Time and the course of Fortune have formed a termination, so different probably from that which we had anticipated. When the rush of the inundation was before our eyes, and in our ears, we were scarce able to remember the state of things before its rage commenced, and when, subsequently, the deluge has subsided within the natural limits of the stream, it is still more difficult to recollect with precision the terrors it inspired when at its height. That which is present possesses such power over our senses and our imagination, that it requires no common effort to recall those sensations which expired with preceding events. Yet, to do this is the peculiar province of history, which will be written and read in vain, unless it can connect with its details an accurate idea of the impression which these produced on men's minds while they were yet in their transit. It is with this view that we attempt to resume the history of France and of Europe, at the conclusion of the American war—a period now only remembered by the more advanced part of the present generation.

STATE OF EUROPE

The peace concluded at Versailles in 1783, was reasonably supposed to augur a long repose to Europe. The high and emulous tone assumed in former times by the rival nations, had been lowered and tamed by recent circumstances. England, under the guidance of a weak, at least a most unlucky administration,[5] had purchased peace at the expense of her North American Empire, and the resignation of supremacy over her colonies; a loss great in itself, but exaggerated in the eyes of the nation, by the rending asunder of the ties of common descent, and exclusive commercial intercourse, and by a sense of the wars waged, and expenses encountered for the protection and advancement of the fair empire which England found herself obliged to surrender. The lustre of the British arms, so brilliant at the Peace of Fontainbleau, had been tarnished, if not extinguished. In spite of the gallant defence of Gibraltar, the general result of the war on land had been unfavourable to her military reputation; and notwithstanding the opportune and splendid victories of Rodney, the coasts of Britain had been insulted, and her fleets compelled to retire into port, while those of her combined enemies rode masters of the channel.[6] The spirit of the country also had been lowered, by the unequal contest which had been sustained, and by the sense that her naval superiority was an object of

---

[5] In consequence of the censure passed on the Peace by the House of Commons, the Shelburne ministry was dissolved on the 26th of February, 1783.

[6] "During nearly twenty years, ever since the termination of the war with France in 1763, the British flag had scarcely been any where triumphant; while the navies of the House of Bourbon, throughout the progress of the American contest, annually insulted us in the Channel, intercepted our mercantile convoys, blocked our harbours, and threatened our coasts."—Wraxall, 1782.

invidious hatred to united Europe. This had been lately made manifest, by the armed alliance of the northern nations, which, though termed a neutrality, was, in fact, a league made to abate the pretensions of England to maritime supremacy. There are to be added to these disheartening and depressing circumstances, the decay of commerce during the long course of hostilities, with the want of credit and depression of the price of land, which are the usual consequences of a transition from war to peace, ere capital has regained its natural channel. All these things being considered, it appeared the manifest interest of England to husband her exhausted resources, and recruit her diminished wealth, by cultivating peace and tranquillity for a long course of time. William Pitt, never more distinguished than in his financial operations, was engaged in new modelling the revenue of the country, and adding to the return of the taxes, while he diminished their pressure. It could scarcely be supposed that any object of national ambition would have been permitted to disturb him in a task so necessary.

Neither had France, the natural rival of England, come off from the contest in such circumstances of triumph and advantage, as were likely to encourage her to a speedy renewal of the struggle. It is true, she had seen and contributed to the humiliation of her ancient enemy, but she had paid dearly for the gratification of her revenge, as nations and individuals are wont to do. Her finances, tampered with by successive sets of ministers, who looked no farther than to temporary expedients for carrying on the necessary expenses of government, now presented an alarming prospect; and it seemed as if the wildest and most enterprising ministers would hardly have dared, in their most sanguine moments, to have recommended either war itself, or any measures of which war might be the consequence.

Spain was in a like state of exhaustion. She had been hurried into the alliance against England, partly by the consequences of the family alliance betwixt her Bourbons and those of France, but still more by the eager and engrossing desire to possess herself once more of Gibraltar. The Castilian pride, long galled by beholding this important fortress in the hands of heretics and foreigners, highly applauded the war, which gave a chance of its recovery, and seconded, with all the power of the kingdom, the gigantic efforts made for that purpose. All these immense preparations, with the most formidable means of attack ever used on such an occasion, had totally failed, and the kingdom of Spain remained at once stunned and mortified by the failure, and broken down by the expenses of so huge an undertaking. An attack upon Algiers, in 1784-5, tended to exhaust the remains of her military ardour. Spain, therefore, relapsed into inactivity and repose, dispirited by the miscarriage of her favourite scheme, and possessing neither the means nor the audacity necessary to meditate its speedy renewal.

Neither were the sovereigns of the late belligerent powers of that ambitious and active character which was likely to drag the kingdoms which they swayed into the renewal of hostilities. The classic eye of the historian Gibbon saw Arcadius and Honorius, the weakest and most indolent of the Roman Emperors, slumbering upon the thrones of the House of Bourbon;[7] and the just and loyal character of George III. precluded any effort on his part to undermine the peace which he signed unwillingly, or to attempt the resumption of those rights which he had formally, though reluctantly, surrendered. His expression to the ambassador of the United States,[8] was a trait of character never to be omitted or forgotten:—"I have been the last man in my dominions to accede to this peace, which separates America from my kingdoms—I will be the first man, now it is made, to resist any attempt to infringe it."

---

[7] "The deepest wounds were inflicted on the empire during the minorities of the sons and grandsons of Theodosius; and after those incapable princes seemed to attain the age of manhood, they abandoned the church to the bishops, the state to the eunuchs, and the provinces to the barbarians. Europe is now divided into twelve powerful, though unequal kingdoms, three respectable commonwealths, and a variety of smaller, though independent states: the chances of royal and ministerial talents are multiplied, at least with the number of its rulers; and a Julian, or Semiramis, may reign in the north, while Arcadius and Honorius again slumber on the thrones of the south."—Gibbon's *Decline and Fall*, vol. iii., p. 636.
"It may not be generally known that Louis the Sixteenth is a great reader, and a great reader of English books. On perusing a passage in my History, which seems to compare him to Arcadius or Honorius, he expressed his resentment to the Prince of B*****, from whom the intelligence was conveyed to me. I shall neither disclaim the allusion, nor examine the likeness; but the situation of the late King of France excludes all suspicion of flattery; and I am ready to declare, that the concluding observations of my third volume were written before his accession to the throne."—Gibbon's *Memoirs*, vol. i., p. 126.
[8] On the occasion of the first audience of Mr. Adams, in June, 1785.—See Wraxall's *Own Time*, vol. i., p. 381.

The acute historian whom we have already quoted seems to have apprehended, in the character and ambition of the northern potentates, those causes of disturbance which were not to be found in the western part of the European republic. But Catherine, the Semiramis of the north, had her views of extensive dominion chiefly turned towards her eastern and southern frontier, and the finances of her immense, but comparatively poor and unpeopled empire, were burdened with the expenses of a luxurious court, requiring at once to be gratified with the splendour of Asia and the refinements of Europe. The strength of her empire also, though immense, was unwieldy, and the empire had not been uniformly fortunate in its wars with the more prompt, though less numerous armies of the King of Prussia, her neighbour. Thus Russia, no less than other powers in Europe, appeared more desirous of reposing her gigantic strength, than of adventuring upon new and hazardous conquests. Even her views upon Turkey, which circumstances seemed to render more flattering than ever, she was contented to resign, in 1784, when only half accomplished; a pledge, not only that her thoughts were sincerely bent upon peace, but that she felt the necessity of resisting even the most tempting opportunities for resuming the course of victory which she had, four years before, pursued so successfully.

GERMANY

Frederick of Prussia himself, who had been so long, by dint of genius and talent, the animating soul of the political intrigues in Europe, had run too many risks, in the course of his adventurous and eventful reign, to be desirous of encountering new hazards in the extremity of life. His empire, extended as it was from the shores of the Baltic to the frontiers of Holland, consisted of various detached portions, which it required the aid of time to consolidate into a single kingdom. And, accustomed to study the signs of the times, it could not have escaped Frederick, that sentiments and feelings were afloat, connected with, and fostered by, the spirit of unlimited investigation, which he himself had termed philosophy, such as might soon call upon the sovereigns to arm in a common cause, and ought to prevent them, in the meanwhile, from wasting their strength in mutual struggles, and giving advantage to a common enemy.

If such anticipations occupied and agitated the last years of Frederick's life, they had not the same effect upon the Emperor Joseph II., who, without the same clear-eyed precision of judgment, endeavoured to tread in the steps of the King of Prussia, as a reformer, and as a conqueror. It would be unjust to deny to this prince the praise of considerable talents, and inclination to employ them for the good of the country which he ruled. But it frequently happens, that the talents, and even the virtues of sovereigns, exercised without respect to time and circumstances, become the misfortune of their government. It is particularly the lot of princes, endowed with such personal advantages, to be confident in their own abilities, and, unless educated in the severe school of adversity, to prefer favourites, who assent to and repeat their opinions, to independent counsellors, whose experience might correct their own hasty conclusions. And thus, although the personal merits of Joseph II. were in every respect acknowledged, his talents in a great measure recognised, and his patriotic intentions scarcely disputable, it fell to his lot, during the period we treat of, to excite more apprehension and discontent among his subjects, than if he had been a prince content to rule by a minister, and wear out an indolent life in the forms and pleasures of a court. Accordingly, the Emperor, in many of his schemes of reform, too hastily adopted, or at least too incautiously and peremptorily executed, had the misfortune to introduce fearful commotions among the people, whose situation he meant to ameliorate, while in his external relations he rendered Austria the quarter from which a breach of European peace was most to be apprehended. It seemed, indeed, as if the Emperor had contrived to reconcile his philosophical professions with the exercise of the most selfish policy towards the United Provinces, both in opening the Scheldt, and in dismantling the barrier towns, which had been placed in their hands as a defence against the power of France. By the first of these measures the Emperor gained nothing but the paltry sum of money for which he sold his pretensions,[9] and the shame of having shown himself ungrateful for

---

[9] "The sum, after long debates, was fixed by the Emperor at ten million guilders."—Coxe's *House of Austria*, vol. ii., p. 583.

the important services which the United Provinces had rendered to his ancestors. But the dismantling of the Dutch barrier was subsequently attended by circumstances alike calamitous to Austria, and to the whole continent of Europe.

In another respect, the reforms carried through by Joseph II. tended to prepare the public mind for future innovations, made with a ruder hand, and upon a much larger scale.[10] The suppression of the religious orders, and the appropriation of their revenues to the general purposes of government, had in it something to flatter the feelings of those of the Reformed religion; but, in a moral point of view, the seizing upon the property of any private individual, or public body, is an invasion of the most sacred principles of public justice, and such spoliation cannot be vindicated by urgent circumstances of state-necessity, or any plausible pretext of state-advantage whatsoever, since no necessity can vindicate what is in itself unjust, and no public advantage can compensate a breach of public faith.[11] Joseph was also the first Catholic sovereign who broke through the solemn degree of reverence attached by that religion to the person of the Sovereign Pontiff. The Pope's fruitless and humiliating visit to Vienna furnished the shadow of a precedent for the conduct of Napoleon to Pius VII.[12]

---

[10] "Joseph the Second borrowed the language of philosophy, when he wished to suppress the monks of Belgium, and to seize their revenues: but there was seen on him a mask only of philosophy, covering the hideous countenance of a greedy despot: and the people ran to arms. Nothing better than another kind of despotism has been seen in the revolutionary powers."—Brissot, *Letter to his Constituents*, 1794.

[11] "In 1780, there were 2024 convents in the Austrian dominions: These were diminished to 700, and 36,000 monks and nuns to 2700. Joseph might have applied to his own reforms the remark he afterwards made to General D'Alten, on the reforms of the French:—'The new constitution of France has not been very polite to the high clergy and nobility; and I still doubt much if all these fine things can be carried into execution!'"—Coxe, vol. ii., p. 578.

[12] "The Pope reached Vienna in February, 1782. He was received with every mark of exterior homage and veneration; but his exhortations and remonstrances were treated with coldness and reserve, and he was so narrowly watched, that the back-door of his apartments was blocked up to prevent him from receiving private visitors. Chagrined with the inflexibility of the Emperor, and mortified by an unmeaning ceremonial, and an affected display of veneration for the Holy See, while it was robbed of its richest possessions, and its most valuable privileges, Pius quitted Vienna at the expiration of a month, equally disgusted and humiliated, after having exhibited himself as a disappointed suppliant at the foot of that throne which had been so often shaken by the thunder of the Vatican."—*Ibid.*, p. 632.

Another and yet less justifiable cause of innovation, placed in peril, and left in doubt and discontent, some of the fairest provinces of the Austrian dominions, and those which the wisest of their princes had governed with peculiar tenderness and moderation. The Austrian Netherlands had been in a literal sense dismantled and left open to the first invader, by the demolition of the barrier fortresses; and it seems to have been the systematic purpose of the Emperor to eradicate and destroy that love and regard for their prince and his government, which in time of need proves the most effectual moral substitute for moats and ramparts. The history of the house of Burgundy bore witness on every page to the love of the Flemings for liberty, and the jealousy with which they have, from the earliest ages, watched the privileges they had obtained from their princes. Yet in that country, and amongst these people, Joseph carried on his measures of innovation with a hand so unsparing, as if he meant to bring the question of liberty or arbitrary power to a very brief and military decision betwixt him and his subjects.

FLEMISH DISTURBANCES

His alterations were not in Flanders, as elsewhere, confined to the ecclesiastical state alone, although such innovations were peculiarly offensive to a people rigidly Catholic, but were extended through the most important parts of the civil government. Changes in the courts of justice were threatened—the great seal, which had hitherto remained with the chancellor of the States, was transferred to the Imperial minister—a Council of State, composed of commissioners nominated by the Emperor, was appointed to discharge the duties hitherto intrusted to a standing committee of the States of Brabant—their universities were altered and new-modelled—and their magistrates subjected to arbitrary arrests and sent to Vienna, instead of being tried in their own country and by their own laws. The Flemish people beheld these innovations with the sentiments natural to freemen, and not a little stimulated certainly by the scenes which had lately passed in North America, where, under circumstances of far less provocation, a large empire had emancipated itself from the mother country. The States remonstrated loudly, and refused submission to the decrees which encroached on their constitutional liberties, and at length arrayed a military force in support of their patriotic opposition.

Joseph, who at the same time he thus wantonly provoked the States and people of Flanders, had been seduced by Russia to join her ambitious plan upon Turkey, bent apparently before the storm he had excited, and for a time yielded to accommodation with his subjects of Flanders, renounced the most obnoxious of his new measures, and confirmed the privileges of the nation, at what was called the Joyous Entry.[13] But this spirit of conciliation was only assumed for the purpose of deception; for so soon as he had assembled in Flanders what was deemed a sufficient armed force to sustain his despotic purposes, the Emperor threw off the mask, and, by the most violent acts of military force, endeavoured to overthrow the constitution he had agreed to observe, and to enforce the arbitrary measures which he had pretended to abandon. For a brief period of two years, Flanders remained in a state of suppressed, but deeply-founded and wide-extended discontent, watching for a moment favourable to freedom and to vengeance. It proved an ample store-house of combustibles, prompt to catch fire, as the flame now arising in France began to expand itself; nor can it be doubted, that the condition of the Flemish provinces, whether considered in a military or in a political light, was one of the principal causes of the subsequent success of the French Republican arms. Joseph himself, broken-hearted and dispirited, died in the very beginning of the troubles he had wantonly provoked.[14] Desirous of fame as a legislator and a warrior, and certainly born with talents to acquire it, he left his arms dishonoured by the successes of the despised Turks, and his fair dominions of the Netherlands and of Hungary upon the very eve of insurrection. A lampoon, written upon the hospital for lunatics at Vienna, might be said to be no unjust epitaph for a monarch, one so hopeful and so beloved—"Josephus, ubique Secundus, hic Primus."

---

[13] The charter by which the privileges of the Flemings were settled, had been promulgated on the *entry* of Philip the Good into Brussels. Hence this name.—See Coxe.

[14] "Joseph expired at Vienna, in February, 1790, at the age of forty-nine, extenuated by diseases, caused or accelerated in their progress by his own irritability of temper, agitation of mind, and the embarrassment of his affairs."—Wraxall, vol. i., p. 277.

These Flemish disturbances might be regarded as symptoms of the new opinions which were tacitly gaining ground in Europe, and which preceded the grand explosion, as slight shocks of an earthquake usually announce the approach of its general convulsion. The like may be said of the short-lived Dutch revolution of 1787, in which the ancient faction of Louvestein, under the encouragement of France, for a time completely triumphed over that of the Stadtholder, deposed him from his hereditary command of Captain-General of the Army of the States, and reduced, or endeavoured to reduce, the confederation of the United States to a pure democracy. This was also a strong sign of the times; for, although totally opposite to the inclination of the majority of the States-General, of the equestrian body, of the landed proprietors, nay, of the very populace, most of whom were from habit and principle attached to the House of Orange, the burghers of the large towns drove on the work of revolution with such warmth of zeal and promptitude of action, as showed a great part of the middling classes to be deeply tinctured with the desire of gaining further liberty, and a larger share in the legislation and administration of the country, than pertained to them under the old oligarchical constitution.

The revolutionary government, in the Dutch provinces, did not, however, conduct their affairs with prudence. Without waiting to organize their own force, or weaken that of the enemy—without obtaining the necessary countenance and protection of France, or co-operating with the malecontents in the Austrian Netherlands, they gave, by arresting the Princess of Orange, (sister of the King of Prussia,) an opportunity of foreign interference, of which that prince failed not to avail himself. His armies, commanded by the Duke of Brunswick, poured into the United Provinces, and with little difficulty possessed themselves of Utrecht, Amsterdam, and the other cities which constituted the strength of the Louvestein or republican faction. The King then replaced the House of Orange in all its power, privileges, and functions. The conduct of the Dutch republicans during their brief hour of authority had been neither so moderate nor so popular as to make their sudden and almost unresisting fall a matter of general regret. On the contrary, it was considered as a probable pledge of the continuance of peace in

Europe, especially as France, busied with her own affairs, declined interference in those of the United States.

INTRIGUES OF RUSSIA

The intrigues of Russia had, in accomplishment of the ambitious schemes of Catherine, lighted up war with Sweden, as well as with Turkey; but in both cases hostilities were commenced upon the old plan of fighting one or two battles, and wresting a fortress of a province from a neighbouring state; and it seems likely, that the intervention of France and England, equally interested in preserving the balance of power, might have ended these troubles, but for the progress of that great and hitherto unheard-of course of events, which prepared, carried on, and matured, the French Revolution.

It is necessary, for the execution of our plan, that we should review this period of history, the most important, perhaps, during its currency, and in its consequences, which the annals of mankind afford; and although the very title is sufficient to awaken in most bosoms either horror or admiration, yet, neither insensible of the blessings of national liberty, nor of those which flow from the protection of just laws, and a moderate but firm executive government, we may perhaps be enabled to trace its events with the candour of one, who, looking back on past scenes, feels divested of the keen and angry spirit with which, in common with his contemporaries, he may have judged them while they were yet in progress.

We have shortly reviewed the state of Europe in general, which we have seen to be either pacific or disturbed by troubles of no long duration; but it was in France that a thousand circumstances, some arising out of the general history of the world, some peculiar to that country herself, mingled, like the ingredients in the witches' cauldron, to produce in succession many a formidable but passing apparition, until concluded by the stern Vision of absolute and military power, as those in the drama are introduced by that of the Armed Head.[15]

The first and most effective cause of the Revolution, was the change which had taken place in the feelings of the French towards their government, and the monarch who was its head. The devoted loyalty of the people to their king had been for several ages the most marked characteristic of the nation; it was their honour in their own eyes, and matter of contempt and ridicule in those of the English, because it seemed in its excess to swallow up all ideas of patriotism. That very excess of loyalty, however, was founded not on a servile, but upon a generous principle. France is ambitious, fond of military glory, and willingly identifies herself with the fame acquired by her soldiers. Down to the reign of Louis XV., the French monarch was, in the eyes of his subjects, a general, and the whole people an army. An army must be under severe discipline, and a general must possess absolute power; but the soldier feels no degradation from the restraint which is necessary to his profession, and without which he cannot be led to conquest.

FRENCH MONARCHY

Every true Frenchman, therefore, submitted, without scruple to that abridgement of personal liberty which appeared necessary to render the monarch great, and France victorious. The King, according to this system, was regarded less as an individual than as the representative of the concentrated honour of the kingdom; and in this sentiment, however extravagant and Quixotic, there mingled much that was generous, patriotic, and disinterested. The same feeling was awakened after all the changes of the Revolution, by the wonderful successes of the Individual of whom the future volumes are to treat, and who transferred, in many instances to his own person, by deeds almost exceeding credibility, the species of devoted attachment with which France formerly regarded the ancient line of her kings.

---

[15] See *Macbeth*, act iv., sc. i.

The nobility shared with the king in the advantages which this predilection spread around him. If the monarch was regarded as the chief ornament of the community, they were the minor gems by whose lustre that of the crown was relieved or adorned. If he was the supreme general of the state, they were the officers attached to his person, and necessary to the execution of his commands, each in his degree bound to advance the honour and glory of the common country. When such sentiments were at their height, there could be no murmuring against the peculiar privileges of the nobility, any more than against the almost absolute authority of the monarch. Each had that rank in the state which was regarded as his birth-right, and for one of the lower orders to repine that he enjoyed not the immunities peculiar to the noblesse, would have been as unavailing, and as foolish, as to lament that he was not born to an independent estate. Thus, the Frenchman, contented, though with an illusion, laughed, danced, and indulged all the gaiety of his national character, in circumstances under which his insular neighbours would have thought the slightest token of patience dishonourable and degrading. The distress or privation which the French plebeian suffered in his own person, was made up to him in imagination by his interest in the national glory.

Was a citizen of Paris postponed in rank to the lowest military officer, he consoled himself by reading the victories of the French arms in the Gazette; and was he unduly and unequally taxed to support the expense of the crown, still the public feasts which were given, and the palaces which were built, were to him a source of compensation. He looked on at the Carousal, he admired the splendour of Versailles, and enjoyed a reflected share of their splendour, in recollecting that they displayed the magnificence of his country. This state of things, however illusory, seemed, while the illusion lasted, to realize the wish of those legislators, who have endeavoured to form a general fund of national happiness, from which each individual is to draw his personal share of enjoyment. If the monarch enjoyed the display of his own grace and agility, while he hunted, or rode at the ring, the spectators had their share of pleasure in witnessing it: if Louis had the satisfaction of beholding the splendid piles of Versailles and the Louvre arise at his command, the subject admired them when raised, and his real portion of pleasure was not, perhaps, inferior to that of the founder. The people were like men inconveniently placed in a crowded theatre, who think little of the personal inconveniences they are subjected to by the heat and pressure, while their mind is engrossed by the splendours of the representation. In short, not only the political opinions of Frenchmen but their actual feelings, were, in the earlier days of the eighteenth century, expressed in the motto which they chose for their national palace—"Earth hath no nation like the French—no Nation a City like Paris, or a King like Louis."

The French enjoyed this assumed superiority with the less chance of being undeceived, that they listened not to any voice from other lands, which pointed out the deficiencies in the frame of government under which they lived, or which hinted the superior privileges enjoyed by the subjects of a more free state. The intense love of our own country, and admiration of its constitution, is usually accompanied with a contempt or dislike of foreign states, and their modes of government. The French, in the reign of Louis XIV., enamoured of their own institutions, regarded those of other nations as unworthy of their consideration; and if they paused for a moment to gaze on the complicated constitution of their great rival, it was soon dismissed as a subject totally unintelligible, with some expression of pity, perhaps, for the poor sovereign who had the ill luck to preside over a government embarrassed by so many restraints and limitations.[16] Yet, into whatever political errors the French people were led by the excess of their loyalty, it would be unjust to brand them as a nation of a mean and slavish spirit. Servitude infers dishonour, and dishonour to a Frenchman is the last of evils. Burke more justly regarded them as a people misled to their disadvantage, by high and romantic ideas of honour and fidelity, and who, actuated by a principle of public spirit in their submission to their monarch, worshipped, in his person, the Fortune of France their common country.

During the reign of Louis XIV., every thing tended to support the sentiment which connected the national honour with the wars and undertakings of the king. His success, in the earlier years of his reign, was splendid, and he might be regarded for many years, as the

---

[16] The old French proverb bore,— "Le roi d'Angleterre, Est le roi d'Enfer."—S.

dictator of Europe. During this period, the universal opinion of his talents, together with his successes abroad, and his magnificence at home, fostered the idea that the Grand Monarque was in himself the tutelar deity, and only representative, of the great nation whose powers he wielded. Sorrow and desolation came on his latter years; but be it said to the honour of the French people, that the devoted allegiance they had paid to Louis in prosperity, was not withdrawn when fortune seemed to have turned her back upon her original favourite. France poured her youth forth as readily, if not so gaily, to repair the defeats of her monarch's old age, as she had previously yielded them to secure and extend the victories of his early reign. Louis had perfectly succeeded in establishing the crown as the sole pivot upon which public affairs turned, and in attaching to his person, as the representative of France, all the importance which in other countries is given to the great body of the nation.

Nor had the spirit of the French monarchy, in surrounding itself with all the dignity of absolute power, failed to secure the support of those auxiliaries which have the most extended influence upon the public mind, by engaging at once religion and literature in defence of its authority. The Gallican Church, more dependent upon the monarch, and less so upon the Pope, than is usual in Catholic countries, gave to the power of the crown all the mysterious and supernatural terrors annexed to an origin in divine right, and directed against those who encroached on the limits of the royal prerogative, or even ventured to scrutinize too minutely the foundation of its authority, the penalties annexed to a breach of the divine law. Louis XIV. repaid this important service by a constant, and even scrupulous attention to observances prescribed by the Church, which strengthened, in the eyes of the public, the alliance so strictly formed betwixt the altar and the throne. Those who look to the private morals of the monarch may indeed form some doubt of the sincerity of his religious professions, considering how little they influenced his practice; and yet, when we reflect upon the frequent inconsistencies of mankind in this particular, we may hesitate to charge with hypocrisy a conduct, which was dictated perhaps as much by conscience as by political convenience. Even judging more severely, it must be allowed that hypocrisy, though so different from religion, indicates its existence, as smoke points out that of pure fire.

Hypocrisy cannot exist unless religion be to a certain extent held in esteem, because no one would be at the trouble to assume a mask which was not respectable, and so far compliance with the external forms of religion is a tribute paid to the doctrines which it teaches. The hypocrite assumes a virtue if he has it not, and the example of his conduct may be salutary to others, though his pretensions to piety are wickedness to Him, who trieth the heart and reins.

On the other hand, the Academy formed by the wily Richelieu served to unite the literature of France into one focus, under the immediate patronage of the crown, to whose bounty its professors were taught to look even for the very means of subsistence. The greater nobles caught this ardour of patronage from the sovereign, and as the latter pensioned and supported the principal literary characters of his reign, the former granted shelter and support to others of the same rank, who were lodged at their hotels, fed at their tables, and were admitted to their society upon terms somewhat less degrading than those which were granted to artists and musicians, and who gave to the Great, knowledge or amusement in exchange for the hospitality they received. Men in a situation so subordinate, could only at first accommodate their compositions to the taste and interest of their protectors. They heightened by adulation and flattery the claims of the king and the nobles upon the community; and the nation, indifferent at that time to all literature which was not of native growth, felt their respect for their own government enhanced and extended by the works of those men of genius who flourished under its protection.

Such was the system of French monarchy, and such it remained, in outward show at least, until the peace of Fontainbleau. But its foundation had been gradually undermined; public opinion had undergone a silent but almost a total change, and it might be compared to some ancient tower swayed from its base by the lapse of time, and waiting the first blast of a hurricane, or shock of an earthquake, to be prostrated in the dust. How the lapse of half a century, or little more, could have produced a change so total, must next be considered; and this can only be done by viewing separately the various changes which the lapse of years had produced on the various orders of the state.

DECAY OF THE NOBILITY

First, then, it is to be observed, that in these latter times the wasting effects of luxury and vanity had totally ruined the greater part of the French nobility, a word which, in respect of that country, comprehended what is called in Britain the nobility and gentry, or natural aristocracy of the kingdom. This body, during the reign of Louis XIV., though far even then from supporting the part which their fathers had acted in history, yet existed, as it were, through their remembrances, and disguised their dependence upon the throne by the outward show of fortune, as well as by the consequence attached to hereditary right. They were one step nearer the days, not then totally forgotten, when the nobles of France, with their retainers, actually formed the army of the kingdom; and they still presented, to the imagination at least, the descendants of a body of chivalrous heroes, ready to tread in the path of their ancestors, should the times ever render necessary the calling forth the Ban, or Arrière-Ban—the feudal array of the Gallic chivalry. But this delusion had passed away; the defence of states was intrusted in France, as in other countries, to the exertions of a standing army; and, in the latter part of the eighteenth century, the nobles of France presented a melancholy contrast to their predecessors.

The number of the order was of itself sufficient to diminish its consequence. It had been imprudently increased by new creations. There were in the kingdom about eighty thousand families enjoying the privileges of nobility; and the order was divided into different classes, which looked on each other with mutual jealousy and contempt.

The first general distinction was betwixt the Ancient, and Modern, or new noblesse. The former were nobles of old creation, whose ancestors had obtained their rank from real or supposed services rendered to the nation in her councils or her battles. The new nobles had found an easier access to the same elevation, by the purchase of territories, or of offices, or of letters of nobility, any of which easy modes invested the owners with titles and rank, often held by men whose wealth had been accumulated in mean and sordid occupations, or by farmers-general, and financiers, whom the people considered as acquiring their fortunes at the expense of the state. These numerous additions to the privileged body of nobles accorded ill with its original composition, and introduced schism and disunion into the body itself. The descendants of the ancient chivalry of France looked with scorn upon the new men, who, rising perhaps from the very lees of the people, claimed from superior wealth a share in the privileges of the aristocracy.

Again, secondly, there was, amongst the ancient nobles themselves, but too ample room for division between the upper and wealthier class of nobility, who had fortunes adequate to maintain their rank, and the much more numerous body, whose poverty rendered them pensioners upon the state for the means of supporting their dignity. Of about one thousand houses, of which the ancient noblesse is computed to have consisted, there were not above two or three hundred families who had retained the means of maintaining their rank without the assistance of the crown. Their claims to monopolize commissions in the army, and situations in the government, together with their exemption from taxes, were their sole resources; resources burdensome to the state, and odious to the people, without being in the same degree beneficial to those who enjoyed them. Even in military service, which was considered as their birth-right, the nobility of the second class were seldom permitted to rise above a certain limited rank. Long service might exalt one of them to the *grade* of lieutenant-colonel, or the government of some small town, but all the better rewards of a life spent in the army were reserved for nobles of the highest order. It followed as a matter of course, that amidst so many of this privileged body who languished in poverty, and could not rise from it by the ordinary paths of industry, some must have had recourse to loose and dishonourable practices; and that gambling-houses and places of debauchery should have been frequented and patronised by individuals, whose ancient descent, titles, and emblems of nobility, did not save them from the suspicion of very dishonourable conduct, the disgrace of which affected the character of the whole body.

There must be noticed a third classification of the order, into the Haute Noblesse, or men of the highest rank, most of whom spent their lives at court, and in discharge of the great offices of the crown and state, and the Noblesse Campagnarde, who continued to reside upon their patrimonial estates in the provinces.

The noblesse of the latter class had fallen gradually into a state of general contempt, which was deeply to be regretted. They were ridiculed and scorned by the courtiers, who despised the rusticity of their manners, and by the nobles of newer creation, who, conscious of their own wealth, contemned the poverty of these ancient but decayed families. The "bold peasant" himself not more a kingdom's pride than is the plain country gentleman, who, living on his own means, and amongst his own people, becomes the natural protector and referee of the farmer and the peasant, and, in case of need, either the firmest assertor of their rights and his own against the aggressions of the crown, or the independent and undaunted defender of the crown's rights, against the innovations of political fanaticism. In La Vendée alone, the nobles had united their interest and their fortune with those of the peasants who cultivated their estates, and there alone were they found in their proper and honourable character of proprietors residing on their own domains, and discharging the duties which are inalienably attached to the owner of landed property. And—mark-worthy circumstance!—in La Vendée alone was any stand made in behalf of the ancient proprietors, constitution, or religion of France; for there alone the nobles and the cultivators of the soil held towards each other their natural and proper relations of patron and client, faithful dependents, and generous and affectionate superiors.[17] In the other provinces of France, the nobility, speaking generally, possessed neither power nor influence among the peasantry, while the population around them was guided and influenced by men belonging to the Church, to the law, or to business; classes which were in general better educated, better informed, and possessed of more talent and knowledge of the world than the poor Noblesse Campagnarde, who seemed as much limited, caged, and imprisoned, within the restraints of their rank, as if they had been shut up within the dungeons of their ruinous chateaux; and who had only their titles and dusty parchments to oppose to the real superiority of wealth and information so generally to be found in the class which

---

[17] See the Memoirs of the Marchioness De La Rochejaquelein, p. 48.

they affected to despise. Hence, Ségur describes the country gentlemen of his younger days as punctilious, ignorant, and quarrelsome, shunned by the better-informed of the middle classes, idle and dissipated, and wasting their leisure hours in coffee-houses, theatres, and billiard-rooms.[18]

The more wealthy families, and the high noblesse, as they were called, saw this degradation of the inferior part of their order without pity, or rather with pleasure. These last had risen as much above their natural duties, as the rural nobility had sunk beneath them. They had too well followed the course which Richelieu had contrived to recommend to their fathers, and instead of acting as the natural chiefs and leaders of the nobility and gentry of the provinces, they were continually engaged in intriguing for charges round the king's person, for posts in the administration, for additional titles and decorations—for all and every thing which could make the successful courtier, and distinguish him from the independent noble. Their education and habits also were totally unfavourable to grave or serious thought and exertion. If the trumpet had sounded, it would have found a ready echo in their bosoms; but light literature at best, and much more frequently silly and frivolous amusements, a constant pursuit of pleasure, and a perpetual succession of intrigues, either of love or petty politics, made their character, in time of peace, approach in insignificance to that of the women of the court, whom it was the business of their lives to captivate and amuse.[19] There were noble exceptions, but in general the order, in every thing but military courage, had assumed a trivial and effeminate character, from which patriotic sacrifices, or masculine wisdom, were scarcely to be expected.

While the first nobles of France were engaged in these frivolous pursuits, their procureurs, bailiffs, stewards, intendants, or by whatever name their agents and managers were designated, enjoyed the real influence which their constituents rejected as beneath them, rose into a degree of authority and credit, which

---

[18] Ségur's Memoirs, vol. i., p. 76.
[19] For a curious picture of the life of the French nobles of fifty years since, see the first volume of Madame Genlis's Memoirs. Had there been any more solid pursuits in society than the gay trifles she so pleasantly describes, they could not have escaped so intelligent an observer.—S.

eclipsed recollection of the distant and regardless proprietor, and formed a rank in the state not very different from that of the middle-men in Ireland. These agents were necessarily of plebeian birth, and their profession required that they should be familiar with the details of public business, which they administered in the name of their seigneurs. Many of this condition gained power and wealth in the course of the Revolution, thus succeeding, like an able and intelligent vizier, to the power which was forfeited by the idle and voluptuous sultan. Of the high noblesse it might with truth be said, that they still formed the grace of the court of France, though they had ceased to be its defence. They were accomplished, brave, full of honour, and in many instances endowed with talent. But the communication was broken off betwixt them and the subordinate orders, over whom, in just degree, they ought to have possessed a natural influence. The chain of gradual and insensible connexion was rusted by time, in almost all its dependencies; forcibly distorted, and contemptuously wrenched asunder, in many. The noble had neglected and flung from him the most precious jewel in his coronet—the love and respect of the country-gentleman, the farmer, and the peasant, an advantage so natural to his condition in a well-constituted society, and founded upon principles so estimable, that he who contemns or destroys it, is guilty of little less than high treason, both to his own rank, and to the community in general. Such a change, however, had taken place in France, so that the noblesse might be compared to a court-sword, the hilt carved, ornamented, and gilded, such as might grace a day of parade, but the blade gone, or composed of the most worthless materials.

It only remains to be mentioned, that there subsisted, besides all the distinctions we have noticed, an essential difference in political opinions among the noblesse themselves, considered as a body. There were many of the order, who, looking to the exigencies of the kingdom, were patriotically disposed to sacrifice their own exclusive privileges, in order to afford a chance of its regeneration. These of course were disposed to favour an alteration or reform in the original constitution of France; but besides these enlightened individuals, the nobility had the misfortune to include many disappointed and desperate men, ungratified by any of the advantages which their rank made them capable of receiving, and whose advantages of birth and education only rendered them more deeply dangerous, or more daringly profligate. A plebeian, dishonoured by his vices, or depressed by the poverty which is their consequence, sinks easily into the insignificance from which wealth or character alone raised him; but the noble often retains the means, as well as the desire, to avenge himself on society, for an expulsion which he feels not the less because he is conscious of deserving it. Such were the debauched Roman youth, among whom were found Cataline, and associates equal in talents and in depravity to their leader; and such was the celebrated Mirabeau, who, almost expelled from his own class, as an irreclaimable profligate, entered the arena of the Revolution as a first-rate reformer, and a popular advocate of the lower orders.

The state of the Church, that second pillar of the throne, was scarce more solid than that of the nobility. Generally speaking, it might be said, that, for a long time, the higher orders of the clergy had ceased to take a vital concern in their profession, or to exercise its functions in a manner which interested the feelings and affections of men.

The Catholic Church had grown old, and unfortunately did not possess the means of renovating her doctrines, or improving her constitution, so as to keep pace with the enlargement of the human understanding. The lofty claims to infallibility which she had set up and maintained during the middle ages, claims which she could neither renounce nor modify, now threatened, in more enlightened times, like battlements too heavy for the foundation, to be the means of ruining the edifice they were designed to defend. *Vestigia nulla retrorsum*, continued to be the motto of the Church of Rome. She could explain nothing, soften nothing, renounce nothing, consistently with her assertion of impeccability. The whole trash which had been accumulated for ages of darkness and ignorance, whether consisting of extravagant pretensions, incredible assertions, absurd doctrines which confounded the understanding, or puerile ceremonies which revolted the taste, were alike incapable of being explained away or abandoned. It would certainly have been—humanly speaking—advantageous, alike for the Church of Rome, and for Christianity in general, that the former had possessed the means of relinquishing her extravagant claims, modifying her more obnoxious doctrines, and retrenching her superstitious ceremonial, as increasing knowledge showed the injustice of the one, and the absurdity of the other. But this power she dared not assume; and hence, perhaps, the great schism which divides the Christian world, which might otherwise never have existed, or at least not in its present extended and embittered state. But, in all events, the Church of Rome, retaining the spiritual empire over so large and fair a portion of the Christian world, would not have been reduced to the alternative of either defending propositions, which, in the eyes of all enlightened men, are altogether untenable, or of beholding the most essential and vital doctrines of Christianity confounded with them, and the whole system exposed to the scorn of the infidel. The more enlightened and better informed part of the French nation had fallen very generally into the latter extreme.

Infidelity, in attacking the absurd claims and extravagant doctrines of the Church of Rome, had artfully availed herself of those abuses, as if they had been really a part of the Christian religion; and they whose credulity could not digest the grossest articles of the Papist creed, thought themselves entitled to conclude, in general, against religion itself, from the abuses engrafted upon it by ignorance and priestcraft. The same circumstances which favoured the assault, tended to weaken the defence. Embarrassed by the necessity of defending the mass of human inventions with which their Church had obscured and deformed Christianity, the Catholic clergy were not the best advocates even in the best of causes; and though there were many brilliant exceptions, yet it must be owned that a great part of the higher orders of the priesthood gave themselves little trouble about maintaining the doctrines, or extending the influence of the Church, considering it only in the light of an asylum, where, under the condition of certain renunciations, they enjoyed, in indolent tranquillity, a state of ease and luxury. Those who thought on the subject more deeply, were contented quietly to repose the safety of the Church upon the restrictions on the press, which prevented the possibility of free discussion. The usual effect followed; and many who, if manly and open debate upon theological subjects had been allowed, would doubtless have been enabled to winnow the wheat from the chaff, were, in the state of darkness to which they were reduced, led to reject Christianity itself, along with the corruptions of the Romish Church, and to become absolute infidels instead of reformed Christians.

THE CLERGY—DUBOIS

The long and violent dispute also betwixt the Jesuits and the Jansenists, had for many years tended to lessen the general consideration for the Church at large, and especially for the higher orders of the clergy. In that quarrel, much had taken place that was disgraceful. The mask of religion has been often used to cover more savage and extensive persecutions, but at no time did the spirit of intrigue, of personal malice, of slander, and circumvention, appear more disgustingly from under the sacred disguise; and in the eyes of the thoughtless and the vulgar, the general cause of religion suffered in proportion.

The number of the clergy who were thus indifferent to doctrine or duty was greatly increased, since the promotion to the great benefices had ceased to be distributed with regard to the morals, piety, talents, and erudition of the candidates, but was bestowed among the younger branches of the noblesse, upon men who were at little pains to reconcile the looseness of their former habits and opinions with the sanctity of their new profession, and who, embracing the Church solely as a means of maintenance, were little calculated by their lives or learning to extend its consideration. Among other vile innovations of the celebrated regent, Duke of Orleans, he set the most barefaced example of such dishonourable preferment, and had increased in proportion the contempt entertained for the hierarchy, even in its highest dignities,—since how was it possible to respect the purple itself, after it had covered the shoulders of the infamous Dubois?[20]

---

[20] "A person of mean extraction, remarkable only for his vices, had been employed in correcting the Regent's tasks, and, by a servile complacence for all his inclinations, had acquired an ascendency over his pupil, which he abused, for the purpose of corrupting his morals, debasing his character, and ultimately rendering his administration an object of

It might have been expected, and it was doubtless in a great measure the case, that the respect paid to the characters and efficient utility of the curates, upon whom, generally speaking, the charge of souls actually devolved, might have made up for the want of consideration withheld from the higher orders of the Church. There can be no doubt that this respectable body of churchmen possessed great and deserved influence over their parishioners; but then they were themselves languishing under poverty and neglect, and, as human beings, cannot be supposed to have viewed with indifference their superiors enjoying wealth and ease, while in some cases they dishonoured the robe they wore, and in others disowned the doctrines they were appointed to teach. Alive to feelings so natural, and mingling with the middling classes, of which they formed a most respectable portion, they must necessarily have become embued with their principles and opinions, and a very obvious train of reasoning would extend the consequences to their own condition. If the state was encumbered rather than benefited by the privileges of the higher order, was not the Church in the same condition? And if secular rank was to be thrown open as a general object of ambition to the able and the worthy, ought not the dignities of the Church to be rendered more accessible to those, who, in humility and truth, discharged the toilsome duties of its inferior offices, and who might therefore claim, in due degree of succession, to attain higher preferment? There can be no injustice in ascribing to this body sentiments, which might have been no less just regarding the Church than advantageous to themselves; and, accordingly, it was not long before this body of churchmen showed distinctly, that their political views were the same with those of the Third Estate, to which they solemnly united themselves, strengthening thereby greatly the first revolutionary movements. But their conduct, when they beheld the whole system of their religion aimed at, should acquit the French clergy of the charge of self-interest, since no body,

---

universal indignation. Soon after his patron's accession to power, Dubois was admitted into the council of state. He asked for the Archbishopric of Cambray. Unaccustomed as he was to delicate scruples, the Regent was startled at the idea of encountering the scandal to which such a prostitution of honours must expose him. He, however, ultimately yielded. This man, one of the most profligate that ever existed, was actually married at the time he received Catholic orders, but he suborned the witnesses, and contrived to have the parish registers, which might have deposed against him, destroyed."—See Lacretelle, tom. i., p. 348.

considered as such, ever showed itself more willing to encounter persecution, and submit to privation for conscience' sake.

TIERS ETAT

While the Noblesse and the Church, considered as branches of the state, were thus divided amongst themselves, and fallen into discredit with the nation at large; while they were envied for their ancient immunities without being any longer feared for their power; while they were ridiculed at once and hated for the assumption of a superiority which their personal qualities did not always vindicate, the lowest order, the Commons, or, as they were at that time termed, the Third Estate, had gradually acquired an extent and importance unknown to the feudal ages, in which originated the ancient division of the estates of the kingdom. The Third Estate no longer, as in the days of Henry IV., consisted merely of the burghers and petty traders in the small towns of a feudal kingdom, bred up almost as the vassals of the nobles and clergy, by whose expenditure they acquired their living. Commerce and colonies had introduced wealth, from sources to which the nobles and the churchmen had no access. Not only a very great proportion of the disposable capital was in the hands of the Third Estate, who thus formed the bulk of the moneyed interest of France, but a large share of the landed property was also in their possession.

There was, moreover, the influence which many plebeians possessed, as creditors, over those needy nobles whom they had supplied with money, while another portion of the same class rose into wealth and consideration, at the expense of the more opulent patricians who were ruining themselves. Paris had increased to a tremendous extent, and her citizens had risen to a corresponding degree of consideration; and while they profited by the luxury and dissipation, both of the court and courtiers, had become rich in proportion as the government and privileged classes grew poor. Those citizens who were thus enriched, endeavoured, by bestowing on their families all the advantages of good education, to counterbalance their inferiority of birth, and to qualify their children to support their part in the scenes, to which their altered fortunes, and the prospects of the country, appeared to call them. In short, it is not too much to say, that the middling classes acquired the advantages of wealth, consequence, and effective power, in a proportion more than equal to that in which the nobility had lost these attributes. Thus, the Third Estate seemed to increase in extent, number, and strength, like a waxing inundation, threatening with every increasing wave to overwhelm the ancient and decayed barriers of exclusions and immunities, behind which the privileged ranks still fortified themselves.

It was not in the nature of man, that the bold, the talented, the ambitious, of a rank which felt its own power and consequence, should be long contented to remain acquiescent in political regulations, which depressed them in the state of society beneath men to whom they felt themselves equal in all respects, excepting the factitious circumstances of birth, or of Church orders. It was no less impossible that they should long continue satisfied with the feudal dogmas, which exempted the noblesse from taxes, because they served the nation with their sword, and the clergy, because they propitiated Heaven in its favour with their prayers. The maxim, however true in the feudal ages when it originated, had become an extravagant legal fiction in the eighteenth century, when all the world knew that both the noble soldier and the priest were paid for the services they no longer rendered to the state, while the *roturier* had both valour and learning to fight his own battles and perform his own devotions; and when, in fact, it was their arms which combated, and their learning which enlightened the state, rather than those of the privileged orders.[21]

Thus, a body, opulent and important, and carrying along with their claims the sympathy of the whole people, were arranged in formidable array against the privileges of the nobles and clergy, and bound to further the approaching changes by the strongest of human ties, emulation and self-interest.

The point was stated with unusual frankness by Emeri, a distinguished member of the National Assembly, and a man of honour and talent. In the course of a confidential communication

---

[21] Thiers, Histoire de la Rév. Franç., tom. i., p. 34.

with the celebrated Marquis de Bouillé, the latter had avowed his principles of royalty, and his detestation of the new constitution, to which he said he only rendered obedience, because the King had sworn to maintain it. "You are right, being yourself a nobleman," replied Emeri, with equal candour; "and had I been born noble, such would have been my principles; but I, a plebeian *Avocat*, must naturally desire a revolution, and cherish that constitution which has called me, and those of my rank, out of a state of degradation."[22]

Considering the situation, therefore, of the three separate bodies, which, before the revolutionary impulse commenced, were the constituent parts of the kingdom of France, it was evident, that in case of a collision, the Nobles and Clergy might esteem themselves fortunate, if, divided as they were among themselves, they could maintain an effectual defence of the whole, or a portion of their privileges, while the Third Estate, confident in their numbers and in their unanimity, were ready to assail and carry by storm the whole system, over the least breach which might be effected in the ancient constitution. Lally Tolendal gave a comprehensive view of the state of parties in these words:—"The commons desired to conquer, the nobles to preserve what they already possessed. The clergy stood inactive, resolved to join the victorious party. If there was a man in France who wished for concord and peace, it was the king."[23]

---

[22] Mémoires de Bouillé, p. 289.
[23] Plaidoyer pour Louis Seize, 1793.

CHAPTER II

State of France continued—State of Public Opinion—Men of Letters encouraged by the Great—Disadvantages attending this Patronage—Licentious tendency of the French Literature—Their Irreligious and Infidel Opinions—Free Opinions on Politics permitted to be expressed in an abstract and speculative, but not in a practical Form—Disadvantages arising from the Suppression of Free Discussion—Anglomania—Share of France in the American War—Disposition of the Troops who returned from America.

STATE OF PUBLIC OPINION

We have viewed France as it stood in its grand political divisions previous to the Revolution, and we have seen that there existed strong motives for change, and that a great force was prepared to level institutions which were crumbling to pieces of themselves. It is now necessary to review the state of the popular mind, and consider upon what principles, and to what extent, the approaching changes were likely to operate, and at what point they might be expected to stop. Here, as with respect to the ranks of society, a tacit but almost total change had been operated in the feelings and sentiments of the public, principally occasioned, doubtless, by the great ascendency acquired by literature—that tree of knowledge of good and evil, which, amidst the richest and most wholesome fruits, bears others, fair in show, and sweet to the taste, but having the properties of the most deadly poison.

The French, the most ingenious people in Europe, and the most susceptible of those pleasures which arise from conversation and literary discussion, had early called in the assistance of men of genius to enhance their relish for society. The nobles, without renouncing their aristocratic superiority,—which, on the contrary, was rendered more striking by the contrast,—permitted literary talents to be a passport into their saloons. The wealthy financier, and opulent merchant, emulated the nobility in this as in other articles of taste and splendour; and their coteries, as well as those of the aristocracy, were open to men of letters, who were in many cases contented to enjoy luxury at the expense of independence. Assuredly this species of patronage, while it often flowed from the vanity or egotism of the patrons, was not much calculated to enhance the character of those who were protected. Professors of literature, thus mingling in the society of the noble and the wealthy upon sufferance, held a rank scarcely higher than that of musicians or actors, from amongst whom individuals have often, by their talents and character, become members of the best society, while the castes, to which such individuals belong, remain in general exposed to the most humiliating contempt. The lady of quality, who smiled on the man of letters, and the man of rank, who admitted him to his intimacy, still retained their consciousness that he was not like themselves, formed out of the "porcelain clay of the earth;" and even while receiving their bounties, or participating in their pleasures, the favourite *savant* must often have been disturbed by the reflection, that he was only considered as a creature of sufferance, whom the caprice of fashion, or a sudden reaction of the ancient etiquette, might fling out of the society where he was at present tolerated. Under this disheartening, and even degrading inferiority, the man of letters might be tempted invidiously to compare the luxurious style of living at which he sat a permitted guest, with his own paltry hired apartment, and scanty and uncertain chance of support. And even those of a nobler mood, when they had conceded to their benefactors all the gratitude they could justly demand, must sometimes have regretted their own situation,

"Condemn'd as needy supplicants to wait, While ladies interpose and slaves debate."[24]

It followed, that many of the men of letters, thus protected, became enemies of the persons, as well as the rank of their patrons; as, for example, no one in the course of the Revolution expressed

---

[24] Johnson's Vanity of Human Wishes.

greater hatred to the nobility than Champfort,[25] the favourite and favoured secretary of the Prince of Condé. Occasions, too, must frequently have occurred, in which the protected person was almost inevitably forced upon comparing his own natural and acquired talents with those of his aristocratic patron, and the result could not be other than a dislike of the institutions which placed him so far behind persons whom, but for those prescribed limits, he must have passed in the career of honour and distinction.

Hence arose that frequent and close inquiry into the origin of ranks, that general system of impugning the existing regulations, and appealing to the original states of society in vindication of the original equality of mankind—hence those ingenious arguments, and eloquent tirades in favour of primitive and even savage independence, which the patricians of the day read and applauded with such a smile of mixed applause and pity, as they would have given to the reveries of a crazed poet, while the inferior ranks, participating the feelings under which they were written, caught the ardour of the eloquent authors, and rose from the perusal with minds prepared to act, whenever action should be necessary to realize a vision so flattering.

It might have been expected that those belonging to the privileged classes at least, would have caught the alarm, from hearing doctrines so fatal to their own interests avowed so boldly, and maintained with so much talent. It might have been thought that they would have started, when Raynal proclaimed to the nations of the earth that they could only be free and happy when they had overthrown every throne and every altar;[26] but no such alarm was taken. Men of rank considered liberal principles as the fashion of the day, and embraced them as the readiest mode of showing that they were above vulgar prejudices. In short, they adopted political

---

[25] See his Maximes et Pensées, &c. &c. He died by his own hand in 1794.
[26] Revolution of America, 1781, pp. 44, 58. When, however, Raynal beheld the abuse of liberty in the progress of the French Revolution, he attempted to retrieve his errors. In May, 1791, he addressed to the Constituent Assembly a most eloquent letter, in which he says, "I am, I own to you, deeply afflicted at the crimes which plunge this empire into mourning. It is true that I am to look back with horror at myself for being one of those who, by feeling a noble indignation against ambitious power, may have furnished arms to licentiousness." Raynal was deprived of all his property during the Revolution, and died in poverty in 1796.

opinions as they put on round hats and jockey-coats, merely because they were current in good society. They assumed the tone of philosophers as they would have done that of Arcadian shepherds at a masquerade, but without any more thoughts of sacrificing their own rank and immunities in the one case, than of actually driving their flocks a-field in the other. Count Ségur gives a most interesting account of the opinions of the young French nobles, in which he himself partook at this eventful period.

"Impeded in this light career by the antiquated pride of the old court, the irksome etiquette of the old order of things, the severity of the old clergy, the aversion of our parents to our new fashions and our costumes, which were favourable to the principles of equality, we felt disposed to adopt with enthusiasm the philosophical doctrines professed by literary men, remarkable for their boldness and their wit. Voltaire seduced our imagination; Rousseau touched our hearts; we felt a secret pleasure in seeing that their attacks were directed against an old fabric, which presented to us a Gothic and ridiculous appearance. We were thus pleased at this petty war, although it was undermining our own ranks and privileges, and the remains of our ancient power; but we felt not these attacks personally; we merely witnessed them. It was as yet but a war of words and paper, which did not appear to us to threaten the superiority of existence we enjoyed, consolidated as we thought it, by a possession of many centuries. * * * We were pleased with the courage of liberty, whatever language it assumed, and with the convenience of equality. There is a satisfaction in descending from a high rank, as long as the resumption of it is thought to be free and unobstructed; and regardless, therefore, of consequences, we enjoyed our patrician advantages, together with the sweets of a plebeian philosophy."[27]

We anxiously desire not to be mistaken. It is not the purport of these remarks to blame the French aristocracy for extending their patronage to learning and to genius. The purpose was honourable to themselves, and fraught with high advantages to the progress of society. The favour of the Great supplied the want of public encouragement, and fostered talent which otherwise might never

---

[27] Ségur's Memoirs, vol. i., p. 39.

have produced its important and inappreciable fruits. But it had been better for France, her nobility, and her literature, had the patronage been extended in some manner which did not intimately associate the two classes of men. The want of independence of circumstances is a severe if not an absolute check to independence of spirit; and thus it often happened, that, to gratify the passions of their protectors, or to advance their interest, the men of letters were involved in the worst and most scandalous labyrinths of *tracasserie*, slander, and malignity; that they were divided into desperate factions against each other, and reduced to practise all those arts of dissimulation, flattery, and intrigue, which are the greatest shame of the literary profession.

FRENCH LITERATURE AND PHILOSOPHY

As the eighteenth century advanced, the men of literature rose in importance, and, aware of their own increasing power in a society which was dependent on them for intellectual gratification, they supported each other in their claims to what began to be considered the dignity of a man of letters. This was soon carried into extremes, and assumed, even in the halls of their protectors, a fanatical violence of opinion, and a dogmatical mode of expression, which made the veteran Fontenelle declare himself terrified for the frightful degree of *certainty* that folks met with every where in society. The truth is, that men of letters, being usually men of mere theory, have no opportunity of measuring the opinions which they have adopted upon hypothetical reasoning, by the standard of practical experiment. They feel their mental superiority to those whom they live with, and become habitual believers in, and assertors of, their own infallibility. If moderation, command of passions and of temper, be part of philosophy, we seldom find less philosophy actually displayed, than by a philosopher in defence of a favourite theory. Nor have we found that churchmen are so desirous of forming proselytes, or soldiers of extending conquests, as philosophers in making converts to their own opinions.

In France they had discovered the command which they had acquired over the public mind, and united as they were—and more especially the Encyclopedists,[28]—they augmented and secured that impression, by never permitting the doctrines which they wished to propagate to die away upon the public ear. For this purpose, they took care these should be echoed, like thunder amongst hills, from a hundred different points, presented in a hundred new lights, illustrated by a hundred various methods, until the public could no longer help receiving that as undeniable which they heard from so many different quarters. They could also direct every weapon of satirical hostility against those who ventured to combat their doctrines, and as their wrath was neither easily endured nor pacified, they drove from the field most of those authors, who, in opposition to their opinions, might have exerted themselves as champions of the Church and Monarchy.

We have already hinted at the disadvantages which literature experiences, when it is under the protection of private individuals of opulence, rather than of the public. But in yet another important respect, the air of *salons*, *ruelles* and *boudoirs* is fatal, in many cases, to the masculine spirit of philosophical self-denial which gives dignity to literary society. They who make part of the gay society of a corrupted metropolis, must lend their countenance to follies and vices, if they do not themselves practise them; and hence, perhaps, French literature, more than any other in Europe, has been liable to the reproach of lending its powerful arm to undermine whatever was serious in morals, or hitherto considered as fixed in principle. Some of their greatest authors, even Montesquieu himself, have varied their deep reasonings on the origin of government, and the most profound problems of philosophy, with licentious tales tending to inflame the passions. Hence, partaking of the license of its professors, the degraded literature of modern times called in to its alliance that immorality, which not only Christian, but even heathen philosophy had considered as the greatest obstacle to a pure, wise, and happy state of existence. The licentiousness which walked abroad in such disgusting and undisguised nakedness, was a part of the unhappy bequest left by the Regent Duke of Orleans to the country which he governed. The decorum of the court during the times of Louis XIV. had prevented such excesses; if there was enough of vice, it was at least decently veiled. But the conduct of

---

[28] Diderot, &c., the conductors of the celebrated Encyclopédie.

Orleans and his minions was marked with open infamy, deep enough to have called down, in the age of miracles, an immediate judgment from Heaven; and crimes which the worst of the Roman emperors would have at least hidden in his solitary Isle of Caprea, were acted as publicly as if men had had no eyes, or God no thunderbolts.[29]

From this filthy Cocytus flowed those streams of impurity which disgraced France during the reign of Louis XV., and which, notwithstanding the example of a prince who was himself a model of domestic virtue, continued in that of Louis XVI. to infect society, morals, and, above all, literature. We do not here allude merely to those lighter pieces of indecency in which humour and fancy outrun the bounds of delicacy. These are to be found in the literature of most nations, and are generally in the hands of mere libertines and men of pleasure, so well acquainted with the practice of vice, that the theory cannot make them worse than they are. But there was a strain of voluptuous and seducing immorality which pervaded not only the lighter and gayer compositions of the French, but tinged the writings of those who called the world to admire them as poets of the highest mood, or to listen as to philosophers of the most lofty pretensions. Voltaire, Rousseau, Diderot, Montesquieu,—names which France must always esteem her highest honour,—were so guilty in this particular, that the young and virtuous must either altogether abstain from the works which are every where the topic of ordinary discussion and admiration, or must peruse much that is hurtful to delicacy, and dangerous to morals, in the formation of their future character. The latter alternative was universally adopted; for the curious will read as the thirsty will drink, though the cup and page be polluted.

So far had an indifference to delicacy influenced the society of France, and so widely spread was this habitual impurity of language and ideas, especially among those who pretended to philosophy, that Madame Roland, a woman admirable for courage and talents, and not, so far as appears, vicious in her private morals, not only mentions the profligate novels of Louvet as replete with the graces of imagination, the salt of criticism, and the tone of philosophy, but

---

[29] Lacretelle Hist. de France, tom. i., p. 105; Mémoires de Mad. Du Barry, tom. ii., p. 3.

affords the public, in her own person, details with which a courtezan of the higher class should be unwilling to season her private conversation.[30]

This license, with the corruption of morals, of which it is both the sign and the cause, leads directly to feelings the most inconsistent with manly and virtuous patriotism. Voluptuousness, and its consequences, render the libertine incapable of relish for what is simply and abstractedly beautiful or sublime, whether in literature or in the arts, and destroy the taste, while they degrade and blunt the understanding. But, above all, such libertinism leads to the exclusive pursuit of selfish gratification, for egotism is its foundation and its essence. Egotism is necessarily the very reverse of patriotism, since the one principle is founded exclusively upon the individual's pursuit of his own peculiar objects of pleasure or advantage, while the other demands a sacrifice, not only of these individual pursuits, but of fortune and life itself, to the cause of the public weal. Patriotism has, accordingly, always been found to flourish in that state of society which is most favourable to the stern and manly virtues of self-denial, temperance, chastity, contempt of luxury, patient exertion, and elevated contemplation; and the public spirit of a nation has invariably borne a just proportion to its private morals.

INFIDELITY

Religion cannot exist where immorality generally prevails, any more than a light can burn where the air is corrupted; and, accordingly, infidelity was so general in France, as to predominate in almost every rank of society. The errors of the Church of Rome, as we have already noticed, connected as they are with her ambitious attempts towards dominion over men, in their temporal as well as spiritual capacity, had long become the argument of the philosopher, and the jest of the satirist; but in exploding these pretensions, and holding them up to ridicule, the philosophers of the age involved

---

[30] The particulars we allude to, though suppressed in the second edition of Madame Roland's Mémoires, are restored in the "Collection des Mémoires rélatifs à la Révolution Française," published at Paris, [56 vols. 8vo.] This is fair play; for if the details be disgusting, the light which they cast upon the character of the author is too valuable to be lost.—S.

with them the general doctrines of Christianity itself; nay, some went so far as not only to deny inspiration, but to extinguish, by their sophistry, the lights of natural religion, implanted in our bosoms as a part of our birth-right. Like the disorderly rabble at the time of the Reformation, (but with infinitely deeper guilt,) they not only pulled down the symbols of idolatry, which ignorance or priestcraft had introduced into the Christian Church, but sacrilegiously defaced and desecrated the altar itself. This work the philosophers, as they termed themselves, carried on with such an unlimited and eager zeal, as plainly to show that infidelity, as well as divinity, hath its fanaticism. An envenomed fury against religion and all its doctrines; a promptitude to avail themselves of every circumstance by which Christianity could be misrepresented; an ingenuity in mixing up their opinions in works, which seemed the least fitting to involve such discussions; above all, a pertinacity in slandering, ridiculing, and vilifying all who ventured to oppose their principles, distinguished the correspondents in this celebrated conspiracy against a religion, which, however it may be defaced by human inventions, breathes only that peace on earth, and good will to the children of men, which was proclaimed by Heaven at its divine origin.

If these prejudiced and envenomed opponents had possessed half the desire of truth, or half the benevolence towards mankind, which were eternally on their lips, they would have formed the true estimate of the spirit of Christianity, not from the use which had been made of the mere name by ambitious priests or enthusiastic fools, but by its vital effects upon mankind at large. They would have seen, that under its influence a thousand brutal and sanguinary superstitions had died away; that polygamy had been abolished, and with polygamy all the obstacles which it offers to domestic happiness, as well as to the due education of youth, and the natural and gradual civilisation of society. They must then have owned, that slavery, which they regarded, or affected to regard, with such horror, had first been gradually ameliorated, and finally abolished by the influence of the Christian doctrines—that there was no one virtue teaching to elevate mankind or benefit society, which was not enjoined by the precepts they endeavoured to misrepresent and weaken—no one vice by which humanity is degraded and society endangered, upon which Christianity hath not imposed a solemn anathema. They might also, in their capacity of philosophers, have considered the peculiar aptitude of the Christian religion, not only to all ranks and conditions of mankind, but to all climates and to all stages of society. Nor ought it to have escaped them, that the system contains within itself a key to those difficulties, doubts, and mysteries, by which the human mind is agitated, so soon as it is raised beyond the mere objects which interest the senses. Milton has made the maze of metaphysics, and the bewildering state of mind which they engender, a part of the employment, and perhaps of the punishment, of the lower regions.[31] Christianity alone offers a clew to this labyrinth, a solution to these melancholy and discouraging doubts; and however its doctrines may be hard to unaided flesh and blood, yet explaining as they do the system of the universe, which without them is so incomprehensible, and through their practical influence rendering men in all ages more worthy to act their part in the general plan, it seems wonderful how those, whose professed pursuit was wisdom, should have looked on religion not alone with that indifference, which was the only feeling evinced by the heathen philosophers towards the gross mythology of their time, but with hatred, malice, and all uncharitableness. One would rather have expected, that, after such a review, men professing the real spirit which searches after truth and wisdom, if unhappily they were still unable to persuade themselves that a religion so worthy of the Deity (if such an expression may be used) had emanated directly from revelation, might have had the modesty to lay their finger on their lip and distrust their own judgment, instead of disturbing the faith of others; or, if confirmed in their incredulity, might have taken the leisure to compute at least what was to be gained by rooting up a tree which bore such goodly fruits, without having the means of replacing it by aught which could produce the same advantage to the commonwealth.

Unhappily blinded by self-conceit, heated with the ardour of controversy, gratifying their literary pride by becoming members of a league, in which kings and princes were included, and procuring

---

[31] "Others apart sat on a hill retired, In thoughts more elevate, and reason'd high Of providence, foreknowledge, will, and fate, Fix'd fate, free-will, foreknowledge absolute, And found no end, in wand'ring mazes lost."
Par. Lost, b. ii.

followers by flattering the vanity of some, and stimulating the cupidity of others, the men of the most distinguished parts in France became allied in a sort of anti-crusade against Christianity, and indeed against religious principles of every kind. How they succeeded is too universally known; and when it is considered that these men of letters, who ended by degrading the morals, and destroying the religion of so many of the citizens of France, had been first called into public estimation by the patronage of the higher orders, it is impossible not to think of the Israelitish champion, who, brought into the house of Dagon to make sport for the festive assembly, ended by pulling it down upon the heads of the guests—and upon his own.

We do not tax the whole nation of France with being infirm in religious faith, and relaxed in morals; still less do we aver that the Revolution, which broke forth in that country, owed its rise exclusively to the license and infidelity, which were but too current there. The necessity of a great change in the principles of the ancient French monarchy, had its source in the usurpations of preceding kings over the liberties of the subject, and the opportunity for effecting this change was afforded by the weakness and pecuniary distresses of the present government. These would have existed had the French court, and her higher orders, retained the simple and virtuous manners of Sparta, united with the strong and pure faith of primitive Christians. The difference lay in this, that a simple, virtuous, and religious people would have rested content with such changes and alterations in the constitution of their government as might remove the evils of which they had just and pressing reason to complain. They would have endeavoured to redress obvious and practical errors in the body politic, without being led into extremes either by the love of realising visionary theories, the vanity of enforcing their own particular philosophical or political doctrines, or the selfish arguments of demagogues, who, in the prospect of bettering their own situation by wealth, or obtaining scope for their ambition, aspired, in the words of the dramatic poet, to throw the elements of society into confusion, and thus

"disturb the peace of all the world, To rule it when 'twas wildest."

It was to such men as these last that Heaven, in punishment of the sins of France and of Europe, and perhaps to teach mankind a dreadful lesson, abandoned the management of the French Revolution, the original movements of which, so far as they went to secure to the people the restoration of their natural liberty, and the abolition of the usurpations of the crown, had become not only desirable through the change of times, and by the influence of public opinion, but peremptorily necessary and inevitable.

FEUDAL SYSTEM

The feudal system of France, like that of the rest of Europe, had, in its original composition, all the germs of national freedom. The great peers, in whose hands the common defence was reposed, acknowledged the king's power as *suzerain*, obeyed his commands as their military leader, and attended his courts as their supreme judge; but recognised no despotic authority in the crown, and were prompt to defend the slightest encroachment upon their own rights. If they themselves were not equally tender of the rights and liberties of their own vassals, their acts of encroachment flowed not from the feudal system, but from its imperfections. The tendency and spirit of these singular institutions, were to preserve to each individual his just and natural rights; but a system, almost purely military, was liable to be frequently abused by the most formidable soldier, and was, besides, otherwise ill fitted to preserve rights which were purely civil. It is not necessary to trace the progress from the days of Louis XIII. downwards, by which ambitious monarchs, seconded by able and subtle ministers, contrived to emancipate themselves from the restraints of their powerful vassals, or by which the descendants of these high feudatories, who had been the controllers of the prince so soon as he outstepped the bounds of legitimate authority, were now ranked around the throne in the capacity of mere courtiers or satellites, who derived their lustre solely from the favour of royalty. This unhappy and shortsighted policy had, however, accomplished its end, and the crown had concentrated within its prerogative almost the entire liberties of the French nation; and now, like an overgorged animal of prey, had reason to repent its fatal voracity, while it lay almost helpless, exposed to the assaults of those whom it had despoiled.

We have already observed, that for a considerable time the Frenchman's love of his country had been transferred to the crown; that his national delight in martial glory fixed his attachment upon the monarch as the leader of his armies; and that this feeling had supported the devotion of the nation to Louis XIV., not only during his victories, but even amid his reverses. But the succeeding reign had less to impose on the imagination. The erection of a palace obtains for the nation the praise of magnificence, and the celebration of public and splendid festivals gives the people at least the pleasure of a holiday; the pensioning artists and men of letters, again, is honourable to the country which fosters the arts; but the court of Louis XV., undiminished in expense, was also selfish in its expenditure. The enriching of needy favourites, their relations, and their parasites, had none of the dazzling munificence of the Grand Monarque; and while the taxes became daily more oppressive on the subjects, the mode in which the revenue was employed not only became less honourable to the court, and less creditable to the country, but lost the dazzle and show which gives the lower orders pleasure as the beholders of a pageant.

The consolation which the imagination of the French had found in the military honour of their nation, seemed also about to fail them. The bravery of the troops remained the same, but the genius of the commanders, and the fortune of the monarch under whose auspices they fought, had in a great measure abandoned them, and the destiny of France seemed to be on the wane. The victory of Fontenoy[32] was all that was to be placed in opposition to the numerous disasters of the Seven Years' War, in which France was almost everywhere else defeated; and it was little wonder, that in a reign attended with so many subjects of mortification, the enthusiastic devotion of the people to the sovereign should begin to give way. The king had engrossed so much power in his own person, that he had become as it were personally responsible for every miscarriage and defeat which the country underwent. Such is

---

[32] The battle was fought May 1, 1745, between the French, under Marshal Saxe, and the allies, under William Duke of Cumberland.

the risk incurred by absolute monarchs, who are exposed to all the popular obloquy for maladministration, from which, in limited governments, kings are in a great measure screened by the intervention of the other powers of the constitution, or by the responsibility of ministers for the measures which they advise; while he that has ascended to the actual peak and extreme summit of power, has no barrier left to secure him from the tempest.

Another and most powerful cause fanned the rising discontent, with which the French of the eighteenth century began to regard the government under which they lived. Like men awakened from a flattering dream, they compared their own condition with that of the subjects of free states, and perceived that they had either never enjoyed, or had been gradually robbed of, the chief part of the most valuable privileges and immunities to which man may claim a natural right. They had no national representation of any kind, and but for the slender barrier offered by the courts of justice, or parliaments, as they were called, were subject to unlimited exactions on the sole authority of the sovereign. The property of the nation was therefore at the disposal of the crown, which might increase taxes to any amount, and cause them to be levied by force, if force was necessary. The personal freedom of the citizen was equally exposed to aggressions by *lettres de cachet*.[33] The French people, in short, had neither, in the strict sense, liberty nor property, and if they did not suffer all the inconveniences in practice which so evil a government announces, it was because public opinion, the softened temper of the age, and the good disposition of the kings themselves, did not permit the scenes of cruelty and despotism to be revived in the eighteenth century, which Louis XI. had practised three ages before.

These abuses, and others arising out of the disproportioned privileges of the noblesse and the clergy, who were exempted from contributing to the necessities of the state; the unequal mode of levying the taxes, and other great errors of the constitution; above all, the total absorption of every right and authority in the person of the sovereign,—these were too gross in their nature, and too

---

[33] Private letters or mandates, issued under the royal *signet*, for the apprehension of individuals who were obnoxious to the court.

destructive in their consequences, to have escaped deep thought on the part of reflecting persons, and hatred and dislike from those who suffered more or less under the practical evils.

SUPPRESSION OF FREE DISCUSSION

They had not, in particular, eluded the observation and censure of the acute reasoners and deep thinkers, who had already become the guiding spirits of the age; but the despotism under which they lived prevented those speculations from assuming a practical and useful character. In a free country, the wise and the learned are not only permitted, but invited, to examine the institutions under which they live, to defend them against the suggestions of rash innovators, or to propose such alterations as the lapse of time and change of manners may render necessary. Their disquisitions are, therefore, usefully and beneficially directed to the repair of the existing government, not to its demolition, and if they propose alteration in parts, it is only for the purpose of securing the rest of the fabric. But in France, no opportunity was permitted of free discussion on politics, any more than on matters of religion.

An essay upon the French monarchy, showing by what means the existing institutions might have been brought more into union with the wishes and wants of the people, must have procured for its author a place in the Bastile; and yet subsequent events have shown, that a system, which might have introduced prudently and gradually into the decayed frame of the French government the spirit of liberty, which was originally inherent in every feudal monarchy, would have been the most valuable present which political wisdom could have rendered to the country. The bonds which pressed so heavily on the subject might thus have been gradually slackened, and at length totally removed, without the perilous expedient of casting them all loose at once. But the philosophers, who had certainly talents sufficient for the purpose, were not permitted to apply to the state of the French government the original principles on which it was founded, or to trace the manner in which usurpations and abuses had taken place, and propose a mode by which, without varying its form, those encroachments might be restrained, and those abuses corrected. An author was indeed at liberty to speculate at any length upon general doctrines of government; he might imagine to himself a Utopia or Atalantis, and argue upon abstract ideas of the rights in which government originates; but on no account was he permitted to render any of his lucubrations practically useful, by adapting them to the municipal regulations of France. The political sage was placed, with regard to his country, in the condition of a physician prescribing for the favourite Sultana of some jealous despot, whom he is required to cure without seeing his patient, and without obtaining any accurate knowledge of her malady, its symptoms, and its progress. In this manner the theory of government was kept studiously separated from the practice. The political philosopher might, if he pleased, speculate upon the former, but he was prohibited, under severe personal penalties, to illustrate the subject by any allusion to the latter. Thus, the eloquent and profound work of Montesquieu professed, indeed, to explain the general rights of the people, and the principles upon which government itself rested, but his pages show no mode by which these could be resorted to for the reformation of the constitution of his country. He laid before the patient a medical treatise on disease in general, instead of a special prescription; applying to his peculiar habits and distemper.

In consequence of these unhappy restrictions upon open and manly political discussion, the French government, in its actual state, was never represented as capable of either improvement or regeneration; and while general and abstract doctrines of original freedom were every where the subject of eulogy, it was never considered for a moment in what manner these new and more liberal principles could be applied to the improvement of the existing system. The natural conclusion must have been, that the monarchical government in France was either perfection in itself, and consequently stood in need of no reformation, or that it was so utterly inconsistent with the liberties of the people as to be susceptible of none. No one was hardy enough to claim for it the former character, and, least of all, those who presided in its councils, and seemed to acknowledge the imperfection of the system, by prohibiting all discussion on the subject. It seemed, therefore, to follow, as no unfair inference, that to obtain the advantages which the new elementary doctrines held forth, and which were so desirable and so much desired, a total abolition of the existing government to its very foundation, was an indispensable preliminary; and there is little doubt that this opinion prevailed so generally at the time of the Revolution, as to prevent any firm or resolute stand being made in defence even of such of the actual institutions of France, as might have been amalgamated with the proposed reform.

ANGLOMANIA

While all practical discussion of the constitution of France, as a subject either above or beneath philosophical inquiry, was thus cautiously omitted in those works which pretended to treat of civil rights, that of England, with its counterpoises and checks, its liberal principle of equality of rights, the security which it affords for personal liberty and individual property, and the free opportunities of discussion upon every topic, became naturally the subject of eulogy amongst those who were awakening their countrymen to a sense of the benefits of national freedom. The time was past, when, as in the days of Louis XIV., the French regarded the institutions of the English with contempt, as fit only for merchants and shopkeepers, but unworthy of a nation of warriors, whose pride was in their subordination to their nobles, as that of the nobles consisted in obedience to their king. That prejudice had long passed away, and Frenchmen now admired, not without envy, the noble system of masculine freedom which had been consolidated by the successive efforts of so many patriots in so many ages. A sudden revulsion seemed to take place in their general feelings towards their neighbours, and France, who had so long dictated to all Europe in matters of fashion, seemed now herself disposed to borrow the more simple forms and fashions of her ancient rival. The spirit of imitating the English, was carried even to the verge of absurdity.[34] Not only did Frenchmen of quality adopt the round hat and frock coat, which set etiquette at defiance—not only had they English carriages, dogs, and horses, but even English butlers were hired, that the wine, which was the growth of France, might be placed on the

---

[34] Ségur, tom. i., p. 268; ii., p. 24.

table with the grace peculiar to England.[35] These were, indeed, the mere ebullitions of fashion carried to excess, but, like the foam on the crest of the billow, they argued the depth and strength of the wave beneath, and, insignificant in themselves, were formidable as evincing the contempt with which the French now regarded all those forms and usages, which had hitherto been thought peculiar to their own country. This principle of imitation rose to such extravagance, that it was happily termed the Anglomania.[36]

While the young French gallants were emulously employed in this mimicry of the English fashions, relinquishing the external signs of rank which always produced some effect on the vulgar, men of thought and reflection were engaged in analyzing those principles of the British government, on which the national character has been formed, and which have afforded her the means of rising from so many reverses, and maintaining a sway among the kingdoms of Europe, so disproportioned to her population and extent.

AMERICAN WAR

To complete the conquest of English opinions, even in France herself, over those of French origin, came the consequences of the American War. Those true Frenchmen who disdained to borrow the sentiments of political freedom from England, might now derive them from a country with whom France could have no rivalry, but

---

[35] One striking feature of this Anglomania was the general institution of *Clubs*, and the consequent desertion of female society. "If our happy inconstancy," wrote Baron de Grimm, in 1790, "did not give room to hope that the fashion will not be everlasting, it might certainly be apprehended that the taste for clubs would lead insensibly to a very marked revolution both in the spirit and morals of the nation; but that disposition, which we possess by nature, of growing tired of every thing, affords some satisfaction in all our follies."—*Correspondence.*

[36] An instance is given, ludicrous in itself, but almost prophetic, when connected with subsequent events. A courtier, deeply infected with the fashion of the time, was riding beside the king's carriage at a full trot, without observing that his horse's heels threw the mud into the royal vehicle. "Vous me crottez, monsieur," said the king. The horseman, considering the words were "Vous trottez," and that the prince complimented his equestrian performance, answered, "Oui, sire, à l'Angloise." The good-humoured monarch drew up the glass, and only said to the gentleman in the carriage, "Voilà une Anglomanie bien forte!" Alas! the unhappy prince lived to see the example of England, in her most dismal period, followed to a much more formidable extent.—S.

in whom, on the contrary, she recognised the enemy of the island, in policy or prejudice termed her own natural foe. The deep sympathy manifested by the French in the success of the American insurgents, though diametrically opposite to the interests of their government, or perhaps of the nation at large, was compounded of too many ingredients influencing all ranks, to be overcome or silenced by cold considerations of political prudence. The nobility, always eager of martial distinction, were in general desirous of war, and most of them, the pupils of the celebrated *Encyclopédie*, were doubly delighted to lend their swords to the cause of freedom. The statesmen imagined that they saw, in the success of the American insurgents, the total downfall of the English empire, or at least a far descent from that pinnacle of dignity which she had attained at the Peace of 1763, and they eagerly urged Louis XVI. to profit by the opportunity, hitherto sought in vain, of humbling a rival so formidable. In the courtly circles, and particularly in that which surrounded Marie Antoinette, the American deputation had the address or good fortune to become popular, by mingling in them with manners and sentiments entirely opposite to those of courts and courtiers, and exhibiting, amid the extremity of refinement, in dress, speech, and manners, a republican simplicity, rendered interesting both by the contrast, and by the talents which Benjamin Franklin and Silas Deane evinced, not only in the business of diplomacy, but in the intercourse of society.[37] Impelled by these and other combining causes, a despotic government, whose subjects were already thoroughly imbued with opinions hostile to its constitution in Church and State, with a discontented people, and a revenue wellnigh bankrupt, was thrust, as if by fatality, into a contest conducted upon principles most adverse to its own existence.

The king, almost alone, whether dreading the expense of a ruinous war, whether alarmed already at the progress of democratic principles, or whether desirous of observing good faith with England, considered that there ought to be a stronger motive for war, than barely the opportunity of waging it with success; the king, therefore, almost alone, opposed this great political error. It was not the only occasion in which, wiser than his counsellors, he nevertheless yielded up to their urgency opinions founded in

---

[37] See Ségur, tom. i., p. 101.

unbiassed morality, and unpretending common sense. A good judgment, and a sound moral sense, were the principal attributes of this excellent prince, and happy it would have been had they been mingled with more confidence in himself, and a deeper distrust of others.

Other counsels prevailed over the private opinion of Louis—the war was commenced—successfully carried on, and victoriously concluded. We have seen that the French auxiliaries brought with them to America minds apt to receive, if not already[38] imbued with, those principles of freedom for which the colonies had taken up arms against the mother country, and it is not to be wondered if they returned to France strongly prepossessed in favour of a cause, for which they had encountered danger, and in which they had reaped honour.[39]

The inferior officers of the French auxiliary army, chiefly men of birth, agreeably to the existing rules of the French service, belonged, most of them, to the class of country nobles, who, from causes, already noticed, were far from being satisfied with the system which rendered their rise difficult, in the only profession which their prejudices, and those of France, permitted them to assume. The proportion of plebeians who had intruded themselves, by connivance and indirect means, into the military ranks, looked with eagerness to some change which should give a free and open career to their courage and their ambition, and were proportionally discontented with regulations which were recently adopted, calculated to render their rise in the army more difficult than before.[40] In these sentiments were united the whole of the non-

---

[38] By some young enthusiasts, the assumption of republican habits was carried to all the heights of revolutionary affectation and extravagance. Ségur mentions a young coxcomb, named Mauduit, who already distinguished himself by renouncing the ordinary courtesies of life, and insisting on being called by his Christian and surname, without the usual addition of Monsieur.—S.—"Mauduit's career was short, and his end an unhappy one; for being employed at St. Domingo, he threw himself among a party of revolters, and was assassinated by the negroes."—Ségur.

[39] "The passion for republican institutions infected even the courtiers of the palace. Thunders of applause shook the theatre of Versailles at the celebrated lines of Voltaire—
"Je suis fils de Brutus, et je porte en mon cœur La liberté gravée et les rois en horreur."
Ségur, tom. i., p. 253.

[40] Plebeians formerly got into the army by obtaining the subscription of four men of noble birth, attesting their patrician descent; and such certificates, however false, could always be

commissioned officers, and the ranks of the common soldiery, all of whom, confiding in their own courage and fortune, now became indignant at those barriers which closed against them the road to military advancement, and to superior command. The officers of superior rank, who derived their descent from the high noblesse, were chiefly young men of ambitious enterprise and warm imaginations, whom not only a love of honour, but an enthusiastic feeling of devotion to the new philosophy, and the political principles which it inculcated, had called to arms. Amongst these were Rochambeau, La Fayette, the Lameths, Chastellux, Ségur, and others of exalted rank, but of no less exalted feelings for the popular cause. They readily forgot, in the full current of their enthusiasm, that their own rank in society was endangered by the progress of popular opinions; or, if they at all remembered that their interest was thus implicated, it was with the generous disinterestedness of youth, prompt to sacrifice to the public advantage whatever of selfish immunities was attached to their own condition.

The return of the French army from America thus brought a strong body of auxiliaries to the popular and now prevalent opinions; and the French love of military glory, which had so long been the safeguard of the throne, became intimately identified with that distinguished portion of the army which had been so lately and so successfully engaged in defending the claims of the people against the rights of an established government.[41] Their laurels were green and newly gathered, while those which had been obtained in the cause of monarchy were of an ancient date, and tarnished by the reverses of the Seven Years' War. The reception of the returned soldiery and their leaders was proportionally enthusiastic; and it became soon evident, that when the eventful struggle betwixt the existing monarchy and its adversaries should commence, the latter were to have the support in sentiment, and probably in action, of that distinguished part of the army, which had of late maintained and recovered the military character of France. It was, accordingly, from its ranks that the Revolution derived many of its most

---

obtained for a small sum. But by a regulation of the Count Ségur, after the American war, candidates for the military profession were obliged to produce a certificate of noble birth from the king's genealogist, in addition to the attestations which were formerly held sufficient.—S.

[41] Lacretelle, tom. v., p. 341.

formidable champions, and it was their example which detached a great proportion of the French soldiers from their natural allegiance to the sovereign, which had been for so many ages expressed in their war-cry of "Vive le Roi," and which was revived, though with an altered object, in that of "Vive l'Empereur."

There remains but to notice the other proximate cause of the Revolution, but which is so intimately connected with its rise and progress, that we cannot disjoin it from our brief review of the revolutionary movements to which it gave the first decisive impulse.

Chapter III

Proximate Cause of the Revolution—Deranged State of the Finances—Reforms in the Royal Household—System of Turgot and Necker—Necker's Exposition of the State of the Public Revenue—The Red-Book—Necker displaced—Succeeded by Calonne—General State of the Revenue—Assembly of the Notables—Calonne dismissed—Archbishop of Sens Administrator of the Finances—The King's Contest with the Parliament—Bed of Justice—Resistance of the Parliament and general Disorder in the Kingdom—Vacillating Policy of the Minister—Royal Sitting—Scheme of forming a Cour Plénière—It proves ineffectual—Archbishop of Sens retires, and is succeeded by Necker—He resolves to convoke the States General—Second Assembly of Notables previous to Convocation of the States—Questions as to the Numbers of which the Tiers Etat should consist, and the Mode in which the Estates should deliberate.

We have already compared the monarchy of France to an ancient building, which, however decayed by the wasting injuries of time, may long remain standing from the mere adhesion of its parts, unless it is assailed by some sudden and unexpected shock, the immediate violence of which completes the ruin which the lapse of ages had only prepared. Or if its materials have become dry and combustible, still they may long wait for the spark which is to awake a general conflagration. Thus, the monarchical government of France, notwithstanding the unsoundness of all its parts, might have for some time continued standing and unconsumed, nay, with timely and judicious repairs, might have been entire at this moment, had the state of the finances of the kingdom permitted the monarch to temporize with the existing discontents and the progress of new opinions, without increasing the taxes of a people already greatly overburdened, and now become fully sensible that these burdens were unequally imposed, and sometimes prodigally dispensed.

DERANGEMENT OF THE FINANCES

A government, like an individual, may be guilty of many acts, both of injustice and folly, with some chance of impunity, provided it possess wealth enough to command partisans and to silence opposition; and history shows us, that as, on the one hand, wealthy and money-saving monarchs have usually been able to render themselves most independent of their subjects, so, on the other, it is from needy princes, and when exchequers are empty, that the people have obtained grants favourable to freedom in exchange for their supplies. The period of pecuniary distress in a government, if it be that when the subjects are most exposed to oppression, is also the crisis in which they have the best chance of recovering their political rights.

It is in vain that the constitution of a despotic government endeavours, in its forms, to guard against the dangers of such conjunctures, by vesting in the sovereign the most complete and unbounded right to the property of his subjects. This doctrine, however ample in theory, cannot in practice be carried beyond certain bounds, without producing either privy conspiracy or open insurrection, being the violent symptoms of the outraged feelings and exhausted patience of the subject, which, in absolute monarchies, supply the want of all regular political checks upon the power of the crown. Whenever the point of human sufferance is exceeded, the despot must propitiate the wrath of an insurgent people with the head of his minister, or he may tremble for his own.[42]

In constitutions of a less determined despotical character, there almost always arises some power of check or control, however

---

[42] When Buonaparte expressed much regret and anxiety on account of the assassination of the Emperor Paul, he was comforted by Fouché with words to the following effect:—"Que voulez vous enfin? C'est une mode de destitution propre à ce pais-là!"—S.

anomalous, which balances or counteracts the arbitrary exactions of the sovereign, instead of the actual resistance of the subjects, as at Fez or Constantinople. This was the case in France.

No constitution could have been more absolute in theory than that of France, for two hundred years past, in the matter of finance; but yet in practice there existed a power of control in the Parliaments, and particularly in that of Paris. These courts, though strictly speaking they were constituted only for the administration of justice, had forced themselves, or been forced by circumstances, into a certain degree of political power, which they exercised in control of the crown, in the imposition of new taxes. It was agreed on all hands, that the royal edicts, enforcing such new impositions, must be registered by the Parliaments; but while the crown held the registering such edicts to be an act purely ministerial, and the discharge of a function imposed by official duty, the magistrates insisted, on the other hand, that they possessed the power of deliberating and remonstrating, nay, of refusing to register the royal edicts. The Parliaments exercised this power of control on various occasions; and as their interference was always on behalf of the subject, the practice, however anomalous, was sanctioned by public opinion; and, in the absence of all other representatives of the people, France naturally looked up to the magistrates as the protectors of her rights, and as the only power which could offer even the semblance of resistance to the arbitrary increase of the burdens of the state. These functionaries cannot be charged with carelessness or cowardice in the discharge of their duty; and as taxes increased and became at the same time less productive, the opposition of the Parliaments became more formidable. Louis XIV. endeavoured to break their spirit by suppression of their court, and banishment of its members from Paris; but, notwithstanding this temporary victory, he is said to have predicted that his successor might not come off from the renewed contest so successfully.

Louis XVI., with the plain well-meaning honesty which marked his character, restored the Parliaments to their constitutional powers immediately on his accession to the throne, having the generosity to regard their resistance to his grandfather as a merit rather than an offence. In the meanwhile, the revenue of the kingdom had fallen into a most disastrous condition. The continued and renewed expense of unsuccessful wars, the supplying the demands of a luxurious court, the gratifying hungry courtiers, and enriching needy favourites, had occasioned large deficits upon the public income of each successive year. The ministers, meanwhile, anxious to provide for the passing moment of their own administration, were satisfied to put off the evil day by borrowing money at heavy interest, and leasing out, in security of these loans, the various sources of revenue to the farmers-general. On their part, these financiers used the government as bankrupt prodigals are treated by usurious money-brokers, who, feeding their extravagance with the one hand, with the other wring out of their ruined fortunes the most unreasonable recompense for their advances. By a long succession of these ruinous loans, and the various rights granted to guarantee them, the whole finances of France appear to have fallen into total confusion, and presented an inextricable chaos to those who endeavoured to bring them into order. The farmers-general, therefore, however obnoxious to the people, who considered with justice that their overgrown fortunes were nourished by the life-blood of the community, continued to be essentially necessary to the state, the expenses of which they alone could find means of defraying;—thus supporting the government, although Mirabeau said with truth, it was only in the sense in which a rope supports a hanged man.

Louis XVI., fully sensible of the disastrous state of the public revenue, did all he could to contrive a remedy. He limited his personal expenses, and those of his household, with a rigour which approached to parsimony, and dimmed the necessary splendour of the throne. He abolished many pensions, and by doing so not only disobliged those who were deprived of the instant enjoyment of those gratuities, but lost the attachment of the much more numerous class of expectants, who served the court in the hope of obtaining similar gratifications in their turn.[43] Lastly, he dismissed a

---

[43] Louis XV. had the arts if not the virtues of a monarch. He asked one of his ministers what he supposed might be the price of the carriage in which they were sitting. The minister, making a great allowance for the monarch's paying *en prince*, yet guessed within two-thirds less than the real sum. When the king named the actual price, the statesman exclaimed, but the monarch cut him short. "Do not attempt," he said, "to reform the expenses of my household. There are too many, and too great men, who have their share in

very large proportion of his household troops and body-guards, affording another subject of discontent to the nobles, out of whose families these corps were recruited, and destroying with his own hand a force devotedly attached to the royal person, and which, in the hour of popular fury, would have been a barrier of inappreciable value. Thus, it was the misfortune of this well-meaning prince, only to weaken his own cause and endanger his safety, by those sacrifices intended to relieve the burdens of the people, and supply the wants of the state.

ECONOMICAL REFORMS

The king adopted a broader and more effectual course of reform, by using the advice of upright and skilful ministers, to introduce, as far as possible, some degree of order into the French finances. Turgot,[44] Malesherbes,[45] and Necker,[46] were persons of unquestionable skill, of sound views, and undisputed integrity; and although the last-named minister finally sunk in public esteem, it was only because circumstances had excited such an extravagant opinion of his powers, as could not have been met and realized by those of the first financier who ever lived. These virtuous and patriotic statesmen did all in their power to keep afloat the vessel of the state, and prevent at least the increase of the deficit, which now

---

that extortion, and to make a reformation would give too much discontent. No minister can attempt it with success or with safety." This is the picture of the waste attending a despotic government: the cup which is filled to the very brim cannot be lifted to the lips without wasting the contents.—S.

[44] Turgot was born at Paris in 1727. Called to the head of the Finances in 1774, he excited the jealousy of the courtiers by his reforms, and of the parliaments by the abolition of the corvées. Beset on all sides, Louis, in 1776, dismissed him, observing at the same time, that "Turgot, and he alone, loved the people." Malesherbes said of him, that "he had the head of Bacon, and the heart of L'Hopital." He died in 1781.

[45] Malesherbes, the descendant of an illustrious family, was born at Paris in 1721. When Louis the Sixteenth ascended the throne, he was appointed minister of the interior, which he resigned on the retirement of his friend Turgot. He was called back into public life, at the crisis of the Revolution, to be the legal defender of his sovereign; but his pleadings only procured for himself the honour of perishing on the same scaffold in 1794, together with his daughter and grand-daughter.

[46] Necker was born at Geneva in 1732; he married, in 1764, Mademoiselle Curchod, the early object of Gibbon's affection, and by her had the daughter so celebrated as the Baroness de Staël Holstein. M. Necker settled in Paris, rose into high reputation as a banker, and was first called to office under the government in 1776. He died in 1804.

arose yearly on the public accounts. They, and Necker in particular, introduced economy and retrenchment into all departments of the revenue, restored the public credit without increasing the national burdens, and, by obtaining loans on reasonable terms, were fortunate enough to find funds for the immediate support of the American war, expensive as it was, without pressing on the patience of the people by new impositions. Could this state of matters have been supported for some years, opportunities might in that time have occurred for adapting the French mode of government to the new lights which the age afforded. Public opinion, joined to the beneficence of the sovereign, had already wrought several important and desirable changes. Many obnoxious and oppressive laws had been expressly abrogated, or tacitly suffered to become obsolete, and there never sate a king upon the French or any other throne, more willing than Louis XVI. to sacrifice his own personal interest and prerogative to whatever seemed to be the benefit of the state. Even at the very commencement of his reign, and when obeying only the dictates of his own beneficence, he reformed the penal code of France, which then savoured of the barbarous times in which it had originated—he abolished the use of torture—he restored to freedom those prisoners of state, the mournful inhabitants of the Bastile, and other fortresses, who had been the victims of his grandfather's jealousy—the compulsory labour called the *corvée*,[47] levied from the peasantry, and one principal source of popular discontent, had been abolished in some provinces and modified in others—and while the police was under the regulation of the sage and virtuous Malesherbes, its arbitrary powers had been seldom so exercised as to become the subject of complaint. In short, the monarch partook the influence of public opinion along with his subjects, and there seemed just reason to hope, that, had times remained moderate, the monarchy of France might have been reformed instead of being destroyed.

Unhappily, convulsions of the state became from day to day more violent, and Louis XVI., who possessed the benevolence and good intentions of his ancestor, Henry IV., wanted his military

---

[47] The corvées, or burdens imposed for the maintenance of the public roads, were bitterly complained of by the farmers. This iniquitous part of the financial system was abolished in 1774, by Turgot.

talents, and his political firmness. In consequence of this deficiency, the king suffered himself to be distracted by a variety of counsels; and vacillating, as all must who act more from a general desire to do that which is right, than upon any determined and well-considered system, he placed his power and his character at the mercy of the changeful course of events, which firmness might have at least combated, if it could not control. But it is remarkable, that Louis resembled Charles I. of England more than any of his own ancestors, in a want of self-confidence, which led to frequent alterations of mind and changes of measures, as well as in a tendency to uxoriousness, which enabled both Henrietta Marie, and Marie Antoinette, to use a fatal influence upon their counsels. Both sovereigns fell under the same suspicion of being deceitful and insincere, when perhaps Charles, but certainly Louis, only changed his course of conduct from a change of his own opinion, or from suffering himself to be over-persuaded, and deferring to the sentiments of others.

Few monarchs of any country, certainly, have changed their ministry, and with their ministry their counsels and measures, so often as Louis XVI.; and with this unhappy consequence, that he neither persevered in a firm and severe course of government long enough to inspire respect, nor in a conciliatory and yielding policy for a sufficient time to propitiate regard and confidence. It is with regret we notice this imperfection in a character otherwise so excellent; but it was one of the leading causes of the Revolution, that a prince, possessed of power too great to be either kept or resigned with safety, hesitated between the natural resolution to defend his hereditary prerogative, and the sense of justice which induced him to restore such part of it as had been usurped from the people by his ancestors. By adhering to the one course, he might have been the conqueror of the Revolution; by adopting the other, he had a chance to be its guide and governor; by hesitating between them, he became its victim.

It was in consequence of this vacillation of purpose that Louis, in 1781, sacrificed Turgot and Necker to the intrigues of the court. These statesmen had formed a plan for new-modelling the financial part of the French monarchy, which, while it should gratify the people by admitting representatives on their part to some influence in the imposition of new taxes, might have released the king from the interference of the parliaments, (whose office of remonstrance, although valuable as a shelter from despotism, was often arbitrarily, and even factiously exercised,) and have transferred to the direct representatives of the people that superintendence, which ought never to have been in other hands.

For this purpose the ministers proposed to institute, in the several provinces of France, convocations of a representative nature, one-half of whom was to be chosen from the Commons, or Third Estate, and the other named by the nobles and clergy in equal proportions, and which assemblies, without having the right of rejecting the edicts imposing new taxes, were to apportion them amongst the subjects of their several provinces. This system contained in it much that was excellent, and might have opened the road for further improvements on the constitution; while, at the same time, it would probably, so early as 1781, have been received as a boon, by which the subjects were called to participate in the royal counsels, rather than as a concession extracted from the weakness of the sovereign, or from his despair of his own resources. It afforded also an opportunity, peculiarly desirable in France, of forming the minds of the people to the discharge of public duty. The British nation owe much of the practical benefits of their constitution to the habits with which almost all men are trained to exercise some public right in head-courts, vestries, and other deliberative bodies, where their minds are habituated to the course of business, and accustomed to the manner in which it can be most regularly despatched. This advantage would have been supplied to the French by Necker's scheme.

But with all the advantages which it promised, this plan of provincial assemblies miscarried, owing to the emulous opposition of the Parliament of Paris, who did not choose that any other body than their own should be considered as the guardians of what remained in France of popular rights.

NECKER'S COMPTE RENDU

Another measure of Necker was of more dubious policy. This was the printing and publishing of his Report to the Sovereign of the state of the revenues of France. The minister probably thought this display of candour, which, however proper in itself, was hitherto unknown in the French administration, might be useful to the King, whom it represented as acquiescing in public opinion, and appearing not only ready, but solicitous, to collect the sentiments of his subjects on the business of the state. Necker might also deem the *Compte Rendu* a prudent measure on his own account, to secure the popular favour, and maintain himself by the public esteem against the influence of court intrigue. Or lastly, both these motives might be mingled with the natural vanity of showing the world that France enjoyed, in the person of Necker, a minister bold enough to penetrate into the labyrinth of confusion and obscurity which had been thought inextricable by all his predecessors, and was at length enabled to render to the sovereign and the people a detailed and balanced account of the state of their finances.

Neither did the result of the national balance-sheet appear so astounding as to require its being concealed as a state mystery. The deficit, or the balance, by which the expenses of government exceeded the revenue of the country, by no means indicated a desperate state of finance, or one which must either demand immense sacrifices, or otherwise lead to national bankruptcy. It did not greatly exceed the annual defalcation of two millions, a sum which, to a country so fertile as France, might even be termed trifling. At the same time, Necker brought forward a variety of reductions and economical arrangements, by which he proposed to provide for this deficiency, without either incurring debt or burdening the subject with additional taxes.

But although this general exposure of the expenses of the state, this appeal from the government to the people, had the air of a frank and generous proceeding, and was, in fact, a step to the great constitutional point of establishing in the nation and its representatives the sole power of granting supplies, there may be doubt whether it was not rather too hastily resorted to. Those from whose eyes the cataract has been removed, are for some time deprived of light, and in the end, it is supplied to them by limited degrees; but that glare which was at once poured on the nation of France, served to dazzle as many as it illuminated. The *Compte Rendu* was the general subject of conversation, not only in coffee-houses and public promenades, but in saloons and ladies' boudoirs, and amongst society better qualified to discuss the merits of the last comedy, or any other frivolity of the day. The very array of figures had something ominous and terrible in it, and the word *deficit* was used, like the name of Marlborough of old, to frighten children with.

To most it intimated the total bankruptcy of the nation, and prepared many to act with the selfish and shortsighted license of sailors, who plunder the cargo of their own vessel in the act of shipwreck. Others saw, in the account of expenses attached to the person and dignity of the prince, a wasteful expenditure, which, in that hour of avowed necessity, a nation might well dispense with. Men began to number the guards and household pomp of the sovereign and his court, as the daughters of Lear did the train of their father. The reduction already commenced might be carried, thought these provident persons, yet farther:—

"What needs he five-and-twenty, ten, or five?"

And no doubt some, even at this early period, arrived at the ultimate conclusion,

"What needs ONE?"

Besides the domestic and household expenses of the sovereign, which, so far as personal, were on the most moderate scale, the public mind was much more justly revolted at the large sum yearly squandered among needy courtiers and their dependents, or even less justifiably lavished upon those whose rank and fortune ought to have placed them far above adding to the burdens of the subjects. The king had endeavoured to abridge this list of gratuities and pensions, but the system of corruption which had prevailed for two centuries, was not to be abolished in an instant; the throne, already tottering, could not immediately be deprived of the band of stipendiary grandees whom it had so long maintained, and who afforded it their countenance in return, and it was perhaps impolitic to fix the attention of the public on a disclosure so peculiarly invidious, until the opportunity of correcting it should arrive;—it was like the disclosure of a wasting sore, useless and disgusting unless when shown to a surgeon, and for the purpose of cure. Yet, though the account rendered by the minister of the finances, while it passed from the hand of one idler to another, and occupied on sofas and toilettes the place of the latest novel, did doubtless engage giddy heads in vain and dangerous speculation, something was to be risked in order to pave the way of regaining for the French subjects the right most essential to freemen, that of granting or refusing their own supplies. The publicity of the distressed state of the finances, induced a general conviction that the oppressive system of taxation could only be removed, and that approaching bankruptcy, which was a still greater evil, avoided, by resorting to the nation itself, convoked in their ancient form of representation, which was called the States-General.

It was true that, through length of time, the nature and powers of this body were forgotten, if indeed they had ever been very thoroughly fixed: and it was also true, that the constitution of the States-General of 1614, which was the last date of their being assembled, was not likely to suit a period when the country was so much changed, both in character and circumstances. The doubts concerning the composition of the medicine, and its probable effects, seldom abate the patient's confidence. All joined in desiring the convocation of this representative body, and all expected that such an assembly would be able to find some satisfactory remedy for the pressing evils of the state. The cry was general, and, as usual in such cases, few who joined in it knew exactly what it was they wanted.

TIERS ETAT

Looking back on the period of 1780, with the advantage of our own experience, it is possible to see a chance, though perhaps a doubtful one, of avoiding the universal shipwreck which was fated to ensue. If the royal government, determining to gratify the general wish, had taken the initiative in conceding the great national measure as a boon flowing from the prince's pure good-will and love of his subjects, and if measures had been taken rapidly and decisively to secure seats in these bodies, but particularly in the Tiers Etat, to men known for their moderation and adherence to the monarchy, it seems probable that the crown might have secured such an interest, in a body of its own creation, as would have silenced the attempts of any heated spirits to hurry the kingdom into absolute revolution. The reverence paid to the throne for so many centuries, had yet all the influence of unassailed sanctity; the king was still the master of an army, commanded under him by his nobles, and as yet animated by the spirit of loyalty, which is the natural attribute of the military profession; the minds of men were not warmed at once, and wearied, by a fruitless and chicaning delay, which only showed the extreme indisposition of the court to grant what they had no means of ultimately refusing; nor had public opinion yet been agitated by the bold discussions of a thousand pamphleteers, who, under pretence of enlightening the people, prepossessed their minds with the most extreme ideas of the popular character of the representation of the Tiers Etat, and its superiority over every other power of the state. Ambitious and unscrupulous men would then hardly have had the time or boldness to form those audacious pretensions which their ancestors dreamed not of, and which the course of six or seven years of protracted expectation, and successive renewals of hope, succeeded by disappointment, enabled them to mature.

Such a fatal interval, however, was suffered to intervene, between the first idea of convoking the States-General, and the period when that measure became inevitable. Without this delay, the king, invested with all his royal prerogatives, and at the head of the military force, might have surrendered with a good grace such parts of his power as were inconsistent with the liberal opinions of the time, and such surrender must have been received as a grace, since it could not have been exacted as a sacrifice. The conduct of the government, in the interim, towards the nation whose representatives it was shortly to meet, resembled that of an insane person, who should by a hundred teazing and vexatious insults irritate into frenzy the lion, whose cage he was about to open, and to whose fury he must necessarily be exposed.

STATE OF THE REVENUE

Necker, whose undoubted honesty, as well as his republican candour, had rendered him highly popular, had, under the influence of the old intriguer Maurepas, been dismissed from his office as minister of finance, in 1781. The witty, versatile, selfish, and cunning Maurepas, had the art to hold his power till the last moment of his long life, and died at the moment when the knell of death was a summons to call him from impending ruin.[48] He made, according to an expressive northern proverb, the "day and way alike long;" and died just about the period when the system of evasion and palliation, of usurious loans and lavish bounties, could scarce have served longer to save him from disgrace. Vergennes,[49] who succeeded him, was, like himself, a courtier rather than a statesman; more studious to preserve his own power, by continuing the same system of partial expedients and temporary shifts, than willing to hazard the king's favour, or the popularity of his administration, by attempting any scheme of permanent utility or general reformation. Calonne,[50] the minister of finance, who had succeeded to that office after the brief administrations of Fleury and d'Ormesson, called on by his duty to the most difficult and embarrassing branch of government, was possessed of a more comprehensive genius, and more determined courage, than his principal Vergennes. So early as the year 1784, the deficiency betwixt the receipts of the whole revenues of the state, and the expenditure, extended to six hundred and eighty-four millions of livres, in British money about equal to twenty-eight millions four hundred thousand pounds sterling; but then a certain large portion of this debt consisted in annuities granted by

---

[48] Maurepas was born in 1701. "At the age of eighty, he presented to the world the ridiculous spectacle of caducity affecting the frivolity of youth, and employed that time in penning a sonnet which would more properly have been devoted to correcting a despatch, or preparing an armament." He died in 1781.—See Lacretelle, tom. v., p. 8.
[49] The Count de Vergennes was born at Dijon in 1717. He died in 1787, greatly regretted by Louis, who was impressed by the conviction that, had his life been prolonged, the Revolution would not have taken place.
[50] Calonne was born at Douay in 1734. After being an exile in England, and other parts of Europe, he died at Paris in 1802.

government, which were annually in the train of being extinguished by the death of the holders; and there was ample room for saving, in the mode of collecting the various taxes. So that large as the sum of deficit appeared, it could not have been very formidable, considering the resources of so rich a country; but it was necessary, that the pressure of new burdens, to be imposed at this exigence, should be equally divided amongst the orders of the state. The Third Estate, or Commons, had been exhausted under the weight of taxes, which fell upon them alone, and Calonne formed the bold and laudable design of compelling the clergy and nobles, hitherto exempted from taxation, to contribute their share to the revenues of the state.

This, however, was, in the present state of the public, too bold a scheme to be carried into execution without the support of something resembling a popular representation. At this crisis, again might Louis have summoned the States-General, with some chance of uniting their suffrages with the wishes of the Crown. The King would have found himself in a natural alliance with the Commons, in a plan to abridge those immunities, which the Clergy and Nobles possessed, to the prejudice of The Third Estate. He would thus, in the outset at least, have united the influence and interests of the Crown with those of the popular party, and established something like a balance in the representative body, in which the Throne must have had considerable weight.

Apparently, Calonne and his principal Vergennes were afraid to take this manly and direct course, as indeed the ministers of an arbitrary monarch can rarely be supposed willing to call in the aid of a body of popular representatives. The ministers endeavoured, therefore, to supply the want of a body like the States-General, by summoning together an assembly of what was termed the Notables, or principal persons in the kingdom. This was in every sense an unadvised measure.[51] With something resembling the form of a great national council, the Notables had no right to represent the nation, neither did it come within their province to pass any resolution whatever. Their post was merely that of an extraordinary body of counsellors, who deliberated on any subject which the King might

---

[51] They were summoned on 29th December, 1786, and met on 22d February of the subsequent year.—S.

submit to their consideration, and were to express their opinion in answer to the Sovereign's interrogatories; but an assembly, which could only start opinions and debate upon them, without coming to any effective or potential decision, was a fatal resource at a crisis when decision was peremptorily necessary, and when all vague and irrelevant discussion was, as at a moment of national fermentation, to be cautiously avoided. Above all, there was this great error in having recourse to the Assembly of the Notables, that, consisting entirely of the privileged orders, the council was composed of the individuals most inimical to the equality of taxes, and most tenacious of those very immunities which were struck at by the scheme of the minister of finance.

Calonne found himself opposed at every point and received from the Notables remonstrances instead of support and countenance. That Assembly censuring all his plans, and rejecting his proposals, he was in their presence like a rash necromancer, who has been indeed able to raise a demon, but is unequal to the task of guiding him when evoked. He was further weakened by the death of Vergennes, and finally obliged to resign his place and his country, a sacrifice at once to court intrigue and popular odium. Had this able but rash minister convoked the States-General instead of the Notables, he would have been at least sure of the support of the Third Estate, or Commons; and, allied with them, might have carried through so popular a scheme, as that which went to establish taxation upon a just and equal principle, affecting the rich as well as the poor, the proud prelate and wealthy noble, as well as the industrious cultivator of the soil.

Calonne having retired to England from popular hatred, his perilous office devolved upon the Archbishop of Sens, afterwards the Cardinal de Loménie,[52] who was raised to the painful pre-eminence [May] by the interest of the unfortunate Marie Antoinette, whose excellent qualities were connected with a spirit of state-intrigue, proper to the sex in such elevated situations, which but too frequently thwarted or bore down the more candid intentions of her

---

[52] M. Loménie de Brienne was born at Paris in 1727. On being appointed Prime Minister, he was made Archbishop of Sens, and on retiring from office, in 1788, he obtained a cardinal's hat. He died in prison in 1794.

husband, and tended, though on her part unwittingly, to give his public measures, sometimes adopted on his own principles, and sometimes influenced by her intrigues and solicitations, an appearance of vacillation, and even of duplicity, which greatly injured them both in the public opinion. The new minister finding it as difficult to deal with the Assembly of Notables as his predecessor, the King finally dissolved that body, without having received from them either the countenance or good counsel which had been expected; thus realizing the opinion expressed by Voltaire concerning such convocations:

"De tous ces Etats l'effet le plus commun, Est de voir tous nos maux, sans en soulager un."[53]

BED OF JUSTICE

After dismission of the Notables, the minister adopted or recommended a line of conduct so fluctuating and indecisive, so violent at one time in support of the royal prerogative, and so pusillanimous when he encountered resistance from the newly-awakened spirit of liberty, that had he been bribed to render the crown at once odious and contemptible, or to engage his master in a line of conduct which should irritate the courageous, and encourage the timid, among his dissatisfied subjects, the Archbishop of Sens could hardly, after the deepest thought, have adopted measures better adapted for such a purpose. As if determined to bring matters to an issue betwixt the King and the Parliament of Paris, he laid before the latter two new edicts for taxes,[54] similar in most respects to those which had been recommended by his predecessor Calonne to the Notables. The Parliament refused to register these edicts, being the course which the minister ought to have expected. He then resolved upon a display of the royal prerogative in its most arbitrary and obnoxious form. A Bed of Justice,[55] as it was termed, was held, [Aug. 6,] where the King, presiding in person over the

---

[53] Such Convocations all our ills descry, And promise much, but no true cure apply.
[54] Viz., One on timber, and one on territorial possessions.—See Thiers, vol. i., p. 14.
[55] "Lit de Justice"—the throne upon which the King was seated when he went to the Parliament.

Court of Parliament, commanded the edicts imposing certain new taxes to be registered in his own presence; thus, by an act of authority emanating directly from the Sovereign, beating down the only species of opposition which the subjects, through any organ whatever, could offer to the increase of taxation.

The Parliament yielded the semblance of a momentary obedience, but protested solemnly, that the edict having been registered solely by the royal command, and against their unanimous opinion, should not have the force of a law. They remonstrated also to the Throne in terms of great freedom and energy, distinctly intimating, that they could not and would not be the passive instruments, through the medium of whom the public was to be loaded with new impositions; and they expressed, for the first time, in direct terms, the proposition, fraught with the fate of France, that neither the edicts of the King, nor the registration of those edicts by the Parliament, were sufficient to impose permanent burdens on the people; but such taxation was competent to the States-General only.[56]

In punishment of their undaunted defence of the popular cause, the Parliament was banished to Troyes; the government thus increasing the national discontent by the removal of the principal court of the kingdom, and by all the evils incident to a delay of public justice. The Provincial Parliaments supported the principles adopted by their brethren of Paris. The Chamber of Accounts, and the Court of Aids, the judicial establishments next in rank to that of the Parliament, also remonstrated against the taxes, and refused to enforce them. They were not enforced accordingly; and thus, for the first time, during two centuries at least, the royal authority of France being brought into direct collision with public opinion and resistance, was, by the energy of the subject, compelled to retrograde and yield ground. This was the first direct and immediate movement of that mighty Revolution, which afterwards rushed to its crisis like a rock rolling down a mountain. This was the first torch which was actually applied to the various combustibles which lay scattered through France, and which we have endeavoured to analyze. The flame soon spread into the provinces. The nobles of Brittany broke

---

[56] Mignet, Hist. de la Rev. Française, tom. i., p. 21.

out into a kind of insurrection; the Parliament of Grenoble impugned, by a solemn decree, the legality of *lettres de cachet*. Strange and alarming fears,—wild and boundless hopes,—inconsistent rumours,—a vague expectation of impending events,—all contributed to agitate the public mind. The quick and mercurial tempers which chiefly distinguish the nation, were half maddened with suspense, while even the dull nature of the lowest and most degraded of the community felt the coming impulse of extraordinary changes, as cattle are observed to be disturbed before an approaching thunder-storm.

The minister could not sustain his courage in such a menacing conjuncture, yet unhappily attempted a show of resistance, instead of leaving the King to the influence of his own sound sense and excellent disposition, which always induced him to choose the means of conciliation. There was indeed but one choice, and it lay betwixt civil war or concession. A despot would have adopted the former course, and, withdrawing from Paris, would have gathered around him the army still his own. A patriotic monarch—and such was Louis XVI. when exercising his own judgment—would have chosen the road of concession; yet his steps, even in retreating, would have been so firm, and his attitude so manly, that the people would not have ventured to ascribe to fear what flowed solely from a spirit of conciliation. But the conduct of the minister, or of those who directed his motions, was an alternation of irritating opposition to the public voice, and of ill-timed submission to its demands, which implied an understanding impaired by the perils of the conjuncture, and unequal alike to the task of avoiding them by concession, or resisting them with courage.

The King, indeed, recalled the Parliament of Paris from their exile, coming, at the same time, under an express engagement to convoke the States-General, and leading the subjects, of course, to suppose that the new imposts were to be left to their consideration. But, as if to irritate men's minds, by showing a desire to elude the execution of what had been promised, the minister ventured, in an evil hour, to hazard another experiment upon the firmness of their nerves, and again to commit the dignity of the sovereign by bringing him personally to issue a command, which experience had shown the Parliament were previously resolved to disobey. By this new proceeding, the King was induced to hold what was called a Royal Sitting of the Parliament, which resembled in all its forms a Bed of Justice, except that it seems as if the commands of the monarch were esteemed less authoritative when so issued, than when they were, as on the former occasion, delivered in this last obnoxious assembly.

Thus, at less advantage than before, and, at all events, after the total failure of a former experiment, the King, arrayed in all the forms of his royalty, once more, and for the last time, convoked his Parliament in person; and again with his own voice commanded the court to register a royal edict for a loan of four hundred and twenty millions of francs, to be raised in the course of five years. This demand gave occasion to a debate which lasted nine hours, and was only closed by the King rising up, and issuing at length his positive and imperative orders that the loan should be registered. To the astonishment of the meeting, the first prince of the blood, the Duke of Orleans, arose, as if in reply, and demanded to know if they were assembled in a Bed of Justice or a Royal Sitting; and receiving for answer that the latter was the quality of the meeting, he entered a solemn protest against the proceedings. [Nov. 19.] Thus was the authority of the King once more brought in direct opposition to the assertors of the rights of the people, as if on purpose to show, in the face of the whole nation, that its terrors were only those of a phantom, whose shadowy bulk might overawe the timid, but could offer no real cause of fear when courageously opposed.

The minister did not, however, give way without such an ineffectual struggle, as at once showed the weakness of the royal authority, and the willingness to wield it with the despotic sway of former times. Two members of the Parliament of Paris[57] were imprisoned in remote fortresses, and the Duke of Orleans was sent in exile to his estate.

A long and animated exchange of remonstrances followed betwixt the King and the Parliament, in which the former

---

[57] Freteau and Sabatier. They were banished to the Hières. In 1794, Freteau was sent to the guillotine by Robespierre.

acknowledged his weakness, even by entering into the discussion of his prerogative; as well as by the concessions he found himself obliged to tender. Meantime, the Archbishop of Sens nourished the romantic idea of getting rid of these refractory courts entirely, and at the same time to evade the convocation of the States-General, substituting in their place the erection of a *Cour-plénière*, or ancient Feudal Court, composed of princes, peers, marshals of France, deputies from the provinces, and other distinguished persons, who should in future exercise all the higher and nobler duties of the Parliaments, thus reduced to their original and proper duties as courts of justice.[58] But a court, or council of the ancient feudal times, with so slight an infusion of popular representation, could in no shape have accorded with the ideas which now generally prevailed; and so much was this felt to be the case, that many of the peers, and other persons nominated members of the *Cour-plénière*, declined the seats proposed to them, and the whole plan fell to the ground.

RIOTS AND INSURRECTIONS

Meantime, violence succeeded to violence, and remonstrance to remonstrance. The Parliament of Paris, and all the provincial bodies of the same description, being suspended from their functions, and the course of regular justice of course interrupted, the spirit of revolt became general through the realm, and broke out in riots and insurrections of a formidable description; while, at the same time, the inhabitants of the capital were observed to become dreadfully agitated.

There wanted not writers to fan the rising discontent; and, what seems more singular, they were permitted to do so without interruption, notwithstanding the deepened jealousy with which free discussion was now regarded in France. Libels and satires of every description were publicly circulated, without an attempt on the part of the government to suppress the publications, or to punish their authors, although the most scandalous attacks on the royal family, and on the queen in particular, were dispersed along with these

---

[58] Mignet, tom. i., p. 22; Thiers, tom. i., p. 19.

political effusions. It seemed as if the arm of power was paralyzed, and the bonds of authority which had so long fettered the French people were falling asunder of themselves; for the liberty of the press, so long unknown was now openly assumed and exercised, without the government daring to interfere.[59]

To conclude the picture, as if God and man had alike determined the fall of this ancient monarchy, a hurricane of most portentous and unusual character burst on the kingdom, and laying waste the promised harvest far and wide, showed to the terrified inhabitants the prospect at once of poverty and famine, added to those of national bankruptcy and a distracted government.[60]

The latter evils seemed fast advancing; for the state of the finances became so utterly desperate, that Louis was under the necessity of stopping a large proportion of the treasury payments, and issuing bills for the deficiency. At this awful crisis, fearing for the King, and more for himself, the Archbishop of Sens retired from administration,[61] and left the monarch, while bankruptcy and famine threatened the kingdom, to manage as he might, amid the storms which the measures of the minister himself had provoked to the uttermost.

STATES-GENERAL CONVOKED

A new premier, and a total alteration of measures were to be resorted to, while Necker, the popular favourite, called to the helm of the state, regretted, with bitter anticipation of misfortune, the time which had been worse than wasted under the rule of the archbishop, who had employed it in augmenting the enemies and diminishing the resources of the crown, and forcing the King on such measures as caused the royal authority to be generally regarded

---

[59] De Staël, tom. i., p. 169.
[60] Thiers, tom. i., p. 37.
[61] 25th August, 1788. The archbishop fled to Italy with great expedition, after he had given in his resignation to his unfortunate sovereign.

as the common enemy of all ranks of the kingdom.[62] To redeem the royal pledge by convoking the States-General, seemed to Necker the most fair as well as most politic proceeding; and indeed this afforded the only chance of once more reconciling the prince with the people, though it was now yielding that to a demand, which two years before would have been received as a boon.

We have already observed that the constitution of this assembly of national representatives was little understood, though the phrase was in the mouth of every one. It was to be the panacea to the disorders of the nation, yet men knew imperfectly the mode of composing this universal medicine, or the manner of its operation. Or rather, the people of France invoked the assistance of this national council, as they would have done that of a tutelary angel, with full confidence in his power and benevolence, though they neither knew the form in which he might appear, nor the nature of the miracles which he was to perform in their behalf. It has been strongly objected to Necker, that he neglected, on the part of the crown, to take the initiative line of conduct on this important occasion, and it has been urged that it was the minister's duty, without making any question or permitting any doubt, to assume that mode of convening the states, and regulating them when assembled, which should best tend to secure the tottering influence of his master. But Necker probably thought the time was past in which this power might have been assumed by the crown without exciting jealousy or opposition. The royal authority, he might recollect, had been of late years repeatedly strained, until it had repeatedly given way, and the issue, first of the Bed of Justice, and then of the Royal Sitting, was sufficient to show that words of authority would be wasted in vain upon disobedient ears, and might only excite a resistance which would prove its own lack of power. It was, therefore, advisable not to trust to the unaided exercise of prerogative, but to strengthen instead the regulations which might be adopted for the constitution of the States-General, by the approbation of some public body independent of the King and his ministers. And with this purpose, Necker convened a second

---

[62] When Necker received the intimation of his recall, his first words were, "Ah! why did they not give me those fifteen months of the Archbishop of Sens? Now it is too late."—De Staël, vol. i., p. 157.

meeting of the Notables, [November,] and laid before them, for their consideration, his plan for the constitution of the States-General.

There were two great points submitted to this body, concerning the constitution of the States-General. I. In what proportion the deputies of the Three Estates should be represented? II. Whether, when assembled, the Nobles, Clergy, and Third Estate, or Commons, should act separately as distinct chambers, or sit and vote as one united body?

THE TIERS ETAT

Necker, a minister of an honest and candid disposition, a republican also, and therefore on principle a respecter of public opinion, unhappily did not recollect, that to be well-formed and accurate, public opinion should be founded on the authority of men of talents and integrity; and that the popular mind must be pre-occupied by arguments of a sound and virtuous tendency, else the enemy will sow tares, and the public will receive it in the absence of more wholesome grain. Perhaps, also, this minister found himself less in his element when treating of state affairs, than while acting in his proper capacity as a financier. However that may be, Necker's conduct resembled that of an unresolved general, who directs his movements by the report of a council of war. He did not sufficiently perceive the necessity that the measures to be taken should originate with himself rather than arise from the suggestion of others, and did not, therefore, avail himself of his situation and high popularity, to recommend such general preliminary arrangements as might preserve the influence of the crown in the States-General, without encroaching on the rights of the subject. The silence of Necker leaving all in doubt, and open to discussion, those arguments had most weight with the public which ascribed most importance to the Third Estate. The talents of the Nobles and Clergy might be considered as having been already in vain appealed to in the two sessions of the Notables, an assembly composed chiefly out of the privileged classes, and whose advice and opinion had been given without producing any corresponding good effect. The Parliament had declared themselves incompetent to the measures necessary for the exigencies of the kingdom. The course adopted by the King indicated doubt and uncertainty, if not incapacity. The Tiers Etat, therefore, was the body of counsellors to whom the nation looked at this critical conjuncture.

"What is the Tiers Etat?" formed the title of a pamphlet by the Abbé Siêyes; and the answer returned by the author was such as augmented all the magnificent ideas already floating in men's minds concerning the importance of this order. "The Tiers Etat," said he, "comprehends the whole nation of France, excepting only the nobles and clergy." This view of the matter was so far successful, that the Notables recommended that the Commons, or Third Estate, should have a body of representatives equal to those of the nobles and the clergy united, and should thus form, in point of relative numbers, the moiety of the whole delegates.

This, however, would have been comparatively of small importance, had it been determined that the three estates were to sit, deliberate, and vote, not as a united body, but in three several chambers.

Necker conceded to the Tiers Etat the right of double representation, but seemed prepared to maintain the ancient order of debating and voting by separate chambers. The crown had been already worsted by the rising spirit of the country in every attempt which it had made to stand through its own unassisted strength; and torn as the bodies of the clergy and nobles were by internal dissensions, and weakened by the degree of popular odium with which they were loaded, it would have required an artful consolidation of their force, and an intimate union betwixt them and the crown, to maintain a balance against the popular claims of the Commons, likely to be at once so boldly urged by themselves, and so favourably viewed by the nation. All this was, however, left, in a great measure, to accident, while every chance was against its being arranged in the way most advantageous to the monarchy.

The minister ought also in policy to have paved the way, for securing a party in the Third Estate itself, which should bear some character of royalism. This might doubtless have been done by the usual ministerial arts of influencing elections, or gaining over to the crown-interests some of the many men of talents, who, determined to raise themselves in this new world, had not yet settled to which side they were to give their support. But Necker, less acquainted with men than with mathematics, imagined that every member had intelligence enough to see the measures best calculated for the public good, and virtue enough to follow them faithfully and exclusively. It was in vain that the Marquis de Bouillé[63] pointed out the dangers arising from the constitution assigned to the States-General, and insisted that the minister was arming the popular part of the nation against the two privileged orders, and that the latter would soon experience the effects of their hatred, animated by self-interest and vanity, the most active passions of mankind. Necker calmly replied, that there was a necessary reliance to be placed on the virtues of the human heart;—the maxim of a worthy man, but not of an enlightened statesman,[64] who has but too much reason to know how often both the virtues and the prudence of human nature are surmounted by its prejudices and passions.[65]

It was in this state of doubt, and total want of preparation, that the King was to meet the representatives of the people, whose elections had been trusted entirely to chance, without even an attempt to influence them in favour of the most eligible persons. Yet surely the crown, hitherto almost the sole acknowledged authority in France, should have been provided with supporters in the new authority which was to be assembled. At least the minister might have been prepared with some system or plan of proceeding, upon which this most important convention was to conduct its deliberations; but there was not even an attempt to take up the reins

---

[63] De Bouillé was a native of Auvergne, and a relative of La Fayette. He died in London, in 1800.
[64] See Mémoires de Bouillé. Madame de Staël herself admits this deficiency in the character of a father, of whom she was justly proud.—"Se fiant trop il faut l'avouer, à l'empire de la raison."—S.—("Confiding, it must be admitted, too much in the power of reason.")—*Rev. Franç.*, tom. i., p. 171.
[65] "The concessions of Necker were the work of a man ignorant of the first principles of the government of mankind. It was he who overturned the monarchy, and brought Louis XVI. to the scaffold. Marat, Danton, Robespierre himself, did less mischief to France: he brought on the Revolution, which they consummated."—Napoleon, as reported by *Bourrienne*, tom. viii., p. 108.

which were floating on the necks of those who were for the first time harnessed to the chariot of the state. All was expectation, mere vague and unauthorised hope, that in this multitude of counsellors there would be found safety.[66]

Hitherto we have described the silent and smooth, but swift and powerful, stream of innovation, as it rolled on to the edge of the sheer precipice. We are now to view the precipitate tumult and terrors of the cataract.

---

[66] A *calembourg* of the period presaged a different result.—"So numerous a concourse of state-physicians assembled to consult for the weal of the nation, argued," it was said, "the imminent danger and approaching death of the patient."—S.

CHAPTER IV

Meeting of the States-General—Predominant Influence of the Tiers Etat—Property not represented sufficiently in that Body—General character of the Members—Disposition of the Estate of the Nobles—And of the Clergy—Plan of forming the Three Estates into two Houses—Its advantages—It fails—The Clergy unite with the Tiers Etat, which assumes the title of the National Assembly—They assume the task of Legislation, and declare all former Fiscal Regulations illegal—They assert their determination to continue their Sessions—Royal Sitting—Terminates in the Triumph of the Assembly—Parties in that Body—Mounier—Constitutionalists—Republicans—Jacobins—Orleans.

INFLUENCE OF THE TIERS ETAT

The Estates-General of France met at Versailles on the 5th May, 1789, and that was indisputably the first day of the Revolution. The Abbé Siêyes, in a pamphlet which we have mentioned, had already asked, "What was the Third Estate?—It was *the whole nation.* What had it been hitherto in a political light?—Nothing. What was it about to become presently?—Something." Had the last answer been *Every thing,* it would have been nearer the truth; for it soon appeared that this Third Estate, which, in the year 1614, the Nobles had refused to acknowledge even as a younger brother[67] of their order, was now, like the rod of the prophet, to swallow up all those who affected to share its power. Even amid the pageantry with which the ceremonial of the first sitting abounded, it

---

[67] The Baron de Senneci, when the estates of the kingdom were compared to three brethren, of which the Tiers Etat was youngest, declared that the Commons of France had no title to arrogate such a relationship with the nobles, to whom they were so far inferior in blood, and in estimation.

was clearly visible that the wishes, hopes, and interest of the public, were exclusively fixed upon the representatives of the Commons. The rich garments and floating plumes of the Nobility, and the reverend robes of the Clergy, had nothing to fix the public eye; their sounding and emphatic titles had nothing to win the ear; the recollection of the high feats of the one, and long sanctified characters of the other order, had nothing to influence the mind of the spectators. All eyes were turned on the members of the Third Estate, in a plebeian and humble costume, corresponding to their lowly birth and occupation, as the only portion of the assembly from whom they looked for the lights and the counsels which the time demanded.[68]

It would be absurd to assert, that the body which thus engrossed the national attention was devoid of talents to deserve it. On the contrary, the Tiers Etat contained a large proportion of the learning, the intelligence, and the eloquence of the kingdom; but unhappily it was composed of men of theory rather than of practice, men more prepared to change than to preserve or repair; and, above all, of men, who, generally speaking, were not directly concerned in the preservation of peace and order, by possessing a large property in the country.

The due proportion in which talents and property are represented in the British House of Commons, is perhaps the best assurance for the stability of the constitution. Men of talents, bold, enterprising, eager for distinction, and ambitious of power, suffer no opportunity to escape of recommending such measures as may improve the general system, and raise to distinction those by whom they are proposed; while men of substance, desirous of preserving the property which they possess, are scrupulous in scrutinizing every new measure, and steady in rejecting such as are not accompanied

---

[68] Madame de Staël, and Madame de Montmorin, wife of the Minister for Foreign Affairs, beheld from a gallery the spectacle. The former exulted in the boundless prospect of national felicity which seemed to be opening under the auspices of her father. "You are wrong to rejoice," said Madame de Montmorin; "this event forebodes much misery to France and to ourselves." Her presentiment was but too well founded. She herself perished on the scaffold with one of her sons; her husband was murdered on September 2d; her eldest daughter died in the hospital of a prison, and her youngest died of a broken heart.— See M. de Staël, vol. i., p. 187.

with the most certain prospect of advantage to the state. Talent, eager and active, desires the means of employment; Property, cautious, doubtful, jealous of innovation, acts as a regulator rather than an impulse on the machine, by preventing its either moving too rapidly, or changing too suddenly. The over-caution of those by whom property is represented, may sometimes, indeed, delay a projected improvement, but much more frequently impedes a rash and hazardous experiment. Looking back on the Parliamentary history of two centuries, it is easy to see how much practical wisdom has been derived from the influence exercised by those members called Country Gentlemen, who, unambitious of distinguishing themselves by their eloquence, and undesirous of mingling in the ordinary debates of the house, make their sound and unsophisticated good sense heard and understood upon every crisis of importance, in a manner alike respected by the Ministry and the opposition of the day,—by the professed statesmen of the house, whose daily business is legislation, and whose thoughts, in some instances, are devoted to public affairs, because they have none of their own much worth looking after. In this great and most important characteristic of representation, the Tiers Etat of France was necessarily deficient; in fact, the part of the French constitution, which, without exactly corresponding to the country gentlemen of England, most nearly resembled them, was a proportion of the Rural Noblesse of France, who were represented amongst the Estate of the Nobility. An edict, detaching these rural proprietors, and perhaps the inferior clergy, from their proper orders, and including their representatives in that of the Tiers Etat, would have infused into the latter assembly a proportional regard for the rights of landholders, whether lay or clerical; and as they must have had a voice in those anatomical experiments, of which their property was about to become the subject, it may be supposed they would have resisted the application of the scalpel, excepting when it was unavoidably necessary. Instead of which, both the Nobles and Clergy came soon to be placed on the anatomical table at the mercy of each state-quack, who, having no interest in their sufferings, thought them excellent subjects on which to exemplify some favourite hypothesis.

While owners of extensive landed property were in a great measure excluded from the representation of the Third Estate, its ranks were filled from those classes which seek novelties in theory, and which are in the habit of profiting by them in practice. There were professed men of letters called thither, as they hoped and expected, to realize theories, for the greater part inconsistent with the present state of things, in which, to use one of their own choicest common-places,—"Mind had not yet acquired its due rank." There were many of the inferior branches of the law; for, unhappily, in this profession also the graver and more enlightened members were called by their rank to the Estate of the Noblesse. To these were united churchmen without livings, and physicians without patients; men, whose education generally makes them important in the humble society in which they move, and who are proportionally presumptuous and conceited of their own powers, when advanced into that which is superior to their usual walk. There were many bankers also, speculators in politics, as in their natural employment of stock-jobbing; and there were intermingled with the classes we have noticed some individual nobles, expelled from their own ranks for want of character, who, like the dissolute Mirabeau, a moral monster for talents and want of principle, menaced, from the station which they had assumed, the rights of the order from which they had been expelled, and, like deserters of every kind, were willing to guide the foes to whom they had fled, into the intrenchments of the friends whom they had forsaken, or by whom they had been exiled. There were also mixed with these perilous elements many individuals, not only endowed with talents and integrity, but possessing a respectable proportion of sound sense and judgment; but who, unfortunately, aided less to counteract the revolutionary tendency, than to justify it by argument or dignify it by example. From the very beginning, the Tiers Etat evinced a determined purpose to annihilate in consequence, if not in rank, the other two orders of the state, and to engross the whole power into their own hands.[69]

---

[69] Lacretelle, tom. i., p. 32; Rivarol, p. 37.

VIEWS OF THE NOBLESSE

It must be allowed to the Commons, that the Noblesse had possessed themselves of a paramount superiority over the middle class, totally inconsistent with the just degree of consideration due to their fellow-subjects, and irreconcilable with the spirit of enlightened times. They enjoyed many privileges which were humiliating to the rest of the nation, and others that were grossly unjust, among which must be reckoned their immunities from taxation. Assembled as an estate of the kingdom, they felt the *esprit-de-corps*, and, attached to the privileges of their order, showed little readiness to make the sacrifices which the times demanded, though at the risk of having what they refused to grant, forcibly wrested from them. They were publicly and imprudently tenacious, when, both on principle and in policy, they should have been compliant and accommodating—for their own sake, as well as that of the sovereign. Yet let us be just to that gallant and unfortunate body of men. They possessed the courage, if not the skill or strength of their ancestors, and while we blame the violence with which they clung to useless and antiquated privileges, let us remember that these were a part of their inheritance, which no man renounces willingly, and no man of spirit yields up to threats. If they erred in not adopting from the beginning a spirit of conciliation and concession, no body of men ever suffered so cruelly for hesitating to obey a summons, which called them to acts of such unusual self-denial.

The Clergy were no less tenacious of the privileges of the Church, than the Noblesse of their peculiar feudal immunities. It had been already plainly intimated, that the property of the clerical orders ought to be subject, as well as all other species of property, to the exigencies of the state; and the philosophical opinions which had impugned their principles of faith, and rendered their persons ridiculous instead of reverend, would, it was to be feared, induce those by whom they were entertained, to extend their views to a general seizure of the whole, instead of a part, of the Church's wealth.

Both the first and second estates, therefore, kept aloof, moved by the manner in which the private interests of each stood committed, and both endeavoured to avert the coming storm, by retarding the deliberations of the States-General. They were particularly desirous to secure their individual importance as distinct orders, and appealed to ancient practice and the usage of the year 1614, by which the three several estates sat and voted in three separate bodies. But the Tiers Etat, who, from the beginning, felt their own strength, were determined to choose that mode of procedure by which their force should be augmented and consolidated. The double representation had rendered them equal in numbers to both the other bodies, and as they were sure of some interest among the inferior Noblesse, and a very considerable party amongst the lower clergy, the assistance of these two minorities, added to their own numbers, must necessarily give them the superiority in every vote, providing the three chambers could be united into one.

On the other hand, the clergy and nobles saw that a union of this nature would place all their privileges and property at the mercy of the Commons, whom the union of the chambers in one assembly would invest with an overwhelming majority in that convocation. They had no reason to expect that this power, if once acquired, would be used with moderation, for not only had their actually obnoxious privileges been assailed by every battery of reason and of ridicule, but the records of former ages had been ransacked for ridiculous absurdities and detestable cruelties of the possessors of feudal power, all which were imputed to the present privileged classes, and mingled with many fictions of unutterable horror, devised on purpose to give a yet darker colouring to the system which it was their object to destroy.[70] Every motive, therefore, of self-interest and self-preservation, induced the two first chambers, aware of the possession which the third had obtained over the public mind, to maintain, if possible, the specific individuality of their separate classes, and use the right hitherto supposed to be vested in them, of protecting their own interests by their own separate votes, as distinct bodies.

---

[70] It was, for example, gravely stated, that a seigneur of a certain province possessed a feudal right to put two of his vassals to death upon his return from hunting, and to rip their bellies open, and plunge his feet into their entrails to warm them.—S.

Others, with a deeper view, and on less selfish reasoning, saw much hazard in amalgamating the whole force of the state, saving that which remained in the crown, into one powerful body, subject to all the hasty impulses to which popular assemblies lie exposed, as lakes to the wind, and in placing the person and authority of the King in solitary and diametrical opposition to what must necessarily, in moments of enthusiasm, appear to be the will of the whole people. Such statesmen would have preferred retaining an intermediate check upon the popular counsels of the Tiers Etat by the other two chambers, which might, as in England, have been united into one, and would have presented an imposing front, both in point of wealth and property, and through the respect which, excepting under the influence of extraordinary emotion, the people, in spite of themselves, cannot help entertaining for birth and rank. Such a body, providing the stormy temper of the times had admitted of its foundations being laid sufficiently strong, would have served as a breakwater betwixt the throne and the streamtide of popular opinion; and the monarch would have been spared the painful and perilous task of opposing himself personally, directly, and without screen or protection of any kind, to the democratical part of the constitution. Above all, by means of such an upper house, time would have been obtained for reviewing more coolly those measures, which might have passed hastily through the assembly of popular representatives. It is observed in the history of innovation, that the indirect and unforeseen consequences of every great change of an existing system, are more numerous and extensive than those which had been foreseen and calculated upon, whether by those who advocated, or those who opposed the alteration. The advantages of a constitution, in which each measure of legislation must necessarily be twice deliberately argued by separate senates, acting under different impressions, and interposing, at the same time, a salutary delay, during which heats may subside, and erroneous views be corrected, requires no further illustration.

INFLUENCE OF THE TIERS ETAT

It must be owned, nevertheless, that there existed the greatest difficulty in any attempt which might have been made to give weight to the Nobles as a separate chamber. The community at large looked to reforms deeply affecting the immunities of the privileged classes, as the most obvious means for the regeneration of the kingdom at large, and must have seen with jealousy an institution like an upper house, which placed the parties who were principally to suffer these changes in a condition to impede, or altogether prevent them. It was naturally to be expected, that the Clergy and Nobles, united in an upper house, must have become somewhat partial judges in the question of retrenching and limiting their own exclusive privileges; and, besides the ill-will which the Commons bore them as the possessors and assertors of rights infringing on the liberties of the people, it might be justly apprehended that, if the scourge destined for them were placed in their own hand, they might use it with the chary moderation of the squire in the romance of Cervantes.[71] There would also have been reason to doubt that, when the nation was so much divided by factions, two houses, so different in character and composition, could hardly have been brought to act with firmness and liberality towards each other—that the one would have been ever scheming for the recovery of their full privileges, supposing they had been obliged to surrender a part of them, while the other would still look forward to the accomplishment of an entirely democratical revolution. In this way, the checks which ought to have acted merely to restrain the violence of either party, might operate as the means of oversetting the constitution which they were intended to preserve.

Still, it must be observed, that while the King retained any portion of authority, he might, with the countenance of the supposed upper chamber, or senate, have balanced the progress of democracy. Difficult as the task might be, an attempt towards it ought to have been made. But, unhappily, the King's ear was successively occupied by two sets of advisers, one of whom counselled him to surrender every thing to the humour of the reformers of the state, while the other urged him to resist their most reasonable wishes;—without considering that he had to deal with those who had the power to take by force what was refused to petition. Mounier and Malouet advocated the establishment of two chambers in the Tiers Etat, and Necker was certainly favourable to

---

[71] See Don Quixote, part ii., chap. lxi., (vol. v., p. 296. Lond., 1822.)

some plan of the kind; but the Noblesse thought it called upon them for too great a sacrifice of their privileges, though it promised to ensure what remained, while the democratical part of the Tiers Etat opposed it obstinately, as tending to arrest the march of the revolutionary impulse.

Five or six weeks elapsed in useless debates concerning the form in which the estates should vote; during which period the Tiers Etat showed, by their boldness and decision, that they knew the advantage which they held, and were sensible that the other bodies, if they meant to retain the influence of their situation in any shape, must unite with them, on the principle according to which smaller drops of water are attracted by the larger. This came to pass accordingly. The Tiers Etat were joined by the whole body of inferior clergy, and by some of the nobles, and on 17th June, 1789, proceeded to constitute themselves a legislative body, exclusively competent in itself to the entire province of legislation; and, renouncing the name of the Third Estate, which reminded men they were only one out of three bodies, they adopted[72] that of the National Assembly, and avowed themselves not merely the third branch of the representative body, but the sole representatives of the people of France, nay, the people themselves, wielding in person the whole gigantic powers of the realm. They now claimed the character of a supreme body, no longer limited to the task of merely requiring a redress of grievances, for which they had been originally appointed, but warranted to destroy and rebuild whatever they thought proper in the constitution of the state. It is not easy, on any ordinary principle, to see how a representation, convoked for a certain purpose, and with certain limited powers, should thus essentially alter their own character, and set themselves in such a different relation to the crown and the nation, from that to which their commissions restricted them; but the National Assembly were well aware, that, in extending their powers far beyond the terms of these commissions, they only fulfilled the wishes of their constituents, and that, in assuming to themselves so ample an authority, they would be supported by the whole nation, excepting the privileged orders.

---

[72] "By a majority of 491 to 90."—Lacretelle.

The National Assembly proceeded to exercise their power with the same audacity which they had shown in assuming it. They passed a sweeping decree, by which they declared all the existing taxes to be illegal impositions, the collection of which they sanctioned only for the present, and as an interim arrangement, until they should have time to establish the financial regulations of the state upon an equal and permanent footing.[73]

ROYAL SITTING

The King, acting under the advice of Necker, and fulfilling the promise made on his part by the Archbishop of Sens, his former minister, had, as we have seen, assembled the States-General; but he was not prepared for the change of the Third Estate into the National Assembly, and for the pretensions which it asserted in the latter character. Terrified, and it was little wonder, at the sudden rise of this gigantic and all-overshadowing fabric, Louis became inclined to listen to those who counselled him to combat this new and formidable authority, by opposing to it the weight of royal power; to be exercised, however, with such attention to the newly-asserted popular opinions, and with such ample surrender of the obnoxious part of the royal prerogative, as might gratify the rising spirit of freedom. For this purpose a Royal Sitting was appointed, at which the King in person was to meet the three estates of his kingdom, and propose a scheme which, it was hoped, might unite all parties, and tranquillize all minds. The name and form of this *Séance Royale* was perhaps not well chosen, as being too nearly allied to those of a Bed of Justice, in which the King was accustomed to exercise imperative authority over the Parliament; and the proceeding was calculated to awaken recollection of the highly unpopular Royal Sitting of the 19th November, 1787, the displacing of Necker, and the banishment of the Duke of Orleans.

But, as if this had not been sufficient, an unhappy accident, which almost resembled a fatality, deranged this project, destroyed all the grace which might, on the King's part, have attended the measure, and in place of it, threw upon the court the odium of

---

[73] Lacretelle, tom. vii., p. 39.

having indirectly attempted the forcible dissolution of the Assembly, while it invested the members of that body with the popular character of steady patriots, whose union, courage, and presence of mind, had foiled the stroke of authority which had been aimed at their existence.

The hall of the Commons was fixed upon for the purposes of the Royal Sitting, as the largest of the three which were occupied by the three estates, and workmen were employed in making the necessary arrangements and alterations. These alterations were imprudently commenced, [June 20,] before holding any communication on the subject with the National Assembly; and it was simply notified to their president, Bailli, by the master of the royal ceremonies, that the King had suspended the meeting of the Assembly until the Royal Sitting should have taken place. Bailli, the president, well known afterwards by his tragical fate, refused to attend to an order so intimated, and the members of Assembly, upon resorting to their ordinary place of meeting, found it full of workmen, and guarded by soldiers. This led to one of the most extraordinary scenes of the Revolution.

The representatives of the nation, thus expelled by armed guards from their proper place of assemblage, found refuge in a common Tennis-court, while a thunder-storm, emblem of the moral tempest which raged on the earth, poured down its terrors from the heavens. It was thus that, exposed to the inclemency of the weather, and with the wretched accommodations which such a place afforded, the members of Assembly took, and attested by their respective signatures, a solemn oath, "to continue their sittings until the constitution of the kingdom, and the regeneration of the public order, should be established on a solid basis."[74] The scene was of a kind to make the deepest impression both on the actors and the spectators; although, looking back at the distance of so many years, we are tempted to ask, at what period the National Assembly would have been dissolved, had they adhered literally to their celebrated oath? But the conduct of the government was, in every respect, worthy of censure. The probability of this extraordinary occurrence might easily have been foreseen. If mere want of consideration gave

---

[74] Lacretelle, tom. vii., p. 41.

rise to it, the King's ministers were most culpably careless; if the closing of the hall, and suspending of the sittings of the Assembly, was intended by way of experiment upon its temper and patience, it was an act of madness equal to that of irritating an already exasperated lion. Be this, however, as it may, the conduct of the court had the worst possible effect on the public mind, and prepared them to view with dislike and suspicion all propositions emanating from the throne; while the magnanimous firmness and unanimity of the Assembly seemed that of men determined to undergo martyrdom, rather than desert the assertion of their own rights, and those of the people.

At the Royal Sitting, which took place three days after the vow of the Tennis-Court, a plan was proposed by the King, offering such security for the liberty of the subject, as would, a year before, have been received with grateful rapture; but it was the unhappy fate of Louis XVI. neither to recede nor advance at the fortunate moment. Happy would it have been for him, for France, and for Europe, if the science of astrology, once so much respected, had in reality afforded the means of selecting lucky days. Few of his were marked with a white stone.

CONCESSIONS OF THE KING

By the scheme which he proposed, the King renounced the power of taxation, and the right of borrowing money, except to a trifling extent, without assent of the States-General; he invited the Assembly to form a plan for regulating *lettres de cachet*, and acknowledged the personal freedom of the subject; he provided for the liberty of the press, but not without a recommendation that some check should be placed upon its license; and he remitted to the States, as the proper authority, the abolition of the *gabelle*,[75] and other unequal or oppressive taxes.

But all these boons availed nothing, and seemed, to the people and their representatives, but a tardy and ungracious mode of

---

[75] The government monopoly of salt, under the name of the *gabelle*, was maintained over about two-thirds of the kingdom.

resigning rights which the crown had long usurped, and only now restored when they were on the point of being wrested from its gripe. In addition to this, offence was taken at the tone and terms adopted in the royal address. The members of the Assembly conceived, that the expression of the royal will was brought forward in too imperative a form. They were offended that the King should have recommended the exclusion of spectators from the sittings of the Assembly; and much displeasure was occasioned by his declaring, thus late, their deliberations and decrees on the subject of taxes illegal. But the discontent was summed up and raised to the height by the concluding article of the royal address, in which, notwithstanding their late declarations, and oath not to break up their sittings until they had completed a constitution for France, the King presumed, by his own sole authority, to dissolve the estates.[76] To conclude, Necker, upon whom alone among the ministers the popular party reposed confidence, had absented himself from the Royal Sitting, and thereby intimated his discontent with the scheme proposed.[77]

This plan of a constitutional reformation was received with great applause by the Clergy and the Nobles, while the Third Estate listened in sullen silence. They knew little of the human mind, who supposed that the display of prerogative, which had been so often successfully resisted, could influence such a body, or induce them to descend from the station of power which they had gained, and to render themselves ridiculous by rescinding the vow which they had so lately taken.

The King having, by his own proper authority, dissolved the Assembly, left the hall, followed by the Nobles and part of the Clergy; but the remaining members, hitherto silent and sullen, immediately resumed their sitting. The King, supposing him resolute to assert the prerogative which his own voice had but just claimed, had no alternative but that of expelling them by force, and thus supporting his order for dissolution of the Assembly; but, always

---

[76] Mignet, tom. i., p. 43.
[77] "The evening before, he had tendered his resignation, which was not accepted, as the measures adopted by the court were not such as he thoroughly approved."—Lacretelle, tom. vii., p. 47.

halting between two opinions, Louis employed no rougher means of removing them than a gentle summons to disperse, intimated by the royal master of ceremonies. To this officer, not certainly the most formidable satellite of arbitrary power, Mirabeau replied with energetic determination,—"Slave! return to thy master, and tell him, that his bayonets alone can drive from their post the representatives of the people."

The Assembly then, on the motion of Camus, proceeded to pass a decree, that they adhered to their oath taken in the Tennis-court; while by another they declared, that their own persons were inviolable, and that whoever should attempt to execute any restraint or violence upon a representative of the people, should be thereby guilty of the crime of high treason against the nation.

Their firmness, joined to the inviolability with which they had invested themselves, and the commotions which had broken out at Paris, compelled the King to give way, and renounce his purpose of dissolving the states, which continued their sittings under their new title of the National Assembly; while at different intervals, and by different manœuvres, the Chambers of the Clergy and Nobles were united with them, or, more properly, were merged and absorbed in one general body. Had that Assembly been universally as pure in its intentions as we verily believe to have been the case with many or most of its members, the French government, now lying dead at their feet, might, like the clay of Prometheus, have received new animation from their hand.

But the National Assembly, though almost unanimous in resisting the authority of the crown, and in opposing the claims of the privileged classes, was much divided respecting ulterior views, and carried in its bosom the seeds of internal dissension, and the jarring elements of at least FOUR parties, which had afterwards their successive entrance and exit on the revolutionary stage; or rather, one followed the other like successive billows, each obliterating and destroying the marks its predecessor had left on the beach.

PARTIES OF THE ASSEMBLY

The First and most practical division of these legislators, was the class headed by Mounier,[78] one of the wisest, as well as one of the best and worthiest men in France,—by Malouet,[79] and others. They were patrons of a scheme at which we have already hinted, and they thought France ought to look for some of the institutions favourable to freedom, to England, whose freedom had flourished so long. To transplant the British oak, with all its contorted branches and extended roots, would have been a fruitless attempt, but the infant tree of liberty might have been taught to grow after the same fashion. Modern France, like England of old, might have retained such of her own ancient laws, forms, or regulations, as still were regarded by the nation with any portion of respect, intermingling them with such additions and alterations as were required by the liberal spirit of modern times, and the whole might have been formed on the principles of British freedom. The nation might thus, in building its own bulwarks, have profited by the plan of those which had so long resisted the tempest. It is true, the French legislature could not have promised themselves, by the adoption of this course, to form at once a perfect and entire system; but they might have secured the personal freedom of the subject, the trial by jury, the liberty of the press, and the right of granting or withholding the supplies necessary for conducting the state,—of itself the strongest of all guarantees for national freedom, and that of which, when once vested in their own representatives, the people will never permit them to be deprived. They might have adopted also other checks, balances, and controls, essential to the permanence of a free country; and having laid so strong a foundation, there would have been time to experience their use as well as their stability, and to introduce gradually such further improvements, additions, or alterations, as the state of France should appear to require, after experience of those which they had adopted.

---

[78] Mounier was born at Grenoble in 1758. He quitted France in 1790, but returned in 1802. He afterwards became one of Napoleon's counsellors of state in 1806.
[79] Malouet was born at Riom in 1740. To escape the massacres of September, 1790, he fled to England; but returned to France in 1801, and, in 1810, was appointed one of Napoleon's counsellors of state. He died in 1814.

But besides that the national spirit might be revolted,—not unnaturally, however unwisely,—at borrowing the essential peculiarities of their new constitution from a country which they were accustomed to consider as the natural rival of their own, there existed among the French a jealousy of the crown, and especially of the privileged classes, with whom they had been so lately engaged in political hostility, which disinclined the greater part of the Assembly to trust the King with much authority, or the nobles with that influence which any imitation of the English constitution must have assigned to them. A fear prevailed, that whatever privileges should be left to the King or nobles, would be so many means of attack furnished to them against the new system. Joined to this was the ambition of creating at once, and by their own united wisdom, a constitution as perfect as the armed personification of wisdom in the heathen mythology. England had worked her way, from practical reformation of abuses, into the adoption of general maxims of government. It was reserved, thought most of the National Assembly, for France, to adopt a nobler and more intellectual course, and, by laying down abstract doctrines of public right, to deduce from these their rules of practical legislation;—just as it is said, that in the French naval yards their vessels are constructed upon the principles of abstract mathematics, while those in England are, or were, chiefly built upon the more technical and mechanical rules.[80] But it seems on this and other occasions to have escaped these acute reasoners, that beams and planks are subject to certain unalterable natural laws, while man is, by the various passions acting in his nature, in contradiction often to the suggestions of his understanding, as well as by the various modifications of society, liable to a thousand variations, all of which call for limitations and exceptions qualifying whatever general maxims may be adopted concerning his duties and his rights.

All such considerations were spurned by the numerous body of the new French legislature, who resolved, in imitation of Medea, to fling into their renovating kettle every existing joint and member

---

[80] "Abstract science will not enable a man to become a ship-wright. The French are perhaps the worst ship-wrights in all Europe, but they are confessedly among the first and best theorists in naval architecture, and it is one of those unaccountable phenomena in the history of man, that they never attempted to combine the two. Happily the English have hit upon that expedient."—Barrow.

of their old constitution, in order to its perfect and entire renovation. This mode of proceeding was liable to three great objections. *First*, That the practical inferences deduced from the abstract principle were always liable to challenge by those, who, in logical language, denied the minor of the proposition, or asserted that the conclusion was irregularly deduced from the premises. *Secondly*, That the legislators, thus grounding the whole basis of their intended constitution upon speculative political opinions, strongly resembled the tailors of Laputa, who, without condescending to take measure of their customers, like brethren of the trade elsewhere, took the girth and altitude of the person by mathematical calculation, and if the clothes did not fit, as was almost always the case, thought it ample consolation for the party concerned to be assured, that, as they worked from infallible rules of art, the error could only be occasioned by his own faulty and irregular conformation of figure. *Thirdly*, A legislature which contents itself with such a constitution as is adapted to the existing state of things, may hope to attain their end, and in presenting it to the people, may be entitled to say, that, although the plan is not perfect, it partakes in that but of the nature of all earthly institutions, while it comprehends the elements of as much good as the actual state of society permits; but from the lawmakers, who begin by destroying all existing enactments, and assume it as their duty entirely to renovate the constitution of a country, nothing short of absolute perfection can be accepted. They can shelter themselves under no respect to ancient prejudices which they have contradicted, or to circumstances of society which they have thrown out of consideration. They must follow up to the uttermost the principle they have adopted, and their institutions can never be fixed or secure from the encroachments of succeeding innovators, while they retain any taint of that fallibility to which all human inventions are necessarily subject.

The majority of the French Assembly entertained, nevertheless, the ambitious view of making a constitution, corresponding in every respect to those propositions they had laid down as embracing the rights of man, which, if it should not happen to suit the condition of their country, would nevertheless be such as *ought* to have suited it, but for the irregular play of human passions, and the artificial habits acquired in an artificial state of society. But this majority differed among themselves in this essential particular, that the SECOND division of the legislature, holding that of Mounier for the first, was disposed to place at the head of their newly-manufactured government the reigning King, Louis XVI. This resolution in his favour might be partly out of regard to the long partiality of the nation to the House of Bourbon, partly out of respect for the philanthropical and accommodating character of Louis. We may conceive also, that La Fayette, bred a soldier, and Bailli, educated a magistrate, had still, notwithstanding their political creed, a natural though unphilosophical partiality to their well-meaning and ill-fated sovereign, and a conscientious desire to relax, so far as his particular interest was concerned, their general rule of reversing all that had previously had a political existence in France.

REPUBLICANS

A THIRD faction, entertaining the same articles of political creed with La Fayette, Bailli, and others, carried them much farther, and set at defiance the scruples which limited the two first parties in their career of reformation. These last agreed with La Fayette on the necessity of reconstructing the whole government upon a new basis, without which entire innovation, they further agreed with him, that it must have been perpetually liable to the chance of a counter-revolution. But carrying their arguments farther than the Constitutional party, as the followers of Fayette, these bolder theorists pleaded the inconsistency and danger of placing at the head of their new system of reformed and regenerated government, a prince accustomed to consider himself, as by inheritance, the legitimate possessor of absolute power. They urged that, like the snake and peasant in the fable, it was impossible that the monarch and his democratical counsellors could forget, the one the loss of his power, the other the constant temptation which must beset the King to attempt its recovery. With more consistency, therefore, than the Constitutionalists, this third party of politicians became decided Republicans, determined upon obliterating from the new constitution every name and vestige of monarchy.

The men of letters in the Assembly were, many of them, attached to this faction. They had originally been kept in the background by the lawyers and mercantile part of the Assembly. Many of them possessed great talents, and were by nature men of honour and of virtue. But in great revolutions, it is impossible to resist the dizzying effect of enthusiastic feeling and excited passion. In the violence of their zeal for the liberty of France, they too frequently adopted the maxim, that so glorious an object sanctioned almost any means which could be used to attain it. Under the exaggerated influence of a mistaken patriotism, they were too apt to forget that a crime remains the same in character, even when perpetrated in a public cause.[81]

It was among these ardent men that first arose the idea of forming a Club, or Society, to serve as a point of union for those who entertained the same political sentiments. Once united, they rendered their sittings public, combined them with affiliated societies in all parts of France, and could thus, as from one common centre, agitate the most remote frontiers with the passionate feelings which electrified the metropolis. This formidable weapon was, in process of time, wrested out of the hands of the Federalists, as the original Republicans were invidiously called, by the faction who were generally termed Jacobins, from their influence in that society, and whose existence and peculiarities as a party, we have now to notice.

---

[81] A singular instance of this overstrained and dangerous enthusiasm is given by Madame Roland. [Memoirs, part i., p. 144.] It being the purpose to rouse the fears and spirit of the people, and direct their animosity against the court party, Grangeneuve agreed that he himself should be murdered, by persons chosen for the purpose, in such a manner that the suspicion of the crime should attach itself to the aristocrats. He went to the place appointed, but Chabot, who was to have shared his fate, neither appeared himself, nor had made the necessary preparations for the assassination of his friend, for which Madame Roland, that high-spirited republican, dilates upon his poltroonery. Yet, what was this patriotic devotion, save a plan to support a false accusation against the innocent, by an act of murder and suicide, which, if the scheme succeeded, was to lead to massacre and proscription? The same false, exaggerated, and distorted views of the public good centering, as it seemed to them, in the establishment of a pure republic, led Barnave and others to palliate the massacres of September. Most of them might have said of the Liberty which they had worshipped, that at their death they found it an empty name.—S.

JACOBINS

As yet this FOURTH, and, as it afterwards proved, most formidable party, lurked in secret among the Republicans of a higher order and purer sentiments, as they, on their part, had not yet raised the mask, or ventured to declare openly against the plan of a constitutional monarchy. The Jacobins[82] were termed, in ridicule, *Les Enragès*, by the Republicans, who, seeing in them only men of a fiery disposition, and violence of deportment and declamation, vainly thought they could halloo them on, and call them off, at their pleasure. They were yet to learn, that when force is solemnly appealed to, the strongest and most ferocious, as they must be foremost in the battle, will not lose their share of the spoil, and are more likely to make the lion's partitions. These Jacobins affected to carry the ideas of liberty and equality to the most extravagant lengths, and were laughed at and ridiculed in the Assembly as a sort of fanatics, too absurd to be dreaded. Their character, indeed, was too exaggerated, their habits too openly profligate, their manners too abominably coarse, their schemes too extravagantly violent, to be produced in open day, while yet the decent forms of society were observed. But they were not the less successful in gaining the lower classes, whose cause they pretended peculiarly to espouse, whose passions they inflamed by an eloquence suited to such hearers, and whose tastes they flattered by affectation of brutal manners and vulgar dress. They soon, by these arts, attached to themselves a large body of followers, violently inflamed with the prejudices which had been infused into their minds, and too boldly desperate to hesitate at any measures which should be recommended by their demagogues. What might be the ultimate object of these men cannot be known. We can hardly give any of them credit for being mad enough to have any real patriotic feeling, however extravagantly distorted. Most probably, each had formed some vague prospect of terminating the affair to his own advantage; but, in the meantime, all agreed in the necessity of sustaining the revolutionary impulse, of deferring the return of quiet, and of resisting and deranging any description of orderly and peaceful government. They were sensible that the return

---

[82] So called, because the first sittings of the Club were held in the ancient convent of the Jacobins.

of law, under any established and regular form whatever, must render them as contemptible as odious, and were determined to avail themselves of the disorder while it lasted, and to snatch at and enjoy such portions of the national wreck as the tempest might throw within their individual reach.

This foul and desperate faction could not, by all the activity it used, have attained the sway which it exerted amongst the lees of the people, without possessing and exercising extensively the power of suborning inferior leaders among the populace. It has been generally asserted, that means for attaining this important object were supplied by the immense wealth of the nearest prince of the blood royal, that Duke of Orleans, whose name is so unhappily mixed with the history of this period. By his largesses, according to the general report of historians, a number of the most violent writers of pamphlets and newspapers were pensioned, who deluged the public with false news and violent abuse. This prince, it is said, recompensed those popular and ferocious orators, who nightly harangued the people in the Palais Royal, and openly stimulated them to the most violent aggressions upon the persons and property of obnoxious individuals. From the same unhappy man's coffers were paid numbers of those who regularly attended on the debates of the Assembly, crowded the galleries to the exclusion of the public at large, applauded, hissed, exercised an almost domineering influence in the national councils, and were sometimes addressed by the representatives of the people, as if they had themselves been the people of whom they were the scum and the refuse.

Fouler accusations even than these charges were brought forward. Bands of strangers, men of wild, haggard, and ferocious appearance, whose persons the still watchful police of Paris were unacquainted with, began to be seen in the metropolis, like those obscene and ill-omened birds which are seldom visible except before a storm. All these were understood to be suborned by the Duke of Orleans and his agents, to unite with the ignorant, violent, corrupted populace of the great metropolis of France, for the purpose of urging and guiding them to actions of terror and cruelty. The ultimate object of these manœuvres is supposed to have been a change of dynasty, which should gratify the Duke of Orleans's revenge by the deposition of his cousin, and his ambition by enthroning himself in his stead, or at least by nominating him Lieutenant of France, with all the royal powers. The most daring and unscrupulous amongst the Jacobins are said originally to have belonged to the faction of Orleans; but as he manifested a want of decision, and did not avail himself of opportunities of pushing his fortune, they abandoned their leader, (whom they continued, however, to flatter and deceive,) and, at the head of the partisans collected for his service, and paid from his finances, they pursued the path of their individual fortunes.

Besides the various parties which we have detailed, and which gradually developed their discordant sentiments as the Revolution proceeded, the Assembly contained the usual proportion of that prudent class of politicians who are guided by events, and who, in the days of Cromwell, called themselves "Waiters upon Providence;"—men who might boast, with the miller in the tale, that though they could not direct the course of the wind, they could adjust their sails so as to profit by it, blow from what quarter it would.

All the various parties in the Assembly, by whose division the King might, by temporizing measures, have surely profited, were united in a determined course of hostility to the crown and its pretensions, by the course which Louis XVI. was unfortunately advised to pursue. It had been resolved to assume a menacing attitude, and to place the King at the head of a strong force. Orders were given accordingly.

TREACHERY OF THE ARMY

Necker, though approving of many parts of the proposal made to the Assembly at the Royal Sitting, had strongly dissented from others, and had opposed the measure of marching troops towards Versailles and Paris to overawe the capital, and, if necessary, the National Assembly. Necker received his dismission,[83] and thus a

---

[83] July 11. "The formal command to quit the kingdom was accompanied by a note from the King, in which he prayed him to depart in a private manner, for fear of exciting

second time the King and the people seemed to be prepared for open war. The force at first glance seemed entirely on the royal side. Thirty regiments were drawn around Paris and Versailles, commanded by Marshal Broglio,[84] an officer of eminence, and believed to be a zealous anti-revolutionist, and a large camp formed under the walls of the metropolis. The town was opened on all sides, and the only persons by whom defence could be offered were an unarmed mob; but this superiority existed only in appearance. The French Guards had already united themselves, or, as the phrase then went, *fraternized* with the people, yielding to the various modes employed to dispose them to the popular cause; and little attached to their officers, most of whom only saw their companies upon the days of parade or duty, an apparent accident, which probably had its origin in an experiment upon the feelings of these regiments, brought the matter to a crisis. The soldiers had been supplied secretly with means of unusual dissipation, and consequently a laxity of discipline was daily gaining ground among them. To correct this license, eleven of the guards had been committed to prison for military offences; the Parisian mob delivered them by violence, and took them under the protection of the inhabitants, a conduct which made the natural impression on their comrades. Their numbers were three thousand six hundred of the best soldiers in France, accustomed to military discipline, occupying every strong point in the city, and supported by its immense though disorderly populace.

The gaining these regiments gave the Revolutionists the command of Paris, from which the army assembled under Broglio might have found it hard to dislodge them; but these last were more willing to aid than to quell any insurrection which might take place. The modes of seduction which had succeeded with the French Guards were sedulously addressed to other corps. The regiments which lay nearest to Paris were not forgotten. They were plied with those temptations which are most powerful with soldiers—wine, women, and money, were supplied in abundance—and it was amidst debauchery and undiscipline that the French army renounced their

---

disturbances. Necker received this intimation just as he was dressing for dinner: he dined quietly, without divulging it to any one, and set out in the evening with Madame Necker for Brussels."—Mignet, tom. i., p. 47.

[84] The Marshal was born in 1718, and died, at the age of eighty-six, in 1804.

loyalty, which used to be even too much the god of their idolatry, and which was now destroyed like the temple of Persepolis, amidst the vapours of wine, and at the instigation of courtezans. There remained the foreign troops, of which there were several regiments, but their disposition was doubtful; and to use them against the citizens of Paris, might have been to confirm the soldiers of the soil in their indisposition to the royal cause, supported as it must then have been by foreigners exclusively.

Meanwhile, the dark intrigues which had been long formed for accomplishing a general insurrection in Paris, were now ready to be brought into action. The populace had been encouraged by success in one or two skirmishes with the gens-d'armes and foreign soldiery. They had stood a skirmish with a regiment of German horse, and had been successful. The number of desperate characters who were to lead the van in these violences, was now greatly increased. Deep had called to deep, and the revolutionary clubs of Paris had summoned their confederates from among the most fiery and forward of every province. Besides troops of galley-slaves and deserters, vagabonds of every order flocked to Paris, like ravens to the spoil. To these were joined the lowest inhabitants of a populous city, always ready for riot and rapine; and they were led on and encouraged by men who were in many instances sincere enthusiasts in the cause of liberty, and thought it could only be victorious by the destruction of the present government. The Republican and Jacobin party were open in sentiment and in action, encouraging the insurrection by every means in their power. The Constitutionalists, more passive, were still rejoiced to see the storm arise, conceiving such a crisis was necessary to compel the King to place the helm of the state in their hands. It might have been expected, that the assembled force of the crown would be employed to preserve the peace at least, and prevent the general system of robbery and plunder which seemed about to ensue. They appeared not, and the citizens themselves took arms by thousands, and tens of thousands, forming the burgher militia, which was afterwards called the National Guard. The royal arsenals were plundered to obtain arms, and La Fayette was adopted the commander-in-chief of this new army, a sufficient sign that they were to embrace what was called the Constitutional party. Another large proportion of the population was hastily armed with pikes, a weapon which was thence termed Revolutionary. The Baron de Besenval, at the head of the Swiss guards, two foreign regiments, and eight hundred horse, after an idle demonstration which only served to encourage the insurgents, retired from Paris without firing a shot, having, he says in his Memoirs, no orders how to act, and being desirous to avoid precipitating a civil war. His retreat was the signal for a general insurrection, in which the French guard, the national guard, and the armed mob of Paris, took the Bastile, and massacred a part of the garrison, [July 14.]

We are not tracing minutely the events of the Revolution, but only attempting to describe their spirit and tendency; and we may here notice two changes, which for the first time were observed to have taken place in the character of the Parisian populace.

The *Baudauds de Paris*,[85] as they were called in derision, had been hitherto viewed as a light, laughing, thoughtless race, passionately fond of news, though not very acutely distinguishing betwixt truth and falsehood, quick in adopting impressions, but incapable of forming firm and concerted resolutions, still more incapable of executing them, and so easily overawed by an armed force, that about twelve hundred police soldiers had been hitherto sufficient to keep all Paris in subjection. But in the attack of the Bastile, they showed themselves resolute, and unyielding, as well as prompt and headlong. These new qualities were in some degree owing to the support which they received from the French guards; but are still more to be attributed to the loftier and more decided character belonging to the revolutionary spirit, and the mixture of men of the better classes, and of the high tone which belongs to them, among the mere rabble of the city. The garrison of this too-famous castle was indeed very weak, but its deep moats, and insurmountable bulwarks, presented the most imposing show of resistance; and the triumph which the popular cause obtained in an exploit seemingly so desperate, infused a general consternation into the King and the Royalists.

---

[85] Cockneys.

MURDER OF FOULON AND BERTHIER

The second remarkable particular was, that from being one of the most light-hearted and kind-tempered of nations, the French seemed, upon the Revolution, to have been animated not merely with the courage, but with the rabid fury of unchained wild-beasts. Foulon and Berthier, two individuals whom they considered as enemies of the people, were put to death, with circumstances of cruelty and insult fitting only at the death-stake of a Cherokee encampment; and, in emulation of literal cannibals, there were men, or rather monsters, found, not only to tear asunder the limbs of their victims, but to eat their hearts, and drink their blood.[86] The intensity of the new doctrines of freedom, the animosity occasioned by civil commotion, cannot account for these atrocities, even in the lowest and most ignorant of the populace. Those who led the way in such unheard-of enormities, must have been practised murderers and assassins, mixed with the insurgents, like old hounds in a young pack, to lead them on, flesh them with slaughter, and teach an example of cruelty too easily learned, but hard to be ever forgotten. The metropolis was entirely in the hands of the insurgents, and civil war or submission was the only resource left to the sovereign. For the former course sufficient reasons might be urged. The whole proceedings in the metropolis had been entirely insurrectionary, without the least pretence of authority from the National Assembly, which continued sitting at Versailles, discussing the order of the day while the citizens of Paris were storming castles, and tearing to pieces their prisoners, without authority from the national representatives, and even without the consent of their own civic rulers. The provost of the merchants[87] was assassinated at the commencement of the disturbance, and a terrified committee of electors were the only persons who preserved the least semblance of authority, which they were obliged to exercise under the control and

---

[86] "M. Foulon, an old man of seventy, member of the former Administration, was seized near his own seat, and with his hands tied behind his back, a crown of thistles on his head, and his mouth stuffed with hay, conducted to Paris, where he was murdered with circumstances of unheard-of cruelty. His son-in-law, Berthier, compelled to kiss his father's head, which was thrust into his carriage on a pike, shortly after shared his fate; and the heart of the latter was torn out of his palpitating body."—Lacretelle, tom. vii., p. 117.

[87] M. de Flesselles. It was alleged that a letter had been found on the Governor of the Bastile, which implicated him in treachery to the public cause.—See Mignet, tom. i., p. 62.

at the pleasure of the infuriated multitude. A large proportion of the citizens, though assuming arms for the protection of themselves and their families, had no desire of employing them against the royal authority; a much larger only united themselves with the insurgents, because, in a moment of universal agitation, they were the active and predominant party. Of these the former desired peace and protection; the latter, from habit and shame, must have soon deserted the side which was ostensibly conducted by ruffians and common stabbers, and drawn themselves to that which protected peace and good order. We have too good an opinion of a people so enlightened as those of France, too good an opinion of human nature in any country, to believe that men will persist in evil, if defended in their honest and legal rights.

CONDUCT OF THE KING

What, in this case, was the duty of Louis XVI.? We answer without hesitation, that which George III. of Britain proposed to himself, when, in the name of the Protestant religion, a violent and disorderly mob opened prisons, destroyed property, burned houses, and committed, though with far fewer symptoms of atrocity, the same course of disorder which now laid waste Paris.[88] It is known that when his ministers hesitated to give an opinion in point of law concerning the employment of military force for protection of life and property against a disorderly banditti, the King, as chief magistrate, declared his own purpose to march into the blazing city at the head of his guards, and with the strong hand of war to subdue the insurgents, and restore peace to the affrighted capital.[89] The same call now sounded loudly in the ear of Louis. He was still the

---

[88] For an account of Lord George Gordon's riots in 1780, see *Annual Register*, vol. xxiii., p. 254; and Wraxall's *Own Time*, vol. i., p. 319.

[89] "If the gardes Françaises, in 1789, had behaved like our regular troops in 1780, the French Revolution might have been suppressed in its birth; but, the difference of character between the two sovereigns of Great Britain and of France, constituted one great cause of the different fate that attended the two monarchies. George the Third, when attacked, prepared to defend his throne, his family, his country, and the constitution intrusted to his care; they were in fact saved by his decision. Louis the Sixteenth tamely abandoned all to a ferocious Jacobin populace, who sent him to the scaffold. No man of courage or of principle could have quitted the former prince. It was impossible to save, or to rescue, the latter ill-fated, yielding, and passive monarch."—Wraxall, vol. i., p. 334.

chief magistrate of the people, whose duty it was to protect their lives and property—still commander of that army levied and paid for protecting the law of the country, and the lives and property of the subject. The King ought to have proceeded to the National Assembly without an instant's delay, cleared himself before that body of the suspicions with which calumny had loaded him, and required and commanded the assistance of the representatives of the people to quell the frightful excesses of murder and rapine which dishonoured the capital. It is almost certain that the whole moderate party, as they were called, would have united with the Nobles and the Clergy. The throne was not yet empty, nor the sword unswayed. Louis had surrendered much, and might, in the course of the change impending, have been obliged to surrender more; but he was still King of France, still bound by his coronation oath to prevent murder and put down insurrection. He could not be considered as crushing the cause of freedom, in answering a call to discharge his kingly duty; for what had the cause of reformation, proceeding as it was by the peaceful discussion of an unarmed convention, to do with the open war waged by the insurgents of Paris upon the King's troops, or with the gratuitous murders and atrocities with which the capital had been polluted? With such members as shame and fear might have brought over from the opposite side, the King, exerting himself as a prince, would have formed a majority strong enough to show the union which subsisted betwixt the Crown and the Assembly, when the protection of the laws was the point in question. With such a support—or without it—for it is the duty of the prince, in a crisis of such emergency, to serve the people, and save the country, by the exercise of his royal prerogative, whether with or without the concurrence of the other branches of the legislature,—the King, at the head of his *gardes du corps*, of the regiments which might have been found faithful, of the nobles and gentry, whose principles of chivalry devoted them to the service of their sovereign, ought to have marched into Paris, and put down the insurrection by the armed hand of authority, or fallen in the attempt, like the representative of Henry IV. His duty called upon him, and the authority with which he was invested enabled him, to act this part; which, in all probability, would have dismayed the factious, encouraged the timid, decided the wavering, and, by obtaining a conquest over lawless and brute violence, would have paved the way for a moderate and secure reformation in the state.

But having obtained this victory, in the name of the law of the realm, the King could only be vindicated in having resorted to arms, by using his conquest with such moderation, as to show that he threw his sword into the one scale, solely in order to balance the clubs and poniards of popular insurrection with which the other was loaded. He must then have evinced that he did not mean to obstruct the quiet course of moderation and constitutional reform, in stemming that of headlong and violent innovation. Many disputes would have remained to be settled between him and his subjects; but the process of improving the constitution, though less rapid, would have been more safe and certain, and the kingdom of France might have attained a degree of freedom equal to that which she now possesses, without passing through a brief but dreadful anarchy to long years of military despotism, without the loss of mines of treasure, and without the expenditure of oceans of blood. To those who object the peril of this course, and the risk to the person of the sovereign from the fury of the insurgents, we can only answer, in the words of the elder Horatius, *Qu'il mourût*.[90] Prince or peasant have alike lived long enough, when the choice comes to be betwixt loss of life and an important duty undischarged. Death, at the head of his troops, would have saved Louis more cruel humiliation, his subjects a deeper crime.

We do not affect to deny, that in this course there was considerable risk of another kind, and that it is very possible that the King, susceptible as he was to the influence of those around him, might have lain under strong temptation to have resumed the despotic authority, of which he had in a great measure divested himself, and have thus abused a victory gained over insurrection into a weapon of tyranny. But the spirit of liberty was so strong in France, the principles of leniency and moderation so natural to the King, his own late hazards so great, and the future, considering the general disposition of his subjects, so doubtful, that we are inclined to think a victory by the sovereign at that moment would have been followed by temperate measures. How the people used theirs is but too well known. At any rate, we have strongly stated our opinion, that Louis would, at this crisis, have been justified in employing

---

[90] "Que voulez-vous qu'il fît contre trois? Qu'il mourût, Ou qu'un beau désespoir alors le secourût." Corneille—*Les Horaces*, Act iii., Sc. 6.

force to compel order, but that the crime would have been deep and inexpiable had he abused a victory to restore despotism.

It may be said, indeed, that the preceding statement takes too much for granted, and that the violence employed on the 14th July was probably only an anticipation of the forcible measures which might have been expected from the King against the Assembly. The answer to this is, that the successful party may always cast on the loser the blame of commencing the brawl, as the wolf punished the lamb for troubling the course of the water, though he drank lowest down the stream. But when we find one party completely prepared and ready for action, forming plans boldly, and executing them skilfully, and observe the other uncertain and unprovided, betraying all the imbecility of surprise and indecision, we must necessarily believe the attack was premeditated on the one side, and unexpected on the other.

The abandonment of thirty thousand stand of arms at the Hôtel des Invalides, which were surrendered without the slightest resistance, though three Swiss regiments lay encamped in the Champs Elysées; the totally unprovided state of the Bastile, garrisoned by about one hundred Swiss and Invalids, and without provisions even for that small number; the absolute inaction of the Baron de Besenval, who—without entangling his troops in the narrow streets, which was pleaded as his excuse—might, by marching along the Boulevards, a passage so well calculated for the manœuvres of regular troops, have relieved the siege of that fortress;[91] and, finally, that general's bloodless retreat from Paris,— show that the King had, under all these circumstances, not only adopted no measures of a hostile character, but must, on the contrary, have issued such orders as prevented his officer from repelling force by force.

---

[91] We have heard from a spectator who could be trusted, that during the course of the attack on the Bastile, a cry arose among the crowd that the regiment of Royales Allemandes were coming upon them. There was at that moment such a disposition to fly, as plainly showed what would have been the effect had a body of troops appeared in reality. The Baron de Besenval had commanded a body of the guards, when, some weeks previously, they subdued an insurrection in the Fauxbourg St. Antoine. On that occasion many of the mob were killed; and he observes in his Memoirs, that, while the citizens of Paris termed him their preserver, he was very coldly received at court. He might be, therefore, unwilling to commit himself, by acting decidedly on the 14th July.—S.

We are led, therefore, to believe, that the scheme of assembling the troops round Paris was one of those half measures, to which, with great political weakness, Louis resorted more than once—an attempt to intimidate by the demonstration of force, which he was previously resolved not to use. Had his purposes of aggression been serious, five thousand troops of loyal principles— and such might surely have been selected—would, acting suddenly and energetically, have better assured him of the city of Paris, than six times that number brought to waste themselves in debauch around its walls, and to be withdrawn without the discharge of a musket. Indeed, the courage of Louis was of a passive, not an active nature, conspicuous in enduring adversity, but not of that energetic and decisive character which turns dubious affairs into prosperity, and achieves by its own exertions the success which Fortune denies.

The insurrection of Paris being acquiesced in by the sovereign, was recognised by the nation as a legitimate conquest, instead of a state crime; and the tameness of the King in enduring its violence, was assumed as a proof that the citizens had but anticipated his intended forcible measures against the Assembly, and prevented the military occupation of the city. In the debates of the Assembly itself, the insurrection was vindicated; the fears and suspicions alleged as its motives were justified as well-founded; the passions of the citizens were sympathized with, and their worst excesses palliated and excused. When the horrors accompanying the murder of Berthier and Foulon were dilated upon by Lally Tolendal in the Assembly, he was heard and answered as if he had made mountains of mole-hills. Mirabeau said, that "it was a time to think, and not to feel." Barnave asked, with a sneer, "If the blood which had been shed was so pure?" Robespierre, rising into animation with acts of cruelty fitted to call forth the interest of such a mind, observed, that "the people, oppressed for ages, had a right to the revenge of a day."

But how long did that day last, or what was the fate of those who justified its enormities? From that hour the mob of Paris, or rather the suborned agitators by whom the actions of that blind multitude were dictated, became masters of the destiny of France. An insurrection was organized whenever there was any purpose to be carried, and the Assembly might be said to work under the impulse of the popular current, as mechanically as the wheel of a water engine is driven by a cascade.

The victory of the Bastile was extended in its consequences to the Cabinet and to the Legislative body. In the former, those ministers who had counselled the King to stand on the defensive against the Assembly, or rather to assume a threatening attitude, suddenly lost courage when they heard the fate of Foulon and Berthier. The Baron de Breteueil, the unpopular successor of Necker, was deprived of his office, and driven into exile; and, to complete the triumph of the people, Necker himself was recalled by their unanimous voice.

The King came, or was conducted to, the Hôtel de Ville of Paris, in what, compared to the triumph of the minister, was a sort of ovation, in which he appeared rather as a captive than otherwise. He entered into the edifice under a vault of steel formed by the crossed sabres and pikes of those who had been lately engaged in combating his soldiers, and murdering his subjects. He adopted the cockade of the insurrection; and in doing so, ratified and approved of the acts done expressly against his command, acquiesced in the victory obtained over his own authority, and completed that conquest by laying down his arms.

The conquest of the Bastile was the first, almost the only appeal to arms during the earlier part of the Revolution; and the popular success, afterwards sanctioned by the monarch, showed that nothing remained save the name of the ancient government. The King's younger brother, the Comte d'Artois, now reigning King of France,[92] had been distinguished as the leader and rallying point of the Royalists. He left the kingdom with his children, and took refuge in Turin. Other distinguished princes, and many of the inferior nobility, adopted the same course, and their departure seemed to announce to the public that the royal cause was indeed desperate, since it was deserted by those most interested in its defence. This was the first act of general emigration, and although, in the circumstances, it may be excused, yet it must still be termed a great political error. For though, on the one hand, it is to be considered,

---

[92] Charles the Tenth.

that these princes and their followers had been educated in the belief that the government of France rested in the King's person, and was identified with him; and that when the King was displaced from his permanent situation of power, the whole social system of France was totally ruined, and nothing remained which could legally govern or be governed; yet, on the other hand, it must be remembered that the instant the emigrants crossed the frontier, they at once lost all the natural advantages of birth and education, and separated themselves from the country which it was their duty to defend.

To draw to a head, and raise an insurrection for the purpose of achieving a counter revolution, would have been the ready and natural resource. But the influence of the privileged classes was so totally destroyed, that the scheme seems to have been considered as hopeless, even if the King's consent could have been obtained. To remain in France, whether in Paris or the departments, must have exposed them, in their avowed character of aristocrats, to absolute assassination. It has been therefore urged, that emigration was their only resource.

But there remained for these princes, nobles, and cavaliers, a more noble task, could they but have united themselves cordially to that portion of the Assembly, originally a strong one, which professed, without destroying the existing state of monarchy in France, to wish to infuse into it the spirit of rational liberty, and to place Louis in such a situation as should have ensured him the safe and honourable station of a limited monarch, though it deprived him of the powers of a despot. It is in politics, however, as in religion—the slighter in itself the difference between two parties, the more tenacious is each of the propositions in which they disagree. The pure Royalists were so far from being disposed to coalesce with those who blended an attachment to monarchy with a love of liberty, that they scarce accounted them fit to share the dangers and distresses to which all were alike reduced.

EMIGRATION

This first emigration proceeded not a little perhaps on the feeling of self-consequence among those by whom it was adopted. The high-born nobles of which it was chiefly composed, had been long the WORLD, as it is termed, to Paris, and to each other, and it was a natural conclusion, that their withdrawing themselves from the sphere which they adorned, must have been felt as an irremediable deprivation. They were not aware how easily, in the hour of need, perfumed lamps are, to all purposes of utility, replaced by ordinary candles, and that, carrying away with them much of dignity, gallantry, and grace, they left behind an ample stock of wisdom and valour, and all the other essential qualities by which nations are governed and defended.

The situation and negotiations of the emigrants in the courts to which they fled, were also prejudicial to their own reputation, and consequently to the royal cause, to which they had sacrificed their country. Reduced "to show their misery in foreign lands," they were naturally desirous of obtaining foreign aid to return to their own, and laid themselves under the heavy accusation of instigating a civil war, while Louis was yet the resigned, if not the contented, sovereign of the newly modified empire. To this subject we must afterwards return.

The conviction that the ancient monarchy of France had fallen for ever, gave encouragement to the numerous parties which united in desiring a new constitution, although they differed on the principles on which it was to be founded. But all agreed that it was necessary, in the first place, to clear away the remains of the ancient state of things. They resolved upon the abolition of all feudal rights, and managed the matter with so much address, that it was made to appear on the part of those who held them a voluntary surrender. The debate in the National Assembly [August 4] was turned by the popular leaders upon the odious character of the feudal rights and privileges, as being the chief cause of the general depression and discontent in which the kingdom was involved. The Nobles understood the hint which was thus given them, and answered it with the ready courage and generosity which has been at all times the attribute of their order, though sometimes these noble qualities have been indiscreetly exercised. "Is it from us personally that the nation expects sacrifices?" said the Marquis de Focault; "be assured that you shall not appeal in vain to our generosity. We are desirous to defend to the last the rights of the monarchy, but we can be lavish of our peculiar and personal interests."

THE DAY OF DUPES

The same general sentiment pervaded at once the Clergy and Nobles, who, sufficiently sensible that what they resigned could not operate essentially to the quiet of the state, were yet too proud to have even the appearance of placing their own selfish interests in competition with the public welfare. The whole privileged classes seemed at once seized with a spirit of the most lavish generosity, and hastened to despoil themselves of all their peculiar immunities and feudal rights. Clergy and laymen vied with each other in the nature and extent of their sacrifices. Privileges, whether prejudicial or harmless, rational or ridiculous, were renounced in the mass. A sort of delirium pervaded the Assembly; each member strove to distinguish the sacrifice of his personal claims by something more remarkable than had yet attended any of the previous renunciations. They who had no rights of their own to resign, had the easier and more pleasant task of surrendering those of their constituents: the privileges of corporations, the monopolies of crafts, the rights of cities, were heaped on the national altar; and the members of the National Assembly seemed to look about in ecstasy, to consider of what else they could despoil themselves and others, as if, like the silly old earl in the civil dissensions of England, there had been an actual pleasure in the act of renouncing.[93] The feudal rights were in many instances odious, in others oppressive, and in others

---

[93] "Is there nothing else we can renounce?" said the old Earl of Pembroke and Montgomery, in the time of the Commonwealth, after he had joined in renouncing Church and King, Crown and Law. "Can no one think of any thing else? I love RENOUNCING." The hasty renunciations of the French nobles and churchmen were brought about in the manner practised of yore in convivial parties, when he who gave a toast burned his wig, had a loose tooth drawn, or made some other sacrifice, which, according to the laws of compotation, was an example necessary to be imitated by all the rest of the company, with whatever prejudice to their wardrobes or their persons.—S.

ridiculous; but it was ominous to see the institutions of ages overthrown at random, by a set of men talking and raving all at once, so as to verify the observation of the Englishman, Williams, one of their own members, "The fools! they would be thought to deliberate, when they cannot even listen." The singular occasion on which enthusiasm, false shame, and mutual emulation, thus induced the Nobles and Clergy to despoil themselves of all their seigneurial rights, was called by some the *day of the sacrifices*, by others, more truly, the *day of the dupes*.

During the currency of this legislative frenzy, as it might be termed, the popular party, with countenances affecting humility and shame at having nothing themselves to surrender, sat praising each new sacrifice, as the wily companions of a thoughtless and generous young man applaud the lavish expense by which they themselves profit, while their seeming admiration is an incentive to new acts of extravagance.

At length, when the sacrifice seemed complete, they began to pause and look around them. Some one thought of the separate distinctions of the provinces of France, as Normandy, Languedoc, and so forth. Most of these provinces possessed rights and privileges acquired by victory or treaty, which even Richelieu had not dared to violate. As soon as mentioned, they were at once thrown into the revolutionary smelting-pot, to be re-modelled after the universal equality which was the fashion of the day. It was not urged, and would not have been listened to, that these rights had been bought with blood, and sanctioned by public faith; that the legislature, though it had a right to extend them to others, could not take them from the possessors without compensation; and it escaped the Assembly no less, how many honest and generous sentiments are connected with such provincial distinctions, which form, as it were, a second and inner fence around the love of a common country; or how much harmless enjoyment the poor man derives from the consciousness that he shares the privileges of some peculiar district. Such considerations might have induced the legislature to pause at least, after they had removed such marks of distinction as tended to engender jealousy betwixt inhabitants of the same kingdom. But her revolutionary level was to be passed over all that tended to distinguish one district, or one individual, from another.

There was one order in the kingdom which, although it had joined largely and readily in the sacrifices of the *day of dupes*, was still considered as indebted to the state, and was doomed to undergo an act of total spoliation. The Clergy had agreed, and the Assembly had decreed, on 4th August, that the tithes should be declared redeemable, at a moderate price, by the proprietors subject to pay them. This regulation ratified, at least, the legality of the Clergy's title. Nevertheless, in violation of the public faith thus pledged, the Assembly, three days afterwards, pretended that the surrender of tithes had been absolute, and that, in lieu of that supposed revenue, the nation was only bound to provide decently for the administration of divine worship. Even the Abbé Sièyes on this occasion deserted the revolutionary party, and made an admirable speech against this iniquitous measure.[94] "You would be free," he exclaimed, with vehemence, "and you know not how to be just!" A curate in the Assembly, recalling to mind the solemn invocation by which the Tiers Etat had called upon the Clergy to unite with them, asked, with similar energy, "Was it to rob us, that you invited us to join with you in the name of the God of Peace?" Mirabeau, on the other hand, forgot the vehemence with which he had pleaded the right of property inherent in religious bodies, and lent his sophistry to defend what his own reasoning had proved in a similar case to be indefensible. The complaints of the Clergy were listened to in contemptuous silence, or replied to with bitter irony, by those who were conscious how little sympathy that body were likely to meet from the nation in general, and who therefore spoke "as having power to do wrong."

We must now revert to the condition of the kingdom of France at large, while her ancient institutions were crumbling to pieces of themselves, or were forcibly pulled down by state innovators. That fine country was ravaged by a civil war of aggravated horrors, waged betwixt the rich and poor, and marked by

---

[94] "Next day Sièyes gave vent to his spleen to Mirabeau, who answered, 'My dear abbé, you have unloosed the bull do you expect he is not to make use of his horns?'"—Dumont, p. 147.

every species of brutal violence. The peasants, their minds filled with a thousand wild suppositions, and incensed by the general scarcity of provisions, were every where in arms, and every where attacked the chateaux of their *seigneurs*, whom they were incited to look upon as enemies of the Revolution, and particularly of the commons. In most instances they were successful, and burnt the dwellings of the nobility, practising all the circumstances of rage and cruelty by which the minds of barbarians are influenced. Men were murdered in presence of their wives; wives and daughters violated before the eyes of their husbands and parents; some were put to death by lingering tortures; others by sudden and general massacre. Against some of these unhappy gentlemen, doubtless, the peasants might have wrongs to remember and to avenge; many of them, however, had borne their faculties so meekly that they did not even suspect the ill intentions of these peasants, until their castles and country-seats kindled with the general conflagration, and made part of the devouring element which raged through the whole kingdom.

What were the National Assembly doing at this dreadful crisis? They were discussing the abstract doctrines of the rights of man, instead of exacting from the subject the respect due to his social duties.

Yet a large party in the Convention, and who had hitherto led the way in the paths of the Revolution, now conceived that the goal was attained, and that it was time to use the curb and forbear the spur. Such was the opinion of La Fayette and his followers, who considered the victory over the Royalists as complete, and were desirous to declare the Revolution ended, and erect a substantial form of government on the ruins of monarchy, which lay prostrate at their feet.

They had influence enough in the Assembly to procure a set of resolutions, declaring the monarchy hereditary in the person of the King and present family, on which basis they proceeded to erect what might be termed a Royal Democracy, or, in plainer terms, a Republic, governed, in truth, by a popular assembly, but encumbered with the expense of a king, to whom they desired to leave no real power, or free will to exercise it, although his name was to remain in the front of edicts, and although he was still to be considered entitled to command their armies, as the executive authority of the state.

THE VETO

A struggle was made to extend the royal authority to an absolute negative upon the decrees of the representative body; and though it was limited by the jealousy of the popular party to a suspensive veto only, yet even this degree of influence was supposed too dangerous in the hands of a monarch who had but lately been absolute. There is indeed an evident dilemma in the formation of a democracy, with a king for its ostensible head. Either the monarch will remain contented with his daily parade and daily food, and thus play the part of a mere pageant, in which case he is a burdensome expense to the state, which a popular government, in prudent economy, as well as from the severity of principle assumed by republicans, are particularly bound to avoid; or else he will naturally endeavour to improve the shadow and outward form of power into something like sinew and substance, and the democracy will be unexpectedly assailed with the spear which they desired should be used only as their standard pole.

To these reasonings many of the deputies would perhaps have answered, had they spoken their real sentiments, that it was yet too early to propose to the French a pure republic, and that it was necessary to render the power of the King insignificant, before abolishing a title to which the public ear had been so long accustomed. In the meantime, they took care to divest the monarch of whatever protection he might have received from an intermediate senate, or chamber, placed betwixt the King and the National Assembly. "One God," exclaimed Rabaut St. Etienne, "one Nation, one King, and one Chamber." This advocate for unity at once and uniformity, would scarce have been listened to if he had added, "one nose, one tongue, one arm, and one eye;" but his first concatenation of unities formed a phrase; and an imposing phrase, which sounds well, and can easily be repeated, has immense force in a revolution. The proposal for a Second, or Upper Chamber, whether hereditary like that of England, or elective like that of America, was rejected as aristocratical. Thus the King of France was placed, in respect to the populace, as Canute of old to the advancing tide—he was entitled to sit on his throne and command the waves to respect him, and take the chance of their obeying his commands, or of being overwhelmed by them. If he was designed to be an integral part of the constitution, this should not have been—if he was considered as something that it was more seemly to abandon to his fate than to destroy by violence, the plan was not ill concerted.

Chapter V

Plan of the Democrats to bring the King and Assembly to Paris—Banquet of the Garde du Corps—Riot at Paris—A formidable Mob of Women assemble to march to Versailles—The National Guard refuse to act against the Insurgents, and demand also to be led to Versailles—The Female Mob arrive—Their behaviour to the Assembly—To the King—Alarming Disorders at Night—La Fayette arrives with the National Guard—Mob force the Palace—Murder the Body Guards—The Queen's safety endangered—Fayette's arrival with his Force restores Order—Royal Family obliged to go to reside at Paris—The Procession—This Step agreeable to the Views of the Constitutionalists, Republicans, and Anarchists—Duke of Orleans sent to England.

We have mentioned the various restrictions upon the royal authority, which had been successively sanctioned by the National Assembly. But the various factions, all of which tended to democracy, were determined upon manœuvres for abating the royal authority, more actively powerful than those which the Assembly dared yet to venture upon. For this purpose, all those who desired to carry the Revolution to extremity, became desirous to bring the sittings of the National Assembly and the residence of the King within the precincts of Paris, and to place them under the influence of that popular frenzy which they had so many ways of exciting, and which might exercise the authority of terror over the body of representatives, fill their galleries with a wild and tumultuous band of partisans, surround their gates with an infuriated populace, and thus dictate the issue of each deliberation. What fate was reserved for the King, after incidents will sufficiently show. To effect an object so important, the Republican party strained every effort, and succeeded in raising the popular ferment to the highest pitch.

Their first efforts were unsuccessful. A deputation, formidable from their numbers and clamorous violence, was about to sally from Paris to petition, as they called it, for the removal of the royal family and National Assembly to Paris, but was dispersed by the address of La Fayette and Bailli. Nevertheless it seemed decreed that the Republicans should carry their favourite measures, less through their own proper strength, great as that was, than by the advantage afforded by the blunders of the Royalists. An imprudence—it seems to deserve no harsher name—which occurred within the precincts of the royal palace at Versailles, gave the demagogues an opportunity, sooner probably than they expected, of carrying their point by a repetition of the violences which had already occurred.

The town of Versailles owed its splendour and wealth entirely to its being the royal residence, yet abounded with a population singularly ill-disposed towards the King and royal family. The national guard of the place, amounting to some thousands, were animated by the same feelings. There were only about four hundred gardes du corps, or life-guards, upon whom reliance could be placed for the defence of the royal family, in case of any popular tumult either in Versailles itself, or directed thither from Paris. These troops consisted of gentlemen of trust and confidence, but their numbers were few in proportion to the extent of the palace, and their very quality rendered them obnoxious to the people as armed aristocrats.

About two-thirds of their number, to avoid suspicion and gain confidence, had been removed to Rambouillets. In these circumstances, the grenadiers of the French guards, so lately in arms, against the royal authority, with an inconsistency not unnatural to men of their profession, took it into their heads to become zealous for the recovery of the posts which they had formerly occupied around the King's person, and threatened openly to march to Versailles, to take possession of the routine of duty at the palace, a privilege which they considered as their due, notwithstanding that they had deserted their posts against the King's command, and were now about to resume them contrary to his consent. The regiment of Flanders was brought up to Versailles, to prevent a movement fraught with so much danger to the royal family. The presence of this corps had been required by the municipality, and the measure had been acquiesced in by the Assembly, though not without some expressive indications of suspicion.

BANQUET AT VERSAILLES

The regiment of Flanders arrived accordingly, and the gardes du corps, according to a custom universal in the French garrisons, invited the officers to an entertainment, at which the officers of the Swiss guards, and those of the national guard of Versailles were also guests. [Oct. 1.] This ill-omened feast was given in the opera hall of the palace, almost within hearing of the sovereigns; the healths of the royal family were drunk with the enthusiasm naturally inspired by the situation. The King and Queen imprudently agreed to visit the scene of festivity, carrying with them the Dauphin. Their presence raised the spirits of the company, already excited by wine and music, to the highest pitch; royalist tunes were played, the white cockade, distributed by the ladies who attended the Queen, was mounted with enthusiasm, and it is said that of the nation was trodden under foot.[95]

If we consider the cause of this wild scene, it seems natural enough that the Queen, timid as a woman, anxious as a wife and a mother, might, in order to propitiate the favour of men who were summoned expressly to be the guard of the royal family, incautiously have recourse to imitate, in a slight degree, and towards one regiment, the arts of conciliation, which in a much grosser shape had been used by the popular party to shake the fidelity of the whole army. But it is impossible to conceive that the King, or ministers, could have hoped, by the transitory and drunken flash of enthusiasm elicited from a few hundred men during a carousal, to commence the counter-revolution, which they dared not attempt when they had at their command thirty thousand troops, under an experienced general.

---

[95] Mignet, tom. i., p. 89; Lacretelle, tom. vii., p. 185.

But as no false step among the Royalists remained unimproved by their adversaries, the military feast of Versailles was presented to the people of Paris under a light very different from that in which it must be viewed by posterity. The Jacobins were the first to sound the alarm through all their clubs and societies, and the hundreds of hundreds of popular orators whom they had at their command, excited the citizens by descriptions of the most dreadful plots, fraught with massacres and proscriptions. Every effort had already been used to heat the popular mind against the King and Queen, whom, in allusion to the obnoxious power granted to them by the law, they had of late learned to curse and insult, under the names of Monsieur and Madame Veto. The King had recently delayed yielding his sanction to the declarations of the Rights of Man, until the constitution was complete. This had been severely censured by the Assembly, who spoke of sending a deputation to extort his consent to these declarations, before presenting him with the practical results which they intended to bottom on them. A dreadful scarcity, amounting nearly to a famine, rendered the populace even more accessible than usual to desperate counsels. The feasts, amid which the aristocrats were represented as devising their plots, seemed an insult on the public misery. When the minds of the lower orders were thus prejudiced, it was no difficult matter to produce an insurrection.

INSURRECTION IN PARIS

That of the 5th October, 1789, was of a singular description, the insurgents being chiefly of the female sex. The market-women, "Dames de la Halle," as they are called, half unsexed by the masculine nature of their employments, and entirely so by the ferocity of their manners, had figured early in the Revolution. With these were allied and associated most of the worthless and barbarous of their own sex, such disgraceful specimens of humanity as serve but to show in what a degraded state it may be found to exist. Females of this description began to assemble early in the morning, in large groups, with the cries for "bread," which so easily rouse a starving metropolis. There were amongst them many men disguised as women, and they compelled all the females they met to go along with them. They marched to the Hôtel de Ville, broke boldly through several squadrons of the national guard, who were drawn up in front of that building for its defence, and were with difficulty dissuaded from burning the records it contained. They next seized a magazine of arms, with three or four pieces of cannon, and were joined by a miscellaneous rabble, armed with pikes, scythes, and similar instruments, who called themselves the conquerors of the Bastile. The still increasing multitude re-echoed the cry of "Bread, bread!—to Versailles! to Versailles!"[96]

The national guard were now called out in force, but speedily showed their officers that they too were infected with the humour of the times, and as much indisposed to subordination as the mob, to disperse which they were summoned. La Fayette put himself at their head, not to give his own, but to receive their orders. They refused to act against women, who, they said, were starving, and in their turn demanded to be led to Versailles, "to dethrone,"—such was their language,—"the King, who was a driveller, and place the crown on the head of his son." La Fayette hesitated, implored, explained; but he had as yet to learn the situation of a revolutionary general. "Is it not strange," said one of his soldiers, who seemed quite to understand the military relation of officer and private on such an occasion, "is it not strange that La Fayette pretends to command the people, when it is his part to receive orders from them?"

Soon afterwards an order arrived from the Assembly of the Commune of Paris, enjoining the commandant's march, upon his own report that it was impossible to withstand the will of the people. He marched accordingly in good order, and at the head of a large force of the national guard, about four or five hours after the departure of the mob, who, while he waited in a state of indecision, were already far on their way to Versailles.

It does not appear that the King, or his ministers, had any information of these hostile movements. Assuredly, there could not have been a royalist in Paris willing to hazard a horse or a groom to carry such intelligence where the knowledge of it must have been so

---

[96] Prudhomme, tom. i., p. 236; Thiers, tom. i., p. 135.

important. The leading members of the Assembly, at Versailles, were better informed. "These gentlemen," said Barbantanne, looking at the part of the hall where the Nobles and Clergy usually sat, "wish more light—they shall have lanterns,[97] they may rely upon it." Mirabeau went behind the chair of Mounier, the president. "Paris is marching upon us," he said.—"I know not what you mean," said Mounier.—"Believe me or not, all Paris is marching upon us—dissolve the sitting."—"I never hurry the deliberations," said Mounier.—"Then feign illness," said Mirabeau,—"go to the palace, tell them what I say, and give me for authority. But there is not a minute to lose—Paris marches upon us."—"So much the better," answered Mounier, "we shall be a republic the sooner."[98]

Shortly after this singular dialogue, occasioned probably by a sudden movement, in which Mirabeau showed the aristocratic feelings from which he never could shake himself free, the female battalion, together with their masculine allies, continued their march uninterruptedly, and entered Versailles in the afternoon, singing patriotic airs, intermingled with blasphemous obscenities, and the most furious threats against the Queen. Their first visit was to the National Assembly, where the beating of drums, shouts, shrieks, and a hundred confused sounds, interrupted the deliberations. A man called Mailliard, brandishing a sword in his hand, and supported by a woman holding a long pole, to which was attached a tambour de basque, commenced a harangue in the name of the sovereign people. He announced that they wanted bread; that they were convinced the ministers were traitors; that the arm of the people was uplifted, and about to strike;—with much to the same purpose, in the exaggerated eloquence of the period.[99] The same sentiments were echoed by his followers, mingled with the bitterest threats,

---

[97] In the beginning of the Revolution, when the mob executed their pleasure on the individuals against whom their suspicions were directed, the lamp-irons served for gibbets, and the lines by which the lamps, or lanterns, were disposed across the street, were ready halters. Hence the cry of "Les Aristocrates à la lanterne." The answer of the Abbé Maury is well known. "Eh! mes amis, et quand vous m'auriez mis à la lanterne, est ce que vous verriez plus clair?"—*Biog. Univ.*—S.

[98] Mounier must be supposed to speak ironically, and in allusion, not to his own opinions, but to Mirabeau's revolutionary tenets. Another account of this singular conversation states his answer to have been, "All the better. If the mob kill all of us—remark, I say *all* of us, it will be the better for the country."—S.—Thiers, tom. i., p. 138.

[99] Prudhomme, tom. i., p. 257.

against the Queen in particular, that fury could contrive, expressed in language of the most energetic brutality.

The Amazons then crowded into the Assembly, mixed themselves with the members, occupied the seat of the president, of the secretaries, produced or procured victuals and wine, drank, sung, swore, scolded, screamed,—abused some of the members, and loaded others with their loathsome caresses.[100]

A deputation of these mad women was at length sent to St. Priest, the minister, a determined Royalist, who received them sternly, and replied, to their demand of bread, "When you had but one king, you never wanted bread—you have now twelve hundred—go ask it of them." They were introduced to the King, however, and were so much struck with the kind interest which he took in the state of Paris, that their hearts relented in his favour, and the deputies returned to their constituents, shouting "Vive le Roi!"[101]

MOB SURROUND THE PALACE

Had the tempest depended on the mere popular breeze, it might now have been lulled to sleep; but there was a secret ground-swell, a heaving upwards of the bottom of the abyss, which could not be conjured down by the awakened feelings or convinced understandings of the deputation. A cry was raised that the deputies had been bribed to represent the King favourably; and, in this humour of suspicion, the army of Amazons stripped their garters, for the purpose of strangling their own delegates. They had by this time ascertained, that neither the national guard of Versailles, nor the regiment of Flanders, whose transitory loyalty had passed away with the fumes of the wine of the banquet, would oppose them by force, and that they had only to deal with the gardes du corps, who dared not to act with vigour, lest they should provoke a general attack on the palace, while the most complete distraction and

---

[100] "In the gallery a crowd of fish women were assembled under the guidance of one virago with stentorian lungs, who called to the deputies familiarly by name, and insisted that their favourite Mirabeau should speak."—Dumont, p. 181.
[101] Mignet, tom. i., p. 92.

indecision reigned within its precincts. Bold in consequence, the female mob seized on the exterior avenues of the palace, and threatened destruction to all within.

The attendants of the King saw it necessary to take measures for the safety of his person, but they were marked by indecision and confusion. A force was hastily gathered of two or three hundred gentlemen, who, it was proposed, should mount the horses of the royal stud, and escort the King to Rambouillet, out of this scene of confusion.[102] The gardes du corps, with such assistance, might certainly have forced their way through a mob or the tumultuary description which surrounded them; and the escape of the King from Versailles, under circumstances so critical, might have had a great effect in changing the current of popular feeling. But those opinions prevailed, which recommended that he should abide the arrival of La Fayette with the civic force of Paris.

It was now night, and the armed rabble of both sexes showed no intention of departing or breaking up. On the contrary, they bivouacked after their own manner upon the parade, where the soldiers usually mustered. There they kindled large fires, ate, drank, sang, caroused, and occasionally discharged their firearms. Scuffles arose from time to time, and one or two of the gardes du corps had been killed and wounded in the quarrel, which the rioters had endeavoured to fasten on them; besides which, this devoted corps had sustained a volley from their late guests, the national guard of Versailles. The horse of a garde du corps, which fell into the hands of these female demons, was killed, torn in pieces, and eaten half raw and half roasted.[103] Every thing seemed tending to a general

---

[102] This was proposed by that Marquis de Favras, whose death upon the gallows, [Feb. 19, 1790,] for a Royalist plot, gave afterwards such exquisite delight to the citizens of Paris. Being the first man of quality whom they had seen hanged, (that punishment having been hitherto reserved for plebeians,) they encored the performance, and would fain have hung him up a second time. The same unfortunate gentleman had previously proposed to secure the bridge at Sevres with a body of cavalry, which would have prevented the women from advancing to Versailles. The Queen signed an order for the horses with this remarkable clause:—"To be used if the King's safety is endangered, but in no danger which affects me only."—S.—"The secret of this intrigue never was known; but I have no doubt Favras was one of those men who, when employed as instruments, are led by vanity much further than their principals intend."—Dumont, p. 174.

[103] Lacretelle, tom. vii., p. 217.

engagement, when late at night the drums announced the approach of La Fayette at the head of his civic army, which moved slowly but in good order.

The presence of this great force seemed to restore a portion of tranquillity, though no one appeared to know with certainty how it was likely to act. La Fayette had an audience of the King, explained the means he had adopted for the security of the palace, recommended to the inhabitants to go to rest, and unhappily set the example by retiring himself.[104] Before doing so, however, he also visited the Assembly, pledged himself for the safety of the royal family and the tranquillity of the night, and with some difficulty, prevailed on the President Mounier to adjourn the sitting, which had been voted permanent. He thus took upon himself the responsibility for the quiet of the night. We are loth to bring into question the worth, honour, and fidelity of La Fayette; and we can therefore only lament, that weariness should have so far overcome him at an important crisis, and that he should have trusted to others the execution of those precautions, which were most grossly neglected.

A band of the rioters found means to penetrate into the palace about three in the morning, through a gate which was left unlocked and unguarded. They rushed to the Queen's apartment, and bore down the few gardes du corps who hastened to her defence. The sentinel knocked at the door of her bedchamber, called to her to escape, and then gallantly exposed himself to the fury of the murderers. His single opposition was almost instantly overcome, and he himself left for dead. Over his bleeding body they forced their way into the Queen's apartment; but their victim, reserved for farther and worse woes, had escaped by a secret passage into the chamber of the King, while the assassins, bursting in, stabbed the bed she had just left with pikes and swords.[105]

---

[104] Rivarol, p. 300; Mignet, tom. i., p. 93.
[105] One of the most accredited calumnies against the unfortunate Marie Antoinette pretends, that she was on this occasion surprised in the arms of a paramour. Buonaparte is said to have mentioned this as a fact, upon the authority of Madame Campan. [O'Meara's *Napoleon in Exile*, vol. ii., p. 172.] We have now Madame Campan's own account, [Memoirs, vol. ii. p. 78.] describing the conduct of the Queen on this dreadful occasion as that of a heroine, and totally excluding the possibility of the pretended anecdote. But let it be farther

MURDER OF THE BODY GUARDS

The gardes du corps assembled in the ante-chamber called the bull's eye, and endeavoured there to defend themselves; but several, unable to gain this place of refuge, were dragged down into the courtyard, where a wretch, distinguished by a long beard, a broad bloody axe, and a species of armour which he wore on his person, had taken on himself, by taste and choice, the office of executioner. The strangeness of the villain's costume, the sanguinary relish with which he discharged his office, and the hoarse roar with which, from time to time, he demanded new victims, made him resemble some demon whom hell had vomited forth, to augment the wickedness and horror of the scene.[106]

Two of the gardes du corps were already beheaded, and the Man with the Beard was clamorous to do his office upon the others who had been taken, when La Fayette, roused from his repose, arrived at the head of a body of grenadiers of the old French guards, who had been lately incorporated with the civic guard, and were probably the most efficient part of his force. He did not think of avenging the unfortunate gentlemen, who lay murdered before his eyes for the discharge of their military duty, but he entreated his soldiers to save him the dishonour of breaking his word, which he had pledged to the King, that he would protect the gardes du corps. It is probable he attempted no more than was in his power, and so far acted wisely, if not generously.

To redeem M. de la Fayette's pledge, the grenadiers did, what they ought to have done in the name of the King, the law, the

---

considered, under what circumstances the Queen was placed—at two in the morning, retired to a privacy liable to be interrupted (as it was) not only by the irruption of the furious banditti who surrounded the palace, demanding her life, but by the entrance of the King, or of others, in whom circumstances might have rendered the intrusion duty; and let it then be judged, whether the dangers of the moment, and the risk of discovery, would not have prevented Messalina herself from choosing such a time for an assignation.—S.

[106] The miscreant's real name was Jourdan, afterwards called *Coupe-Tête*, distinguished in the massacres of Avignon. He gained his bread by sitting as an academy-model to painters, and for that reason cultivated his long beard. In the depositions before the Chatelet, he is called *L'Homme à la barbe*—an epithet which might distinguish the ogre or goblin of some ancient legend.—S.

nation, and insulted humanity,—they cleared, and with perfect ease, the court of the palace from these bands of murderous bacchantes, and their male associates. The instinct of ancient feelings, was, in some degree, awakened in the grenadiers. They experienced a sudden sensation of compassion and kindness for the gardes du corps, whose duty on the royal person they had in former times shared. There arose a cry among them,—"Let us save the gardes du corps, who saved us at Fontenoy." They took them under their protection, exchanged their caps with them in sign of friendship and fraternity, and a tumult, which had something of the character of joy, succeeded to that which had announced nothing but blood and death.[107]

The outside of the palace was still besieged by the infuriated mob, who demanded, with hideous cries, and exclamations the most barbarous and obscene, to see "the Austrian," as they called the Queen. The unfortunate princess appeared on the balcony[108] with one of her children in each hand. A voice from the crowd called out, "No children," as if on purpose to deprive the mother of that appeal to humanity which might move the hardest heart. Marie Antoinette, with a force of mind worthy of Maria Theresa, her mother, pushed her children back into the room, and, turning her face to the tumultuous multitude, which tossed and roared beneath, brandishing their pikes and guns with the wildest attitudes of rage, the reviled, persecuted, and denounced Queen stood before them, her arms folded on her bosom, with a noble air of courageous resignation.[109] The secret reason of this summons—the real cause of repelling the children—could only be to afford a chance of some desperate hand among the crowd executing the threats which resounded on all sides. Accordingly, a gun was actually levelled, but one of the bystanders struck it down; for the passions of the mob had taken an opposite turn, and, astonished at Marie Antoinette's noble presence, and graceful firmness of demeanour, there arose, almost in spite of themselves, a general shout of "Vive la Reine!"[110]

---

[107] Lacretelle, tom. vii., p. 238.
[108] Thiers, tom. i., p. 182; Lacretelle, tom. vii., p. 241.
[109] Rivarol, p. 312; Campan, vol. ii., p. 81.
[110] Mémoires de Weber, vol. ii., p. 457.—S.

But if the insurgents, or rather those who prompted them, missed their first point, they did not also lose their second. A cry arose, "To Paris!" at first uttered by a solitary voice, but gathering strength, until the whole multitude shouted, "To Paris—to Paris!"[111] The cry of these blood-thirsty bacchanals, such as they had that night shown themselves, was, it seems, considered as the voice of the people, and as such, La Fayette neither remonstrated himself, nor permitted the King to interpose a moment's delay in yielding obedience to it; nor was any measure taken to put some appearance even of decency on the journey, or to disguise its real character, of a triumphant procession of the sovereign people, after a complete victory over their nominal monarch.

PROCESSION TO PARIS.

The carriages of the royal family were placed in the middle of an immeasurable column, consisting partly of La Fayette's soldiers, partly of the revolutionary rabble, whose march had preceded his, amounting to several thousand men and women of the lowest and most desperate description, intermingling in groups amongst the bands of French guards and civic soldiers, whose discipline could not enable them to preserve even a semblance of order. Thus they rushed along, howling their songs of triumph. The harbingers of the march bore the two bloody heads of the murdered gardes du corps, paraded on pikes, at the head of the column, as the emblems of their prowess and success.[112] The rest of this body, worn down by fatigue, most of them despoiled of their arms, and many without hats, anxious for the fate of the royal family, and harassed with apprehensions for themselves, were dragged like captives in the midst of the mob, while the drunken females around them bore aloft in triumph their arms, their belts, and their hats. These wretches, stained with the blood in which they had bathed

---

[111] "The Queen, on returning from the balcony, approached my mother, and said to her, with stifled sobs, 'They are going to force the King and me to Paris, with the heads of our body-guards carried before us, on the point of their pikes.' Her prediction was accomplished."—M. de Staël, vol. i., p. 344.

[112] It has been said that they were borne immediately before the royal carriage; but this is an exaggeration where exaggeration is unnecessary. These bloody trophies preceded the royal family a great way on the march to Paris.—S.

themselves, were now singing songs, of which the burden bore—"We bring you the baker, his wife, and the little apprentice!"[113] as if the presence of the unhappy royal family, with the little power they now possessed, had been in itself a charm against scarcity. Some of these Amazons rode upon the cannon, which made a formidable part of the procession. Many of them were mounted on the horses of the gardes du corps, some in masculine fashion, others *en croupe*. All the muskets and pikes which attended this immense cavalcade, were garnished, as if in triumph, with oak boughs, and the women carried long poplar branches in their hands, which gave the column, so grotesquely composed in every respect, the appearance of a moving grove.[114] Scarcely a circumstance was omitted which could render this entrance into the capital more insulting to the King's feelings—more degrading to the royal dignity.

After six hours of dishonour and agony, the unfortunate Louis was brought to the Hôtel de Ville, where Bailli, then mayor,[115] complimented him upon the "beau jour," the "splendid day," which restored the monarch of France to his capital; assured him that order, peace, and all the gentler virtues, were about to revive in the country under his royal eye, and that the King would henceforth become powerful through the people, the people happy through the King; and, "what was truest of all," that as Henry IV. had entered Paris by means of reconquering his people, Louis XVI. had done so, because his people had reconquered their King.[116] His wounds salved with this lip-comfort, the unhappy and degraded prince was at length permitted to retire to the palace of the Tuileries, which,

---

[113] "Nous ne manquerons plus de pain; nous amenons le boulanger, la boulangère, et le petit mitron!"—Prudhomme, tom. i., p. 244.
[114] Prudhomme, tom. i., p. 243.
[115] "The King said to the mayor, 'I come with pleasure to my good city of Paris;' the Queen added, 'and with confidence.' The expression was happy, but the event, alas! did not justify it."—M. de Staël, vol. i., p. 344.
[116] The Mayor of Paris, although such language must have sounded like the most bitter irony, had no choice of words on the 6th October, 1789. But if he seriously termed that "a glorious day," what could Bailli complain of the studied insults and cruelties which he himself sustained, when, in Oct. 1792, the same banditti of Paris, who forced the King from Versailles, dragged himself to death, with every circumstance of refined cruelty and protracted insult?—S.—It was not on the 6th October, but the 17th July, three days after the capture of the Bastile, that Bailli, on presenting Louis with the keys of Paris, made use of this expression.—See Prudhomme, tom. i., p. 203.

long uninhabited, and almost unfurnished, yawned upon him like the tomb where alone he at length found repose.[117]

The events of the 14th July, 1789, when the Bastile was taken, formed the first great stride of the Revolution, actively considered. Those of the 5th and 6th of October, in the same year, which we have detailed at length, as peculiarly characteristic of the features which it assumed, made the second grand phasis. The first had rendered the inhabitants of the metropolis altogether independent of their sovereign, and indeed of any government but that which they chose to submit to; the second deprived the King of that small appearance of freedom which he had hitherto exercised, and fixed his dwelling in the midst of his metropolis, independent and self-regulated as we have described it. "It is wonderful," said Louis, "that with such love of liberty on all sides, I am the only person that is deemed totally unworthy of enjoying it." Indeed, after the march from Versailles, the King could only be considered as the signet of royal authority, used for attesting public acts at the pleasure of those in whose custody he was detained, but without the exercise of any free-will on his own part.

All the various parties found their account, less or more, in this state of the royal person, excepting the pure Royalists, whose effective power was little, and their comparative numbers few. There remained, indeed, attached to the person and cause of Louis, a party of those members, who, being friends to freedom, were no less so to regulated monarchy, and who desired to fix the throne on a firm and determined basis. But their numbers were daily thinned, and their spirits were broken. The excellent Mounier, and the eloquent Lally Tolendal, emigrated after the 9th October, unable to endure the repetition of such scenes as were then exhibited. The indignant adieus of the latter to the National Assembly, were thus forcibly expressed:—

---

[117] "As the arrival of the royal family was unexpected, very few apartments were in a habitable state, and the Queen had been obliged to get tent-beds put up for her children in the very room where she received us; she apologized for it, and added, 'You know that I did not expect to come here.' Her physiognomy was beautiful, but irritated; it was not to be forgotten after having been seen."—M. de Staël, vol. i., p. 345.

"It is impossible for me, even my physical strength alone considered, to discharge my functions amid the scenes we have witnessed. Those heads borne in trophy; that Queen half assassinated; that King dragged into Paris by troops of robbers and assassins; the 'splendid day' of M. Bailli; the jests of Barnave, when blood was floating around us; Mounier escaping, as if by miracle, from a thousand assassins; these are the causes of my oath never again to enter that den of cannibals. A man may endure a single death; he may brave it more than once, when the loss of life can be useful—but no power under Heaven shall induce me to suffer a thousand tortures every passing minute—while I am witnessing the progress of cruelty, the triumph of guilt, which I must witness without interrupting it. They may proscribe my person, they may confiscate my fortune; I will labour the earth for my bread, and I will see them no more."[118]

The other parties into which the state was divided, saw the events of the 5th October with other feelings, and if they did not forward, at least found their account in them.

VIEWS OF THE CONSTITUTIONALISTS.

The Constitutional party, or those who desired a democratical government with a king at its head, had reason to hope that Louis, being in Paris, must remain at their absolute disposal, separated from those who might advise counter-revolutionary steps, and guarded only by national troops, embodied in the name, and through the powers, of the Revolution. Every day, indeed, rendered Louis more dependent on La Fayette and his friends, as the only force which remained to preserve order; for he soon found it a necessary, though a cruel measure, to disband his faithful gardes du corps, and that perhaps as much with a view to their safety as to his own.

The Constitutional party seemed strong both in numbers and reputation. La Fayette was commandant of the national guards, and

---

[118] Lacretelle, tom. vii., p. 265.

they looked up to him with that homage and veneration with which young troops, and especially of this description, regard a leader of experience and bravery, who, in accepting the command, seems to share his laurels with the citizen-soldier, who has won none of his own. Bailli was Mayor of Paris, and, in the height of a popularity not undeserved, was so well established in the minds of the better class of citizens, that, in any other times than those in which he lived, he might safely have despised the suffrages of the rabble, always to be bought, either by largesses or flattery. The Constitutionalists had also a strong majority in the Assembly, where the Republicans dared not yet throw off the mask, and the Assembly, following the person of the King, came also to establish its sittings in their stronghold, the metropolis.[119] They seemed, therefore, to assume the ascendency in the first instance, after the 5th and 6th of October, and to reap all the first fruits of the victory then achieved, though by their connivance rather than their active co-operation.

It is wonderful, that, meaning still to assign to the regal dignity a high constitutional situation, La Fayette should not have exerted himself to preserve its dignity undegraded, and to save the honour, as he certainly saved the lives, of the royal family. Three reasons might prevent his doing what, as a gentleman and a soldier, he must otherwise at least have attempted. First, although he boasted highly of his influence with the national guard of Paris, it may be doubted whether all his popularity would have borne him through, in any endeavour to deprive the good people of that city of such a treat as the Joyous Entry of the 6th of October, or whether the civic power would, even for the immediate defence of the King's person, have used actual force against the band of Amazons who directed that memorable procession. Secondly, La Fayette might fear the revival of the fallen colossus of despotism, more than the rising spirit of anarchy, and thus be induced to suppose that a conquest in the King's cause over a popular insurrection, might be too active a cordial to the drooping spirits of the Royalists. And lastly, the revolutionary general, as a politician, might not be unwilling that the King and his consort should experience in their own persons, such a

---

[119] "On being informed of the King's determination to quit Versailles for Paris, the Assembly hastily passed a resolution, that it was inseparable from the King, and would accompany him to the capital."—Thiers, tom. i., p. 182.

specimen of popular power, as might intimidate them from further opposition to the popular will, and incline Louis to assume unresistingly his diminished rank in the new constitution.

The Republican party, with better reason than the Constitutionalists, exulted in the King's change of residence. It relieved them as well as Fayette's party from all apprehension of Louis raising his standard in the provinces, and taking the field on his own account, like Charles of England in similar circumstances. Then they already foresaw, that whenever the Constitutionalists should identify themselves with the crown, whom all parties had hitherto laboured to represent as the common enemy, they would become proportionally unpopular with the people at large, and lose possession of the superior power as a necessary consequence. Aristocrats, the only class which was sincerely united to the King's person, would, they might safely predict, dread and distrust the Constitutionalists, while with the Democrats, so very much the more numerous party, the King's name, instead of "a tower of strength," as the poet has termed it,[120] must be a stumbling-block and a rock of offence. They foresaw, finally, either that the King must remain the mere passive tool of the Constitutionalists, acting unresistingly under their order,—in which case the office would be soon regarded as an idle and expensive bauble, without any force or dignity of free-will, and fit only to be flung aside as an unnecessary incumbrance on the republican forms,—or, in the event of the King attempting, either by force or escape, to throw off the yoke of the Constitutionalists, he would equally furnish arms to the pure Democrats against his person and office, as the source of danger to the popular cause. Some of the Republican chiefs had probably expected a more sudden termination to the reign of Louis from an insurrection so threatening; at least these leaders had been the first to hail and to encourage the female insurgents, on their arrival at Versailles.[121] But though the issue of that insurrection may have fallen short of their hopes, it could not but be highly acceptable to them so far as it went.

---

[120] See Richard the Third, act v., sc. iii.
[121] Barnave, as well as Mirabeau, the Republican as well as the Orleanist, was heard to exclaim, "Courage, brave Parisians—liberty for ever—fear nothing—we are for you!"—See *Mémoires de Ferrieres*, li., iv.—S.

ORLEANS SENT TO ENGLAND.

The party of Orleans had hitherto wrapt in its dusky folds many of those names which were afterwards destined to hold dreadful rank in the Revolutionary history. The prince whose name they adopted is supposed to have been animated partly by a strong and embittered spirit of personal hatred against the Queen, and partly, as we have already said, by an ambitious desire to supplant his kinsman. He placed, according to general report, his treasures, and all which his credit could add to them, at the disposal of men, abounding in those energetic talents which carry their owners forward in times of public confusion, but devoid alike of fortune, character, and principle; who undertook to serve their patron by enlisting in his cause the obscure and subordinate agents, by whom mobs were levied, and assassins subsidized. It is said, that the days of the 5th and 6th of October were organized by the secret agents of Orleans, and for his advantage; that had the enterprise succeeded, the King would have been deposed, and the Duke of Orleans proclaimed Lieutenant-General of the kingdom, while his revenge would probably have been satiated with the Queen's assassination. He is stated to have skulked in disguise about the outskirts of the scene when the tumult was at the highest, but never to have had courage to present himself boldly to the people, either to create a sensation by surprise, or to avail himself of that which his satellites had already excited in his favour.[122] His resolution having thus failed him at the point where it was most necessary, and the tumult having ended without any thing taking place in his favour, the Duke of Orleans was made a scape-goat, and the only one, to atone for the whole insurrection. Under the title of an embassy to England, he was honourably exiled from his native country. [Oct. 14.] Mirabeau spoke of him in terms of the utmost contumely, as being base-minded as a lackey, and totally unworthy the trouble which had been taken on his account. His other adherents gradually and successively dropped away, in proportion as the wealth, credit, and character of this besotted prince rendered him incapable of maintaining his gratuities; and they sailed henceforth under their own flag, in the

---

[122] See the proceedings before the Chatelet.—S.—See also Thiers, tom. i., p. 184; Lacretelle, tom. vii.; and M. de Staël, vol. i., p. 350.

storms he had fitted them to navigate. These were men who had resolved to use the revolutionary axe for cutting out their own private fortunes, and, little interesting themselves about the political principles which divided the other parties of the state, they kept firm hold of all the subordinate machinery despised by the others in the abstraction of metaphysical speculation, but which gave them the exclusive command of the physical force of the mob of Paris—Paris, the metropolis of France, and the prison-house of her monarch.

Chapter VI

La Fayette resolves to enforce order—A Baker is murdered by the Rabble—One of his Murderers executed—Decree imposing Martial Law—Introduction of the Doctrines of Equality—They are in their exaggerated sense inconsistent with Human Nature and the progress of Society—The Assembly abolish titles of Nobility, Armorial bearings, and phrases of Courtesy—Reasoning on these Innovations—Disorder of Finance—Necker becomes unpopular—Seizure of Church-Lands—Issue of Assignats—Necker leaves France in unpopularity—New Religious Institution—Oath imposed on the Clergy—Resisted by the greater part of the Order—General view of the operations of the Constituent Assembly—Enthusiasm of the People for their new Privileges—Limited Privileges of the Crown—King is obliged to dissemble—His Negotiations with Mirabeau—With Bouillé—Attack on the Palace—Prevented by Fayette—Royalists expelled from the Tuileries—Escape of Louis—He is captured at Varennes—Brought back to Paris—Riot in the Champ de Mars—Louis accepts the Constitution.

La Fayette followed up his victory over the Duke of Orleans by some bold and successful attacks upon the revolutionary right of insurrection, through which the people of late had taken on themselves the office of judges at once and executioners. This had hitherto been thought one of the sacred privileges of the Revolution; but, determined to set bounds to its farther progress, La Fayette resolved to restore the dominion of the law over the will of the rabble.

A large mob, in virtue of the approbation, the indulgence at least, with which similar frolics had been hitherto treated, had seized upon and hanged an unhappy baker, named Denis François, who fell under their resentment as a public enemy, because he sold bread dear when he could only purchase grain at an enormous price. They varied the usual detail with some additional circumstances, causing many of his brethren in trade to salute the bloody head, which they paraded according to their wont; and finally, by pressing the dead lips to those of the widow, as she lay fainting before them. This done, and in the full confidence of impunity, they approached the Hall of the Assembly, in order to regale the representatives of the people with the same edifying spectacle.[123]

MARTIAL LAW PROCLAIMED

The baker being neither an aristocrat nor nobleman, the authorities ventured upon punishing the murder, without fearing the charge of *incivisme*. La Fayette, at the head of a detachment of the national guards, attacked and dispersed the assassins, and the active citizen who carried the head, was tried, condemned, and hanged, just as if there had been no revolution in the kingdom. There was much surprise at this, as there had been no such instance of severity since the day of the Bastile.[124] This was not all:

La Fayette, who may now be considered as at the head of affairs, had the influence and address to gain from the Assembly a decree, empowering the magistracy, in case of any rising, to declare martial law by displaying a red flag; after which signal, those who refused to disperse should be dealt with as open rebels. This edict, much to the purpose of the British Riot Act, did not pass without opposition, as it obviously tended to give the bayonets of the national guard a decided ascendency over the pikes and clubs of the rabble of the suburbs. The Jacobins, meaning the followers of Marat, Robespierre, and Danton, and even the Republicans, or Brissotines, had hitherto considered these occasional insurrections and murders like affairs of posts in a campaign, in which they themselves had enjoyed uniformly the advantage; but while La Fayette was followed and obeyed by the national guard, men of

---

[123] Thiers, tom. i., p. 192; Lacretelle, tom. vii., p. 262.
[124] "The indignant populace murmured at the severity. 'What!' they exclaimed, 'is this our liberty? We can no longer hang whom we please!'"—Toulongeon, tom. i., p. 168.

substance, and interested in maintaining order, it was clear that he had both the power and will to stop in future these revolutionary excesses.

This important advantage in some degree balanced the power which the Republican and Revolutionary party had acquired. These predominated, as has been already said, in the Club of Jacobins, in which they reviewed the debates of the Assembly, denouncing at their pleasure those who opposed them; but they had besides a decided majority among the daily attendants in the tribunes, who, regularly paid and supplied with food and liquors, filled the Assembly with their clamours of applause or disapprobation, according to the rules they had previously received. It is true, the hired auditors gave their voices and applause to those who paid them, but nevertheless they had party feelings of their own, which often dictated unbought suffrages, in favour of those who used the most exaggerated tone of revolutionary fury. They shouted with sincere and voluntary zeal for such men as Marat, Robespierre, and Danton, who yelled out for the most bloody measures of terror and proscription, and proclaimed war against the nobles with the same voice with which they flattered the lowest vices of the multitude.

By degrees the Revolution appeared to have assumed a different object from that for which it was commenced. France had obtained Liberty, the first, and certainly the worthiest, object which a nation can desire. Each individual was declared as free as it was possible for him to be, retaining the least respect to the social compact. It is true, the Frenchman was not practically allowed the benefit of this freedom; for though the Rights of Man permitted the citizen to go where he would, yet, in practice, he was apt to find his way to the next prison unless furnished with a municipal passport, or to be murdered by the way, if accused of aristocracy. In like manner, his house was secure as a castle, his property sacred as the ornaments of a temple;—excepting against the Committee of Research, who might, by their arbitrary order, break into the one and dilapidate the other at pleasure. Still, however, the general principle of Liberty was established in the fullest metaphysical extent, and it remained to place on as broad a footing the sister principle of Equality.

To this the attention of the Assembly was now chiefly directed. In the proper sense, equality of rights and equality of laws, a constitution which extends like protection to the lowest and the highest, are essential to the existence and to the enjoyment of freedom. But, to erect a levelling system designed to place the whole mass of the people on the same footing as to habits, manners, tastes, and sentiments, is a gross and ridiculous contradiction of the necessary progress of society. It is a fruitless attempt to wage war with the laws of Nature. She has varied the face of the world with mountain and valley, lake and torrent, forest and champaign, and she has formed the human body in all the different shapes and complexions we behold, with all the various degrees of physical force and weakness. She has avoided equality in all her productions, as she was formerly said to have abhorred a vacuum; even in those of her works which present the greatest apparent similarity, exact equality does not exist; no one leaf of a tree is precisely similar to another, and among the countless host of stars, each differs from the other in glory. But, what are these physical varieties to the endless change exhibited in the human character, with all its various passions, powers, and prejudices, so artfully compounded in different proportions, that it is probable there has not existed, since Adam's time to ours, an exact resemblance between any two individuals? As if this were not enough, there came to aid the diversity, the effects of climate, of government, of education, and habits of life, all of which lead to endless modifications of the individual. The inequalities arising from the natural differences of talent and disposition are multiplied beyond calculation, as society increases in civilisation.

The savage may, indeed, boast a rude species of equality in some patriarchal tribes, but the wiliest and strongest, the best hunter, and the bravest warrior, soon lords it over the rest, and becomes a king or a chief. One portion of the nation, from happy talents or happy circumstances, rises to the top, another sinks, like dregs, to the bottom; a third portion occupies a mid place between them. As society advances, the difference of ranks advances with it. And can it be proposed seriously, that any other equality, than that of rights, can exist between those who think and those who labour; those "whose talk is of bullocks," and those whose time permits them to study the paths of wisdom? Happy, indeed, is the country and constitution, where those distinctions, which must necessarily exist in every society, are not separated by insurmountable barriers, but where the most distinguished rank is open to receive that precious supply of wisdom and talent, which so frequently elevates individuals from the lowest to the highest classes; and, so far as general equality can be attained, by each individual having a fair right to raise himself to the situation which he is qualified to occupy, by his talents, his merits, or his wealth, the gates cannot be thrown open too widely. But the attempt of the French legislators was precisely the reverse, and went to establish the proposed equality of ranks, by depressing the upper classes into the same order with those who occupy the middle of society, while they essayed the yet more absurd attempt to crush down these last, by the weight of legislative authority, into a level with the lowest orders,—men whose education, if it has not corrupted their hearts, must necessarily have blunted their feelings, and who, in a great city like Paris, exchange the simplicity which makes them respectable under more favourable circumstances, for the habitual indulgence of the coarsest and grossest pleasures. Upon the whole, it must be admitted, that in every state far advanced in the progress of civilisation, the inequality of ranks is a natural and necessary attribute. Philosophy may comfort those who regret this necessity, by the assurance that the portions of individual happiness and misery are divided amongst high and low with a very equal hand; and religion assures us, that there is a future state, in which, with amended natures and improved faculties, the vain distinctions of this world will no longer subsist. But any practical attempt to remedy the inequality of rank in civilized society by forcible measures, may indeed degrade the upper classes, but cannot improve those beneath them. Laws may deprive the gentleman of his title, the man of education of his books, or, to use the French illustration, the *muscadin* of his clothes; but this cannot make the clown a man of breeding, or give learning to ignorance, or decent attire to the Sans Culottes. Much will be lost to the grace, the information, and the decency of society in general, but nothing can possibly be gained by any individual. Nevertheless, it was in this absolutely impracticable manner, that the exaggerated feelings of the French legislators, at this period of total change, undertook to equalize the nation which they were regenerating.

ABOLITION OF TITLES OF HONOUR

With a view to this great experiment upon human society, the Assembly abolished all titles of honour,[125] all armorial bearings, and even the insignificant titles of Monsieur and Madame; which, meaning nothing but phrases of common courtesy, yet, with other expressions of the same kind, serve to soften the ordinary intercourse of human life, and preserve that gentleness of manners which the French, by a happy name, were wont to call "La petite morale." The first of these abrogations affected the nobles in particular. In return for their liberal and unlimited surrender of their essential powers and privileges, they were now despoiled of their distinction and rank in society;—as if those who had made prisoner and plundered a cavalier, should, last of all, have snatched away in derision the plume from his hat. The aristocracy of France, so long distinguished as the flower of European chivalry, were now, so far as depended on the legislature, entirely abolished. The voice of the nation had pronounced against them a general sentence of degradation, which, according to the feelings of the order, could only be the punishment of some foul and disgraceful crime; and the condition of the ex-nobles might justly have been described as Bolingbroke paints his own,

"Eating the bitter bread of banishment, Whilst you have fed upon my signories, Dispark'd my parks, and fell'd my forest woods, From my own windows torn my household coat, Razed out my impress, leaving me no sign, Save men's opinions and my living blood, To show the world I was a gentleman."[126]

It was a fatal error, that, in search of that equality which it is impossible to attain, the Assembly should have torn down the ancient institutions of chivalry. Viewing them philosophically, they are indeed of little value; but where are the advantages beyond the means, first, of mere subsistence, secondly, of information, which ought not to be indifferent to true philosophers? And yet, where

---

[125] "A simple decree, proposed, June 20th, by Lameth, that the titles of duke, count, marquis, viscount, baron, and chevalier, should be suppressed, was carried by an overwhelming majority."—Mignet, tom. ii., p. 114.
[126] Richard the Second, act iii., sc. i.

exists the true philosopher, who has been able effectually to detach himself from the common mode of thinking on such subjects? The estimation set upon birth or rank, supposing its foundation illusory, has still the advantage of counterbalancing that which is attracted by wealth only; the prejudice has something generous and noble in it, is connected with historical recollections and patriotic feelings, and if it sometimes gives rise to extravagances, they are such as society can restrain and punish by the mere effect of ridicule.[127] It is curious, even in the midst of the Revolution, and amongst those who were its greatest favourers, what difficulties were found to emancipate themselves from those ancient prejudices which affected the difference of ranks.[128]

As for the proscription of the phraseology of civilized society, it had an absurd appearance of affectation in the eyes of most people of understanding; but, on some enthusiastic minds, it produced a worse effect than that of mere disgust. Let a man place himself in the attitude of fear or of rage, and he will in some measure feel the passion arise in his mind which corresponds with the gesture he has assumed. In like manner, those who affected the brutal manners, coarse language, and slovenly dress of the lower orders, familiarized their imaginations with the violent and savage thoughts and actions proper to the class whose costume they had thus adopted. Above all, when this sacrifice was made to the very taste and phraseology of that class, (the last points in which one would think them deserving of imitation,) it appeared to intimate the progressive strength of the revolutionary tide, which, sweeping before it all distinctions, trivial as well as important, seemed soon destined to overthrow the throne, now isolated and wellnigh

---

[127] "One of the most singular propositions of this day was, that of renouncing the names of estates, which many families had borne for ages, and obliging them to resume their patronymic appellations. In this way the Montmorencies would have been called Bouchard; La Fayette, Mottié; Mirabeau, Riquetti. This would have been stripping France of her history; and no man, how democratic soever, either would or ought to renounce in this manner the memory of his ancestors."—M. de Staël, vol. i., p. 364.

[128] The Comte de Mirabeau was furious at being called *Riquetti l'ainé*, and said, with great bitterness, when his speeches were promulgated under that name, "*Avec votre Riquetti, vous avez désorienté l'Europe pour trois jours.*" Mirabeau was at heart an aristocrat. But what shall we say of Citoyenne Roland, who piques herself on the plebeian sound of her name, *Manon Philipon*, yet inconsequentially upbraids Citoyen Pache with his father's having been a porter!—S.—*Memoirs*, part i., p. 140.

undefended. The next step was necessarily to fix the executive government in the same body which enjoyed the powers of legislation,—the surest of all roads to tyranny. But although the doctrine of equality, thus understood, is absurd in theory and impossible in practice, yet it will always find willing listeners when preached to the lower classes, whose practical view of it results into an agrarian law, or a general division of property.

There was one order yet remaining, however, which was to be levelled,—the destruction of the Church was still to be accomplished; and the Republican party proceeded in the work of demolition with infinite address, by including the great object in a plan for restoring finance, and providing for the expenses of the state, without imposing further burdens on the people.

DISORDER OF FINANCES

It must be remembered, that the States-General had been summoned to restore the finances of the country. This was the cause of their convocation. But although they had exercised almost every species of power—had thrown down and rebuilt every constituted authority in the kingdom, still the finances were as much embarrassed as ever, or much more so; since most men in France judged the privilege of refusing to pay taxes, the most unequivocal, and not the least pleasing part, of their newly-acquired freedom.

Necker, so often received among the populace as a saviour of the country, was here totally at a loss. The whole relative associations which bind men together in the social contract, seemed to be rent asunder; and where public credit is destroyed, a financier, however able, resembles Prospero, after his wand is broken, and his book sunk in the deep sea. Accordingly, Necker in vain importuned the Assembly, by representing the pressure of the finances. They became wearied with his remonstrances, and received them with manifest symptoms of coldness and disrespect. What service, indeed, could the regulated advice, and deep-calculated and combined schemes of a financier, have rendered to men, who had already their resources in their eye, and were determined that no idle scruple should prevent their pouncing upon them? Necker's expostulations, addressed to their ears, were like a lecture upon thrift and industry to Robin Hood and his merry-men, when they were setting forth to rob the rich in the name of the poor.

The Assembly had determined, that, all prejudices apart, the property of the Church should come under confiscation for the benefit of the nation.[129] It was in vain that the Clergy exclaimed against these acts of rapine and extortion—in vain that they stated themselves as an existing part of the nation, and that as such they had coalesced with the Assembly, under the implied ratification of their own rights—in vain that they resounded in the hall the declaration solemnly adopted, that property was inviolable, save upon full compensation. It was to as little purpose that Mirabeau was reminded of his language, addressed to the Emperor Joseph upon a similar occasion.—"Despise the monks," he had said, "as much as you will, but do not rob them. Robbery is equally a crime, whether perpetrated on the most profligate atheist, or the most bigoted capuchin." The Clergy were told, with insulting gravity, that the property belonging to a community was upon a different footing from that belonging to individuals, because the state might dissolve the community or body-corporate, and resume the property attached to it; and, under this sophism, they assumed for the benefit of the public the whole right of property belonging to the Church of France.[130]

---

[129] This proposition was made by Talleyrand, then Bishop of Autun. In support of it he argued, that "the clergy were not proprietors, but depositories of their estates; that no individual could maintain any right of property, or inheritance in them; that they were bestowed originally by the munificence of kings or nobles, and might now be resumed by the nation, which had succeeded to *their* rights." To this Maury and Sièyes replied, "that it was an unfounded assertion that the property of the Church was at the disposal of the state; that it flowed from the munificence or piety of individuals in former ages, and was destined to a peculiar purpose, totally different from secular concerns; that, if the purposes originally intended could not be carried into effect it should revert to the heirs of the donors, but certainly not accrue to the legislature."—Thiers, tom. i., p. 193.

[130] M. de Chateaubriand says, "The funds thus acquired were enormous, the church-lands were nearly one-half of the whole landed property of the kingdom."

CONFISCATION OF CHURCH LANDS

As it was impossible to bring these immense subjects at once to sale, the Assembly adopted a system of paper-money, called *Assignats*, which were secured or hypothecated upon the church-lands. The fluctuation of this paper, which was adopted against Necker's earnest cautions, created a spirit of stock-jobbing and gambling, nearly resembling that which distinguished the famous scheme of the Mississippi. Spelman would have argued, that the taint of sacrilege attached to funds raised upon the spoils of the Church;[131] yet it must be admitted that these supplies enabled the National Assembly not only to avoid the gulf of general bankruptcy, but to dispense with many territorial exactions which pressed hard on the lower orders, and to give relief and breath to that most useful portion of the community. These desirable results, however, flowed from that divine alchymy which calls good out of evil, without affording a justification to the perpetrators of the latter.

Shortly after the adoption of this plan, embraced against his opinion and his remonstrances, Necker saw his services were no longer acceptable to the Assembly, and that he could not be useful to the King. He tendered his resignation, [Sept. 4,] which was received with cold indifference by the Assembly; and even his safety was endangered on his return to his native country, by the very people who had twice hailed him as their deliverer. This accomplished statesman discovered too late, that public opinion requires to be guided and directed towards the ends of public good, which it will not reach by its own unassisted and misdirected efforts; and that his own popularity had only been the stalking-horse, through means of which, men less honest, and more subtle than himself, had taken aim at their own objects.[132]

But the majority of the National Assembly had yet another and even a more violent experiment to try upon the Gallican Church establishment. It was one which touched the consciences of

---

[131] See Sir Henry Spelman's treatise on the "History of Sacrilege."
[132] See M. de Staël, vol. i., p. 384. "The retreat of Necker produced a total change in the ministry. Of those who now came into office two were destined to perish on the scaffold, and a third by the sword of the revolutionary assassins."—Lacretelle, tom. viii., p. 92.

the French clergy in the same degree as the former affected their fortunes, and was so much the less justifiable, that it is difficult to suggest any motive except the sweeping desire to introduce novelty in every department of the state, and to have a constitutional clergy as they had a constitutional king, which should have instigated them to such a measure.

When the Assembly had decreed the assumption of the church-lands, it remained to be settled on what foundation religion was to be placed within the kingdom. A motion was made for decreeing, that the Holy Apostolical religion was that of France, and that its worship alone should be permitted. A Carthusian monk, named Dom Gerle, made this proposal, alarmed too late lest the popular party, to which he had so long adhered, should now be about to innovate in the matters of the Church, as they had already in those of the state. The debate was conducted with decency for one day, but on the second the hall of the Assembly was surrounded by a large and furious multitude, who insulted, beat, and maltreated all who were known to favour the measure under consideration. It was represented within the house, that the passing the decree proposed would be the signal for a religious war; and Dom Gerle withdrew his motion in terror and despair.

The success of this opposition showed, that almost any experiment on the Church might be tried with effect, since the religion which it taught seemed no longer to interest the national legislators. A scheme was brought forward, in which the public worship (*culte publique*) as it was affectedly termed, without any addition of reverence, (as if to give it the aid of a mere code of formal enactments,) was provided for on the narrowest and most economical plan. But this was not all. A civil constitution was, by the same code, framed for the clergy, declaring them totally independent of the See of Rome, and vesting the choice of bishops in the departmental authorities. To this constitution each priest and prelate was required to adhere by a solemn oath. A subsequent decree of the Assembly declared forfeiture of his benefice against whomsoever should hesitate; but the clergy of France showed in that trying moment, that they knew how to choose betwixt sinning against their conscience, and suffering wrong at the hands of man.

Their dependence on the See of Rome was a part of their creed, an article of their faith, which they would not compromise. The noble attitude of firmness and self-denial adopted by prelates and richly-beneficed clergymen, who had hitherto been thought more governed by levities of every kind than by regard to their profession, commanded for a time the respect of the Assembly, silenced the blasphemies of the hired assistants in the tribunes, and gave many to fear that, in depriving the Church of its earthly power, the Assembly might but give them means to extend their spiritual dominion more widely, and awake an interest in their fate which slumbered during their prosperity. "Beware what you do," said Montlosier. "You may expel the bishop from his episcopal residence, but it will be only to open to him the cabins of the poor. If you take from his hands the cross of gold, he will display a cross of wood; and it was by a cross of wood that the world was saved."[133]

Summoned, one by one, to take the oath, or refuse it under the consequences menaced, the Assembly, fearful of the effect of their firmness, would scarce hear these sufferers speak a syllable, save Yes or No. Their tumult on the occasion resembled the beating of drums to drown the last words of a martyr. Few, indeed, were the priests who accepted the constitutional oath. There were in the number only three bishops. One had been a person of note—it was that Archbishop of Sens—that very cardinal, whose maladministration of fifteen months had led to this mighty change. Another of the three Constitutional prelates was destined to be much more remarkable—it was the celebrated Talleyrand, whose talents as a statesman have been so distinguished.

The National Assembly failed totally in their attempts to found a national Church. The priests who took the oaths received neither reverence nor affection, and were only treated with decency by such as considered religion in the light of a useful political institution. They were alike despised by the sincere Catholic, and the declared infidel. All of real religious feeling or devotion that was left in France turned towards their ancient pastors, and though the impulse was not strong enough to counteract the revolutionary movement, it served, on many occasions, to retard and embarrass

---

[133] Lacretelle, tom. viii., p. 38.

it.[134] The experiment which had thus signally miscarried, was indeed as impolitic as it was unnecessary. It can only be imputed, on the one hand, to the fanaticism of the modern philosophers,[135] who expected, by this indirect course, to have degraded the Christian religion; and, on the other, to the preconcerted determination of the Revolutionists, that no consideration should interfere with the plan of new-modelling the nation through all its institutions, as well of Church as of State.

Victorious at once over altar and throne, mitre and coronet, King, Nobles, and Clergy, the National Assembly seemed, in fact, to possess, and to exert, that omnipotence, which has been imputed to the British Parliament. Never had any legislature made such extensive and sweeping changes, and never were such changes so easily accomplished. The nation was altered in all its relations; its flag and its emblems were changed—every thing of a public character was destroyed and replaced, down to the very title of the sovereign, who, no longer termed King of France and Navarre, was now called King of the French. The names and divisions of the provinces, which had existed for many years, were at once obliterated, and were supplied by a geographical partition of the territory into eighty-three departments, subdivided into six hundred districts, and these again portioned out into forty-eight thousand communities or municipalities. By thus recasting, as it were, the whole geographical relations of the separate territories of which France consisted, the Abbé Sièyes designed to obliterate former recollections and distinctions, and to bring every thing down to the general level of liberty and equality. But it had an effect beyond what was proposed. While the provinces existed they had their separate capitals, their separate privileges; and those capitals, though in a subordinate rank, being yet the seats of provincial parliaments, had a separate consequence, inferior to, but yet distinct from, that of Paris. But when France became one single province, the importance of its sole capital, Paris, was increased to a most formidable degree; and during the whole Revolution, and through all its changes, whatever

---

[134] Mignet, tom. i., pp. 107, 121; Thiers, tom. i., pp. 240, 266.
[135] Mignet says, "The Constitutional Church establishment was not the work of the modern philosophers, but was devised by the Jansenists, or rigid party." No doubt, the Jansenists, dupes of the philosophers, fancied themselves guides instead of blind instruments.

party held the metropolis was sure speedily to acquire the supreme power through the whole departments; and woe to those who made the fruitless attempt to set the sense or feelings of the nation in opposition to those of the capital! Republican or royalist was equally sure to perish in the rash attempt.

TRIAL BY JURY

The Parliaments of France, long the strongholds of liberty, now perished unnoticed, as men pull down old houses to clear the ground for modern edifices. The sale of offices of justice was formally abolished; the power of nominating the judges was taken from the crown; the trial by jury, with inquests of accusation and conviction, corresponding to the grand and petty juries of England, were sanctioned and established. In thus clearing the channels of public justice, dreadfully clogged as they had become during the decay of the monarchy, the National Assembly rendered the greatest possible services to France, the good effects of which will long be felt. Other alterations were of a more doubtful character. There might be immediate policy, but there was certainly much harshness, in wresting from the crown the power of granting pardons. If this was for fear lest grace should be extended to those condemned for the new crime of leeze-nation, or treason against the Constitution, the legislators might have remembered how seldom the King dares to exercise this right of mercy in favour of an unpopular criminal. It requires no small courage to come betwixt the dragon and his wrath, the people and their victim. Charles I. dared not save Strafford.

The National Assembly also recognised the freedom of the press; and, in doing so, conferred on the nation a gift fraught with much good and some evil, capable of stimulating the worst passions, and circulating the most atrocious calumnies, and occasioning frequently the most enormous deeds of cruelty and injustice; but ever bearing along with it the means of curing the very evils caused by its abuses, and of transmitting to futurity the sentiments of the good and the wise, so invaluable when the passions are silenced, and the calm slow voice of reason and reflection comes to obtain a hearing. The press stimulated massacres and proscriptions during the frightful period which we are approaching; but the press has also held up to horror the memory of the perpetrators, and exposed the artifices by which the actors were instigated. It is a rock on which a vessel may be indeed, and is often wrecked; but that same rock affords the foundation of the brightest and noblest beacon.

We might add to the weight of benefits which France unquestionably owes to the Constituent Assembly, that they restored liberty of conscience by establishing universal toleration. But against this benefit must be set the violent imposition of the constitutional oath upon the Catholic clergy, which led afterwards to such horrible massacres of innocent and reverend victims, murdered in defiance of those rules of toleration, which, rather in scorn of religion of any kind than regard to men's consciences, the Assembly had previously adopted.

Faithful to their plan of forming not a popular monarchy, but a species of royal republic, and stimulated by the real Republicans, whose party was daily gaining ground among their ranks, as well as by the howls and threats of those violent and outrageous demagogues, who, from the seats they had adopted in the Assembly, were now known by the name of the "Mountain,"[136] the framers of the Constitution had rendered it democratical in every point, and abridged the royal authority, till its powers became so dim and obscure as to merit Burke's happy illustration, when he exclaimed, speaking of the new-modelled French government,—

"——What *seem'd* its head, The *likeness* of a kingly crown had on."

The crown was deprived of all appointments to civil offices, which were filled up by popular elections, the Constitutionalists being, in this respect, faithful to their own principles, which made the will of the people the source of all power. Never was such an immense patronage vested in the body of any nation at large, and the arrangement was politic in the immediate sense, as well as in conformity with the principles of those who adopted it; for it attached to the new Constitution the mass of the people, who felt

---

[136] It was their custom to sit on the highest rows of benches in the hall.

themselves elevated from villanage into the exercise of sovereign power. Each member of the elective assembly of a municipality, through whose collective votes bishops, administrators, judges, and other official persons received their appointments, felt for the moment, the importance which his privilege bestowed, and recognised in his own person, with corresponding self-complacency, a fraction, however small, of the immense community, now governed by those whom they themselves elected into office. The charm of power is great at all times, but exquisite to intoxication to those to whom it is a novelty.

Called to the execution of these high duties, which hitherto they had never dreamed of, the people at large became enamoured of their own privileges, carried them into every department of society, and were legislators and debaters, in season and out of season. The exercise even of the extensive privilege committed to them, seemed too limited to these active citizens. The Revolution appeared to have turned the heads of the whole lower classes, and those who had hitherto thought least of political rights, were now seized with the fury of deliberating, debating, and legislating, in all possible times and places. The soldiers on guard debated at the Oratoire—the journeymen tailors held a popular assembly at the Colonnade—the peruke-makers met at the Champs-Elysées. In spite of the opposition of the national guard, three thousand shoemakers deliberated on the price of shoes in the Place Louis Quinze; every house of call was converted into the canvassing hall of a political body; and France for a time presented the singular picture of a country, where every one was so much involved in public business, that he had little leisure to attend to his own.

There was, besides, a general disposition to assume and practise the military profession; for the right of insurrection having been declared sacred, each citizen was to be prepared to discharge effectually so holy a duty. The citizens procured muskets to defend their property—the rabble obtained pikes to invade that of others—the people of every class every where possessed themselves of arms, and the most peaceful burgesses were desirous of the honours of the epaulet. The children, with mimicry proper to their age, formed battalions on the streets, and the spirit in which they were formed was intimated by the heads of cats borne upon pikes in front of the juvenile revolutionists.[137]

FEVER OF LEGISLATION

In the departments, the fever of legislation was the same. Each district had its permanent committee, its committee of police, its military committee, civil committee, and committee of subsistence. Each committee had its president, its vice-president, and its secretaries. Each district was desirous of exercising legislative authority, each committee of usurping the executive power.[138] Amid these subordinate conclaves, every theme of eulogy and enthusiasm referred to the Revolution which had made way for the power they enjoyed, every subject of epidemic alarm to the most distant return towards the ancient system which had left the people in insignificance. Rumour found a ready audience for every one of her thousand tongues; Discord a prompt hand, in which she might place each of her thousand snakes.

The Affiliation, as it was called, or close correspondence of the Jacobin Clubs in all their ramifications, tended to influence this political fever, and to direct its fury against the last remains of royalty. Exaggerated and unfounded reports of counter-revolutionary plots and aristocratical conspiracies, not a little increased by the rash conversation and impotent efforts of the nobility in some districts, were circulated with the utmost care; and the falsehood, which had been confuted at Paris, received new currency in the departments; as that which was of departmental growth was again circulated with eagerness in the metropolis. Thus, the minds of the people were perpetually kept in a state of excitation, which is not without its pleasures. They are of a nature peculiarly incompatible with soundness in judgment and moderation in action, but favourable, in the same degree, to audacity of thought, and determination in execution.

---

[137] Mémoires du Marquis des Ferrieres, l. iii.
[138] Mémoires de Bailli, 16 Août.

CROWN PRIVILEGES

The royal prerogative of the King, so closely watched, was in appearance formidable enough to be the object of jealousy and suspicion, but in reality a mere pageant which possessed no means either of attack or resistance. The King was said to be the organ of the executive power, yet he had named but a small proportion of the officers in the army and navy, and those who received their appointments from a source so obnoxious, possessed little credit amongst those whom they commanded. He was the nominal head of six ministers, who were perpetually liable to be questioned by the Assembly, in which they might be called to defend themselves as criminals, but had no seat or vote to enable them to mingle in its debates. This was, perhaps, one of the greatest errors of the constitution; for the relation which the ministers bore to the legislative body, was of such a limited and dependent nature, as excluded all ideas of confidence and cordiality. The King's person was said to be inviolable, but the frowning brows of a large proportion of his subjects, their public exclamations, and the pamphlets circulated against him, intimated very different doctrine. He might propose to the Assembly the question of peace or war, but it remained with them to decide upon it. Lastly, the King had the much-grudged privilege of putting a veto on any decree of the legislative body, which was to have the effect of suspending the passing of the law until the proposition had been renewed in two successive Assemblies; after which the royal sanction was held as granted. This mode of arresting the progress of any favourite law was likely to be as dangerous to the sovereign in its exercise, as the attempt to stop a carriage by catching hold of the wheel. In fact, whenever the King attempted to use this sole relic of monarchical power, he risked his life, and it was by doing so that he at length forfeited it. Among these mutilated features of sovereignty, it is scarcely worth while to mention, that the King's effigy was still struck upon the public coin, and his name prefixed to public edicts.

Small as was the share of public power which the new Constitution of France afforded to the crown, Louis, in outward semblance at least, appeared satisfied. He made it a rule to adopt the advice of the Assembly on all occasions, and to sanction every decree which was presented to him. He accepted even that which totally changed the constitution of the Gallican Church. He considered himself, doubtless, as under forcible restraint, ever since he had been dragged in triumph from Versailles to Paris, and therefore complied with what was proposed to him, under the tacit protest that his acquiescence was dictated by force and fear. His palace was guarded by eight hundred men, with two pieces of cannon; and although this display of force was doubtless intended by La Fayette to assure Louis's personal safety, yet it was no less certain that it was designed also to prevent his escape from the metropolis. The King had, therefore, good cause to conceive himself possessed of the melancholy privilege of a prisoner, who cannot incur any legal obligation by acts which do not flow from free-will, and therefore finds a resource against oppression in the incapacities which attend it. It was, however, carrying this privilege to the verge of dissimulation, nay, beyond it, when the King went, [Feb. 4,] apparently freely and voluntarily, down to the National Assembly, and, in a dignified and touching speech, (could it have been thought a sincere one,) accepted the Constitution, made common cause with the regenerated nation, and declared himself the head of the Revolution.[139] Constrained as he was by circumstances, anxious for his own safety, and that of his family, the conduct of Louis must not be too severely criticised; but this step was unkingly as well as impolitic, and the unfortunate monarch gained nothing by abasing himself to the deceit which he practised at the urgency of his ministers, excepting the degradation attending a deception by which none are deceived. No one, when the heat of the first enthusiasm was over, gave the King credit for sincerity in his acceptance of the Constitution: the Royalists were revolted, and the Revolutionists could only regard the speech and accession as the acts of royal hypocrisy. Louis was openly spoken of as a prisoner; and the public voice, in a thousand different forms, announced that his life would be the penalty of any attempt to his deliverance.

---

[139] Prudhomme, tom. ii., p. 297.

LOUIS'S NEGOTIATIONS

Meanwhile, the King endeavoured to work out his escape from Paris and the Revolution at once, by the means of two separate agents in whom alone he confided.

The first was no other than Mirabeau—that very Mirabeau who had contributed so much to the Revolution, but who, an aristocrat at heart, and won over to the royal party by high promises of wealth and advancement, at length laboured seriously to undo his own work.[140] His plan was, to use the Assembly itself, in which his talents, eloquence, and audacity, gave him so much influence, as the means of re-establishing the royal authority. He proposed, as the final measure, that the King should retire from Paris to Compiegne, then under the government of the Marquis de Bouillé, and he conceived his own influence in the Assembly to be such, that he could have drawn thither, upon some reasonable terms of accommodation, a great majority of the members. It is certain he had the highest ascendency which any individual orator exercised over that body, and was the only one who dared to retort threats and defiance to the formidable Jacobins. "I have resisted military and ministerial despotism," said he, when opposing a proposed law against the emigrants; "can it be supposed I will yield to that of a club?"—"By what right?" exclaimed Goupil, "does Mirabeau act as a dictator in the Assembly?"—"Goupil," replied Mirabeau, "is as much mistaken when he calls me a dictator, as formerly when he termed me a Cataline."—The indignant roar of the Jacobins bellowing from their boasted mountain, in vain endeavoured to interrupt him.—"Silence these thirty voices," said Mirabeau, at the full pitch of his thundering voice; and the volcano was silent at his

---

[140] See Mignet, tom. i., p. 126; Lacretelle, tom. viii., p. 128.
"I have had in my hands a letter of Mirabeau, written for the purpose of being shown to the King. He there made offer of all his means to restore to France an efficient and respected, but a limited monarchy; he made use, among others, of this remarkable expression: 'I should lament to have laboured at nothing but a vast destruction.'"—M. de Staël, vol. i., p. 401.
"He (Mirabeau) received for a short time a pension of 20,000 francs, or £800 a-month, first from the Comte D'Artois, and afterwards the King; but he considered himself an agent intrusted with their affairs, and he accepted those pensions not to be governed by, but to govern, those who granted them."—Dumont, p. 230.

bidding.[141] Yet, possessed as he was of this mighty power, Mirabeau did not, perhaps, reflect how much less it would have availed him on the royal side, than when he sailed with all the wind and tide which the spirit of a great and general revolution could lend him. He was a man, too, as remarkable for his profligacy as his wonderful talents, and the chance which the King must have risked in embarking with him, was like that of the prince in the tale, who escaped from a desert island by embarking on board a skiff drifting among dangerous eddies, and rowed by a figure half human and half tiger.[142] The experiment was prevented by the sudden and violent illness and death of Mirabeau, who fell a victim to his debaucheries.[143] His death [April 2, 1791] was greatly lamented, though it is probable that, had the Apostle of the Revolution lived much longer, he would either have averted its progress, or his dissevered limbs would have ornamented the pikes of those multitudes, who, as it was, followed him to the grave with weapons trailed, and howling and lamentation.[144]

The King's other confidant was the Marquis de Bouillé, a person entirely different from Mirabeau. He was a French soldier of the old stamp, a Royalist by birth and disposition; had gained considerable fame during the American war, and at the time of the Revolution was governor of Metz and Alsace. Bouillé was endowed with a rare force of character, and proved able without having recourse to disguise of any kind, to keep the garrison of Metz in tolerable discipline during the general dissolution of the army. The

---

[141] Lacretelle, tom. viii., p. 126.

[142] Mirabeau bore much of his character imprinted on his person and features. He was short, bull-necked, and very strongly made. A quantity of thick matted hair hung round features of a coarse and exaggerated character, strongly scarred and seamed. "Figure to your mind," he said, describing his own countenance to a lady who knew him not, "a tiger who has had the small-pox." When he talked of confronting his opponents in the Assembly, his favourite phrase was, "I will show them *La Hure*," that is, the boar's head, meaning his own tusked and shaggy countenance.—S.

[143] "Mirabeau knew that his end was approaching. 'After my death,' said he, 'the factions will share among themselves the shreds of the monarchy.' He suffered cruelly in the last days of his life; and, when no longer able to speak, wrote to his physician for a dose of opium, in these words of Hamlet, 'to die—to sleep.' He received no consolation from religion."—M. de Staël, vol. i., p. 402.

[144] "His funeral obsequies were celebrated with extraordinary pomp by torchlight; 20,000 national guards, and delegates from all the sections of Paris, accompanied the corpse to the Pantheon, where it was placed by the remains of Des Cartes."—Lacretelle, tom. viii., p. 135.

state of military insubordination was so great, that La Fayette, and his party in the Assembly, not only hesitated to dismiss a general who was feared and obeyed by the regiments under his command, but, Royalist as he was, they found themselves obliged to employ the Marquis de Bouillé and his troops in subduing the formidable revolt of three regiments quartered at Nancy, which he accomplished with complete success, and such slaughter among the insurgents, as was likely to recommend subordination in future. The Republican party of course gave this act of authority the name of a massacre of the people, and even the Assembly at large, though Bouillé acted in consequence of their authority, saw with anxiety the increased importance of an avowed Royalist. La Fayette, who was Bouillé's relation, spared no pains to gain him to the Constitutional side, while Bouillé avowed publicly that he only retained his command in obedience to the King, and in the hope of serving him.[145]

With this general, who had as yet preserved an authority that was possessed by no other Royalist in France, the King entered into a close though secret correspondence in cipher, which turned chiefly on the best mode of facilitating the escape of the royal family from Paris, where late incidents had rendered his abode doubly odious, and doubly dangerous.

La Fayette's strength consisted in his popularity with the middle classes of the Parisians, who, in the character of national guards, looked up to him as their commandant, and in general obeyed his orders in dispersing those tumultuous assemblies of the lower orders, which threatened danger to persons and property. But La Fayette, though fixed in his principle to preserve monarchy as a part of the constitution, seems to have been always on cold and distrustful terms with the monarch personally. He was perpetually trying his own feelings, and those whom he influenced, by the thermometer, and became alarmed if his own loyalty or theirs arose above the most tepid degree.

---

[145] Toulongeon, tom. i., p. 242; Mignet, tom. i., p. 132.

Two marked incidents served to show that the civic guard were even less warm than their commandant in zeal for the royal person.

PROJECTED ATTACK ON VINCENNES

The national guard, headed by La Fayette, together with the edict respecting martial law, had, as we have observed, greatly contributed to the restoration of order in Paris, by checking, and dispersing, upon various occasions, those disorderly assemblies of rioters, whose violence and cruelty had dishonoured the commencement of the Revolution. But the spirit which raised these commotions was unabated, and was carefully nourished by the Jacobins and all their subordinate agents, whose popularity lay among the rabble, as that of the Constitutionalists did with the citizens. Among the current falsehoods of the day, arose a report that the old castle of Vincennes, situated about three miles from Paris, was to be used as a state prison in place of the Bastile. A large mob marched from the suburb called Saint Antoine, the residence of a great number of labourers of the lowest order, already distinguished by its zeal for the revolutionary doctrines. [Feb. 20.] They were about to commence the destruction of the ancient castle, when the vigilant commandant of Paris arrived, and dispersed them, not without bloodshed. In the meantime, the few Royalists whom Paris still contained, became alarmed lest this tumult, though beginning in another quarter, might be turned against the person of the King. For his protection about three hundred gentlemen repaired to the Tuileries, armed with sword canes, short swords, pistols, and such other weapons as could be best concealed about their persons, as they went through the streets. Their services and zeal were graciously acknowledged by the unfortunate Louis, little accustomed of late to such marks of devotion. But when La Fayette returned to the palace, at the head of his grenadiers of the national guard, he seems not to have been ill pleased that the intrusion of these gentlemen gave him an opportunity of showing, that if he had dispersed the revolutionary mob of the Fauxbourgs, it was without any undue degree of affection to the royal cause. He felt, or affected, extreme jealousy of the armed aristocrats whom he found in the

Tuileries, and treated them as men who had indecently thrust themselves into the palace, to usurp the duty of defending the King's person, by law consigned to the national guard. To appease the jealousy of the civic soldiers, the King issued his commands upon the Royalists to lay down their arms. He was no sooner obeyed by those, to whom alone out of so many millions he could still issue his commands, than a most scandalous scene ensued. The soldiers, falling upon the unfortunate gentlemen, expelled them from the palace with blows and insult, applying to them the name of "Knights of the Poniard," afterwards often repeated in revolutionary objurgation. The vexation and sorrow of the captive prince had a severe effect on his health, and was followed by indisposition.

The second incident we have alluded to intimated even more directly the personal restraint in which he was now held. Early in spring [April 18,] Louis had expressed his purpose of going to Saint Cloud, under the pretext of seeking a change of air, but in reality, it may be supposed, for the purpose of ascertaining what degree of liberty he would be permitted to exercise. The royal carriages were drawn out, and the King and Queen had already mounted theirs, when the cries of the spectators, echoed by those of the national guards who were upon duty, declared that the King should not be permitted to leave the Tuileries. La Fayette arrived—commanded, implored, threatened the refractory guards, but was answered by their unanimous refusal to obey his orders. After the scene of tumult had lasted more than an hour, and it had been clearly proved that La Fayette's authority was unable to accomplish his purpose, the royal persons returned to the palace, now their absolute and avowed prison.[146]

La Fayette was so much moved by this affront, that he laid down his commission as commandant of the national guard; and although he resumed it, upon the general remonstrances and excuses of the corps, it was not without severely reproaching them for their want of discipline, and intimating justly, that the respect they showed ought to be for his rank and office, not for his person.

---

[146] Lacretelle, tom. viii., p. 220.

Meantime, the natural inferences from these cruel lessons, drove the King and Queen nearly desperate. The events of the 28th of February had shown that they were not to be permitted to introduce their friends or defenders within the fatal walls which inclosed them; those of the 18th April proved, that they were not allowed to leave their precincts. To fly from Paris, to gather around him such faithful subjects as might remain, seemed, though a desperate resource, the only one which remained to the unhappy monarch, and the preparations were already made for the fatal experiment.

The Marquis de Bouillé had, under various pretences, formed a camp at Montmedy, and had drawn thither some of the troops he could best depend upon; but such was the universal indisposition, both of the soldiery and the people of every description, that the general seems to have entertained almost no hope of any favourable result for the royal cause.[147] The King's life might have been saved by his escaping into foreign parts, but there was hardly any prospect of restoring the monarchy.

The history of the unhappy Journey to Varennes is well known. On the night between the 20th and 21st of June, Louis and his Queen, with their two children, attended by the Princess Elizabeth and Madame de Tourzel, and escorted by three gentlemen of the gardes du corps, set out in disguise from Paris. The King left behind him a long manifesto, inculpating the Assembly for various political errors, and solemnly protesting against the acts of government to which he had been compelled, as he stated, to give his assent, during what he termed his captivity, which he seemed to have dated from his compulsory residence in the Tuileries.[148]

ESCAPE OF THE KING

The very first person whom the Queen encountered in the streets was La Fayette himself, as he crossed the Place du

---

[147] Mignet, tom. i., p. 132; Thiers, tom. i., p. 287.
[148] See Annual Register, vol. xxxiii., p. 131.

Carousel.[149] A hundred other dangers attended the route of the unfortunate fugitives, and the hair-breadth escapes by which they profited, seemed to intimate the favour of fortune, while they only proved her mutability. An escort placed for them at the Pont de Sommeville, had been withdrawn, after their remaining at that place for a time had excited popular suspicion. At Saint Menehould they met a small detachment of dragoons, stationed there by Bouillé, also for their escort. But while they halted to change horses, the King, whose features were remarkable, was recognised by Drouet, a son of the postmaster. The young man was a keen revolutionist, and resolving to prevent the escape of the sovereign, he mounted a horse, and pushed forwards to Varennes to prepare the municipality for the arrival of the King.

Two remarkable chances seemed to show that the good angel of Louis still strove in his favour. Drouet was pursued by a resolute Royalist, a quartermaster of dragoons, who suspected his purpose, and followed him with the design of preventing it, at all hazards. But Drouet, better acquainted with the road, escaped a pursuit which might have been fatal to him. The other incident was, that Drouet for a time pursued the road to Verdun, instead of that to Varennes, concluding the King had taken the former direction, and was only undeceived by an accident.

He reached Varennes, and found a ready disposition to stop the flight of the unhappy prince. The King was stopped at Varennes and arrested; the national guards were called out—the dragoons refused to fight in the King's defence—an escort of hussars, who might have cut a passage, arrived too late, acted with reluctance, and finally deserted the town. Still there remained one last throw for their freedom. If the time could have been protracted but for an hour and a half, Bouillé would have been before Varennes at the head of such a body of faithful and disciplined troops as might easily have dispersed the national militia. He had even opened a correspondence with the royal prisoners through a faithful emissary

---

[149] "To deceive any one that might follow, we drove about several streets: at last we returned to the Little Carousel. My brother was fast asleep at the bottom of the carriage. We saw M. de la Fayette go by, who had been at my father's *coucher*. There we remained, waiting a full hour, ignorant of what was going on. Never did time appear so tedious."—Duchess of Angoulême's *Narrative*, p. 9.

who ventured into Varennes, and obtained speech of the King; but could obtain no answer more decided than that, being a prisoner, Louis declined giving any orders. Finally, almost all the troops of the Marquis de Bouillé declared against the King and in favour of the nation, tending to show the little chance which existed of a favourable issue to the King's attempt to create a Royalist force. The Marquis himself made his escape with difficulty into the Austrian territories.[150]

The Parisians in general, but especially the Legislative Assembly, had been at first astounded, as if by an earthquake. The King's escape seemed to menace his instant return at the head of aristocratical levies, supported by foreign troops. Reflection made most men see, as a more probable termination, that the dynasty of the Bourbons could no longer hold the crown; and that the government, already so democratical in principle, must become a republic in all its forms.[151] The Constitutionalists grieved that their constitution required a monarchical head; the Republicans rejoiced, for it had long been their object to abolish the kingly office. Nor did the anarchists of the Jacobin Club less exult; for the events which had taken place, and their probable consequences, were such as to animate the revolutionary spirit, exasperate the public mind, prevent the return of order, and stimulate the evil passions of lawless ambition, and love of blood and rapine.

---

[150] Bouillé's Memoirs, pp. 275-290; Lacretelle, tom. viii., p. 258.
[151] The following anecdote will serve to show by what means this conclusion was insinuated into the public mind. A group in the Palais Royal were discussing in great alarm the consequences of the King's flight, when a man, dressed in a thread-bare great-coat, leaped upon a chair and addressed them thus:—"Citizens, listen to a tale, which shall not be a long one. A certain well-meaning Neapolitan was once on a time startled in his evening walk, by the astounding intelligence that the Pope was dead. He had not recovered his astonishment, when behold he is informed of a new disaster,—the King of Naples was also no more. 'Surely,' said the worthy Neapolitan, 'the sun must vanish from heaven at such a combination of fatalities.' But they did not cease here. The Archbishop of Palermo, he is informed, has also died suddenly. Overcome by this last shock he retired to bed, but not to sleep. In the morning he was disturbed in his melancholy reverie by a rumbling noise, which he recognised at once to be the motion of the wooden instrument which makes macaroni. 'Aha!' says the good man, starting up, 'can I trust my ears?—The Pope is dead—the King of Naples is dead—the Bishop of Palermo is dead—yet my neighbour the baker makes macaroni! Come! The lives of these great folk are not then so indispensable to the world after all.'" The man in the great-coat jumped down and disappeared. "I have caught his meaning," said a woman amongst the listeners. "He has told us a tale, and it begins like all tales—*There was ONCE a King and a Queen.*"—S.

But La Fayette was determined not to relinquish the constitution he had formed, and, in spite of the unpopularity of the royal dignity, rendered more so by this frustrated attempt to escape, he was resolved to uphold it; and was joined in this purpose by Barnave and others, who did not always share his sentiments, but who thought it shame, apparently, to show to the world, that a constitution, framed for immortality upon the best political principles of the most accomplished statesmen in France, was so slightly built, as to part and go asunder at the first shock. The purpose of the commandant of Paris, however, was not to be accomplished without a victory over the united strength of the Republican and Jacobinical parties, who on their part might be expected to put in motion on the occasion their many-handed revolutionary engine, an insurrection of the people.

Such was the state of political opinions, when the unfortunate Louis was brought back to Paris.[152] He was, with his wife and children, covered with dust, dejected with sorrow, and exhausted with fatigue. The faithful gardes du corps who had accompanied their flight, sate bound like felons on the driving seat of the carriage. His progress was at first silent and unhonoured. The guard did not present arms—the people remained covered—no man said God bless him. At another part of the route, a number of the rabble precipitated themselves on the carriage, and it was with the utmost difficulty that the national guards and some deputies, could assure it a safe passage.[153] Under such auspices were the royal family committed once more to their old prison of the Tuileries.

---

[152] Three commissioners, Petion, La Tour Maubourg, and Barnave, were sent to reconduct the fugitives to Paris. They met them at Epernay, and travelled with them to the Tuileries. During the journey, Barnave, though a stern Republican, was so melted by the graceful dignity of the Queen, and impressed with the good sense and benevolence of the King, that he became inclined to the royal cause, and ever after supported their fortunes. His attentions to the Queen were so delicate, and his conduct so gentle, that she assured Madame Campan, that she forgave him all the injuries he had inflicted on her family.—Thiers, tom. i., p. 299.

[153] "Count de Dampierre, a nobleman inhabiting a chateau near the road, approaching to kiss the hand of the King, was instantly pierced by several balls from the escort; his blood sprinkled the royal carriage, and his remains were torn to pieces by the savages."—Lacretelle, tom. viii., p. 271; M. de Campan, tom. ii., p. 154.

Meantime the crisis of the King's fate seemed to be approaching. It was not long ere the political parties had an opportunity of trying their respective force. A meeting was held, upon the motion of the Republican and Jacobinical leaders, in the Champ de Mars, [July 17,] to subscribe a petition[154] for the dethronement of the King, couched in the boldest and broadest terms. There was in this plain a wooden edifice raised on scaffolding, called the Altar of the Country, which had been erected for the ceremony of the Federation of 14th July, 1790, when the assembled representatives of the various departments of France took their oath to observe the constitution. On this altar the petition was displayed for signature; but each revolutionary act required a preliminary libation of blood, and the victims on this occasion were two wretched invalids, whom the rabble found at breakfast under the scaffolding which supported the revolutionary altar, and accused of a design to blow up the patriots. To accuse was to condemn. They were murdered without mercy, and their heads paraded on pikes, became as usual the standards of the insurgent citizens.[155]

REVOLT IN THE CHAMP DE MARS

The municipal officers attempted to disperse the assemblage, but to no purpose. Bailli, mayor of Paris, together with La Fayette, resolved to repel force by force; martial law was proclaimed, and its signal, the red flag, was displayed from the Hôtel de Ville. La Fayette, with a body of grenadiers, arrived in the Champ de Mars. He was received with abuse, and execrations of "Down with La Fayette! Down with martial law!" followed by a volley of stones. The commandant gave orders to fire, and was on this occasion most promptly obeyed; for the grenadiers pouring their shot directly into the crowd, more than a hundred men lay dead at the first volley. The Champ de Mars was empty in an instant, and the constituted authority, for the first time since the Revolution commenced, remained master of a contested field. La Fayette ought to have followed up this triumph of the legal force, by giving a triumph to the law itself, in the trial and conviction of some of his prisoners,

---

[154] Drawn up by Brissot, author of the *Patriot Française*.
[155] Lacretelle, tom. viii., p. 311.

selecting particularly the agitators employed by the Club of Jacobins; but he thought he had done enough in frightening these harpies back to their dens. Some of their leaders sought and found refuge among the Republicans, which was not, in that hour of danger, very willingly granted.[156] Marat, and many others who had been hitherto the undaunted and unwearied instigators of the rabble, were compelled to skulk in obscurity for some time after this victory of the Champ de Mars, which the Jacobins felt severely at the time, and forgot not afterwards to avenge most cruelly.[157]

This victory led to the triumph of the Constitutionalists in the Assembly. The united exertions of those who argued against the deposition of Louis, founding their reasoning upon that constitutional law, which declares the King inviolable in his person, overpowered the party who loudly called on the Assembly to proclaim his forfeiture, or appoint his trial. The Assembly clogged, however, the future inviolability of the King with new penalties. If the King, having accepted the constitution, should retract, they decreed he should be considered as abdicated. If he should order his army, or any part of it, to act against the nation, this should, in like manner, be deemed an act of abdication; and an abdicated monarch, it was farther decreed, should become an ordinary citizen, answerable to the laws for every act he had done since the act of abdication.

The constitution, with the royal immunity thus curtailed and maimed, was now again presented to the King, who again accepted it purely and simply, in terms which, while they excited acclamation from the Assembly, were but feebly echoed from the gallery, [September 14.] The legislators were glad to make a virtue of necessity, and complete their constitutional code, though in a precarious manner; but the hearts of the people were now decidedly alienated from the King, and, by a strange concurrence of misfortune, mixed with some errors, Louis, whose genuine and disinterested good intentions ought to have made him the darling of his subjects, had now become the object of their jealousy and detestation.

---

[156] Mémoires de Mad. Roland, art. *"Robert,"* —[part i., p. 157.]—S.
[157] Thiers, tom. i. , p. 312.

LOUIS ACCEPTS THE CONSTITUTION

Upon reviewing the measures which had been adopted on the King's return to Paris, historians will probably be of opinion, that it was impolitic in the Assembly to offer the constitutional crown to Louis, and imprudent in that unhappy prince to accept it under the conditions annexed. On the former point it must be remembered, that these innovators, who had changed every thing else in the state, could, upon principle, have had no hesitation to alter the person or the dynasty of their sovereign. According to the sentiments which they had avowed, the King, as well as the Nobles and Clergy, was in their hands, as clay in that of the potter, to be used or thrown away at pleasure. The present King, in the manifesto left behind him on his flight, had protested to all Europe against the system of which he was made the head, and it was scarcely possible that his sentiments could be altered in its favour, by the circumstances attending his unwilling return from Varennes. The Assembly, therefore, acting upon their own principles, should have at once proceeded on the idea that his flight was a virtual abdication of the crown—they should have made honourable provision for a prince placed in so uncommon a situation, and suffered him to enjoy in Spain or Italy an honourable independence, so soon as the storm was ended which threatened them from abroad. In the meanwhile, the person of the King would have been a pledge in their hands, which might have given them some advantage in treating with the foreign princes of his family, and the potentates of Europe in general. The general policy of this appears so obvious, that it was probably rather the difficulty of arranging in what hands the executive authority should be lodged, than any preference of Louis XVI., which induced the Assembly again to deposit it in his hands, shorn, in a great measure, even of the limited consequence and privileges constitutionally annexed to it.[158] La Fayette and his party perhaps reckoned on the

---

[158] "Mr. Fox told me in England, in 1793, that at the time of the King's departure to Varennes, he should have wished that he had been allowed to quit the kingdom in peace."—M. de Staël, vol. i., p. 408.
Napoleon said at St. Helena:—"The National Assembly never committed so great an error as in bringing back the King from Varennes. A fugitive and powerless, he was hastening to the frontier, and in a few hours would have been out of the French territory. What should they have done in these circumstances? Clearly facilitated his escape, and declared the

King's spirit having given way, from observing how unanimously the people of France were disposed in favour of the new state of things, and may have trusted to his accommodating himself, therefore, without further resistance, to act the part of the unsubstantial pageant which the constitution assigned him.

If it was impolitic in the Constitutionalists to replace the crown upon the head of Louis, it was certainly unworthy of that monarch to accept it, unless invested with such a degree of power as might give him some actual weight and preponderance in the system. Till his flight to Varennes, the King's dislike to the constitution was a secret in his own bosom, which might indeed be suspected from circumstances, but which could not be proved; and which, placed as he was, the King was entitled to conceal, since his real sentiments could not be avowed consistently with his personal safety. But now this veil was torn aside, and he had told all Europe in a public declaration, that he had been acting under constraint, since the time he was brought in triumph from Versailles to Paris. It would certainly have been most dignified in Louis to have stood or fallen in conformity with this declaration, made on the only occasion which he had enjoyed for such a length of time, of speaking his own free sentiments. He should not, when brought back to his prison, have resumed the submission of a prisoner, or affected to accept as a desirable boon, the restoration, as it might be called, and that in a mutilated state, of a sovereignty, which he had voluntarily abandoned, at such extreme personal risk. His resolutions were too flexible, and too much at the mercy of circumstances, to be royal or noble. Charles I., even in the Isle of Wight, treated with his subjects, as a prisoner indeed, but still as a King, refusing to accede to such articles as, in his own mind, he was determined not to abide by. Louis, we conceive, should have returned the same answer to the Assembly which he did to the royalist officer at Varennes, "that a prisoner could give no orders, and make no concessions." He should not, like a bird which has escaped and been retaken, forget the notes which he uttered when at freedom, and return to his set and prescribed prison-song the instant that the cage again enclosed him. No man, above all, no king, should place the language of his

---

throne vacant by his desertion. They would thus have avoided the infamy of a regicide government, and attained their great object of republican institutions."

feelings and sentiments so much at the disposal of fortune. An adherence to the sentiments expressed in his voluntary declaration, might, it is possible, have afforded him the means of making some more favourable composition; whereas, the affectation of willing submission to the same force which his own voice had so lately proclaimed illegal, could but make the unhappy King suspected of attempting a deceit, by which no one could be deceived. But the difficulties of his situation were great, and Louis might well remember the proverb, which places the grave of deposed sovereigns close to their prison-gates. He might be persuaded to temporize with the party which still offered to preserve a show of royalty in the constitution, until time or circumstances permitted him to enlarge its basis. In the meantime, if we can believe Bertrand de Moleville, Louis avowed to him the determination to act under the constitution with all sincerity and good faith; but it must be owned, that it would have required the virtues of a saint to have enabled him to make good this pledge, had the success of the Austrians, or any strong counter-revolutionary movement, tempted him to renounce it. At all events, the King was placed in a doubtful and suspicious position towards the people of France, who must necessarily have viewed with additional jealousy the head of a government, who, avowedly discontented with the share of power allotted to him, had nevertheless accepted it,—like the impoverished gamester, who will rather play for small stakes than be cut out of the game.

CONSTITUTIONAL ASSEMBLY

The work of the constitution being thus accomplished, the National, or, as it is usually called, the Constituent Assembly, dissolved itself, [Sept. 29,] agreeably to the vow they had pronounced in the Tennis-court at Versailles. The constitution, that structure which they raised for immortality, soon afterwards became ruinous; but in few assemblies of statesmen have greater and more varied talents been assembled. Their debates were often fierce and stormy, their mode of arguing wild and vehement, their resolutions sudden and ill-considered. These were the faults partly of the French character, which is peculiarly open to sudden impulses, partly to the great changes perpetually crowding upon them, and to the exciting progress of a revolution which hurried all men into extravagance. On the other hand, they respected freedom of debate; and the proscription of members of their body, for maintaining and declaring their sentiments, in opposition to that of the majority, is not to be found in their records, though so fearfully frequent in those of their successors. Their main and master error was the attempt to do too much, and to do it all at once. The parties kept no terms with each other, would wait for no conviction, and make no concession. It was a war for life and death betwixt men, who, had they seen more calmly for their country and for themselves, would rather have sacrificed some part of the theoretical exactness of principle on which they insisted, to the opportunity of averting practical evil, or attaining practical good. The errors of the Assembly were accordingly those of extremes. They had felt the weight of the feudal chains, and they destroyed the whole nobility. The monarch had been too powerful for the liberties of the subject—they now bound him as a slave at the feet of the legislative authority. Their arch of liberty gave way, because they hesitated to place upon it, in the shape of an efficient executive government, a weight sufficient to keep it steady. Yet to these men France was indebted for the first principles of civil liberty. They kindled the flame, though they could not regulate it; and such as now enjoy its temperate warmth should have sympathy for the errors of those to whom they owe a boon so inestimable;—nor should this sympathy be the less, that so many perished in the conflagration, which, at the commencement, they had fanned too rashly. They did even more, for they endeavoured to heal the wounds of the nation by passing an act of general amnesty, which at once placed in security the Jacobins of the Champ de Mars, and the unfortunate companions of the King's flight. This was one of their last and wisest decrees, could they have enforced its observance by their successors.

The adieus which they took of power were anything but prophetic. They pronounced the Revolution ended, and the Constitution completed—the one was but commencing, and the other was baseless as a morning dream.

Chapter VII

Legislative Assembly—Its Composition—Constitutionalists—Girondists or Brissotins—Jacobins—Views and Sentiments of Foreign Nations—England—Views of the Tories and Whigs—Anacharsis Clootz—Austria—Prussia—Russia—Sweden—Emigration of the French Princes and Clergy—Increasing Unpopularity of Louis from this Cause—Death of the Emperor Leopold, and its Effects—France declares War—Views and Interests of the different Parties in France at this Period—Decree against Monsieur—Louis interposes his Veto—Decree against the Priests who should refuse the Constitutional Oath—Louis again interposes his Veto—Consequences of these Refusals—Fall of De Lessart—Ministers now chosen from the Brissotins—All Parties favourable to War.

The first, or Constituent Assembly, in destroying almost all which existed as law in France, when they were summoned together as States-General, had preserved, at least in form, the name and power of a monarch. The Legislative Assembly, which succeeded them, seemed preparing to destroy the symbol of royalty which their predecessors had left standing, though surrounded by republican enactments.

The composition of this second body of representatives was much more unfavourable to the royal cause than that of those whom they succeeded. In a bad hour for France and themselves, the Constituent Assembly had adopted two regulations, which had the same disabling effect on their own political interest, as the celebrated self-denying ordinance in the Long Parliament had upon that of the Presbyterians. By the first of these decrees, the members of the Constituent Assembly were rendered incapable of being elected to that which should succeed its dissolution: by the second, they were declared ineligible to be ministers of the crown, until two years had elapsed after their sitting as legislators.[159] Those individuals who had already acquired some political knowledge and information, were thus virtually excluded from the counsels of the state, and pronounced inadmissible into the service of the crown. This exclusion was adopted upon the wild principle of levelling, which was one prime moving spring of the Revolution, and which affected to destroy even the natural aristocracy of talents. "Who are the *distinguished members* whom the speaker mentions?" said a Jacobin orator, in the true spirit of this imaginary equality;—"There are no members of the Assembly more distinguished than others by talents or skill, any more than by birth or rank—We are all EQUAL."[160] Rare words indeed, and flattering, doubtless, to many in the Assembly. Unhappily no legislative decree can give sense to folly, or experience to ignorance; it could only prevent a certain portion of wisdom and talent from being called into the service of the country. Both King and people were necessarily obliged to put their confidence in men of inexperience in business, liable to act with all the rashness by which inexperience is generally attended. As the Constituent Assembly contained the first and readiest choice among the men of ability whom France had in her bosom, it followed that the second Assembly could not be equal to the first in abundance of talent; but still the Legislative Assembly held in its ranks many men of no ordinary acquirements, and a few of a corresponding boldness and determination of character. A slight review of the parties into which it was divided, will show how much the influence of the crown was lowered in the scale.

CONSTITUTIONALISTS

There was no party remained which could be termed strictly or properly Royalist. Those who were attached to the old monarchy of France were now almost all exiles, and there were left but few even of that second class of more moderate and more reasonable

---

[159] Mignet, tom. i., p. 141; Dumont, p. 244.
[160] "One evening M. de Narbonne made use of this expression: 'I appeal to the most distinguished members of this Assembly.' At that moment the whole party of the Mountain rose up in a fury, and Merlin, Bazire, and Chabot, declared, that 'all the deputies were equally distinguished.'"—M. de Staël, tom. ii., p. 39.

Royalists, who desired to establish a free constitution on the basis of an effective monarchy, strong enough to protect the laws against license, but not sufficiently predominant to alter or overthrow them. Cazalès,[161] whose chivalrous defence of the nobility,—Maury,[162] whose eloquent pleadings for the Church,—had so often made an honourable but vain struggle against the advances of revolution, were now silent and absent, and the few feeble remnants of their party had ranged themselves with the Constitutionalists, who were so far favourers of monarchy as it made part of their favourite system—and no farther. La Fayette continued to be the organ of that party, and had assembled under his banners Duport,[163] Barnave, Lameth, all of whom had striven to keep pace with the headlong spirit of the Revolution, but, being outstripped by more active and forward champions of the popular cause, now shifted ground, and formed a union with those who were disposed to maintain, that the present constitution was adapted to all the purposes of free and effectual government, and that, by its creation, all farther revolutionary measures were virtually superseded.

In stern opposition to those admirers of the constitution, stood two bodies of unequal numbers, strength, and efficacy; of which the first was determined that the Revolution should never stop until the downfall of the monarchy, while the second entertained the equally resolved purpose of urging these changes still farther onwards, to the total destruction of all civil order, and the establishment of a government, in which terror and violence should be the ruling principles, to be wielded by the hands of the demagogues who dared to nourish a scheme so nefarious. We have indicated the existence of both these parties in the first, or Constituent Assembly; but in the second, called the Legislative, they assumed a more decided form, and appeared united towards the abolition of royalty as a common end, though certain, when it was

---

[161] Cazalès, one of the most brilliant orators of the Assembly, was born at Grenade-sur-la-Garonne in 1752. He died in 1805. In 1821, *Les Discours et Opinions de Cazalès* were published at Paris, in an octavo volume.

[162] Shortly after the dissolution of the Constituent Assembly, Maury retired to Italy, where he became a cardinal. In 1806, he returned to France, and in 1810 was made, by Napoleon, Archbishop of Paris. He died at Rome in 1817.

[163] After the 10th of August, 1792, Duport fled to Switzerland, where he died in 1798.

attained, to dispute with each other the use which was to be made of the victory. In the words of Shakspeare, they were determined

"To lay this Angiers even with the ground, Then, after, fight who should be king of it."[164]

The first of these parties took its most common denomination from the Gironde, a department which sent most of its members to the Convention. Condorcet, dear to science, was one of this party, and it was often named from Brissot, another of its principal leaders. Its most distinguished champions were men bred as lawyers in the south of France, who had, by mutual flattery, and the habit of living much together, acquired no small portion of that self-conceit and overweening opinion of each other's talents, which may be frequently found among small provincial associations for political or literary purposes. Many had eloquence, and most of them a high fund of enthusiasm, which a classical education, and their intimate communication with each other, where each idea was caught up, lauded, re-echoed, and enhanced, had exalted into a spirit of republican zeal. They doubtless had personal ambition, but in general it seems not to have been of a low or selfish character. Their aims were often honourable though visionary, and they marched with great courage towards their proposed goal, with the vain purpose of erecting a pure republic, in a state so disturbed as that of France, and by hands so polluted as those of their Jacobin associates.[165] It will be recorded, however, to the disgrace of their pretensions to stern republican virtue, that the Girondists were willing to employ, for the accomplishment of their purpose, those base and guilty tools which afterwards effected their own destruction. They were for using the revolutionary means of insurrection and violence, until the republic should be established, and no longer; or in the words of the satirist,

---

[164] King John, act ii., sc. i.
[165] Dumont, p. 272; Mignet, tom. i., p. 151.

"For letting Rapine loose, and Murther, To rage just so far, but no further; And setting all the land on fire To burn t' a scantling, but no higher."[166]

JACOBINS

The Jacobins,—the second of these parties,—were allies of the Brissotins, with the ulterior purpose of urging the revolutionary force to the uttermost, but using as yet the shelter of their republican mantle. Robespierre, who, by an affectation of a frugal and sequestered course of life, preserved among the multitude the title of the Incorruptible, might be considered as the head of the Jacobins, if they had indeed a leader more than wolves have, which tune their united voices to the cry of him who bays the loudest. Danton, inexorable as Robespierre himself, but less prudent because he loved gold and pleasure as well as blood and power, was next in authority. Marat, who loved to talk of murder as soldiers do of battles; the wretched Collot d'Herbois, a broken-down player; Chabot, an ex-capuchin;[167] with many other men of desperate character, whose moderate talents were eked out by the most profligate effrontery, formed the advanced-guard of this party, soiled with every species of crime, and accustomed to act their parts in the management of those dreadful insurrections, which had at once promoted and dishonoured the Revolution. It is needless to preserve from oblivion names such as Santerre and Hebert, distinguished for cruelty and villany above the other subaltern villains. Such was the party who, at the side of the Brissotins, stood prompt to storm the last bulwarks of the monarchy, reserving to themselves the secret determination, that the spoil should be all their own.[168]

---

[166] Hudibras, part iii., c. 2.
[167] Chabot was the principal editor of a paper entitled *Journal Populaire, ou le Catéchisme des Sans Culottes*. He was guillotined in April, 1794.
[168] Thiers, tom. ii., p. 12; Mignet, tom. i., p. 152.

FORCE OF PARTIES

The force of these three parties was as variously composed as their principles. That of La Fayette, as we have repeatedly observed, lay amongst the better order of shopkeepers and citizens, and other proprietors, who had assumed arms for their own protection, and to maintain something like general good order. These composed the steadiest part of the national guard, and, generally speaking, were at the devotion of their commandant, though his authority was resisted by them on some occasions, and seemed daily to grow more precarious. The Royalists might perhaps have added some force to the Constitutional party, but La Fayette did not now possess such an unsuspected character with the so called friends of freedom, as could permit him to use the obnoxious assistance of those who were termed its enemies. His high character as a military man still sustained an importance, which, nevertheless, was already somewhat on the wane.

The party of the Gironde had in their favour the theoretical amateurs of liberty and equality, young men, whose heated imaginations saw the Forum of ancient Rome in the gardens of the Palais Royal, and yielded a ready assent to whatever doctrine came recommended by a flourishing and eloquent peroration, and was rounded off in a sounding sentence, or a quaint apothegm. The partisans of Brissot had some interest in the southern departments, which had sent them to the capital, and conceived that they had a great deal more. They pretended that there existed in those districts a purer flame of freedom than in the metropolis itself, and held out, that Liberty, if expelled from Paris, would yet find refuge in a new republic, to be founded on the other side of the Loire. Such day-dreams did not escape the Jacobins, who carefully treasured them to be the apology of future violence, and finally twisted them into an accusation which bestowed on the Brissotins the odious name of Federalists, and charged them with an intention to dismember France, by splitting it into a league of petty commonwealths, like those of Holland and Switzerland.

The Brissotins had a point of union in the saloon of Madame Roland, wife to one of their number. The beauty, talents, courage, and accomplishments of this remarkable woman, pushed forward into public notice a husband of very middling abilities, and preserved a high influence over the association of philosophical rhapsodists, who hoped to oppose pikes with syllogisms, and to govern a powerful country by the discipline of an academy.

The substantial and dreadful support of the Jacobins lay in the club so named, with the yet more violent association of Cordeliers and their original affiliated societies, which reigned paramount over those of the municipal bodies, which in most departments were fain to crouch under their stern and sanguinary dominion. This club had more than once changed masters, for its principal and leading feature being the highest point of democratical ardour, it drove from its bosom in succession those who fell short of the utmost pitch of extravagant zeal for liberty and equality, manifested by the most uncompromising violence. The word *moderation* was as odious in this society as could have been that of slavery, and he who could affect the most exaggerated and outrageous strain of patriotism was sure to outstrip their former leaders. Thus the Lameths took the guidance of the club out of the hands of La Fayette; Robespierre, and Marat, wrenched the management from the Lameths; and, considering their pitch of extravagant ferocity, there was little chance of *their* losing it, unless an Avatar of the Evil Spirit had brought Satan himself to dispute the point in person.

The leaders, who were masters of this club, had possession, as we have often remarked, of the master-keys to the passions of the populace, could raise a forest of pikes with one word, and unsheath a thousand daggers with another. They directly and openly recommended the bloodiest and most ruffian-like actions, instead of those which, belonging to open and manly warfare, present something that is generous even in the midst of violence. "Give me," said the atrocious Marat, when instructing Barbaroux in his bloody science,—"Give me two-hundred Neapolitans—the knife in their right hand, in their left a *muff*, to serve for a target—with these I will traverse France, and complete the revolution." At the same lecture he made an exact calculation, (for the monster was possessed of some science,) showing in what manner two hundred and sixty thousand men might be put to death in one day.[169] Such were the means, the men, and the plans of the Jacobins, which they were now, in the Legislative Assembly, to oppose to the lukewarm loyalty of the Constitutionalists, and, in the hour of need, to the fine-spun republican theories of the Brissotins. But ere we proceed in our review of the internal affairs of the nation, it becomes now necessary to glance at her external relations.

Hitherto France had acted alone in this dreadful tragedy, while the other nations of Europe looked on in amazement, which now began to give place to a desire of action. No part of public law is more subtle in argument than that which pretends to define the exact circumstances in which, according to the proper interpretation of the *Jus Gentium*, one nation is at liberty, or called upon, to interfere in the internal concerns of another. If my next neighbour's house is on fire, I am not only entitled, but obliged, by the rules alike of prudence and humanity, to lend my aid to extinguish it; or, if a cry of murder arises in his household, the support due to the law, and the protection of the innocent, will excuse my forcible entrance upon his premises. These are extreme cases, and easily decided; they have their parallels in the laws of nations, but they are of rare occurrence. But there lies between them and the general maxim, prohibiting the uncalled-for interference of one party in what primarily and principally concerns another, a whole *terra incognita* of special cases, in which it may be difficult to pronounce any satisfactory decision.

In the history of nations, however, little practical difficulty has been felt, for wherever the jurisconsults have found a Gordian knot, the sword of the sovereign has severed it without ceremony. The doubt has usually been decided on the practical questions, What benefit the neutral power is like to derive from his interference? And whether he possesses the power of using it effectually, and to his own advantage? In free countries, indeed, the public opinion must be listened to; but man is the same in every situation, and the same desire of aggrandizement, which induces an arbitrary monarch to shut his ears to the voice of justice, is equally powerful with senates and popular assemblies; and aggressions have been as frequently

---

[169] Mémoires de Barbaroux, p. 47; Mignet, tom. i., p. 220.

made by republics and limited monarchs on the independence of their neighbours, as by those princes who have no bounds to their own royal pleasure. The gross and barefaced injustice of the partition of Poland had gone far to extinguish any remains of hesitation upon such subjects, and might be said to be a direct recognition of the right of the strongest. There would not, therefore, have wanted pretexts for interference in the affairs of France, of the nations around her, had any of them been at the time capable of benefiting by the supposed opportunity.

VIEWS OF ENGLAND

England, the rival of France, might, from the example of that country, have exercised a right of interfering with her domestic concerns, in requital of the aid which she afforded to the Americans; but besides that the publicity of the Parliamentary debates must compel the most ambitious British minister to maintain at least an appearance of respect to the rights of other countries, England was herself much divided upon the subject of the French Revolution.

This was not the case when the eventful scene first commenced. We believe that the first display of light, reason, and rational liberty in France, was hailed as a day-spring through all Britain, and that there were few if any in that country, who did not feel their hearts animated and enlarged by seeing such a great and noble nation throwing aside the fetters, which at once restrained and dishonoured them, and assuming the attitude, language, and spirit of a free people. All men's thoughts and eyes were bent on struggles, which seemed to promise the regeneration of a mighty country, and the British generally felt as if days of old hate and mutual rivalry would thereafter be forgotten, and that in future the similarity of liberal institutions, and the possession of a just portion of rational liberty on either side, would throw kindness and cordiality into the intercourse between the two countries, since France would no longer have ground to contemn England as a country of seditious and sullen clowns, or Britain to despise France as a nation of willing slaves.

This universal sympathy was not removed by the forcible capture of the Bastile, and the violences of the people on that occasion. The name of that fortress was so unpopular, as to palliate and apologize for the excesses which took place on its fall, and it was not to be expected that a people so long oppressed, when exerting their power for the first time, should be limited by the strict bounds of moderation. But in England there always have been, and must exist, two parties of politicians, who will not long continue to regard events of such an interesting nature with similar sensations.

The Revolutionists of France were naturally desirous to obtain the applause of the elder-born of freedom, and the societies in Britain, which assumed the character of the peculiar admirers and protectors of liberty, conceived themselves obliged to extend their countenance to the changes in the neighbouring nation. Hence there arose a great intercourse between the clubs and self-constituted bodies in Britain, which assumed the extension of popular freedom as the basis of their association, and the Revolutionists in France, who were realizing the systems of philosophical theorists upon the same ground. Warm tributes of applause were transmitted from several of these associations; the ambassadors sent to convey them were received with great distinction by the National Assembly; and the urbane intercourse which took place on these occasions led to exaggerated admiration of the French system on the part of those who had thus unexpectedly become the medium of intercourse between a great nation and a few private societies.[170] The latter were gradually induced to form unfavourable comparisons betwixt the Temple of French freedom, built, as it seemed to them, upon the most perfect principles of symmetry and uniformity, and that in which the goddess had been long worshipped in England, and which, on the contrast, appeared to them like an ancient edifice constructed in barbaric times, and incongruously encumbered with Gothic ornaments and emblems, which modern political architects had discarded. But these political sages overlooked the important circumstance, that the buttresses, which seemed in some respects encumbrances to the English edifice, might, on examination, be found to add to its stability; and that in fact they furnished evidence to show, that the venerable pile was built with cement, fitted to

---

[170] See Annual Register, vol. xxxiv., pp. 70-72, 73.

endure the test of ages, while that of France, constructed of lath daubed with untempered mortar, like the pageants she exhibited on the revolutionary festivals, was only calculated to be the wonder of a day.

The earnest admiration of either party of the state is sure in England to be balanced by the censure of the other, and leads to an immediate trial of strength betwixt them. The popular side is always the more loud, the more active, the more imposing of the two contending parties. It is formidable, from the body of talents which it exhibits, (for those ambitious of distinction are usually friends to innovation,) and from the unanimity and vigour with which it can wield them. There may be, and indeed always are, great differences in the point to which each leader is desirous to carry reformation; but they are unanimous in desiring its commencement. The Opposition, also, as it is usually termed, has always included several of the high aristocracy of the country, whose names ennoble their rank, and whose large fortunes are a pledge that they will, for their own sakes, be a check upon eager and violent experimentalists. The Whigs, moreover, have the means of influencing assemblies of the lower orders, to whom the name of liberty is, and ought to be dear, since it is the privilege which must console them for narrow circumstances and inferiority of condition; and these means the party, so called, often use successfully, always with industry and assiduity.

The counterbalance to this active and powerful body is to be found, speaking generally, in the higher classes at large—the great mass of nobility and gentry—the clergy of the Established Church—the superior branches of the law—the wealthier of the commercial classes—and the bulk of those who have property to lose, and are afraid of endangering it. This body is like the Ban of the Germanic empire, a formidable force, but slow and diffident in its operations, and requiring the stimulus of sudden alarm to call it into effective exercise. To one or other of these great national parties, every Englishman, of education enough to form an opinion, professes to belong; with a perfect understanding on the part of all men of sense and probity, that the general purpose is to ballast the vessel of the state, not to overset it, and that it becomes a state-treason in any one to follow his party when they carry their doctrines to extremity.

From the nature of this grand national division, it follows, that the side which is most popular should be prompt in adopting theories, and eager in recommending measures of alteration and improvement. It is by such measures that men of talents rise into importance, and by such that the popular part of the constitution is maintained in its integrity. The other party is no less useful, by opposing to each successive attempt at innovation the delays of form, the doubts of experience, the prejudices of rank and condition, legal objections, and the weight of ancient and established practice. Thus, measures of a doubtful tendency are severely scrutinized in Parliament, and if at length adopted, it is only when public opinion has long declared in their favour, and when, men's minds having become habituated to the discussion, their introduction into our system cannot produce the violent effect of absolute novelty. If there were no Whigs, our constitution would fall to pieces for want of repair; if there were no Tories, it would be broken in the course of a succession of rash and venturous experiments.

BURKE'S "REFLECTIONS"

It followed, as a matter of course, that the Whigs of Britain looked with complacence, the Tories with jealousy, upon the progress of the new principles in France; but the latter had a powerful and unexpected auxiliary in the person of Edmund Burke, whose celebrated *Reflections on the Revolution in France*[171] had the most

---

[171] This work made its appearance in November, 1790; about 30,000 copies were sold; and a French translation, by M. Dupont, quickly spread its reputation throughout Europe. "The publication of Burke towards the close of the year 1790," says Lacretelle, "was one of the most remarkable events of the eighteenth century. It is a history, by anticipation, of the first fifteen years of the French Revolution."—Tom. viii., p. 182. "However the arguments of Burke may seem to have been justified by posterior events, it yet remains to be shown, that the war-cry then raised against France did not greatly contribute to the violence which characterised that period. It is possible that had he merely roused the attention of the governments and wealthy classes to the dangers of this new political creed, he might have proved the saviour of Europe; but he made such exaggerated statements, and used

striking effect on the public mind, of any work in our time. There was something exaggerated at all times in the character as well as the eloquence of that great man; and upon reading at this distance of time his celebrated composition, it must be confessed that the colours he has used in painting the extravagances of the Revolution, ought to have been softened, by considering the peculiar state of a country, which, long labouring under despotism, is suddenly restored to the possession of unembarrassed license. On the other hand, no political prophet ever viewed futurity with a surer ken. He knew how to detect the secret purpose of the various successive tribes of revolutionists, and saw in the constitution the future republic; in the republic the reign of anarchy; from anarchy he predicted military despotism; and from military despotism, last to be fulfilled, and hardest to be believed, he prophesied the late but secure resurrection of the legitimate monarchy. Above all, when the cupidity of the French rulers aspired no farther than the forcible possession of Avignon and the Venaissin territories, he foretold their purpose of extending the empire of France by means of her new political theories, and, under pretext of propagating the principles of freedom, her project of assailing with her arms the states, whose subjects had been already seduced by her doctrines.

The work of Burke raised a thousand enemies to the French Revolution, who had before looked upon it with favour, or at least with indifference. A very large portion of the talents and aristocracy of the Opposition party followed Burke into the ranks of the Ministry, who saw with pleasure a member, noted for his zeal in the cause of the Americans, become an avowed enemy of the French Revolution, and with equal satisfaction heard him use arguments, which might, in their own mouths, have assumed an obnoxious and suspicious character.

But the sweeping terms in which the author reprobated all attempts at state-reformation, in which he had himself been at one time so powerful an agent, subjected him to the charge of inconsistency among his late friends, many of whom, and Fox in particular, declared themselves favourable to the progress of the

---

arguments so alarming to freedom, that on many points he was not only plausibly, but victoriously refuted."—Dumont, p. 137.

Revolution in France, though they did not pretend to excuse its excesses. Out of Parliament it met more unlimited applause; for England, as well as France, had talent impatient of obscurity, ardour which demanded employment, ambition which sought distinction, and men of headlong passions, who expected, in a new order of things, more unlimited means of indulging them. The middling classes were open in England as elsewhere, though not perhaps so much so, to the tempting offer of increased power and importance; and the populace of London and other large towns loved license as well as the sans culottes of France. Hence the division of the country into Aristocrats and Democrats, the introduction of political hatred into the bosom of families, and the dissolution of many a band of friendship which had stood the strain of a lifetime. One part of the kingdom looked upon the other with the stern and relentless glance of keepers who are restraining madmen, while the others bent on them the furious glare of madmen conspiring revenge on their keepers.

From this period the progress of the French Revolution seemed in England like a play presented upon the stage, where two contending factions divide the audience, and hiss or applaud as much from party spirit as from real critical judgment, while every instant increases the probability that they will try the question by actual force.

Still, though the nation was thus divided on account of French politics, England and France observed the usual rules of amity, and it seemed that the English were more likely to wage hostility with each other than to declare war against France.

There was, in other kingdoms and states upon the Continent, the same diversity of feelings respecting the Revolution which divided England. The favour of the lower and unprivileged classes, in Germany especially, was the more fixed upon the progress of the French Revolution, because they lingered under the same incapacities from which the changes in France had delivered the Commons, or Third Estate, of that country. Thus far their partiality was not only natural and innocent, but praiseworthy. It is as reasonable for a man to desire the natural liberty from which he is unjustly excluded, as it is for those who are in an apartment where the air is polluted, to wish for the wholesome atmosphere.

Unhappily, these justifiable desires were connected with others of a description less harmless and beneficial. The French Revolution had proclaimed war on castles, as well as peace to cottages.[172] Its doctrine and practice held out the privileged classes in every country as the natural tyrants and oppressors of the poor, whom it encouraged by the thousand tongues of its declaimers to pull down their thrones, overthrow their altars, renounce the empire of God above, and of kings below, and arise, like regenerated France, alike from thraldom and from superstition. And such opinions, calling upon the other nations of Europe to follow them in their democratic career, were not only trumpeted forth in all affiliated clubs of the Jacobins, whose influence in the National Assembly was formidable, but were formally recognised by that body itself upon an occasion, which, but for the momentous omen it presented, might have been considered as the most ridiculous scene ever gravely acted before the legislators of a great nation.

There was in Paris a native of Prussia, an exile from his country, whose brain, none of the soundest by nature, seems to have been affected by the progress of the Revolution, as that of ordinary madmen is said to be influenced by the increase of the moon. This personage having become disgusted with his baptismal name, had adopted that of the Scythian philosopher, and uniting it with his own Teutonic family appellation, entitled himself—"Anacharsis Clootz, Orator of the Human Race."[173]

FEAST OF FEDERATION

It could hardly be expected, that the assumption of such a title should remain undistinguished by some supreme act of folly. Accordingly, the self-dubbed Anacharsis set on foot a procession, which was intended to exhibit the representatives of delegates from

---

[172] "Guerre aux châteaux, paix aux hamaux."
[173] Clootz was born at Cleves in 1755. Being suspected by Robespierre, he was, in May, 1794, sent to the guillotine.

all nations upon earth, to assist at the Feast of the Federation of the 14th July, 1790, by which the French nation proposed to celebrate the Revolution. In recruiting his troops, the orator easily picked up a few vagabonds of different countries in Paris; but as Chaldeans, Illinois, and Siberians, are not so common, the delegates of those more distant tribes were chosen among the rabble of the city, and subsidized at the rate of about twelve francs each. We are sorry we cannot tell whether the personage, whose dignity was much insisted upon as "a Miltonic Englishman," was genuine, or of Parisian manufacture. If the last, he must have been worth seeing.

Anacharsis Clootz, having got his ragged regiment equipped in costume at the expense of the refuse of some theatrical wardrobe, conducted them in solemn procession to the bar of the National Assembly, presented them as the representatives of all the nations on earth, awakened to a sense of their debased situation by the choral voices of twenty-five millions of freemen, and demanding that the sovereignty of the people should be acknowledged, and their oppressors destroyed, through all the universe, as well as in France.

So far this absurd scene was the extravagance of a mere madman, and if the Assembly had sent Anacharsis to bedlam, and his train to the Bicêtre, it would have ended as such a farce ought to have done. But *the President, in the name of the Assembly*, M. de Menou, (the same, we believe, who afterwards turned Turk when in Egypt,)[174] applauded the zeal of the orator, and received the homage of his grotesque attendants as if they had been what they pretended, the deputies of the four quarters of the globe. To raise the jest to the highest, Alexander Lameth proposed,—as the feelings of these august pilgrims must necessarily be hurt to see, in the land of freedom, those kneeling figures representing conquered nations, which surround the statue of Louis XV.,—that, from respect to this body of charlatans, these figures should be forthwith demolished. This was done accordingly, and the destruction of these symbols

---

[174] Menou was born at Boussay de Loches in 1750. After Buonaparte's flight from Egypt, he turned Mahometan, submitted to the peculiar rites of Islamism, and called himself Abdallah James Menou. He died at Venice in 1810; of which place he had been appointed Governor by Napoleon.

was regarded as a testimony of the assistance which France was ready to render such states as should require her assistance, for following in the revolutionary course. The scene, laughable in itself, became serious when its import was considered, and went far to persuade the governments of the neighbouring countries, that the purpose of France was to revolutionize Europe, and spread the reign of liberty and equality over all the civilized nations of the globe. Hopes so flattering as these, which should assign to the commons not merely freedom from unjust restraints and disqualifications, (and that granted with reserve, and only in proportion as they became qualified to use it with advantage,) but their hour of command and sovereignty, with the privilege of retaliation on those who had so long kept them in bondage, were sure to find a general good reception among all to whom they were addressed, in whatever country; while, on the contrary, the fears of existing governments for the propagation of doctrines so seductive in themselves, and which France seemed apparently prepared to support with arms, were excited in an equal proportion.

It is true that the National Assembly had formally declared, that France renounced the unphilosophical practices of extending her limits by conquest, but although this disavowal spoke to the ear, it was contradicted by the annexation of those desirable possessions, the ancient city of Avignon, and the district called the Comtat Venaissin, to the kingdom of France; while the principle on which the annexation was determined on, seemed equally applicable in all similar cases.

A dispute had broken out betwixt the aristocrats and democrats in the town and province in question [Oct. 30]; blood had flowed; a part of the population had demanded to become citizens of regenerated France.[175] Would it be worthy of the Protectress of Liberty, said the advocates for the annexation, to repel from her bosom supplicants, who panted to share the freedom they had achieved? And so Avignon and the Comtat Venaissin were declared lawful prize, and *reunited* to France, (so went the phrase,) as Napoleon afterwards reunited the broken fragments of the empire of Charlemagne. The prescient eye of Burke easily detected, in these

---

[175] Lacretelle, tom. ix., p. 52.

petty and surreptitious acquisitions, the gigantic plan by which France afterwards encircled herself by dependent states, which, while termed allies and auxiliaries, were, in fact, her most devoted subjects, and the governments of which changed their character from monarchical to popular, like the Great Nation.[176]

AUSTRIA—PRUSSIA—SWEDEN

The princes at the head of despotic governments were, of course, most interested in putting an end, if it were possible, to the present Revolution of France, and extinguishing a flame which appeared so threatening to its neighbours. Yet there was a long hesitation ere any thing to this purpose was attempted. Austria, whom the matter concerned as so near an ally of France, was slow ere she made any decisive step towards hostility. The Emperor Joseph was too much embroiled by the dissensions which he had provoked in the Netherlands, to involve himself in war with France. His successor, Leopold, had been always reckoned to belong to the philosophical party. He put down, without much trouble, the insurrection which had nearly cost his brother the dominion of Flanders, and as he used the victory with moderation, it seemed unlikely that the tranquillity of his government should be again disturbed. Still, it would have been hazardous to expose the allegiance of the subjects, so newly restored to order, to the temptations which must have opened to the Flemings by engaging in a war with France, and Leopold, far from seeking for a ground of quarrel with the favourers of the Revolution, entered into friendly relations with the government which they established; and, with anxiety, doubtless, for the safety of his brother-in-law, and an earnest desire to see the government of France placed on something like a steady footing, the Emperor continued in amicable terms with the existing rulers of that country down till his death. Francis, his successor, for some time seemed to adopt the same pacific policy.

Prussia, justly proud of her noble army, her veteran commanders, and the bequest of military fame left her by the Great Frederick, was more eager than Austria to adopt what began to be

---
[176] See Burke's Works, vol. viii., p. 272.

called the cause of Kings and Nobles, though the sovereign of the latter kingdom was so nearly connected with the unfortunate Louis. Frederick William had been taught to despise revolutionary movements by his cheap victory over the Dutch democracy, while the resistance of the Low Countries had induced the Austrians to dread such explosions.

Russia declared herself hostile to the French Revolution, but hazarded no effective step against them. The King of Sweden, animated by the adventurous character which made Gustavus, and after him Charles, sally forth from their frozen realms to influence the fates of Europe, showed the strongest disposition to play the same part, though the limited state of his resources rendered his valour almost nugatory.

Thus, while so many increasing discontents and suspicions showed that a decision by arms became every day more inevitable, Europe seemed still reluctant to commence the fatal encounter, as if the world had anticipated the long duration of the dreadful struggle, and the millions of lives which it must cost to bring it to a termination.

There can be no doubt that the emigration of the French princes, followed by a great part of the nobles of France, a step ill-judged in itself, as removing beyond the frontiers of the country all those most devotedly interested in the preservation of the monarchy, had the utmost effect in precipitating the impending hostilities. The presence of so many noble exiles,[177] the respect and sympathy which their misfortunes excited in those of the same rank, the exaggerated accounts which they gave of their own consequence; above all, the fear that the revolutionary spirit should extend beyond the limits of France, and work the same effects in other nations, produced through the whole aristocracy of Germany a general desire to restore them to their country and to their rights by the force of arms, and to extinguish by main force a spirit which seemed destined to wage war against all established governments,

---

[177] Their number was at this time, with their families, nearly a hundred thousand.—See Burke, vol. viii., p. 72, and Lacretelle, tom. viii., p. 117.

and to abolish the privileges which they recognised in their higher classes.

The state of the expatriated French clergy, driven from their home, and deprived of their means of subsistence, because they refused an oath imposed contrary to their ecclesiastical vows, and to their conscience, added religious zeal to the general interest excited by the spectacle, yet new to Europe, of thousands of nobility and clergy compelled to forsake their country, and take refuge among aliens.

Several petty princes of the empire made a show of levying forces, and complained of a breach of public faith, from the forfeiture of rights which individual princes of the Germanic body possessed in Alsace and Lorraine, and which, though sanctioned by the treaty of Westphalia, the National Assembly had not deemed worthy of exception from their sweeping abolition of feudal tenures. The emigrants formed themselves into armed corps at Treves and elsewhere, in which the noblest youths in France carried arms as privates, and which, if their number and resources had been in any proportion to their zeal and courage, were qualified to bear a distinguished part in deciding the destinies of the nation. Thus united, they gave way but too much to the natural feelings of their rank and country, menaced the land from which they had emigrated, and boasted aloud that it needed but one thrust (*botte*) of an Austrian general, to parry and pay home all the decrees of the National Assembly.[178] This ill-timed anticipation of success was founded in a great measure on the disorganization of the French army, which had been begun by the decay of discipline during the progress of the Revolution, and was supposed to be rendered complete by the emigration of such numbers of officers as had joined the princes and their standards. It was yet to be learned how soon such situations can be filled up, from the zeal and talent always found among the lower classes, when critical circumstances offer a reward to ambition.

---

[178] See Lacretelle, tom. viii., p. 117.

DECLARATION OF PILNITZ

Yet, while confident of success, the position of the emigrants was far from being flattering. Notwithstanding their most zealous exertions, the princes found their interest with foreign courts unable to bring either kings or ministers willingly or hastily to the point which they desired. The nearest approach was by the declaration of Pilnitz, [August 27,] in which, with much diplomatical caution, the Emperor and King of Prussia announced the interest which they took in the actual condition of the King of France; and intimated, that, supposing the other nations appealed to, should entertain feelings of the same kind, they would, conjoined with those other powers, use the most efficacious means to place Louis in a situation to establish in his dominions, on the basis of the most perfect liberty, a monarchical government, suitable to the rights of the sovereign, and the welfare of the people.[179]

This implied threat, which was to be conditionally carried into effect in case other powers not named should entertain the same sentiments with the two sovereigns by whom it was issued, was well calculated to irritate, but far too vague to intimidate, such a nation as France. It showed the desire to wound, but showed it accompanied by the fear to strike, and instead of inspiring respect, only awakened indignation, mingled with contempt.

The emigrants were generally represented among the people of France as men who, to recover their own vain privileges, were willing to lead a host of foreigners into the bosom of their country; and lest some sympathy with their situation, as men suffering for the cause to which they had devoted themselves, and stimulated by anxiety for the fate of their imprisoned King, should have moderated the severity of this judgment, forgery was employed to render their communication with the foreign monarchs still more odious and unpopular.

The secret articles of a pretended treaty were referred to, by which it was alleged that Monsieur and the Comte d'Artois had

---

[179] Jomini, tom. i., p. 265; Lacretelle, tom. viii., pp. 334, 439; De Bouillé, p. 422.

agreed to a dismemberment of France; Lorraine and Alsace being to be restored to Austria, in consequence of her entering into the counter-revolutionary league. The date of this supposed treaty was first placed at Pavia, and afterwards transferred to Pilnitz; but although it was at one time assumed as a real document in the British House of Commons, it is now generally allowed to have had no existence.[180] In the meanwhile, as a calumny well adapted to the prejudices of the time, the belief in such a secret compact became generally current, and excited the utmost indignation against the selfish invaders, and against the exiles who were supposed willing to dismember their native country, rather than submit to a change in its constitution adverse to their own selfish interests.

A great deal of this new load of unpopularity was transferred to the account of the unfortunate Louis, who was supposed to instigate and support in private the attempts of his brothers for engaging foreign courts in his favour, while the Queen, from her relationship to the Emperor of Austria, was universally represented as a fury, urging him to revenge her loss of power on the rebellious people of France. An Austrian committee was talked of as managing the correspondence between these royal persons on the one part, and the foreign courts and emigrant princes on the other. This was totally groundless; but it is probable and natural that some intercourse was maintained between Louis and his brothers, as, though their warlike schemes suited the King's temper too little, he might wish to derive advantage from the dread which it was vainly supposed their preparations would inspire. The royal pair were indeed in a situation so disastrous, that they might have been excused for soliciting rescue by almost any means. But, in fact, Louis and Leopold seem to have agreed in the same system of temporizing politics. Their correspondence, as far as can be judged from the

---

[180] See two articles on the pretended treaties of Pavia and Pilnitz, signed Detector, in the Anti-jacobin Newspaper, July 2, 1798. They were, we believe, written by the late Mr. Pitt. [Since this work was published it seems to have become certain that the letters there referred to were the productions of Lord Grenville, at that time Secretary of State for Foreign Affairs.]—"As far as we have been able to trace," said Mr. Pitt, in 1800, "the declaration signed at Pilnitz referred to the imprisonment of Louis: its immediate view was to effect his deliverance, if a concert sufficiently extensive could be formed for that purpose. I left the internal state of France to be decided by the King restored to his liberty, with the free consent of the states of the kingdom, and it did not contain one word relative to the dismemberment of the country."—*Parliamentary History*, vol. xxxiv., p. 1316.—S.

letters of De Lessart, Louis' trusted minister for foreign affairs, seems always to point to a middle course; that of suffering the Constitution of France to remain such as it had been chosen by the people, and sanctioned by the National Assembly, while the ministers attempted, by the influence of fear of dangers from abroad, to prevent any future assaults upon the power of the Crown, and especially against the King's person. On condition that such further aggression should be abstained from, the Emperor seems to have been willing to prohibit the mustering of the emigrant forces in his dominions. But Leopold demanded that, on their part, the French nation should release themselves from the clubs of Jacobins and Cordeliers, (another assembly of the same nature,) which, pretending to be no more than private associations, without public character or responsibility, nevertheless dictated to the National Assembly, the King, and all France, in virtue of the power of exciting the insurrectional movements, by which their denunciations and proposed revolutions had been as regularly seconded, as the flash is followed by the thunderbolt.

On the death of Leopold, [March 1, 1792,] and the succession of the Emperor Francis to the imperial throne, the disposition of Austria became much more turned towards war. It became the object of Francis to overcome the revolutionists, and prevent, if possible, the impending fate of the royal family. In adopting these warlike counsels, the mind of the new Emperor was much influenced by the desire of Prussia to take the field. Indeed, the condition of the royal family, which became every day more precarious, seemed to both powers to indicate and authorise hostile measures, and they were at no pains to conceal their sentiments. It is not probable that peace would have remained long unbroken, unless some change, of an unexpected and unhoped-for character, in favour of royalty, had taken place in France; but, after all the menaces which had been made by the foreign powers, it was France herself, who, to the surprise of Europe, first resorted to arms. The ostensible reason was, that, in declaring war, she only anticipated, as became a brave and generous nation, the commencement of hostilities which Austria had menaced. But each party in the state had its own private views for concurring in a measure, which, at the time, seemed of a very audacious character.

LA FAYETTE

La Fayette now felt his influence in the national guard of Paris was greatly on the wane. With the democrats he was regarded as a denounced and devoted man, for having employed the armed force to disperse the people in the Champ de Mars, upon the 17th of July, 1791. Those who countenanced him on that occasion were Parisian citizens of substance and property, but timorous, even from the very consciousness of their wealth, and unwilling, either for the sake of La Fayette, or the Constitution which he patronised, to expose themselves to be denounced by furious demagogues, or pillaged by the hordes of robbers and assassins whom they had at their disposal. This is the natural progress in revolutions. While order continues, property has always the superior influence over those who may be desirous of infringing the public peace; but when law and order are in a great measure destroyed, the wealthy are too much disposed to seek, in submission, or change of party, the means of securing themselves and their fortunes. The property which, in ordinary times, renders its owners bold, becomes, in those of imminent danger, the cause of their selfish cowardice. La Fayette tried, however, one decisive experiment, to ascertain what share remained of his once predominant influence over the Parisians. He stood an election for the mayoralty of Paris against Pétion, [Nov. 17,] a person attached to the Brissotin, or Republican faction, and the latter was preferred. Unsuccessful in this attempt, La Fayette became desirous of foreign war. A soldier, and an approved one, he hoped his fortune would not desert him, and that, at the head of armies, which he trusted to render victorious over the public enemy, he might have a better chance of being listened to by those factions who began to hold in disrespect the red flag, and the decaying efforts of the national guard of Paris; and thus gaining the power of once more enforcing submission to the constitution, which he had so large a share in creating. Unquestionably, also, La Fayette remembered the ardour of the French for national glory, and welcomed the thoughts of shifting the scene to combat against a public and avowed enemy, from his obscure and unsatisfactory struggle with the clubs of Paris. La Fayette, therefore, desired war, and was followed in his opinion by most of the Constitutional party.

VIEWS OF THE PARTIES

The Girondists were not less eager for a declaration of hostilities. Either the King must, in that case, place his veto upon the measure, or he must denounce hostilities against his brother-in-law and his brothers, subjecting himself to all the suspicions of bad faith which such a measure inferred. If the arms of the nation were victorious, the risk of a revolution in favour of royalty by insurrections within, or invasions from without the kingdom, was ended at once and for ever. And if the foreigners obtained advantages, it would be easy to turn the unpopularity of the defeat upon the monarch, and upon the Constitutionalists, who had insisted, and did still insist, on retaining him as the ostensible head of the executive government.

The Jacobins, those whose uniform object it was to keep the impulse of forcible and revolutionary measures in constant action, seemed to be divided among themselves on the great question of war or peace. Robespierre himself struggled, in the club, against the declaration of hostilities, probably because he wished the Brissotins to take all the responsibility of that hazardous measure, secure beforehand to share the advantage which it might afford those Republicans against the King and Constitutionalists. He took care that Louis should profit nothing by the manner in which he pleaded the cause of justice and humanity. He affected to prophesy disasters to the ill-provided and ill-disciplined armies of France, and cast the blame beforehand on the known treachery of the King and the Royalists, the arbitrary designs of La Fayette and the Constitutionalists, and the doubtful patriotism of Brissot and Condorcet. His arguments retarded, though they could not stop, the declaration of war, which probably they were not intended seriously to prevent; and the most violent and sanguinary of men obtained a temporary character for love of humanity, by adding hypocrisy to his other vices. The Jacobins in general, notwithstanding Robespierre's remonstrances, moved by the same motives which operated with the Brissotins, declared ultimately in favour of hostilities.[181]

The resolution for war, therefore, predomated in the Assembly, and two preparatory measures served, as it were, to sound the intentions of the King on the subject, and to ascertain how far he was disposed to adhere to the constitutional government which he had accepted, against those who, in his name, seemed prepared by force of arms to restore the old system of monarchy. Two decrees were passed against the emigrants in the Assembly, [Nov. 9.] The first was directed against the King's brother, and summoned Xavier Stanislaus, Prince of France, to return into France in two months, upon pain of forfeiting his right to the regency. The King consented to this decree: he could not, indeed, dissent from it with consistency, being, as he had consented to be, the holder of the crown under a constitution, against which his exiled brother had publicly declared war. The second decree denounced death against all emigrants who should be found assembled in arms on the 1st of January next.[182] The right of a nation to punish with extreme pains those of its native subjects who bear arms against her, has never been disputed. But although, on great changes of the state, the vanquished party, when essaying a second struggle, stand in the relation of rebels against the existing government, yet there is generally wisdom as well as humanity, in delaying to assert this right in its rigour, until such a period shall have elapsed, as shall at once have established the new government in a confirmed state of possession, and given those attached to the old one time to forget their habits and predilections in its favour.

Under this defence, Louis ventured to use the sole constitutional weapon with which he was intrusted. He refused his consent to the decree. Sensible of the unpopularity attending this rejection, the King endeavoured to qualify it, by issuing a severe proclamation against the emigrants, countermanding their proceedings;—which was only considered as an act of dissimulation and hypocrisy.

---

[181] Lacretelle, tom. ix., p. 61; Thiers, tom. ii., p. 48.
[182] Lacretelle, tom. ix., p. 48.

The decree last proposed, jarred necessarily on the heart and sensibility of Louis; the next affected his religious scruples. The National Assembly had produced a schism in the Church, by imposing on the clergy a constitutional oath, inconsistent with their religious vows. The philosophers in the present legislative body, with all the intolerance which they were in the habit of objecting against the Catholic Church, resolved to render the breach irreparable.

They had, they thought, the opportunity of striking a death's blow at the religion of the state, and they remembered, that the watch-word applied by the Encyclopedists to Christianity, had been *Ecrasez l'Infame*. The proposed decree bore, that such priests as refused the constitutional oath should forfeit the pension allowed them for subsistence, when the government seized upon the estates of the clergy; that they should be put into a state of surveillance, in the several departments where they resided, and banished from France the instant they excited any religious dissensions.[183]

A prince, with the genuine principles of philosophy, would have rejected this law as unjust and intolerant; but Louis had stronger motives to interpose his constitutional *veto*, as a Catholic Christian, whose conscience would not permit him to assent to the persecution of the faithful servants of his Church. He refused his assent to this decree also.

In attempting to shelter the emigrants and the recusant churchmen, the King only rendered himself the more immediate object of the popular resentment. His compassion for the former was probably mingled with a secret wish, that the success of their arms might relieve him from his present restraint; at any rate, it was a motive easily imputed, and difficult to be disproved. He was, therefore, represented to his people as in close union with the bands of exiled Frenchmen, who menaced the frontiers of the kingdom, and were about to accompany the foreign armies on their march to

---

[183] "The adoption of this oppressive decree was signalized by the first open expression of *atheistical* sentiments in the Assembly. 'My God is the Law; I acknowledge no other,' was the expression of Isnard. The remonstrance of the constitutional bishops had no effect. The decree was carried amidst tumult and acclamation."—Lacretelle, tom. ix., p. 46.

the metropolis. The royal rejection of the decree against the orthodox clergy was imputed to Louis's superstition, and his desire of rebuilding an ancient Gothic hierarchy unworthy of an enlightened age. In short, that was now made manifest, which few wise men had ever doubted, namely, that so soon as the King should avail himself of his constitutional right, in resistance to the popular will, he was sure to incur the risk of losing both his crown and life.[184]

Meantime this danger was accelerated by the consequences of a dissension in the royal cabinet. It will scarcely be believed, that situations in the ministry of France, so precarious in its tenure, so dangerous in its possession, so enfeebled in its authority, should have been, even at this time, the object of ambition; and that to possess such momentary and doubtful eminence, men, and wise men too, employed all the usual arts of intrigue and circumvention, by which rival statesmen, under settled governments and in peaceful times, endeavour to undermine and supplant each other. We have heard of criminals in the Scottish Highlands, who asserted with obstinacy the dignity of their clans, when the only test of preeminence was the priority of execution. We have read, too, of the fatal raft, where shipwrecked men in the midst of the Atlantic, contended together with mortal strife for equally useless preferences. But neither case is equal in extravagance to the conduct of those rivals, who struggled for power in the cabinet of Louis XVI. in 1792, when, take what party they would, the jealousy of the Assembly, and the far more fatal proscription of the Jacobins, was sure to be the reward of their labours. So, however, it was, and the fact serves to show, that a day of power is more valuable in the eyes of ambition, than a lifetime of ease and safety.

CHANGE OF MINISTRY

De Lessart, the Minister of Foreign Affairs already mentioned, had wished to avoid war, and had fed Leopold and his ministers with hopes, that the King would be able to establish a constitutional power, superior to that of the dreadful Jacobins. The Comte de

---

[184] Lacretelle, tom. ix., p. 46.

Narbonne, on the other side, being Minister of War, was desirous to forward the views of La Fayette, who, as we have said, longed to be at the head of the army. To obtain his rival's disgrace, Narbonne combined with La Fayette and other generals to make public the opposition which De Lessart and a majority of the cabinet ministers had opposed to the declaration of hostilities. Louis, justly incensed at an appeal to the public from the interior of his own cabinet, displaced Narbonne.[185]

The legislative body immediately fell on De Lessart. He was called to stand on his defence, and imprudently laid before the Assembly his correspondence with Kaunitz, the Austrian minister. In their communications De Lessart and Kaunitz had spoken with respect of the constitution, and with moderation even of their most obnoxious measures; but they had reprobated the violence of the Jacobins and Cordeliers, and stigmatized the usurpations of those clubs over the constitutional authorities of the state, whom they openly insulted and controlled. These moderate sentiments formed the real source of De Lessart's fall. He was attacked on all sides—by the party of Narbonne and his friends from rivalry—by Brissot and his followers from policy, and in order to remove a minister too much of a royalist for their purpose—by the Jacobins, from hatred and revenge. Yet, when Brissot condescended upon the following evidence of his guilt, argument and testimony against him must have indeed been scarce. De Lessart, with the view of representing the present affairs of France under the most softened point of view to the Emperor, had assured him that the constitution of 1791 was firmly adhered to by a *majority* of the nation.[186] "Hear the atrocious calumniator!" said the accuser. "The inference is plain. He dares to insinuate the existence of a minority, which is not attached to the

---

[185] Mignet, tom. i., p. 164; Lacretelle, tom. ix., p. 74. "The war department was intrusted, in December, 1791, to M. de Narbonne. He employed himself with unfeigned zeal in all the preparations necessary for the defence of the kingdom. Possessing rank and talents, the manners of a court, and the views of a philosopher, that which was predominant in his soul was military honour and French valour. To oppose the interference of foreigners under whatever circumstances, always seemed to him the duty of a citizen and a gentleman. His colleagues combined against him, and succeeded in obtaining his removal. He lost his life at the siege of Torgau, in 1813."—M. de Staël, vol. ii., p. 39.
[186] Lacretelle, tom. ix., p. 77.

Constitution."[187] Another accusation, which in like manner was adopted as valid by the acclamation of the Assembly, was formed thus. A most horrible massacre[188] had taken place during the tumults which attended the union of Avignon with the kingdom of France. Vergniaud, the friend and colleague of Brissot, alleged, that if the decree of union had been early enough sent to Avignon, the dissensions would not have taken place; and he charged upon the unhappy De Lessart that he had not instantly transmitted the official intelligence. Now the decree of reunion was, as the orator knew, delayed on account of the King's scruples to accede to what seemed an invasion of the territory of the Church; and, at any rate, it could no more have prevented the massacre of Avignon, which was conducted by that same Jourdan, called Coupe-tête, the Bearded Man of the march to Versailles, than the subsequent massacre of Paris, perpetrated by similar agents. The orator well knew this; yet, with eloquence as false as his logic, he summoned the ghosts of the murdered from the glacière, in which their mangled remains had been piled, to bear witness against the minister, to whose culpable neglect they owed their untimely fate. All the while he was imploring for justice on the head of a man, who was undeniably ignorant and innocent of the crime, Vergniaud and his friends secretly meditated extending the mantle of safety over the actual perpetrators of the massacre, by a decree of amnesty; so that the whole charge against De Lessart can only be termed a mixture of hypocrisy and cruelty. In the course of the same discussion, Gauchon, an orator of the suburb of Saint Antoine, in which lay the strength of the Jacobin interest, had already pronounced sentence in the cause, at the very

---

[187] This strange argument reminds us of an Essay read before a literary society in dispraise of the east wind, which the author supported by quotations from every poem or popular work, in which Eurus is the subject of invective. The learned auditors sustained the first part of this infliction with becoming fortitude, but declined submitting to the second, understanding that the accomplished author had there fortified himself by the numerous testimonies of almost all poets in favour of the west, and which, with logic similar to that of M. Brissot in the text, he regarded as indirect testimony against the east wind.—S.

[188] "On Sunday, the 30th October, 1791, the gates were closed, the walls guarded so as to render escape impossible, and a band of assassins, commanded by the barbarous Jourdan, sought out in their own houses the individuals destined for death. Sixty unhappy wretches were speedily thrust into prison, where, during the obscurity of night, the murderers wreaked their vengeance with impunity. One young man put fourteen to death with his own hand, and only desisted from excess of fatigue. Twelve women perished, after having undergone tortures which my pen cannot describe. When vengeance had done its worst, the remains of the victims were torn and mutilated, and heaped up in a ditch, or thrown into the Rhone."—Lacretelle, tom. ix., p. 54.

bar of the Assembly which was engaged in trying it. "Royalty may be struck out of the Constitution," said the demagogue, "but the unity of the legislative body defies the touch of time. Courtiers, ministers, kings, and their civil lists, may pass away, but the sovereignty of the people, and the pikes which enforce it, are perpetual."

This was touching the root of the matter. De Lessart was a royalist, though a timid and cautious one, and he was to be punished as an example to such ministers as should dare to attach themselves to their sovereign and his personal interest. A decree of accusation was passed against him, and he was sent to Orleans to be tried before the High Court there. Other royalists of distinction were committed to the same prison, and, in the fatal month of September, 1792, were involved in the same dreadful fate.[189]

Pétion, the Mayor of Paris, appeared next day, at the bar, at the head of the municipality, to congratulate the Assembly on a great act of justice, which he declared resembled one of those thunder-storms by which nature purifies the atmosphere from noxious vapours. The ministry was dissolved by this severe blow on one of the wisest, at least one of the most moderate, of its members. Narbonne and the Constitutional party who had espoused his cause, were soon made sensible, that he or they were to gain nothing by the impeachment, to which their intrigues led the way. Their claims to share the spoils of the displaced ministry were passed over with contempt, and the King was compelled, in order to have the least chance of obtaining a hearing from the Assembly, to select his ministers from the Brissotin, or Girondist faction, who, though averse to the existence of a monarchy, and desiring a republic instead, had still somewhat more of principle and morals than the mere Revolutionists and Jacobins, who were altogether destitute of both.

---

[189] Lacretelle, tom. ix., p. 75.

WAR WITH AUSTRIA

With the fall of De Lessart, all chance of peace vanished; as indeed it had been gradually disappearing before that event. The demands of the Austrian court went now, when fully explained, so far back upon the Revolution, that a peace negotiated upon such terms, must have laid France and all its various parties, (with the exception perhaps of a few of the first Assembly,) at the foot of the sovereign, and, what might be more dangerous, at the mercy of the restored emigrants. The Emperor demanded the establishment of monarchy in France, on the basis of the royal declaration of 23d June, 1789, which had been generally rejected by the Tiers Etat when offered to them by the King. He farther demanded the restoration of the effects of the Church, and that the German princes having rights in Alsace and Lorraine should be replaced in those rights, agreeably to the treaty of Westphalia.

The Legislative Assembly received these extravagant terms as an insult on the national dignity; and the King, whatever might be his sentiments as an individual, could not, on this occasion, dispense with the duty his office as Constitutional Monarch imposed upon him. Louis, therefore, had the melancholy task [April 20] of proposing to an Assembly, filled with the enemies of his throne and person, a declaration of war against his brother-in-law the Emperor, in his capacity of King of Hungary and Bohemia,[190] involving, as matter of course, a civil war with his own two brothers, who had taken the field at the head of that part of his subjects from birth and principle the most enthusiastically devoted to their sovereign's

---

[190] "After a long exposition by Dumouriez, the King, with a tremulous voice, pronounced these words:—'You have heard, gentlemen, the result of my negotiations with the Court of Vienna: they are conformable to the sentiments more than once expressed to me by the National Assembly, and confirmed by the great majority of the kingdom. All prefer a war to the continuance of outrages to the national honour, or menaces to the national safety. I have exhausted all the means of pacification in my power; I now come, in terms of the Constitution, to propose to the Assembly, that we should declare war against the King of Hungary and Bohemia.'"—Mignet, tom. i., p. 168; *Annual Register*, vol. xxxiv., p. 201; Dumouriez, vol. ii., p. 272.

person, and who, if they had faults towards France, had committed them in love to him.[191]

The proposal was speedily agreed to by the Assembly; for the Constitutionalists saw their best remaining chance for power was by obtaining victory on the frontiers,—the Girondists had need of war, as what must necessarily lead the way to an alteration in the constitution, and the laying aside the regal government,—and the Jacobins, whose chief, Robespierre, had just objected enough to give him the character and credit of a prophet if any reverses were sustained, resisted the war no longer, but remained armed and watchful, to secure the advantage of events as they might occur.

---

[191] "I was present at the sitting in which Louis was forced to a measure which was necessarily painful to him in so many ways. His features were not expressive of his thoughts, but it was not from dissimulation that he concealed them; a mixture of resignation and dignity repressed in him every outward sign of his sentiments. On entering the Assembly, he looked to the right and left, with that kind of vacant curiosity which is usual to persons who are so shortsighted that their eyes seem to be of no use to them. He proposed war in the same tone of voice as he might have used in requiring the most indifferent decree possible."—M. de Staël, vol. ii., p. 40.

Chapter VIII

Defeats of the French on the Frontier—Decay of Constitutionalists—They form the Club of Feuillans, and are dispersed by the Jacobins—The Ministry—Dumouriez—Breach of confidence betwixt the King and his Ministers—Dissolution of the King's Constitutional Guard—Extravagant measures of the Jacobins—Alarms of the Girondists—Departmental Army proposed—King puts his Veto on the decree, against Dumouriez's representations—Decree against the recusant Priests—King refuses it— Letter of the Ministers to the King—He dismisses Roland, Clavière, and Servan—Dumouriez, Duranton, and Lacoste, appointed in their stead— King ratifies the decree concerning the Departmental Army—Dumouriez resigns, and departs for the Frontiers—New Ministers named from the Constitutionalists—Insurrection of 20th June—Armed Mob intrude into the Assembly—Thence into the Tuileries—La Fayette repairs to Paris— Remonstrates in favour of the King—But is compelled to return to the Frontiers—Marseillois appear in Paris—Duke of Brunswick's manifesto.

It is not our purpose here to enter into any detail of military events. It is sufficient to say, that the first results of the war were more disastrous than could have been expected, even from the want of discipline and state of mutiny in which this call to arms found the troops of France. If Austria, never quick at improving an opportunity, had possessed more forces on the Flemish frontier, or had even pressed her success with the troops she had, events might have occurred to influence, if not to alter, the fortunes of France and her King. They were inactive, however, and La Fayette, who was at the head of the army, exerted himself, not without effect, to rally the spirits of the French, and infuse discipline and confidence into their ranks. But he was able to secure no success of so marked a character, as to correspond with the reputation he had acquired in America; so that as the Austrians were few in number, and not very decisive in their movements, the war seemed to languish on both sides.

In Paris, the absence of La Fayette had removed the main stay from the Constitutional interests, which were now nearly reduced to that state of nullity to which they had themselves reduced the party, first of pure Royalists, and then that of the *Moderés*, or friends of limited monarchy, in the first Assembly. The wealthier classes, indeed, continued a fruitless attachment to the Constitutionalists, which gradually diminished with their decreased power to protect their friends. At length this became so contemptible, that their enemies were emboldened to venture upon an insult, which showed how little they were disposed to keep measures with a feeble adversary.

CLUB OF FEUILLANS

Among other plans, by which they hoped to counterpoise the omnipotence of the Jacobin Club, the Constitutionalists had established a counter association, termed, from its place of meeting,[192] Les Feuillans. In this club,—which included about two hundred members of the Legislative Body, the ephemeral rival of the great Jacobinical forge in which the Revolutionists had their strength and fabricated their thunders,—there was more eloquence, argument, learning, and wit, than was necessary; but the Feuillans wanted the terrible power of exciting the popular passions, which the orators of the Jacobin Club possessed and wielded at pleasure. These opposed factions might be compared to two swords, of which one had a gilded and ornamented hilt, but a blade formed of glass or other brittle substance, while the brazen handle of the other corresponded in strength and coarseness to the steel of the weapon itself. When two such weapons came into collision, the consequence may be anticipated, and it was so with the opposite clubs. The Jacobins, after many preparatory insults, went down upon and assailed their adversaries with open force, insulting and dispersing

---

[192] The site of the old convent of the Feuillans.

them with blows and violence; while Pétion, the mayor of Paris, who was present on the occasion, consoled the fugitives, by assuring them that the law indeed protected them, but the people having pronounced against them, it was not for him to enforce the behests of the law, in opposition to the will of that people, from whom the law originated.[193] A goodly medicine for their aching bones!

The Constitutional party amidst their general humiliation, had lost almost all influence in the ministry, and could only communicate with the King underhand, and in a secret manner,—as if they had been, in fact, his friends and partisans, not the cause of, or willing consenters to, his present imprisoned and disabled condition. Of six ministers, by whom De Lessart and his comrades had been replaced, the husband of Madame Roland, and two others, Servan[194] and Clavière,[195] were zealous republicans; Duranthon[196] and Lacoste[197] were moderate in their politics, but timorous in character; the sixth, Dumouriez, who held the war department, was the personal rival of La Fayette, both in civil and military matters, and the enemy, therefore, of the Constitutional party. It is now, for the first time, that we mention one of those names renowned in military history, which had the address to attract Victory to the French banners, to which she so long appeared to adhere without shadow of changing. Dumouriez passed early from the scene, but left his name strongly written in the annals of France.

---

[193] Lacretelle, tom. ix., p. 76.
[194] Servan was born at Romans in 1741, and died at Paris in 1808. "He was," says Madame Roland, "an honest man in the fullest signification of the term; an enlightened patriot, a brave soldier, and an active minister; he stood in need of nothing but a more sober imagination, and a more flexible mind."—*Memoirs*, part i., p. 72.
[195] Clavière was born at Geneva in 1735, "where," says M. Dumont, "he became one of the popular leaders: shrewd and penetrating, he obtained the credit of being also cunning and artful: he was a man of superior intellect: deaf from his youth, and, deprived by this infirmity of the pleasures of society, he had sought a compensation in study, and formed his education by associating politics and moral philosophy with trade."—Being denounced by Robespierre, to avoid the guillotine, he stabbed himself in his prison, June 9, 1793. His wife poisoned herself on the following day.
[196] Duranthon was born at Massedon in 1736. In December, 1793, he was dragged before the revolutionary tribunal, and guillotined. "He was an honest man, but very indolent: his manner indicated vanity, and his timid disposition and pompous prattle made him always appear to me no better than an old woman."—Mad. Roland, part i., p. 71.
[197] "A true jack-in-office of the old order of things, of which he had the insignificant and awkward look, cold manner, and dogmatic tone. He was deficient both in the extensive views and activity necessary for a minister."—Mad. Roland, p. 70. He died in 1803.

Dumouriez was little in person, but full of vivacity and talent; a brave soldier, having distinguished himself in the civil dissensions of Poland; an able and skilful intriguer, and well-fitted to play a conspicuous part in times of public confusion. He has never been supposed to possess any great firmness of principle, whether public or private; but a soldier's honour, and a soldier's frankness, together with the habits of good society, led him to contemn and hate the sordid treachery, cruelty, and cynicism of the Jacobins; while his wit and common sense enabled him to see through and deride the affected and pedantic fanaticism of republican zeal of the Girondists, who, he plainly saw, were amusing themselves with schemes to which the country of France, the age, and the state of manners, were absolutely opposed. Thus, he held the situation of minister at war, coquetting with all parties; wearing one evening in the Jacobin Club the red night-cap, which was the badge of breechless freedom, and the next, with better sincerity, advising the King how he might avoid the approaching evils; though the by-roads he pointed out were often too indirect to be trodden by the good and honest prince, to whom Providence had, in Dumouriez, assigned a counsellor better fitted to a less scrupulous sovereign. The King nevertheless reposed considerable confidence in the general, which, if not answered with all the devotion of loyalty, was at least never betrayed.[198]

The Republican ministers were scarcely qualified by their talents, to assume the air of Areopagites, or Roman tribunes. Roland, by himself, was but a tiresome pedant, and he could not bring his wife to the cabinet council, although it is said she attempted to make her way to the ministerial dinners.[199] His colleagues were of the same character, and affected in their intercourse with the King a stoical contempt of the forms of the court,[200] although in effect, these are like other courtesies of society,

---

[198] Thiers, tom. ii., p. 59; Mignet, tom. i., p. 64; Lacretelle, tom. ix., p. 89.
[199] So says Des Ferrieres, and pretends that Madame Roland's pretensions to be presented at the ministerial parties being rejected, was the first breach to the amicable understanding of the ministers. But nothing of this sort is to be found in her Memoirs, and we are confident she would have recorded it, had the fact been accurate.—S.
[200] The court nicknamed the new ministry, "Le Ministère sans culottes."

which it costs little to observe, and is brutal to neglect.[201] Besides petty insults of this sort, there was a total want of confidence on both sides, in the intercourse betwixt them and the King. If the ministers were desirous to penetrate his sentiments on any particular subject, Louis evaded them by turning the discourse on matters of vague and general import; and did he, on the other hand, press them to adopt any particular measure, they were cold and reserved, and excused themselves under the shelter of their personal responsibility. Indeed, how was it possible that confidence could exist betwixt the King and his Republican ministers, when the principal object of the latter was to procure the abolition of the regal dignity, and when the former was completely aware that such was their purpose?

KING'S GUARD DISBANDED

The first step adopted by the factions of Girondists and Jacobins, who moved towards the same object side by side, though not hand in hand, was to deprive the King of a guard, assigned him by the Constitution, in lieu of his disbanded *gardes du corps*. It was, indeed, of doubtful loyalty, being partly levied from soldiers of the line, partly from the citizens, and imbued in many cases with the revolutionary spirit of the day; but they were officered by persons selected for their attachment to the King, and even their name of Guards expressed and inspired an *esprit de corps*, which might be formidable. Various causes of suspicion were alleged against this guard—that they kept in their barracks a white flag (which proved to be the ornament of a cake presented to them by the Dauphin)—that their sword-hilts were formed into the fashion of a cock, which announced some anti-revolutionary enigma—that attempts were made to alienate them from the Assembly, and fix their affections on the King. The guard contained several spies, who had taken that service for the purpose of betraying its secrets to the Jacobins. Three or four of these men, produced at the bar, affirmed much that

---

[201] When Roland, whose dress was somewhat like that of a Quaker, appeared at court in shoestrings, the usher approached him with a severe look, and addressed him, "How, sir, no buckles?"—"Ah," said Dumouriez, who laughed at all and every thing, "all is lost."—S.—Roland, part ii., p. 8; Mignet, tom. i., p. 166.

was, and much that was not true; and amid the causes they had for distrusting the King, and their reasons for desiring to weaken him, the Assembly decreed the reduction of the Constitutional Guard. The King was with difficulty persuaded not to oppose his *veto*, and was thus left almost totally undefended to the next blast of the revolutionary tempest.[202]

Every successive proceeding of the factions tended to show more strongly that the storm was speedily to arise. The invention of the Jacobins exhausted itself in proposing and adopting revolutionary measures so extravagant, that very shame prevented the Girondists from becoming parties to them. Such was the carrying the atrocious cut-throat Jourdan in triumph through the streets of Avignon, where he had piled eighty carcasses into a glacière in the course of one night.[203] A less atrocious, but no less insolent proceeding, was the feast given in honour of the regiment of Chateauvieux, whose mutiny had been put down at Nancy by M. de Bouillé, acting under the express decree of the first National Assembly.[204]

In a word, understanding much better than the Brissotins the taste of the vulgar for what was most violent, gross, and exaggerated, the Jacobins purveyed for them accordingly, filled their ears with the most incredible reports, and gulled their eyes by the most absurd pageants.

ALARM OF THE GIRONDISTS

The Girondists, retaining some taste and some principle, were left far behind in the race of vulgar popularity, where he that throws off every mark of decency bids most fair to gain the prize. They beheld with mortification feats which they could not emulate, and felt that their own assertions of their attachment to freedom, emphatic as they were, seemed cold and spiritless compared to the extravagant and flaming declamations of the Jacobins. They

---

[202] Lacretelle, tom. ix., p. 109.
[203] Prudhomme, tom. ii., p. 271.
[204] Bouillé's Memoirs, p. 215.

regarded with envy the advantages which their rivals acquired by those exaggerated proceedings, and were startled to find how far they were like to be outstripped by those uncompromising and unhesitating demagogues. The Girondists became sensible that a struggle approached, in which, notwithstanding their strength in the Assembly, they must be vanquished, unless they could raise up some body of forces, entirely dependent on themselves, to be opposed in time of need to the Jacobin insurgents. This was indeed essentially necessary to their personal safety, and to the stability of their power. If they looked to the national guard, they found such of that body as were no longer attached to La Fayette wearied of revolutions, unmoved by the prospect of a republic, and only desirous to protect their shops and property. If they turned their eyes to the lower orders, and especially the suburbs, the myriads of pikemen which they could pour forth were all devoted to the Jacobins, from whom their leaders received orders and regular pay.

The scheme of a departmental army was resorted to by the Girondists as the least startling, yet most certain mode of bringing together a military force sufficient to support the schemes of the new administration. Five men were to be furnished by every canton in France, which would produce a body of 20,000 troops, to be armed and trained under the walls of Paris. This force was to serve as a central army to reinforce the soldiers on the frontier, and maintain order in the capital, as occasion should demand. The measure, proposed by the Girondists, was unexpectedly furthered by the Jacobins, who plainly saw, that through the means of their affiliated societies which existed in every canton, they would be able to dictate the choice of so large a part of the departmental army, that, when assembled, it should add to the power of their insurrectionary bands at Paris, instead of controlling them.[205]

The citizens of Paris were disposed to consider this concourse of undisciplined troops under the walls of the city as dangerous to its safety, and an insult to the national guard, hitherto thought adequate to the defence of the metropolis. They petitioned the Assembly against the measure, and even invoked the King to reject the decree, when it should pass through that body.

---

[205] Mignet, tom. i., p. 172; Lacretelle, tom. ix., p. 114; Dumouriez, vol. ii., p. 350.

To this course Louis was himself sufficiently inclined; for neither he nor any one doubted that the real object of the Girondists was to bring together such an army, as would enable them to declare their beloved republic without fear of La Fayette, even if he should find himself able to bring the army which he commanded to his own sentiments on the subject.

Dumouriez warned Louis against following this course of direct opposition to the Assembly. He allowed, that the ultimate purpose of the proposal was evident to every thinking person, but still its ostensible object being the protection of the country and capital, the King, he said, would, in the eyes of the vulgar, be regarded as a favourer of the foreign invasion, if he objected to a measure represented as essential to the protection of Paris. He undertook, as Minister of War, that as fast as a few hundreds of the departmental forces arrived, he would have them regimented and dismissed to the frontier, where their assistance was more necessary than at home. But all his remonstrances on this subject were in vain. Louis resolved at all risks to place his *veto* on the measure.[206] He probably relied on the feelings of the national guard, of which one or two divisions were much attached to him, while the dispositions of the whole had been certainly ameliorated, from their fear of fresh confusion by means of these new levies. Perhaps, also, the King could not bring himself at once to trust the versatile disposition of Dumouriez, whose fidelity, however, we see no reason for suspecting.

Another renewed point of discussion and disagreement betwixt the King and his ministers, respected the recusant clergy. A decree was passed in the Assembly, that such priests as might be convicted of a refusal to subscribe the oath to the civil Constitution, should be liable to deportation. This was a point of conscience with Louis, and was probably brought forward in order to hasten him into a resignation of the crown. He stood firm accordingly, and determined to oppose his *veto* to this decree also, [June 12,] in spite at once of all the arguments which the worldly prudence of

---

[206] Dumouriez, vol. ii., p. 353.

Dumouriez could object, and of the urgency of the Republican ministers.[207]

DISMISSAL OF ROLAND, ETC

The firm refusal of the King disconcerted the measures of the Girondist counsellors. Madame Roland undertook to make the too scrupulous monarch see the errors of his ways; and composed, in name of her husband and two of his colleagues, a long letter, to which Dumouriez and the other two refused to place their names. It was written in what the Citoyenne termed "an austere tone of truth;"[208] that is to say, without any of the usual marks of deference and respect, and with a harshness calculated to jar all the feelings, affectionate or religious, of him whom they still called King. Alas! the severest and most offensive truths, however late in reaching the ears of powerful and prosperous monarchs, make themselves sternly loud to those princes who are captive and unfriended. Louis might have replied to this rude expostulation, like the knight who received a blow from an enemy when he was disarmed, and a prisoner,— "There is little bravery in this *now*." The King, however, gave way to his resentment as far as he could. He dismissed Roland, Servan, and Clavière, and with difficulty prevailed on Dumouriez, Duranthon, and Lacoste, to retain their situations, and endeavour to supply the place of those whom he had deprived of office; but he was obliged to purchase their adherence, by ratifying the decree concerning the federal or departmental army of twenty thousand men, on condition that they should rendezvous at Soissons, not at Paris. On the decree against the priests, his resolution continued unmoved and immovable. Thus Religion, which had for half a century been so slightly regarded in France, at length interposed her influence in deciding the fate of the King and the kingdom.

The three discarded ministers affected to congratulate each other on being released from scenes so uncongenial to their republican virtues and sentiments, as the ante-chambers of a court,

---

[207] Lacretelle, tom. ix., p. 116; Mignet, tom. i., p. 173; Dumouriez, vol. ii., p. 360.
[208] "Je sais que le langage austère de la vérité est rarement accueillé près du trone."—See the Letter in Prudhomme, tom. iii., p. 82.

where men were forced to wear buckles instead of shoe-strings, or undergo the frowns of ushers and masters of ceremonies, and where patriotic tongues were compelled to practise court-language, and to address a being of the same flesh and blood as their own, with the titles of Sire, and your Majesty. The unhappy pedants were not long in learning that there are constraints worse to undergo than the etiquette of a court, and sterner despots to be found in the ranks of a republic, than the good-humoured and lenient Louis. As soon as dismissed, they posted to the Assembly, to claim the applause due to suffering virtue, and to exhibit their letter to those for whose ears it was really written—the sympathizing democrats and the tribunes.[209]

They were, accordingly, as victims of their democratic zeal, received with acclamation; but the triumph of those who bestowed it, was unexpectedly qualified and diminished. Dumouriez, who spoke fluently, and had collected proofs for such a moment, overwhelmed the Assembly by a charge of total neglect and incapacity, against Roland and his two colleagues. He spoke of unrecruited armies, ungarrisoned forts, unprovided commissariats, in a tone which compelled the Assembly to receive his denunciations against his late associates in the ministry.

But although his unpleasant and threatening communications made a momentary impression on the Assembly, almost in spite of themselves, the wily and variable orator saw that he could only maintain his ground as minister, by procuring, if possible, the assent of the King to the decree against the recusant clergy. He made a final attempt, along with his ephemeral colleagues; stated his conviction, that the refusal of the King, if persisted in, would be the cause of insurrection; and, finally, tendered his resignation, in case their urgent advice should be neglected. "Think not to terrify me by threats," replied Louis. "My resolution is fixed." Dumouriez was not a man to perish under the ruins of the throne which he could not preserve. His resignation was again tendered and accepted, not without marks of sensibility on the King's part and his own; and having thus saved a part of his credit with the Assembly, who respected his talents, and desired to use them against the invaders,

---

[209] Prudhomme, tom. iii., p. 92.

he departed from Paris to the frontiers, to lead the van among the French victors.[210]

Louis was now left to the pitiless storm of revolution, without the assistance of any one who could in the least assist him in piloting through the tempest. The few courtiers—or, much better named—the few ancient and attached friends, who remained around his person, possessed neither talents nor influence to aid him; they could but lament his misfortunes and share his ruin. He himself expressed a deep conviction, that his death was near at hand, yet the apprehension neither altered his firmness upon points to which he esteemed his conscience was party, nor changed the general quiet placidity of his temper. A negotiation to resign his crown was, perhaps, the only mode which remained, affording even a chance to avert his fate; but the days of deposed monarchs are seldom long, and no pledge could have assured Louis that any terms which the Girondists might grant, would have been ratified by their sterner and uncompromising rivals of the Jacobin party. These men had been long determined to make his body the step to their iniquitous power. They affected to feel for the cause of the people, with the zeal which goes to slaying. They had heaped upon the crown, and its unhappy wearer, all the guilt and all the misfortunes of the Revolution; it was incumbent on them to show that they were serious in their charge, by rendering Louis a sin-offering for the nation. On the whole, it was the more kingly part not to degrade himself by his own voluntary act, but to await the period which was to close at once his life and his reign. He named his last Ministry from the dispirited remnants of the Constitutional party, which still made a feeble and unsupported struggle against the Girondists and Jacobins in the Assembly. They did not long enjoy their precarious office.

The factions last named were now united in the purpose of precipitating the King from his throne by actual and direct force. The voice of the Girondists Vergniaud had already proclaimed in the Assembly. "Terror," he said, "must, in the name of the people,

---

[210] Dumouriez, tom. ii., p. 392; Mignet, tom. i., p. 173; Lacretelle, tom. i., p. 240.

burst her way into yonder palace, whence she has so often sallied forth at the command of monarchs."[211]

Though the insurrection was resolved upon, and thus openly announced, each faction was jealous of the force which the other was to employ, and apprehensive of the use which might be made of it against themselves, after the conquest was obtained. But however suspicious of each other, they were still more desirous of their common object, the destruction of the throne, and the erection of a republic, which the Brissotins supposed they could hold under their rule, and which the Jacobins were determined to retain under their misrule. An insurrection was at length arranged, which had all the character of that which brought the King a prisoner from Versailles, the Jacobins being the prime movers of their desperate followers, and the actors on both occasions; while the Girondists, on the 20th June, 1792, hoped, like the Constitutionalists on the 6th October, 1789, to gain the advantage of the enterprise which their own force would have been unable to accomplish. The community, or magistracy, of Paris, which was entirely under the dominion of Robespierre, Danton, and the Jacobins, had been long providing for such an enterprise, and under pretext that they were arming the lower classes against invasion, had distributed pikes and other weapons to the rabble, who were to be used on this occasion.

THE TWENTIETH OF JUNE

On the 20th of June, the Sans Culottes of the suburbs of Saint Marçeau and Saint Antoine assembled together, armed with pikes, scythes, hay-forks, and weapons of every description, whether those actually forged for the destruction of mankind, or those which, invented for peaceful purposes, are readily converted by popular fury into offensive arms. They seemed, notwithstanding their great numbers to act under authority, and amid their cries, their songs, their dances, and the wild intermixture of grotesque and fearful revel, appeared to move by command, and to act with a unanimity that gave the effect of order to that which was in itself confusion. They were divided into bodies, and had their leaders. Standards also

---

[211] Lacretelle, tom. ix., p. 136.

were displayed, carefully selected to express the character and purpose of the wretches who were assembled under them. One ensign was a pair of tattered breeches, with the motto, "Vivent les Sans Culottes." Another ensign-bearer, dressed in black, carried on a long pole a hog's harslet, that is, part of the entrails of that animal, still bloody, with the legend, "La fressure d'un Aristocrat." This formidable assemblage was speedily recruited by the mob of Paris, to an immense multitude, whose language, gestures, and appearance, all combined to announce some violent catastrophe.

The terrified citizens, afraid of general pillage, concentrated themselves,—not to defend the King or protect the National Assembly, but for the preservation of the Palais Royal, where the splendour of the shops was most likely to attract the cupidity of the Sans Culottes. A strong force of armed citizens guarded all the avenues to this temple of Mammon, and, by excluding the insurgents from its precincts, showed what they could have done for the Hall of the Legislature, or the palace of the monarch, had the cause of either found favour in their eyes.[212]

The insurrection rolled on to the hall of the Assembly, surrounded the alarmed deputies, and filled with armed men every avenue of approach; talked of a petition which they meant to present, and demanded to file through the hall to display the force by which it was supported. The terrified members had nothing better to reply, than by a request that the insurgents should only enter the Assembly by a representative deputation—at least that, coming in a body, they should leave their arms behind. The formidable petitioners laughed at both proposals, and poured through the hall, shaking in triumph their insurrectionary weapons.[213] The Assembly, meanwhile, made rather an ignoble figure; and their attempts to preserve an outward appearance of indifference, and even of cordiality towards their foul and frightful visitors, have been aptly compared to a band of wretched

---

[212] Lacretelle, tom. ix., p. 131.
[213] The passage of the procession lasted three hours.—See Lacretelle, tom. ix., p. 135; Thiers, tom. ii., p. 133.

comedians, endeavouring to mitigate the resentment of a brutal and incensed audience.[214]

MOB FORCE THE TUILERIES

From the hall of the Assembly, the populace rushed to the Tuileries. Preparations had been made for defence, and several bodies of troops were judiciously placed, who, with the advantages afforded by the gates and walls, might have defended their posts against the armed rabble which approached. But there was neither union, loyalty, nor energy, in those to whom the defence was intrusted, nor did the King, by placing himself at their head, attempt to give animation to their courage.

The national guards drew off at the command of the two municipal officers, decked with their scarfs of office, who charged them not to oppose the will of the people. The grates were dashed to pieces with sledge hammers. The gates of the palace itself were shut, but the rabble, turning a cannon upon them, compelled entrance, and those apartments of royal magnificence, so long the pride of France, were laid open to the multitude, like those of Troy to her invaders:—

Apparet domus intus, et atria longa patescunt, Apparent Priami et veterum penetralia regum.[215]

---

[214] It may be alleged in excuse, that the Assembly had no resource but submission. Yet, brave men in similar circumstances have, by a timely exertion of spirit, averted similar insolencies. When the furious Anti-Catholic mob was in possession of the avenues to, and even the lobbies of, the House of Commons, in 1780, General Cosmo Gordon, a member of the House, went up to the unfortunate nobleman under whose guidance they were supposed to act, and addressed him thus: "My lord, is it your purpose to bring your rascally adherents into the House of Commons? for if so, I apprise you, that the instant one of them enters, I pass my sword, not through his body, but your lordship's." The hint was sufficient, and the mob was directed to another quarter. Undoubtedly there were, in the French Legislative Assembly, men capable of conjuring down the storm they had raised, and who might have been moved to do so, had any man of courage made them directly and personally responsible for the consequences.—See Wraxall, vol. i., p. 247, for the story of Lord George Gordon and General Gordon; but the Editor is informed, that the person who really threatened Lord George in the manner described, was Colonel Holroyd, now Lord Sheffield.

The august palace of the proud house of Bourbon lay thus exposed to the rude gaze, and vulgar tread, of a brutal and ferocious rabble. Who dared have prophesied such an event to the royal founders of this stately pile—to the chivalrous Henry of Navarre, or the magnificent Louis XIV.!—The door of the apartment entering into the vestibule was opened by the hand of Louis himself, the ill-fated representative of this lofty line. He escaped with difficulty the thrust of a bayonet, made as the door was in the act of expanding. There were around him a handful of courtiers, and a few of the grenadiers of the national guard belonging to the section of Filles Saint Thomas, which had been always distinguished for fidelity. They hurried and almost forced the King into the embrazure of a window, erected a sort of barricade in front with tables, and stood beside him as his defenders. The crowd, at their first entrance, levelled their pikes at Madame Elizabeth, whom they mistook for the Queen. "Why did you undeceive them?" said the heroic princess to those around her—"It might have saved the life of my sister."[216] Even the insurgents were affected by this trait of heroism. They had encountered none of those obstacles which chafe such minds and make them thirsty of blood, and it would seem that their leaders had not received decided orders, or, having received them, did not think the time served for their execution. The insurgents defiled through the apartments, and passed the King, now joined by the Queen with her children. The former, though in the utmost personal danger, would not be separated from her husband, exclaiming, that her post was by his side; the latter were weeping with terror at a scene so horrible.

The people seemed moved, or rather their purpose was deprived of that energetic unanimity which had hitherto carried them so far. Some shouted against the veto—some against the unconstitutional priests, some more modestly called out for

---

[215] Dryden has expanded these magnificent lines, without expressing entirely either their literal meaning or their spirit. But he has added, as usual, beautiful ideas of his own, equally applicable to the scene described in the text:— "A mighty breach is made; the rooms conceal'd Appear, and all the palace is reveal'd; The halls of audience, and of public state— And where the lovely Queen in secret sate, Arm'd soldiers now by trembling maids are seen With not a door, and scarce a space between." *Æneid*, book ii.—S.
[216] Prudhomme, tom. iii., p. 117; Lacretelle, tom. ix., p. 139; Madame Campan, vol. ii., p. 212.

lowering the price of bread and butcher-meat. One of them flung a red cap to the King, who quietly drew it upon his head; another offered him a bottle, and commanded him to drink to the Nation. No glass could be had, and he was obliged to drink out of the bottle. These incidents are grotesque and degrading, but they are redeemed by one of much dignity. "Fear nothing, Sire," said one of the faithful grenadiers of the national guard who defended him. The King took his hand, and pressing it to his heart, replied, "Judge yourself if I fear."[217]

Various leaders of the Republicans were present at this extraordinary scene, in the apartments, or in the garden,[218] and expressed themselves according to their various sentiments. "What a figure they have made of him with the red night-cap and the bottle!" said Manuel, the Procureur of the Commune of Paris.—"What a magnificent spectacle!" said the artist David, looking out upon the tumultuary sea of pikes, agitated by fifty thousand hands, as they rose and sunk, welked and waved;—"Tremble, tremble, tyrants!"—"They are in a fair train," said the fierce Gorsas; "we shall soon see their pikes garnished with several heads." The crowds who thrust forward into the palace and the presence, were pressed together till the heat increased almost to suffocation, nor did there appear any end to the confusion.

Late and slow, the Legislative Assembly did at length send a deputation of twenty-five members, headed by Vergniaud and

---

[217] Prudhomme, tom. iii., p. 117; Mignet, tom. i., p. 178; Lacretelle, tom. ix., p. 142; Campan, vol. ii., p. 212.

[218] Napoleon was a witness of this scene from the gardens of the Tuileries. "While we were leading," says De Bourrienne, "a somewhat idle life, the 20th June arrived. We met that morning, as usual, in a coffee-room, Rue St. Honoré. On going out we saw approaching a mob, which Buonaparte computed at five or six thousand men, all in rags, and armed with every sort of weapon, vociferating the grossest abuse, and proceeding with rapid pace towards the Tuileries. 'Let us follow that rabble,' said Buonaparte to me. We got before them, and went to walk in the gardens, on the terrace overlooking the water. From this station he beheld the disgraceful occurrences that ensued. I should fail in attempting to depict the surprise and indignation aroused within him. He could not comprehend such weakness and forbearance. But when the King showed himself at one of the windows fronting the garden, with the red cap which one of the mob had just placed upon his head, Buonaparte could no longer restrain his indignation. 'What madness!' exclaimed he; 'how could they allow these scoundrels to enter? They ought to have blown four or five hundred of them into the air with cannon; the rest would then have taken to their heels.'"—De Bourrienne, tom. i., p. 49.

Isnard, to the palace. Their arrival put an end to the tumult; for Pétion, the Mayor of Paris, and the other authorities, who had hitherto been wellnigh passive, now exerted themselves to clear away the armed populace from the palace and gardens, and were so readily obeyed, that it was evident similar efforts would have entirely prevented the insurrection. The "poor and virtuous people," as Robespierre used to call them, with an affected unction of pronunciation, retired for once with their pikes unbloodied, not a little marvelling why they had been called together for such a harmless purpose.[219]

That a mine so formidable should have exploded without effect, gave some momentary advantages to the party at whose safety it was aimed. Men of worth exclaimed against the infamy of such a gratuitous insult to the crown, while it was still called a Constitutional authority. Men of substance dreaded the recurrence of such acts of revolutionary violence, and the commencement of riots, which were likely to end in pillage. Petitions were presented to the Assembly, covered with the names of thousands, praying that the leaders of the insurgents should be brought to punishment; while the King demanded, in a tone which seemed to appeal to France and to Europe, some satisfaction for his insulted dignity, the violation of his palace, and the danger of his person.[220] But La Fayette, at the head of an army whose affections he was supposed to possess, was the most formidable intercessor. He had, two or three days before, [June 16,] transmitted to the Assembly a letter, or rather a remonstrance,[221] in which, speaking in the name of the army, as well as his own, he expressed the highest dissatisfaction with the recent events at Paris, complaining of the various acts of violation of the constitution, and the personal disrespect offered to the King. This letter of itself had been accounted an enormous offence, both by the Jacobins and the Girondists; but the tumult of the 20th of June roused the general to bolder acts of intercession.

---

[219] "By eight o'clock in the evening they had all departed, and silence and astonishment reigned in the palace."—Mignet, tom. i., p. 178.
[220] Jomini, Hist. des Guerres de la Révolution, tom. ii., p. 53; Dumont, p. 343.
[221] For the letter itself, see Annual Register, vol. xxxiv., p. 206.

LA FAYETTE ARRIVES AT PARIS

On the 28th of the same month of June, all parties heard with as much interest as anxiety, that General La Fayette was in Paris. He came, indeed, only with a part of his staff. Had he brought with him a moderate body of troops upon whom he could have absolutely depended, his presence so supported, in addition to his influence in Paris, would have settled the point at issue. But the general might hesitate to diminish the French army then in front of the enemy, and by doing so to take on himself the responsibility of what might happen in his absence; or, as it appeared from subsequent events, he may not have dared to repose the necessary confidence in any corps of his army, so completely had they been imbued with the revolutionary spirit. Still his arrival, thus slightly attended, indicated a confidence in his own resources, which was calculated to strike the opposite party with anxious apprehension.

He appeared at the bar of the Assembly, and addressed the members in a strain of decision, which had not been lately heard on the part of those who pleaded the royal cause in that place. He denounced the authors of the violence committed on the 20th of June, declared that several corps of his army had addressed him, and that he came to express their horror, as well as his own, at the rapid progress of faction; and to demand that such measures should be taken as to ensure the defenders of France, that while they were shedding their blood on the frontiers, the Constitution, for which they combated, should not be destroyed by traitors in the interior. This speech, delivered by a man of great courage and redoubted influence, had considerable effect. The Girondists, indeed, proposed to inquire, whether La Fayette had permission from the minister of war to leave the command of his army; and sneeringly affirmed, that the Austrians must needs have retreated from the frontier, since the general of the French army had returned to Paris: but a considerable majority preferred the motion of the Constitutionalist Ramond, who, eulogizing La Fayette as the eldest son of liberty, proposed an inquiry into the causes and object of those factious proceedings of which he had complained.²²²

Thus happily commenced La Fayette's daring enterprise; but those by whom he expected to be supported did not rally around him. To disperse the Jacobin club was probably his object, but no sufficient force gathered about him to encourage the attempt. He ordered for the next day a general review of the national guards, in hopes, doubtless, that they would have recognised the voice which they had obeyed with such unanimity of submission; but this civic force was by no means in the state in which he had left them at his departure. The several corps of grenadiers, which were chiefly drawn from the more opulent classes, had been, under pretence of the general principle of equality, melted down and united with those composed of men of an inferior description, and who had a more decided revolutionary tendency. Many officers, devoted to La Fayette and the Constitution, had been superseded; and the service was, by studied contumely and ill usage, rendered disgusting to those who avowed the same sentiments, or displayed any remaining attachment to the sovereign. By such means Pétion, the mayor of Paris, had now authority enough with the civic army to prevent the review from taking place. A few grenadiers of different sections did indeed muster, but their number was so small that they dispersed in haste and alarm.

The Girondists and Jacobins, closely united at this crisis, began to take heart, yet dared not on their part venture to arrest the general. Meantime La Fayette saw no other means of saving the King than to propose his anew attempting an escape from Paris, which he offered to further by every means in his power. The plan was discussed, but dismissed in consequence of the Queen's prejudices against La Fayette, whom, not unnaturally, (though as far as regarded intention certainly unjustly,) she looked upon as the original author of the King's misfortunes.²²³ After two days lingering

---

[222] Thiers, tom. ii., p. 154; Lacretelle, tom. ix., p. 153.
[223] Madame Campan, tom. ii., p. 224.

in Paris, La Fayette found it necessary to return to the army which he commanded, and leave the King to his fate.[224]

La Fayette's conduct on this occasion may always be opposed to any aspersions thrown on his character at the commencement of the Revolution; for, unquestionably, in June 1792, he exposed his own life to the most imminent danger, in order to protect that of the King, and the existence of royalty. Yet he must himself have felt a lesson, which his fate may teach to others; how perilous, namely, it is, to set the example of violent and revolutionary courses, and what dangerous precedents such rashness may afford to those who use similar means for carrying events to still further extremities. The march to Versailles, 6th October, 1789, in which La Fayette to a certain degree co-operated, and of which he reaped all the immediate advantage, had been the means of placing Louis in that precarious situation from which he was now so generously anxious to free him. It was no less La Fayette's own act, by means of his personal aid-de-camp, to bring back the person of the King to Paris from Varennes; whereas he was now recommending, and offering to further his escape, by precisely such measures as his interference had then thwarted.

PETION AND MANUEL SUSPENDED

Notwithstanding the low state of the royal party, one constituted authority, amongst so many, had the courage to act offensively on the weaker and the injured side. The Directory of the Department (or province) of Paris, declared against the mayor, imputed to him the blame of the scandalous excesses of the 20th of June, and suspended him and Manuel, the Procureur of the Community of Paris, from their offices, [July 6.] This judgment was affirmed by the King. But, under the protection of the Girondists and Jacobins, Pétion appealed to the Assembly, where the demon of discord seemed now let loose, as the advantage was contended for by at least three parties, avowedly distinct from each other, together with innumerable subdivisions of opinion. And yet, in the midst of

---

[224] "He was burnt in effigy by the Jacobins, in the garden of the Palais Royal."—Prudhomme, tom. iii., p. 131.

such complicated and divided interests, such various and furious passions, two individuals, a lady and a bishop, undertook to restore general concord, and, singular to tell, they had a momentary success. Olympia de Gouges was an ardent lover of liberty, but she united with this passion an intense feeling of devotion, and a turn like that entertained by our friends the Quakers, and other sects who affect a transcendental love of the human kind, and interpret the doctrines of Christian morality in the most strict and literal sense. This person had sent abroad several publications recommending to all citizens of France, and the deputies especially of the Assembly, to throw aside personal views, and form a brotherly and general union with heart and hand, in the service of the public.

The same healing overture, as it would have been called in the civil dissensions of England, was brought before the Assembly, [July 9,] and recommended by the constitutional Bishop of Lyons, the Abbé L'Amourette. This good-natured orator affected to see, in the divisions which rent the Assembly to pieces, only the result of an unfortunate error—a mutual misunderstanding of each other's meaning. "You," he said to the Republican members, "are afraid of an undue attachment to aristocracy; you dread the introduction of the English system of two Chambers into the Constitution. You of the right hand, on the contrary, misconstrue your peaceful and ill-understood brethren, so far as to suppose them capable of renouncing monarchy, as established by the Constitution. What then remains to extinguish these fatal divisions, but for each party to disown the designs falsely imputed to them, and for the Assembly united to swear anew their devotion to the Constitution, as it has been bequeathed to us by the Constituent Assembly!"

This speech, wonderful as it may seem, had the effect of magic. The deputies of every faction, Royalist, Constitutionalist, Girondist, Jacobin, and Orleanist, rushed into each other's arms, and mixed tears with the solemn oaths by which they renounced the innovations supposed to be imputed to them. The King was sent for to enjoy this spectacle of concord, so strangely and so unexpectedly renewed. But the feeling, though strong,—and it might be with many overpowering for the moment,—was but like oil spilt on the raging sea, or rather like a shot fired across the waves of a torrent, which, though it counteracts them by its momentary impulse, cannot for a second alter their course. The factions, like Le Sage's demons, detested each other the more for having been compelled to embrace, and from the name and country of the benevolent bishop, the scene was long called, in ridicule, "*Le Baiser d'Amourette*," and "*La réconciliation Normande.*"[225]

The next public ceremony showed how little party spirit had been abated by this singular scene. The King's acceptance of the Constitution was repeated in the Champ de Mars before the Federates, or deputies sent up to represent the various departments of France; and the figure made by the King during that pageant, formed a striking and melancholy parallel with his actual condition in the state. With hair powdered and dressed, with clothes embroidered in the ancient court-fashion, surrounded and crowded unceremoniously by men of the lowest rank, and in the most wretched garbs, he seemed something belonging to a former age, but which in the present has lost its fashion and value. He was conducted to the Champ de Mars under a strong guard, and by a circuitous route, to avoid the insults of the multitude, who dedicated their applauses to the Girondist Mayor of Paris, exclaiming "Pétion or death!" When he ascended the altar to go through the ceremonial of the day, all were struck with the resemblance to a victim led to sacrifice, and the Queen so much so, that she exclaimed, and nearly fainted. A few children alone called, "Vive le Roi!" This was the last time Louis was seen in public until he mounted the scaffold.[226]

The departure of La Fayette renewed the courage of the Girondists, and they proposed a decree of impeachment against him

---

[225] Lacretelle, tom. ix., p. 161. After the dissolution of the Legislative Assembly, L'Amourette returned to Lyons, and continued there during the siege. He was afterwards conducted to Paris, condemned to death, and decapitated in January, 1794. The abbé was the author of several works, among others, "Les Délices de la Religion, ou Le Pouvoir de l'Evangile de nous rendre heureux."

[226] "The expression of the Queen's countenance on this day will never be effaced from my remembrance; her eyes were swollen with tears; the splendour of her dress, the dignity of her deportment, formed a contrast with the train that surrounded her. It required the character of Louis XVI., that character of martyr which he ever upheld, to support, as he did, such a situation. When he mounted the steps of the altar, he seemed a sacred victim, offering himself as a voluntary sacrifice. He descended; and, crossing anew the disordered ranks, returned to take his place beside the Queen and his children."—M. De Staël, vol. ii., p. 53.

in the Assembly [Aug. 8]; but the spirit which the general's presence had awakened was not yet extinguished, and his friends in the Assembly undertook his defence with a degree of unexpected courage, which alarmed their antagonists.[227] Nor could their fears be termed groundless. The constitutional general might march his army upon Paris, or he might make some accommodation with the foreign invaders, and receive assistance from them to accomplish such a purpose. It seemed to the Girondists, that no time was to be lost. They determined not to trust to the Jacobins, to whose want of resolution they seem to have ascribed the failure of the insurrection on the 20th of June. They resolved upon occasion of the next effort, to employ some part of that departmental force, which was now approaching Paris in straggling bodies, under the name of Federates. The affiliated clubs had faithfully obeyed the mandates of the parent society of the Jacobins, by procuring that the most stanch and exalted Revolutionists should be sent on this service. These men, or the greater part of them, chose to visit Paris, rather than to pass straight to their rendezvous at Soissons. As they believed themselves the armed representatives of the country, they behaved with all the insolence which the consciousness of bearing arms gives to those who are unaccustomed to discipline. They walked in large bodies in the garden of the Tuileries, and when any persons of the royal family appeared, they insulted the ladies with obscene language and indecent songs, the men with the most hideous threats. The Girondists resolved to frame a force, which might be called their own, out of such formidable materials.

BARBAROUX

Barbaroux, one of the most enthusiastic admirers of the Revolution, a youth, like the Séide of Voltaire's tragedy,[228] filled with the most devoted enthusiasm for a cause of which he never suspected the truth, offered to bring up a battalion of Federates from his native city of Marseilles, men, as he describes them, who knew how to die, and who, as it proved, understood at least as well

---

[227] "To the astonishment of both parties, the accusation against La Fayette was thrown out by a majority of 446 to 224,"—Lacretelle, tom. ix., p. 190.
[228] Le Fanatisme.

how to kill. In raking up the disgusting history of mean and bloody-minded demagogues it is impossible not to dwell on the contrast afforded by the generous and self-devoted character of Barbaroux, who, young, handsome,[229] generous, noble-minded, and disinterested, sacrificed his family happiness, his fortune, and finally his life, to an enthusiastic though mistaken zeal for the liberty of his country. He had become from the commencement of the Revolution one of its greatest champions at Marseilles, where it had been forwarded and opposed by all the fervour of faction, influenced by the southern sun. He had admired the extravagant writings of Marat and Robespierre; but when he came to know them personally, he was disgusted with their low sentiments and savage dispositions, and went to worship Freedom amongst the Girondists, where her shrine was served by the fair and accomplished Citoyenne Roland.

The Marseillois, besides the advantage of this enthusiastic leader, marched to the air of the finest hymn to which liberty or the Revolution had yet given birth. They appeared in Paris, where it had been agreed between the Jacobins and the Girondists, that the strangers should be welcomed by the fraternity of the suburbs, and whatever other force the factions could command. Thus united, they were to march to secure the municipality, occupy the bridges and principal posts of the city with detached parties, while the main body should proceed to form an encampment in the garden of the Tuileries, where the conspirators had no doubt they should find themselves sufficiently powerful to exact the King's resignation, or declare his forfeiture.

This plan failed through the cowardice of Santerre, the chief leader of the insurgents of the suburbs, who had engaged to meet the Marseillois with forty thousand men. Very few of the promised auxiliaries appeared; but the undismayed Marseillois, though only about five hundred in number, marched through the city to the terror of the inhabitants, their keen black eyes seeming to seek out aristocratic victims, and their songs partaking of the wild Moorish

---

[229] Madame Roland describes him as one "whose features no painter would disdain to copy for the head of an Antinous."—*Memoirs*, part i., p. 146.

character that lingers in the south of France, denouncing vengeance on kings, priests, and nobles.[230]

In the Tuileries, the Federates fixed a quarrel on some grenadiers of the national guard, who were attached to the Constitution, and giving instant way to their habitual impetuosity, attacked, defeated, and dispersed them. In the riot, Espremenil, who had headed the opposition to the will of the King in Parliament, which led the way to the Convocation of Estates, and who had been once the idol of the people, but now had become the object of their hate, was cut down and about to be massacred. "Assist me," he called out to Pétion, who had come to the scene of confusion,—"I am Espremenil—once as you are now, the minion of the people's love." Pétion, not unmoved, it is to be supposed, at the terms of the appeal, hastened to rescue him. Not long afterwards both suffered by the guillotine,[231] which was the bloody conclusion of so many popular favourites. The riot was complained of by the Constitutional party, but as usual it was explained by a declaration on the part of ready witnesses, that the forty civic soldiers had insulted and attacked the five hundred Marseillois, and therefore brought the disaster upon themselves.

DUKE OF BRUNSWICK'S MANIFESTO

Meanwhile, though their hands were strengthened by this band of unscrupulous and devoted implements of their purpose, the Girondists failed totally in their attempt against La Fayette in the Assembly, the decree of accusation against him being rejected by a victorious majority. They were therefore induced to resort to measures of direct violence, which unquestionably they would willingly have abstained from, since they could not attempt them without giving a perilous superiority to the Jacobin faction. The Manifesto of the Duke of Brunswick, and his arrival on the French

---

[230] "I never," says Madame de la Rochejaquelein, "heard any thing more impressive and terrible than their songs."

[231] Espremenil suffered by the guillotine in June, 1793; but Pétion, becoming at that time an object of suspicion to Robespierre, took refuge in the department of the Calvados, where he is supposed to have perished with hunger; his body being found in a field half devoured by wolves.

frontier at the head of a powerful Prussian army, acted upon the other motives for insurrection, as a high pressure upon a steam-engine, producing explosion.

It was the misfortune of Louis, as we have often noticed, to be as frequently injured by the erroneous measures of his friends as by the machinations of his enemies; and this proclamation, issued [July 25] by a monarch who had taken arms in the King's cause, was couched in language intolerable to the feelings even of such Frenchmen as might still retain towards their King some sentiments of loyalty. All towns or villages which should offer the slightest resistance to the allies, were in this ill-timed manifesto menaced with fire and sword. Paris was declared responsible for the safety of Louis, and the most violent threats of the total subversion of that great metropolis were denounced as the penalty.[232]

The Duke of Brunswick was undoubtedly induced to assume this tone, by the ease which he had experienced in putting down the revolution in Holland; but the cases were by no means parallel. Holland was a country much divided in political opinions, and there was existing among the constituted authorities a strong party in favour of the Stadtholder. France, on the contrary, excepting only the emigrants who were in the Duke's own army, was united, like the Jews of old, against foreign invasion, though divided into many bitter factions within itself. Above all, the comparative strength of France and Holland was so different, that a force which might overthrow the one country without almost a struggle, would scarce prove sufficient to wrest from such a nation as France even the most petty of her frontier fortresses. It cannot be doubted, that this haughty and insolent language on the part of the invaders, irritated the personal feelings of every true Frenchman, and determined them to the most obstinate resistance against invaders, who were confident enough to treat them as a conquered people, even before a skirmish had been fought. The imprudence of the allied general recoiled on the unfortunate Louis, on whose account he used this menacing language. Men began to consider his cause as identified with that of the invaders, of course as standing in diametrical opposition to that of the country; and these opinions spread

---

[232] See Annual Register, vol. xxxiv., p. 229.

generally among the citizens of Paris. To animate the citizens to their defence, the Assembly declared, that the country was in danger; and in order that the annunciation might be more impressive, cannon were hourly discharged from the hospital of the Invalids—bands of military music traversed the streets—bodies of men were drawn together hastily, as if the enemy were at the gates—and all the hurried and hasty movements of the constituted authorities seemed to announce, that the invaders were within a day's march of Paris.[233]

These distracting and alarming movements, with the sentiments of fear and anxiety which they were qualified to inspire, aggravated the unpopularity of Louis, in whose cause his brothers and his allies were now threatening the metropolis of France. From these concurring circumstances the public voice was indeed so strongly against the cause of monarchy, that the Girondists ventured by their organ, Vergniaud, to accuse the King in the Assembly of holding intelligence with the enemy, or at least of omitting sufficient defensive preparations, and proposed in express terms that they should proceed to declare his forfeiture. The orator, however, did not press this motion, willing, doubtless, that the power of carrying through and enforcing such a decree should be completely ascertained, which could only be after a mortal struggle with the last defenders of the Crown;[234] but when a motion like this could be made and seconded, it showed plainly how little respect was preserved for the King in the Assembly at large. For this struggle all parties were arranging their forces, and it became every hour more evident, that the capital was speedily to be the scene of some dreadful event.

---

[233] Thiers, tom. ii., p. 145.
[234] Lacretelle, tom. ix., p. 172.

WALTER SCOTT

Chapter IX

The Day of the Tenth of August—Tocsin sounded early in the Morning—Swiss Guards, and relics of the Royal Party, repair to the Tuileries—Mandat assassinated—Dejection of Louis, and energy of the Queen—King's Ministers appear at the Bar of the Assembly, stating the peril of the Royal Family, and requesting a Deputation might be sent to the Palace—Assembly pass to the Order of the Day—Louis and his Family repair to the Assembly—Conflict at the Tuileries—Swiss ordered to repair to the King's Person—and are many of them shot and dispersed on their way to the Assembly—At the close of the Day almost all of them are massacred—Royal Family spend the Night in the Convent of the Feuillans.

The King had, since the insurrection of the 20th of June, which displayed how much he was at the mercy of his enemies, renounced almost all thoughts of safety or escape. Henry IV. would have called for his arms—Louis XVI. demanded his confessor. "I have no longer any thing to do with earth," he said; "I must turn all my thoughts on Heaven." Some vain efforts were made to bribe the leaders of the Jacobins, who took the money, and pursued, as might have been expected, their own course with equal rigour. The motion for the declaration of the King's forfeiture[235] still lingered in the Convention, its fate depending upon the coming crisis. At length the fatal Tenth of August approached, being the day which, after repeated adjournments, had been fixed by the Girondists and their rivals for the final rising.

---

[235] "The question of abdication was discussed with a degree of frenzy. Such of the deputies as opposed the motion were abused, ill-treated, and surrounded by assassins. They had a battle to fight at every step they took; and at length they did not dare to sleep in their houses."—Montjoie.

The King was apprised of their intention, and had hastily recalled from their barracks at Courbe-Voie about a thousand Swiss guards, upon whose fidelity he could depend. The formidable discipline and steady demeanour of these gallant mountaineers, might have recalled the description given by historians, of the entrance of their predecessors into Paris under similar circumstances, the day before the affair of the Barricades, in the reign of Henry II.[236] But the present moment was too anxious to admit of reflections upon past history.

TENTH OF AUGUST

Early on the morning of the 10th of August, the tocsin rung out its alarm-peal over the terrified city of Paris, and announced that the long-menaced insurrection was at length on foot. In many parishes the Constitutional party resisted those who came to sound this awful signal; but the well-prepared Jacobins were found every where victorious, and the prolonged mournful sound was soon tolled out from every steeple in the metropolis.[237]

To this melancholy music the contending parties arranged their forces for attack and defence, upon a day which was doomed to be decisive.

The Swiss guards got under arms, and repaired to their posts in and around the palace. About four hundred grenadiers of the loyal section of Filles Saint Thomas, joined by several from that of Les Petits Pères, in whom all confidence could justly be reposed, were posted in the interior of the palace, and associated with the Swiss for its defence. The relics of the Royalist party, undismayed at the events of the 28th of February in the year preceding,[238] had repaired to the palace on the first signal given by the tocsin. Joined

---

[236] Thus imitated by the dramatist Lee, from the historian Davila:— "Have you not heard—the King, preventing day, Received the guards within the city gates; The jolly Swisses marching to their pipes, The crowd stood gaping heedless and amazed, Shrunk to their shops, and left the passage free."—S.
[237] M. de Staël, tom. ii., p. 59.
[238] When they were, in similar circumstances, maltreated by the national guard.—See *ante*. —S.

to the domestic attendants of the royal family, they might amount to about four hundred persons. Nothing can more strongly mark the unprepared state of the court, than that there were neither muskets nor bayonets for suitably arming these volunteers, nor any supply of ammunition, save what the Swiss and national grenadiers had in their pouches. The appearance also of this little troop tended to inspire dismay rather than confidence. The chivalrous cry of "Entrance for the Noblesse of France," was the signal for their filing into the presence of the royal family. Alas! instead of the thousand nobles whose swords used to gleam around their monarch at such a crisis, there entered but veteran officers of rank, whose strength, though not their spirit, was consumed by years, mixed with boys scarce beyond the age of children, and with men of civil professions, several of whom, Lamoignon Malesherbes for example, had now for the first time worn a sword. Their arms were as miscellaneous as their appearance. Rapiers, hangers, and pistols, were the weapons with which they were to encounter bands well provided with musketry and artillery.[239] Their courage, however, was unabated. It was in vain that the Queen conjured, almost with tears, men aged fourscore and upwards, to retire from a contest where their strength could avail so little. The veterans felt that the fatal hour was come, and, unable to fight, claimed the privilege of dying in the discharge of their duty.[240]

The behaviour of Marie Antoinette was magnanimous in the highest degree. "Her majestic air," says Peltier, "her Austrian lip, and aquiline nose, gave her an air of dignity, which can only be conceived by those who beheld her in that trying hour."[241] Could she have inspired the King with some portion of her active spirit, he might even at that extreme hour have wrested the victory from the Revolutionists; but the misfortunes which he could endure like a

---

[239] "M. de St. Souplet, one of the King's equerries, and a page, instead of muskets, carried upon their shoulders the tongs belonging to the King's ante-chamber, which they had broken and divided between them."—Mad. Campan. vol. ii., p. 246.
[240] Lacretelle, tom. ix., p. 201.
[241] Dernier Tableau de Paris, tom. i., p. 176.

saint, he could not face and combat like a hero; and his scruples about shedding human blood wellnigh unmanned him.[242]

The distant shouts of the enemy were already heard, while the gardens of the Tuileries were filled by the successive legions of the national guard, with their cannon. Of this civic force, some, and especially the artillerymen, were as ill-disposed towards the King as was possible; others were well inclined to him; and the greater part remained doubtful. Mandat, their commander, was entirely in the royal interests. He had disposed the force he commanded to the best advantage for discouraging the mutinous, and giving confidence to the well-disposed, when he received an order to repair to the municipality for orders. He went thither accordingly, expecting the support of such Constitutionalists as remained in that magistracy, but he found it entirely in possession of the Jacobin party. Mandat was arrested, and ordered a prisoner to the Abbaye, which he never reached, being pistoled by an assassin at the gate of the Hôtel de Ville. His death was an infinite loss to the King's party.[243]

A signal advantage had, at the same time, been suffered to escape. Pétion, the Brissotin Mayor of Paris, was now observed among the national guards. The Royalists possessed themselves of his person, and brought him to the palace, where it was proposed to detain this popular magistrate as an hostage. Upon this, his friends in the Assembly moved that he should be brought to the bar, to render an account of the state of the capital. A message was despatched accordingly requiring his attendance, and Louis had the weakness to permit him to depart.

---

[242] "The King ought then to have put himself at the head of his troops, and opposed his enemies. The Queen was of this opinion, and the courageous counsel she gave on this occasion does honour to her memory."—M. de Staël, tom. ii., p. 60.
"This invasion of the 10th of August, was another of those striking occasions on which the King, by suddenly changing his character, and assuming firmness, might have recovered his throne. The mass of the French people were weary of the excesses of the Jacobins, and the outrage of the 20th of June roused the general indignation. Had he ordered the clubs of the Jacobins and Cordeliers, to be shut up, dissolved the Assembly, and seized upon the factions, that day had restored his authority: but this weak prince, unmindful that the safety of his kingdom depended upon the preservation of his own authority, chose rather to expose himself to certain death, than give orders for his defence."—Dumont, p. 362.
[243] Mignet, tom. i., p. 190; Lacretelle, tom. ix., p. 208.

The motions of the assailants were far from being so prompt and lively as upon former occasions, when no great resistance was anticipated. Santerre, an eminent brewer, who, from his great capital, and his affectation of popular zeal, had raised himself to the command of the suburb forces, was equally inactive in mind and body, and by no means fitted for the desperate part which he was called on to play.[244] Westerman, a zealous republican, and a soldier of skill and courage, came to press Santerre's march, informing him, that the Marseillois and Breton Federates were in arms in the Place du Carousel, and expected the advance of the pikemen from the suburbs of Saint Antoine and St. Marçeau. On Santerre's hesitating, Westerman placed his sword-point at his throat, and the citizen commandant, yielding to the nearer terror, put his bands at length in motion. Their numbers were immense. But the real strength of the assault was to lie on the Federates of Marseilles and Bretagne, and other provinces, who had been carefully provided with arms and ammunition. They were also secure of the gens-d'armes, or soldiers of police, although these were called out and arranged on the King's side. The Marseillois and Bretons were placed at the head of the long columns of the suburb pikemen, as the edge of an axe is armed with steel, while the back is of coarser metal to give weight to the blow. The charge of the attack was committed to Westerman.

DEJECTION OF LOUIS

In the meantime, the defenders of the palace advised Louis to undertake a review of the troops assembled for his defence. His appearance and mien were deeply dejected, and he wore, instead of a uniform, a suit of violet, which is the mourning colour of sovereigns. His words were broken and interrupted, like the accents of a man in despair, and void of the energy suitable to the occasion. "I know not," he said, "what they would have from me—I am willing to die with my faithful servants—Yes, gentlemen, we will at

---

[244] "The muscular expansion of his tall person, the sonorous hoarseness of his voice, his rough manners, and his easy and vulgar eloquence, made him, of course, a hero among the rabble. In truth, he had gained a despotic empire over the dregs of the Fauxbourgs. He could excite them at will; but that was the extent of his skill and capacity."—Montjoie, *Hist. de Marie Antoinette*, p. 295.

length do our best to resist."[245] It was in vain that the Queen laboured to inspire her husband with a tone more resolved—in vain that she even snatched a pistol from the belt of the Comte d'Affray, and thrust it into the King's hand, saying, "Now is the moment to show yourself as you are."[246] Indeed, Barbaroux, whose testimony can scarce be doubted, declares his firm opinion, that had the King at this time mounted his horse, and placed himself at the head of the national guards, they would have followed him, and succeeded in putting down the Revolution.[247] History has its strong parallels, and one would think we are writing of Margaret of Anjou, endeavouring in vain to inspire determination into her virtuous but feeble-minded husband.

Within the palace, the disposition of the troops seemed excellent, and there, as well as in the courts of the Tuileries, the King's address was answered with shouts of "Vive le Roi!" But when he sallied out into the garden, his reception from the legions of the national guard was at least equivocal, and that of the artillerymen, and of a battalion from Saint Marçeau, was decidedly unfavourable. Some cried, "Vive la nation!"[248] Some, "Down with the tyrant!" The King did nothing to encourage his own adherents, or to crush his enemies, but retired to hold counsel in the palace, around which the storm was fast gathering.

CONDUCT OF THE MINISTRY

It might have been expected that the Assembly, in which the Constitutionalists possessed so strong a majority as to throw out the accusation against La Fayette by a triumphant vote, might now, in the hour of dread necessity, have made some effort to save the crown which that constitution recognised, and the innocent life of

---

[245] "I was at a window looking on the garden. I saw some of the gunners quit their posts, go up to the King, and thrust their fists in his face, insulting him by the most brutal language. He was as pale as a corpse. When the royal family came in again, the Queen told me that all was lost; that the King had shown no energy, and that this sort of review had done more harm than good."—Mad. Campan, vol. ii., p. 245.
[246] Lacretelle, tom. ix., p. 214.
[247] Mémoires de Barbaroux, p. 69.
[248] "And I," exclaimed the King, "I, too, say '*Vive la Nation*!'—its happiness has ever been the dearest object of my heart."—Lacretelle, tom. ix., p. 214.

the prince by whom it was occupied. But fear had laid strong possession upon these unworthy and ungenerous representatives. The ministers of the King appeared at the bar, and represented the state of the city and of the palace, conjuring the Assembly to send a deputation to prevent bloodshed. This was courageous on the part of those faithful servants; for to intimate the least interest in the King's fate, was like the bold swimmer who approaches the whirlpool caused by the sinking of a gallant vessel. The measure they proposed had been resorted to on the 20th June preceding, and was then successful, even though the deputation consisted of members the most unfriendly to the King. But now, the Assembly passed to the order of the day, and thereby left the fate of the King and capital to chance, or the result of battle.[249]

In the meantime, the palace was completely invested. The bridge adjacent to the Tuileries, called the Pont Royale, was occupied by the insurgents, and the quai on the opposite side of the river was mounted with cannon, of which the assailants had about fifty pieces, served by the most determined Jacobins; for the artillerymen had, from the beginning, embraced the popular cause with unusual energy.

At this decisive moment Rœderer, the procureur-general syndic, the depositary and organ of the law, who had already commanded the Swiss and armed Royalists not to make any offensive movement, but to defend themselves when attacked, began to think, apparently, that his own safety was compromised, by this implied grant of permission to use arms, even in defence of the King's person. He became urgent with the King to retire from the palace, and put himself under the protection of the National Assembly. The Queen felt at once all the imbecility and dishonour of throwing themselves as suppliants on the protection of a body, which had not shown even a shadow of interest in their safety, surrounded as they knew the royal family to be with the most inveterate enemies. Ere she consented to such infamy, she said, she would willingly be nailed to the walls of the palace.[250] But the

---

[249] Prudhomme, tom. iii., p. 198; Mad. Campan, vol. ii., p. 247.
[250] "'Oui,' disait-elle à MM. de Briges et de Saint Priest, 'j'aimerais mieux me faire clouer aux murs du château que de choisir cet indigne refuge.'"—Lacretelle, tom. ix., p. 216.

counsel which promised to avert the necessity of bloodshed on either part, suited well with the timorous conscience and irresolution of Louis. Other measures were hastily proposed by those who had devoted themselves to secure his safety. There was, however, no real alternative but to fight at the head of his guards, or to submit himself to the pleasure of the Assembly, and Louis preferred the latter.[251]

His wife, his sister, and his children, accompanied him on this occasion; and the utmost efforts of an escort of three hundred Swiss and national grenadiers were scarce able to protect them, and a small retinue, consisting of the ministers and a few men of rank, the gleanings of the most brilliant court of Christendom, who accompanied their master in this last act of humiliation, which was, indeed, equal to a voluntary descent from his throne. They were, at every moment of their progress, interrupted by the deadliest threats and imprecations, and the weapons of more than one ruffian were levelled against them. The Queen was robbed even of her watch and purse—so near might the worst criminals approach the persons of the royal fugitives.[252] Louis showed the greatest composure amidst all these imminent dangers. He was feeble when called upon to kill, but strong in resolution when the question was only to die.[253]

The King's entrance into the Assembly was not without dignity. "My family and I are come among you," he said, "to prevent the commission of a great crime." Vergniaud, who was president at the time, answered with propriety, though ambiguously. He assured the King, that the Assembly knew its duties, and was ready to perish in support of them. A member of the Mountain[254] observed, with bitter irony, that it was impossible for the Assembly to deliberate freely in presence of the monarch, and proposed he should retreat into one of the most remote committee rooms—a place where

---

[251] Lacretelle, tom. ix., p. 219; Mad. Campan, vol. ii., p. 247.
[252] Mad. Campan, vol. ii., p. 429; Lacretelle, tom. ix., p. 220.
[253] "The Queen told me, that the King had just refused to put on the under-waistcoat of mail which she had prepared for him; that he had consented to wear it on the 14th of July, because it was merely going to a ceremony, where the blade of an assassin was to be apprehended; but that, on a day in which his party might have to fight against the revolutionists, he thought there was something cowardly in preserving his life by such means."—Mad. Campan, vol. ii., p. 243.
[254] Chabot.

assassination must have been comparatively easy. The Assembly rejected this proposal, alike insulting and insidious, and assigned a box, or small apartment, called the Logographe, used for the reporters of the debates, for the place of refuge of this unhappy family. This arrangement was scarce made, ere a heavy discharge of musketry and cannon announced that the King's retreat had not prevented the bloodshed he so greatly feared.[255]

It must be supposed to have been Louis's intention, that his guards and defenders should draw off from the palace, as soon as he himself had abandoned it; for to what purpose was it now to be defended, when the royal family were no longer concerned; and at what risk, when the garrison was diminished by three hundred of the best of the troops, selected as the royal escort? But no such order of retreat, or of non-resistance, had, in fact, been issued to the Swiss guards, and the military discipline of this fine corps prevented their retiring from an assigned post without command. Captain Durler is said to have asked the Maréchal Mailly for orders, and to have received for answer, "Do not suffer your posts to be forced." "You may rely on it," replied the intrepid Swiss.[256]

Meantime, to give no unnecessary provocation, as well as on account of their diminished numbers, the court in front of the palace was abandoned, and the guards were withdrawn into the building itself; their outermost sentinels being placed at the bottom of the splendid staircase, to defend a sort of barricade which had been erected there, ever since the 20th June, to prevent such intrusions as distinguished that day.

The insurgents, with the Marseillois and Breton Federates at their heads, poured into the court-yard without opposition, planted their cannon where some small buildings gave them advantage, and advanced without hesitation to the outposts of the Swiss. They had already tasted blood that day, having massacred a patrol of Royalists, who, unable to get into the Tuileries, had attempted to assist the defence, by interrupting, or at least watching and discovering, the

---

[255] Lacretelle, tom. ix., p. 223.
[256] Lacretelle, tom. ix., p. 227.

measures adopted by the insurgents. These men's heads were, as usual, borne on pikes among their ranks.

CONFLICT AT THE TUILERIES

They pushed forward, and it is said the Swiss at first offered demonstrations of truce. But the assailants thronged onward, crowded on the barricade, and when the parties came into such close collision, a struggle ensued, and a shot was fired. It is doubtful from what side it came, nor is it of much consequence, for, on such an occasion, that body must be held the aggressors who approach the pickets of the other, armed and prepared for assault; and although the first gun be fired by those whose position is endangered, it is no less defensive than if discharged in reply to a fire from the other side.

This unhappy shot seems to have dispelled some small chance of a reconciliation between the parties. Hard firing instantly commenced from the Federates and Marseillois, whilst the palace blazed forth fire from every window, and killed a great many of the assailants. The Swiss, whose numbers were now only about seven hundred men, determined, notwithstanding, upon a sally, which, in the beginning, was completely successful. They drove the insurgents from the court-yard, killed many of the Marseillois and Bretons, took some of their guns, and turning them along the streets, compelled the assailants to actual flight, so that word was carried to the National Assembly that the Swiss were victorious. The utmost confusion prevailed there; the deputies upbraided each other with their share in bringing about the insurrection; Brissot showed timidity; and several of the deputies, thinking the guards were hastening to massacre them, attempted to escape by the windows of the hall.[257]

If, indeed, the sally of the Swiss had been supported by a sufficient body of faithful cavalry, the Revolution might have been

---

[257] Lacretelle, tom. ix., p. 231; Mignet, tom. i., p. 195; Thiers, tom. ii., p. 263.

that day ended.²⁵⁸ But the gens-d'armes, the only horsemen in the field, were devoted to the popular cause, and the Swiss, too few to secure their advantage, were obliged to return to the palace, where they were of new invested.

Westerman posted his forces and artillery with much intelligence, and continued a fire on the Tuileries from all points. It was now returned with less vivacity, for the ammunition of the defenders began to fail. At this moment D'Hervilly arrived from the Assembly, with the King's commands that the Swiss should cease firing, evacuate the palace, and repair to the King's person. The faithful guards obeyed at once, not understanding that the object was submission, but conceiving they were summoned elsewhere, to fight under the King's eye. They had no sooner collected themselves into a body, and attempted to cross the garden of the Tuileries, than, exposed to a destructive fire on all sides, the remains of that noble regiment, so faithful to the trust assigned to it, diminished at every step; until, charged repeatedly by the treacherous gens-d'armes, who ought to have supported them, they were separated into platoons, which continued to defend themselves with courage, even till the very last of them was overpowered, dispersed, and destroyed by multitudes. A better defence against such fearful odds scarce remains on historical record—a more useless one can hardly be imagined.²⁵⁹

The rabble, with their leaders the Federates, now burst into the palace, executing the most barbarous vengeance on the few defenders who had not made their escape; and, while some massacred the living, others, and especially the unsexed women who were mingled in their ranks, committed the most shameful butchery on the corpses of the slain.²⁶⁰

Almost every species of enormity was perpetrated upon that occasion excepting pillage, which the populace would not permit,

---

[258] "S'il y avait eu trois cents cavaliers fidèles pour marcher à la poursuite des rebelles, Paris était soumis au roi, et l'Assemblée tombait aux pieds de son captif."—Lacretelle, tom. ix., p. 230.
[259] Lacretelle, tom. ix., p. 233; Toulongeon, tom. ii., p. 253.
[260] "L'histoire ne peut dire les obscènes et atroces mutilations que d'impudiques furies firent subir aux cadavres des Suisses."—Lacretelle, tom. ix., p. 240.

even amid every other atrocity.²⁶¹ There exist in the coarsest minds, nay, while such are engaged in most abominable wickedness, redeeming traits of character, which show that the image of the Deity is seldom totally and entirely defaced even in the rudest bosoms. An ordinary workman of the suburbs, in a dress which implied abject poverty, made his way into the place where the royal family were seated, demanding the King by the name of Monsieur Veto. "So you are here," he said, "beast of a Veto! There is a purse of gold I found in your house yonder. If you had found mine, you would not have been so honest."²⁶² There were, doubtless, amongst that dreadful assemblage many thousands, whose natural honesty would have made them despise pillage, although the misrepresentations by which they were influenced to fury easily led them to rebellion and murder.

Band after band of these fierce men, their faces blackened with powder, their hands and weapons streaming with blood, came to invoke the vengeance of the Assembly on the head of the King and royal family, and expressed in the very presence of the victims whom they claimed, their expectations and commands how they should be dealt with.

FALL OF THE MONARCHY

Vergniaud, who, rather than Brissot, ought to have given name to the Girondists, took the lead in gratifying the wishes of these dreadful petitioners. He moved, 1st, That a National Convention should be summoned. 2d, That the King should be suspended from his office. 3d, That the King should reside at the Luxembourg palace under safeguard of the law,—a word which they were not ashamed to use. These proposals were unanimously assented to.²⁶³

---

²⁶¹ Prudhomme, tom. iii., p. 202; but see Lacretelle, tom. ix., p. 241.
²⁶² Mémoires de Barbaroux. "L'anecdote," says Lacretelle, "est fausse; mais quelle fiction atroce!" tom. ix., p. 243.
²⁶³ Mignet, tom. i., p. 195; Thiers, tom. i., p. 263; Lacretelle, tom. ix., p. 244.

An almost vain attempt was made to save the lives of that remaining detachment of Swiss which had formed the King's escort to the Assembly, and to whom several of the scattered Royalists had again united themselves. Their officers proposed, as a last effort of despair, to make themselves masters of the Assembly, and declare the deputies hostages for the King's safety. Considering the smallness of their numbers, such an attempt could only have produced additional bloodshed, which would have been ascribed doubtless to the King's treachery. The King commanded them to resign their arms, being the last order which he issued to any military force. He was obeyed; but, as they were instantly attacked by the insurgents, few escaped slaughter, and submission preserved but a handful. About seven hundred and fifty fell in the defence, and after the storm of the Tuileries. Some few were saved by the generous exertions of individual deputies—others were sent to prison, where a bloody end awaited them—the greater part were butchered by the rabble, so soon as they saw them without arms. The mob sought for them the whole night, and massacred many porters of private families, who, at Paris, are generally termed Swiss, though often natives of other countries.

The royal family were at length permitted to spend the night, which, it may be presumed, was sleepless, in the cells of the neighbouring convent of the Feuillans.[264]

---

[264] "For fifteen hours the royal family were shut up in the short-hand writer's box. At length, at one in the morning, they were transferred to the Feuillans. When left alone, Louis prostrated himself in prayer. 'Thy trials, O God! are dreadful; give us courage to bear them. We bless thee in our afflictions, as we did in the day of prosperity: receive into thy mercy all those who have died fighting in our defence.'"—Lacretelle, tom. ix., p. 250.

"The royal family remained three days at the Feuillans. They occupied a small suite of apartments, consisting of four cells. In the first were the gentlemen who had accompanied the King. In the second we found the King: he was having his hair dressed; he took two locks of it, and gave one to my sister and one to me. In the third was the Queen, in bed, and in an indescribable state of affliction. We found her attended only by a bulky woman, who appeared tolerably civil; she waited upon the Queen, who, as yet, had none of her own people about her. I asked her Majesty what the ambassadors from foreign powers had done under existing circumstances? She told me that they could do nothing, but that the lady of the English ambassador had just given her a proof of the private interest she took in her welfare by sending her linen for her son."—Mad. Campan, vol. ii., p. 259.

"At this frightful period, Lady Sutherland," [the present Duchess and Countess of Sutherland,] "then English ambassadress at Paris, showed the most devoted attentions to the royal family."—Mad. de Staël, tom. ii., p. 69.

Thus ended, for the period of twenty years and upwards, the reign of the Bourbons over their ancient realm of France.

CHAPTER X

La Fayette compelled to Escape from France—Is made Prisoner by the Prussians, with three Companions—Reflections—The Triumvirate, Danton, Robespierre, and Marat—Revolutionary Tribunal appointed—Stupor of the Legislative Assembly—Longwy, Stenay, and Verdun, taken by the Prussians—Mob of Paris enraged—Great Massacre of Prisoners in Paris, commencing on the 2d, and ending 6th September—Apathy of the Assembly during and after these Events—Review of its Causes.

The success of the 10th of August had sufficiently established the democratic maxim, that the will of the people, expressed by their insurrections, was the supreme law; the orators of the clubs its interpreters; and the pikes of the suburbs its executive power. The lives of individuals and their fortunes were, from that time, only to be regarded as leases at will, subject to be revoked so soon as an artful, envious, or grasping demagogue should be able to turn against the lawful owners the readily-excited suspicions of a giddy multitude, whom habit and impunity had rendered ferocious. The system established on these principles, and termed liberty, was in fact an absolute despotism, far worse than that of Algiers; because the tyrannic dey only executes his oppression and cruelties within a certain sphere, affecting a limited number of his subjects who approach near to his throne; while, of the many thousand leaders of the Jacobins of France, every one had his peculiar circle in which he claimed right, as full as that of Robespierre or Marat, to avenge former slights or injuries, and to gratify his own individual appetite for plunder and blood.

All the departments of France, without exception, paid the most unreserved submission to the decrees of the Assembly, or rather to those which the Community of Paris, and the insurgents, had dictated to that legislative body; so that the hour seemed arrived when the magistracy of Paris, supported by a democratic force, should, in the name and through the influence of the Assembly, impose its own laws upon France.

La Fayette, whose headquarters was at this juncture at Sedan, in vain endeavoured to animate his soldiers against this new species of despotism. The Jacobins had their friends and representatives in the very trustiest of his battalions. He made an effort, however, and a bold one. He seized on the persons of three deputies, sent to him as commissioners by the Assembly, to compel submission to their decrees, and proposed to reserve them as hostages for the King's safety. Several of his own general officers, the intrepid Desaix amongst others, seemed willing to support him. Dumouriez, however, the personal enemy of La Fayette, and ambitious of being his successor in the supreme command, recognised the decrees of the Assembly in the separate army which he commanded. His example drew over Luckner, who also commanded an independent corps d'armée, and who at first seemed disposed to join with La Fayette.[265]

LA FAYETTE ESCAPES FROM FRANCE

That unfortunate general was at length left unsupported by any considerable part even of his own army; so that with three friends, whose names were well known in the Revolution,[266] he was fain to attempt an escape from France, and, in crossing a part of the enemy's frontier, they were made prisoners by a party of Prussians.

Fugitives from their own camp for the sake of royalty, they might have expected refuge in that of the allied kings, who were in arms for the same object; but, with a littleness of spirit which augured no good for their cause, the allies determined that these unfortunate gentlemen should be consigned as state prisoners to different fortresses. This conduct on the part of the monarchs, however irritated they might be by the recollection of some part of

---

[265] Lacretelle, tom. ix., p. 265; Mignet, tom. i., p. 197.
[266] Bursau de Pucy, Latour Maubourg, and Alexander Lameth. Their intention was to proceed to the United States of America.

La Fayette's conduct in the outset of the Revolution, was neither to be vindicated by morality, the law of nations, nor the rules of sound policy. We are no approvers of the democratic species of monarchy which La Fayette endeavoured to establish, and cannot but be of opinion, that if he had acted upon his victory in the Champ de Mars, he might have shut up the Jacobin Club, and saved his own power and popularity from being juggled out of his hands by those sanguinary charlatans. But errors of judgment must be pardoned to men placed amidst unheard-of difficulties; and La Fayette's conduct on his visit to Paris, bore testimony to his real willingness to save the King and preserve the monarchy. But even if he had been amenable for a crime against his own country, we know not what right Austria or Prussia had to take cognizance of it. To them he was a mere prisoner of war, and nothing farther. Lastly, it is very seldom that a petty and vindictive line of policy can consist with the real interest either of great princes or of private individuals. In the present case, the arrest of La Fayette was peculiarly the contrary. It afforded a plain proof to France and to all Europe, that the allied monarchs were determined to regard as enemies all who had, in any manner, or to any extent, favoured the Revolution, being indeed the whole people of France, excepting the emigrants now in arms. The effect must necessarily have been, to compel every Frenchman, who was desirous of enjoying more liberty than the ancient despotism permitted, into submission to the existing government, whatever it was, so long as invading armies of foreigners, whose schemes were apparently as inconsistent with the welfare as with the independence of the country, were hanging on the frontiers of France.

For a short space, like hounds over the carcass of the prey they have jointly run down, the Girondists and Jacobins suspended their dissensions; but when the Constitutional party had ceased to show all signs of existence, their brawl soon recommenced, and the Girondists early discovered, that in the allies whom they had called on to assist them in the subjugation of royalty, they had already to strive with men, who, though inferior to them in speculative knowledge, and in the eloquence which was to sway the Assembly, possessed in a much higher degree the practical energies by which revolutions are accomplished, were in complete possession of the community (or magistracy) of Paris, and maintained despotic authority over all the bands of the metropolis. Three men of terror, whose names will long remain, we trust, unmatched in history by those of any similar miscreants, had now the unrivalled leading of the Jacobins, and were called the Triumvirate.

Danton deserves to be named first, as unequalled by his colleagues in talent and audacity. He was a man of gigantic size, and possessed a voice of thunder. His countenance was that of an Ogre on the shoulders of a Hercules.[267] He was as fond of the pleasures of vice as of the practice of cruelty; and it was said there were times when he became humanized amidst his debauchery, laughed at the terror which his furious declamations excited, and might be approached with safety, like the Maelstrom at the turn of tide. His profusion was indulged to an extent hazardous to his popularity, for the populace are jealous of a lavish expenditure, as raising their favourites too much above their own degree; and the charge of peculation finds always ready credit with them, when brought against public men.[268]

ROBESPIERRE

Robespierre possessed this advantage over Danton, that he did not seem to seek for wealth, either for hoarding or expending, but lived in strict and economical retirement, to justify the name of the Incorruptible, with which he was honoured by his partisans. He appears to have possessed little talent, saving a deep fund of hypocrisy, considerable powers of sophistry, and a cold exaggerated strain of oratory, as foreign to good taste, as the measures he recommended were to ordinary humanity. It seemed wonderful, that even the seething and boiling of the revolutionary cauldron should have sent up from the bottom, and long supported on the surface, a

---

[267] "I never saw any countenance that so strongly expressed the violence of brutal passions, and the most astonishing audacity, half-disguised by a jovial air, an affectation of frankness, and a sort of simplicity."—Mad. Roland, part i., p. 88.

[268] "In 1789, he was a miserable lawyer, more burdened with debts than causes. He went to Belgium to augment his resources, and now had the hardihood to avow a fortune of 1,400,000 livres, (£58,333,) and to wallow in luxury, whilst preaching sans-culottism, and sleeping on heaps of slaughtered men. O, Danton! cruel as Marius, and more terrible than Cataline, you surpass their misdeeds, without possessing their good qualities."—Mad. Roland, part ii., p. 59.

thing so miserably void of claims to public distinction; but Robespierre had to impose on the minds of the vulgar, and he knew how to beguile them, by accommodating his flattery to their passions and scale of understanding, and by acts of cunning and hypocrisy, which weigh more with the multitude than the words of eloquence, or the arguments of wisdom. The people listened as to their Cicero, when he twanged out his apostrophes of "Pauvre Peuple! Peuple vertueux!" and hastened to execute whatever came recommended by such honied phrases, though devised by the worst of men for the worst and most inhuman of purposes.[269]

Vanity was Robespierre's ruling passion, and though his countenance was the image of his mind, he was vain even of his personal appearance, and never adopted the external habits of a Sans Culotte. Amongst his fellow Jacobins, he was distinguished by the nicety with which his hair was arranged and powdered; and the neatness of his dress was carefully attended to, so as to counterbalance, if possible, the vulgarity of his person. His apartments, though small, were elegant, and vanity had filled them with representations of the occupant. Robespierre's picture at length hung in one place, his miniature in another, his bust occupied a niche, and on the table were disposed a few medallions, exhibiting his head in profile.[270] The vanity which all this indicated was of the coldest and most selfish character, being such as considers neglect as insult, and receives homage merely as a tribute; so that, while praise is received without gratitude, it is withheld at the risk of mortal hate. Self-love of this dangerous character is closely allied with envy, and Robespierre was one of the most envious and vindictive men that ever lived. He never was known to pardon any opposition, affront, or even rivalry; and to be marked in his tablets on such an account was a sure, though perhaps not an immediate, sentence of death. Danton was a hero, compared with this cold, calculating, creeping miscreant; for his passions, though exaggerated, had at least some touch of humanity, and his brutal ferocity was supported by brutal courage. Robespierre was a coward, who signed death-warrants with a hand that shook, though his heart was relentless. He possessed no

---

[269] "Il avait une manière de prononcer *pauvre peuple et peuple vertueux*, qui ne manqua jamais son effet sur de feroces spectateurs."—Lacretelle, tom. ix., p. 15.
[270] Mémoires de Barbaroux, p. 63.

passions on which to charge his crimes; they were perpetrated in cold blood, and upon mature deliberation.[271]

Marat, the third of this infernal triumvirate, had attracted the attention of the lower orders, by the violence of his sentiments in the journal which he conducted from the commencement of the Revolution, upon such principles that it took the lead in forwarding its successive changes. His political exhortations began and ended like the howl of a blood-hound for murder; or, if a wolf could have written a journal, the gaunt and famished wretch could not have ravened more eagerly for slaughter. It was blood which was Marat's constant demand, not in drops from the breast of an individual, not in puny streams from the slaughter of families, but blood in the profusion of an ocean. His usual calculation of the heads which he demanded amounted to two hundred and sixty thousand; and though he sometimes raised it as high as three hundred thousand, it never fell beneath the smaller number.[272] It may be hoped, and, for the honour of human nature, we are inclined to believe, there was a touch of insanity in this unnatural strain of ferocity; and the wild and squalid features of the wretch appear to have intimated a degree of alienation of mind. Marat was, like Robespierre, a coward. Repeatedly denounced in the Assembly, he skulked instead of defending himself, and lay concealed in some obscure garret or cellar, among his cut-throats, until a storm appeared, when, like a bird of ill omen, his death-screech was again heard. Such was the strange and fatal triumvirate, in which the same degree of cannibal cruelty existed under different aspects. Danton murdered to glut his rage; Robespierre, to avenge his injured vanity, or to remove a rival whom he envied; Marat, from the same instinctive love of blood, which induces a wolf to continue his ravage of the flocks long after his hunger is appeased.[273]

---

[271] "I once conversed with Robespierre at my father's house, in 1789. His features were mean, his complexion pale, his veins of a greenish hue."—Mad. de Staël, vol. ii., p. 140.
"I had twice occasion to converse with Robespierre. He had a sinister expression of countenance, never looked you in the face, and had a continual and unpleasant winking of the eyes."—Dumont, p. 202.
[272] Mémoires de Barbaroux, p. 57.
[273] Mignet, tom. i., p. 220; Garat, p. 174.

These three men were in complete possession of the Community of Paris, which was filled with their adherents exclusively, and which, now in command of the armed force that had achieved the victory of the 10th of August, held the Assembly as absolutely under their control, as the Assembly, prior to that period, had held the person of the King. It is true, Pétion was still Mayor of Paris; but, being considered as a follower of Roland and Brissot, he was regarded by the Jacobins as a prisoner, and detained in a sort of honourable restraint, having a body of their most faithful adherents constantly around him, as a guard which they pretended was assigned for his defence and protection. The truth is, that Pétion, a vain man, and of very moderate talents, had already lost his consequence. His temporary popularity arose almost solely out of the enmity entertained against him by the court, and his having braved on one or two occasions the King's personal displeasure, particularly on the 20th of June. This merit was now forgotten, and Pétion was fast sinking into his natural nullity. Nothing could be more pitiful than the appearance of this magistrate, whose name had been so lately the theme of every tongue in Paris, when brought to the bar of the Assembly, pale and hesitating, to back, by his appearance among his terrible revolutionary associates, petitions for measures, as distasteful to himself as to his friends of the Gironde party, who had apparently no power to deliver him from his state of humiliating restraint.[274]

REVOLUTIONARY TRIBUNALS

The demands of the Community of Paris, now the Sanhedrim of the Jacobins, were of course for blood and vengeance, and revolutionary tribunals to make short and sharp execution upon constitutionalist and royalist, soldier and priest—upon all who acted on the principle, that the King had some right to defend his person and residence against a furious mob, armed with muskets and cannon—and upon all who could, by any possible implication, be charged with having approved such doctrines as leaned towards monarchy, at any time during all the changes of this changeful-featured Revolution.

---

[274] Lacretelle, tom. ix., pp. 292, 316.

A Revolutionary Tribunal was appointed accordingly; but the Girondists, to impose some check on its measures, rendered the judgment of a jury necessary for condemnation—an encumbrance which seemed to the Jacobins a needless and uncivic restriction of the rights of the people. Robespierre was to have been appointed president of this tribunal, but he declined the office, on account of his philanthropic principles![275] Meantime, the sharpness of its proceedings was sufficiently assured by the nomination of Danton to the office of minister of justice, which had fallen to his lot as a Jacobin, while Roland, Servan, and Clavière, alike fearing and detesting their dreadful colleague, assumed, with Monge and Lebrun, the other offices, in what was now called a Provisionary Executive. These last five ministers were Girondists.

It was not the serious intention of the Assembly to replace Louis in a palace, or to suffer him to retain the smallest portion of personal freedom or political influence. It had, indeed, been decreed on the night of the 10th of August, that he should inhabit the Luxembourg palace, but, on the 13th, his residence was transferred, with that of the royal family, to an ancient fortress called the Temple, from the Knights Templars, to whom it once belonged.[276] There was in front a house, with some more modern apartments, but the dwelling of Louis was the donjon or ancient keep, itself a huge square tower of great antiquity, consisting of four stories. Each story contained two or three rooms or closets; but these apartments were unfurnished, and offered no convenience for the accommodation of an ordinary family, much less to prisoners of such distinction. The royal family were guarded with a strictness, of which every day increased the rigour.

DANTON'S PLAN OF EXTERMINATION

In the meanwhile, the revolutionary tribunal was proceeding against the friends and partisans of the deposed monarch with no

---

[275] "Un emploi si rigoureux répugnerait trop à mes principes philanthropiques."—Lacretelle, tom. ix., p. 274.
[276] "The carriage which conveyed the royal family to the Temple, was stopped on the Place Vendôme, in order that the King might see the fragments of the statue of Louis the Great."—Lacretelle, tom. ix., p. 262.

lack, one would have thought, of zeal or animosity. De la Porte, intendant of the King's civil list, D'Augrémont, and Durosoi, a Royalist author, were with others condemned and executed. But Montmorin, the brother of the royal minister, was acquitted; and even the Comte d'Affri, though Colonel of the Swiss guards, found grace in the eyes of this tribunal;—so lenient it was, in comparison to those which France was afterwards doomed to groan under. Danton, baulked of his prey, or but half-supplied with victims, might be compared to the spectre-huntsman of Boccaccio,—

"Stern look'd the fiend, as frustrate of his will, Not half sufficed, and greedy yet to kill."

But he had already devised within his soul, and agitated amongst his compeers, a scheme of vengeance so dark and dreadful, as never ruffian before or since had head to contrive, or nerve to execute. It was a measure of extermination which the Jacobins resolved upon—a measure so sweeping in its purpose and extent, that it should at once drown in their own blood every Royalist or Constitutionalist who could raise a finger, or even entertain a thought, against them.

Three things were indispensably essential to their execrable plan. In the first place, they had to collect and place within reach of their assassins, the numerous victims whom they sought to overwhelm with this common destruction. Secondly, it was necessary to intimidate the Assembly, and the Girondist party in particular; sensible that they were likely to interfere, if it was left in their power, to prevent acts of cruelty incompatible with the principles of most or all of their number. Lastly, the Jacobin chiefs were aware, that ere they could prepare the public mind to endure the massacres which they meditated, it was necessary they should wait for one of those critical moments of general alarm, in which fear makes the multitude cruel, and when the agitations of rage and terror combine to unsettle men's reason, and drown at once their humanity and their understanding.

To collect prisoners in any numbers was an easy matter, when the mere naming a man, however innocent, as an aristocrat or a suspected person, especially if he happened to have a name indicative of gentle blood, and an air of decency in apparel, was sufficient ground for sending him to prison. For the purpose of making such arrests upon suspicion, the Commune of Paris openly took upon themselves the office of granting warrants for imprisoning individuals in great numbers, and at length proceeded so far in their violent and arbitrary conduct, as to excite the jealousy of the Legislative Body.

This Assembly of National Representatives seemed to have been stunned by the events of the 10th of August. Two-thirds of the deputies had a few days before exculpated La Fayette for the zeal with which he impeached the unsuccessful attempt of the 20th of June, designed to accomplish the same purpose which had been effected on this last dread epoch of the Revolution. The same number, we must suppose, were inimical to the revolution achieved by the taking of the Tuileries, and the dethronement of the monarch, whom it had been La Fayette's object to protect and defend, in dignity and person. But there was no energy left in that portion of the Assembly, though by far the largest, and the wisest. Their benches were left deserted, nor did any voice arise, either to sustain their own dignity, or, as a last resource, to advise a union with the Girondists, now the leading force in the Representative Body, for the purpose of putting a period to the rule of revolutionary terror over that of civil order. The Girondists themselves proposed no decisive measures, and indeed appear to have been the most helpless party, (though possessing in their ranks very considerable talent,) that ever attempted to act a great part in the convulsions of a state. They seem to have expected, that, so soon as they had accomplished the overthrow of the throne, their own supremacy should have been established in its room. They became, therefore, liable to the disappointment of a child, who, having built his house of boughs after his own fashion, is astonished to find those bigger and stronger than himself throw its materials out of their way, instead of attempting, according to his expectations, to creep into it for the purpose of shelter.

COMMUNE OF PARIS

Late and timidly, they at length began to remonstrate against the usurped power of the Commune of Paris, who paid them as little regard, as they were themselves doing to the constituted authorities of the executive power.

The complaints which were laid before them of the violent encroachments made on the liberty of the people at large, the Girondists had hitherto answered by timid exhortations to the Commune to be cautious in their proceedings. But, on the 29th of August, they were startled out of their weak inaction, by an assumption of open force, and open villany, on the part of those formidable rivals, under which it was impossible to remain silent.[277] On the night previous, the Commune, proceeding to act upon their own sole authority, had sent their satellites, consisting of the municipal officers who were exclusively attached to them, (who were selected from the most determined Jacobins, and had been augmented to an extraordinary number,) to seize arms of every description, and to arrest suspicious persons in every corner of Paris. Hundreds and thousands of individuals had been, under these usurped powers, committed to the various prisons of the city, which were now filled, even to choking, with all persons of every sex and age, against whom political hatred could allege suspicion, or private hatred revive an old quarrel, or love of plunder awake a thirst for confiscation.

The deeds of robbery, of license, and of ferocity, committed during these illegal proceedings, as well as the barefaced contempt which they indicated of the authority of the Assembly, awakened the Girondists, but too late, to some sense of the necessity of exertion. They summoned the Municipality to their bar. They came, not to deprecate the displeasure of the Assembly, not to submit themselves to its mercy,—they came to triumph; and brought the speechless and trembling Pétion in their train, as their captive, rather than their

---

[277] "Nuit de terreur! prelude affreux de plusieurs jours de sang! nuit où une capitale perdue dans la mollesse, infectée des maximes de l'égoïsme philosophique, expia le sort honteux de s'être laissé asservir par tout ce que sa population offrait de plus abjèct et de plus criminel!"—Lacretelle, tom. ix., p. 288.

mayor. Tallien explained the defence of the Commune, which amounted to this: "The provisional representatives of the city of Paris," he said, "had been calumniated; they appeared, to justify what they had done, not as accused persons, but as triumphing in having discharged their duty. The Sovereign People," he said, "had committed to them full powers, saying, Go forth, save the country in our name—whatever you do we will ratify." This language was, in effect, that of defiance, and it was supported by the shouts and howls of assembled multitudes, armed as for the attack on the Tuileries, and their courage, it may be imagined, not the less, that there were neither aristocrats nor Swiss guards between them and the Legislative Assembly. Their cries were, "Long live our Commune—our excellent commissioners—we will defend them or die!"[278]

The satellites of the same party, in the tribunes or galleries, joined in the cry, with invectives on those members of the Assembly, who were supposed, however republican in principle, to be opposed to the revolutionary measures of the Commune. The mob without soon forced their way into the hall—joined with the mob within,—and left the theoretical Republicans of the Assembly the choice of acquiescence in their dictates, flight, or the liberty of dying on their posts, like the senators of that Rome which they admired. None embraced this last alternative. They broke up the meeting in confusion, and left the Jacobins secure of impunity in whatever they might next choose to attempt.

Thus, Danton and his fell associates achieved the second point necessary to the execution of the horrors which they meditated: the Legislative Assembly were completely subdued and intimidated. It remained to avail themselves of some opportunity which might excite the people of Paris, in their present feverish state, to participate in, or to endure crimes, at which, in calm moments, the rudest would probably have shuddered. The state of affairs on the frontier aided them with such an opportunity—*aided* them, we say, because every step of preparation beforehand, shows that the horrors acted on the 3d September were premeditated; nay,

---

[278] Lacretelle, tom. ix., p. 296.

the very trenches destined to inhume hundreds and thousands of prisoners, yet alive, untried and undoomed, were already excavated.

A temporary success of the allied monarchs fell upon the mine already prepared, and gave fire to it, as lightning might have fired a powder magazine. Longwy, Stenay, and Verdun, were announced to have fallen into the hands of the King of Prussia. The first and last were barrier fortresses of reputed strength, and considerable resistance had been expected. The ardent and military spirit of the French was awakened in the resolute, upon learning that their frontier was thus invaded; fear and discomfiture took possession of others, who thought they already heard the allied trumpets at the gates of Paris. Between the eager desire of some to march against the army of the invaders, and the terror and dismay of others, there arose a climax of excitation and alarm, favourable to the execution of every desperate design; as ruffians ply their trade best, and with least chance of interruption, in the midst of an earthquake or a conflagration.

On the 2d September, the Commune of Paris announced the fall of Longwy, and the approaching fate of Verdun, and, as if it had been the only constituted authority in the country, commanded the most summary measures for the general defence. All citizens were ordered to keep themselves in readiness to march on an instant's warning. All arms were to be given up to the Commune, save those in the hands of active citizens, armed for the public protection. Suspected persons were to be disarmed, and other measures were announced, all of which were calculated to call men's attention to the safety of themselves and their families, and to destroy the interest which at ordinary times the public would have taken in the fate of others.[279]

The awful voice of Danton astounded the Assembly with similar information, hardly deigning to ask their approbation of the measures which the Commune of Paris had adopted on their own sole authority. "You will presently hear," he said, "the alarm-guns—falsely so called—for they are the signal of a charge. Courage—courage—and once again courage, is all that is necessary to conquer

---

[279] Lacretelle, tom. ix., p. 298.

our enemies." These words, pronounced with the accent and attitude of an exterminating spirit, appalled and stupified the Assembly. We find nothing that indicated in them either interest in the imminent danger of the public from without, or in the usurpation from within. They appeared paralysed with terror.[280]

The armed bands of Paris marched in different quarters, to seize arms and horses, to discover and denounce suspected persons; the youth fit for arms were every where mustered, and amid shouts, remonstrances, and debates, the general attention was so engaged, each individual with his own affairs, in his own quarter, that, without interference of any kind, whether from legal authority, or general sympathy, a universal massacre of the numerous prisoners was perpetrated, with a quietness and deliberation, which has not its parallel in history. The reader, who may be still surprised that a transaction so horrid should have passed without opposition or interruption, must be again reminded of the astounding effects of the popular victory of the 10th of August; of the total quiescence of the Legislative Assembly; of the want of an armed force of any kind to oppose such outrages; and of the epidemic panic which renders multitudes powerless and passive as infants. Should these causes not appear to him sufficient, he must be contented to wonder at the facts we are to relate, as at one of those dreadful prodigies by which Providence confounds our reason, and shows what human nature can be brought to, when the restraints of morality and religion are cast aside.

The number of individuals accumulated in the various prisons of Paris, had increased by the arrests and domiciliary visits subsequent to the 10th of August, to about eight thousand persons. It was the object of this infernal scheme to destroy the greater part of these under one general system of murder, not to be executed by the sudden and furious impulse of an armed multitude, but with a certain degree of cold blood and deliberate investigation. A force of armed banditti, Marseillois partly, and partly chosen ruffians of the Fauxbourgs, proceeded to the several prisons, into which they either forced their passage, or were admitted by the jailors, most of whom had been apprised of what was to take place, though some even of

---

[280] Mignet, tom. i., p. 204; Thiers, tom. ii., p. 61; Lacretelle, tom. ix., p. 293.

these steeled officials exerted themselves to save those under their charge. A revolutionary tribunal was formed from among the armed ruffians themselves, who examined the registers of the prisons, and summoned the captives individually to undergo the form of a trial. If the judges, as was almost always the case, declared for death, their doom, to prevent the efforts of men in despair, was expressed in the words, "Give the prisoners freedom."[281] The victim was then thrust out into the street, or yard; he was despatched by men and women, who, with sleeves tucked up, arms dyed elbow-deep in blood, hands holding axes, pikes, and sabres, were executioners of the sentence; and, by the manner in which they did their office on the living, and mangled the bodies of the dead, showed that they occupied their post as much from pleasure as from love of hire. They often exchanged places; the judges going out to take the executioners' duty, the executioners, with their reeking hands, sitting as judges in their turn. Maillard, a ruffian alleged to have distinguished himself at the siege of the Bastile, but better known by his exploits upon the march to Versailles,[282] presided during these brief and sanguinary investigations. His companions on the bench were persons of the same stamp. Yet there were occasions when they showed some transient gleams of humanity, and it is not unimportant to remark, that boldness had more influence on them than any appeal to mercy or compassion. An avowed Royalist was occasionally dismissed uninjured, while the Constitutionalists were sure to be massacred. Another trait of a singular nature is, that two of the ruffians who were appointed to guard one of these intended victims home in safety, as a man acquitted, insisted upon seeing his meeting with his family, seemed to share in the transports of the moment, and on taking leave, shook the hand of their late prisoner, while their own were clotted with the gore of his friends, and had been just raised to shed his own. Few, indeed, and brief, were these symptoms of relenting. In general, the doom of the prisoner was death, and that doom was instantly accomplished.

In the meanwhile, the captives were penned up in their dungeons like cattle in a shambles, and in many instances might, from windows which looked outwards, mark the fate of their

---

[281] Lacretelle, tom. ix., p. 314.
[282] See *ante*.

comrades, hear their cries, and behold their struggles, and learn from the horrible scene, how they might best meet their own approaching fate. They observed, according to Saint Meard, who, in his well-named "Agony of Thirty-Six Hours," has given the account of this fearful scene, that those who intercepted the blows of the executioners, by holding up their hands, suffered protracted torment, while those who offered no show of struggle were more easily despatched; and they encouraged each other to submit to their fate, in the manner least likely to prolong their sufferings.[283]

MASSACRES OF SEPTEMBER

Many ladies, especially those belonging to the court, were thus murdered. The Princess de Lamballe, whose only crime seems to have been her friendship for Marie Antoinette, was literally hewn to pieces, and her head, and that of others, paraded on pikes through the metropolis. It was carried to the Temple on that accursed weapon, the features yet beautiful in death, and the long fair curls of the hair floating around the spear. The murderers insisted that the King and Queen should be compelled to come to the window to view this dreadful trophy. The municipal officers who were upon duty over the royal prisoners, had difficulty, not merely in saving them from this horrible inhumanity, but also in preventing the prison from being forced. Three-coloured ribbons were extended across the street, and this frail barrier was found sufficient to intimate that the Temple was under the safeguard of the nation. We do not read that the efficiency of the three-coloured ribbons was tried for the protection of any of the other prisons. No doubt the executioners had their instructions where and when they should be respected.[284]

The Clergy, who had declined the Constitutional oath from pious scruples, were, during the massacre, the peculiar objects of insult and cruelty, and their conduct was such as corresponded with their religious and conscientious professions. They were seen confessing themselves to each other, or receiving the confessions of

---

[283] Mon Agonie de Trente-six Heures, p. 30.
[284] Thiers, tom. iii., p. 8; Lacretelle, tom. ix., p. 325.

their lay companions in misfortune, and encouraging them to undergo the evil hour, with as much calmness as if they themselves had not been to share its bitterness. As Protestants, we cannot abstractedly approve of the doctrines which render the established clergy of one country dependent upon a sovereign pontiff, the prince of an alien state: but these priests did not make the laws for which they suffered; they only obeyed them; and as men and Christians we must regard them as martyrs, who preferred death to what they considered as apostasy.[285]

In the brief intervals of this dreadful butchery, which lasted for four days, the judges and executioners ate, drank, and slept; and awoke from slumber, or rose from their meal, with fresh appetite for murder. There were places arranged for the male and for the female murderers, for the work had been incomplete without the intervention of the latter. Prison after prison was invested, entered, and under the same form of proceeding, made the scene of the same inhuman butchery. The Jacobins had reckoned on making the massacre universal over France. But the example was not generally followed. It required, as in the case of Saint Bartholomew, the only massacre which can be compared to this in atrocity, the excitation of a large capital, in a violent crisis, to render such horrors possible.

The Commune of Paris were not in fault for this. They did all they could to extend the sphere of murder. Their warrant brought from Orleans near sixty persons, including the Duke de Cossé-Brissac, De Lessart the late minister, and other Royalists of distinction, who were to have been tried before the high court of that department. A band of assassins met them, by appointment of the Commune, at Versailles, who, uniting with their escort, murdered almost the whole of these unhappy men.[286]

MASSACRE IN THE BICETRE

From the 2d to the 6th of September, these infernal crimes proceeded uninterrupted, protracted by the actors for the sake of

---

[285] Thiers, tom. iii., p. 64.
[286] Thiers, tom. iii., p. 127; Lacretelle, tom. ix., p. 348.

the daily pay of a louis to each, openly distributed amongst them, by order of the Commune.[287] It was either from a desire to continue as long as possible a labour so well requited, or because these beings had acquired an insatiable lust of murder, that, when the jails were emptied of state criminals, the assassins attacked the Bicêtre, a prison where ordinary delinquents were confined. These unhappy wretches offered a degree of resistance which cost the assailants dearer than any they had experienced from their proper victims. They were obliged to fire on them with cannon, and many hundreds of the miserable creatures were in this way exterminated, by wretches worse than themselves.

No exact account was ever made of the number of persons murdered during this dreadful period; but not above two or three hundred of the prisoners arrested for state offences were known to escape, or be discharged, and the most moderate computation raises the number of those who fell to two or three thousand, though some carry it to twice the extent. Truchod announced to the Legislative Assembly, that four thousand had perished. Some exertion was made to save the lives of persons imprisoned for debt, whose numbers, with those of common felons, may make up the balance betwixt the number slain, and eight thousand who were prisoners when the massacre began. The bodies were interred in heaps, in immense trenches, prepared beforehand by order of the Commune of Paris; but their bones have since been transferred to the subterranean Catacombs, which form the general charnel-house of the city. In those melancholy regions, while other relics of mortality lie exposed all around, the remains of those who perished in the massacres of September are alone secluded from the eye. The vault in which they repose is closed with a screen of freestone, as if relating to crimes unfit to be thought of even in the proper abode of death, and which France would willingly hide in oblivion.

---

[287] The books of the Hôtel de Ville preserve evidence of this fact. Billaud-Varennes appeared publicly among the assassins, and distributed the price of blood.—S.—"I am authorised," he said, "to offer to each of you twenty-four francs, which shall be instantly paid. Respectable citizens, continue your good work, and acquire new titles to the homage of your country! Let every thing on this great day be fitting the sovereignty of the people, who have committed their vengeance to your hands."—Sicard, p. 135; Thiers, tom. iii., p. 74.

In the meanwhile, the reader may be desirous to know what efforts were made by the Assembly to save the lives of so many Frenchmen, or to put a stop to a massacre carried on in contempt of all legal interference, and by no more formidable force than that of two or three hundred atrocious felons, often, indeed, diminished to only fifty or sixty.[288] He might reasonably expect that the national representatives would have thundered forth some of those decrees which they formerly directed against the crown, and the noblesse; that they should have repaired by deputations to the various sections, called out the national guards, and appealed to all, not only that were susceptible of honour or humanity, but to all who had the breath and being of man, to support them in interrupting a series of horrors disgraceful to mankind. Such an appeal to the feelings of their fellow-citizens made them at last successful in the overthrow of Robespierre. But the Reign of Terror was now but in its commencement, and men had not yet learned that there lay a refuge in the efforts of despair.

Instead of such energy as might have been expected from the principles of which they boasted, nothing could be more timid than the conduct of the Girondists, being the only party in the Assembly who had the power, and might be supposed to have the inclination, to control the course of crime.

We looked carefully through the *Moniteurs* which contain the official account of the sittings of the Assembly on these dreadful days. We find regular entries of many patriotic gifts, of such importance as the following:—A fusee from an Englishman—a pair of hackney-coach horses from the coachman—a map of the country around Paris from a lady. While engaged in receiving and registering these civic donations, their journal bears few and doubtful references to the massacres then in progress. The Assembly issued no decree against the slaughter—demanded no support from the public force, and restricted themselves to sending to the murderers a pitiful deputation of twelve of their number, whose commission seems to have been limited to petition for the safety of one of their colleagues, belonging to the Constitutional faction. With difficulty they saved him, and the celebrated Abbé Sicard, the philanthropic

---

[288] Louvet's Memoirs, p. 73; Barbaroux, p. 57; Thiers, tom. iii., p. 77.

instructor of the deaf and dumb, imprisoned as a non-juring priest, for whom the wails and tears of his hapless pupils had procured a reprieve even from the assassins.[289] Dussault, one of that deputation, distinguished himself by the efforts which he used to persuade the murderers to desist. "Return to your place," said one of the ruffians, his arms crimsoned with blood. "You have made us lose too much time. Return to your own business, and leave us to ours."

APATHY OF THE ASSEMBLY

Dussault went back, to recount to those who had sent him what he had witnessed, and how he had been received; and concluded with the exclamation, "Woe's me, that I should have lived to see such horrors, without the power of stopping them!" The Assembly heard the detail, and remained timid and silent as before.[290]

Where, in that hour, were the men who formed their judgment upon the models presented by Plutarch, their feelings on the wild eloquence of Rousseau? Where were the Girondists, celebrated by one of their admirers,[291] as distinguished by good morals, by severe probity, by a profound respect for the dignity of man, by a deep sense of his rights and his duties, by a sound, constant, and immutable love of order, of justice, and of liberty? Were the eyes of such men blind, that they could not see the blood which flooded for four days the streets of the metropolis? were their ears deadened, that they could not hear the shouts of the murderers, and the screams of the victims? or were their voices mute, that they called not upon God and man—upon the very stones of Paris, to assist them in interrupting such a crime? Political reasons have, by royalist writers, been supposed to furnish a motive for their acquiescence; for there is, according to civilians, a certain degree of careless or timid imbecility, which can only be explained as having its origin in fraud. They allege that the Girondists saw, rather with

---

[289] "The abbé would have been instantly murdered, had not a courageous watchmaker, of the name of Monnot, rushed between them, and staid the lance already raised to be plunged in his bosom."—Thiers, tom. iii., p. 71.
[290] Lacretelle, tom. ix., p. 317.
[291] Mémoires de Buzot, p. 82.

pleasure than horror, the atrocities which were committed, while their enemies the Jacobins, exterminating their equally hated enemies the Constitutionalists and Royalists, took on themselves the whole odium of a glut of blood, which must soon, they might naturally expect, disgust the sense and feelings of a country so civilized as France. We remain, nevertheless, convinced, that Vergniaud, Brissot, Roland, and, to a certainty, his high-minded wife, would have stopped the massacres of September, had their courage and practical skill in public affairs borne any proportion to the conceit which led them to suppose, that their vocation lay for governing such a nation as France.

But whatever was the motive of their apathy, the Legislative Assembly was nearly silent on the subject of the massacres, not only while they were in progress, but for several days afterwards. On the 16th of September, when news from the army on the frontiers was beginning to announce successes, and when the panic of the metropolis began to subside, Vergniaud adroitly charged the Jacobins with turning on unhappy prisoners of state the popular resentment, which should have animated them with bravery to march out against the common enemy. He upbraided also the Commune of Paris with the assumption of unconstitutional powers, and the inhuman tyranny with which they had abused them; but his speech made little impression, so much are deeds of cruelty apt to become familiar to men's feelings, when of frequent recurrence. When the first accounts were read in the Constituent Assembly, of the massacres perpetrated at Avignon, the president fainted away, and the whole body manifested a horror, as well of the senses as of the mind; and now, that a far more cruel, more enduring, more extensive train of murders was perpetrated under their own eye, the Legislative Assembly looked on in apathy. The utmost which the eloquence of Vergniaud could extract from them was a decree, that in future the Commune should be answerable with their own lives for the security of the prisoners under their charge. After passing this decree, the Legislative Assembly, being the second representative body of the French nation, dissolved itself according to the resolutions of the 10th of August, to give place to the National Convention.[292]

The Legislative Assembly was, in its composition and its character, of a caste greatly inferior to that which it succeeded. The flower of the talents of France had naturally centred in the National Assembly, and, by an absurd regulation, its members were incapacitated from being re-elected; which necessarily occasioned their situation being in many instances supplied by persons of inferior attainments. Then the destinies of the first Assembly had been fulfilled in a more lofty manner. They were often wrong, often absurd, often arrogant and presumptuous, but never mean or servile. They respected the liberty of debate, and even amidst the bitterest political discussions, defended the persons of their colleagues, however much opposed to them in sentiment, and maintained their constitutional inviolability. They had also the great advantage of being, as it were, free born. They were indeed placed in captivity by their removal to Paris, but their courage was not abated; nor did they make any concessions of a personal kind to the ruffians, by whom they were at times personally ill-used.

But the second, or Legislative Assembly, had, on the contrary been captive from the moment of their first convocation. They had never met but in Paris, and were inured to the habit of patient submission to the tribunes and the refuse of the city, who repeatedly broke into their hall, and issued their mandates in the form of petitions. On two memorable occasions, they showed too distinctly, that considerations of personal safety could overpower their sense of public duty. Two-thirds of the representatives joined in acquitting La Fayette, and declared, by doing so, that they abhorred the insurrection of the 20th of June; yet, when that of the 10th of August had completed what was before attempted in vain upon the occasion preceding, the Assembly unanimously voted the deposition of the monarch, and committed him to prison. Secondly, they remained silent and inactive during all the horrors of September, and suffered the executive power to be wrenched out of their hands by the Commune of Paris, and used before their eyes for the

---

[292] Lacretelle, tom. ix., p. 359.

destruction of many thousands of Frenchmen whom they represented.

It must be, however, remembered, that the Legislative Assembly were oppressed by difficulties and dangers the most dreadful that can threaten a government;—the bloody discord of contending factions, the arms of foreigners menacing the frontier, and civil war breaking out in the provinces. In addition to these sources of peril and dismay, there were three divided parties within the Assembly itself; while a rival power, equally formidable from its audacity and its crimes, had erected itself in predominating authority, like that of the maires du palais over the feeble monarchs of the Merovingian dynasty.

Chapter XI

Election of Representatives for the National Convention—Jacobins are very active—Right hand Party—Left hand side—Neutral Members—The Girondists are in possession of the ostensible Power—They denounce the Jacobin Chiefs, but in an irregular and feeble manner—Marat, Robespierre, and Danton, supported by the Commune and Populace of Paris—France declared a Republic—Duke of Brunswick's Campaign—Neglects the French Emigrants—Is tardy in his Operations—Occupies the poorest part of Champagne—His Army becomes sickly—Prospects of a Battle—Dumouriez's Army recruited with Carmagnoles—The Duke resolves to Retreat—Thoughts on the consequences of that measure—The Retreat disastrous—The Emigrants disbanded in a great measure—Reflections on their Fate—The Prince of Condé's Army.

NATIONAL CONVENTION

It was, of course, the object of each party to obtain the greatest possible majority in the National Convention now to be assembled, for arranging upon some new footing the government of France, and for replacing that Constitution to which faith had been so repeatedly sworn.

The Jacobins made the most energetic exertions. They not only wrote missives through their two thousand affiliated societies, but sent three hundred commissaries, or delegates, to superintend the elections in the different towns and departments; to exhort their comrades not only to be firm, but to be enterprising; and to seize with strong hand the same power over the public force, which the mother society possessed in Paris. The advice was poured into willing ears; for it implied the sacred right of insurrection, with the concomitant privileges of pillage and slaughter.

The power of the Jacobins was irresistible in Paris, where Robespierre, Danton, and Marat, who shared the high places in their synagogue, were elected by an immense majority;[293] and of the twenty deputies who represented Paris, there were not above five or six unconnected with the massacres. Nor were they any where unsuccessful, where there existed enough of their adherents to overawe by threats, clamour, and violence, the impartial voice of the public.

But in every state there is a great number of men who love order for itself, and for the protection it affords to property. There were also a great many persons at heart Royalists, either pure or constitutional, and all these united in sending to the National Convention deputies, who, if no opportunity occurred of restoring the monarchy, might at least co-operate with the Girondists and more moderate Republicans in saving the life of the unfortunate Louis, and in protecting men's lives, and property in general, from the infuriate violence of the Jacobins. These supporters of order— we know no better name to assign to them—were chiefly representatives of the departments, where electors had more time to discriminate and reflect, than when under the influence of the revolutionary societies and clubs of the towns. Yet Nantes, Bourdeaux, Marseilles, Lyons, and other towns, chiefly in the west and south, were disposed to support the Girondists, and sent deputies favourable to their sentiments. Thus the Convention, when assembled, still presented the appearance of two strong parties; and the feebleness of that, which, being moderate in its views, only sought to act defensively consisted not in want of numbers, but in want of energy.

It was no good omen, that, on taking their places in the Assembly, these last assumed the Right Side; a position which seemed doomed to defeat, since it had been successively occupied

---

[293] Among others of the same party thus elected were David, the painter, Camille Desmoulins, Collot d'Herbois, and the Duke of Orleans, who had abdicated his titles, and was now called Philip Egalité.—See Thiers, tom. iii., p. 133.

by the suppressed parties of moderate Royalists and Constitutionalists. There was defeat in the very sound of the *parti droit*, whereas the left-hand position had always been that of victory. Men's minds are moved by small incidents in dubious times. Even this choice of seats made an impression upon spectators and auditors unfavourable to the Girondists, as all naturally shrink from a union with bad fortune. There was a considerable party of neutral members, who, without joining themselves to the Girondists, affected to judge impartially betwixt the contending parties. They were chiefly men of consciences too timid to go all the lengths of the Jacobins, but also of too timid nerves to oppose them openly and boldly. These were sure to succumb on all occasions, when the Jacobins judged it necessary to use their favourite argument of popular terror.

The Girondists took possession, however, of all ostensible marks of power. Danton was dismissed from his place as minister of justice; and they were, as far as mere official name and title could bestow it on them, in possession of the authority of government. But the ill-fated regulation which excluded ministers from seats in the Assembly, and consequently from any right save that of defence, proved as fatal to those of the new system, as it had done to the executive government of Louis.

FRANCE DECLARED A REPUBLIC

Our remarks upon the policy of the great change from Monarchy to a Republic, will be more in place elsewhere.[294] Indeed, violent as the change sounded in words, there was not such an important alteration in effect as to produce much sensation. The Constitution of 1791 was a democracy to all intents and purposes, leaving little power with the King, and that little subject to be so much cramped and straitened in its operation, that the royal authority was even smaller in practice than it had been limited in theory. When to this is added, that Louis was a prisoner amongst his

---

[294] "The first measure of the Convention was to abolish Monarchy and proclaim a Republic. The calendar was changed; it was no longer the fourth year of Liberty, but the first of the French Republic."—Mignet, tom. i., p. 212.

subjects, acting under the most severe restraint, and endangering his life every time he attempted to execute his constitutional power, he must long have been held rather an incumbrance on the motions and councils of the state, than as one of its efficient constituted authorities. The nominal change of the system of government scarcely made a greater alteration in the internal condition of France, than the change of a sign makes upon a house of entertainment, where the business of the tavern is carried on in the usual way, although the place is no longer distinguished as the King's Head.

DUKE OF BRUNSWICK'S CAMPAIGN

While France was thus alarmed and agitated within, by change, by crime, by the most bitter political factions, the dawn of that course of victory had already risen on the frontiers, which, in its noonday splendour, was to blaze fiercely over all Europe. It is not our purpose to detail military events at present; we shall have but too many of them to discuss hereafter. We shall barely state, that the Duke of Brunswick's campaign, considered as relative to his proclamation, forms too good an illustration of the holy text, "Pride goeth before destruction, and a haughty spirit before a fall." The duke was at the head of a splendid army, which had been joined by fifteen thousand emigrants in the finest state of equipment, burning with zeal to rescue the King, and avenge themselves on those by whom they had been driven from their country. From what fatality it is hard to conceive, but the Duke of Brunswick seems to have looked with a certain degree of coldness and suspicion on those troops, whose chivalrous valour and high birth called them to the van, instead of the rear, in which the generalissimo was pleased to detain them. The chance of success that might justly have been expected from the fiery energy which was the very soul of French chivalry, from the fear which such an army might have inspired, or perhaps from the friends whom they might have found, was altogether lost. There was something in this extraordinary conduct, which almost vindicated the suspicion, that Prussia was warring on her own account, and was not disposed to owe too much of the expected success to the valour of the emigrants. And it escaped not the remark, both of the emigrants and the French at large, that

Longwy and Verdun were ostentatiously taken possession of by the allies, not under the name of the King of France, or the Comte d'Artois, but in that of the Emperor; which appeared to give colour to the invidious report, that the allies were to be indemnified for the cost of their assistance, at the expense of the French line of frontier towns. Neither did the duke use his fine army of Prussians, or direct the motions of the Austrians under Clairfait, to any greater advantage. He had, indeed, the troops of the Great Frederick; but under the command of an irresolute and incapable leader, it was the sword of Scanderbeg in the hands of a boy.

This tardiness of the Duke of Brunswick's movements intimated a latent doubt of his own capacity to conduct the campaign. The superiority of his veteran and finely disciplined forces over the disorganized army of Dumouriez, reinforced as it was by crowds of Federates, who were perfect strangers to war, would have been best displayed by bold and rapid movements, evincing at once activity and combination, and alarming raw troops by a sense of danger, not in front alone, but on every point. Each day which these new soldiers spent unfought, was one step towards military discipline, and what is more, towards military confidence. The general who had threatened so hard, seemed to suspend his blow in indecision; and he remained trifling on the frontiers, "when Frederick, had he been in our front," said the French general, "would long since have driven us back upon Chalons."[295]

The result of so many false steps began soon to appear. Brunswick, whose army was deficient in battering guns, though entering France on a frontier of fortifications, was arrested by the obstinate defence of Thionville. Having at length decided to advance, he spent nine days in marching thirty leagues, but omitted to possess himself of the defiles of Argonnes, by which alone the army of Luckner could co-operate with that of Dumouriez. The allied general now found himself in the most elevated part of the province of Champagne, branded for its poverty and sterility with the unseemly name "La Champagne Pouilleuse," where he found difficulty to subsist his army. Meantime, if corn and forage were scarce, grapes and melons were, unfortunately, plenty. These last

---

[295] Dumouriez, vol. ii., p. 387.

fruits are so proverbially unwholesome, that the magistrates of Liege, and some other towns, forbid the peasants to bring them to market under pain of confiscation. It was the first time such delicacies had been presented to the hyperborean appetites of the Prussians; and they could not resist the temptation, though the same penalty was annexed to the banquet, as to that which produced the first transgression. They ate and died. A fatal dysentery broke out in the camp, which swept the soldiers away by hundreds in a day, sunk the spirits of the survivors, and seems to have totally broken the courage of their commander.[296]

Two courses remained to the embarrassed general. One was, to make his way by giving battle to the French, by attacking them in the strong position which they had been permitted to occupy, notwithstanding the ease with which they might have been anticipated. It is true, Dumouriez had been very strongly reinforced. France, from all her departments, had readily poured forth many thousands of her fiery youth, from city and town, village and grange and farm, to protect the frontiers, at once, from the invasion of foreigners, and the occupation of thousands of vengeful emigrants. They were undisciplined, indeed, but full of zeal and courage, heated and excited by the scenes of the republic, and inflamed by the florid eloquence, the songs, dances, and signal-words with which it had been celebrated. Above all, they were of a country, which, of all others in Europe, has been most familiar with war, and the youth of which are most easily rendered amenable to military discipline.

But to these new levies the Duke of Brunswick might have safely opposed the ardent valour of the emigrants, men descended of families whose deeds of chivalry fill the registers of Europe; men by whom the road to Paris was regarded as that which was to conduct them to victory, to honour, to the rescue of their King, to reunion with their families, to the recovery of their patrimony; men accustomed to consider disgrace as more dreadful by far than death, and who claimed as their birth-right, military renown and the use of arms. In one skirmish, fifteen hundred of the emigrant cavalry had defeated, with great slaughter, a column of the Carmagnoles, as the republican levies were called. They were routed with great slaughter,

---

[296] Jomini, tom. ii., p. 133.

and their opponents had the pleasure to count among the slain a considerable number of the assassins of September.

But the French general had more confidence in the Carmagnole levies, from which his military genius derived a valuable support, than Brunswick thought proper to repose in the chivalrous gallantry of the French noblesse. He could only be brought to engage in one action, of artillery, near Valmy, which was attended with no marked consequence, and then issued his order for a retreat. It was in vain that the Comte d'Artois, with a spirit worthy of the line from which he was descended, and the throne to which he has now succeeded, entreated, almost implored, a recall of this fatal order; in vain that he offered in person to head the emigrant forces, and to assume with them the most desperate post in the battle, if the generalissimo would permit it to be fought. But the duke, obstinate in his desponding in proportion to his former presumption, was not of that high mind which adopts hazardous counsels in desperate cases. He saw his army mouldering away around him, beheld the French forming in his rear, knew that the resources of Prussia were unequal to a prolonged war, and, after one or two feeble attempts to negotiate for the safety of the captive Louis, he was at length contented to accept an implied permission to retreat without molestation. He raised his camp on the 29th of September,[297] and left behind him abundant marks of the dreadful state to which his army was reduced.[298]

When we look back on these events, and are aware of Dumouriez's real opinions, and the interest which he took in the fate of the King, we have little reason to doubt, that the Duke of Brunswick might, by active and prompt exertions, have eluded that general's defensive measures; nay, that judicious negotiation might have induced him, on certain points being conceded, to have united a part at least of his forces with those of the emigrants in a march to Paris, for the King's rescue, and the punishment of the Jacobins.

---

[297] Dumouriez, vol. iii., p. 63; Jomini, tom. ii., p. 138.
[298] "All the villages were filled with dead and the dying; without any considerable fighting, the allies had lost, by dysentery and fevers, more than a fourth of their numbers."—Toulongeon, tom. ii., p. 357.

But had the restoration of Louis XVI. taken place by the armed hand of the emigrants and the allies, the final event of the war must still have been distant. Almost the whole body of the kingdom was diametrically opposed to the restoration of the absolute monarchy, with all its evils; and yet it must have been the object of the emigrants, in case of success, again to establish, not only royalty in its utmost prerogative, but all the oppressive privileges and feudal subjections which the Revolution had swept away. Much was to have been dreaded too, from the avidity of the strangers, whose arms had assisted the imprisoned Louis, and much more from what has since been aptly termed the Reaction, which must have taken place upon a counter-revolution. It was greatly to be apprehended, that the emigrants, always deeming too lightly of the ranks beneath them, incensed by the murder of their friends, and stung by their own private wrongs and insults, would, if successful, have treated the Revolution not as an exertion of the public will of France to free the country from public grievances, but as a *Jacquerie*, (which in some of its scenes it too much resembled,) a domestic treason of the vassals against their liege lords. It was the will of Providence, that the experience of twenty years and upwards should make manifest, that in the hour of victory itself, concessions to the defeated, as far as justice demands them, is the only mode of deriving permanent and secure peace.

EMIGRANT REGIMENTS DISBANDED

The retreat of the Prussians was executed in the best possible order, and in the most leisurely manner. But if to them it was a measure of disgrace, it was to the unfortunate emigrants who had joined their standard, the signal of utter despair and ruin. These corps were composed of gentlemen, who, called suddenly and unprovided from their families and homes, had only brought with them such moderate sums of money as could be raised in an emergency, which they had fondly conceived would be of very brief duration. They had expended most of their funds in providing themselves with horses, arms, and equipments—some part must have been laid out in their necessary subsistence, for they served chiefly at their own expense—and perhaps, as might have been expected among high-spirited and high-born youths, their slender funds had not been managed with an economical view of the possibility of the reverses which had taken place. In the confusion and disorder of the retreat, their baggage was plundered by their auxiliaries, that is to say, by the disorderly Prussian soldiers, who had shaken loose all discipline; and they were in most cases reduced for instant maintenance to sell their horses at such paltry prices as they could obtain. To end the history of such of this devoted army as had been engaged in the Duke of Brunswick's campaign, they were disbanded at Juliers, in November 1792.

The blindness of the sovereigns, who, still continuing a war on France, suffered such fine troops to be dissolved for want of the means of support, was inexcusable; their cold and hard-hearted conduct towards a body of gentlemen, who, if politically wrong, were at least devoted to the cause for which Austria asserted that she continued in arms, was equally unwise and ungenerous. These gallant gentlemen might have upbraided the Kings who had encouraged, and especially the general who led, this ill-fated expedition, in the words of Shakspeare, if he had been known to them,—

"Hast thou not spoke like thunder on our side, Been sworn our soldier—bidding us depend Upon thy stars, thy fortune, and thy strength?"[299]

But the reproaches of those who have no remedy but the exposition of their wrongs, seldom reach the ears of the powerful by whom these wrongs have been committed.

It is not difficult to conceive the agony with which these banished gentlemen abandoned all hopes of saving the life of their King, and the recovery of their rank and fortune. All their proud vaunts of expected success were lost, or converted into serpents to sting them. They had no hope before them, and, what is worst to men of high spirit, they had fallen with scarce a blow struck for honour, far less for victory. They were now doomed, such as could, to exercise for mere subsistence the prosecution of sciences and

---

[299] King John, act iii., sc. i.

arts, which they had cultivated to adorn prosperity—to wander in foreign lands, and live upon the precarious charity of foreign powers, embittered every where by the reflections of some, who pitied the folly that could forfeit rank and property for a mere point of honour; and of others, who saw in them the enemies of rational liberty, and upbraided them with the charge, that their misfortunes were the necessary consequence of their arbitrary principles.

It might have in some degree mitigated their calamity, could some gifted sage have shown them, at such distance as the Legislator of Israel beheld the Promised Land from Mount Pisgah, the final restoration of the royal house, in whose cause they had suffered shipwreck of their all. But how many perished in the wilderness of misfortune which intervened—how few survived the twenty years wandering which conducted to this promised point! and of those few, who, war-worn and wearied by misfortunes, survived the restoration of royalty, how very few were rewarded by more than the disinterested triumph which they felt on that joyful occasion! and how many might use the simile of a royalist of Britain on a similar occasion,—"The fleece of Gideon remained dry, while the hoped-for restoration shed showers of blessing on all France beside!"

The emigrant regiments under the command of the Prince of Condé had another and nobler fate. They retained their arms, and signalized themselves by their exertions; were consumed by the sword, and in toils of service, and died at least the death of soldiers, mourned, and not unrevenged. But they were wasting their devoted courage in the service of foreigners; and if their gallantry was gratified by the defeat of those whom they regarded as the murderers of their king and as usurpers of their rights, they might indeed feel that their revenge was satiated, but scarce in any sense could they regard their victories as serviceable to the cause to which they had sacrificed their country, their possessions, their hopes, their lives. Their fate, though on a much more extensive scale, much resembles that of the officers of the Scottish army in 1690, who, following the fortunes of James II. to France, were at length compelled to form themselves into a battalion of privates, and, after doing many feats of gallantry in the service of the country where they found refuge, at length melted away under the sword of the enemy, and the privations of military service. History, while she is called upon to censure or commend the actions of mankind according to the rules of immutable justice, is no less bound to lament the brave and generous, who, preferring the dictates of honourable feeling to those of prudence, are hurried into courses which may be doubtful in policy, and perhaps in patriotism, but to which they are urged by the disinterested wish of discharging what they account a conscientious duty. The emigrants were impolitic, perhaps, in leaving France, though that conduct had many apologies; and their entrance into their country in arms to bring back the despotic system, which Louis XVI. and the whole nation, save themselves, had renounced, was an enterprise unwisely and unjustly undertaken. But the cause they embraced was one dear to all the prejudices of the rank and sentiments in which they had been brought up; their loyal purpose in its defence is indisputable; and it would be hard to condemn them for following one extreme, when the most violent and tyrannical proceedings were, in the sight of all Europe, urging another, so bloody, black, and fatal as that of the faction which now domineered in Paris, and constrained men, whose prejudices of birth or education were in favour of freedom, to loathe the very name of France, and of the Revolution.

The tame and dishonourable retreat of the Duke of Brunswick and his Prussians, naturally elated the courage of a proud and martial people. Recruits flowed into the Republican ranks from every department; and the generals, Custine on the Rhine, and Montesquiou on the side of Savoy, with Dumouriez in the Netherlands, knew how to avail themselves of these reinforcements, which enabled them to assume the offensive on all parts of the extensive south-eastern frontier of France.

ATTACK OF SAVOY

The attack of Savoy, whose sovereign, the King of Sardinia, was brother-in-law of the Comte d'Artois, and had naturally been active in the cause of the Bourbons, was successfully commenced, and carried on by General Montesquiou already mentioned, a

French noble, and an aristocrat of course by birth, and as it was believed by principle, but to whom, nevertheless, the want of experienced leaders had compelled the ruling party at Paris to commit the command of an army. He served them well, possessed himself of Nice and Chamberi, and threatened even Italy.[300]

On the centre of the same line of frontier, Custine, an excellent soldier and a fierce republican, took Spires, Oppenheim, Worms, finally the strong city of Mentz, and spread dismay through that portion of the Germanic empire. Adopting the republican language of the day, he thundered forth personal vengeance, denounced in the most broad and insulting terms, against such princes of the Germanic body as had distinguished themselves by zeal against the Revolution; and, what was equally formidable, he preached to their subjects the flattering and exciting doctrines of the Republicans, and invited them to join in the sacred league of the oppressed people against princes and magistrates, who had so long held over them a usurped power.[301]

But the successes of Dumouriez were of a more decided and more grateful character to the ruling men in the Convention. He had a heavier task than either Custine or Montesquiou; but his lively and fertile imagination had already devised modes of conquest with the imperfect means he possessed. The difference between commanders is the same as between mechanics. A workman of commonplace talents, however expert custom and habit may have made him in the use of his ordinary tools, is at a loss when deprived of those which he is accustomed to work with. The man of invention and genius finds out resources, and contrives to make such implements as the moment supplies answer his purpose, as well, and perhaps better, than a regular chest of working utensils. The ideas of the ordinary man are like a deep-rutted road, through which his imagination moves slowly, and without departing from the track; those of the man of genius are like an avenue, clear, open, and smooth, on which he may traverse as occasion requires.

---

[300] Botta, tom. i., p. 88; Jomini, tom. ii., p. 190.
[301] Thiers, tom. iii., p. 182; Jomini, tom. ii., p. 151.

Dumouriez was a man of genius, resource, and invention. Clairfait, who was opposed to him, a brave and excellent soldier, but who had no idea of strategie or tactics, save those current during the Seven Years' War. The former knew so well how to employ the fire and eagerness of his Carmagnoles, of whose blood he was by no means chary, and how to prevent the consequences of their want of discipline, by reserves of his most steady and experienced troops, that he gave Clairfait a signal defeat at Jemappes, on the 6th November, 1792.[302]

It was then that both Austria and Europe had reason to regret the absurd policy of Joseph II., both in indisposing the inhabitants towards his government, and, in the fine provinces of the Austrian Netherlands, dismantling the iron girdle of fortified towns, with which the wisdom of Europe had invested that frontier. Clairfait, who, though defeated, was too good a disciplinarian to be routed, had to retreat on a country unfriendly to the Austrians, from recollection of their own recent insurrection, and divested of all garrison towns; which must have been severe checks, particularly at this period, to the incursion of a revolutionary army, more fitted to win battles by its impetuosity, than to overcome obstacles which could only be removed by long and patient sieges.

As matters stood, the battle of Jemappes was won, and the Austrian Netherlands were fully conquered without further combat by the French general. We shall leave him in his triumph, and return to the fatal scenes acting in Paris.

---

[302] Dumouriez, vol. iii., p. 169; Toulongeon, tom. iii., p. 47; Jomini, tom. ii., p. 217.

Walter Scott

Chapter XII

Jacobins determine upon the Execution of Louis—Progress and Reasons of the King's Unpopularity—Girondists taken by surprise, by a proposal for the Abolition of Royalty made by the Jacobins—Proposal carried—Thoughts on the New System of Government—Compared with that of Rome, Greece, America, and other Republican States—Enthusiasm throughout France at the Change—Follies it gave birth to—And Crimes—Monuments of Art destroyed—Madame Roland interposes to save the Life of the King—Barrère—Girondists move for a Departmental Legion—Carried—Revoked—and Girondists defeated—The Authority of the Community of Paris paramount even over the Convention—Documents of the Iron-Chest—Parallel betwixt Charles I. and Louis XVI.—Motion by Pétion, that the King should be Tried before the Convention.

It is generally to be remarked, that Crime, as well as Religion, has her sacramental associations, fitted for the purposes to which she desires to pledge her votaries. When Cataline imposed an oath on his fellow-conspirators, a slave was murdered, and his blood mingled with the beverage in which they pledged each other to their treason against the republic. The most desperate mutineers and pirates too have believed, that by engaging their associates in some crime of a deep and atrocious nature, so contrary to the ordinary feelings of humanity as to strike with horror all who should hear of it, they made their allegiance more completely their own; and, as remorse is useless where retreat is impossible, that they thus rendered them in future the desperate and unscrupulous tools, necessary for the designs of their leaders.

In like manner, the Jacobins—who had now full possession of the passions and confidence of the lower orders in France, as well as of all those spirits among the higher classes, who, whether desirous of promotion by exertions in the revolutionary path, or whether enthusiasts whose imagination had become heated with the extravagant doctrines that had been current during these feverish times,—the Jacobins resolved to engage their adherents, and all whom they influenced, in proceeding to the death of the unfortunate Louis. They had no reason to doubt that they might excite the populace to desire and demand that final sacrifice, and to consider the moment of its being offered as a time of jubilee. Nor were the better classes likely to take a warm or decisive interest in the fate of their unhappy prince, so long the object of unpopularity.

UNPOPULARITY OF LOUIS XVI

From the beginning of the Revolution, down to the total overthrow of the throne, first the power of the King, and afterwards his person and the measures to which he resorted, were the constant subject of attack by the parties who successively forced themselves into his administration. Each faction accused the other, during the time of their brief sway, of attempts to extend the power and the privileges of the crown; which was thus under a perpetual siege, though carried on by distinct and opposite factions, one of whom regularly occupied the lines of attack, to dislodge the others, as fast as they obtained successively possession of the ministry. Thus the Third Estate overcame the two privileged classes, in behalf of the people and against the crown; La Fayette and the Constitutionalists triumphed over the Moderates, who desired to afford the King the shelter and bulwark of an intermediate senate; and then, after creating a constitution as democratical as it could be, leaving a name and semblance of royalty, they sunk under the Girondists, who were disposed altogether to dispense with that symbol. In this way it appeared to the people, that the King was their natural enemy, and that the royal interest was directly opposed to a revolution which had brought them sundry advantages, besides giving them the feelings and consequence of freemen. In this manner, one of the mildest and best disposed monarchs that ever swayed a sceptre, became exposed to general suspicion and misconstruction in his measures, and (as is sure speedily to follow) to personal contempt, and even hatred. Whatever the King did in compliance with the current tide of revolution was accounted as fraudful complaisance, designed to blind the nation. Whatever opposition he made to that powerful impulse, was accounted an act of open treason against the sovereignty of the people.

His position, with regard to the invading powers, was enough of itself to load him with obloquy and suspicion. It is true, that he was called, and professed himself, the willing king of a popular, or democratic monarchy; but in the proclamations of his allies, he was described as a monarch imprisoned, degraded, and almost dethroned. To achieve his liberty (as they affirmed,) and to re-establish his rights, the Emperor, his brother-in-law, the King of Prussia, his ally, and above all, his brothers, the princes of the blood of France, were in arms, and had sent numerous armies to the frontiers.[303] It was scarcely possible, in the utmost extent of candour, that the French people should give Louis credit for desiring the success of the revolutionary cause, by which not only his power had been circumscribed, but his person had been placed under virtual restraint, against forces armed avowedly for his safety and liberty, as well as the restoration of his power. We can allow as much to the disinterestedness of Louis, as to any whose feelings and rights were immediately concerned with the point at issue; and we admit that all concessions which he made to the popular cause, before the National Assembly had asserted a paramount authority over his, were willingly and freely granted. But, after the march from Versailles, he must have been an enthusiast for public liberty of a very uncommon character, if we could suppose him seriously wishing the defeat of his brothers and allies, and the victory of those who had deprived him first of authority, and then of freedom.

A single glance at his situation must have convinced the people of France, that Louis could scarcely be sincere in desiring the continuance of the system to which he had given his adhesion as sovereign; and the consciousness that they could not expect confidence where they themselves had made ungenerous use of their power, added force to their suspicions, and acrimony to the deep resentments which arose out of them. The people had

---

[303] Annual Register, vol xxxiv., pp. 230, 236.

identified themselves and their dearest interests (right or wrong, it signifies little to the result) with the Revolution, and with the increasing freedom which it bestowed, or rather promised to bestow, in every succeeding change. The King, who had been the regular opponent of every one of these innovations, was in consequence regarded as the natural enemy of the country, who, if he continued to remain at the helm of the executive government, did so with the sole view of running the vessel upon the rocks.

If there had been any men in France generous enough to give the King credit for complete good faith with the Constitutionalists, his flight from Paris, and the manifestoes which he left behind him, protesting against the measures in which he had acquiesced, as extorted from him by constraint, gave open proof of Louis's real feelings. It is true, the King denied any purpose of leaving the kingdom, or throwing himself into the hands of the foreign powers; but it could escape no one, that such a step, however little it was calculated upon in the commencement of his flight, might very easily have become inevitable before its completion. It does not appear from the behaviour of the escorts of dragoons and hussars, that there was any attachment among the troops to the King's person; and had the mutiny of Bouillé's forces against that general's authority taken place after the King reached the camp, the only safety of Louis must have been in a retreat into the Austrian territory. This chance was so evident, that Bouillé himself had provided for it, by requesting that the Austrian forces might be so disposed as to afford the King protection should the emergency occur.[304] Whatever, therefore, might be the King's first experiment, the point to which he directed his flight bore out those, who supposed and asserted that it must have ultimately terminated in his re-union with his brothers; and that such a conclusion must have repeatedly occurred to the King's thoughts.

But if the King was doubted and suspected before he gave this decisive proof of his disinclination to the constitution, there had surely happened nothing in the course of his being seized at Varennes, or the circumstances of his reception at Paris, tending to reconcile him to the constitutional crown, which was a second time

---

[304] Bouillé's Memoirs, p. 250.

proffered him, and which he again, with all its duties and acts of self-denial, solemnly accepted.

We have before hinted, that the King's assuming of new the frail and barren sceptre, proffered to him under the most humiliating circumstances, was a piece of indifferent policy. There occurred almost no course of conduct by which, subjected as he was to general suspicion, he could show himself once more to his people in a clear and impartial point of view—each of his measures was sure to be the theme of the most malignant commentary. If his conduct assumed a popular aspect, it was accounted an act of princely hypocrisy; if it was like his opposition to the departmental army, it would have been held as intended to weaken the defence of the country; if it resembled his rejection of the decrees against the emigrants and refractory priests, then it might be urged as inferring a direct intention of bringing back the old despotic system.

In short, all confidence was lost between the sovereign and the people, from a concurrence of unhappy circumstances, in which it would certainly be unjust to cast the blame exclusively on either party, since there existed so many grounds for distrust and misunderstanding on both sides. The noble and generous confidence which Frenchmen had been wont to repose in the personal character of their monarch—a confidence, which the probity of no man could deserve more than that of Louis—was withered, root and branch; or those in whose breasts it still flourished were banished men, and had carried the Oriflamme, and the ancient spirit of French chivalry, into a camp not her own. The rest of the nation, a scattered and intimidated remnant of Royalists excepted, were Constitutionalists, who, friends rather to the crown than to the King as an individual, wished to preserve the form of government, but without either zeal or attachment to Louis; or Girondists, who detested his office as Republicans; or Jacobins, who hated his person. Every one, therefore, assailed Louis; and it was held enrolling himself amongst aristocrats, the most avowed and hated enemies of the new order of things, if any one lifted a voice in his defence, or even apology.

To this the influence of the revolutionary clubs, amounting to so many thousands, and of the daily press, almost the only kind of literature which France had left, added the full tribute of calumny and inculpation. The Jacobins attacked the person of the King from the very commencement of the Revolution; for they desired that Louis should be destroyed, even when some amongst them were leagued for placing Orleans in his room. The Girondists, on the contrary, would have been well contented to spare the person of Louis; but they urged argument after argument, in the journal which they directed, against the royal office. But upon the whole, the King, whether in his royal or personal character, had been so long and uniformly calumniated and misinterpreted, that through most parts of France he was esteemed the enemy whom the people had most to dread, and whom they were most interested to get rid of. In evidence of which it may be added, that during all successive changes of parties, for the next year or two, the charge of a disposition towards royalty was always made an aggravation of the accusations which the parties brought against each other, and was considered as so necessary an ingredient, that it was not omitted even when circumstances rendered it impossible.

ABOLITION OF ROYALTY

Both parties in the Convention were thus prepared to acquire popularity, by gratifying the almost universal prejudices against monarchy, and against the King. The Girondists, constant to the Republican principles they entertained, had resolved to abolish the throne; but their audacious rivals were prepared to go a step beyond them, by gratifying the popular spirit of vengeance which their own calumnies had increased to such a pitch, by taking the life of the dethroned monarch. This was the great national crime which was to serve France for a republican baptism, and which, once committed, was to be regarded as an act of definitive and deadly adhesion to the cause of the Revolution. But not contented with taking measures for the death of the monarch, this desperate but active faction resolved to anticipate their rivals in the proposal for the abolition of royalty.

The Girondists, who counted much on the popularity which they were to attain by this favourite measure, were so far from fearing the anticipation of the Jacobins, that, under the idea of Orleans having some interest remaining with Danton and others, they rather expected some opposition on their part. But what was their surprise and mortification when, on the 21st September, Manuel[305] arose, and demanded that one of the first proposals submitted to the Convention should be the abolition of royalty! Ere the Girondists could recover from their surprise, Collot d'Herbois, a sorry comedian, who had been hissed from the stage, desired the motion to be instantly put to the vote. The Girondists, anticipated in their scheme, had no resource left but to be clamorous in applauding the motion, lest their hesitation should bring their republican zeal into question. Thus all they could do was but to save their credit with the popular party, at a time when they had expected to increase it to such a height. Their antagonists had been so alert as to steal the game out of their hands.[306]

The violence with which the various orators expressed themselves against monarchy of every complexion, and kings in general, was such as to show, either that they were in no state of mind composed enough to decide on a great national measure, or that the horrors of the massacres, scarce ten days remote, impressed on them the danger of being lukewarm in the cause of the sovereign people, who were not only judges without resort, but the prompt executioners of their own decrees.

The Abbé Grégoire declared, that the dynasties of kings were a race of devouring animals, who fed on the blood of the people; and that kings were in the moral order of things what monsters are in the physical—that courts were the arsenals of crimes, and the centre of corruption—and that the history of princes was the

---

[305] Manuel was born at Montargis in 1751. On the trial of the King he voted for imprisonment and banishment in the event of peace. When the Queen's trial came on, he was summoned as a witness against her; but only expressed admiration of her fortitude, and regret for her misfortunes. In November, 1793, he was condemned to death by the Revolutionary Tribunal, and executed. Among other works, Manuel published "Coup d'œil Philosophique sur le Règne de St. Louis," "Voyages de l'Opinion dans les Quatres Parties du Monde," and "Lettres sur la Révolution."
[306] Lacretelle, tom. x., p. 12; Mignet, tom. iii., p. 150.

martyrology of the people. Finally, that all the members of the Convention being fully sensible of these self-evident truths, it was needless to delay, even for a moment, the vote of abolition, reserving it to more leisure to put their declaration into better form. Ducos[307] exclaimed, that the crimes of Louis alone formed a sufficient reason for the abolition of monarchy. The motion was received and passed unanimously; and each side of the hall, anxious to manifest their share in this great measure, echoed back to the other the new war-cry of "Vive la Republique!"[308] Thus fell, at the voice of a wretched player and cut-throat, backed by that of a renegade priest, the most ancient and most distinguished monarchy of Europe. A few remarks may be permitted upon the new government, the adoption of which had been welcomed with so much gratulation.

NEW SYSTEM OF GOVERNMENT

It has been said, that the government which is best administered is best. This maxim is true for the time, but for the time only; as good administration depends often on the life of individuals, or other circumstances in themselves mutable. One would rather incline to say, that the government is best calculated to produce the happiness of a nation, which is best adapted to the existing state of the country which it governs, and possesses, at the same time, such internal means of regeneration as may enable it to keep pace with the changes of circumstances, and accommodate itself to the unavoidable alterations which must occur in a progressive state of society. In this point of view, and even in the patriarchal circle, the most natural forms of government, in the early periods of society, are Monarchy, or a Republic. The father is head of his own family; the assembled council of the fathers governs the Republic; or the *patria potestas* of the whole state is bestowed upon some successful warrior or eminent legislator, who becomes king of the tribe. But a republic, in the literal acceptation, which supposes all the individuals subject to its government to be consulted in council

---

[307] Born at Bordeaux in 1765. He voted for the death of the King—and was guillotined, Oct., 1793.
[308] Lacretelle, tom. x., p. 16.

upon all affairs of the public, cannot survive the most early period of existence. It is only to be found around the council-fire of a North American tribe of Indians; and even there, the old men, forming a sort of senate, have already established a species of aristocracy. As society advances, and the little state extends itself, ordinary matters of government are confided to delegates, or exclusively grasped by some of the higher orders of the community. Rome, when she dismissed the Tarquins, the period to which the Girondists were fond of assimilating that of the French Revolution, had already a privileged body of patricians, the senate, from which were exclusively chosen the consuls; until at a later period, and at the expense of many feuds with the patricians, the plebeians succeeded in obtaining for their order many advantages. But the state of Rome was not more republican, in the proper sense, than before these concessions. The corporate citizens of Rome were indeed admitted into some of the privileges of the nobles; but the quantity of territory and of population over which these citizens extended their dominion, was so great, that the rural and unrepresented part of the inhabitants quite outnumbered that of the citizens who voted in the Comitia, and constituted the source of authority. There was the whole body of slaves, who neither were nor could be represented, being considered by the law as no farther capable of political or legal rights, than a herd of so many cattle; and there were the numerous and extensive dominions, over which, under the name of auxiliaries, Rome exercised a right of absolute sovereignty. In fact, the so called democracy was rather an oligarchy, dispersed more widely than usual, and vesting the government of an immense empire in a certain limited number of the inhabitants of Rome called citizens, bearing a very small proportion in bulk to the gross number of the inhabitants. These privileged persons in some degree lived upon their votes;—the ambitious caressed them, fed them, caught their eyes with magnificent exhibitions, and their ears with extravagant eloquence, and by corrupting their principles, at last united the small class of privileged citizens themselves, under the very bondage in which they had long kept their extensive empire. There is no one period of the Roman republic, in which it can be said, considering the number of the persons governed relatively to those who had as citizens a share of that government by vote, or capacity of bearing office, that the people, as a whole, were fairly and fully represented.

All other republics of which we have any distinct account, including the celebrated states of Greece, were of so small a size, that it was by no means difficult to consult the citizens to a considerable extent in the affairs of the state. Still this right of being consulted was retained among the *free* citizens of Greece. Slaves, who amounted to a very large proportion of the inhabitants, were never permitted any interference there, more than in Rome. Now, as it was by slaves that the coarser, more debasing, and more sordid parts of the labour of the community were performed, there were thus excluded from the privilege of citizens almost all those, who, by constant toil, and by the sordid character of the employments to which their fate condemned them, might be supposed incapable of exercising political rights with due feelings of reflection and of independence. It is not too much to say, in conclusion, that, excepting in the earliest stage of human society, there never existed a community in which was to be found that liberty and equality, which the French claimed for each individual in the whole extent of their empire.

Not only the difficulty or impossibility of assigning to every person in France an equal portion of political power, was one against which antiquity had never attempted to struggle, but the wealth and size of the late French empire were circumstances which experience induced wise statesmen to conclude against the favourable issue of the experiment. Those memorable republics, which Montesquieu eulogizes[309] as being formed upon *virtue*, as the leading principle, inhabited the modest and sequestered habitations where virtue is most often found. In mountainous countries like those of the Swiss, where the inhabitants are nearly of the same rank, and not very much disproportioned in substance, and where they inhabit a small district or territory, a republic seems the most natural form of government. Nature has, to a certain extent, established an equality among the fathers of such a society, and there is no reason why policy should supplant it. In their public meetings, they come together upon the same general footing, and possess nearly the same opportunity of forming a judgment; and the affairs of such a state are too little complicated to require frequent or prolonged discussions. The same applies to small states, like

---

[309] Esprit des Lois, liv. iii., c. 9.

Genoa, and some of the Dutch provinces, where the inequality of wealth, if it exists in some instances, is qualified by the consideration, that it is gained in the same honourable pursuit of mercantile traffic, where all fortunes are founded on the same commercial system, and where the chance that has made one man rich yesterday, may to-morrow depress him and raise another. Under such favourable circumstances, republics may exist long and happy, providing they can prevent luxury from working the secret dissolution of their moral principles, or the exterior force of more powerful neighbours from swallowing up their little community in the rage of conquest.

America must certainly be accounted a successful attempt to establish a republic on a much larger scale than those we have mentioned. But that great and flourishing empire consists, it must be remembered, of a federative union of many states, which, though extensive in territory, are comparatively thin in occupants. There do not exist in America, in the same degree, those circumstances of a dense and degraded population, which occasion in the old nations of Europe such an infinite difference of knowledge and ignorance, of wealth the most exuberant, and indigence the most horrible. No man in America need be poor, if he has a hatchet and arms to use it. The wilderness is to him the same retreat which the world afforded to our first parents. His family, if he has one, is wealth; if he is unencumbered with wife or children, he is the more easily provided for. A man who wishes to make a large fortune, may be disappointed in America; but he who seeks, with a moderate degree of industry, only the wants which nature demands, is certain to find them. An immense proportion of the population of the United States consists of agriculturists, who live upon their own property, which is generally of moderate extent, and cultivate it by their own labour. Such a situation is peculiarly favourable to republican habits. The man who feels himself really independent,—and so must each American who can use a spade or an axe,—will please himself with the mere exertion of his freewill, and form a strong contrast to the hollowing, bawling, blustering rabble of a city, where a dram of liquor, or the money to buy a meal, is sure to purchase the acclamation of thousands, whose situation in the scale of society is too low to permit their thinking of their political right as a thing more valuable than to be bartered against the degree of advantage they may procure, or of a license which they may exercise, by placing it at the disposal of one candidate or another.

Above all, before considering the case of America as parallel with that of France, the statesmen of the latter country should have observed one grand and radical difference. In America, after the great change in their system had been effected by shaking off the sovereignty of the mother country, the states arranged their new government so as to make the least possible alteration in the habits of their people. They left to a future and more convenient opportunity, what farther innovation this great change might render necessary; being more desirous to fix the general outlines of a firm and orderly government, although containing some anomalies, than to cast all existing authorities loose, in order that they might produce a constitution more regular in theory, but far less likely to be put into effectual execution, than those old forms under which the people had grown up, and to which they were accustomed to render regular obedience. They abolished no nobility, for they had none in the colonies to abolish; but in fixing the basis of their constitution, they balanced the force and impulse of the representative body of the states by a Senate, designed to serve the purposes answered by the House of Lords in the British Constitution. The governors of the different states also, in whose power the executive administration of each was reposed, continued to exercise the same duties as before, without much other change, than that they were named by their fellow-citizens, instead of being appointed by the sovereign of the mother country. The Congress exercised the rights which success had given them over the loyalists, with as much temperance as could be expected after the rage of a civil war. Above all, the mass of the American population was in a sound healthy state, and well fitted to bear their share in the exercise of political rights. They were independent, as we have noticed, and had comparatively few instances amongst them of great wealth, contrasted with the most degrading indigence. They were deeply imbued with a sense of religion, and the morality which is its fruit. They had been brought up under a free government, and in the exercise of the rights of freemen; and their fancies were not liable to be excited, or their understandings made giddy, with a sudden elevation to privileges, the nature of which was unknown to them. The republic of America, moreover, did not consist of one huge and populous country, with an overgrown capital, where the legislative body, cooped up in its precincts like prisoners, were liable to be acted upon by the applauses or threats of a desperate rabble. Each state of America carries on its own immediate government, and enjoys unmolested the privilege of adopting such plans as are best suited to their own peculiar situation, without embarrassing themselves with that ideal uniformity, that universal equality of rights, which it was the vain object of the French Constituent Assembly to establish. The Americans know that the advantage of a constitution, like that of a garment, consists, neither in the peculiarity of the fashion, nor in the fineness of the texture, but in its being well adapted to the person who receives protection from it. In short, the sagacity of Washington was not more apparent in his military exploits, than in the manly and wise pause which he made in the march of revolution, so soon as peace gave an opportunity to interrupt its impulse. To replace law and social order upon an established basis was as much the object of this great general, as it seems to have been that of the statesmen of Paris, civilians as they were, to protract a period of insurrection, murder, and revolutionary tyranny.

FRANCE, A REPUBLIC

To such peculiarities and advantages as those we have above stated, France opposed a direct contrast. Not only was the exorbitant influence of such a capital as Paris a bar to the existence of that republican virtue which is the essence of a popular form of government, but there was nothing like fixed or settled principles in the minds of the people of France at large. Every thing had, within the last few years, been studiously and industriously altered, from the most solemn rites of the Church of Rome, to the most trifling article of dress; from the sacrament of the mass to the fashion of a shoe-tie. Religion was entirely out of the question, and the very slightest vestiges of an established church were about to be demolished. Republican virtue (with the exception of that of the soldiers, whose valour did honour to the name) consisted in wearing a coarse dress and foul linen, swearing the most vulgar oaths, obeying without scruple the most villanous mandates of the Jacobin Club, and assuming the title, manner, and sentiments of a real sans-culotte. The country was besides divided into an infinite variety of factions, and threatened with the plague of civil war. The streets of the metropolis had been lately the scene of a desperate conflict, and yet more recently of a horrible massacre. On the frontiers, the country was pressed by armies of invaders. It was a crisis in which the Romans, with all their love of freedom, would have called in the assistance of a dictator; yet it was then, when, without regarding either the real wants of the country, or the temper of its inhabitants, France was erected into a Republic, a species of government the most inconsistent with energetic, secret, and successful councils.

These considerations could not have escaped the Girondists. Neither could they be blind to the fact, that each republic, whatever its pretensions to freedom, has committed to some high officer of the state, under the name of doge, stadtholder, president, or other title, the custody of the executive power; from the obvious and undeniable principle, that, with safety to freedom, it cannot be lodged in the hands of the legislative body. But, knowing this to be the case, they dared not even hint that such a separation of powers was indispensable, aware that their fierce enemies, the Jacobins, while they would have seized on the office without scruple, would, with the other hand, sign an accusation of leze-nation against them for proposing it. Thus crude, raw, and ill considered, did one of the most important changes that could be wrought upon a country, pass as hastily through this legislative body as the change of a decoration in the theatre.

The alteration was, notwithstanding, hailed by the community at large, as the consummation of the high fortunes to which France was called. True, half Europe was in arms at her gates—but the nation who opposed their swords to them were become Republicans. True, the most frightful disorder had stalked abroad, in the shape of armed slaughter—it was but the effervescence and delirium of a republican consciousness of freedom. Peculation had crept into the finance, and theft had fingered the diamonds of the state[310]—but the name of a republic was of itself sufficient to restore to the blackest Jacobin of the gang, the moral virtues of a Cincinnatus. The mere word *Republic* was now the universal medicine for all evils which France could complain of, and its regenerating operations were looked for with as much faith and confidence, as if the salutary effects of the convocation of the estates of the kingdom, once worshipped as a panacea with similar expectations, had not deceived the hopes of the country.

Meantime, the actors in the new drama began to play the part of Romans with the most ludicrous solemnity. The name of *citizen* was now the universal salutation to all classes; even when a deputy spoke to a shoe-black, that fond symbol of equality was regularly exchanged betwixt them; and, in the ordinary intercourse of society, there was the most ludicrous affectation of republican brevity and simplicity. "When thou conquerest Brussels," said Collot d'Herbois, the actor, to General Dumouriez, "my wife, who is in that city, has my permission to reward thee with a kiss." Three weeks afterwards the general took Brussels, but he was ungallant enough not to profit by this flattering permission.[311] His quick wit caught the ridicule of such an ejaculation as that which Camus addressed to him: "Citizen-general," said the deputy, "thou dost meditate the part of Cæsar; but remember I will be Brutus, and plunge a poniard in thy bosom."—"My dear Camus," said the lively soldier, who had been in worse dangers than were involved in this classical threat, "I am no more like Cæsar than you are like Brutus; and an assurance that I should live till you kill me, would be equal to a brevet of immortality."

With a similar assumption of republican dignity, men graced their children, baptized or unbaptized, with the formidable names of Roman heroes, and the folly of Anacharsis Clootz seemed to become general throughout the nation.

Republican virtues were of course adopted or affected. The duty of mothers nursing their own children, so eloquently insisted

---

[310] "One night the jewel-office, in the Tuileries, was pillaged, and all the splendid ornaments of the crown disappeared. The seals affixed on the locks were removed, but no marks of violence appeared on them, which showed that the abstraction was by order of the authorities, and not by popular violence."—Thiers, tom. iii., p. 103.
[311] Dumouriez, vol. iii., p. 262; Journal des Jacobins, 14th Oct., 1792.

on by Rousseau,[312] and nevertheless so difficult to practise under the forms of modern life, was generally adopted in Paris; and as the ladies had no idea that this process of parental attention was to interfere with the usual round of entertainment, mothers, with their infants dressed in the most approved Roman costume, were to be seen at the theatre, with the little disastrous victims of republican affectation, whose wailings, as well as other embarrassments occasioned by their presence, formed sometimes disagreeable interruptions to the amusements of the evening, and placed the inexperienced matrons in an awkward situation.

These were follies to be laughed at. But when men read Livy, for the sake of discovering what degree of private crime might be committed under the mask of public virtue, the affair became more serious. The deed of the younger Brutus served any man as an apology to betray to ruin and to death a friend, or a patron, whose patriotism might not be of the pitch which suited the time. Under the example of the elder Brutus, the nearest ties of blood were repeatedly made to give way before the ferocity of party zeal—a zeal too often assumed for the most infamous and selfish purposes. As some fanatics of yore studied the Old Testament for the purpose of finding examples of bad actions to vindicate those which themselves were tempted to commit, so the Republicans of France, we mean the desperate and outrageous bigots of the Revolution, read history, to justify, by classical instances, their public and private crimes. Informers, those scourges of a state, were encouraged to a degree scarce known in ancient Rome in the time of the emperors, though Tacitus has hurled his thunders against them, as the poison and pest of his time. The duty of lodging such informations was unblushingly urged as indispensable. The safety of the republic being the supreme charge of every citizen, he was on no account to hesitate in *denouncing*, as it was termed, any one whomever, or however connected with him,—the friend of his counsels, or the wife of his bosom,—providing he had reason to suspect the devoted individual of the crime of *incivism*,—a crime the more mysteriously dreadful, that no one knew exactly its nature.

---

[312] Emile, liv. i.

The virtue, even of comparatively good men, gave way under the temptations held out by these fearful innovations on the state of morals. The Girondists themselves did not scruple to avail themselves of the villany of others, when what they called the cause of the country, in reality that of their own faction, could be essentially served by it; but it was reserved for the Jacobins to carry to the most hideous extremity the principle which made an exclusive idol of patriotism, and demanded that every other virtue, as well as the most tender and honourable dictates of feeling and conscience, should be offered up at the shrine of the Republic, as children were of old made to pass through the fire to Moloch.

SACRILEGE OF SAINT DENIS

Another eruption of republican zeal was directed against the antiquities, and fine arts of France. The name of king being pronounced detestable, all the remembrances of royalty were, on the motion of Barrère, ordered to be destroyed. This task was committed to the rabble; and although a work dishonourable to their employers, and highly detrimental both to history and the fine arts, it was nevertheless infinitely more harmless than those in which the same agents had been lately employed. The royal sepulchres at Saint Denis, near Paris, the ancient cemetery of the Bourbons, the Valois, and all the long line of French monarchs, were not only defaced on the outside, but utterly broken down, the bodies exposed, the bones dispersed, and the poor remains, even of Henry IV. of Navarre, so long the idol of the French nation, exposed to the rude gaze, and irreverent grasp, of the banditti who committed the sacrilege.[313]

---

[313] "The first vault opened was that of Turenne. The body was found dry like a mummy, the features perfectly resembling the portrait of this distinguished general. Relics were sought after with eagerness, and Camille Desmoullins cut off one of the little fingers. The body, at the intercession of M. Desfontaines, was removed to the Jardin des Plantes. The features of Henry the Fourth were also perfect. A soldier cut off a lock of the beard with his sabre, and putting it upon his upper lip, exclaimed, 'Et moi aussi, je suis soldat Français! désormais je n'aurai pas d'autre moustache!' The body was placed upright upon a stone for the rabble to divert themselves with it; and a woman, reproaching the dead Henry with the crime of having been a king, knocked down the corpse, by giving it a blow in the face. Two large pits had been dug in front of the north entrance of the church, and quick lime laid in

Le Noire, an artist, had the courage to interpose for preventing the total dispersion of the materials of those monuments, so valuable to history and to literature. He procured, with difficulty, permission to preserve and collect them in a house and garden in the *Rue des Petits Augustins*, where their mutilated remains continued in safety till after the restoration of the Bourbons. The enterprise was accomplished at much personal risk; for if the people he had to deal with had suspected that the zeal which he testified for the preservation of the monuments, was rather that of a royalist than of an antiquary, his idolatry would have been punished by instant death.

But the demolition of those ancient and sacred monuments, was comparatively a trivial mode of showing hatred to royalty. The vengeance of the Republicans was directed against the emigrants, who, armed or unarmed, or from whatever cause they were absent from France, were now to be at once confounded in a general set of decrees. 1. All emigrants taken in arms were to suffer death within twenty-four hours. 2. Foreigners who had quitted the service of France since the 14th July, 1789, were, contrary to the law of nations, subjected to the same penalty. 3. All Frenchmen who had sought refuge in foreign parts, were banished for ever from their native country, without any distinction, or inquiry into the cause of their absence. The effects of these unfortunate exiles were already under sequestration, and by the assignats which were issued on the strength of this spoliation, Cambon, who managed the finances, carried on the war, and supplied the expenses of government.

The emigrants who had fled abroad, were not more severely treated than those supposed to share their sentiments who had remained at home. Persons suspected, from whatever cause, or denounced by private malice as disinclined to the new system, were piled anew into the prisons, which had been emptied on the 2d and 3d of September, and where the blood of their predecessors in misfortune was yet visible on the walls. The refractory priests were

---

them; into those pits the bodies were thrown promiscuously; the leaden coffins were then carried to a furnace, which had been erected in the cemetery, and cast into balls, destined to punish the enemies of the republic."—See Promenade aux Sépultures Royales de Saint Denis, par M. P. St. A. G., and Lacretelle, tom. xi., p. 264.

particularly the objects of this species of oppression, and at length a summary decree was made for transporting them in the mass from the land of France to the unhealthy colony of Guiana, in South America. Many of these unfortunate men came to a more speedy fate.

But the most august victims destined to be sacrificed at the altar of republican virtue, were the royal family in the Temple, whose continuing in existence seemed, doubtless, to the leaders, a daily reproach to their procrastination, and an object to which, when the present spirit should abate, the affections of the bewildered people might return with a sort of reaction. The Jacobins resolved that Louis should die, were it only that the world might see they were not ashamed to attest, with a bloody seal, the truth of the accusations they had brought against him.

On the other hand, there was every reason to hope that the Girondists would exert, in protection of the unhappy prince, whatever vigour they derived from their predominating influence in the Convention. They were, most of them, men, whose philosophy, though it had driven them on wild political speculations, had not destroyed the sense of moral right and wrong, especially now that the struggle was ended betwixt monarchy and democracy, and the only question remaining concerned the use to be made of their victory. Although they had aided the attack on the Tuileries, on the 10th of August, which they considered as a combat, their hands were unstained with the massacres of September, which, as we shall presently see, they urged as an atrocious crime against their rivals, the Jacobins. Besides, they had gained the prize, and were in possession of the government; and, like the Constitutionalists before them, the Girondists now desired that here, at length, the revolutionary career should terminate, and that the ordinary forms of law and justice should resume their usual channels through France; yielding to the people protection for life, personal liberty, and private property, and affording themselves, who held the reins of government, the means of guiding these honourably safely, and with advantage to the community.

The philosophical statesmen, upon whom these considerations were not lost, felt nevertheless great embarrassment in the mode of interposing their protection in the King's favour. Their republicanism was the feature on which they most prided themselves. They delighted to claim the share in the downfall of Louis, which was due to their colleague Barbaroux, and the Federates of Marseilles and Brest. It was upon their accession to this deed that the Girondists rested their claims to popularity; and with what front could they now step forward the defenders, at the least the apologists, of the King whom they had aided to dethrone; or what advantages would not the Jacobins obtain over them, when they represented them to the people as lukewarm in their zeal, and as falling off from the popular cause, in order to preserve the life of the dethroned tyrant? The Girondist ministers felt these embarrassments, and suffered themselves to be intimidated by them from making any open, manly, and direct interference in the King's cause.

MADAME ROLAND

A woman, and, although a woman, not the least distinguished among the Girondist party, had the courage to urge a decisive and vigorous defence of the unhappy prince, without having recourse to the veil of a selfish and insidious policy. This was the wife of Roland, one of the most remarkable women of her time. A worthless, at least a careless father, and the doating folly of her mother, had left her when young to pick out such an education as she could, among the indecencies and impieties of French philosophy. Yet, though her Memoirs afford revolting specimens of indelicacy, and exaggerated sentiments in politics, it cannot be denied that the tenor of her life was innocent and virtuous in practice, and her sentiments unperverted, when left to their natural course.[314] She saw the great question in its true and real position; she

---

[314] "To a very beautiful person, Madame Roland united great powers of intellect; her reputation stood very high, and her friends never spoke of her but with the most profound respect. In character she was a Cornelia; and had she been blessed with sons, would have educated them like the Gracchi. The simplicity of her dress did not detract from her natural grace and elegance, and though her pursuits were more adapted to the other sex, she adorned them with all the charms of her own. Her personal memoirs are admirable. They

saw, that it was only by interposing themselves betwixt the legislative body of France and the commission of a great crime, that the Girondists could either remain firm in the government, attract the confidence of honest men of any description, or have the least chance of putting a period to the anarchy which was devouring their country. "Save the life of Louis," she said;[315] "save him by an open and avowed defence. It is the only measure that can assure your safety—the only course which can fix the stamp of public virtue on your government." Those whom she addressed listened with admiration; but, like one who has rashly climbed to a height where his brain grows giddy, they felt their own situation too tottering to permit their reaching a willing hand to support another, who was in still more imminent peril.

Their condition was indeed precarious. A large party in the Convention avowedly supported them; and in *"the Plain,"* as it was called, a position held by deputies affecting independence, both of the Girondists and the Jacobins, and therefore occupying the neutral ground betwixt them, sate a large number, who, from the timidity of temper which makes sheep and other weak animals herd together in numbers, had formed themselves into a faction, which could at any time cast decision into either scale which they favoured. But they exercised this power of inclining the balance, less with a view to carrying any political point, than with that of securing their own safety. In ordinary debates, they usually gave their votes to the ministers, both because they were ministers, and also because the milder sentiments of the Girondists were more congenial to the feelings of men, who would gladly have seen peace and order restored. But then these timid members of the Plain also assiduously courted the Jacobins, avoided joining in any measure which should give them mortal offence, and purchased a sort of immunity from their revenge, by showing plainly that they deserved only contempt. In this neutral party the gleanings of the defeated factions of Moderates and of Constitutionalists were chiefly to be found; resigning themselves to the circumstances of the moment, consulting their own safety, as they gave their votes, and waiting,

---

are an imitation of Rousseau's Confessions, and often not unworthy of the original."—Dumont, p. 326.
[315] At the bar of the National Convention, Dec. 7, 1792.

perhaps, till less disorderly days might restore to them the privilege of expressing their actual sentiments. The chief of these trucklers to fortune was Barrère, a man of wit and eloquence, prompt invention, supple opinions, and convenient conscience.[316] His terror of the Jacobins was great, and his mode of disarming their resentment, so far as he and the neutral party were concerned, was often very ingenious. When by argument or by eloquence the Girondists had obtained some triumph in the Assembly, which seemed to reduce their adversaries to despair, it was then Barrère, and the members of *the Plain*, threw themselves between the victors and vanquished, and, by some proposal of an insidious and neutralizing nature, prevented the completion of the conquest, and afforded a safe retreat to the defeated.

The majorities, therefore, which the Girondists obtained in the Assembly, being partly eked out by this heartless and fluctuating band of auxiliaries, could never be supposed to arm them with solid or effective authority. It was absolutely necessary that they should exhibit such a power of protecting themselves and those who should join them, as might plainly show that the force was on their side. This point once established, they might reckon Barrère and his party as faithful adherents. But while the Jacobins retained the power of surrounding the Convention at their pleasure with an insurrection of the suburbs, without the deputies possessing other means of defence than arose out of their inviolability, the adherence of those whose chief object in voting was to secure their personal safety, was neither to be hoped nor expected. The Girondists, therefore, looked anxiously round, to secure, if it were possible, the possession of such a force, to protect themselves and their timorous allies.

---

[316] "I used to meet Barrère at a table d'hôte. I considered him of a mild and amiable temper. He was very well-bred, and seemed to love the Revolution from a sentiment of benevolence. His association with Robespierre, and the court which he paid to the different parties he successively joined and afterwards deserted, were less the effect of an evil disposition, than of a timid and versatile character, and a conceit, which made it incumbent upon him to appear as a public man. His talents as an orator were by no means of the first order. He was afterwards surnamed the Anacreon of the guillotine; but when I knew him he was only the Anacreon of the Revolution, upon which, in his 'Point du Jour,' he wrote some very amorous strains."—Dumont, p. 199.

DANTON—ROBESPIERRE—MARAT

It has been thought, that a more active, more artful body of ministers, and who were better acquainted with the mode of carrying on revolutionary movements, might at this period have secured an important auxiliary, by detaching the formidable Danton from the ranks of the enemy, and receiving him into their own. It must be observed, that the camp of the Jacobins contained three separate parties, led each by one of the triumvirs whom we have already described, and acting in concert, for the common purpose of propelling the Revolution by the same violent means which had begun it—of unsheathing the sword of terror, and making it pass for that of justice—and, in the name of liberty, of letting murder and spoil, under the protection of armed ruffians of the basest condition, continue to waste and ravage the departments of France. But, although agreed in this main object, the triumvirs were extremely suspicious of each other, and jealous of the rights each might claim in the spoil which they contemplated. Danton despised Robespierre for his cowardice, Robespierre feared the ferocious audacity of Danton; and with him to fear was to hate—and to hate was—when the hour arrived—to destroy. They differed in their ideas also of the mode of exercising their terrible system of government. Danton had often in his mouth the sentence of Machiavel, that when it becomes necessary to shed blood, a single great massacre has a more dreadful effect than a series of successive executions. Robespierre, on the contrary, preferred the latter process as the best way of sustaining the Reign of Terror. The appetite of Marat could not be satiated, but by combining both modes of murder. Both Danton and Robespierre kept aloof from the sanguinary Marat. This position of the chiefs of the Jacobins towards each other seemed to indicate, that one of the three at least might be detached from the rest, and might bring his ruffians in opposition to those of his late comrades, in case of any attempt on the Assembly; and policy recommended Danton, not averse, it is said, to the alliance, as the most useful auxiliary.

MARAT

Among the three monsters mentioned, Danton had that energy which the Girondists wanted, and was well acquainted with the secret movements of those insurrections to which they possessed no key. His vices of wrath, luxury, love of spoil, dreadful as they were, are attributes of mortal men;—the envy of Robespierre, and the instinctive blood-thirstiness of Marat, were the properties of fiends. Danton, like the huge serpent called the boa, might be approached with a degree of safety when gorged with prey—but the appetite of Marat for blood was like the horse-leech, which says, "Not enough"—and the slaughterous envy of Robespierre was like the gnawing worm that dieth not, and yields no interval of repose. In glutting Danton with spoil, and furnishing the means of indulging his luxury, the Girondists might have purchased his support; but nothing under the supreme rule in France would have gratified Robespierre; and an unlimited torrent of the blood of that unhappy country could alone have satiated Marat. If a colleague was to be chosen out of that detestable triumvirate, unquestionably Danton was to be considered as the most eligible.

On the other hand, men like Brissot, Vergniaud, and others, whose attachment to republicanism was mixed with a spirit of virtue and honour, might be well adverse to the idea of contaminating their party with such an auxiliary, intensely stained as Danton was by his share in the massacres of September. They might well doubt, whether any physical force which his revolutionary skill, and the arms it could put in motion, might bring to their standard, would compensate for the moral horror with which the presence of such a grisly proselyte must strike all who had any sense of honour or justice. They, therefore, discouraged the advances of Danton, and resolved to comprise him with Marat and Robespierre in the impeachment against the Jacobin chiefs, which they designed to bring forward in the Assembly.

The most obvious means by which the Girondists could ascertain their safety and the freedom of debate, was by levying a force from the several departments, each contributing its quota, to be called a Departmental Legion, which was to be armed and paid to act as a guard upon the National Convention. The subject was introduced by Roland, [Sept. 24,] in a report to the Assembly, and renewed on the next day by Kersaint, a spirited Girondist, who candidly declared the purpose of his motion: "It was time," he said, "that assassins and their prompters should see that the law had scaffolds."

The Girondists obtained, that a committee of six members should be named, to report on the state of the capital, on the encouragement afforded to massacre, and on the mode of forming a departmental force for the defence of the metropolis. The decree was carried for a moment; but, on the next day, the Jacobins demanded that it should be revoked, denying that there was any occasion for such a defence to the Convention, and accusing the ministers of an intention to surround themselves with a force of armed satellites, in order to overawe the good city of Paris, and carry into effect their sacrilegious plan of dismembering France.[317] Rebecqui and Barbaroux replied to this charge by impeaching Robespierre, on their own testimony, of aspiring to the post of dictator. The debate became more tempestuous the more that the tribunes or galleries of the hall were filled with the violent followers of the Jacobin party, who shouted, cursed, and yelled, to back the exclamations and threats of their leaders in the Assembly. While the Girondists were exhausting themselves to find out terms of reproach for Marat, that prodigy stepped forth, and raised the disorder to the highest, by avowing himself the author and advocate for a dictatorship. The anger of the Convention seemed thoroughly awakened, and Vergniaud read to the deputies an extract from Marat's journal, in which, after demanding two hundred and sixty thousand heads, which was his usual stint, he abused the Convention in the grossest terms, and exhorted the people to ACT[318]—words, of which the import was by this time perfectly understood.

This passage excited general horror, and the victory for a moment seemed in the hands of the Girondists; but they did not pursue it with sufficient vigour. The meeting passed to the order of

---

[317] Lacretelle, tom. x., p. 41.
[318] "O! peuple babillard, si tu savais agir!"

the day; and Marat, in ostentatious triumph, produced a pistol, with which he said he would have blown out his brains, had a decree of accusation been passed against him. The Girondists not only lost the advantage of discomfiting their enemies by the prosecution of one of their most noted leaders, but were compelled for the present to abandon their plan of a departmental guard, and resign themselves to the guardianship of the faithful citizens of Paris.[319]

This city of Paris was at the time under the power of the intrusive community, or Common Council, many of whom had forced themselves into office on the 10th of August. It was the first act of their administration to procure the assassination of Mandat, the commandant of the national guard; and their accompts, still extant, bear testimony, that it was by their instrumentality that the murderers of September were levied and paid. Trained Jacobins and pitiless ruffians themselves, this civic body had raised to be their agents and assistants an unusual number of municipal officers, who were at once their guards, their informers, their spies, their jailors, and their executioners. They had, besides, obtained a majority of the inhabitants in most of the sections, whose votes placed them and their agents in command of the national guard; and the pikemen of the suburbs were always ready to second their excellent community, even against the Convention itself, which, in point of freedom of action, or effective power, made a figure scarcely more respectable than that of the King after his return from Varennes.

Roland almost every day carried to the Convention his vain complaints, that the course of the law for which he was responsible, was daily crossed, thwarted, and impeded, by the proceedings of this usurping body. The considerable funds of the city itself, with those of its hospitals and other public establishments of every kind, were dilapidated by these revolutionary intruders, and applied to their own purposes. The minister at length, in a formal report to the Convention, inculpated the Commune in these and such like offences. In another part of the report, he intimated a plot of the Jacobins to assassinate the Girondists, possess themselves of the government by arms, and choose Robespierre dictator. Louvet denounced Robespierre as a traitor, and Barbaroux proposed a

---

[319] Thiers, tom. iii., p. 170; Lacretelle, tom. x., p. 23.

series of decrees; the first declaring the Convention free to leave any city, where they should be exposed to constraint and violence; the second resolving to form a conventional guard; the third declaring, that the Convention should form itself into a court of justice, for trial of state crimes; the fourth announcing, that in respect the sections of Paris had declared their sittings permanent, that resolution should be abrogated.

Instead of adopting the energetic measures proposed by Barbaroux, the Convention allowed Robespierre eight days for his defence against Louvet's accusation, and ordered to the bar, [Nov. 5,] ten members of the Community, from whom they were contented to accept such slight apologies, and evasive excuses, for their unauthorised interference with the power of the Convention, as these insolent demagogues condescended to offer.

The accusation of Robespierre though boldly urged by Louvet and Barbaroux, was also eluded, by passing to the order of the day; and thus the Convention showed plainly, that however courageous they had been against their monarch, they dared not protect the liberty which they boasted of, against the encroachment of fiercer demagogues than themselves.[320]

Barbaroux endeavoured to embolden the Assembly, by bringing once more from his native city a body of those fiery Marseillois, who had formed the vanguard of the mob on the 10th of August. He succeeded so far in his scheme, that a few scores of those Federates again appeared in Paris, where their altered demeanour excited surprise. Their songs were again chanted, their wild Moresco dances and gestures again surprised the Parisians; and the more, as in their choruses they imprecated vengeance on the Jacobins, called out for mercy to the "poor tyrant," so they termed the King, and shouted in the cause of peace, order, and the Convention.[321]

. The citizens of Paris, who could not reconcile the songs and exclamations of the Marseillois with their appearance and character,

---

[320] Mignet, tom. i., p. 224; Thiers, tom. iii., p. 213; Lacretelle, tom. x., p. 54.
[321] "Point de procès au roi! épargnons le pauvre tyran!"—Lacretelle, tom. x., p. 47.

concluded that a snare was laid for them, and abstained from uniting themselves with men, whose sincerity was so suspicious. The Marseillois themselves, discouraged with their cold reception, or not liking their new trade of maintaining order so well as their old one of oversetting it, melted away by degrees, and were soon no more seen nor heard of. Some of the Breton Federates, kept in the interest of the Girondists, by their countrymen the deputies Kersaint and Kervclagan, remained still attached to the Convention, though their numbers were too few to afford them protection in any general danger.

If the Memoirs of Dumouriez are to be relied on, that active and intriguing general presented to the Girondists another resource, not free certainly from hazard or difficulty to the republican government, which was the idol of these theoretical statesmen, but affording, if his means had proved adequate to the execution of his plans, a certain bulwark against the encroachments of the hideous anarchy threatened by the Jacobin ascendency.

DUMOURIEZ'S PROPOSAL

General Dumouriez was sufficiently hated by the Jacobins, notwithstanding the successes which he had gained on the part of France over foreign enemies, to induce him to feel the utmost desire of putting down their usurped power; but he was under the necessity of acting with great caution. The bad success of La Fayette, deserted by his army as soon as he attempted to lead them against Paris, was in itself discouraging; but Dumouriez was besides conscious that the Jacobin clubs, together with the commissioners of the Convention, with Danton at their head, had been actively engaged in disorganizing his army, and diminishing his influence over them. Thus circumstanced, he naturally resolved to avoid hazarding any violent measure without the support of the Convention, in case of being deserted by his army. But he affirms, that he repeatedly informed the Girondists, then predominant in the Assembly, that if they could obtain a decree, but of four lines, authorising such a measure, he was ready to march to Paris at the head of a chosen body of troops, who would have been willing to obey such a summons; and that he would by this means have placed the Convention in a situation, when they might have set the Jacobins and their insurrectionary forces at absolute defiance.[322]

Perhaps the Girondists entertained the fear, first, that Dumouriez's influence with his troops might prove as inefficient as that of La Fayette, and leave them to atone with their heads for such a measure attempted and unexecuted. Or, secondly, that if the manœuvre proved successful, they would be freed from fear of the Jacobins, only to be placed under the restraint of a military chief, whose mind was well understood to be in favour of monarchy of one kind or other. So that, conceiving they saw equal risk in the alternative, they preferred the hazard of seeing their fair and favourite vision of a republic overthrown by the pikes of the Jacobins, rather than by the bayonets of Dumouriez's army. They turned, therefore, a cold ear to the proposal, which afterwards they would gladly have accepted, when the general had no longer the power to carry it into execution.

Thus the factions, so intimately united for the destruction of royalty, could not, when that step was gained, combine for any other purpose save the great crime of murdering their deposed sovereign. Nay, while the Jacobins and Girondists seemed moving hand in hand to the ultimate completion of that joint undertaking, the union was only in outward appearance; for the Girondists, though apparently acting in concert with their stern rivals, were in fact dragged after them by compulsion, and played the part less of actors than subdued captives in this final triumph of democracy. They were fully persuaded of the King's innocence as a man, of his inviolability and exemption from criminal process as a constitutional authority. They were aware that the deed meditated would render France odious to all the other nations of Europe; and that the Jacobins, to whom war and confusion were natural elements, were desirous for that very reason to bring Louis to the scaffold. All this was plain to them, and yet their pride as philosophers made them ashamed to be thought capable of interesting themselves in the fate of a tyrant; and their desire of getting the French nation under their own exclusive government, induced them to consent to any thing rather than

---

[322] Dumouriez, vol. iii., p. 273.

protect the obnoxious though innocent sovereign, at the hazard of losing their popularity, and forfeiting their dearly won character of being true Republicans.

A committee of twenty-four persons had been appointed early in the session of the Convention, to inquire into, and report upon, the grounds for accusing Louis. Their report was brought up on the 1st of November, 1792, and a more loathsome tissue of confusion and falsehood never was laid upon the table of such an assembly. All acts that had been done by the Ministers in every department, which could be twisted into such a shape as the times called criminal, were charged as deeds, for which the sovereign was himself responsible; and the burden of the whole was to accuse the King, when he had scarcely a single regiment of guards even at his nominal disposal, of nourishing the intention of massacring the Convention, defended by thirty thousand national guards, besides the federates, and the militia of the suburbs.[323]

DOCUMENTS OF THE IRON CHEST

The Convention were rather ashamed of this report, and would scarce permit it to be printed. So soon as it appeared, two or three persons, who were therein mentioned as accomplices of particular acts charged against the King, contradicted the report upon their oath.[324] An additional charge was brought under the following mysterious circumstances:—Gamin, a locksmith of Versailles, communicated to Roland, about the latter end of December, that, in the beginning of May, 1792, he had been employed by the King to secrete an iron chest, or cabinet, in the wall of a certain apartment in the Tuileries, which he disclosed to the ministers of justice. He added a circumstance which throws discredit on his whole story, namely, that the King gave him with his own hand a glass of wine, after taking which he was seized with a cholic, followed by a kind of paralysis, which deprived him for

---

[323] Mignet, tom. i., p. 228.
[324] M. de Septueil, in particular, quoted as being the agent by whom Louis XVI. was said to have transmitted money to his brothers when in exile, positively denied the fact, and made affidavit accordingly.—S.

fourteen months of the use of his limbs, and the power of working for his bread. The inference of the wretch was, that the King had attempted to poison him; which those may believe who can number fourteen months betwixt the beginning of May and the end of December in the same year. This gross falsehood utterly destroys Gamin's evidence; and as the King always denied his knowledge of the existence of such a chest with such papers, we are reduced to suppose, either that Gamin had been employed by one of the royal ministers, and had brought the King personally into the tale for the greater grace of his story, or that the papers found in some other place of safety had been selected, and put into the chest by the Jacobin commissioners, then employed in surveying and searching the palace, with the purpose of trumping up evidence against the King.

Roland acted very imprudently in examining the contents of the chest alone, and without witness, instead of calling in the commissioners aforesaid, who were in the palace at the time. This was perhaps done with the object of putting aside such papers as might, in that hour of fear and uncertainty, have brought into danger some of his own party or friends. One of importance, however, was found, which the Jacobins turned into an implement against the Girondists. It was an overture from that party addressed to Louis XVI., shortly before the 10th of August, engaging to oppose the motion for his forfeiture, providing Louis would recall to his councils the three discarded ministers of their faction.

The contents of the chest were of a very miscellaneous nature. The documents consisted of letters, memorials, and plans, from different persons, and at different dates, offering advice, or tendering support to the King, and proposing plans for the freedom of his person. The Royalist project of Mirabeau, in his latter days, was found amongst the rest; in consequence of which his body was dragged out of the Pantheon, formerly the Church of Saint Genevieve, now destined to receive the bodies of the great men of the Revolution, but whose lodgings shifted as often as if they had been taken by the month.

The documents, as we have said, consisted chiefly of projects for the King's service, which he certainly never acted on, probably never approved of, and perhaps never saw. The utmost to which he could be liable, was such penalty as may be due to one who retains possession of plans submitted to his consideration, but which have in no shape obtained his assent. It was sufficiently hard to account Louis responsible for such advice of his ministers as he really adopted; but it was a dreadful extension of his responsibility to make him answerable for such as he had virtually rejected. Besides which, the story of Gamin was so self-contradictory in one circumstance, and so doubtful in others, as to carry no available proof that the papers had been in the King's possession; so that this new charge was as groundless as those brought up by the first committee; and, arguing upon the known law of any civilized country, the accusations against him ought to have been dismissed, as founded on the most notorious injustice.[325]

CHARLES I AND LOUIS XVI

There was one circumstance which probably urged those into whose hands Louis had fallen, to proceed against his person to the uttermost. They knew that, in English history, a king had been condemned to death by his subjects, and were resolved that France should not remain behind England in the exhibition of a spectacle so interesting and edifying to a people newly regenerated. This parallel case would not perhaps have been thought a worthy precedent in other countries; but in France there is a spirit of wild enthusiasm, a desire of following out an example even to the most exaggerated point, and of outdoing, if possible, what other nations have done before them. This had doubtless its influence in causing Louis to be brought to the bar in 1792, like Charles of England in 1648.

The French statesmen did not pause to reflect, that the violent death of Charles only paved the way for a series of years spent in servitude under military despotism, and then to restoration of the

---

[325] Mignet, tom. i., p. 229; Montgaillard, tom. iii., p. 265; Thiers, tom. iii., p. 259; Lacretelle, tom. x., p. 164; Madame Campan, vol. ii., p. 222.

legitimate sovereign. Had they regarded the precedent on this side, they would have obtained a glimpse into futurity, and might have presaged what were to be the consequences of the death of Louis. Neither did the French consider, that by a great part of the English nation the execution of Charles Stuart is regarded as a national crime, and the anniversary still observed as a day of fasting and penitence; that others who condemn the King's conduct in and preceding the Civil War, do, like the Whig Churchill, still consider his death as an unconstitutional action;[326] that the number is small indeed who think it justifiable even on the precarious grounds of state necessity; and that it is barely possible a small portion of enthusiasts may still exist, who glory in the deed as an act of popular vengeance.

But even among this last description of persons, the French regicides would find themselves entirely at a loss to vindicate the execution of Louis by the similar fate of Charles; and it would be by courtesy only, if at all, that they could be admitted to the honours of a sitting at a Calves-Head Club.[327]

The comparison between these unhappy monarchs fails in almost every point, excepting in the closing scene; and no parallel can, with justice to either, be drawn betwixt them. The most zealous Cavalier will, in these enlightened days, admit, that the early government of Charles was marked by many efforts to extend the prerogative beyond its legal bounds; that there were instances of oppressive fines, cruel punishment by mutilation, long and severe imprisonments in distant forts and castles; exertions of authority which no one seeks to justify, and which those who are the King's

---

[326] "Unhappy Stuart! harshly though that name Grates on my ear, I should have died with shame, To see my King before his subjects stand, And at their bar hold up his royal hand; At their command to hear the monarch plead, By their decrees to see that monarch bleed. What though thy faults were many, and were great— What though they shook the fabric of the state? In royalty secure thy person stood, And sacred was the fountain of thy blood. Vile ministers, who dared abuse their trust, Who dared seduce a king to be unjust, Vengeance, with justice leagued, with power made strong, Had nobly crush'd—The King can do no wrong." *Gotham.*—S.

[327] This club used to meet on the 30th January, at a tavern near Charing Cross, to celebrate the anniversary of the death of Charles I. Their toasts were, "The glorious year, 1648." "D———n to the race of the Stuarts." "The pious memory of Oliver Cromwell," &c.—See *Gent.'s Mag.*, vol. v., p. 105; and "*History of the Calves-Head Club.*"

apologists can only endeavour to mitigate, by alleging the precedents of arbitrary times, or the interpretation of the laws by courtly ministers, and time-serving lawyers. The conduct of Louis XVI., from the hour he assumed the throne, was, on the contrary, an example of virtue and moderation.[328] Instead of levying ship-money and benevolences, Louis lightened the feudal services of the vassals, and the *corvée* among the peasantry. Where Charles endeavoured to enforce conformity to the Church of England by pillory and ear-slitting, Louis allowed the Protestants the free use of their religion, and discharged the use of torture in all cases whatever. Where Charles visited his Parliament to violate their freedom by arresting five of their members, Louis may be said to have surrendered himself an unresisting prisoner to the representatives of the people, whom he had voluntarily summoned around him. But above all, Charles, in person, or by his generals, waged a long and bloody war with his subjects, fought battles in every county of England, and was only overcome and made prisoner, after a lengthened and deadly contest, in which many thousands fell on both sides. The conduct of Louis was in every respect different. He never offered one blow in actual resistance, even when he had the means in his power. He ordered up, indeed, the forces under Maréchal Broglio; but he gave them command to retire, so soon as it was evident that they must either do so, or act offensively against the people. In the most perilous situations of his life, he showed the utmost reluctance to shed the blood of his subjects. He would not trust his attendants with pistols, during the flight to Varennes; he would not give the officer of hussars orders to clear the passage, when his carriage was stopped upon the bridge. When he saw that the martial array of the Guards did not check the audacity of the assailants on the 10th of August, he surrendered himself to the Legislative Assembly, a prisoner at discretion, rather than mount his horse and place himself at the head of his faithful troops and subjects. The blood that was shed that day was without command of his. He could have no reason for encouraging such a strife, which, far from defending his person, then in the custody of the Assembly, was likely to place it in the most imminent danger. And in the very last stage, when he

---

[328] "No one act of tyranny can be laid to Louis's charge: and, far from restraining the liberty of the press, it was the Archbishop of Sens, the King's prime minister, who, in the name of his Majesty, invited all writers to make known their opinions upon the form and manner of assembling the States-General."—De Staël, vol. ii., p. 94.

received private notice that there were individuals determined to save his life at peril of their own, he forbade the enterprise. "Let not a drop of blood be shed on my account," he said; "I would not consent to it for the safety of my crown: I never will purchase mere life at such a rate." These were sentiments perhaps fitter for the pious sectaries of the community of Friends, than for the King of a great nation; but such as they were, Louis felt and conscientiously acted on them. And yet his subjects could compare his character, and his pretended guilt, with the bold and haughty Stuart, who, in the course of the Civil War, bore arms in person, and charged at the head of his own regiment of guards!

Viewed in his kingly duty, the conduct of Louis is equally void of blame; unless it be that blame which attaches to a prince, too yielding and mild to defend the just rights of his crown. He yielded, with feeble struggling, to every demand in succession which was made upon him, and gave way to every inroad on the existing state of France. Instead of placing himself as a barrier between his people and his nobility, and bringing both to some fair terms of composition, he suffered the latter to be driven from his side, and by the ravaging their estates, and the burning of their houses, to be hurried into emigration. He adopted one popular improvement after another, each innovating on the royal authority, or derogatory to the royal dignity. Far from having deserved the charge of opposing the nation's claim of freedom, it would have been well for themselves and him, had he known how to limit his grant to that quantity of freedom which they were qualified to make a legitimate use of; leaving it for future princes to slacken the reins of government, in proportion as the public mind in France should become formed to the habitual exercise of political rights.

PREPARATIONS FOR THE KING'S TRIAL

The King's perfect innocence was therefore notorious to the whole world, but especially to those who now usurped the title of arraigning him; and men could hardly persuade themselves, that his life was seriously in danger. An ingenious contrivance of the Jacobins seems to have been intended to drive the wavering

Girondists into the snare of voting for the King's trial. Saint Just, one of their number, made a furious speech against any formality being observed, save a decree of death, on the urgency of the occasion. "What availed," said the supporters of this brief and sure measure, "the ceremonies of grand and petty jury? The cannon which made a breach in the Tuileries, the unanimous shout of the people on the 10th of August, had come in place of all other solemnities. The Convention had no farther power to inquire; its sole duty was to pronounce, or rather confirm and execute, the doom of the sovereign people."

This summary proposal was highly applauded, not only by the furious crowds by whom the galleries were always occupied, but by all the exaggerations of the more violent democrats. They exclaimed that every citizen had the same right over the life of Louis which Brutus possessed over that of Cæsar. Others cried out, that the very fact of having reigned, was in itself a crime notorious enough to dispense with further investigation, and authorise instant punishment.[329]

Stunned by these clamours, the Girondists and neutral party, like all feeble-minded men, chose a middle course, and instead of maintaining the King's innocence, adopted measures, calculated to save him indeed from immediate slaughter, but which ended by consigning him to a tribunal too timid to hear his cause justly. They resolved to urge the right of the National Convention to judge in the case of Louis.

There were none in the Convention who dared to avow facts to which their conscience bore witness, but the consequences of admitting which, were ingeniously urged by the sophist Robespierre, as a condemnation of their own conduct. "One party," said the wily logician, "must be clearly guilty; either the King, or the Convention, who have ratified the actions of the insurgent people. If you have dethroned an innocent and legal monarch, what are you but traitors? and why sit you here—why not hasten to the Temple, set Louis at liberty, install him again in the Tuileries, and beg on your knees for a pardon you have not merited? But if you have, in the great popular

---

[329] Lacretelle, tom. x., p. 145.

act which you have ratified, only approved of the deposition of a tyrant, summon him to the bar, and demand a reckoning for his crimes." This dilemma pressed on the mind of many members, who could not but see their own condemnation the necessary consequence of the King's acquittal. And while some felt the force of this argument, all were aware of the obvious danger to be encountered from the wrath of the Jacobins and their satellites, should they dare to dissent from the vote which these demagogues demanded from the Assembly.

When Robespierre had ended, Pétion arose and moved that the King should be tried before the Convention. It is said, the Mayor of Paris took the lead in this cruel persecution, because Louis had spoken to him sharply about the tumultuary inroad of the Jacobin rabble into the Tuileries on the 20th of June; and when Pétion attempted to reply, had pointed to the broken grating through which the entrance had been forced, and sternly commanded him to be silent. If this was true, it was a bitter revenge for so slight an offence, and the subsequent fate of Pétion is the less deserving of pity.

The motion was carried [Dec. 3] without opposition,[330] and the next chapter affords us the melancholy results.

---

[330] Thiers, tom. iii., p. 257.

WALTER SCOTT

Chapter XIII

The Trial of Louis—Indecision of the Girondists, and its Effects—The Royal Family insulted by the Agents of the Community—The King deprived of his Son's society—The King brought to trial before the Convention—His first Examination—Carried back to Prison amidst Insult and Abuse—Tumult in the Assembly—The King deprived of Intercourse with his Family—Malesherbes appointed as Counsel to defend the King—and De Seze—Louis again brought before the Convention—Opening Speech of De Seze—King remanded to the Temple—Stormy Debate—Eloquent Attack of Vergniaud on the Jacobins—Sentence of Death pronounced against the King—General Sympathy for his Fate—Dumouriez arrives in Paris—Vainly tries to avert the King's Fate—Louis XVI. Beheaded on 21st January, 1793—Marie Antoinette on the 16th October thereafter—The Princess Elizabeth in May 1794—The Dauphin perishes, by cruelty, June 8th, 1795—The Princess Royal exchanged for La Fayette, 19th December, 1795.

INDECISION OF THE GIRONDISTS

We have already said, that the vigorous and masculine, as well as virtuous exhortations of Madame Roland, were thrown away upon her colleagues, whose fears were more than female. The Girondists could not be made to perceive that, though their ferocious adversaries were feared through France, yet they were also hated. The moral feeling of all Frenchmen who had any left, detested the authors of a long train of the most cold-blooded murders; the suspicions of all men of property were attached to the conduct of a party, whose leaders rose from indigence to affluence by fines, confiscations, sequestrations, besides every other kind of plunder, direct and indirect. If the majority of the Convention had adopted the determination of boldly resisting their unprincipled tyrants, and preventing, at whatever hazard, the murder of the King, the strength of the country would probably have supported a constituted authority against the usurpations of the Community of Paris, which had no better title to tyrannize over the Convention, and by so doing to govern France at pleasure, than had the council of the meanest town in the kingdom.

The Girondists ought to have been sensible, that, even by thwarting this favourite measure, they could not increase the hatred which the Jacobins already entertained against them, and should have known that further delay to give open battle would only be regarded as a timid indecision, which must have heated their enemies, in proportion as it cooled their friends. The truckling, time-serving policy which they observed on this occasion, deprived the Girondists of almost all chance of forming a solid and substantial interest in the country. By a bold, open, and manly defence of the King, they would have done honour to themselves as public men, willing to discharge their duty at the risk of their lives. They would have been sure of whatever number could be gathered, either of Royalists, who were beginning to raise a head in Bretagne and La Vendée, or of Constitutionalists, who feared the persecution of the Jacobins. The materials were already kindled for those insurrections, which afterwards broke out at Lyons, Marseilles, Toulon, and generally through the south and west of France. They might have brought up five or six thousand Federates from the departments, and the force would then have been in their own hands. They might, by showing a bold and animated front, have regained possession of the national guard, which was only prevented by a Jacobin commander and his staff officers, as well as by their timidity, from throwing off a yoke so bloody and odious as that which they were groaning under. But to dare this, it was necessary that they should have the encouragement of the Convention; and that body, managed as it was by the Girondists, showed a timorous unwillingness to support the measures of the Jacobins, which implied their dislike indeed, but also evinced their fear.

ROYAL FAMILY IN THE TEMPLE

Meantime the King, with the Queen, his sister, and their children, the Dauphin and the Princess Royal, remained in the tower of the Temple, more uncomfortably lodged, and much more harshly treated than state prisoners before the Revolution had been in the execrable Bastile.[331] The royal prisoners were under the especial charge of the Commune of Paris, who, partly from their gross ignorance, partly from their desire to display their furious Jacobinical zeal, did all in their power to embitter their captivity.

Pétion, whose presence brought with it so many cruel recollections, studiously insulted him by his visits to the prison. The municipal officers, sent thither to ensure the custody of the King's person, and to be spies upon his private conversation, were selected among the worst and most malignant Jacobins. His efforts at equanimity, and even civility, towards these brutal jailors, were answered with the most gross insolence. One of them, a mason, in his working dress, had thrown himself into an arm-chair, where, decorated with his municipal scarf, he reposed at his ease. The King condescended to ask him, by way of conversation, where he wrought. He answered gruffly, "at the church of Saint Genevieve."—"I remember," said the King, "I laid the foundation stone—a fine edifice; but I have heard the foundation is insecure."—"It is more sure," answered the fellow, "than the thrones of tyrants." The King smiled and was silent. He endured with the same patience the insolent answer of another of these officials. The man not having been relieved at the usual and regular hour, the King civilly expressed his hopes that he would find no inconvenience from the delay. "I am come here," answered the ruffian, "to watch your conduct, not for you to trouble yourself with mine. No one," he added, fixing his hat firm on his brow, "least of all you, have any business to concern themselves with it." We have seen prisons, and are sure that even the steeled jailor, accustomed as he is to scenes of distress, is not in the habit, unprovoked and wantonly, of answering with reproach and insult such ordinary

---

[331] The reader may compare the account which Marmontel gives of his residence in the Bastile, with the faithful Cléry's narrative of Louis's captivity in the Temple.—S.

expressions of civility, when offered by the worst criminals. The hearts of these men, who, by chance as it were, became dungeon-keepers, and whose first captive had been many years their King, must have been as hard as the nether millstone.[332]

While such scenes occurred within the prison, those who kept watch without, either as sentinels or as patrols of the Jacobins, (who maintained stern vigilance in the environs of the prison,) were equally ready to contribute their share of vexation and insult. Pictures and placards, representing the royal family under the hands of the executioner, were pasted up where the King and Queen might see them. The most violent patriotic songs, turning upon the approaching death of Monsieur and Madame Veto, were sung below their windows, and the most frightful cries for their blood disturbed such rest as prisoners can obtain. The head of the Princess of Lamballe was brought under their window on the 3d September, and one of the municipal officers would have enticed the royal family to the window that they might see this ghastly spectacle, had not the other, "of milder mood," prevented them from complying. When questioned concerning the names of these two functionaries by some less savage persons, who wished to punish the offending ruffian, Louis would only mention that of the more humane of the two; so little was this unhappy prince addicted to seek revenge, even for the most studied cruelties practised against him.[333]

The conduct of the Community increased in rigour, as the process against Louis seemed to draw nearer. The most ordinary points of personal accommodation were made subjects of debate ere they could be granted, and that upon the King's being permitted to shave himself, lasted a long while. Every article was taken from him, even to his toothpick and penknife, and the Queen and princesses

---

[332] Cléry, p. 55; Thiers, tom. iii., p. 223; Mignet, tom. i., p. 234; Lacretelle, tom. x., p. 141.

[333] "The 3d of September, at three o'clock, just after dinner, the most horrid shouts were heard. The officer on guard in the room behaved well: he shut the door and the window, and even drew the curtains, to prevent their seeing any thing. Several officers of the guard and of the municipality now arrived: the former insisted that the King should show himself at the windows; fortunately, the latter opposed it; but, on his Majesty's asking what was the matter, a young officer of the guard replied, 'Well! since you will know, it is the head of Madame de Lamballe that they want to show you.' At these words the Queen was overcome with horror: it was the only occasion in which her firmness abandoned her."—Duchesse d'Angoulême, *Private Memoirs*, p. 18.

were deprived of their scissors and housewives. This led to a touching remark of Louis. He saw his sister, while at work, obliged to bite asunder a thread which she had no means of cutting, and the words escaped him, "Ah! you wanted nothing in your pretty house at Montreuil."—"Dearest brother," answered the princess, whose character was that of sanctity, purity of thought, and benevolence, "can I complain of any thing, since Heaven has preserved me to share and to comfort, in some degree, your hours of captivity?" It was, indeed, in the society of his family that the character of Louis shone to the greatest advantage; and if, when on the throne, he did not always possess the energies demanded of his high situation, in the dungeon of the Temple misfortune threw around him the glories of a martyr. His morning hours were spent in instructing or amusing the young dauphin, a task for which the King's extensive information well qualified him. The captives enjoyed, as they best might, a short interval, when they were permitted to walk in the gardens of the Temple, sure to be insulted (like Charles I. in the same situation) by the sentinels, who puffed volumes of tobacco-smoke in their faces as they passed them, while others annoyed the ears of the ladies with licentious songs, or the most cruel denunciations.[334]

All this Louis and his family endured with such sainted patience, that several who obtained access to his person were moved by the spectacle of royalty reduced to a situation so melancholy, yet sustained with such gentleness and fortitude. Some of the municipal officers themselves became melted, and changed their ideas of the King, when they beheld him in so new and singular a light.

Stories of the insults which he daily received, and of the meekness with which he sustained them, began to circulate among the citizens of the higher classes; and, joined to their fear of falling completely under the authority of the Sans-Culottes, led many of the Republicans to cast back their thoughts to the constitution of 1791, with all its faults, and with its monarchical executive government.

The more wise and sensible of the Girondists began to suspect that they had been too hasty in erecting their favourite

---

[334] Cléry, pp. 60, 142.

republic, on ground incapable of affording a sound and secure foundation for such an edifice. Buzot gives testimony to this, dated later, no doubt, than the period we are treating of; but the grounds of the reasoning existed as much at the King's trial as after the expulsion of the Girondists. The passage is remarkable. "My friends," says this distinguished Girondist, "preserved a long time the hopes of establishing a republic in France, even when all seemed to demonstrate that the enlightened classes, whether from prejudice or from just reasoning, felt indisposed to that form of government. That hope did not forsake my friends when the most wicked and the vilest of men obtained possession of the minds of the inferior classes, and corrupted them by the opportunities they offered of license and pillage. My friends reckoned on the lightness and aptitude to change proper to the French character, and which they considered to be peculiarly suitable to a republican nation. I have always considered that conclusion as entirely false, and have repeatedly in my heart despaired of my darling wish to establish a republic in my country." In another place he says, "It must not be dissembled that the majority of Frenchmen earnestly desired royalty, and the constitution of 1791. In Paris, the wish was general, and was expressed most freely, though only in confidential society, and among private friends. There were only a few noble and elevated minds who felt themselves worthy to be Republicans, and whom the example of the Americans had encouraged to essay the project of a similar government in France, the country of frivolity and mutability. The rest of the nation, with the exception of the ignorant wretches, without either sense or substance, who vomited abuse against royalty, as at another time they would have done against a commonwealth, and all without knowing why,—the rest of the nation were all attached to the constitution of 1791, and looked on the pure Republicans as a very well-meaning kind of madmen."[335]

In these lines, written by one of the most sincere of their number, we read the condemnation of the Girondists, who, to adventure the precarious experiment of a republic, in which they themselves saw so many difficulties, were contented to lend their arms and countenance to the destruction of that very government, which they knew to be desired by all the enlightened classes of

---

[335] See Mémoires de Buzot, par Guadet, p. 87.

France except themselves, and which demolition only made room for the dreadful triumvirate,—Danton, Robespierre, and Marat.

LOUIS SEPARATED FROM HIS SON

But we also see, from this and other passages, that there existed feelings, both in Paris and in the departments, which, if the Convention had made a manly appeal to them, might have saved the King's life, and prevented the Reign of Terror. There began to arise more obvious signs of disaffection to the rulers, and of interest in the King's fate. These were increased when he was brought before the Convention for examination—an occasion upon which Louis was treated with the same marked appearance of premeditated insult, which had been offered to him when in his dungeon. He had as yet been allowed to enjoy the society of his son, though his intercourse with the other members of the family had been much abridged. He was passionately attached to this unhappy son, who answered his affection, and showed early token of talents which were doomed never to blossom. It was the cruel resolution of his jailors to take the boy from his father on the very morning [December 11] when Louis was to undergo an interrogatory before the Convention. In other words, to give the deepest blow to his feelings, at the very moment when it was necessary he should combine his whole mental powers for defending his life against his subtle and powerful enemies.

This cruel measure produced in some respect the effect desired. The King testified more deep affliction than he had yet manifested. The child was playing at the game called Siam with his father, and by no effort could the dauphin get beyond the number *sixteen*. "That is a very unlucky number," said the child. This petty omen seemed soon accomplished by the commissioners of the Assembly, who, without deigning further explanation than that Louis must prepare to receive the Mayor of Paris, tore the child from his father, and left him to his sorrow. In about two hours, during which the trampling of many horses was heard, and a formidable body of troops with artillery were drawn up around the prison, the mayor appeared, a man called Chambon, weak and illiterate, the willing tool of the ferocious Commune in which he presided. He read to the King the decree of the Convention, that Louis Capet should be brought to their bar. "Capet," answered Louis, "is not my name—it was that of one of my ancestors. I could have wished, sir, that I had not been deprived of the society of my son during the two hours I have expected you, but it is only of a piece with the usage I have experienced for four months. I will attend you to the Convention, not as acknowledging their right to summon me, but because I yield to the superior power of my enemies."[336]

The crowd pressed much on the King during the passage from the Temple to the Tuileries, where the Convention had now established their sittings, as men who had slain and taken possession. Loud cries were heard, demanding the life of the tyrant; yet Louis preserved the most perfect composure, even when he found himself standing as a criminal before an assembly of his native subjects, born most of them in a rank which excluded them from judicial offices, till he himself had granted the privilege.[337]

"Louis," said the president—the versatile, timorous, but subtle Barrère, "be seated."[338] The King sat down accordingly, and listened without apparent emotion to a long act of accusation, in which every accident that had arisen out of the Revolution was gravely charged as a point of indictment against the King. He replied by short laconic answers, which evinced great presence of mind and composure, and alleged the decrees of the National Assembly as authority for the affair of Nancy, and the firing on the people in the Champ-de-Mars, both of which were urged against him as aggressions on the people. One or two replies we cannot omit inserting.

---

[336] Cléry, p. 153.
[337] "Before the King entered, Barrère recommended tranquillity to the Assembly, 'in order that the guilty man might be awed by the silence of the tomb.'"—Lacretelle, tom. x., p. 174.
[338] "When the president said to his King, '*Louis, asseyez vous!*' we feel more indignation even than when he is accused of crimes which he had never committed. One must have sprung from the very dust not to respect past obligations, particularly when misfortune has rendered them sacred; and vulgarity joined to crime inspires us with as much contempt as horror."—De Staël, vol. ii., p. 84.

"You are accused," said the president, "of having authorised money to be distributed to poor unknowns in the suburb of Saint Antoine. What have you to reply?"—"That I know no greater pleasure," answered Louis, "than in giving assistance to the needy."—"You held a review of the Swiss at five o'clock in the morning of the 10th of August."—"I did," replied the King, "review the troops that were about my person. It was in presence of the constituted authorities, the department, and the Mayor of Paris. I had sent in vain to request from the Convention a deputation of its members, and I came with my family to place myself in their hands."—"Why did you double the strength of the Swiss Guards at that time!" demanded the president.—"It was done with the knowledge of all the constituted authorities," said the King, in a tone of perfect composure; "I was myself a constituted authority, it was my duty to defend my office."—"You have caused," said the president, "the blood of Frenchmen to be shed. What have you to reply?"—"It was not *I* who caused it," answered Louis, speaking with more emphasis than he had before used.

The King was carried back to his prison, amid threats and abuse from the same banditti whose ranks he had before traversed.

In replying to the articles alleged against him, Louis had followed a different course from Charles, who refused to plead before the tribunal at which he was arraigned. The latter acted with the high spirit of a prince, unwilling to derogate from the honour of the crown he had worn; the former, as a man of honour and probity, was desirous of defending his character wherever it should be attacked, without stopping to question the authority of the court which was met to try him.

A great tumult followed in the Assembly the moment the King had withdrawn. The Jacobins became sensible that the scene which had just passed had deeply affected many of the neutral party, and was not unlikely to influence their final votes. They demanded an instant decree of condemnation, and that in the name of the oppressed people. "You who have heard the tyrant," said Billaud-Varennes, "ought in justice to hear the people whom he has oppressed." The Convention knew well what was meant by the appearance of the people at the bar, and while they trembled at this threat, Duhem[339] exclaimed, "I move that Louis be hung this very night." Some received this with a triumphant laugh; the majority, however, retained too much sense of shame to permit themselves to be hurried farther that evening. They indulged the King with the selection of counsel to defend him.[340]

The monarch, on returning to his prison, had found he was doomed to solitary confinement. All intercourse with his family was denied him. He wept, but neither wife, sister, nor child, was permitted to share his tears. It was for the fate of his son that he showed the deepest interest. Yet, anxious as his apprehensions were, they could not reach the extremities to which the child was reduced. The heart of man could not have imagined the cruelty of his lot.

LOUIS CHOOSES HIS COUNSEL

Louis chose for his counsel two lawyers of celebrity, carefully selecting such as he thought would incur least risk of danger by the task imposed. One of these, Tronchet,[341] was too sensible to the honour of his profession to hesitate a moment in accepting the perilous office; but the other, Target, refused to undertake it. The phrase used by this unworthy jurisconsult, in his letter to the President of the Convention, seemed to involve the King's condemnation. "A free Republican," he said, "ought not to undertake functions of which he feels himself incapable." Timid as the Convention was, this excuse was heard with disapprobation. It

---

[339] Duhem was born at Lille in 1760. He afterwards practised physic at Quesnoi. After the amnesty of Oct., 1795, he returned to his profession, and died in 1807, at Mentz.
[340] Mignet, tom. i., p. 235; Lacretelle, tom. x., p. 179.
[341] One of Napoleon's first acts on becoming first consul, was to place Tronchet at the head of the Court of Cassation. "Tronchet," he said, "was the soul of the civil code, as I was its demonstrator. He was gifted with a singularly profound and correct understanding, but he could not descend to developements."-Las Cases, vol. ii., p. 234. Tronchet died in 1806, and was buried in the Pantheon.

was declaring, that the defence of the King was untenable by any friend of the present system.[342]

Several persons offered their services[343] with voluntary devotion, but the preference was claimed by Lamoignon-Malesherbes,[344] who, twice called by Louis to be a member of his council, when the office was the object of general ambition, alleged his right to a similar function, when others might reckon it dangerous.[345] This burst of honourable self-devotion awakened a sentiment of honour in the Convention, which, could it have lasted, might have even yet prevented a great national crime.

Paris began to show symptoms of returning interest in the person of Louis. The oft-repeated calumnies against him seemed to lose their influence on all but the ignorant multitude, and hired bandits. The honest devotion of Malesherbes, whose character was known through the nation as a man of talent, honour, and probity, reflected a forcible light on that of his royal client, who had, in the hour of need, found such a defender.[346] Desèze, an excellent lawyer, was afterwards added to the King's band of counsel;[347] but the King gained little more by this indulgence, excepting the consolation of communicating with such men as Malesherbes and his two

---

[342] "Cambacérès declared, that Target's example endangered public morality. Target attempted in vain to repair the disgrace, by publishing a short defence of the King."—Lacretelle, tom. x., p. 182.

[343] "Tronson du Coudrai, who perished in the deserts of Sinamari; Guillaume, the courageous author of the petition of the twenty thousand; Huet de Guerville; Sourdat de Troyes; and Madame Olympe de Gouges.—Lalli de Tolendal, Malouet, and Necker published admirable pleadings for Louis, but the Convention would not allow them to be read."—Lacretelle, tom. x., p. 185.

[344] See *ante*.

[345] "Je lui dois le même service, lorsque c'est une fonction que bien des gens trouvent dangereuse."—See his letter to the President of the Convention in Lacretelle, tom. x., p. 182.

[346] "The first time M. Malesherbes entered the Temple, the King clasped him in his arms, and exclaimed, with tears in his eyes, 'Ah! is it you, my friend! you see to what the excess of my love for the people has brought me, and the self-denial which induced me to consent to the removal of the troops intended to protect my throne and person, against the designs of a factious assembly: you fear not to endanger your own life to save mine; but all will be useless: they will bring me to the scaffold: no matter; I shall gain my cause, if I leave an unspotted memory behind me."—Hue, *Dernières Années de la Vie de Louis XVI.*, p. 42.

[347] Desèze was born at Bourdeaux in 1750. He accepted no office under Napoleon; but on the restoration of the Bourbons he was appointed First President of the Court of Cassation, and afterwards created a peer of France. He died at Paris in 1828.

associates, at a time when no other friend was suffered to approach him, excepting the faithful Cléry, his valet-de-chambre.[348]

The lawyers entertained some hopes, and, in the spirit of their profession, exulted when they saw how facts contradicted the charges of the prosecutors. "Moderate your satisfaction, my friends," said Louis; "all these favourable circumstances are well known to the gentlemen of the Convention, and if they considered them as entitled to weight in my favour, I should not be in this difficulty. You take, I fear, a fruitless task in hand, but let us perform it as a last duty." When the term of his second appearance at the Convention arrived, he expressed anxiety at the thoughts of appearing before them with his beard and hair overgrown, owing to his being deprived of razors and scissors. "Were it not better your Majesty went as you are at present," said the faithful Cléry, "that all men may see the usage you have received?"—"It does not become me," answered the King, "to seek to obtain pity."[349] With the same spirit, he commanded his advocates to avoid all appeals to the passions or the feelings of the judges and audience, and to rest his defence exclusively upon logical deductions from the evidence produced.[350]

When summoned to the Convention, [Dec. 26,][351] Louis was compelled to wait for a time in the outer hall, where he walked about conversing with his counsel. A deputy who passed, heard Malesherbes during this intercourse use to his royal client the

---

[348] Cléry we have seen and known, and the form and manners of that model of pristine faith and loyalty can never be forgotten. Gentlemanlike and complaisant in his manners, his deep gravity and melancholy features announced that the sad scenes in which he had acted a part so honourable, were never for a moment out of his memory.—S.—Cléry died at Hitzing, near Vienna, in 1809. In 1817, Louis XVIII. gave letters of nobility to his daughter.
[349] Cléry, p. 187.
[350] "When the pathetic peroration of M. Desèze was read to the King, the evening before it was to be delivered to the Assembly, 'I have to request of you,' he said, 'to make a painful sacrifice; strike out of your pleading the peroration. It is enough for me to appear before such judges, and show my entire innocence; I will not move their feelings.'"—Lacretelle, tom. x., p. 197.
[351] "The King was conveyed in the mayor's carriage. He evinced, on the way, as much coolness as on former occasions; spoke of Seneca, Livy, and the public hospitals; and addressed himself, in a delicate vein of pleasantry, to one of the municipality, who sat in his carriage with his hat on."—Thiers, tom. iii., p. 277.

courtesies of "*Sire—Your Majesty.*" "What renders you so bold," he said, "that you utter these prohibited expressions?"—"Contempt of life," answered the generous Malesherbes.[352]

OPENING SPEECH OF DESEZE

Deséze opened his case with great ability. He pleaded with animation the right which the King had to the character of inviolability, a right confirmed to him by the Legislative Assembly after the flight to Varennes, and which implied a complete indemnity for that crime, even supposing a journey from his capital in a post carriage, with a few attendants, could be deemed criminal. But he urged that, if the Convention did not respect his inviolability—if, in a word, they did not consider him as a King, he was then entitled to the formal securities provided for every citizen by the laws. He ridiculed the idea that, with a trifling force of Swiss, Louis could meditate any serious injury against the Convention. "He prepared," said Deséze, "for his defence, as you citizens would doubtless do, when you heard that an armed multitude were on their way to surprise you in your sanctuary." He closed an excellent pleading with an enumeration of the benefits which Louis had conferred on the French nation, and reminded them that their King had given them liberty so soon as they desired to be free. Louis himself said a few words with much firmness.[353] He was remanded to the Temple, and a stormy debate commenced.

---

[352] Lacretelle, tom. x., p. 199.
[353] "You have heard my defence; I will not recapitulate it; when addressing you, probably for the last time, I declare that my conscience has nothing to reproach itself with, and that my defenders have said nothing but the truth. I have no fears for the public examination of my conduct; but my heart bleeds at the accusation brought against me, of having been the cause of the misfortunes of my people; and, most of all, of having shed their blood on the 10th of August. The multiplied proofs I have given, in every period of my reign, of my love for my people, and the manner in which I have conducted myself towards them, might, I had hoped, have saved me from so cruel an imputation."—Thiers. tom. iii., p. 281.
"The King withdrew with his defenders. He embraced M. Deséze, and exclaimed, 'This is indeed true eloquence! I am tranquil.—I shall at least have an honoured memory.—The French will regret my death.'"—Lacretelle, tom. x., p. 210.

DEBATE

At first, the Jacobins attempted to carry all by a clamorous demand of the vote. Lanjuinais replied to them with unexpected spirit, charged them with planning and instigating the assault on the 10th of August, and then with turning on the King the blame which justly lay with themselves alone. Dreadful outcries followed this true and intrepid speech. "Let the friends of the despot die with him!" was the general exclamation of the Jacobins; "to the Abbaye—to the scaffold with the perjured deputy, who slanders the glorious 10th of August!"—"Be it so," answered Lanjuinais; "better death, than the crime of pronouncing an unjust sentence."

The Girondists were too much themselves accessory to the attack on the Tuileries to follow this bold and manly line of defence, and Lanjuinais stood unsupported in his opinion.

Saint Just and Robespierre eagerly called for a doom of death. The former accused the King of a design to cheat the people out of their liberties by a pretended show of submission to their will, and an affected moderation in exercising his authority. On the 10th of August, (he had the effrontery to state this,) the King, entering the hall of the Legislature with armed followers, (the small escort who had difficulty in protecting him through the armed crowd,) had violated the asylum of the laws. "Besides," as he triumphantly concluded, "was it for a people who had declared war against all tyrants, to sorrow for the fate of their own?"[354] Robespierre openly disowned the application of legal forms, and written rubrics of law, to such a case as was before the Convention.[355] The people who had asserted their own right in wresting the sceptre from the hands of Louis, had a right to punish him for having swayed it. He talked of the case being already decided by the unanimous voice and act of

---

[354] "St. Just, after having searched in vain for authentic facts against the King, finished by declaring, that 'no one could reign innocently: and nothing could better prove the necessity of the inviolability of kings than this maxim; for there is no king who might not be accused in some way or another, if there were no constitutional barrier placed around him.'"—De Staël, vol. ii., p. 86.

[355] "Il est des principes indestructibles, supérieurs aux rubriques consacrées par l'habitude et les préjugés."

the people, from whom all legal authority emanated, and whose authority was paramount to that of the Convention, which were only their representatives.

Vergniaud, the most eloquent of the Girondists, found nothing better to propose, than that the case of Louis should be decided by an appeal to the nation. He alleged that the people, who, in solemn federation had sworn, in the Champ-de-Mars, to recognise the Constitution, had thereby sworn the inviolability of the King. This was truly said; but, such being the case, what right had the Convention to protract the King's trial by sending the case from before themselves to the people? If his inviolability had been formally admitted and sworn to by the nation, what had the Convention more to do than recognise the inviolability with which the nation had invested the monarch, and dismiss him from the bar accordingly?

The explanation lay here;—that the eloquent orator was hampered and constrained in his reasoning, by the difficulty of reconciling his own conduct, and that of his associates, to the principles which he was now willing to adopt as those that were just and legal. If the person of the King was indeed inviolable, what was to be thought of their consistency, who, by the means of their daring and devoted associates, Barbaroux and Rebecque, had actually brought up the force of Marseillois, who led the van, and were, in fact, the efficient and almost the only means by which the palace of that inviolable sovereign was stormed, his guards slaughtered, his person committed to prison, and, finally, his life brought in danger? It was the obvious and personal answer arising out of their own previous manœuvres, the *argumentum ad hominem*, as it is called by logicians, which hung a padlock on the lips of the eloquent Vergniaud, while using the argument which, in itself most just and true, was irreconcilable with the revolutionary measures to which he had been an express party. "Do not evil, that good may come of it," is a lesson which may be learned, not indeed in the transcendental philosophy which authorises the acting of instant and admitted wrong, with the view of obtaining some distant, hypothetical, and contingent good; but in the rules of Christian faith and true philosophy, which commands that each case be weighed on its own circumstances, and decided upon the immutable rules of right or wrong, without admitting any subterfuge founded on the hope of remote contingencies and future consequences.

But Vergniaud's oratory was freed from these unhappy trammels, when, with the fervour of a poet, and the inspiration of a prophet, he declaimed against the faction of Jacobins, and announced the consequences of that sanguinary body's ascending to supreme power, by placing their first step on the body of Louis. The picture which he drew of the coming evil seemed too horrible for reality; and yet the scenes which followed even more than realized the predictions of the baffled Republican, who saw too late and too clearly the tragic conclusion of the scenes in which he had borne so active a part.

The appeal to the people or to the nation, had been argued against by the Jacobin speakers, as opening the nearest road to civil war. Indeed it was one of the many objections to this intermediate and evasive plan, that the people of France, convened in their different bodies, were likely to come to very different conclusions on the King's impeachment. Where the Jacobin clubs were strong and numerous, they would have been sure, according to the maxim of their union, to use the compulsory but ready means of open violence, to disturb the freedom of voting on this important question, and would thus have carried by forcible measures the vote of death. In departments in which Constitutionalists and Royalists had strong interest, it was probable that force would have been repelled by force; and, upon the whole, in France, where the law had been long a dead letter, the arbitrement of the nation on the King's fate must and would have proved a bloody one.

But from that picture which must have followed the success of his party on this memorable occasion, Vergniaud endeavoured to avert the thoughts of his hearers, while he strove to fix them on the crimes and criminal ambition of the Jacobins. "It is *they* who wish civil war," he exclaimed, "who threaten with daggers the National Convention of France—they who preach in the tribune, and in the market-place, doctrines subversive of all social order. *They* are the men who desire civil war, who accuse justice of pusillanimity, because she will not strike before conviction—who call common humanity a proof of conspiracy, and accuse all those as traitors to their country who will not join in acts of robbery and assassination—those, in fine, who pervert every sentiment and principle of morality, and by the grossest flatteries endeavour to gain the popular assent and countenance to the most detestable crimes."

He dissected the arts of the demagogues in terms equally just and severe. They had been artfully referred to the Temple as the cause of every distress under which the populace laboured; after the death of Louis, which they so eagerly pursued, they would have the same reasons and the same power for directing the odium of every distress or misfortune against the Convention, and making the representatives of France equally obnoxious to the people, as they had now rendered the dethroned King. He concluded with a horrible picture of Paris under the domination of Jacobinism, which was, however, exceeded by the facts that ensued. "To what horrors," he said, "will not Paris be delivered, when she becomes the prey of a horde of desperate assassins? Who will inhabit a city, where Death and Desolation will then fix their court? Who will console the ruined citizen, stripped of the wealth he has honourably acquired, or relieve the wants of his family, which his exertions can no longer supply? Go in that hour of need," he continued, "and ask bread of those who have precipitated you from competence into ruin, and they will answer, 'Hence! dispute with hungry hounds for the carcasses of those we have last murdered—or, if you would drink, here is the blood we have lately shed—other nourishment we have none to afford you!'"

The eloquence of Vergniaud,[356] and the exertions of his associates, were in vain. Barrère, the auxiliary of the Jacobins, though scarcely the partaker of their confidence, drew off as usual many of the timid host of neutrals, by alleging specious reasons, of which the convincing power lay in this, that they must consult their own safety rather than the cause of justice. The appeal to the people, on which the Girondists relied as the means of reprieving rather than saving the King—of giving their consciences the quieting

---

[356] "Vergniaud was an indolent man, and required to be stimulated; but when excited, his eloquence was true, forcible, penetrating, and sincere."—Dumont, p. 321.

opiate, that he died not by their direct agency—was rejected by 423 voices against 281. A decisive appeal was made to the Convention on the question, to what punishment the dethroned monarch should be subjected.[357]

LOUIS CONDEMNED

The bravoes of the Jacobins surrounded the place of meeting on every point of access while this final vote was called, and, to men already affrighted with their situation, added every motive of terror that words, and sometimes acts of violence, could convey. "Think not," they said, "to rob the people of their prey. If you acquit Louis, we go instantly to the Temple to destroy him with his whole family, and we add to his massacre that of all who befriended him." Undoubtedly, among the terrified deputies, there were some moved by these horrible arguments, who conceived that, in giving a vote for Louis's life, they would endanger their own, without saving him. Still, however, among this overawed and trembling band of judges, there were many whose hearts failed them as they reflected on the crime they were about to commit, and who endeavoured to find some evasion stopping short of regicide. Captivity till the peace was in general proposed as a composition. The philosophic humanity of Condorcet threw in fetters, to make the condition more acceptable to the Jacobins. Others voted for death conditionally. The most intense anxiety prevailed during the vote; and even the banditti in the tribunes suspended their usual howls, and only murmured death to the voter, when the opinion given was for the more lenient punishment. When the Duke of Orleans, who had returned from England on the fall of La Fayette, and sat as a member of the Convention, under the absurd name of Citizen L'Egalité—when this base prince was asked his vote, there was a deep pause; and when the answer proved Death, a momentary horror electrified the auditors.[358] When the voices were numbered, the direct doom was carried by a majority of fifty-three, being the difference between 387

---

[357] Thiers, tom. iii., p. 290; Lacretelle, tom. x., p. 213; Toulongeon, tom. iii., p. 187.
[358] His own death, by the guillotine, in the same year, was hardly sufficient retribution for his fiendlike conduct on this afflicting occasion.—S.

and 334. The president, Vergniaud, announced that the doom of Death was pronounced against Louis Capet.[359]

Let none, we repeat, dishonour the parallel passage in England's history, by comparing it with this disgraceful act of murder, committed by a few in rabid fury of gain, by the greater part in mere panic and cowardice. That deed, which Algernon Sidney pronounced the bravest and justest ever done in England—that *facinus tam illustre* of Milton—was acted by men, from whose principles and feelings we differ entirely; but not more than the ambition of Cromwell differed from that of the bloodthirsty and envious Robespierre, or the political views of Hutchinson and his associates, who acted all in honour, from those of the timid and pedantic Girondists.

DUMOURIEZ ARRIVES IN PARIS

In Paris there was a general feeling for the King's condition, and a wish that he might be saved; but never strong enough to arise into the resolution to effect his safety.[360] Dumouriez himself came to Paris with all the splendour of a conqueror, whose victory at Jemappes had added Belgium, as Flanders began to be called, to the

---

[359] "When, on the 17th January, M. de Malesherbes went to the Temple to announce the result of the vote, he found Louis with his forehead resting on his hands, and absorbed in a deep reverie. Without inquiring concerning his fate, he said, 'For two hours I have been considering whether, during my whole reign, I have voluntarily given any cause of complaint to my subjects; with perfect sincerity I declare, that I deserve no reproach at their hands, and that I have never formed a wish but for their happiness.'"—Lacretelle, tom. x., p. 244.
"On the 18th, the King desired me to look in the library for the volume of Hume's History which contained the death of Charles I., which he read the following days. I found, on this occasion, that, since his coming to the Temple, his Majesty had perused two hundred and fifty volumes."—Cléry, p. 216.—"On the 20th, Santerre appeared with the Executive Council. The sentence of death was read by Carat. No alteration took place in the King's countenance; I observed only, at the word 'conspiracy,' a smile of indignation appear upon his lips; but at the words, 'shall suffer the punishment of death,' the heavenly expression of his face, when he looked on those around him, showed them that death had no terrors for innocence."—Cléry, p. 222.
[360] "At the representation of the comedy called 'L'Ami des Lois' at the Français, every allusion to the King's trial was caught and received with unbounded applause. At the Vaudeville, on one of the characters in 'La Chaste Susanne' saying to the two Elders, 'You cannot be accusers and judges at the same time,' the audience obliged the actor to repeat the passage several times."—Cléry, p. 204.

French nation; and there can be no doubt, that whatever might be his ulterior design, which his situation and character render somewhat doubtful, his purpose was, in the first place, to secure the person of Louis from farther danger or insult. But conqueror as he was, Dumouriez, though more favourably placed than La Fayette had been upon a similar attempt, was far from being, with respect to Paris, in the same independent situation in which Cromwell had been to London, or Cæsar to Rome.

The army with which he had accomplished his victories was yet but half his own. Six commissioners from the Convention, Danton himself being the principal, had carefully remained at his head quarters, watching his motions, controlling his power, encouraging the private soldiers of each regiment to hold Jacobin clubs exclusive of the authority of the general, studiously placing in their recollection at every instant, that the doctrines of liberty and equality rendered the soldier to a certain point independent of his commander; and reminding them that they conquered by the command of Dumouriez, indeed, but under the auspices of the Republic, to whom the general, as they themselves, was but a servant and factor.[361] The more absolute the rule of a community, the more do its members enjoy any relaxation of such severe bonds; so that he who can with safety preach a decay of discipline to an army, of which discipline is the very essence, is sure to find willing listeners. A great part of Dumouriez's army was unsettled in their minds by doctrines, which taught an independence of official authority inconsistent with their situation as soldiers, but proper, they were assured, to their quality of citizens.

The manner in which Pache, the minister of war, who, brought into office by Roland, deserted his benefactor to join the Jacobin faction, had conducted his branch of the administration, was so negligent, that it had given ground for serious belief that it was his intention to cripple the resources of the armed force (at whatever risk of national defeat) in such a manner, that if, in their disorganized state, Dumouriez had attempted to move them towards Paris for ensuring the safety of Louis, he should find them

---

[361] Dumouriez, vol. iii., p. 278; Jomini, tom. ii., p. 265.

unfit for such a march.³⁶² The army had no longer draught-houses for the artillery, and was in want of all with which a regular body of forces should be supplied. Dumouriez, according to his own account, both from the want of equipments of every kind, and from the manner in which the Jacobin commissioners had enfeebled the discipline of his troops, could not have moved towards Paris without losing the command of the army, and his head to boot, before he had got beyond the frontiers of Belgium.

Dumouriez had detached, however, according to his own statement, a considerable number of officers and confidential persons, to second any enterprise which he might find himself capable of undertaking in the King's behalf. While at Paris, he states that he treated with every faction in turn, attempting even to move Robespierre; and through means of his own intimate friend Gensonné³⁶³ he renewed his more natural connexions with the Girondists. But the one party were too determined on their bloody object to be diverted from it; the other, disconcerted in viewing the result of their timid and ambiguous attempt to carry through an appeal to the people, saw no further chance of saving the King's life otherwise than by the risk of their own, and chose rather to be executioners than victims.

Among the citizens of Paris, many of whom Dumouriez states himself to have urged with the argument, that the Convention, in assuming the power of judging the King, had exceeded the powers granted to them by the nation, he found hearers, not indeed uninterested or unmoved, but too lukewarm to promise efficient assistance. The citizens were in that state, in which an English poet has said of them,—

---

³⁶² "The peculation, or the profuse expenditure, at least, that took place in the war department during Pache's administration, was horrible. In the twenty-four hours that preceded his dismission, he filled up sixty different places with all the persons he knew of who were base enough to pay their court to him, down to his very hair-dresser, a blackguard boy of nineteen, whom he made a muster-master."—Mad. Roland, part i., p. 140.
³⁶³ Born at Bourdeaux in 1758—he was involved in the fall of the Girondists, and guillotined 31st Oct., 1793.

"Cold burghers must be struck, and struck like flints, Ere their hid fire will sparkle."

With the natural sense of right and justice, they perceived what was expected of them; but felt not the less the trammels of their situation, and hesitated to incur the fury of a popular insurrection, which passiveness on their own part might postpone or avert. They listened to the general with interest, but without enthusiasm; implored him to choose a less dangerous subject of conversation; and spoke of the power of the Jacobins, as of the influence of a tempest, which mortal efforts could not withstand. With one man of worth and confidence, Dumouriez pressed the conversation on the meanness of suffering the city to be governed by two or three thousand banditti, till the citizen looked on the ground and blushed, as he made the degrading confession,—"I see, citizen-general, to what conclusion your argument tends; but we are cowards, and the King MUST perish. What exertion of spirit can you expect from a city, which, having under arms eighty thousand well-trained militia, suffered themselves, notwithstanding, to be domineered over and disarmed by a comparative handful of rascally Federates from Brest and Marseilles?" The hint was sufficient. Dumouriez, who was involved in much personal danger, desisted from efforts, in which he could only compromise his own safety without ensuring that of the King. He affirms, that during twenty days' residence near Paris, he witnessed no effort, either public or private, to avert the King's fate; and that the only feelings which prevailed among the higher classes, were those of consternation and apathy.

It was then especially to be regretted, that an emigration, certainly premature, had drained the country of those fiery and gallant nobles, whose blood would have been so readily ventured in defence of the King. Five hundred men of high character and determined bravery would probably have been seconded by the whole burgher-force of Paris, and might have bid open defiance to the Federates, or, by some sudden and bold attempt, snatched from their hands their intended victim. Five hundred—but five hundred—of those who were winning barren laurels under Condé, or, yet more unhappily, were subsisting on the charity of foreign nations, might at this moment, could they have been collected in Paris, have accomplished the purpose for which they themselves most desired to live, by saving the life of their unhappy sovereign. But although powerful reasons, and yet more aggrieved feelings, had recommended the emigration from that country, it operated like the common experiment of the Leyden phial, one side of which being charged with an uncommon quantity of the electrical fluid, has the effect of creating a deficiency of the same essence upon the other. In the interior of France, the spirit of loyalty was at the lowest ebb; because those upon whom it especially acted as a principle, were divided from the rest of the nation, to whom they would otherwise have afforded both encouragement and example.

The sacrifice, therefore, was to be made—made in spite of those who certainly composed the great majority of Paris, at least of such as were capable of reflection,—in spite of the commander of the army, Dumouriez,—in spite of the consciences of the Girondists, who, while they affected an air of republican stoicism, saw plainly, and were fully sensible of the great political error, the great moral sin, they were about to commit.

Undoubtedly they expected, that by joining in, or acquiescing in at least, if not authorising, this unnecessary and wanton cruelty, they should establish their character with the populace as firm and unshaken Republicans, who had not hesitated to sacrifice the King, since his life was demanded at the shrine of freedom. They were not long of learning, that they gained nothing by their mean-spirited acquiescence in a crime which their souls must have abhorred. All were sensible that the Girondists had been all along, notwithstanding their theoretical pretensions in favour of a popular government, lingering and looking back with some favour to the dethroned prince, to whose death they only consented in sheer coldness and cowardice of heart, because it required to be defended at some hazard to their own safety. The faults at once of duplicity and cowardice were thus fixed on this party; who, detested by the Royalists, and by all who in any degree harboured opinions favourable to monarchy, had their lives and offices sought after by the whole host of Jacobins in full cry, and that on account of faint-spirited wishes, which they had scarcely dared even to attempt to render efficient.

DEATH OF LOUIS XVI

On the 21st of January, 1793,[364] Louis XVI. was publicly beheaded in the midst of his own metropolis, in the *Place Louis Quinze*, erected to the memory of his grandfather. It is possible for the critical eye of the historian to discover much weakness in the conduct of this unhappy monarch; for he had neither the determination necessary to fight for his rights, nor the power of submitting with apparent indifference to circumstances, where resistance inferred danger. He submitted, indeed, but with so bad a grace, that he only made himself suspected of cowardice, without getting credit for voluntary concession. But yet his behaviour, on many trying occasions, effectually vindicated him from the charge of timidity, and showed that the unwillingness to shed blood, by which he was peculiarly distinguished, arose from benevolence, not from pusillanimity.

Upon the scaffold, he behaved with the firmness which became a noble spirit, and the patience beseeming one who was reconciled to Heaven. As one of the few marks of sympathy with which his sufferings were softened, the attendance of a confessor, who had not taken the constitutional oath, was permitted to the dethroned monarch. He who undertook the honourable but

---

[364] "At seven, the King said to me, 'You will give this seal to my son, this ring to the Queen, and assure her that it is with pain I part with it;—this little packet contains the hair of all my family, you will give her that too. Tell the Queen, my dear children, and my sister, that although I promised to see them again this morning, I have resolved to spare them the pangs of so cruel a separation; tell them how much it costs me to go without receiving their embraces once more!' He wiped away some tears; then added, in the most mournful accents, 'I charge you to bear them my last farewell.'"—Cléry, p. 249.

"On the morning of this terrible day, the princesses rose at six. The night before, the Queen had scarcely strength enough to put her son to bed. She threw herself, dressed as she was, upon her own bed, where she was heard shivering with cold and grief all night long. At a quarter-past six, the door opened; the princesses believed that they were sent for to see the King, but it was only the officers looking for a prayer-book for the King's mass; they did not, however, abandon the hope of seeing him, till the shouts of joy of the unprincipled populace came to tell them that all was over."—Duchesse d'Angoulême, p. 52.

dangerous office, was a gentleman of the gifted family of Edgeworth of Edgeworthstown; and the devoted zeal with which he rendered the last duties to Louis, had like in the issue to have proved fatal to himself.[365] As the instrument of death descended, the confessor pronounced the impressive words,—"Son of Saint Louis, ascend to Heaven!"

LOUIS'S LAST TESTAMENT

There was a last will of Louis XVI. circulated upon good authority, bearing this remarkable passage:—"I recommend to my son, should he have the misfortune to become King, to recollect, that his whole faculties are due to the service of the public; that he ought to consult the happiness of his people, by governing according to the laws, forgetting all injuries and misfortunes, and in particular those which I may have sustained. But, while I exhort him to govern under the authority of the laws, I cannot but add, that this will be only in his power, in so far as he shall be endowed with authority to cause right to be respected, and wrong punished; and

---

[365] "The procession from the Temple to the place of execution lasted nearly two hours. As soon as the carriage stopped, the King whispered to me, 'We are at the end of our journey, if I mistake not.' My silence answered that we were. One of the guards came to open the door, and the gens-d'armes would have jumped out, but the King stopped them, and leaning his arm on my knee, 'Gentlemen,' said he, with the tone of majesty, 'I recommend to you this good man; take care that after my death no insult be offered to him—I charge you to prevent it.' As soon as the King had left the carriage, three guards surrounded him, and would have taken off his clothes, but he repulsed them with dignity; he undressed himself, untied his neckcloth, opened his shirt, and arranged it himself. The path leading to the scaffold was extremely rough, and from the slowness with which the King proceeded, I feared for a moment that his courage might be failing; but what was my astonishment, when, arrived at the last step, I felt him suddenly let go my arm, and saw him cross with a firm foot the breadth of the whole scaffold; he silenced, by his look alone, fifteen or twenty drums; and I heard him, in a loud voice, pronounce distinctly these memorable words, 'I die innocent of all the crimes laid to my charge; I pardon those who have occasioned my death; and I pray to God that the blood you are going to shed may never be visited on France.' He was proceeding, when a man on horseback, in the national uniform, (Santerre,) waved his sword, and ordered the drums to beat. Upon which, the executioners, seizing the King with violence, dragged him under the axe of the guillotine, which, with one stroke, severed his head from his body."—Abbé Edgeworth, *Last Hours of Louis XVI.*, p. 84.

that, without such authority, his situation in the government must be more hurtful than advantageous to the state."[366]

Not to mingle the fate of the illustrious victims of the royal family with the general tale of the sufferers under the Reign of Terror, we must here mention the deaths of the rest of that illustrious house, which closed for a time a monarchy, that, existing through three dynasties, had given sixty-six kings to France.

It was not to be supposed, that the Queen was to be long permitted to survive her husband. She had been even more than he the object of revolutionary detestation; nay, many were disposed to throw on Marie Antoinette, almost exclusively, the blame of those measures, which they considered as counter-revolutionary. She came to France a gay, young, and beautiful princess—she found in her husband a faithful, affectionate, almost an uxorious husband. In the early years of her reign she was guilty of two faults.

In the first place, she dispensed too much with court-etiquette, and wished too often to enjoy a retirement and freedom, inconsistent with her high rank and the customs of the court. This was a great though natural mistake. The etiquette of a court places round the great personages whom it regards, a close and troublesome watch, but that very guard acts as a barrier against calumny; and when these formal witnesses are withdrawn, evil tongues are never wanting to supply with infamous reports a blank, which no testimony can be brought to fill up with the truth. No individual suffered more than Marie Antoinette from this species of slander, which imputed the most scandalous occupations to hours that were only meant to be stolen from form and from state, and devoted to the ease which crowned heads ought never to dream of enjoying.

Another natural, yet equally false step, was her interfering more frequently with politics than became her sex; exhibiting thus her power over the King, and at the same time lowering him in the eyes of his subjects, who, whatever be the auspices under which

---

[366] "The day after the execution, the municipality published the will, as a proof of the fanaticism and crimes of the King."—Lacretelle, tom. x., p. 254.

their own domestic affairs are conducted, are always scandalized if they see, or think they see, any thing like female influence directing the councils of their sovereigns. We are uncertain what degree of credit is to be given to the Memoirs of Bezenval, but we believe they approach near the truth in representing the Queen as desirous of having a party of her own, and carrying points in opposition to the ministers; and we know that a general belief of this sort was the first foundation of the fatal report, that an Austrian cabal existed in the Court of France, under the direction of the Queen, which was supposed to sacrifice the interests of France to favour those of the Emperor of Germany.

The terms of her accusation were too basely depraved to be even hinted at here. She scorned to reply to it, but appealed to all who had been mothers, against the very possibility of the horrors which were stated against her.[367] The widow of a king, the sister of an emperor, was condemned to death, dragged in an open tumbril to the place of execution, and beheaded on the 16th October, 1793. She suffered death in her thirty-ninth year.[368]

The Princess Elizabeth, sister of Louis, of whom it might be said, in the words of Lord Clarendon, that she resembled a chapel in a king's palace, into which nothing but piety and morality enter, while all around is filled with sin, idleness, and folly, did not, by the most harmless demeanour and inoffensive character, escape the miserable fate in which the Jacobins had determined to involve the whole family of Louis XVI. Part of the accusation redounded to the honour of her character. She was accused of having admitted to the apartments of the Tuileries some of the national guards, of the section of Filles de Saint Thomas, and causing the wounds to be

---

[367] "Si je n'ai pas répondu, c'est que la nature se refuse à répondre a une pareille inculpation faite à une mère." (Ici l'accusée paroit vivement émue,) "J'en appelle à toutes celles qui peuvent se trouver ici."—*Procès de Marie Antoinette*, p. 29.

[368] "Sorrow had blanched her once beautiful hair; but her features and air still commanded the admiration of all who beheld her. Her cheeks, pale and emaciated, were occasionally tinged with a vivid colour at the mention of those she had lost. When led out to execution, she was dressed in white; she had cut off her hair with her own hands. Placed in a tumbril, with her arms tied behind her, she was taken by a circuitous route to the Place de la Révolution, and she ascended the scaffold with a firm and dignified step, as if she had been about to take her place on a throne, by the side of her husband."—Lacretelle, tom. xi, p. 261.

looked to which they had received in a skirmish with the Marseillois, immediately before the 10th of August. The princess admitted her having done so, and it was exactly in consistence with her whole conduct. Another charge stated the ridiculous accusation, that she had distributed bullets chewed by herself and her attendants, to render them more fatal, to the defenders of the castle of the Tuileries; a ridiculous fable, of which there was no proof whatever. She was beheaded in May, 1794, and met her death as became the manner in which her life had been spent.[369]

We are weary of recounting these atrocities, as others must be of reading them. Yet it is not useless that men should see how far human nature can be carried, in contradiction to every feeling the most sacred, to every pleading whether of justice or of humanity. The Dauphin we have already described as a promising child of seven years old, an age at which no offence could have been given, and from which no danger could have been apprehended. Nevertheless, it was resolved to destroy the innocent child, and by means to which ordinary murders seem deeds of mercy.

DEATH OF THE DAUPHIN

The unhappy boy was put in charge of the most hard-hearted villain whom the Community of Paris, well acquainted where such agents were to be found, were able to select from their band of Jacobins. This wretch, a shoemaker called Simon, asked his employers, "What was to be done with the young wolf-whelp was he to be slain?"—"No."—"Poisoned?"—"No."—"Starved to death?"—"No."—"What then?"—"He was to be got rid of."[370] Accordingly, by a continuance of the most severe treatment; by

---

[369] "Madame Elizabeth was condemned, with many other individuals of rank. When on the tumbril, she declared that Madame de Serilli, one of the victims, had disclosed to her that she was pregnant, and was thus the means of saving her life."—Lacretelle, tom. xi., p. 424. "The assassination of the Queen and of Madame Elizabeth excited perhaps still more astonishment and horror than the crime which had been perpetrated against the person of the King; for no other object could be assigned for these horrible enormities, than the very terror which they were fitted to inspire."—De Staël, vol. ii., p. 125.
[370] Lacretelle, tom. xi., p. 233.

beating, cold, vigils, fasts, and ill usage of every kind, so frail a blossom was soon blighted. He died on the 8th of June, 1795.[371]

After this last horrible crime, there was a relaxation in favour of the daughter, and now the sole child, of this unhappy house. The Princess Royal, whose qualities have since honoured even her birth and blood, experienced, from this period, a mitigated captivity. Finally, on the 19th December, 1795, this last remaining relic of the family of Louis was permitted to leave her prison and her country, in exchange for La Fayette and others, whom, on that condition, Austria delivered from captivity. She became afterwards the wife of her cousin the Duke d'Angoulême, eldest son of the reigning monarch of France, and obtained, by the manner in which she conducted herself at Bourdeaux in 1815, the highest praise for gallantry and spirit.

---

[371] "Simon had had the cruelty to leave the poor child, absolutely alone. Unexampled barbarity! to leave an unhappy and sickly infant of eight years old, in a great room, locked and bolted in, with no other resource than a broken bell, which he never rang, so greatly did he dread the people whom its sound would have brought to him; he preferred wanting any thing and every thing to the sight of his persecutors. His bed had not been touched for six months, and he had not strength to make it himself; it was alive with bugs, and vermin still more disgusting. His linen and his person were covered with them. For more than a year he had had no change of shirt or stockings; every kind of filth was allowed to accumulate about him, and in his room; and during all that period, nothing of that kind had been removed. His window, which was locked as well as grated, was never opened; and the infectious smell of this horrid room was so dreadful, that no one could bear it for a moment. He passed his days without any kind of occupation. They did not even allow him light in the evening. This situation affected his mind as well as his body; and it is not surprising that he should have fallen into a frightful atrophy."—Duchesse d'Angoulême, p. 109.

CHAPTER XIV

Dumouriez—His displeasure at the Treatment of the Flemish Provinces by the Convention—His projects in consequence—Gains the ill-will of his Army—and is forced to fly to the Austrian Camp—Lives many years in retreat, and finally dies in England—Struggles betwixt the Girondists and Jacobins—Robespierre impeaches the Leaders of the Girondists—and is denounced by them—Decree of Accusation against Marat—Commission of Twelve—Marat acquitted—Terror of the Girondists—Jacobins prepare to attack the Palais Royal, but are repulsed—Repair to the Convention, who recall the Commission of Twelve—Louvet and other Girondist Leaders fly from Paris—Convention go forth in procession to expostulate with the People—Forced back to their Hall, and compelled to Decree the Accusation of Thirty of their Body—Girondists finally ruined—and their principal Leaders perish—Close of their History.

While the Republic was thus indulging the full tyranny of irresistible success over the remains of the royal family, it seemed about to sustain a severe shock from one of its own children, who had arisen to eminence by its paths. This was Dumouriez, whom we left victor at Jemappes, and conqueror, in consequence, of the Flemish provinces. These fair possessions, the Convention, without a moment's hesitation, annexed to the dominions of France; and proceeded to pour down upon them their tax-gatherers, commissaries, and every other denomination of spoilers, who not only robbed without ceremony the unfortunate inhabitants, but insulted their religion by pillaging and defacing their churches, set their laws and privileges at contempt, and tyrannized over them in the very manner, which had so recently induced the

Flemings to offer resistance to their own hereditary princes of the House of Austria.

Dumouriez, naturally proud of his conquest, felt for those who had surrendered to his arms upon assurance of being well treated, and was sensible that his own honour and influence were aimed at; and that it was the object of the Convention to make use of his abilities only as their implements, and to keep his army in a state of complete dependence upon themselves.

PROJECTS OF DUMOURIEZ

The general, on the contrary, had the ambition as well as the talents of a conqueror: he considered his army as the means of attaining the victories, which, without him, it could not have achieved, and he desired to retain it under his own immediate command, as a combatant wishes to keep hold of the sword which he has wielded with success. He accounted himself strongly possessed of the hearts of his soldiers, and therefore thought himself qualified to play the part of military umpire in the divisions of the state, which La Fayette had attempted in vain; and it was with this view, doubtless, that he undertook that expedition to Paris, in which he vainly attempted a mediation in behalf of the King.

After leaving Paris, Dumouriez seems to have abandoned Louis personally to his fate, yet still retaining hopes to curb the headlong course of the Revolution.

Two plans presented themselves to his fertile invention, nor can it be known with certainty to which of them he most inclined. He may have entertained the idea of prevailing upon the army to decide for the youthful Dauphin to be their Constitutional King; or, as many have thought, it may better have suited his personal views to have recommended to the throne a gallant young prince of the blood, who had distinguished himself in his army, the eldest son of the miserable Duke of Orleans.[372] Such a change of dynasty might

---

[372] Louis-Philippe, of Orleans, chosen King of the French at the Revolution of July, 1830.

be supposed to limit the wishes of the proposed sovereign to that share of power entrusted to him by the Revolution, since he would have had no title to the crown save what arose from the Constitution. But, to qualify himself in either case to act as the supreme head of the army, independent of the National Convention, it was necessary that Dumouriez should pursue his conquests, act upon the plan laid down by the ministers at Paris, and in addition to his title of victor in Belgium, add that of conqueror of Holland. He commenced, accordingly, an invasion of the latter country, with some prospect of success. But though he took Gertruydenberg, and blockaded Bergen-op-Zoom, he was repulsed from Williamstadt; and at the same time he received information that an army of Austrians, under the Prince of Saxe-Cobourg, a general of eminence, though belonging to the old military school of Germany, was advancing into Flanders. Dumouriez retreated from Holland to make a stand against these new enemies, and was again unfortunate. The French were defeated at Aix-la-Chapelle, and their new levies almost entirely dispersed. Chagrined with this disaster, Dumouriez gave an imprudent loose to the warmth of his temper. Following the false step of La Fayette, in menacing before he was prepared to strike, he wrote a letter to the Convention, threatening the Jacobin party with the indignation of his army. This was on the 12th March, 1793, and six days afterwards he was again defeated in the battle of Neerwinden.[373]

It must have been extremely doubtful, whether, in the very pitch of victory, Dumouriez possessed enough of individual influence over his army, to have inclined them to declare against the National Convention. The forces which he commanded were not to be regarded in the light of a regular army, long embodied, and engaged perhaps for years in difficult enterprises, and in foreign countries, where such a force exists as a community only by their military relations to each other; where the common soldiers knew no other home than their tents, and no other direction than the voice of their officers; and the officers no other laws than the pleasure of the general. Such armies, holding themselves independent of the civil authorities of their country, came at length, through the habit of long wars and distant conquests, to exist in the

---

[373] Dumouriez, vol. ii., p. 287; Toulongeon, tom. iii., p. 293; Lacretelle, tom. x., p. 284.

French empire, and upon such rested the foundation-stone of the imperial throne; but as yet, the troops of the Republic consisted either of the regiments revolutionized, when the great change had offered commissions to privates, and batons to subalterns,—or of new levies, who had their very existence through the Revolution, and whose common nickname of Carmagnoles,[374] expressed their Republican origin and opinions. Such troops might obey the voice of the general on the actual field of battle, but were not very amenable even to the ordinary course of discipline elsewhere, and were not likely to exchange their rooted political principles, with all the ideas of license connected with them, at Dumouriez's word of command, as they would have changed their front, or have adopted any routine military movement. Still less were they likely implicitly to obey this commander, when the *prestige* of his fortune seemed in the act of abandoning him, and least of all, when they found him disposed to make a compromise with the very foe who had defeated him, and perceived that he negotiated, by abandoning his conquests to the Austrians, to purchase the opportunity or permission of executing the counter-revolution which he proposed.

Nevertheless, Dumouriez, either pushed on by an active and sanguine temper, or being too far advanced to retreat, endeavoured, by intrigues in his own army, and an understanding with the Prince of Saxe-Cobourg, to render himself strong enough to overset the reigning party in the Convention, and restore, with some modifications, the Constitution of 1791. He expressed this purpose with imprudent openness. Several generals of division declared against his scheme. He failed in obtaining possession of the fortresses of Lisle, Valenciennes, and Condé. Another act of imprudence aggravated the unpopularity into which he began to fall with his army. Four commissioners of the Convention[375] remonstrated publicly on the course he was pursuing. Dumouriez, not contented with arresting them, had the imprudence to send them to the camp of the Austrians prisoners, thus delivering up to the public enemy the representatives of the government under

---

[374] Carmagnole was the name applied in the early period of the Revolution to a certain dance, and the song connected with it. It was afterwards given to the French soldiers who first engaged in the cause of Republicanism, and who wore a dress of a peculiar cut.
[375] Camus, Quinette, Bancal, and Lamarque.

which he was appointed, and for which he had hitherto acted, and proclaiming his alliance with the invaders whom he was commissioned to oppose.

DUMOURIEZ DEFEATED

All this rash conduct disunited the tie between Dumouriez and his army. The resistance to his authority became general, and finally, it was with great difficulty and danger that he made his escape to the Austrian camp, with his young friend the Duke de Chartres.[376]

All that this able and ambitious man saved in his retreat was merely his life, of which he spent some years afterwards in Germany, concluding it in England, a few years ago, without again making any figure in the political horizon.[377] Thus, the attempt of Dumouriez, to use military force to stem the progress of the Revolution, failed, like that of La Fayette, some months before. To use a medical simile, the imposthume, was not yet far enough advanced, and sufficiently come to a head, to be benefited by the use of the lancet.

Meanwhile, the Convention, though triumphant over the schemes of the revolted general, was divided by the two parties to whom its walls served for an arena, in which to aim against each other the most deadly blows. It was now manifest that the strife must end tragically for one of the parties, and all circumstances pointed out the Girondists as the victims. They had indeed still the command of majorities in the Convention, especially when the votes were taken by scrutiny or ballot; on which occasions the feebler deputies of the Plain could give their voice according to their consciences, without its being known that they had done so. But in open debate, and when the members voted *vivâ voce*, amongst the

---

[376] Thiers, tom. iv., p. 118; Toulongeon, tom. iii., p. 316; Mignet, tom. i., p. 258. Shortly after the flight of Dumouriez, the French army was placed by the Convention under the command of General Dampierre.

[377] Dumouriez was a man of pleasing manners and lively conversation. He lived in retirement latterly at Turville Park, near Henley upon Thames, and died, March 14, 1823, in his eighty-fifth year.—S.

intimidating cries and threats of tribunes filled by an infuriated audience, the spirit of truth and justice seemed too nearly allied to that of martyrdom, to be prevalent generally amongst men who made their own safety the rule of their own political conduct. The party, however, continued for several months to exercise the duties of administration, and to make such a struggle in the Convention as could be achieved by oratory and reasoning, against underhand intrigue, supported by violent declamation, and which was, upon the least signal, sure of the aid of actual brutal violence.

The Girondists, we have seen, had aimed decrees of the Assembly at the triumvirate, and a plot was now laid among the Jacobins, to repay that intended distinction by the actual strokes of the axe, or, failing that, of the dagger.

When the news of Dumouriez's defection arrived, the Jacobins, always alert in prepossessing the public mind, held out the Girondists as the associates of the revolted general. It was on them that they directed the public animosity, great and furious in proportion to the nature of the crisis. That majority of the Convention, which the traitor Dumouriez affirmed was sound, and with which he acted in concert, intimated, according to the Jacobins, the Girondists the allies of his treasons. They called out in the Convention, on the 8th of March, for a tribunal of judgment fit to decide on such crimes, without the delays arising from ordinary forms of pleading and evidence, and without even the intervention of a jury. The Girondists opposed this measure, and the debate was violent. In the course of the subsequent days, an insurrection of the people was prepared by the Jacobins, as upon the 20th June and 10th of August. It ought to have broken out upon the 10th of March, which was the day destined to put an end to the ministerial party by a general massacre. But the Girondists received early intelligence of what was intended, and absented themselves from the Convention on the day of peril. A body of Federates from Brest, about four hundred strong, were also detached in their favour by Kevelegan, one of the deputies from the ancient province of Bretagne, and who was a zealous Girondist. The precaution, however slight, was sufficient for the time. The men who were prepared to murder, were unwilling to fight, however strong the odds on their side; and the mustering of the Jacobin bravoes proved, on this occasion, an empty menace.

Duly improved, a discovered conspiracy is generally of advantage to the party against which it was framed. But Vergniaud, when in a subsequent sitting he denounced to the Convention the existence of a conspiracy to put to death a number of the deputies, was contented to impute it to the influence of the aristocracy, of the nobles, the priests, and the emissaries of Pitt and Cobourg; thus suffering the Jacobins to escape every imputation of that blame, which all the world knew attached to them, and to them only. He was loudly applauded. Marat, who rose after him, was applauded as loudly, and the Revolutionary Tribunal was established.[378]

Louvet, who exclaims against Vergniaud for his pusillanimity, says, that the orator alleged in his excuse, "the danger of incensing violent men, already capable of all excesses." They had come to the boar chase, they had roused him and provoked his anger, and now they felt, too late, that they lacked weapons with which to attack the irritated monster. The plot of the 10th March had been compared to that of the Catholics on the 5th November, in England. It had been described in the *Moniteur* as a horrible conspiracy, by which a company of ruffians, assuming the title of *de la Glacière*, in remembrance of the massacre of Avignon, surrounded the hall for two days, with the purpose of dissolving the National Convention by force, and putting to death a great proportion of the deputies. Yet the Convention passed over, without effective prosecution of any kind, a crime of so enormous a dye; and in doing so, showed themselves more afraid of immediate personal consequences, than desirous of seizing an opportunity to rid France of the horrible faction by whom they were scourged and menaced.

DECREE AGAINST MARAT

In the midst of next month the Jacobins became the assailants, proud, it may be supposed, of the impunity under which

---

[378] Thiers, tom. iv., p. 66; Mignet, tom. i., p. 248; Lacretelle, tom. x., p. 311.

they had been sheltered. Robespierre impeached by name the leaders of the Girondists, as accomplices of Dumouriez. But it was not in the Convention where Robespierre's force lay. Guadet, with great eloquence, repelled the charge, and in his turn denounced Robespierre and the Jacobins. He proclaimed to the Convention, that they sat and debated under raised sabres and poniards, which a moment's signal could let loose on them; and he read from the journal conducted by Marat,[379] an appeal, calling on the people to rise in insurrection. Fear and shame gave the Convention momentary courage. They passed a decree of accusation against Marat, who was obliged to conceal himself for a few days.[380]

Buzot, it may be remarked, censures this decree against Marat as impolitic, seeing it was the first innovation affecting the inviolability of the persons of the deputies. In point of principle, he is certainly right; but as to any practical effects resulting from this breach of privilege, by reprisals on the other side, we are quite sceptical. Whatever violence was done to the Girondists, at the end of the conflict, was sure to have befallen them, whether Marat had been arrested or not. Precedents were as useless to such men, as a vizard to one of their ruffians. Both could do their business barefaced.

The Convention went farther than the decree of accusation against Marat; and for the first time showed their intention to make a stand against the Jacobins. On the motion of Barrère, they nominated a commission of twelve members, some Girondists, some neutrals, to watch over and repress the movements of such citizens as should seem disposed to favour anarchy.[381]

INSURRECTION AGAINST GIRONDISTS

The Convention were not long of learning the character of the opposition which they had now defied. Pache, Mayor of Paris, and

---

[379] L'Ami du Peuple.
[380] Mignet, tom. i., p. 259; Thiers, tom. iv., p. 145; Montgaillard, tom. iv., p. 9; Lacretelle, tom. x., p. 332.
[381] Mignet, tom. i., p. 261; Lacretelle, tom. x., p. 346.

one of the worst men of the Revolution, appeared at the bar of the Convention with two thousand petitioners, as they were called. They demanded, in the name of the sections, the arrest of twenty-two of the most distinguished of the Girondist leaders. The Convention got rid of the petition by passing to the order of the day. But the courage of the anarchists was greatly increased; and they saw that they had only to bear down with repeated attacks an enemy who had no fortification save the frail defences of the law, which it was the pride of the Jacobins to surmount and to defy. Their demand of proscription against these unfortunate deputies was a measure from which they never departed; and their audacity in urging it placed that party on the defensive, who ought, in all reason to have been active in the attack.

The Girondists, however, felt the extremity to which they were reduced, and sensible of the great advantage to be attained by being the assailants in such a struggle, they endeavoured to regain the offensive.

The Revolutionary Tribunal to which Marat had been sent by the decree of accusation, knew their business too well to convict any one, much less such a distinguished patriot, who was only accused of stimulating the people to exercise the sacred right of insurrection. He was honourably acquitted, after scarcely the semblance of a trial, and brought back to his place in the Convention, crowned with a civic coronet, and accompanied by a band of such determined ruffians as were worthy to form his body-guard. They insisted on filing through the hall, while a huge pioneer, their spokesman, assured the Convention that the people loved Marat, and that the cause of Marat and the people would always be the same.[382]

Meanwhile, the committee of twelve proceeded against the Terrorists with some vigour. One of the most furious provokers of insurrection and murder was Hébert, a devoted Jacobin, substitute of the Procureur Syndic of the Community.[383] Speaking to this body, who now exercised the whole powers of magistracy in Paris, this

---

[382] Thiers, tom. iv., p. 151; Lacretelle, tom. x., p. 343.
[383] Hébert was also editor of an obscene and revolting revolutionary journal, entitled the "Père Duchêsne" which had obtained an immense circulation.

man had not blushed to demand the heads of three hundred deputies. He was arrested and committed to prison.

This decisive action ought in policy to have been followed by other steps equally firm. The Girondists, by displaying confidence, might surely have united to themselves a large number of the neutral party; and might have established an interest in the sections of Paris, consisting of men who, though timid without leaders, held in deep horror the revolutionary faction, and trembled for their families and their property, if put under the guardianship, as it had been delicately expressed, of the rabble of the Fauxbourgs. The very show of four hundred Bretons had disconcerted the whole conspiracy of the 10th of March; and therefore, with a moderate support of determined men, statesmen of a more resolute and practised character than these theoretical philosophers, might have bid defiance to the mere mob of Paris, aided by a few hundreds of hired ruffians. At the worst they would have perished in attempting to save their country from the most vile and horrible tyranny.

The Girondists, however, sat in the Convention, like wild-fowl when the hawk is abroad, afraid either to remain where they were, or to attempt a flight. Yet, as they could make no armed interest in Paris, there was much to induce them to quit the metropolis, and seek a place of free deliberation elsewhere. France, indeed, was in such a state, that had these unfortunate experimentalists possessed any influence in almost any department, they could hardly have failed to bring friends around them, if they had effected a retreat to it. Versailles seems to have been thought of as the scene of their adjournment, by those who nourished such an idea; and it was believed that the inhabitants of that town, repentant of the part they had played in driving from them the royal family and the legislative body, would have stood in their defence. But neither from the public journals and histories of the time, nor from the private memoirs of Buzot, Barbaroux, or Louvet, does it appear that these infatuated philosophers thought either of flight or defence. They appear to have resembled the wretched animal, whose chance of escape from its enemies rests only in the pitiful cries which it utters when seized. Their whole system was a castle in the air, and when it vanished they could only sit down and lament over it. On the other hand, it must be allowed to the Girondists, that the inefficiency and imbecility of their conduct was not to be attributed to personal cowardice. Enthusiasts in their political opinions, they saw their ruin approaching, waited for it, and dared it; but like that of the monarch they had been so eager to dethrone, and by dethroning whom they had made way for their own ruin, their resolution was of a passive, not an active character; patient and steady to endure wrong, but inefficient where the object was to do right towards themselves and France.

For many nights, these unhappy and devoted deputies, still possessed of the ministerial power, were so far from being able to ensure their own safety, or that of the country under their nominal government, that they had shifted about from one place of rendezvous to another, not daring to occupy their own lodgings, and usually remaining, three or four together, armed for defence of their lives, in such places of secrecy and safety as they could devise.

It was on the night preceding the 30th of May, that Louvet, with five of the most distinguished of the Girondist party, had absconded into such a retreat, more like robbers afraid of the police than legislators, when the tocsin was rung at dead of night. Rabaud de Saint Etienne, a Protestant clergyman, and one of the most distinguished of the party for humanity and resolution, received it as a death-knell, and continued to repeat, *Illa suprema dies.*

INSURRECTION OF THE 31ST OF MAY

The alarm was designed to raise the suburbs; but in this task the Jacobins do not seem to have had the usual facilities—at least, they began by putting their bloodhounds on a scent, upon which they thought them likely to run more readily than the mere murder or arrest of twenty or thirty deputies of the Convention. They devised one which suited admirably, both to alarm the wealthier citizens, and teach them to be contented with looking to their own safety, and to animate the rabble with the hope of plunder. The rumour was spread, that the section of La Butte-des-Moulins, comprehending the Palais Royal, and the most wealthy shops in

Paris, had become counter-revolutionary—had displayed the white cockade, and were declaring for the Bourbons.

Of this not a word was true. The citizens of the Palais Royal were disposed perhaps to royalty—certainly for a quiet and established government—but loved their own shops much better than the House of Bourbon, and had no intention of placing them in jeopardy either for king or kaisar. They heard with alarm the accusation against them, mustered in defence of their property, shut the gates of the Palais Royal, which admits of being strongly defended, turned cannon with lighted matches upon the mob as they approached their precincts, and showed, in a way sufficient to intimidate the rabble of Saint Antoine, that though the wealthy burgesses of Paris might abandon to the mob the care of killing kings and changing ministers, they had no intention whatever to yield up to them the charge of their counters and tills. Five sections were under arms and ready to act. Not one of the Girondist party seems to have even attempted to point out to them, that by an exertion to preserve the independence of the Convention, they might rid themselves for ever of the domination under which all who had property, feeling, or education, were rendered slaves by these recurring insurrections. This is the more extraordinary, as Raffé, the commandant of the section of La Butte-des-Moulins, had actually marched to the assistance of the Convention on the 10th of March, then, as now, besieged by an armed force.

Left to themselves, the sections who were in arms to protect order, thought it enough to provide against the main danger of the moment. The sight of their array, and of their determined appearance, far more than their three-coloured cockades, and cries of "Vive la Republique," were sufficient to make the insurgents recognise those as good citizens, who could not be convicted of *incivism* without a bloody combat.

They were, however, at length made to comprehend by their leaders, that the business to be done lay in the Hall of the Convention, and that the exertions of each active citizen were to entitle him to forty *sous* for the day's work. In the whole affair there was so much of cold trick, and so little popular enthusiasm, that it is difficult to believe that the plotters might not have been countermined and blown to the moon with their own petard, had there been active spirit or practical courage on the side of those who were the assailed party. But we see no symptoms of either. The Convention were surrounded by the rabble, and menaced in the grossest terms. Under the general terror inspired by their situation, they finally recalled the Commission of Twelve, and set Hébert at liberty;—concessions which, though short of those which the Jacobins had determined to insist upon, were such as showed that the power of the Girondists was entirely destroyed, and that the Convention itself might be overawed at the pleasure of whoever should command the mob of Paris.[384]

The Jacobins were now determined to follow up their blow, by destroying the enemy whom they had disarmed. The 2d of June was fixed for this purpose. Louvet, and some others of the Girondist party, did not choose to await the issue, but fled from Paris. To secure the rest of the devoted party, the barriers of the city were shut.

On this decisive occasion, the Jacobins had not trusted entirely to the efficiency of their suburb forces. They had also under their orders about two thousand Federates, who were encamped in the Champs-Elysées, and had been long tutored in the part they had to act. They harnessed guns and howitzers, prepared grape-shot and shells, and actually heated shot red-hot, as if their purpose had been to attack some strong fortress, instead of a hall filled with the unarmed representatives of the people. Henriot, commander-general of the armed force of Paris, a fierce, ignorant man, entirely devoted to the Jacobin interest, took care, in posting the armed force which arrived from all hands around the Convention, to station those nearest to the legislative body, whose dispositions with regard to them were most notoriously violent. They were thus entirely surrounded as if in a net, and the Jacobins had little more to do than to select their victims.

The universal cry of the armed men who surrounded the Convention, was for a decree of death or outlawry against twenty-

---

[384] Thiers, tom. iv., p. 251; Toulongeon, tom. iii., p. 414; Lacretelle, tom. x., p. 356.

two members of the Girondist party, who had been pointed out, by the petition of Pache, and by subsequent petitions of the most inflammatory nature, as accomplices of Dumouriez, enemies of the good city of Paris, and traitors who meditated a federative instead of an indivisible republic. This list of proscription included the ministers.

The Convention were in a dreadful situation; it was manifest that the arm of strong force was upon them. Those who were supposed to belong to the Girondist party, were struck and abused as they entered the hall, hooted and threatened as they arose to deliver their opinion. The members were no longer free to speak or vote. There could be no deliberation within the Assembly, while such a scene of tumult and fury continued and increased without.

Barrère, leader, as we have said, of the Plain, or neutral party, who thought with the Girondists in conscience, and acted with the Jacobins in fear, proposed one of those seemingly moderate measures, which involve as sure destruction to those who adopt them, as if their character were more decisively hostile. With compliments to their good intentions, with lamentations for the emergency, he entreated the proscribed Girondists to sacrifice themselves as the unhappy subjects of disunion in the Republic, and to resign their character of deputies. The Convention, he said, "would then declare them under the protection of the law,"—as if they were not invested with that protection, while they were convicted of no crime, and clothed at the same time with the inviolability, of which he advised them to divest themselves. It was as if a man were requested to lay aside his armour, on the promise that the ordinary garments which he wore under it should be rendered impenetrable.

But a Frenchman is easily induced to do that to which he is provoked, as involving a point of honour. This treacherous advice was adopted by Isnard, Dussaux, and others of the proscribed deputies, who were thus persuaded to abandon what defences remained to them, in hopes to soften the ferocity of an enemy, too inveterate to entertain feelings of generosity.

Lanjuinais maintained a more honourable struggle. "Expect not from me," he said to the Convention, "to hear either of submission or resignation of my official character. Am I free to offer such a resignation, or are you free to receive it?" As he would have turned his eloquence against Robespierre and the Jacobins, an attempt was made by Legendre and Chabot to drag him from the tribune. While he resisted he received several blows. "Cruel men!" he exclaimed—"The Heathens adorned and caressed the victims whom they led to the slaughter—you load them with blows and insult."

Shame procured him a moment's hearing, during which he harangued the Assembly with much effect on the baseness, treachery, cruelty, and impolicy, of thus surrendering their brethren to the call of a bloodthirsty multitude from without, stimulated by a vengeful minority of their own members. The Convention made an effort to free themselves from the toils in which they were entangled. They resolved to go out in a body, and ascertain what respect would be paid to their persons by the armed force assembled around them.

FALL OF THE GIRONDISTS

They sallied forth accordingly, in procession, into the gardens of the Tuileries, the Jacobins alone remaining in the hall; but their progress was presently arrested by Henriot, at the head of a strong military staff, and a large body of troops. Every passage leading from the gardens was secured by soldiers. The president read the decree of the Assembly, and commanded Henriot's obedience. The commandant of Paris only replied by reining back his horse, and commanding the troops to stand to their arms. "Return to your posts," he said to the terrified legislators; "the people demand the traitors who are in the bosom of your assembly, and will not depart till their will is accomplished." Marat came up presently afterwards at the head of a select band of a hundred ruffians. He called on the multitude to stand firm to their purpose, and commanded the

Convention, in the name of the people, to return to their place of meeting, to deliberate, and, above all, to obey.[385]

The Convention re-entered their hall in the last degree of consternation, prepared to submit to the infamy which now seemed inevitable, yet loathing themselves for their cowardice, even while obeying the dictates of self-preservation. The Jacobins meanwhile enhanced their demand, like her who sold the books of the Sibyls. Instead of twenty-two deputies, the accusation of thirty was now demanded. Amid terror mingled with acclamations, the decree was declared to be carried. This doom of proscription passed on the motion of Couthon; a decrepid being whose lower extremities were paralysed,—whose benevolence of feeling seemed to pour itself out in the most gentle expressions, uttered in the most melodious tones,—whose sensibility led him constantly to foster a favourite spaniel in his bosom, that he might have something on which to bestow kindness and caresses,—but who was at heart as fierce as Danton, and as pitiless as Robespierre.

Great part of the Convention did not join in this vote, protesting loudly against the force imposed on them. Several of the proscribed deputies were arrested, others escaped from the hall by the connivance of their brethren; and of the official persons attached to the Convention, some, foreseeing their fate, had absented themselves from the meeting, and were already fled from Paris.

Thus fell, without a blow struck, or sword drawn in their defence, the party in the Convention which claimed the praise of acting upon pure Republican principles—who had overthrown the throne, and led the way to anarchy, merely to perfect an ideal theory. They fell, as the wisest of them admitted, dupes to their own system, and to the vain and impracticable idea of ruling a large and corrupt empire, by the motives which may sway a small and virtuous community. They might, as they too late discovered, have as well attempted to found the Capitol on a bottomless and quaking marsh, as their pretended Republic in a country like France. The violent Revolutionary expedients, the means by which they acted, were

---

[385] Thiers, tom. iv., p. 270; Lacretelle, tom. x., p. 375; Mignet, tom. i., p. 272.

turned against them by men, whose ends were worse than their own. The Girondists had gloried in their share of the triumphs of the 10th of August; yet what was that celebrated day, save an insurrection of the populace against the constituted authority of the time, as those of the 31st of May, and 2d of June, 1793, under which the Girondists succumbed, were directed against them as successors in the government? In the one case, a king was dethroned; in the other, a government, or band of ministers dismissed. And if the people had a right, as the Girondists claimed in their behalf, to act as the executioners of their own will in the one instance, it is difficult to see upon what principle their power should be trammelled in the other.

In the important process against the King, the Girondists had shown themselves pusillanimous;—desirous to save the life of a guiltless man, they dared not boldly vouch his innocence, but sheltered themselves under evasions which sacrificed his character, while they could not protect his life. After committing this great error, they lost every chance of rallying with efficacy under their standard what might remain of well-intentioned individuals in Paris and in France, who, if they had seen the Girondists, when in power, conduct themselves with firmness, would probably rather have ranked themselves in the train of men who were friends to social order, however republican their tenets, than have given way to the anarchy which was doomed to ensue.[386]

Upon all their own faults, whether of act or of omission, the unfortunate Girondists had now ample time to meditate. Twenty-two of their leading members, arrested on the fatal 2d of June, already waited their doom in prison, while the others wandered on, in distress and misery, through the different departments of France.

The fate of those who were prisoners was not very long suspended. In October they were brought to trial, and convicted of

---

[386] "The Girondists felt without doubt, at the bottom of their hearts, a keen remorse for the means which they had employed to overturn the throne; and when those very means were directed against themselves, when they recognised their own weapons in the wounds which they received, they must have reflected without doubt on that rapid justice of revolutions, which concentrates on a few instants the events of several ages."—De Staël, vol. ii., p. 122.

royalism! Such was the temper of France at the time, and so gross the impositions which might be put upon the people, that the men in the empire, who, upon abstract principle, were most averse to monarchy, and who had sacrificed even their consciences to join with the Jacobins in pulling down the throne, were now accused and convicted of being Royalists; and that at a time when what remained of the royal family was at so low an ebb, that the imprisoned Queen could not obtain the most ordinary book for the use of her son, without a direct and formal application to the Community of Paris.[387]

FATE OF THE GIRONDIST LEADERS

When the Girondists were brought before the tribunal, the people seem to have shown more interest in men, whose distinguished talents had so often swayed the legislative body, than was altogether acceptable to the Jacobins, who were induced to fear some difficulty in carrying through their conviction. They obtained a decree from the Convention, declaring that the president of the Revolutionary Tribunal should be at liberty to close the procedure so soon as the jury should have made up their minds, and without hearing the accused in their defence.[388] This frightful expedient of cutting short the debate, (*couper la parole* was the phrase,) was often resorted to on those revolutionary trials. Unquestionably, they dreaded the reasoning of Brissot, and the eloquence of Vergniaud, of which they had so long and so often experienced the thunders. One crime,—and it was a fatal offence, considering before what judicature they stood,—seems to have been made out by Brissot's own letters. It was that by which the late members attempted to effect a combination among the departments, for the purpose of counterpoising, if possible, the tremendous influence which the capital and the revolutionary part of its magistracy exercised over the Convention, whom Paris detained prisoners within her walls. This delinquency alone was well calculated to remove all scruples

---

[387] Witness the following entry in the minutes of the *Commune*, on a day, be it remarked, betwixt the 29th May and the 2d June: "Antoinette fait demander pour son fils le roman de Gil Blas de Santillane—Accordé."—S.
[388] Toulongeon, tom. iv., p. 114; Thiers, tom. iv., p. 389.

from the minds of a jury, selected from that very class of Parisians, whose dreadful importance would have been altogether annihilated by the success of such a scheme. The accused were found guilty, as conspirators against the unity and indivisibility of the Republic, and the liberty and safety of the French people.

When the sentence of death was pronounced, one of their number, Valazé, plunged a dagger in his bosom.[389] The rest suffered in terms of the sentence, and were conveyed to the place of execution in the same tumbril with the bloody corpse of their suicide colleague. Brissot seemed downcast and unhappy. Fauchet, a renegade priest, showed signs of remorse. The rest affected a Roman resolution, and went to execution singing a parody on the hymn of the Marseillois, in which that famous composition was turned against the Jacobins.[390] They had long rejected the aids of religion, which, early received and cherished, would have guided their steps in prosperity, and sustained them in adversity. Their remaining stay was only that of the same vain and speculative philosophy, which had so deplorably influenced their political conduct.

Those members of the Girondist party, who, escaping from Paris to the departments, avoided their fate somewhat longer, saw little reason to pride themselves on the political part they had chosen to act. They found the eastern and southern departments in a ferment against Paris and the Jacobins, and ready to rise in arms; but they became aware, at the same time, that no one was thinking of or regretting their system of a pure republic, the motives by which the malecontents were agitated being of a very different, and far more practical character. Great part of the nation, all at least of better feelings, had been deeply affected by the undeserved fate of the King, and the cruelty with which his family had been, and were still treated. The rich feared to be pillaged and murdered by the Jacobins; the poor suffered no less under scarcity of grain, under the depreciation of assignats, and a compulsory levy of no less than

---

[389] "The court immediately ordered that his dead body should be borne on a car to the place of execution, and beheaded with the other prisoners."—Lacretelle, tom. xi., p. 269.
[390] "Allons, enfans de la patrie, Le jour de gloire est arrivé; Contre nous, de la tyrannie Le couteau sanglant est levé." Lacretelle, tom. xi., p. 270.

three hundred thousand men over France, to supply the enormous losses of the French army. But every where the insurrections took a Royalist, and not a Republican character; and although the Girondists were received at Caen and elsewhere with compassion and respect, the votes they had given in the King's trial, and their fanatic zeal for a kind of government for which France was totally unfitted, and which those from whom they obtained refuge were far from desiring, prevented their playing any distinguished part in the disturbed districts of the West.

Buzot seems to see this in the true sense. "It is certain," he says, "that if we could have rested our pretensions upon having wished to establish in France a moderate government of that character, which, according to many well-instructed persons, best suited the people of France," (indicating a limited monarchy,) "we might have entertained hopes of forming a formidable coalition in the department of Calvados, and rallying around us all whom ancient prejudices attached to royalty."[391] As it was, they were only regarded as a few enthusiasts, whom the example of America had induced to attempt the establishment of a republic, in a country where all hopes and wishes, save those of the Jacobins, and the vile rabble whom they courted and governed, were turned towards a moderate monarchy. Buzot also observed, that the many violences and atrocities, forced levies, and other acts of oppression practised in the name of the Republic, had disgusted men with a form of government, where cruelty seemed to rule over misery by the sole aid of terror. With more candour than some of his companions, he avows his error, and admits that he would, at this closing scene, have willingly united with the moderate monarchists, to establish royalty under the safeguard of constitutional restraints.

LOUVET—RIOUFFE—BARBAROUX

Several of the deputies, Louvet, Riouffe, Barbaroux, Pétion, and others, united themselves with a body of Royalists of Bretagne, to whom General Wimpfen had given something of the name of an

---

[391] Mémoires de Buzot, p. 98.

army, but which never attained the solidity of one. It was defeated at Vernon, and never afterwards could be again assembled.

The proscribed deputies, at first with a few armed associates, afterwards entirely deserted, wandered through the country, incurring some romantic adventures, which have been recorded by the pen of their historian, Louvet. At length, six of the party succeeded in obtaining the means of transportation to Bourdeaux, the capital of that Gironde from which their party derived its name, and which those who were natives of it, remembering only the limited society in which they had first acquired their fame, had described as possessing and cherishing the purest principles of philosophical freedom. Guadet had protested to his companions in misfortune a thousand times, that if liberal, honourable, and generous sentiments were chased from every other corner of France, they were nevertheless sure to find refuge in *La Gironde*. The proscribed wanderers had wellnigh kissed the land of refuge, when they disembarked, as in a country of assured protection. But Bourdeaux was by this time no more than a wealthy trading town, where the rich, trembling before the poor, were not willing to increase their own imminent danger, by intermeddling with the misfortunes of others. All doors, or nearly so, of La Gironde itself, were shut against the Girondists, and they wandered outcasts in the country, suffering every extremity of toil and hunger, and bringing, in some cases, death upon the friends who ventured to afford them refuge.

Louvet alone escaped, of the six Girondists who took refuge in their own peculiar province. Guadet, Sailes, and the enthusiastic Barbaroux, were seized and executed at Bourdeaux, but not till the last had twice attempted suicide with his pistols. Buzot and Pétion killed themselves in extremity, and were found dead in a field of corn. This was the same Pétion who had been so long the idol of the Parisians, and who, when the forfeiture of the King was resolved on, had been heard to say with simple vanity, "If they should force *me* to become regent now, I cannot see any means by which I can avoid it." Others of this unhappy party shared the same melancholy fate. Condorcet, who had pronounced his vote for the King's life, but in perpetual fetters, was arrested, and poisoned himself. Rabaud de Saint Etienne was betrayed by a friend in whom he trusted, and was executed. Roland was found dead on the high-road, between Paris and Rouen,[392] accomplishing a prophecy of his wife, whom the Jacobins had condemned to death, and who had declared her conviction that her husband would not long survive her. That remarkable woman, happy if her high talents had, in youth, fallen under the direction of those who could better have cultivated them, made before the revolutionary tribunal a defence more manly than the most eloquent of the Girondists. The bystanders, who had become amateurs in cruelty, were as much delighted with her deportment, as the hunter with the pulling down a noble stag. "What sense," they said; "what wit, what courage! What a magnificent spectacle it will be to behold such a woman upon the scaffold!" She met her death with great firmness, and, as she passed the Statue of Liberty, on her road to execution, she exclaimed, "Ah, Liberty! what crimes are committed in thy name!"[393]

About forty-two of the Girondist deputies perished by the guillotine, by suicide, or by the fatigue of their wanderings. About twenty-four escaped these perils, and were, after many and various sufferings, recalled to the Convention, when the Jacobin influence was destroyed. They owed their fall to the fantastic philosophy and visionary theories which they had adopted, not less than to their presumptuous confidence, that popular assemblies, when actuated by the most violent personal feelings, must yield to the weight of argument, as inanimate bodies obey the impulse of external force; and that they who possess the highest powers of oratory, can, by mere elocution, take the weight from clubs, the edge from sabres, and the angry and brutal passions from those who wield them. They made no further figure as a party in any of the state changes in France; and, in relation to their experimental Republic, may remind the reader of the presumptuous champion of antiquity, who was caught in the cleft of oak, which he in vain attempted to rend

---

[392] "He had stabbed himself with a knife, concealed in his walking stick. In his pocket was found a paper, containing these words: 'Whoever you are, oh passenger! who discover my body, respect the remains of the unfortunate. They are those of a man who devoted his whole life to the service of his country. Not fear, but indignation, made me quit my retreat when I heard of the murder of my wife. I loathed a world stained with so many crimes.'"—Roland, tom. i., p. 46.

[393] Lacretelle, tom. xi., p. 277.

asunder. History has no more to say on the subject of La Gironde, considered as a party name.

Chapter XV

Views of Parties in Britain relative to the Revolution—Affiliated Societies—Counterpoised by Aristocratic Associations—Aristocratic Party eager for War with France—The French proclaim the Navigation of the Scheldt—British Ambassador recalled from Paris, and French Envoy no longer accredited in London—France declares War against England—British Army sent to Holland, under the Duke of York—State of the Army—View of the Military Positions of France—in Flanders—on the Rhine—in Piedmont—Savoy—on the Pyrenees—State of the War in La Vendée—Description of the Country—Le Bocage—Le Louroux—Close Union betwixt the Nobles and Peasantry—Both strongly attached to Royalty, and abhorrent of the Revolution—The Priests—The Religion of the Vendéans outraged by the Convention—A general Insurrection takes place in 1793—Military Organization and Habits of the Vendéans—Division in the British Cabinet on the Mode of conducting the War—Pitt—Windham—Reasoning upon the Subject—Vendéans defeated—They defeat, in their turn, the French Troops at Laval—But are ultimately destroyed and dispersed—Unfortunate Expedition to Quiberon—La Charette defeated and executed, and the War of La Vendée finally terminated—Unsuccessful Resistance of Bourdeaux, Marseilles, and Lyons, to the Convention—Siege of Lyons—Its surrender and dreadful Punishment—Siege of Toulon.

The Jacobins, by their successive victories on the 31st May and 2d June, 1793, had vanquished and driven from the field their adversaries; and we have already seen with what fury they had pursued their scattered enemies, and dealt among them vengeance and death. But the situation of the country, both in regard to external and internal relations, was so precarious, that it required the exertion of men as bold and unhesitating as those who now assumed the guidance of the power of France, to exert the energies necessary to repel foreign force, and at the same time to subdue internal dissension.

STATE OF PARTIES IN BRITAIN

We have seen that England had become, in a great measure, divided into two large parties, one of which continued to applaud the French Revolution, although the wise and good among them reprobated its excesses; while the other, with eyes fixed in detestation upon the cruelties, confiscations, and horrors of every description which it had given rise to, looked on the very name of this great change,—though, no doubt, comprehending much good as well as evil,—with the unmixed feelings of men contemplating a spectacle equally dreadful and disgusting.

The affair of the 10th of August, and the approaching fate of the King, excited general interest in Britain; and a strong inclination became visible among the higher and middling classes, that the nation should take up arms, and interfere in the fate of the unhappy Louis.

Mr. Pitt had been making up his mind to the same point; but, feeling how much his own high talents were turned to the improvement of the internal regulations and finances of the country, he hesitated for some time to adopt a hostile course, though approved by the sovereign, and demanded by a large proportion of his subjects. But new circumstances arose every day to compel a decision on this important point.

The French, whether in their individual or collective capacities, have been always desirous to take the lead among European nations, and to be considered as the foremost member of the civilized republic. In almost all her vicissitudes, France has addressed herself as much to the citizens of other countries as to those of her own; and it was thus, that in the speeches of her statesmen, invitations were thrown out to the subjects of other states, to imitate the example of the Republic, cast away the rubbish of their old institutions, dethrone their Kings, demolish their nobility, divide the lands of the Church and the aristocracy among the lower classes, and arise a free and regenerated people. In Britain, as elsewhere, these doctrines carried a fascinating sound; for Britain as well as France had men of parts, who thought themselves neglected,—men of merit, who conceived themselves oppressed,—experimentalists, who would willingly put the laws in their revolutionary crucible,—and men desirous of novelties in the Church and in the State, either from the eagerness of restless curiosity, or the hopes of bettering by the change. Above all, Britain had a far too ample mass of poverty and ignorance, subject always to be acted upon by the hope of license. Affiliated societies were formed in almost all the towns of Great Britain. They corresponded with each other, held very high and intimidating language, and seemed to frame themselves on the French model. They addressed the National Convention of France directly in the name of their own bodies, and of societies united for the same purpose; and congratulated them on their freedom, and on the manner in which they had gained it, with many a broad hint that their example would not be lost on Britain. The persons who composed these societies had, generally speaking, little pretension to rank or influence; and though they contained some men of considerable parts, there was a deficiency of any thing like weight or respectability in their meetings. Their consequence lay chiefly in the numbers who were likely to be influenced by their arguments; and these were extraordinarily great, especially in large towns, and in the manufacturing districts. That state of things began to take place in Britain, which had preceded the French Revolution; but the British aristocracy, well cemented together, and possessing great weight in the State, took the alarm sooner, and adopted precautions more effectual, than had been thought of in France. They associated together in political unions on their side, and, by the weight of influence, character, and fortune, soon obtained a superiority, which made it dangerous, or at least inconvenient, to many, whose situations in society rendered them, in some degree, dependent upon the favour of the aristocracy, to dissent violently from their opinions. The political Shibboleth, used by these associations, was a renunciation of the doctrines of the French Revolution; and they have been reproached, that this abhorrence was expressed by some of them in terms so strong, as if designed to withhold the subscribers from attempting any reformation in their own government, even by the most constitutional means. In short, while the democratical party made, in their clubs, the most violent and furious speeches against the aristocrats, the others became doubly prejudiced against reform of every description, and all who attempted to assert its propriety. After all, had this political ferment broke out in Britain at any other period, or on any other occasion, it would have probably passed away like other heart-burnings of the same description, which interest for a time, but weary out the public attention, and are laid aside and forgotten. But the French Revolution blazed in the neighbourhood like a beacon of hope to the one party, of fear and caution to the other. The shouts of the democratic triumphs—the foul means by which their successes were obtained, and the cruel use which was made of them, increased the animosity of both parties in England. In the fury of party zeal, the democrats excused many of the excesses of the French Revolution, in respect of its tendency; while the other party, in condemning the whole Revolution, both root and branch, forgot that, after all, the struggle of the French nation to recover their liberty, was, in its commencement, not only justifiable, but laudable.

The wild and inflated language addressed by the French statesmen to mankind in general, and the spirit of conquest which the nation had lately evinced, mixed with their marked desire to extend their political principles, and with the odium which they had heaped upon themselves by the King's death, made the whole aristocratic party, commanding a very large majority in both Houses of Parliament, become urgent that war should be declared against France; a holy war, it was said, against treason, blasphemy, and murder, and a necessary war, in order to break off all connexion betwixt the French Government and the discontented part of our own subjects, who could not otherwise be prevented from the most close, constant, and dangerous intercourse with them.

Another reason for hostilities, more in parallel with similar cases in history, occurred, from the French having, by a formal decree, proclaimed the Scheldt navigable. In so doing, a point had been assumed as granted, upon the denial of which the States of Holland had always rested as the very basis of their national prosperity. It is probable that this might, in other circumstances, have been made the subject of negotiation; but the difference of opinion on the general politics of the Revolution, and the mode in which it had been carried on, set the governments of France and England in such direct and mortal opposition to each other, that war became inevitable.

BRITISH AMBASSADOR RECALLED
WAR WITH ENGLAND

Lord Gower,[394] the British ambassador, was recalled from Paris, immediately on the King's execution. The prince to whom he was sent was no more; and, on the same ground, Chauvelin, the French envoy at the Court of St. James's, though not dismissed by his Majesty's government, was made acquainted that the ministers no longer considered him as an accredited person.[395] Yet, through Maret,[396] a subordinate agent, Pitt continued to keep up some correspondence with the French Government, in a lingering desire to preserve peace, if possible. What the British minister chiefly wished was, to have satisfactory assurances, that the strong expressions of a decree, which the French Convention had passed on the 19th November, were not to be considered as applicable to England. The decree was in these words: "The National Convention declares, in the name of the French nation, that it will grant fraternity and assistance to all people who wish to recover their liberty; and it charges the executive power to send the necessary orders to the generals, to give succours to such people, and to defend those citizens who have suffered, or may suffer, in the cause of liberty."—"That this decree might not remain a secret to those for whose benefit it was intended, a translation of it, in every foreign

---

[394] Afterwards Marquis of Stafford, and created Duke of Sutherland. He died in 1833.
[395] Annual Register, vol. xxxv., p. 128.
[396] In 1789, Maret published the proceedings of the States-General, under the title of "Bulletin de l'Assemblée," taking Woodfall's Parliamentary Register for his model. The success of the experiment was so great, that when Pankouke, the bookseller, projected the plan of the *"Moniteur,"* he prevailed on Maret to transfer his labours to the new journal. Such was the origin of Napoleon's well-known Duke of Bassano.

language, was ordered to be printed."[397] The Convention, as well as the ministers of France, refused every disavowal of the decree as applicable to Great Britain; were equally reluctant to grant explanation of any kind on the opening of the Scheldt; and finally, without one dissentient voice, the whole Convention, in a full meeting, [Feb. 1,] declared war upon England;[398]—which last nation is, nevertheless, sometimes represented, even at this day, as having declared war upon France.

In fact, Mr. Pitt came unwillingly into the war. With even more than his great father's ministerial talents, he did not habitually nourish the schemes of military triumph, which were familiar to the genius of Chatham, and was naturally unwilling, by engaging in an expensive war, to derange those plans of finance by which he had retrieved the revenues of Great Britain from a very low condition. It is said of Chatham, that he considered it as the best economy, to make every military expedition which he fitted out, of such a power and strength, as to overbear, as far as possible, all chance of opposition. A general officer, who was to be employed in such a piece of service, having demanded a certain body of troops, as sufficient to effect his purpose,—"Take double the number," said Lord Chatham, "and answer with your head for your success." His son had not the same mode of computation, and would, perhaps, have been more willing to have reduced the officer's terms, chaffered with him for the lowest number, and finally despatched him at the head of as small a body as the general could have been prevailed on to consider as affording any prospect of success. This untimely economy of resources arose from the expense attending the British army. They are certainly one of the bravest, best appointed, and most liberally paid in Europe; but in forming demands on their valour, and expectations from their exertions, their fellow-subjects are apt to indulge extravagant computations, from not being in the habit of considering military calculations, or being altogether aware of the numerical superiority possessed by other countries. That one Englishman will fight two Frenchmen is certain; but that he will beat them, though a good article of the popular creed, must be allowed to be more dubious; and it is not

---

[397] Annual Register, vol. xxxv., p. 153.
[398] See the Declaration, Annual Register, vol. xxxv., p. 139.

wise to wage war on such odds, or to suppose that, because our soldiers are infinitely valuable to us, and a little expensive besides, it is therefore judicious to send them in small numbers against desperate odds.

Another point, well touched by Sheridan, during the debate on the question of peace or war, was not sufficiently attended to by the British Administration. That statesman, whose perception of the right and wrong of any great constitutional question was as acute as that of any whomever of his great political contemporaries, said, "He wished every possible exertion to be made for the preservation of peace. If, however, that were impracticable, in such case, but in such case only, he proposed to vote for a vigorous war. Not a war of shifts and scraps, of timid operation, or protracted effort; but a war conducted with such energy as might convince the world that we were contending for our dearest and most valuable privileges."[399]

Of this high-spirited and most just principle, the policy of Britain unfortunately lost sight during the first years of the war, when there occurred more than one opportunity in which a home and prostrating blow might have been aimed at her gigantic adversary.

A gallant auxiliary army was, however, immediately fitted out, and embarked for Holland, with his Royal Highness the Duke of York at their head; as if the King had meant to give to his allies the dearest pledge in his power, how serious was the interest which he took in their defence.

But, though well equipped, and commanded, under the young prince, by Abercromby, Dundas, Sir William Erskine, and many other officers of gallantry and experience, it must be owned that the British army had not then recovered the depressing and disorganizing effects of the American war. The soldiers were, indeed, fine men on the parade; but their external appearance was acquired by dint of a thousand minute and vexatious attentions, exacted from them at the expense of private comfort, and which, after all, only gave them the exterior appearance of high drilling, in

---

[399] Annual Register, vol. xxxv., p. 250.—S.

exchange for ease of motion and simplicity of dress. No general system of manœuvres, we believe, had been adopted for the use of the forces; each commanding officer managed his regiment according to his own pleasure. In a field-day, two or three battalions could not act in concert, without much previous consultation; in action, they got on as chance directed. The officers, too, were acquainted both with their soldiers and with their duty, in a degree far inferior to what is now exacted from them. Our system of purchasing commissions, which is necessary to connect the army with the country, and the property of the country, was at that time so much abused, that a mere beardless boy might be forced at once through the subordinate and subaltern steps into a company or a majority, without having been a month in the army. In short, all those gigantic abuses were still subsisting, which the illustrious prince whom we have named eradicated from the British army, by regulations, for which his country can never be sufficiently grateful, and without which they could never have performed the distinguished part finally destined to them in the terrible drama, which was about to open under less successful auspices.

There hung also, like a cloud, upon the military fame of England, the unfortunate issue of the American struggle; in which the advantages obtained by regulars, against less disciplined forces, had been trifled with in the commencement, until the genius of Washington, and the increasing spirit and numbers of the continental armies, completely over-balanced, and almost annihilated, that original preponderance.

Yet the British soldiery did not disgrace their high national character, nor show themselves unworthy of fighting under the eye of the son of their monarch; and when they joined the Austrian army, under the Prince of Saxe-Cobourg, gave many demonstrations both of valour and discipline. The storming the fortified camp of the French at Famars—the battle of Lincelles—the part they bore in the sieges of Valenciennes and Condé, both of which surrendered successively to the allied forces, upheld the reputation of their country, and amounted, indeed, to what, in former wars, would have been the fruits of a very successful campaign.[400] But Europe was

---

[400] Jomini, tom. iii., pp. 163-181; Toulongeon, tom. iv., pp. 6-43.

now arrived at a time when war was no longer to be carried on according to the old usage, by the agency of standing armies of moderate numbers; when a battle lost and won, or a siege raised or successful, was thought sufficient for the active exertions of the year, and the troops on either side were drawn off into winter quarters, while diplomacy took up the contest which tactics had suspended. All this was to be laid aside; and instead of this drowsy state of hostility, nations were to contend with each other like individuals in mortal conflict, bringing not merely the hands, but every limb of the body into violent and furious struggle. The situation of France, both in internal and external relations, required the most dreadful efforts which had ever been made by any country; and the exertions which she demanded, were either willingly made by the enthusiasm of the inhabitants, or extorted by the energy and severity of the revolutionary government. We must bestow a single glance on the state of the country, ere we proceed to notice the measures adopted for its defence.

MILITARY POSITION OF FRANCE

On the north-eastern frontier of France, considerable advances had been made by the English and Hanoverian army, in communication and conjunction with the Austrian force under the Prince of Saxe-Cobourg, an excellent officer, but who, belonging to the old school of formal and prolonged war, never sufficiently considered, that a new description of enemies were opposed to him, who were necessarily to be combated in a different manner from those whom his youth had encountered, and who, unenterprising himself, does not appear either to have calculated upon, or prepared to counteract, strokes of audacity and activity on the part of the enemy.

The war on the Rhine was furiously maintained by Prussians and Austrians united. The French lost the important town of Mentz, were driven out of other places, and experienced many reverses, although Custine,[401] Moreau, Houchard,[402] Beauharnais,[403] and other general officers of high merit, had already given lustre to the arms of the Republic. The loss of the strong lines of Weissenburgh, which were carried by General Wurmser, a distinguished Austrian officer, completed the shade of disadvantage which here hung on the Republican banners.[404]

In Piedmont, the French were also unsuccessful, though the scale was less grand and imposing. The republican general Brunet[405] was unfortunate, and he was forced from his camp at Belvidere; while, on the side of Savoy, the King of Sardinia also obtained several temporary advantages.

On the Pyrenees, the Republican armies had been equally unsuccessful. A Spanish army, conducted with more spirit than had been lately the case with the troops of that once proud monarchy, had defeated the republican general Servan, and crossed the Bidassoa. On the eastern extremity of these celebrated mountains, the Spaniards had taken the towns of Port Vendre and Ollioulles.[406]

Assailed on so many sides, and by so many enemies, all of whom, excepting the Sardinians, had more or less made impression upon the frontiers of the Republic, it might seem, that the only salvation which remained for France, must have been sought for in the unanimity of her inhabitants. But so far was the nation from possessing this first of requisites for a successful opposition to the overpowering coalition which assailed her, that a dreadful civil war was already waged in the western provinces of France, which threatened, from its importance and the success of the insurgents, to

---

[401] On the loss of Mentz, the Convention ordered Custine to Paris to answer for his conduct, and delivered him over to the revolutionary tribunal, by whom, in August, 1793, he was condemned and executed.

[402] Accused of not having followed up the advantages at Hondscoote, by an immediate attack upon the British force. Houchard was brought before the revolutionary tribunal, condemned, and executed, 17th Nov., 1793.

[403] Alexander, Viscount de Beauharnais, first husband of Josephine. Denounced as an aristocrat by his own troops, he was, in July, 1794, dragged before the revolutionary tribunal, which instantly condemned him to death.

[404] Toulongeon, tom. iv., p. 142; Jomini, tom. iv., pp. 86-165.

[405] Condemned to death, Nov. 6, 1793, by the revolutionary tribunal.

[406] Jomini, tom. iv., p. 273.

undo in a great measure the work of the Revolution; while similar discords breaking out on different points in the south, menaced conclusions no less formidable.

LA VENDEE

It does not belong to us to trace the interesting features of the war in La Vendée with a minute pencil, but they mingle too much with the history of the period to be altogether omitted.

We have elsewhere said, that, speaking of La Vendée as a district, it was there alone, through the whole kingdom of France, that the peasants and the nobles, in other words, the proprietors and cultivators of the soil, remained in terms of close and intimate connexion and friendship, which made them feel the same undivided interest in the great changes created by the Revolution. The situation of La Vendée, its soil and character, as well as the manners of the people, had contributed to an arrangement of interests and habits of thinking, which rendered the union betwixt these two classes indissoluble.

La Vendée is a wooded and pastoral country, not indeed mountainous, but abounding in inequalities of ground, crossed by brooks, and intersected by a variety of canals and ditches, made for drainage, but which become, with the numerous and intricate thickets, posts of great strength in the time of war. The enclosures seemed to be won, as it were, out of the woodland; and the paths which traversed the country were so intricate and perplexed, as to render it inaccessible to strangers, and not easily travelled through by the natives themselves. There were almost no roads practicable for ordinary carriages during the rainy season; and the rainy season in La Vendée is a long one. The ladies of rank, when they visited, went in carriages drawn by bullocks; the gentlemen, as well as the peasants, travelled chiefly on foot; and by assistance of the long leaping-poles, which they carried for that purpose, surmounted the ditches and other obstacles which other travellers found impassable.

The whole tract of country is about one hundred and fifty miles square, and lies at the mouth and on the southern bank of the Loire. The internal part is called Le Bocage (the Thicket,) because partaking in a peculiar degree of the wooded and intricate character which belongs to the whole country. That portion of La Vendée which lies close to the Loire, and nearer its mouth, is called Le Louroux. The neighbouring districts partook in the insurrection; but the strength and character which it assumed was derived chiefly from La Vendée.

The union betwixt the noblesse of La Vendée and their peasants, was of the most intimate character. Their chief exportations from the district consisted in the immense herds of cattle which they reared in their fertile meadows, and which supplied the consumption of the metropolis. These herds, as well as the land on which they were raised, were in general the property of the seigneur; but the farmer possessed a joint interest in the latter. He managed the stock, and disposed of it at market, and there was an equitable adjustment of their interests in disposing of the produce.

Their amusements were also in common. The chase of wolves, not only for the sake of sport, but to clear the woods of those ravenous animals, was pursued as of yore by the seigneur at the head of his followers and vassals. Upon the evenings of Sundays and holydays, the young people of each village and métairie repaired to the court-yard of the chateau, as the natural and proper scene for their evening amusement, and the family of the baron often took part in the pastime.

In a word, the two divisions of society depended mutually on each other, and were strongly knit together by ties, which, in other districts of France, existed only in particular instances. The Vendéan peasant was the faithful and attached, though humble friend of his lord; he was his partner in bad and good fortune; submitted to his decision the disputes which might occur betwixt him and his neighbours; and had recourse to his protection if he sustained wrong, or was threatened with injustice from any one.

This system of simple and patriarchal manners could not have long subsisted under any great inequality of fortune. Accordingly, we find that the wealthiest of the Vendéan nobility did not hold estates worth more than twelve or fifteen hundred a-year, while the lowest might be three or four hundred. They were not accordingly much tempted by exuberance of wealth to seek to display magnificence; and such as went to court, and conformed to the fashions of the capital, were accustomed to lay them aside in all haste when they returned to the Bocage, and to reassume the simple manners of their ancestors.

All the incentives to discord which abounded elsewhere through France, were wanting in this wild and wooded region, where the peasant was the noble's affectionate partner and friend, the noble the natural judge and protector of the peasant. The people had retained the feelings of the ancient French in favour of royalty; they listened with dissatisfaction and disgust to the accounts of the Revolution as it proceeded; and feeling themselves none of the evils in which it originated, its whole tendency became the object of their alarm and suspicion. The neighbouring districts, and Bretagne in particular, were agitated by similar commotions; for although the revolutionary principles predominated in the towns of the west, they were not relished by the country people any more than by the nobles. Great agitation had for some time taken place through the provinces of Bretagne, Anjou, Maine, and Poitou, to which the strength of the insurrection in La Vendée gave impulse. It was not, however, a political impulse which induced the Vendéans to take the field. The influence of religion, seconded by that of natural affection, was the immediate stimulating motive.

In a country so simple and virtuous in its manners as we have described La Vendée, religious devotion must necessarily be a general attribute of the inhabitants, who, conscious of loving their neighbours as themselves, are equally desirous, to the extent of their strength and capacity, to love and honour the Great Being who created all. The Vendéans were therefore very regular in the performance of their prescribed religious duties; and their parish priest, or curé, held an honoured and influential rank in their little society, was the attendant of the sick-bed of the peasant, as well for rendering medical as religious aid; his counsellor in his family affairs, and often the arbiter of disputes not of sufficient importance to be carried before the seigneur. The priests were themselves generally natives of the country, more distinguished for the primitive duty with which they discharged their office, than for talents and learning. The curé took frequent share in the large hunting parties, which he announced from the pulpit, and after having said mass, attended in person with the fowling-piece on his shoulder. This active and simple manner of life rendered the priests predisposed to encounter the fatigues of war. They accompanied the bands of Vendéans with the crucifix displayed, and promised, in the name of the Deity, victory to the survivors, and honour to those who fell in the patriotic combat. But Madame La Roche-Jacquelein repels, as a calumny, their bearing arms, except for the purpose of self-defence.[407]

Almost all these parish priests were driven from their cures by the absurd and persecuting fanaticism of that decree of the Assembly, which, while its promoters railed against illiberality, and intolerance, deprived of their office and of their livelihood, soon after of liberty and life, those churchmen who would not renounce the doctrines in which they had been educated, and which they had sworn to maintain.[408] In La Vendée, as elsewhere, where the curates resisted this unjust and impolitic injunction of the legislature, persecution followed on the part of the government, and was met in its turn by violence on that of the people.

The peasants maintained in secret their ancient pastors, and attended their ministry in woods and deserts; while the intruders, who were settled in the livings of the recusants, dared hardly appear in the churches without the protection of the national guards.

So early as 1791, when Dumouriez commanded the forces at Nantes, and the districts adjacent, the flame of dissension had begun to kindle. That general's sagacity induced him to do his best to appease the quarrel by moderating betwixt the parties. His military eye detected in the inhabitants and their country an alarming scene

---

[407] La Roche-Jacquelein, p. 35; Guerres des Vendéans et des Chouans, tom. i., p. 31.
[408] See *ante*.

for civil war. He received the slightest concessions on the part of the parish priests as satisfactory, and appears to have quieted the disturbances of the country, at least for a time.[409]

But in 1793, the same cause of discontent, added to others, hurried the inhabitants of La Vendée into a general insurrection of the most formidable description. The events of the 10th of August, 1792, had driven from Paris a great proportion of the Royalist nobility, who had many of them carried their discontents and their counter-revolutionary projects into a country prepared to receive and adopt them.

Then followed the Conventional decree, which supported their declaration of war by a compulsory levy of three hundred thousand men throughout France. This measure was felt as severe by even those departments in which the revolutionary principles were most predominant, but was regarded as altogether intolerable by the Vendéans, averse alike to the republican cause and principles. They resisted its exaction by main force, delivered the conscripts in many instances, defeated the national guards in others, and finding that they had incurred the vengeance of a sanguinary government, resolved by force to maintain the resistance which in force had begun. Thus originated that celebrated war, which raged so long in the very bosom of France, and threatened the stability of her government, even while the Republic was achieving the most brilliant victories over her foreign enemies.[410]

It is remote from our purpose to trace the history of these hostilities; but a sketch of their nature and character is essential to a general view of the Revolution, and the events connected with it.

LA CHARETTE

The insurgents, though engaged in the same cause, and frequently co-operating, were divided into different bodies, under leaders independent of each other. Those of the right bank of the

---

[409] Dumouriez, vol. ii., p. 144.
[410] Guerres des Vendéans, tom. i., p. 65; La Roche-Jacquelein, p. 38.

Loire were chiefly under the orders of the celebrated La Charette, who, descended from a family distinguished as commanders of privateers, and himself a naval officer, had taken on him this dangerous command. An early wandering disposition, not unusual among youth of eager and ambitious character, had made him acquainted with the inmost recesses of the woods, and his native genius had induced him to anticipate the military advantages which they afforded.[411] In his case, as in many others, either the sagacity of these uninstructed peasants led them to choose for command men whose talents best fitted them to enjoy it, or perhaps the perils which environed such authority prevented its being aspired to, save by those whom a mixture of resolution and prudence led to feel themselves capable of maintaining their character when invested with it. It was remarkable also, that in choosing their leaders, the insurgents made no distinction between the noblesse and the inferior ranks. Names renowned in ancient history—Talmont, D'Autichamp, L'Escure, and La Roche-Jacquelein, were joined in equal command with the gamekeeper Stoflet; Cathelineau, an itinerant wool-merchant; La Charette, a roturier of slight pretensions; and others of the lowest order, whom the time and the public voice called into command, but who, nevertheless, do not seem, in general, to have considered their official command as altering the natural distinction of their rank in society.[412] In their success, they formed a general council of officers, priests, and others, who held their meetings at Chatillon, and directed the military movements of the different bodies; assembled them at pleasure on particular points, and for particular objects of service; and dispersed them to their homes when these were accomplished.

WAR OF LA VENDEE

With an organization so simple, the Vendéan insurgents, in about two months, possessed themselves of several towns and an

---

[411] Thiers, tom. iv., p. 175.
[412] Madame La Roche-Jacquelein mentions an interesting anecdote of a young plebeian, a distinguished officer, whose habits of respect would scarce permit him to sit down in her presence. This cannot be termed servility. It is the noble pride of a generous mind, faithful to its original impressions, and disclaiming the merits which others are ready to heap on it.—S.

extensive tract of country; and though repeatedly attacked by regular forces, commanded by experienced generals, they were far more frequently victors than vanquished, and inflicted more loss on the Republicans by gaining a single battle, than they themselves sustained in repeated defeats.

Yet at first their arms were of the most simple and imperfect kind. Fowling-pieces, and fusees of every calibre, they possessed from their habits as huntsmen and fowlers; for close encounter they had only scythes, axes, clubs, and such weapons as anger places most readily in the hands of the peasant. Their victories, latterly, supplied them with arms in abundance, and they manufactured gunpowder for their own use in great quantity.

Their tactics were peculiar to themselves, but of a kind so well suited to their country and their habits, that it seems impossible to devise a better and more formidable system. The Vendéan took the field with the greatest simplicity of military equipment. His scrip served as a cartridge box, his uniform was the country short jacket and pantaloons, which he wore at his ordinary labour; a cloth knapsack contained bread and some necessaries, and thus he was ready for service. They were accustomed to move with great secrecy and silence amongst the thickets and enclosures by which their country is intersected, and were thus enabled to choose at pleasure the most favourable points of attack or defence. Their army, unlike any other in the world, was not divided into companies, or regiments, but followed in bands, and at their pleasure, the chiefs to whom they were most attached. Instead of drums or military music, they used, like the ancient Swiss and Scottish soldiers, the horns of cattle for giving signals to their troops. Their officers wore, for distinction, a sort of chequered red handkerchief, knotted round their head, with others of the same colour tied round their waist, by way of sash, in which they stuck their pistols.[413]

---

[413] The adoption of this wild costume, which procured them the name of *brigands*, from its fantastic singularity, originated in the whim of Henri La Roche-Jacquelein, who first used the attire. But as this peculiarity, joined to the venturous exposure of his person, occasioned a general cry among the Republicans, of "Aim at the red handkerchief," other officers assumed the fashion to diminish the danger of the chief whom they valued so highly, until at length it became a kind of uniform.—S.

The attack of the Vendéans was that of sharpshooters. They dispersed themselves so as to surround their adversaries with a semicircular fire, maintained by a body of formidable marksmen, accustomed to take aim with fatal precision, and whose skill was the more dreadful, because, being habituated to take advantage of every tree, bush, or point of shelter, those who were dealing destruction amongst others, were themselves comparatively free from risk. This manœuvre was termed *s'égaler*; and the execution of it resembling the Indian bush-fighting, was, like the attack of the red warriors, accompanied by whoops and shouts, which seemed, from the extended space through which they resounded, to multiply the number of the assailants.

When the Republicans, galled in this manner, pressed forward to a close attack, they found no enemy on which to wreak their vengeance; for the loose array of the Vendéans gave immediate passage to the head of the charging column, while its flanks, as it advanced, were still more exposed than before to the murderous fire of their invisible enemies. In this manner they were sometimes led on from point to point, until the regulars, meeting with a barricade, or an *abatis*, or a strong position in front, or becoming perhaps involved in a defile, the Vendéans exchanged their fatal musketry for a close and furious onset, throwing themselves with the most devoted courage among the enemy's ranks, and slaughtering them in great numbers. If, on the other hand, the insurgents were compelled to give way, a pursuit was almost as dangerous to the Republicans as an engagement. The Vendéan, when hard pressed, threw away his clogs, or wooden shoes, of which he could make himself a new pair at the next resting-place, sprang over a fence or canal, loaded his fusee as he ran, and discharged it at the pursuer with a fatal aim, whenever he found opportunity of pausing for that purpose.

This species of combat, which the ground rendered so advantageous to the Vendéans, was equally so in case of victory or defeat. If the Republicans were vanquished, their army was nearly destroyed; for the preservation of order became impossible, and without order their extermination was inevitable, while baggage, ammunition, carriages, guns, and all the material part, as it is called, of the defeated army, fell into possession of the conquerors. On the other hand, if the Vendéans sustained a loss, the victors found nothing on the field but the bodies of the slain, and the *sabots*, or wooden shoes of the fugitives. The few prisoners whom they made had generally thrown away or concealed their arms, and their army having no baggage or carriages of any kind, could of course lose none. Pursuit was very apt to convert an advantage into a defeat; for the cavalry could not act, and the infantry, dispersed in the chase, became frequent victims to those whom they pursued.

In the field, the Vendéans were courageous to rashness. They hesitated not to attack and carry artillery with no other weapons than their staves; and most of their worst losses proceeded from their attacking fortified towns and positions with the purpose of carrying them by main force. After conquest they were in general humane and merciful: but this depended on the character of their chiefs. At Machecoul, the insurgents conducted themselves with great ferocity in the very beginning of the civil war; and towards the end of it, mutual and reciprocal injuries had so exasperated the parties against each other, that quarter was neither given nor taken on either side. Yet until provoked by the extreme cruelties of the Revolutionary party, and unless when conducted by some peculiarly ferocious chief, the character of the Vendéans united clemency with courage. They gave quarter readily to the vanquished, but having no means of retaining prisoners, they usually shaved their heads before they set them at liberty, that they might be distinguished if found again in arms, contrary to their parole. A no less striking feature, was the severity of a discipline respecting property, which was taught them only by their moral sense. No temptation could excite them to pillage; and Madame La Roche-Jacquelein has preserved the following singular instance of their simple honesty:—After the peasants had taken the town of Bressuire by storm, she overheard two or three of them complain of the want of tobacco, to the use of which they were addicted, like the natives of moist countries in general. "What," said the lady, "is there no tobacco in the shops?"— "Tobacco enough," answered the simple-hearted and honest peasants, who had not learned to make steel supply the want of gold,—"tobacco enough; but we have no money to pay for it."[414]

---

[414] La Roche-Jacquelein, p. 90.

Amidst these primitive warriors were mingled many gentlemen of the first families in France, who, Royalists from principle, had fled to La Vendée rather than submit to the dominion of the Convention, or the Convention's yet more cruel masters. There were found many men, the anecdotes told of whom remind us continually of the age of Henri Quatre, and the heroes of chivalry. In these ranks, and almost on a level with the valiant peasants of which they were composed, fought the calm, steady, and magnanimous L'Escure,—D'Elbée, a man of the most distinguished military reputation,—Bonchamp, the gallant and the able officer, who, like the Constable Montmorency, with all his talent, was persecuted by fortune,—the chivalrous Henry La Roche-Jacquelein, whose call upon his soldiers was—"If I fly, slay me—if I advance, follow me—if I fall, avenge me;" with other names distinguished[415] in the roll of fame, and not the less so, that they have been recorded by the pen of affection.

The object of the insurrection was announced in the title of The Royal and Catholic Army, assumed by the Vendéans. In their moments of highest hope their wishes were singularly modest. Had they gained Paris, and replaced the royal authority in France, they meditated the following simple boons:—1. They had resolved to petition, that the name of La Vendée be given to the Bocage and its dependencies, which should be united under a separate administration, instead of forming, as at present, a part of three distinct provinces. 2. That the restored monarch would honour the Bocage with a visit. 3. That in remembrance of the loyal services of the country, a white flag should be displayed from each steeple, and the King should add a cohort of Vendéans to his body-guard. 4. That former useful projects of improving the navigation of the Loire and its canals, should be perfected by the government. So little of selfish hope or ambition was connected with the public spirit of these patriarchal warriors.

---

[415] The Memoirs of Madame Bonchamp, and still more those of Madame La Roche-Jacquelein, are remarkable for the virtues of the heart, as well as the talents which are displayed by their authors. Without affectation, without vanity, without violence or impotent repining, these ladies have described the sanguinary and irregular warfare, in which they and those who were dearest to them were engaged for so long and stormy a period; and we arise from the perusal sadder and wiser, by having learned what the brave can dare, and what the gentle can endure with patience.—S.

The war of La Vendée was waged with various fate for nearly two years, during which the insurgents, or brigands as they were termed, gained by far the greater number of advantages, though with means infinitely inferior to those of the government, which detached against them one general after another, at the head of numerous armies, with equally indifferent success. Most of the Republicans intrusted with this fatal command suffered by the guillotine, for not having done that which circumstances rendered impossible.

Upwards of two hundred battles and skirmishes were fought in this devoted country. The revolutionary fever was in its access; the shedding of blood seemed to have become positive pleasure to the perpetrators of slaughter, and was varied by each invention which cruelty could invent to give it new zest. The habitations of the Vendéans were destroyed, their families subjected to violation and massacre, their cattle houghed and slaughtered, and their crops burnt and wasted. One Republican column assumed and merited the name of the Infernal, by the horrid atrocities which they committed. At Pillau, they roasted the women and children in a heated oven. Many similar horrors could be added, did not the heart and hand recoil from the task. Without quoting any more special instances of horror, we use the words of a Republican eyewitness, to express the general spectacle presented by the theatre of civil conflict:—

"I did not see a single male being at the towns of Saint Hermand, Chantonnay, or Herbiers. A few women alone had escaped the sword. Country-seats, cottages, habitations of whichever kind, were burnt. The herds and flocks were wandering in terror around their usual places of shelter, now smoking in ruins. I was surprised by night, but the wavering and dismal blaze of conflagration afforded light over the country. To the bleating of the disturbed flocks, and bellowing of the terrified cattle, was joined the deep hoarse notes of carrion crows, and the yells of wild animals coming from the recesses of the woods to prey on the carcasses of the slain. At length a distant column of fire, widening and increasing as I approached, served me as a beacon. It was the town of Mortagne in flames. When I arrived there, no living creatures were to be seen, save a few wretched women who were striving to save some remnants of their property from the general conflagration."[416]

Such is civil war! and to this pass had its extremities reduced the smiling, peaceful, and virtuous country, which we have described a few pages before!

It is no wonder, after such events, that the hearts of the peasants became hardened in turn, and that they executed fearful vengeance on those who could not have the face to expect mercy. We read, therefore, without surprise, that the Republican General Haxo,[417] a man of great military talent, and who had distinguished himself in the Vendéan war, shot himself through the head, when he saw his army defeated by the insurgents, rather than encounter their vengeance.

During the superiority of the Vendéans, it may be asked why their efforts, so gigantic in themselves, never extended beyond the frontier of their own country; and why an insurrection, so considerable and so sustained, neither made any great impression on the French Convention, where they were spoken of only as a handful of brigands, nor on foreign nations, by whom their existence, far less their success, seems hardly to have been known? On the former subject, it is perhaps sufficient to observe, that the war of the Vendéans, and their mode of conducting it, so formidable in their own country, became almost nugatory when extended into districts of an open character, and affording highroads and plains, by which cavalry and artillery could act against peasants, who formed no close ranks, and carried no bayonets. Besides, the Vendéans remained bound to their ordinary occupation—they were necessarily children of the soil—and their army usually dispersed after the battle was over, to look after their cattle, cultivate the plot of arable land, and attend to their families. The discipline of their array, in which mere good-will supplied the place of the usual distinctions of rank, would not have been sufficient to keep them united in long and distant marches, and they must have found the want of a commissariat, a train of baggage,

---

[416] Mémoires d'un Ancien Administrateur des Armées Republicaines.—S.
[417] Haxo died at Roche-sur-yon, April 26, 1794.

field-pieces, a general staff, and all the other accompaniments of a regular army, which, in the difficult country of La Vendée, familiar to the natives, and unknown to strangers, could be so easily dispensed with. In a word, an army which, under circumstances of hope and excitation, might one day amount to thirty or forty thousand, and on the next be diminished to the tenth part of the number, might be excellent for fighting battles, but could not be relied on for making conquests, or securing the advantages of victory.

It is not but that a man of D'Elbée's knowledge in the art of war, who acted as one of their principal leaders, meditated higher objects for the Vendéans than merely the defence of their own province.

A superb prospect offered itself to them by a meditated attack on the town of Nantes. Upon the success of this attempt turned, perhaps, the fate of the Revolution. This beautiful and important commercial city is situated on the right bank of the Loire, which is there a fine navigable river, about twenty-seven miles from its junction with the sea. It is without fortifications of any regular description, but had a garrison of perhaps ten thousand men, and was covered by such hasty works of defence as time had permitted them to erect. The force of the Vendéans by which it was attacked, has been estimated so high as thirty or forty thousand men under D'Elbée, while the place was blockaded on the left bank by Charette, and an army of Royalists equal in number to the actual assailants. Had this important place been gained, it would probably have changed the face of the war. One or more of the French princes might have resorted there with such adherents as they had then in arms. The Loire was open to succours from England, the indecision of whose cabinet might have been determined by a success so important. Bretagne and Normandy, already strongly disposed to the royal cause, would have, upon such encouragement, risen in mass upon the Republicans; and as Poitou and Anjou were already in possession of the Royal and Catholic Army, they might probably have opened a march upon Paris, distracted as the capital then was by civil and foreign war.[418]

Accordingly, [June 18th,] the rockets which were thrown up, and the sound of innumerable bugle-horns, intimated to General Canclaux, who commanded the town, that he was to repel a general attack of the Vendéans. Fortunately, for the infant republic, he was a man of military skill and high courage, and by his dexterous use of such means of defence as the place afforded, and particularly by a great superiority of artillery, he was enabled to baffle the attacks of the Vendéans, although they penetrated, with the utmost courage, into the suburbs, and engaged at close quarters the Republican troops. They were compelled to retreat after a fierce combat, which lasted from three in the morning till four in the afternoon.[419]

At different times after the failure of this bold and well-imagined attempt, opportunities occurred during which the allies, and the English government in particular, might have thrown important succours into La Vendée. The island of Noirmoutier was for some time in possession of the Royalists, when arms and money might have been supplied to them to any amount. Auxiliary forces would probably have been of little service, considering in what sort of country they were to be engaged, and with what species of troops they were to act. At least it would have required the talents of a Peterborough or a Montrose, in a foreign commander, to have freed himself sufficiently from the trammels of military pedantry, and availed himself of the peculiar qualities of such troops as the Vendéans, irresistible after their own fashion, but of a character the most opposite possible to the ideas of excellence entertained by a mere martinet.

---

[418] See Jomini, tom. vi., p 400.
[419] A picture by Vernet, representing the attack on Nantes, estimable as a work of art, but extremely curious in an historical point of view, used to be in the Luxembourg palace, and is probably now removed to the Louvre. The Vendéans are presented there in all their simplicity of attire, and devoted valour; the priests who attended them displaying their crosses, and encouraging the assault, which is, on the other hand, repelled by the regular steadiness of the Republican forces.—S.—[This picture is still in the Luxembourg. The paintings of living artists are never admitted to the Louvre.]

DIVISIONS IN THE BRITISH CABINET

But it is now well known, there was a division in the British Cabinet concerning the mode of carrying on the war. Pitt was extremely unwilling to interfere with the internal government of France. He desired to see the barrier of Flanders, so foolishly thrown open by the Emperor Joseph, again re-established, and he hoped from the success of the allied arms, that this might be attained,—that the French lust for attacking their neighbours might be ended—their wildness for crusading in the cause of innovation checked, and some political advances to a regular government effected. On the other hand, the enthusiastic, ingenious, but somewhat extravagant opinions of Windham, led him to espouse those of Burke in their utmost extent; and he recommended to England, as to Europe, the replacing the Bourbons, with the ancient royal government and constitution, as the fundamental principle on which the war should be waged. This variance of opinion so far divided the British counsels, that, as it proved, no sufficient efforts were made, either on the one line of conduct or the other.

Indeed, Madame La Roche-Jacquelein (who, however, we are apt to think, has been in some degree misled in her account of that matter) says, the only despatches received by the Vendéans from the British Cabinet, indicated a singular ignorance of the state of La Vendée, which was certainly near enough to Jersey and Guernsey, to have afforded the means of obtaining accurate information upon the nature and principles of the Vendéan insurrection.

The leaders of *The Royal and Catholic Army* received their first communication from Britain through a Royalist emissary, the Chevalier de Tinténiac, who carried them concealed in the wadding of his pistols, addressed to a supposed chief named Gaston, whose name had scarce been known among them. In this document they were required to say for what purpose they were in arms, whether in behalf of the old government, or of the constitution of 1791, or the principles of the Girondists? These were strange questions to be asked of men who had been in the field as pure Royalists for more than five months, who might have reasonably hoped that the news of their numerous and important victories had resounded through all Europe, but must at least have expected they should be well known to those neighbours of France who were at war with her present government. Assistance was promised, but in a general and indecisive way; nor did the testimony of M. de Tinténiac give his friends much assurance that it was seriously proposed. In fact, no support ever arrived until after the first pacification of La Vendée. The ill-fated expedition to Quiberon, delayed until the cause of royalty was nigh hopeless, was at length undertaken, when its only consequence was that of involving in absolute destruction a multitude of brave and high-spirited men. But on looking back on a game so doubtful, it is easy to criticize the conduct of the players; and perhaps no blunder in war or politics is so common, as that which arises from missing the proper moment of exertion.[420]

The French, although more able to seize the advantageous opportunity than we, (for their government being always in practice something despotic, is at liberty to act more boldly, secretly, and decisively, than that of England,) are nevertheless chargeable with similar errors. If the English Cabinet missed the opportunities given by the insurrection of La Vendée, the French did not more actively improve those afforded by the Irish rebellion; and if we had to regret the too tardy and unhappy expedition to Quiberon, they in their turn might repent having thrown away the troops whom they landed at Castlehaven, after the pacification of Ireland, for the sole purpose, it would seem, of surrendering at Ballinamuck.

It is yet more wonderful, that a country whose dispositions were so loyal, and its local advantages so strong, should not have been made by the loyalists in general the centre of those counter-revolutionary exertions which were vainly expended on the iron eastern frontier, where the fine army of Condé wasted their blood about paltry frontier redoubts and fortresses. The nobles and gentlemen of France, fighting abreast with the gallant peasants of La Vendée, inspired with the same sentiments of loyalty with themselves, would have been more suitably placed than in the mercenary ranks of foreign nations. It is certain that the late King Louis XVIII., and also his present Majesty,[421] were desirous to have

---

[420] La Roche-Jacquelein, p. 69; Lacretelle, tom. x., p. 143.
[421] King Charles the Tenth.

exposed their persons in the war of La Vendée. The former wrote to the Duke d'Harcourt—"What course remains for me but La Vendée? Who can place me there?—England—Insist upon that point; and tell the English ministers in my name, that I demand from them a crown or a tomb."[422] If there were a serious intention of supporting these unfortunate princes, the means of this experiment ought to have been afforded them, and that upon no stinted scale. The error of England, through all the early part of the war, was an unwillingness to proportion her efforts to the importance of the ends she had in view.

Looking upon the various chances which might have befriended the unparalleled exertions of the Vendéans, considering the generous, virtuous, and disinterested character of those primitive soldiers, it is with sincere sorrow that we proceed to trace their extermination by the bloodthirsty ruffians of the Reign of Terror. Yet the course of Providence, after the lapse of time, is justified even in our weak and undiscerning eyes. We should indeed have read with hearts throbbing with the just feelings of gratified vengeance, that La Charette or La Roche-Jacquelein had successfully achieved, at the head of their gallant adherents, the road to Paris— had broke in upon the committees of public safety and public security, like Thalaba the Destroyer[423] into the Dom-daniel; and with the same dreadful result to the agents of the horrors with which these revolutionary bodies had deluged France. But such a reaction, accomplished solely for the purpose of restoring the old despotic monarchy, could not have brought peace to France or to Europe; nay, could only have laid a foundation for farther and more lasting quarrels. The flame of liberty had been too widely spread in France to be quenched even by such a triumph of royalty as we have supposed, however pure the principles and high the spirit of the Vendéans. It was necessary that the nation should experience both the extremes of furious license and of stern despotism, to fix the hopes of the various contending parties upon a form of government, in which a limited power in the monarch should be united to the enjoyment of all rational freedom in the subject. We return to our sad task.

---

[422] Lacretelle, tom. xi., p. 145.
[423] See Southey's Thalaba, b. 12.

WAR OF LA VENDÉE

Notwithstanding the desolating mode in which the Republicans conducted the war, with the avowed purpose of rendering La Vendée uninhabitable, the population seemed to increase in courage, and even in numbers, as their situation became more desperate. Renewed armies were sent into the devoted district, and successively destroyed in assaults, skirmishes, and ambuscades, where they were not slaughtered in general actions. More than a hundred thousand men were employed at one time, in their efforts to subjugate this devoted province. But this could not last for ever; and a chance of war upon the frontiers, which threatened reverses to the Convention, compensated them by furnishing new forces, and of a higher description in point of character and discipline, for the subjection of La Vendée.

This was the surrender of the town of Mentz to the Prussians. By the capitulation, a garrison of near fifteen thousand experienced soldiers, and some officers of considerable name, were debarred from again bearing arms against the allies. These troops were employed in La Vendée, where the scale had already begun to preponderate against the dauntless and persevering insurgents. At the first encounters, the soldiers of Mentz, unacquainted with the Vendéan mode of fighting, sustained loss, and were thought lightly of by the Royalists.[424] This opinion of their new adversaries was changed, in consequence of a defeat [Oct. 17] near Chollet, more dreadful in its consequences than any which the Vendéans had yet received, and which determined their generals to pass the Loire with their whole collected force, leave their beloved Bocage to the axes and brands of the victors, and carry the war into Bretagne, where they expected either to be supported by a descent of the English, or by a general insurrection of the inhabitants.[425]

In this military emigration the Royalists were accompanied by their aged people, their wives, and their children; so that their

---

[424] They punned on the word *Mayence* (Mentz,) and said, the newly arrived Republicans were soldiers of *fayence* (potter' ware,) which could not endure the fire.—S.
[425] Beauchamp, Hist. de la Guerre de la Vendée, tom. ii., p. 99; Jomini, tom. iv., p. 318; La Roche-Jacquelein, p. 239; Lacretelle, tom. xi., p. 151.

melancholy march resembled that of the Cimbrians or Helvetians of old, when abandoning their ancient dwellings, they wandered forth to find new settlements in a more fertile land. They crossed the river near Saint Florent, and the banks were blackened with nearly a hundred thousand pilgrims of both sexes, and of every age. The broad river was before them, and behind them their burning cottages and the exterminating sword of the Republicans. The means of embarkation were few and precarious; the affright of the females almost ungovernable; and such was the tumult and terror of the scene, that, in the words of Madame La Roche-Jacquelein, the awe-struck spectators could only compare it to the day of judgment.[426] Without food, directions, or organization of any kind—without the show of an army, saving in the front and rear of the column, the centre consisting of their defenceless families marching together in a mass—these indomitable peasants defeated a Republican army under the walls of Laval.

The garrison of Mentz, whose arrival in La Vendée had been so fatal to the insurgents, and who had pursued them in a state of rout, as they thought, out of their own country, across the Loire, were almost exterminated in this most unexpected defeat. An unsuccessful attack upon Granville more than counterbalanced this advantage, and although the Vendéans afterwards obtained a brilliant victory at Dol, it was the last success of what was termed the Great Army of La Vendée, and which well deserved that title, on more accounts than in its more ordinary sense. They had now lost, by the chances of war, most of their best chiefs; and misfortunes, and the exasperating feelings attending them, had introduced disunion, which had been so long a stranger to their singular association. Charette was reflected upon as being little willing to aid La Roche-Jacquelein; and Stoflet seems to have set up an independent standard. The insurgents were defeated at Mons, where of three Republican generals of name, Westermann, Marçeau, and Kleber, the first disgraced himself by savage cruelty, and the other two gained honour by their clemency. Fifteen thousand male and

---

[426] Mémoires, p. 240.

female natives of La Vendée perished in the battle and the massacre which ensued.[427]

But though La Vendée, after this decisive loss, which included some of her best troops and bravest generals, could hardly be said to exist, La Charette continued, with indefatigable diligence, and undaunted courage, to sustain the insurrection of Lower Poitou and Bretagne. He was followed by a division of peasants from the Marais, whose activity in marshy grounds gave them similar advantages to those possessed by the Vendéans in their woodlands. He was followed also by the inhabitants of Morbihan, called, from their adherence to royalism, the Little La Vendée. He was the leader, besides, of many of the bands called Chouans, a name of doubtful origin given to the insurgents of Bretagne, but which their courage has rendered celebrated.[428] La Charette himself, who, with these and other forces, continued to sustain the standard of royalty in Bretagne and Poitou, was one of those extraordinary characters, made to shine amidst difficulties and dangers. As prudent and cautious as he was courageous and adventurous, he was at the same time so alert and expeditious in his motions, that he usually appeared at the time and place where his presence was least expected and most formidable. A Republican officer, who had just taken possession of a village, and was speaking of the Royalist leader as of a person at twenty leagues' distance, said publicly,—"I should like to see this famous Charette."—"There he is," said a woman, pointing with her finger. In fact, he was at that moment in the act of charging the Republican troops, who were all either slain or made prisoners.

TREATY WITH LA CHARETTE

After the fall of Robespierre, the Convention made offers of pacification to La Charette, which were adjusted betwixt the

---

[427] Jomini, tom. iv., p. 319. Beauchamp, tom. ii., p. 102.
[428] Some derived it from *Chat-huant*, as if the insurgents, like owls, appeared chiefly at night; others traced it to *Chouin*, the name of two brothers, sons of a blacksmith, said to have been the earliest leaders of the Breton insurgents.—S.

Vendéan chief and General Canclaux,[429] the heroic defender of Nantes. The articles of treaty were subscribed in that place, which La Charette entered at the head of his military staff, with his long white plume streaming in the wind. He heard with coldness shouts of welcome from a city, to which his name had been long a terror; and there was a gloom on his brow as he signed his name to the articles agreed upon. He certainly suspected the faith of those with whom he transacted, and they did not by any means confide in his. An armistice was agreed on until the Convention should ratify the pacification. But this never took place. Mutual complaints and recriminations followed, and the soldiers of La Charette and of the Republic began once more to make a petty war on each other.

Meantime, that party in the British Cabinet which declared for a descent on France, in name and on behalf of the successor to the crown, had obtained the acquiescence of their colleagues in an experiment of this nature; but unhappily it had been postponed until its success had become impossible. The force, too, which composed this experimental operation, was injudiciously selected. A certain proportion consisted of emigrants, in whom the highest confidence might be with justice reposed; but about two battalions of this invading expedition were vagrant foreigners of various descriptions, many or most of them enlisted from among the prisoners of war, who readily took any engagement to get out of captivity, with the mental resolution of breaking it the first opportunity. Besides these imprudences, the purpose and time of executing a project, which, to be successful, should have been secret and sudden, were generally known in France and England before the expedition weighed anchor.

The event, as is universally known, was most disastrous: The mercenaries deserted to the Republicans as soon as they got ashore; and the unfortunate emigrants, who became prisoners in great numbers, were condemned and executed without mercy. The ammunition and muskets, of which a quantity had been landed, fell into the hands of the enemy; and what was worse, England did not,

---

[429] Canclaux was born at Paris in 1740. After the revolution of the 18th Brumaire, Napoleon gave him the command of the 14th military division, and made him a senator. At the restoration he was created a peer. He died in 1817.

among other lighter losses, entirely save her honour. She was severely censured as giving up her allies to destruction, because she had yielded to the wishes which enthusiastic and courageous men had elevated into hope.

Nothing, indeed, can be more difficult, than to state the just extent of support, which can prudently be extended by one nation to a civil faction in the bosom of another. Indeed, nothing short of success—absolute success—will prove the justification of such enterprises in the eyes of some, who will allege, in the event of failure, that men have been enticed into perils, in which they have not been adequately supported; or of others, who will condemn such measures as squandering the public resources, in enterprises which ought not to have been encouraged at all. But in fair judgment, the expedition of Quiberon ought not to be summarily condemned. It was neither inadequate, nor, excepting as to the description of some of the forces employed, ill calculated for the service proposed. Had such reinforcements and supplies arrived while the Royalists were attacking Nantes or Grenoble, or while they yet held the island of Noirmoutier, the good consequences to the royal cause might have been incalculable. But the expedition was ill-timed, and that was in a great measure owing to those unfortunate gentlemen engaged, who, impatient of inactivity, and sanguine by character, urged the British Ministry, or rather Mr. Windham, to authorise the experiment, without fully considering more than their own zeal and courage. We cannot, however, go so far as to say, that their impatience relieved ministers from the responsibility attached to the indifferent intelligence on which they acted. There could be no difficulty in getting full information on the state of Bretagne by way of Jersey; and they ought to have known that there was a strong French force collected from various garrisons, for the purpose of guarding against a descent at Quiberon.[430]

---

[430] We can and ought to make great allowances for national feeling; yet it is a little hard to find a well-informed historian, like M. Lacretelle, [tom. xi., p. 146,] gravely insinuate, that England threw the unfortunate Royalists on the coast of Quiberon to escape the future burden of maintaining them. Her liberality towards the emigrants, honourable and meritorious to the country, was entirely gratuitous. She might have withdrawn when she pleased a bounty conferred by her benevolence; and it is rather too hard to be supposed capable of meditating their murder, merely to save the expense of supporting them. The

After this unfortunate affair, and some subsequent vain attempts to throw in supplies on the part of the English, La Charette still continued in open war. But Hoche, an officer of high reputation, was now sent into the disturbed districts, with a larger army than had yet been employed against them. He was thus enabled to form moveable columns, which acted in concert, supporting each other when unsuccessful, or completing each other's victory when such was obtained. La Charette, after his band was almost entirely destroyed, was himself made prisoner. Being condemned to be shot, he refused to have his eyes covered, and died as courageously as he had lived. With him and Stoflet, who suffered a similar fate, the war of La Vendée terminated.

To trace this remarkable civil war, even so slightly as we have attempted the task, has carried us beyond the course of our narrative. It broke out in the beginning of March 1793, and La Charette's execution, by which it was closed, took place at Nantes, 29th March, 1796. The astonishing part of the matter is, that so great a conflagration should not have extended itself beyond a certain limited district, while within that region it raged with such fury, that for a length of time no means of extinguishing it could be discovered.

STATE OF THE PROVINCES

We now return to the state of France in spring 1793, when the Jacobins, who had possessed themselves of the supreme power of the Republic, found that they had to contend, not only with the allied forces on two frontiers of France, and with the Royalists in the west, but also with more than one of the great commercial towns, which, with less inclination to the monarchical cause, than a general terror of revolutionary measures, prepared for resistance, after the proscription of the Girondists upon the 31st of May.

Bourdeaux, Marseilles, Toulon, and Lyons, had declared themselves against the Jacobin supremacy. Rich from commerce and

---

expedition was a blunder; but one in which the unfortunate sufferers contributed to mislead the British Government.—S.

their maritime situation, and, in the case of Lyons, from their command of internal navigation, the wealthy merchants and manufacturers of those cities foresaw the total insecurity of property, and in consequence their own ruin, in the system of arbitrary spoliation and murder upon which the government of the Jacobins was founded. But property, for which they were solicitous, though, if its natural force is used in time, the most powerful barrier to withstand revolution, becomes, after a certain period of delay, its most helpless victim. If the rich are in due season liberal of their means, they have the power of enlisting in their cause, and as adherents, those among the lower orders, who, if they see their superiors dejected and despairing, will be tempted to consider them as objects of plunder. But this must be done early, or those who might be made the most active defenders of property will join with such as are prepared to make a prey of it.

We have already seen that Bourdeaux, in which the Brissotines or Girondists had ventured to hope for a zeal purely republican, at once adverse to royalty and to Jacobin domination, had effectually disappointed their expectations, and succumbed with little struggle under the ferocious victors.

Marseilles showed at once her good-will and her impotency of means. The utmost exertions of that wealthy city, whose revolutionary band had contributed so much to the downfall of the monarchy in the attack on the Tuileries, were able to equip only a small and doubtful army of about three thousand men, who were despatched to the relief of Lyons. This inconsiderable army threw themselves into Avignon, and were defeated with the utmost ease, by the republican general Cartaux,[431] despicable as a military officer, and whose forces would not have stood a single *également* of the Vendéan sharp-shooters. Marseilles received the victors, and bowed her head to the subsequent horrors which it pleased Cartaux, with

---

[431] "This man, originally a painter, had become an adjutant in the Parisian corps; he was afterwards employed in the army; and, having been successful against the Marseillois, the deputies of the Mountain had, in the same day, obtained him the appointments of brigadier-general and general of division. He was extremely ignorant, and had nothing military about him, otherwise he was not ill-disposed."—Napoleon, *Memoirs*, vol. i., p. 19.

two formidable Jacobins, Barras and Fréron,[432] to inflict on that flourishing city. The place underwent the usual terrors of Jacobin purification, and was for a time affectedly called, "the nameless commune."[433]

REVOLT OF LYONS

Lyons made a more honourable stand. That noble city had been subjected for some time to the domination of Châlier, one of the most ferocious, and at the same time one of the most extravagantly absurd, of the Jacobins. He was at the head of a formidable club, which was worthy of being affiliated with the mother society, and ambitious of treading in its footsteps; and he was supported by a garrison of two revolutionary regiments, besides a numerous artillery, and a large addition of volunteers, amounting in all to about ten thousand men, forming what was called a revolutionary army. This Châlier was an apostate priest, an atheist, and a thorough-paced pupil in the school of terror. He had been created Procureur of the Commune, and had imposed on the wealthy citizens a tax, which was raised from six to thirty millions of livres. But blood as well as gold was his object. The massacre of a few priests and aristocrats confined in the fortress of Pierre-Seize, was a pitiful sacrifice; and Châlier, ambitious of deeds more decisive, caused a general arrest of an hundred principal citizens, whom he destined as a hecatomb more worthy of the demon whom he served.

This sacrifice was prevented by the courage of the Lyonnois a courage which, if assumed by the Parisians, might have prevented most of the horrors which disgraced the Revolution. The meditated

---

[432] Stanislaus Fréron was son of the well-known victim of Voltaire, and godson of the unfortunate King of Poland. He accompanied the French expedition to St. Domingo in 1802, and being appointed sub-prefect at the Cayes, soon sunk under the influence of the climate. His portfolio falling into the hands of the black government, some of its contents were published by the authority of Dessaline, and subjoined to a work entitled "Mémoires pour servir à l'Histoire de Hayti." Among them are several amatory epistles from Napoleon's second sister Pauline, by which it appears that Fréron was the earliest object of her choice, but that Napoleon and Josephine would not hear of an alliance with the friend of Robespierre, and ready instrument of his atrocities.
[433] Jomini, tom. iv., p. 208; Toulongeon, tom. iv., p. 63.

slaughter was already announced by Châlier to the Jacobin Club. "Three hundred heads," he said, "are marked for slaughter. Let us lose no time in seizing the members of the departmental office-bearers, the presidents and secretaries of the sections, all the local authorities who obstruct our revolutionary measures. Let us make one fagot of the whole, and deliver them at once to the guillotine."

But ere he could execute his threat, terror was awakened into the courage of despair. The citizens rose in arms, [May 29,] and besieged the Hôtel de Ville, in which Châlier, with his revolutionary troops, made a desperate, and for some time a successful, yet ultimately a vain defence. But the Lyonnois unhappily knew not how to avail themselves of their triumph. They were not sufficiently aware of the nature of the vengeance which they had provoked, or of the necessity of supporting the bold step which they had taken, by measures which precluded a compromise. Their resistance to the violence and atrocity of the Jacobins had no political character, any more than that offered by the traveller against robbers who threaten him with plunder and murder. They were not sufficiently aware, that, having done so much, they must necessarily do more. They ought, by declaring themselves Royalists, to have endeavoured to prevail on the troops of Savoy, if not on the Swiss, who had embraced a species of neutrality, (which, after the 10th of August, was dishonourable to their ancient reputation,) to send in all haste soldiery to the assistance of a city which had no fortifications or regular troops to defend it; but which possessed, nevertheless, treasures to pay their auxiliaries, and strong hands and able officers to avail themselves of the localities of their situation, which, when well defended, are sometimes as formidable as the regular protection erected by scientific engineers.

The people of Lyons vainly endeavoured to establish a revolutionary character for themselves, upon the system of the Gironde; two of whose proscribed deputies, Biroteau and Chasset, tried to draw them over to their unpopular and hopeless cause; and they inconsistently sought protection by affecting a republican zeal, even while resisting the decrees, and defeating the troops of the Jacobins. There were undoubtedly many of royalist principles among the insurgents, and some of their leaders were decidedly such; but these were not numerous or influential enough to establish the true principle of open resistance, and the ultimate chance of rescue, by a bold proclamation of the King's interest. They still appealed to the Convention as their legitimate sovereign, in whose eyes they endeavoured to vindicate themselves, and at the same time tried to secure the interest of two Jacobin deputies, who had countenanced every violence attempted by Châlier, that they might prevail upon them to represent their conduct favourably. Of course they had enough of promises to this effect, while Messrs. Guathier and Nioche, the deputies in question, remained in their power; promises, doubtless, the more readily given, that the Lyonnois, though desirous to conciliate the favour of the Convention, did not hesitate in proceeding to the punishment of the Jacobin Châlier. He was condemned and executed, along with one of his principal associates, termed Ribard.[434]

To defend these vigorous proceedings, the unhappy insurgents placed themselves under the interim government of a council, who, still desirous to temporize and maintain the revolutionary character, termed themselves "The Popular and Republican Commission of Public Safety of the Department of the Rhone and Loire;" a title which, while it excited no popular enthusiasm, and attracted no foreign aid, noways soothed, but rather exasperated, the resentment of the Convention, now under the absolute domination of the Jacobins, by whom every thing short of complete fraternization was accounted presumptuous defiance. Those who were not with them, it was their policy to hold as their most decided enemies.

The Lyonnois had, indeed, letters of encouragement, and promised concurrence, from several departments; but no effectual support was ever directed towards their city, excepting the petty reinforcement from Marseilles, which we have seen was intercepted and dispersed with little trouble by the Jacobin General Cartaux.

Lyons had expected to become the patroness and focus of an Anti-jacobin league, formed by the great commercial towns, against Paris and the predominant part of the Convention. She found

---

[434] Lacretelle, tom. xi., p. 98; Thiers, tom. iv., p. 161.

herself isolated and unsupported, and left to oppose her own proper forces and means of defence, to an army of sixty thousand men, and to the numerous Jacobins contained within her own walls. About the end of July, after a lapse of an interval of two months, a regular blockade was formed around the city, and in the first week of August hostilities took place. The besieging army was directed in its military character by General Kellerman, who, with other distinguished soldiers, had now begun to hold an eminent rank in the Republican armies. But for the purpose of executing the vengeance for which they thirsted, the Jacobins relied chiefly on the exertions of the deputies they had sent along with the commander, and especially of the representative Dubois-Crancé, a man whose sole merit appears to have been his frantic Jacobinism. General Précy, formerly an officer in the Royal service, undertook the almost hopeless task of defence, and by forming redoubts on the most commanding situations around the town, commenced a resistance against the immensely superior force of the besiegers, which was honourable if it could have been useful. The Lyonnois, at the same time, still endeavoured to make fair weather with the besieging army, by representing themselves as firm Republicans. They celebrated as a public festival the anniversary of the 10th of August, while Dubois-Crancé, to show the credit he gave them for their republican zeal, fixed the same day for commencing his fire on the place, and caused the first gun to be discharged by his own concubine, a female born in Lyons. Bombs and red-hot bullets were next resorted to, against the second city of the French empire; while the besieged sustained the attack with a constancy, and on many parts repelled it with a courage, highly honourable to their character.

But their fate was determined. The deputies announced to the Convention their purpose of pouring their instruments of havoc on every quarter of the town at once, and when it was on fire in several places to attempt a general storm. "The city," they said, "must surrender, or there shall not remain one stone upon another, and this we hope to accomplish in spite of the suggestions of false compassion. Do not then be surprised when you shall hear that Lyons exists no longer." The fury of the attack threatened to make good these promises.

In the meantime the Piedmontese troops made a show of descending from their mountains to the succour of the city, and it is probable their interference would have given a character of royalism to the insurrection. But the incursion of the Piedmontese and Sardinians was speedily repelled by the skill of Kellerman, and produced no effect in favour of the city of Lyons, except that of supporting for a time the courage of its defenders.

The sufferings of the citizens became intolerable. Several quarters of the city were on fire at the same time, immense magazines were burnt to the ground, and a loss incurred, during two nights' bombardment, which was calculated at two hundred millions of livres. A black flag was hoisted by the besieged on the Great Hospital, as a sign that the fire of the assailants should not be directed on that asylum of hopeless misery. The signal seemed only to draw the republican bombs to the spot where they could create the most frightful distress, and outrage, in the highest degree, the feelings of humanity. The devastations of famine were soon added to those of slaughter; and after two months of such horrors had been sustained, it became obvious that farther resistance was impossible.

The military commandant of Lyons, Précy, resolved upon a sally, at the head of the active part of the garrison, hoping that, by cutting his way through the besiegers, he might save the lives of many of those who followed him in the desperate attempt, and gain the neutral territory of Switzerland, while the absence of those who had been actual combatants during the siege, might, in some degree, incline the Convention to lenient measures towards the more helpless part of the inhabitants. A column of about two thousand men made this desperate attempt. But, pursued by the Republicans, and attacked on every side by the peasants, to whom they had been represented in the most odious colours by the Jacobin deputies, and who were stimulated besides by the hope of plunder, scarcely fifty of the devoted body reached, with their leader, the protecting soil of Switzerland. Lyons reluctantly opened her gates after the departure of her best and bravest. The rest may be described in the words of Horace,—

"Barbarus heu cineres insistet victor, et urbem, ——dissipabit insolens."

The paralytic Couthon, with Collot D'Herbois,[435] and other deputies, were sent to Lyons by the Committee of Public Safety, to execute the vengeance which the Jacobins demanded; while Dubois-Crancé was recalled for having put, it was thought, less energy in his proceedings than the prosecution of the siege required. Collot D'Herbois had a personal motive of a singular nature for delighting in the task intrusted to him and his colleagues. In his capacity of a play-actor, he had been hissed from the stage at Lyons, and the door to revenge was now open. The instructions of this committee enjoined them to take the most satisfactory revenge for the death of Châlier, and the insurrection of Lyons, not merely on the citizens, but on the town itself. The principal streets and buildings were to be levelled with the ground, and a monument erected where they stood, was to record the cause;—"*Lyons rebelled against the Republic—Lyons is no more.*" Such fragments of the town as might be permitted to remain were to bear the name of *Commune Affranchie*. It will scarcely be believed, that a doom like that which might have passed the lips of some Eastern despot, in all the frantic madness of arbitrary power and utter ignorance, could have been seriously pronounced, and as seriously enforced in one of the most civilized nations in Europe; and that in the present enlightened age, men who pretended to wisdom and philosophy, should have considered the labours of the architect as a proper subject of punishment. So it was, however; and to give the demolition more effect, the impotent Couthon was carried from house to house, devoting each to ruin, by striking the door with a silver hammer, and pronouncing these words—"House of a rebel, I condemn thee in the name of the Law." Workmen followed in great multitudes, who executed the sentence by pulling the house down to the foundations. This wanton demolition continued for six months, and is said to have been carried on at an expense equal to that which the superb military hospital, the Hôtel des Invalides, cost its founder, Louis

---

[435] Before the arrival of Collot d'Herbois, Fouché (afterwards Duke of Otranto) issued a decree, directing that all religious emblems should be destroyed, and that the words "Death is an eternal sleep!" should be placed over the entrance of every burial ground.—See *Moniteur*, Nos. 57, 64.

XIV. But republican vengeance did not waste itself exclusively upon senseless lime and stone—it sought out sentient victims.

The deserved death of Châlier had been atoned by an apotheosis,[436] executed after Lyons had surrendered; but Collot D'Herbois declared that every drop of that patriotic blood fell as if scalding his own heart, and that the murder demanded atonement. All ordinary process, and every usual mode of execution, was thought too tardy to avenge the death of a Jacobin proconsul. The judges of the revolutionary commission were worn out with fatigue—the arm of the executioner was weary—the very steel of the guillotine was blunted. Collot d'Herbois devised a more summary mode of slaughter. A number of from two to three hundred victims at once were dragged from prison to the Place de Brotteaux, one of the largest squares in Lyons, and there subjected to a fire of grape-shot.[437] Efficacious as this mode of execution may seem, it was neither speedy nor merciful. The sufferers fell to the ground like singed flies, mutilated but not slain, and imploring their executioners to despatch them speedily. This was done with sabres and bayonets, and with such haste and zeal, that some of the jailors and assistants were slain along with those whom they had assisted in dragging to death; and the mistake was not discerned, until, upon counting the dead bodies, the military murderers found them amount to more than the destined tale. The bodies of the dead were thrown into the Rhone, to carry news of the Republican vengeance, as Collot d'Herbois expressed himself, to Toulon, then also in a state of revolt. But the sullen stream rejected the office imposed on it, and heaved back the dead in heaps upon the banks; and the Committee of Representatives were compelled at length to allow the

---

[436] An ass formed a conspicuous part of the procession, having a mitre fastened between his ears, and dragging in the dirt a Bible tied to its tail; which Bible was afterwards burnt, and its ashes scattered to the winds. Fouché wrote to the Convention—"The shade of Châlier is satisfied. Yes, we swear that the people shall be avenged. Our severe courage shall keep pace with their just impatience."—*Moniteur*, Montgaillard, tom. iv., pp. 113, 138.

[437] Fouché, on the 19th December, wrote to Collot d'Herbois—"Let us show ourselves terrible: let us annihilate in our wrath, and at one blow, every conspirator, every traitor, that we may not feel the pain, the long torture, of punishing them as kings would do. We this evening send two hundred and thirteen rebels before the thunder of our cannon. Farewell, my friend! tears of joy stream from my eyes, and overflow my heart.—(Signed) Fouché."—*Moniteur*, No. 85.

relics of their cruelty to be interred, to prevent the risk of contagion.[438]

The people of the south of France have always been distinguished by the vivacity of their temperament. As cruelties beget retaliation, it may be as well here mentioned, that upon the fall of the Jacobins, the people of Lyons forgot not what indeed was calculated for eternal remembrance, and took by violence a severe and sanguinary vengeance on those who had been accessary to the atrocities of Couthon and Collot d'Herbois. They rose on the Jacobins after the fall of Robespierre, and put to death several of them.

Toulon, important by its port, its arsenals, and naval-yard, as well as by its fortifications both on the sea and land side, had partaken deeply in the feelings which pervaded Marseilles, Bourdeaux, and Lyons. But the insurgents of Toulon were determinedly royalist. The place had been for some time subjected to the administration of a Jacobin club, and had seen the usual quantity of murders and excesses with the greater pain, that the town contained many naval officers and others who had served under the King, and retained their affection for the royal cause. Their dissatisfaction did not escape the notice of men, to whom every sullen look was cause of suspicion, and the slightest cause of suspicion a ground of death. The town being threatened with a complete purification after the Jacobin fashion, the inhabitants resolved to anticipate the blow.

At the dead of night the tocsin was sounded by the citizens, who dispersed the Jacobin club, seized on the two representatives who had governed its proceedings, arrested seven or eight Jacobins, who had been most active in the previous assassinations, and, in spite of some opposition, actually executed them. With more decision than the inhabitants of Lyons, they proceeded to proclaim Louis XVII. under the constitution of 1791. Cartaux presently marched upon the insurgent city, driving before him the Marseillois,

---

[438] Guillon de Montléon, Mémoires pour servir à l'Hist. de la Ville de Lyon, tom. ii., p. 405; Toulongeon, tom. iv., p. 68; Jomini, tom. iv., p. 186; Thiers, tom. v., p. 310; Lacretelle, tom. ix., p. 109.

whom, as before mentioned, he had defeated upon their march towards Lyons. Alarmed at this movement, and destitute of a garrison which they could trust, the Toulonnois implored the assistance of the English and Spanish admirals, Lord Hood and Gravina, who were cruising off their port. It was instantly granted, and marines were sent on shore for their immediate protection, while efforts were made to collect from the different allied powers such a supply of troops as could be immediately thrown into the place. But the event of the siege of Toulon brings our general historical sketch into connexion with the life of that wonderful person, whose actions we have undertaken to record. It was during this siege that the light was first distinguished, which, broadening more and more, and blazing brighter and brighter, was at length to fill with its lustre the whole hemisphere of Europe, and was then to set with a rapidity equal to that with which it had arisen.

Ere, however, we produce this first-rate actor upon the stage, we must make the reader still more particularly acquainted with the spirit of the scene.

Chapter XVI

Views of the British Cabinet regarding the French Revolution—Extraordinary Situation of France—Explanation of the Anomaly which it exhibited—System of Terror—Committee of Public Safety—Of Public Security—David the Painter—Law against suspected Persons—Revolutionary Tribunal—Effects of the Emigration of the Princes and Nobles—Causes of the Passiveness of the French People under the Tyranny of the Jacobins—Singular Address of the Committee of Public Safety—General Reflections.

It has been a maxim with great statesmen, that evil governments must end by becoming their own destruction, according to the maxim, *Res nolunt diù male administrari.* Pitt himself was of opinion, that the fury of the French Revolution would wear itself out; and that it already presented so few of the advantages and privileges of social compact, that it seemed as if its political elements must either altogether dissolve, or assume a new form more similar to that on which all other states and governments rest their stability. It was on this account that this great English statesman declined assisting, in plain and open terms the royal cause, and desired to keep England free from any pledge concerning the future state of government in France, aware of the danger of involving her in any declared and avowed interference with the right of a people to choose their own system. However anxious to prevent the revolutionary opinions, as well as arms, from extending beyond their own frontier, it was thought in the British Cabinet, by one large party, that the present frantic excess of Republican principles must, of itself, produce a reaction in favour of more moderate sentiments. Some steady system for the protection of life and property, was, it was said, essential to the very existence of society. The French nation must assume such, and renounce the prosecution of those revolutionary doctrines, for the sake of their own as well as of other countries. The arrangement must, it was thought, take place, from the inevitable course of human affairs, which, however they may fluctuate, are uniformly determined at length by the interest of the parties concerned.

Such was the principle assumed by many great statesmen, whose sagacity was unhappily baffled by the event. In fact, it was calculating upon the actions and personal exertions of a raving madman, as if he had been under the regulation of his senses, and acting upon principles of self-regard and self-preservation. France continued not only to subsist, but to be victorious, without a government, unless the revolutionary committees and Jacobin clubs could be accounted such—for the Convention was sunk into a mere engine of that party, and sanctioned whatever they proposed; without religion, which, as we shall see, they formally abolished; without municipal laws or rights, except that any one of the ruling party might do what mischief he would, while citizens, less distinguished for patriotism, were subjected, for any cause, or no cause, to loss of liberty, property, and life itself; without military discipline, for officers might be dragged from their regiments, and generals from their armies, on the information of their own soldiers; without revenues of state, for the depression of the assignats was extreme; without laws, for there were no ordinary tribunals left to appeal to; without colonies, ships, manufactories, or commerce; without fine arts, any more than those which were useful;—in short, France continued to subsist, and to achieve victories, although apparently forsaken of God, and deprived of all the ordinary resources of human wisdom.

The whole system of society, indeed, seemed only to retain some appearances of cohesion from mere habit, the same which makes trained horses draw up in something like order, even without their riders, if the trumpet is sounded. And yet in foreign wars, notwithstanding the deplorable state of the interior, the Republic was not only occasionally, but permanently and triumphantly victorious. She was like the champion in Berni's romance, who was so delicately sliced asunder by one of the Paladins, that he went on fighting, and slew other warriors, without discovering for a length of time that he was himself killed.

All this extraordinary energy, was, in one word, the effect of TERROR. Death—a grave—are sounds which awaken the strongest efforts in those whom they menace. There was never anywhere, save in France during this melancholy period, so awful a comment on the expression of Scripture, "All that a man hath will he give for his life." Force, immediate and irresistible force, was the only logic used by the government—Death was the only appeal from their authority—the Guillotine[439] the all sufficing argument, which settled each debate betwixt them and the governed.

Was the exchequer low, the Guillotine filled it with the effects of the wealthy, who were judged aristocratical, in exact proportion to the extent of their property. Were these supplies insufficient, diminished as they were by peculation ere they reached the public coffers, the assignats remained, which might be multiplied to any quantity. Did the paper medium of circulation fall in the market to fifty under the hundred, the Guillotine was ready to punish those who refused to exchange it at par. A few examples of such jobbers in the public funds made men glad to give one hundred franks for state money, which they knew to be worth no more than fifty. Was bread awanting, corn was to be found by the same compendious means, and distributed among the Parisians, as among the ancient citizens of Rome, at a regulated price. The Guillotine was a key to storehouses, barns, and granaries.

Did the army want recruits, the Guillotine was ready to exterminate all conscripts who should hesitate to march. On the generals of the Republican army, this decisive argument, which, *à priori*, might have been deemed less applicable, in all its rigour, to them than to others, was possessed of the most exclusive authority. They were beheaded for want of success, which may seem less

---

[439] The Convention having, by a decree of the 17th March, 1792, come to the determination to substitute decapitation for hanging, this instrument was adopted, on the proposition of Dr. Guillotin, an eminent physician of Paris; who regretted to the hour of his death, in 1814, that his name should have been thus associated with the instrument of so many horrors. He had devised it with a view to humanity.

different from the common course of affairs;[440] but they were also guillotined when their successes were not improved to the full expectations of their masters.[441] Nay, they were guillotined, when, being too successful, they were suspected of having acquired over the soldiers who had conquered under them, an interest dangerous to those who had the command of this all-sufficing reason of state.[442] Even mere mediocrity, and a limited but regular discharge of duty, neither so brilliant as to incur jealousy, nor so important as to draw down censure, was no protection.[443] There was no rallying point against this universal, and very simple system—of main force.

The Vendéans, who tried the open and manly mode of generous and direct resistance, were, as we have seen, finally destroyed, leaving a name which will live for ages. The commercial towns, which, upon a scale more modified, also tried their strength with the revolutionary torrent, were successively overpowered. One can, therefore, be no more surprised that the rest of the nation gave way to predominant force, than we are daily at seeing a herd of strong and able-bodied cattle driven to the shambles before one or two butchers, and as many bull-dogs. As the victims approach the slaughter-house, and smell the blood of those which have suffered the fate to which they are destined, they may be often observed to hesitate, start, roar, and bellow, and intimate their dread of the fatal spot, and instinctive desire to escape from it; but the cudgels of their drivers, and the fangs of the mastiffs, seldom fail to compel them forward, slavering, and snorting, and trembling, to the destiny which awaits them.

---

[440] The fate of Custine illustrates this,—a general who had done much for the Republic, and who, when his fortune began to fail him, excused himself by saying, "Fortune was a woman, and his hairs were growing grey."—S.—He was guillotined in August, 1793.

[441] Witness Houchard, who performed the distinguished service of raising the siege of Dunkirk, and who, during his trial, could be hardly made to understand that he was to suffer for not carrying his victory still farther.—S.—Guillotined, Nov., 1793.

[442] Several generals of reputation sustained capital punishment, from no other reason than the jealousy of the committees of their influence with the army.—S.

[443] Luckner, an old German thick-headed soldier, who was of no party, and scrupulously obeyed the command of whichever was uppermost at Paris, had no better fate than others.—S.—He was guillotined in Nov., 1793.

The power of exercising this tremendous authority over a terrified nation, was vested in few hands, and rested on a very simple basis.

The Convention had, after the fall of the Girondists, remained an empty show of what it had once some title to call itself,—the Representative Body of the French Nation. The members belonging to The Plain, who had observed a timid neutrality betwixt The Mountain and the Girondists, if not without talent, were without courage to make any opposition to the former when triumphant. They crouched to their fate, were glad to escape in silence, and to yield full passage to the revolutionary torrent. They consoled themselves with the usual apology of weak minds—that they submitted to what they could not prevent; and their adversaries, while despising them, were yet tolerant of their presence, and somewhat indulgent to their scruples, because, while these timid neutrals remained in their ranks, they furnished to the eye at least the appearance of a full senate, filled the ranks of the representative body as a garment is stuffed out to the required size by buckram, and countenanced by their passive acquiescence the measures which they most detested in their hearts. It was worth the while of The Mountain to endure the imbecility of such associates, and even to permit occasionally some diffident opposition on their part, had it only been to preserve appearances, and afford a show of a free assembly debating on the affairs of the nation. Thus, although the name of the National Convention was generally used, its deputies, carefully selected from the Jacobin or ruling party, were every where acting in their name, with all the authority of Roman proconsuls; while two-thirds of the body sate with submitted necks and padlocked lips, unresisting slaves to the minor proportion, which again, under its various fierce leaders, was beginning to wage a civil war within its own limited circle.

But the young reader, to whom this eventful history is a novelty, may ask in what hands was the real power of the government lodged, of which the Convention, considered as a body, was thus effectually deprived, though permitted to retain, like the apparition in Macbeth,—

"upon its baby brow the round And type of sovereignty?"

France had, indeed, in 1792, accepted, with the usual solemnities, a new constitution, which was stated to rest on the right republican basis, and was, of course, alleged to afford the most perfect and absolute security for liberty and equality, that the nation could desire. But this constitution was entirely superseded in practice by the more compendious mode of governing by means of a junto, selected out of the Convention itself, without observing any farther ceremony. In fact, two small Committees vested with the full authority of the state, exercised the powers of a dictatorship; while the representatives of the people, like the senate under the Roman empire, retained the form and semblance of supreme sway, might keep their curule chairs, and enjoy the dignity of fasces and lictors, but had in their possession and exercise scarcely the independent powers of an English vestry, or quarter-sessions.

The Committee of Public Safety dictated every measure of the Convention, or more frequently acted without deigning to consult the legislative body at all. The number of members who exercised this executive government fluctuated betwixt ten and twelve; and, as they were all chosen Jacobins, and selected as men capable of going all the lengths of their party, care was taken, by re-elections from time to time, to render the situation permanent. This body deliberated in secret, and had the despotic right of interfering with and controlling every other authority in the state; and before its absolute powers, and the uses which were made of them, the Council of Ten of the Venetian government sunk into a harmless and liberal institution. Another committee, with powers of the same revolutionary nature, and in which the members were also renewed from time to time, was that of Public Security. It was inferior in importance to that of Public Safety, but was nevertheless as active within its sphere. We regret to record of a man of genius, that David, the celebrated painter,[444] held a seat in the Committee of Public Security. The fine arts, which he studied, had not produced on his mind the softening and humanizing effect ascribed to them. Frightfully ugly in his exterior, his mind seemed to correspond with

---

[444] David is generally allowed to have possessed great merit as a draughtsman. Foreigners do not admire his composition and colouring, so much as his countrymen.—S.

the harshness of his looks. "Let us grind enough of the Red," was the professional phrase of which he made use, when sitting down to the bloody work of the day.

That these revolutionary committees might have in their hands a power subject to no legal defence or evasion on the part of the accused, Merlin of Douay, a lawyer, it is said, of eminence, framed what was termed the law against suspected persons, which was worded with so much ingenuity, that not only it enveloped every one who, by birth, friendship, habits of life, dependencies, or other ties, was linked, however distantly, with aristocracy, whether of birth or property, but also all who had, in the various changes and phases of the Revolution, taken one step too few in the career of the most violent patriotism, or had, though it were but for one misguided and doubtful moment, held opinions short of the most extravagant Jacobinism. This crime of suspicion was of the nature of the cameleon; it derived its peculiar shade or colour from the person to whom it attached for the moment. To have been a priest, or even an assertor of the rights and doctrines of Christianity, was fatal; but in some instances, an overflow of atheistical blasphemy was equally so. To be silent on public affairs, betrayed a culpable indifference; but it incurred darker suspicion to speak of them otherwise than in the most violent tone of the ruling party. By a supplementary law, this spider's web was so widely extended, that it appeared no fly could be found insignificant enough to escape its meshes. Its general propositions were of a nature so vague, that it was impossible they could ever be made subjects of evidence. Therefore they were assumed without proof; and at length, definition of the characteristics of suspicion seems to have been altogether dispensed with, and all those were suspected persons whom the revolutionary committees and their assistants chose to hold as such.

The operation of this law was terrible. A suspected person, besides being thrown into prison, was deprived of all his rights, his effects sealed up, his property placed under care of the state, and he himself considered as civilly dead. If the unfortunate object of suspicion had the good fortune to be set at liberty, it was no security whatever against his being again arrested on the day following. There was, indeed, no end to the various shades of sophistry which brought almost every kind of person under this oppressive law, so ample was its scope, and undefined its objects.

That the administrators of this law of suspicion might not have too much trouble in seeking for victims, all householders were obliged to publish on the outside of their doors a list of the names and description of their inmates. Domestic security, the most precious of all rights to a people who know what freedom really is, was violated on every occasion, even the slightest, by domiciliary visits. The number of arrests which took place through France, choked the prisons anew which had been so fearfully emptied on the 2d and 3d of September, and is said to have been only moderately computed at three hundred thousand souls, one-third of whom were women. The Jacobins, however, found a mode of jail-delivery less summary than by direct massacre; although differing so little from it in every other respect, that a victim might have had pretty nearly the same chance of a fair trial before Maillard and his men of September, as from the Revolutionary Tribunal. It requires an effort even to write that word, from the extremities of guilt and horror which it recalls. But it is the lot of humanity to record its own greatest disgraces; and it is a wholesome and humbling lesson to exhibit a just picture of those excesses, of which, in its unassisted movements, and when agitated by evil and misguided passions, human nature can be rendered capable.

REVOLUTIONARY TRIBUNAL

The extraordinary criminal court, better known by the name of the Revolutionary Tribunal, was first instituted upon the motion of Danton. Its object was to judge of state crimes, plots, and attempts against liberty, or in favour of royalty, or affecting the rights and liberty of man, or in any way, more or less, tending to counteract the progress of the Revolution. In short, it was the business of this court to execute the laws, or inflict the sentence rather, upon such as had been arrested as suspected persons; and they generally saw room to punish in most of the instances where the arresting functionaries had seen ground for imprisonment.

This frightful court consisted of six judges or public accusers, and two assistants. There were twelve jurymen; but the appointment of these was a mere mockery. They were official persons, who held permanent appointments; had a salary from the state; and were in no manner liable to the choice or challenge of the party tried. Jurors and judges were selected for their Republican zeal and steady qualities, and were capable of seeing no obstacle either of law or humanity in the path of their duty. This tribunal had the power of deciding without proof,—or cutting short evidence when in the progress of being adduced,—or stopping the defence of the prisoners at pleasure; privileges which tended greatly to shorten the forms of court, and aid the despatch of business.[445]

The Revolutionary Tribunal was in a short time so overwhelmed with work, that it became necessary to divide it into four sections, all armed with similar powers. The quantity of blood which it caused to be shed was something unheard of, even during the proscriptions of the Roman Empire; and there were involved in its sentences crimes the most different, personages the most opposed, and opinions the most dissimilar. When Henry VIII. roused the fires of Smithfield both against Protestant and Papist, burning at the same stake one wretch for denying the King's supremacy, and another for disbelieving the divine presence in the Eucharist, the association was consistency itself, compared to the scenes presented at the Revolutionary tribunal, in which Royalist, Constitutionalist, Girondist, Churchman, Theophilanthropist, Noble and Roturier, Prince and Peasant, both sexes and all ages, were involved in one general massacre, and sent to execution by scores together, and on the same sledge.

Supporting by their numerous associations the government as exercised by the Revolutionary Committees, came the mass of Jacobins, who, divided into a thousand clubs, emanating from that which had its meetings at Paris, formed the strength of the party to which they gave the name.

The sole principle of the Jacobinical institutions was to excite against all persons who had any thing to lose, the passions of those

---

[445] Thiers, tom. iv., p. 6; Mignet, tom. i., p. 248.

who possessed no property, and were, by birth and circumstances, brutally ignorant, and envious of the advantages enjoyed by the higher classes. All other governments have made individual property the object of countenance and protection; but in this strangely inverted state of things, it seemed the object of constant suspicion and persecution, and exposed the owner to perpetual danger. We have elsewhere said that Equality (unless in the no less intelligible than sacred sense of equal submission to the law) is a mere chimera, which can no more exist with respect to property, than in regard to mental qualifications, or personal strength, beauty, or stature. Divide the whole property of a country equally among its inhabitants, and a week will bring back the inequality which you have endeavoured to remove; nay, a much shorter space will find the industrious and saving richer than the idle and prodigal. But in France, at the period under discussion, this equality, in itself so unattainable, had completely superseded even the principle of liberty, as a watch-word for exciting the people. It was to sin against this leading principle to be possessed of, and more especially to enjoy ostentatiously, any thing which was wanting to your neighbour. To be richer, more accomplished, better bred, or better taught, subjected you to the law of suspicion, and you were conducted instantly before a Revolutionary Committee, where you were probably convicted of incivism; not for interfering with the liberty and property of others, but for making what use you pleased of your own.

The whole of the terrible mystery is included in two regulations, communicated by the Jacobin Club of Paris to the Committee of Public Safety.—1. That when, by the machinations of opulent persons, seditions should arise in any district, it should be declared in a state of rebellion.—2. That the Convention shall avail themselves of such opportunity *to excite the poor to make war on the rich*, and to restore order at any price whatever.—This was so much understood, that one of the persons tried by the Revolutionary Tribunal, when asked what he had to say in his defence, answered,—"I am wealthy—what avails it to me to offer any exculpation when such is my offence?"

AFFILIATED SOCIETIES

The committees of government distributed large sums of money to the Jacobin Club and its affiliated societies, as being necessary to the propagation of sound political principles. The clubs themselves took upon them in every village the exercise of the powers of government; and while they sat swearing, drinking, and smoking, examined passports, imprisoned citizens, and enforced to their full extent the benefits of liberty and equality. "Death or Fraternity" was usually inscribed over their place of assembly; which some one translated,—"Become my brother, or I will kill thee."

These clubs were composed of members drawn from the lees of the people, that they might not, in their own persons, give an example contradicting the equality which it was their business to enforce. They were filled with men without resources or talents, but towards whom the confidence of the deceived people was directed, from the conviction that, because taken from among themselves, they would have the interest of the lower orders constantly in view. Their secretaries, however, were generally selected with some attention to alertness of capacity; for on them depended the terrible combination which extended from the mother society of Jacobins in Paris, down into the most remote villages of the most distant provinces, in which the same tyranny was maintained by the influence of similar means. Thus rumours could be either circulated or collected with a speed and uniformity, which enabled a whisper from Robespierre to regulate the sentiments of the Jacobins at the most distant part of his empire; for his it unquestionably was, for the space of two dreadful years.

France had been subjected to many evils ere circumstances had for a time reduced her to this state of passive obedience to a yoke, which, after all, when its strength was fairly tried, proved as brittle as it was intolerable. Those who witnessed the tragedies which then occurred, look back upon that period as the delirium of a national fever, filled with visions too horrible and painful for recollection, and which, being once wiped from the mind, we recall with difficulty and reluctance, and dwell upon with disgust. A long course of events, tending each successively to disorganize society more and more, had unhappily prevented a brave, generous, and accomplished people from combining together in mutual defence. The emigration and forfeiture of the nobles and clergy had deprived the country at once of those higher classes, that right-hand file, who are bred up to hold their lives light if called on to lay them down for religion, or in defence of the rights of their country, or the principles of their own honour or conscience. Whatever may be thought of the wisdom or necessity of emigration, its evils were the same. A high-spirited and generous race of gentry, accustomed to consider themselves as peculiar depositaries of the national honour—a learned and numerous priesthood, the guardians of religious opinion—had been removed from their place, and society was so much the more weak and more ignorant for the want of them. Whether voluntarily abandoning or forcibly driven from the country, the expulsion of so large a mass, belonging entirely to the higher orders, tended instantly to destroy the balance of society, and to throw all power into the hands of the lower class; who, deceived by bad and artful men, abused it to the frightful excess we have described.

We do not mean to say, that the emigrants had carried with them beyond the frontiers all the worth and courage of the better classes in France, or that there were not, among men attached to the cause of liberty, many who would have shed their blood to have prevented its abuse. But these had been, unhappily, during the progress of the Revolution, divided and subdivided among themselves, were split up into a variety of broken and demolished parties which had repeatedly suffered proscription; and, what was worse, sustained it from the hand of each other. The Constitutionalist could not safely join in league with the Royalist, or either with the Girondist; and thus there existed no confidence on which a union could be effected, among materials repulsive of each other. There extended, besides, through France, far and near, that sorrow and sinking of the heart, which prevails amid great national calamities, where there is little hope. The state of oppression was so universal, that no one strove to remedy its evils, more than they would have struggled to remedy the *malaria* of an infected country. Those who escaped the disorder contented themselves with their individual safety, without thinking of the general evil, as one which human art could remedy, or human courage resist.

Moreover, the Jacobinical rulers had surrounded themselves with such a system of espionage and delation, that the attempt to organize any resistance to their power, would have been in fact, to fall inevitably and fatally under their tyranny. If the bold conspirator against this most infernal authority did not bestow his confidence on a false friend or a concealed emissary of the Jacobin party, he was scarce the safer on that account; for if he breathed forth in the most friendly ear any thing tending to reflect on the free, happy, and humane government under which he had the happiness to live, his hearer was bound, equally as a hired spy, to carry the purport of the conversation to the constituted authorities—that is, to the Revolutionary Committees or Republican Commissioners; and above all, to the Committee of Public Safety. Silence on public affairs, and acquiescence in democratic tyranny, became, therefore, matter of little wonder; for men will be long mute, when to indulge the tongue may endanger the head. And thus, in the kingdom which boasts herself most civilized in Europe, and with all that ardour for liberty which seemed but of late to animate every bosom, the general apathy of terror and astonishment, joined to a want of all power of combination, palsied every effort at resistance. They who make national reflections on the French for remaining passive under circumstances so hopeless, should first reflect, that our disposition to prevent or punish crime, and our supposed readiness to resist oppression, have their foundation in a strong confidence in the laws, and in the immediate support which they are sure to receive from the numerous classes who have been trained up to respect them, as protectors of the rich equally and of the poor. But in France, the whole system of the administration of justice was in the hands of brutal force; and it is one thing to join in the hue and cry against a murderer, seconded by the willing assistance of a whole population—another to venture upon withstanding him in his den, he at the head of his banditti, the assailant defenceless, excepting in the justice of his cause.

FEROCITY OF THE POPULACE

It has further been a natural subject of wonder, not only that the richer and better classes, the avowed objects of Jacobin persecution, were so passively resigned to this frightful tyranny, but also why the French populace, whose general manners are so civilized and so kindly, that they are, on ordinary occasions, the gayest and best humoured people in Europe, should have so far changed their character as to delight in cruelty, or at least to look on, without expressing disgust, at cruelties perpetrated in their name.

But the state of a people in ordinary times and peaceful occupations, is in every country totally different from the character which they manifest under strong circumstances of excitation. Rousseau says, that no one who sees the ordinary greyhound, the most sportive, gentle, and timid perhaps of the canine race, can form an idea of the same animal pursuing and strangling its screaming and helpless victim. Something of this sort must plead the apology of the French people in the early excesses of the Revolution; and we must remember, that men collected in crowds, and influenced with a sense of wrongs, whether real or imaginary, are acted upon by the enthusiasm of the moment, and are, besides, in a state of such general and undistinguishing fury, that they adopt, by joining in the clamours and general shouts, deeds of which they hardly witness the import, and which perhaps not one of the assembled multitude out of a thousand would countenance, were that import distinctly felt and known. In the revolutionary massacres and cruelties, there was always an executive power, consisting of a few well-breathed and thorough-paced ruffians, whose hands perpetrated the actions, to which the ignorant vulgar only lent their acclamations.

This species of assentation became less wonderful when instant slaughter, without even the ceremony of inquiry, had been exchanged for some forms, however flimsy and unsubstantial, of regular trial, condemnation, and execution. These served for a time to satisfy the public mind. The populace saw men dragged to the guillotine, convicted of criminal attempts, as they were informed, against the liberty of the people; and they shouted as at the punishment of their own immediate enemies.

But as the work of death proceeded daily, the people became softened as their passions abated; and the frequency of such sacrifices having removed the odious interest which for a while attended them, the lower classes, whom Robespierre desired most to conciliate, looked on, first with indifference, but afterwards with shame and disgust, and at last with the wish to put an end to cruelties, which even the most ignorant and prejudiced began to regard in their own true, undisguised light.

Yet the operation of these universal feelings was long delayed. To support the Reign of Terror, the revolutionary committees had their own guards and executioners, without whom they could not have long withstood the general abhorrence of mankind. All official situations were scrupulously and religiously filled up by individuals chosen from the Sans-Culottes, who had rendered themselves, by their zeal, worthy of that honourable appellation. Were they of little note, they were employed in the various capacities of guards, officers, and jailors, for which the times created an unwearied demand. Did they hold places in the Convention, they were frequently despatched upon commissions to different parts of France, to give new edge to the guillotine, and superintend in person the punishment of conspiracy or rebellion, real or supposed. Such commissioners or proconsuls, as they were frequently termed, being vested with unlimited power, and fresh in its exercise, signalized themselves by their cruelty, even more than the tyrants whose will they discharged.

We may quote in illustration, a remarkable passage in an address, by the Commissioners of Public Safety, to the representatives absent upon commissions, in which there occur some gentle remarks on their having extended capital punishment to cases where it was not provided by law, although the lustre of their services to the Republic far outshone the shade of such occasional peccadiloes. For their future direction they are thus exhorted. "Let your energy awaken anew as the term of your labour approaches. The Convention charges you to complete the purification and reorganization of the constituted authorities with the least possible delay, and to report the conclusion of these two operations before the end of the next month. A simple measure may effect the desired purification. *Convoke the people in the popular societies—Let the public functionaries appear before them—Interrogate the people on the subject of their conduct, and let their judgment dictate yours.*"[446] Thus the wildest prejudices arising in the Jacobin Club, consisting of the lowest, most ignorant, most prejudiced, and often most malicious members in society, were received as evidence, and the populace declared masters, at their own pleasure, of the property, honour, and life of those who had held any brief authority over them.

Where there had occurred any positive rising or resistance, the duty of the commissioners was extended by all the powers that martial law, in other words, the rule of superior force, could confer. We have mentioned the murders committed at Lyons; but even these, though hundreds were swept away by volleys of musket-shot, fell short of the horrors perpetrated by Carrier at Nantes,[447] who, in avenging the Republic on the obstinate resistance of La Vendée, might have summoned hell to match his cruelty, without a demon venturing to answer his challenge. Hundreds, men, women, and children, were forced on board of vessels which were scuttled and sunk in the Loire, and this was called Republican Baptism. Men and women were stripped, bound together, and thus thrown into the river, and this was called Republican Marriage.[448] But we have said enough to show that men's blood seems to have been converted into poison, and their hearts into stone, by the practices in which

---

[446] Moniteur, No. 995, 25th December, 1793.—S.
[447] Carrier was born at Yolay, near Aurillac, in 1756, and, previous to the Revolution, was an attorney. During his mission to Nantes, not less than thirty-two thousand human beings were destroyed by *noyades* and *fusillades*, and by the horrors of crowded and infected prisons. Being accused by Merlin de Thionville, Carnot, and others, he declared to the Convention, 23d November, 1794, that by trying him it would ruin itself, and that if all the crimes committed in its name were to be punished, "not even the little bell of the president was free from guilt." He was convicted of having had children of thirteen and fourteen years old shot, and of having ordered drownings, and this with counter-revolutionary intentions. He ascended the scaffold with firmness and said, "I die a victim and innocent: I only executed the orders of the committees."
[448] See Montgaillard, tom. iv., p. 42; Toulongeon, tom. v., p. 120; Thiers, tom. vi., p. 373; Lacretelle, tom. xii., p. 165; Vie et Crimes de Carrier, par Gracchus Babœuf; Dénonciation des Crimes de Carrier, par Philippes Tronjolly; Procès de Carrier; Bulletin du Tribunal Révolutionnaire de Nantes.

they were daily engaged. Many affected even a lust of cruelty, and the instrument of punishment was talked of with the fondness and gaiety with which we speak of a beloved and fondled object. It had its pet name of "the Little National Window," and others equally expressive; and although saints were not much in fashion, was, in some degree canonized by the name of "the Holy Mother Guillotine."[449] That active citizen, the executioner, had also his honours, as well as the senseless machine which he directed. This official was admitted to the society of some of the more emphatic patriots, and, as we shall afterwards see, shared in their civic festivities. It may be questioned whether even *his* company was not too good for the patrons who thus regaled him.

REVOLUTIONARY ARMY

There was also an armed force raised among the most thorough-paced and hardened satellites of the lower order, termed by pre-eminence "the Revolutionary Army." They were under the command of Ronsin, a general every way worthy of such soldiers.[450] These troops were produced on all occasions, when it was necessary to intimidate the metropolis and the national guard. They were at the more immediate disposal of the Commune of Paris, and were a ready, though not a great force, which always could be produced at a moment's notice, and were generally joined by the more active democrats, in the capacity of a Jacobin militia. In their own ranks they mustered six thousand men.

It is worthy of remark, that some of the persons whose agency was distinguished during this disgraceful period, and whose hands were deeply dyed in the blood so unrelentingly shed, under whatever frenzy of brain, or state of a generally maddening impulse they may

---

[449] Lacretelle, tom. xi., p. 309. "In 1793, a bookseller, (a *pure* Royalist in 1814,) had this inscription painted over his shop door, 'A Notre Dame de la Guillotine.'"—Montgaillard, tom. iv., p. 189.

[450] Ronsin was born at Soissons in 1752. He figured in the early scenes of the Revolution, and in 1789, brought out, at one of the minor Paris theatres, a tragedy called "La Ligue des Fanatiques et des Tyrans," which, though despicable in point of style, had a considerable run. Being denounced by Robespierre, he was guillotined, March 24, 1794. His dramatic pieces have been published under the title of "Théâtre de Ronsin."

have acted, nevertheless made amends, in their after conduct, for their enormities then committed. This was the case with Tallien, with Barras, with Fouché, Legendre, and others, who, neither good nor scrupulous men, were yet, upon many subsequent occasions, much more humane and moderate than could have been expected from their early acquaintance with revolutionary horrors. They resembled disbanded soldiers, who, returned to their native homes, often resume so entirely the habits of earlier life, that they seem to have forgotten the wild, and perhaps sanguinary character of their military career. We cannot, indeed, pay any of these reformed Jacobins the compliment ascribed to Octavius by the Romans, who found a blessing in the emperor's benevolent government, which compensated the injuries inflicted by the triumvir. But it is certain that, had it not been for the courage of Tallien and Barras in particular, it might have been much longer ere the French had been able to rid themselves of Robespierre, and that the revolution of 9th Thermidor, as they called the memorable day of his fall, was, in a great measure, brought about by the remorse or jealousy of the dictator's old comrades. But, ere we arrive at that more auspicious point of our story, we have to consider the train of causes which led to the downfall of Jacobinism.

Periods which display great national failings or vices, are those also which bring to light distinguished and redeeming virtues. France unfortunately, during the years 1793 and 1794, exhibited instances of extreme cruelty, in principle and practice, which make the human blood curdle. She may also be censured for a certain abasement of spirit, for sinking so long unresistingly under a yoke so unnaturally horrible. But she has to boast that, during this fearful period, she can produce as many instances of the most high and honourable fidelity, of the most courageous and devoted humanity, as honour the annals of any country whatever.

The cruelty of the laws denounced the highest penalties against those who relieved proscribed fugitives. These were executed with the most merciless rigour. Madame Boucquey and her husband were put to death at Bourdeaux for affording shelter to the members of the Gironde faction; and the interdiction of fire and water to outlawed persons, of whatever description, was enforced with the heaviest penalty. Yet, not only among the better classes, but among the poorest of the poor, were there men of noble minds found, who, having but half a morsel to support their own family, divided it willingly with some wretched fugitive, though death stood ready to reward their charity.

In some cases, fidelity and devotion aided the suggestions of humanity. Among domestic servants, a race whose virtues should be the more esteemed, that they are practised sometimes in defiance of strong temptation, were found many distinguished instances of unshaken fidelity. Indeed, it must be said, to the honour of the French manners, that the master and his servant live on a footing of much more kindliness than attends the same relation in other countries, and especially in Britain. Even in the most trying situations, there were not many instances of domestic treason, and many a master owed his life to the attachment and fidelity of a menial. The feelings of religion sheltered others. The recusant and exiled priests often found among their former flock the means of concealment and existence, when it was death to administer them. Often this must have flowed from grateful recollection of their former religious services—sometimes from unmingled veneration for the Being whose ministers they professed themselves.[451] Nothing short of such heroic exertions, which were numerous, (and especially in the class where individuals, hard pressed on account of their own wants, are often rendered callous to the distress of others,) could have prevented France, during this horrible period,

---

[451] Strangers are forcibly affected by the trifling incidents which sometimes recall the memory of those fearful times. A venerable French ecclesiastic being on a visit at a gentleman's house in North Britain, it was remarked by the family, that a favourite cat, rather wild and capricious in its habits, paid particular attention to their guest. It was explained, by the priest giving an account of his lurking in the waste garret, or lumber-room, of an artisan's house, for several weeks. In this condition, he had no better amusement than to study the manners and habits of the cats which frequented his place of retreat, and acquire the mode of conciliating their favour. The difficulty of supplying him with food, without attracting suspicion, was extreme, and it could only be placed near his place of concealment, in small quantities, and at uncertain times. Men, women, and children knew of his being in that place; there were rewards to be gained by discovery, life to be lost by persevering in concealing him; yet he was faithfully preserved, to try upon a Scottish cat, after the restoration of the Monarchy, the arts which he had learned in his miserable place of shelter during the Reign of Terror. The history of the time abounds with similar instances.

from becoming a universal charnel-house, and her history an unvaried calendar of murder.

Chapter XVII

Marat, Danton, Robespierre—Marat poniarded—Danton and Robespierre become Rivals—Commune of Paris—their gross Irreligion—Gobel—Goddess of Reason—Marriage reduced to a Civil Contract—Views of Danton—and of Robespierre—Principal Leaders of the Commune arrested—and Nineteen of them executed—Danton arrested by the Influence of Robespierre—and, along with Camille Desmoulins, Westermann, and La Croix, taken before the Revolutionary Tribunal, condemned, and executed—Decree issued, on the motion of Robespierre, acknowledging a Supreme Being—Cécilée Regnault—Gradual Change in the Public Mind—Robespierre becomes unpopular—Makes every effort to retrieve his power—Stormy Debate in the Convention—Collot D'Herbois, Tallien, &c., expelled from the Jacobin Club at the instigation of Robespierre—Robespierre denounced in the Convention on the 9th Thermidor, (27th July, 1794,) and, after furious struggles, arrested, along with his brother, Couthon, and Saint Just—Henriot, Commandant of the National Guard, arrested—Terrorists take refuge in the Hôtel de Ville—Attempt their own lives—Robespierre wounds himself—but lives, along with most of the others, long enough to be carried to the Guillotine, and executed—His character—Struggles that followed his Fate—Final Destruction of the Jacobinical System—and return of Tranquillity—Singular colour given to Society in Paris—Ball of the Victims.

The reader need not be reminded, that the three distinguished champions who assumed the front in the Jacobin ranks, were Marat, Danton, and Robespierre. The first was poniarded by

Charlotte Corday[452] an enthusiastic young person, who had nourished, in a feeling betwixt lunacy and heroism, the ambition of ridding the world of a tyrant.[453] Danton and Robespierre, reduced to a Duumvirate, might have divided the power betwixt them. But Danton, far the more able and powerful-minded man, could not resist temptations to plunder and to revel; and Robespierre, who took care to preserve proof of his rival's peculations, a crime of a peculiarly unpopular character, and from which he seemed to keep his own hands pure, possessed thereby the power of ruining him whenever he should find it convenient. Danton married a beautiful woman, became a candidate for domestic happiness, withdrew himself for some time from state affairs, and quitted the stern and menacing attitude which he had presented to the public during the earlier stages of the Revolution. Still his ascendency, especially in the Club of Cordeliers, was formidable enough to command

---

[452] Charlotte Corday was born, in 1768, near Séez, in Normandy. She was twenty-five years of age, and resided at Caen, when she conceived and executed the design of ridding the world of this monster. She reached Paris on the 11th July, and on the 12th wrote a note to Marat, soliciting an interview, and purchased in the Palais Royal a knife to plunge into the bosom of the tyrant. On the 13th, she obtained admission to Marat, whom she found in his bath-room. He enquired after the proscribed deputies at Caen. Being told their names—"They shall soon," he said, "meet with the punishment they deserve."—"Thine is at hand!" exclaimed she, and stabbed him to the heart. She was immediately brought to trial, and executed on the 17th.—Lacretelle, tom. xi., p. 47; Montgaillard, tom. iv., p. 55.—Charlotte Corday was descended, in a direct line, from the great Corneille. See the genealogical table of the Corneille family, prefixed to Lepan's *Chefs d'Œuvres de Corneille*, tom. v., 8vo, 1816.

[453] Marat was born at Neuchatel in 1744. He was not five feet high. His countenance was equally ferocious and hideous, and his head monstrous in size. "He wore," says Madame Roland, "boots, but no stockings, a pair of old leather breeches, and a white silk waistcoat. His dirty shirt, open at the bosom, exhibited his skin of yellow hue; while his long and dirty nails displayed themselves at his fingers' ends, and his horrid face accorded perfectly with his whimsical dress."—*Mémoires*, part i., p. 176.

"After Marat's death, honours, almost divine, were decreed to him. In all the public places in Paris triumphal arches and mausoleums were erected to him: in the Place du Carousel a sort of pyramid was raised in celebration of him, within which were placed his bust, his bathing-tub, his writing desk, and his lamp. The honours of the Pantheon were decreed him, and the poets celebrated him on the stage and in their works. But at last France indignantly broke the busts which his partisans had placed in all the theatres, his filthy remains were torn from the Pantheon, trampled under foot, and dragged through the mud, by the same populace who had deified him."—*Biog. Mod.*, tom. ii., p. 355; Mignet, tom. ii., p. 279.

"In 1774, Marat resided at Edinburgh, where he taught the French language, and published, in English, a volume entitled 'The Chains of Slavery;' a work wherein the clandestine and villanous attempts of princes to ruin liberty are pointed out, and the dreadful scenes of despotism disclosed; to which is prefixed an address to the electors of Great Britain.'"—*Biog. Univ.*

Robespierre's constant attention, and keep awake his envy, which was like the worm that dieth not, though it did not draw down any indication of his immediate and active vengeance. A power, kindred also in crime, but more within his reach for the moment, was first to be demolished, ere Robespierre was to measure strength with his great rival.

COMMUNE OF PARIS

This third party consisted of those who had possessed themselves of official situations in the Commune of Paris, whose civic authority, and the implement which they commanded in the Revolutionary army, commanded by Ronsin, gave them the power of marching, at a moment's warning, upon the Convention, or even against the Jacobin Club. It is true, these men, of whom Hébert, Chaumette, and others, were leaders, had never shown the least diffidence of Robespierre, but, on the contrary, had used all means to propitiate his favour. But the man whom a tyrant fears, becomes, with little farther provocation, the object of his mortal enmity. Robespierre watched, therefore, with vigilance, the occasion of overreaching and destroying this party, whose power he dreaded; and, singular to tell, he sought the means of accomplishing their ruin in the very extravagance of their revolutionary zeal, which shortly before he might have envied, as pushed farther than his own. But Robespierre did not want sense; and he saw with pleasure Hébert, Chaumette, and their followers, run into such inordinate extravagances, as he thought might render his own interference desirable, even to those who most disliked his principles, most abhorred the paths by which he had climbed to power, and most feared the use which he made of it.

It was through the subject of religion that this means of ruining his opponents, as he hoped, arose. A subject, which one would have thought so indifferent to either, came to be on both sides the occasion of quarrel between the Commune of Paris and the Jacobin leader. But there is a fanaticism of atheism, as well as of superstitious belief; and a philosopher can harbour and express as much malice against those who persevere in believing what he is pleased to denounce as unworthy of credence, as an ignorant and bigoted priest can bear against a man who cannot yield faith to dogmata which he thinks insufficiently proved. Accordingly, the throne being wholly annihilated, it appeared to the philosophers of the school of Hébert,[454] that, in totally destroying such vestiges of religion and public worship as were still retained by the people of France, there was room for a splendid triumph of liberal opinions. It was not enough, they said, for a regenerate nation to have dethroned earthly kings, unless she stretched out the arm of defiance towards those powers which superstition had represented as reigning over boundless space.[455]

An unhappy man, named Gobel, constitutional bishop of Paris, was brought forward to play the principal part in the most impudent and scandalous farce ever acted in the face of a national representation.

It is said that the leaders of the scene had some difficulty in inducing the bishop to comply with the task assigned him; which, after all, he executed, not without present tears and subsequent remorse.[456] But he did play the part prescribed. He was brought forward in full procession, [Nov. 7,] to declare to the Convention, that the religion which he had taught so many years, was, in every respect, a piece of priestcraft, which had no foundation either in history or sacred truth. He disowned, in solemn and explicit terms, the existence of the Deity to whose worship he had been consecrated, and devoted himself in future to the homage of Liberty, Equality, Virtue, and Morality. He then laid on the table his Episcopal decorations, and received a fraternal embrace from the

---

[454] See Note, *ante*.
[455] "Pache, Hébert, and Chaumette, the leaders of the municipality, publicly expressed their determination to dethrone the King of Heaven, as well as the kings of the earth!"—Lacretelle, tom. xi., p. 300.
[456] Gobel was born at Thann, in Upper Alsace, in 1727. In January, 1791, he took the oath of fidelity to the new constitution, and in March following was installed Bishop of Paris, by the Bishop of Autun, M. de Talleyrand. In April, 1794, he was dragged before the revolutionary tribunal, accused (with Chaumette, and the actor Grammont,) of conspiracy and atheism, and executed. See, in the *Annales Catholiques*, tom. iii., p. 466, a letter from the Abbé Lothringer, one of his vicars, showing that Gobel died penitent.

president of the Convention.[457] Several apostate priests followed the example of this prelate.[458]

The gold and silver plate of the churches was seized upon and desecrated; processions entered the Convention, travestied in priestly garments, and singing the most profane hymns; while many of the chalices and sacred vessels were applied by Chaumette and Hébert to the celebration of their own impious orgies. The world, for the first time, heard an assembly of men, born and educated in civilisation, and assuming the right to govern one of the finest of the European nations, uplift their united voice to deny the most solemn truth which man's soul receives, and renounce unanimously the belief and worship of a Deity. For a short time, the same mad profanity continued to be acted upon.

GODDESS OF REASON

One of the ceremonies of this insane time stands unrivalled for absurdity, combined with impiety. The doors of the Convention [Nov. 10] were thrown open to a band of musicians; preceded by whom, the members of the municipal body entered in solemn procession, singing a hymn in praise of liberty, and escorting, as the object of their future worship, a veiled female, whom they termed the Goddess of Reason. Being brought within the bar, she was unveiled with great form, and placed on the right hand of the president; when she was generally recognised as a dancing-girl of the Opera,[459] with whose charms most of the persons present were acquainted from her appearance on the stage, while the experience of individuals was farther extended. To this person, as the fittest

---

[457] "On présente le bonnet rouge à Gobel; il le met sur la tête. Un grand nombre de membres—'L'accolade à l'évêque de Paris.'—*Le Président.* 'D'après l'abjuration qui vient d'être faite, l'évêque de Paris est un être de raison: mais je vais embrasser Gobel.'—Le président donne l'accolade à Gobel."—*Moniteur*, No. 49, 2d décade de Brumaire, 9th November.

[458] Toulongeon, tom. iv., p. 124; Montgaillard, tom. iv., p. 157. "Gaivernon, one of the constitutional bishops, exclaimed, 'I want no other god, and no other king, but the will of the people.'"—Lacretelle, tom. xi., p. 302.

[459] A Mademoiselle Maillard, at that time the mistress of Mormoro.

representative of that Reason whom they worshipped, the National Convention of France rendered public homage.[460]

This impious and ridiculous mummery had a certain fashion; and the installation of the Goddess of Reason was renewed and imitated throughout the nation, in such places where the inhabitants desired to show themselves equal to all the heights of the Revolution. The churches were, in most districts of France, closed against priests and worshippers—the bells were broken and cast into cannon—the whole ecclesiastical establishment destroyed—and the Republican inscription over the cemeteries, declaring Death to be perpetual Sleep,[461] announced to those who lived under that dominion, that they were to hope no redress even in the next world.

Intimately connected with these laws affecting religion, was that which reduced the union of marriage, the most sacred engagement which human beings can form, and the permanence of which leads most strongly to the consolidation of society, to the state of a mere civil contract of a transitory character, which any two persons might engage in, and cast loose at pleasure, when their taste was changed, or their appetite gratified.[462] If fiends had set themselves to work to discover a mode of most effectually destroying whatever is venerable, graceful, or permanent in domestic life, and of obtaining, at the same time, an assurance that the mischief which it was their object to create should be perpetuated from one generation to another, they could not have invented a more effectual plan than the degradation of marriage into a state of mere occasional cohabitation, or licensed concubinage. Sophie Arnould,[463] an actress famous for the witty things she said, described the Republican marriage as "the Sacrament of Adultery."

---

[460] "The goddess, after receiving the fraternal hug of the president, was mounted on a magnificent car, and conducted, amidst an immense crowd, to the church of Notre-Dame, to take the place of the Holy of Holies. Thenceforward that ancient and imposing cathedral was called 'the Temple of Reason.'"—Lacretelle, tom. xi., p. 306; Thiers, tom. v., p. 342; Toulongeon, tom. iv., p. 124.
[461] "C'est ici l'asile du sommeil eternel."
[462] Lacretelle, tom. xi., p. 333.
[463] Sophie Arnould, born at Paris in 1740, was not less celebrated for her native wit than her talents on the stage. Shortly after her death, in 1803, appeared "Arnouldiana, ou Sophie Arnould et ses contemporaines."

These anti-religious and anti-social regulations did not answer the purpose of the frantic and inconsiderate zealots, by whom they had been urged forward. Hébert and Chaumette had outrun the spirit of the time, evil as that was, and had contrived to get beyond the sympathy even of those, who, at heart as vicious and criminal as they, had still the sagacity to fear, or the taste to be disgusted with, this overstrained tone of outrageous impiety. Perhaps they might have other motives for condemning so gross a display of irreligion. The most guilty of men are not desirous, generally speaking, totally to disbelieve and abandon all doctrines of religious faith. They cannot, if they would, prevent themselves from apprehending a future state of retribution; and little effect as such feeble glimmering of belief may have on their lives, they will not, in general, willingly throw away the slight chance, that it may be possible on some occasion to reconcile themselves to the Church or to the Deity. This hope, even to those on whom it has no salutary influence, resembles the confidence given to a sailor during a gale of wind, by his knowing that there is a port under his lee. His purpose may be never to run for the haven, or he may judge there is great improbability that by doing so he should reach it in safety; yet still, such being the case, he would esteem himself but little indebted to any one who should blot the harbour of refuge out of the chart. To all those, who, in various degrees, received and believed the great truths of religion, on which those of morality are dependent, the professors of those wild absurdities became objects of contempt, dislike, hatred, and punishment.

Danton regarded the proceedings of Hébert and his philosophers of the Commune with scorn and disgust. However wicked he had shown himself, he was too wise and too proud to approve of such impolitic and senseless folly. Besides, this perpetual undermining whatever remained of social institutions, prevented any stop being put to the revolutionary movements, which Danton, having placed his party at the head of affairs, and himself nearly as high as he could promise to climb, was now desirous should be done.

ROBESPIERRE

Robespierre looked on these extravagant proceedings with a different and more watchful eye. He saw what Hébert and his associates had lost in popularity, by affecting the doctrines of atheism and utter profaneness; and he imagined a plan, first, for destroying these blasphemers, by the general consent of the nation, as noxious animals, and then of enlarging, and, as it were, sanctifying his own power, by once more connecting a spirit of devotion of some modified kind or other with the revolutionary form of government, of which he desired to continue the head.

It has even been supposed, that Robespierre's extravagant success in rising so much above all human expectation, had induced him to entertain some thoughts of acting the part of a new Mahomet, in bringing back religious opinion into France, under his own direct auspices. He is said to have countenanced in secret the extravagances of a female called Catherine Theos, or Theost,[464] an enthusiastic devotee, whose doctrines leaned to Quietism. She was a kind of Joanna Southcote,[465] and the Aaron of her sect was Dom Gerle, formerly a Carthusian monk, and remarkable for the motion he made in the first National Assembly, that the Catholic religion should be recognised as that of France.[466] Since that time he had become entirely deranged. A few visionaries of both sexes attended secret and nightly meetings, in which Theos and Dom Gerle[467] presided. Robespierre was recognised by them as one of the elect, and is said to have favoured their superstitious doctrines. But, whether the dictator saw in them any thing more than tools, which might be applied to his own purpose, there seems no positive authority to decide. At any rate, whatever religious opinions he might have imbibed himself, or have become desirous of infusing

---

[464] This miserable visionary passed herself off at one time as the mother of God, and at another as a second Eve, destined to regenerate mankind. In 1794, she was arrested and sent to the Conciergerie, where she died, at the age of seventy.—See *Les Mystères de la Mère de Dieu devoilés*, in the *Collection des Mémoires relatifs à la Rev. Franç.*, tom. xx., p. 271.

[465] This aged lunatic, who fancied herself to be with child of a new Messiah, died in 1815.

[466] See *ante*.

[467] Gerle was imprisoned in the Conciergerie, but liberated through the interference of Robespierre. He was employed, during the reign of Napoleon, in the office of the home department.

into the state, they were not such as were qualified to modify either his ambition, his jealousy, or his love of blood.

The power of Hébert, Chaumette, and of the Commune of Paris, was now ripe for destruction. Ronsin, with the other armed satellites of the revolutionary army, bullied indeed, and spoke about taking the part of the magistracy of Paris against the Convention; but though they had the master and active ruffians still at their service, they could no longer command the long sable columns of pikes, which used to follow and back them, and without whose aid they feared they might not be found equal in number to face the National Guard. So early as 27th December, 1793, we find Chaumette[468] expressing himself to the Commune, as one who had fallen on evil times and evil days. He brought forward evidence to show that it was not he who had conducted the installation of the Goddess of Reason in his native city of Nevers; and he complains heavily of his lot, that the halls were crowded with women demanding the liberty of their husbands, and complaining of the conduct of the Revolutionary societies. It was plain, that a change was taking place in the political atmosphere, when Chaumette was obliged to vindicate himself from the impiety which used to be his boast, and was subjected, besides, to female reproach for his republican zeal, in imprisoning and destroying a few thousand suspected persons.

The spirit of reaction increased, and was strengthened by Robespierre's influence now thrown into the scale against the Commune. The principal leaders in the Commune, many of whom seem to have been foreigners, and among the rest the celebrated Anacharsis Clootz, were [22d March] arrested.

---

[468] Chaumette was born at Nevers in 1763. For some time he was employed as a transcriber by the journalist Prudhomme, who describes him as a very ignorant man. In 1792, he was appointed attorney of the Commune of Paris, upon which occasion he changed his patronymic of Pierre-Gaspard for that of Anaxagoras—"a saint," he said, "who had been hanged for his republicanism." He it was who prepared the charges and arranged the evidence against Marie Antoinette. On being committed to the prison of the Luxembourg, "he appeared," says the author of the Tableau des Prisons de Paris, "oppressed with shame, like a fox taken in a net: he hung his head, his eye was mournful and cast down, his countenance sad, his voice soft and supplicating. He was no longer the terrible attorney of the Commune." He was guillotined, 13th April, 1794, with the apostate bishop, Gobel, and the actor Grammont.

The case of these men was singular, and would have been worthy of pity had it applied to any but such worthless wretches. They were accused of almost every species of crime, which seemed such in the eyes of a Sans-Culotte. Much there was which could be only understood metaphysically; much there was of literal falsehood; but little or nothing like a distinct or well-grounded accusation of a specific criminal fact. The charge bore, that they were associates of Pitt and Cobourg, and had combined against the sovereignty of the people—loaded them with the intention of starving thereby Paris—with that of ridiculing the Convention, by a set of puppets dressed up to imitate that scarce less passive assembly—and much more to the same purpose, consisting of allegations that were totally unimportant, or totally unproved. But nothing was said of their rivalry to Robespierre, which was the true cause of their trial, and as little of their revolutionary murders, being the ground on which they really deserved their fate. Something was talked of pillage, at which Ronsin, the commandant of the revolutionary army, lost all patience. "Do they talk to me of pilfering?" he says. "Dare they accuse such a man as I am of a theft of bed and body linen? Do they bring against me a charge of petty larceny—against *me*, who have had all their throats at my disposal?"[469]

The accused persons were convicted and executed, [23d March,] to the number of nineteen.[470] From that time the city of Paris lost the means of being so pre-eminent in the affairs of France, as her Commune had formerly rendered her. The power of the magistracy was much broken by the reduction of the revolution army, which the Convention dissolved, as levied upon false principles, and as being rather a metropolitan than a national force, and one which was easily applied to serve the purposes of a party.

---

[469] Lacretelle, tom. xi., p. 363.
[470] "Such was the public avidity to witness the execution of Hébert and his companions, that considerable sums were realized by the sale of seats. Hébert wept from weakness, and made no attempt to conceal his terrors. He sunk down at every step; while the populace, who had so recently endeavoured to deliver him from the fangs of the Convention, loaded him with execrations, mimicking the cry of the newsmen who hawked his journal about the streets."—Thiers, tom. vi., p. 142.

DANTON ARRESTED

The Hébertists being removed, Robespierre had yet to combat and defeat a more formidable adversary. The late conspirators had held associations with the Club of Cordeliers, with which Danton was supposed to have particular relations, but they had not experienced his support, which in policy he ought to have extended to them. He had begun to separate his party and his views too distinctly from his old friends and old proceedings. He imagined, falsely as it proved, that his bark could sail as triumphantly upon waves composed only of water, as on those of blood. He and others seem to have been seized with a loathing against these continued acts of cruelty, as if they had been gorged and nauseated by the constant repetition. Danton spoke of mercy and pardon; and his partisan, Camille Desmoulins, in a very ingenious parody upon Tacitus,[471] drew a comparison between the tyrants and informers of the French Jacobin government, and those of the Roman Imperial Court. The parallels were most ably drawn, and Robespierre and his agents might read their own characters in those of the most odious wretches of that odious time. From these aggressions Danton seemed to meditate the part which Tallien afterwards adopted, of destroying Robespierre and his power, and substituting a mode of government which should show some regard at least to life and to property. But he was too late in making his movement; Robespierre was beforehand with him; and, on the morning of the 31st of March, the Parisians and the members of the Convention hardly dared whisper to each other, that Danton, whose name had been as formidable as the sound of the tocsin, had been arrested like any poor ex-noble, and was in the hands of the fatal lictors.

There was no end of exclamation and wonder; for Danton was the great apostle, the very Mahomet of Jacobinism. His gigantic stature, his huge and ferocious physiognomy, his voice, which struck terror in its notes of distant thunder, and the energies of talent and vehemence mingled, which supplied that voice with language worthy

---

[471] Of the pamphlet, entitled "Le Vieux Cordelier," one hundred thousand copies, Lacretelle says, were sold in a few days. It was reprinted, in 1825, in the *Collection des Mémoires sur la Révolution*.

of its deep tones, were such as became the prophet of that horrible and fearful sect. Marat was a madman, raised into consequence only by circumstances,—Robespierre a cold, creeping, calculating hypocrite, whose malignity resembled that of a paltry and second-rate fiend,—but Danton was a character for Shakspeare or Schiller to have drawn in all its broad lights and shades; or Bruce could have sketched from him a yet grander Ras Michael than he of Tigré. His passions were a hurricane, which, furious, regardless, and desolating in its course, had yet its intervals of sunshine and repose. Neither good by nature, nor just by principle or political calculation, men were often surprised at finding he still possessed some feelings of generosity, and some tendency even towards magnanimity. Early habits of profligate indulgence, the most complete stifler of human virtue, and his implication at the beginning of his career with the wretched faction of Orleans, made him, if not a worse certainly a meaner villain than nature had designed him; for his pride must have saved him from much, which he yielded to from the temptations of gross indulgence, and from the sense of narrow circumstances. Still, when Danton fell under Robespierre, it seemed as if the "mousing-owl" had hawked at and struck an eagle, or at least a high-soaring vulture. His avowed associates lamented him, of course; nay, Legendre and others, by undertaking his defence in the Convention, and arrogating for him the merit of those violent measures which had paved the way to the triumph of Jacobinism, showed more consistency in their friendship than these ferocious demagogues manifested on any other occasion.[472]

Danton, before his fall, seemed to have lost much of his sagacity as well as energy. He had full warning of his danger from La Croix, Westermann, and others, yet took no steps either for escape or defence, though either seemed in his power.[473] Still, his courage was in no degree abated, or his haughty spirit tamed; although he seemed to submit passively to his fate, with the disheartening

---

[472] Mignet, tom. ii., p. 308; Thiers, tom. vi., p. 189.
[473] "Sneak into exile!" said he, "can a man carry his country at the sole of his shoe?"—Thiers, tom. vi., p. 148.

conviction, which often unmans great criminals, that his hour was come.[474]

DANTON'S TRIAL

Danton's process was, of course, a short one. He and his comrades, Camille Desmoulins, Westermann, and La Croix,[475] were dragged before the Revolutionary Tribunal—a singular accomplishment of the prophecy of the Girondist, Boyer Fonfrède.[476] This man had exclaimed to Danton, under whose auspices that engine of arbitrary power was established, "You insist, then, upon erecting this arbitrary judgment-seat? Be it so; and, like the tormenting engine devised by Phalaris, may it not fall to consume its inventors?" As judges, witnesses, accusers, and guards, Danton was now surrounded by those who had been too humble to aspire to be companions of his atrocities, and held themselves sufficiently honoured in becoming his agents. They looked on his unstooping pride and unshaken courage, as timid spectators upon a lion in a cage, while they still doubt the security of the bars, and have little confidence in their own personal safety. He answered to the formal interrogatories concerning his name and dwelling, "My dwelling will be soon with annihilation—my name will live in the Pantheon of History."[477] Camille Desmoulins,[478] Hérault Séchelles,[479]

---

[474] Riouffe, a fellow captive, states, that when Danton entered his prison, he exclaimed, "At last I perceive, that in revolutions the supreme power rests with the most abandoned."—*Mémoires*, p. 67.

"Seeing Thomas Payne, he said to him, 'What you have accomplished for the happiness and freedom of your country, I have in vain endeavoured to effect for mine. I have been less successful, but am not more culpable.' At another time he exclaimed, 'It is just about a year since I was the means of instituting the revolutionary tribunal. I ask pardon of God and man for what I did: my object was to prevent a new September, and not to let loose a scourge of humanity.' ... 'My treacherous brethren (mes frères Caïn) understand nothing of government: I leave every thing in frightful confusion.' ... 'It were better to be a poor fisherman than a ruler of men.'"—Thiers, tom. vi., p. 155; Mignet, tom. ii., p. 312.

[475] La Croix was born, in 1754, at Pont-Audemer. His destruction being resolved on by Robespierre, he was arrested with Danton, 31st March, and executed 5th April, 1794. When the act of accusation was brought, Danton asked him what he said to it. "That I am going to cut off my hair," said he, "that Samson [the executioner] may not touch it."

[476] Boyer Fonfrède was born at Bordeaux. Being appointed deputy from the Gironde to the Convention, he vigorously opposed Marat and the Mountain. He escaped the first proscription of the Girondists, but perished on the scaffold in 1793.

[477] Lacretelle, tom. xi., p. 380.

Fabre d'Eglantine,[480] men of considerable literary talent, and amongst the few Jacobins who had any real pretension to such accomplishments, shared his fate. Westermann was also numbered with them, the same officer who directed the attack on the palace of the Tuileries on the 10th August, and who afterwards was

---

[478] Camille Desmoulins was born at Guise in 1762, and educated with Robespierre, at the College of Louis-le-Grand. He it was who, in 1789, began the practice of collecting groups of people to harangue them in the streets, and who advised the revolutionists to distinguish themselves by a badge. Hence the tricolor cockade. After the taking of the Bastile, he published, under the name of "Attorney-General of the Lantern," a periodical paper, called "Révolutions de France et de Brabant." "It must not, however," says M. Dumont, "be imagined, that he excited the people to use the lantern-posts instead of the gallows, an abomination attributed to him by Bertrand de Moleville—quite the reverse: he pointed out the danger and injustice of such summary executions, but in a tone of lightness and badinage, by no means in keeping with so serious a subject. Camille appeared to me what is called a good fellow; of rather exaggerated feelings, devoid of reflection or judgment, as ignorant as he was unthinking, not deficient in wit, but in politics possessing not even the first elements of reason."—P. 135. On his trial, being interrogated as to his age, he answered, "I am thirty-three, the same age as the Sans-Culotte Jesus Christ when he died." On the day of execution he made the most violent efforts to avoid getting into the fatal cart. His shirt was in tatters, and his shoulders bare; his eyes glared, his mouth foamed at the moment when he was bound, and on seeing the scaffold, he exclaimed, "This, then, is the reward reserved for the first apostle of liberty!" His wife, a beautiful creature, by whom he was tenderly beloved, was arrested a few days after his death, and sent to the scaffold.— Thiers, tom. vi., p. 169; *Biog. Mod.*, tom. i., p. 364; Lacretelle, tom. xi., p. 380.

[479] Hérault Séchelles was born at Paris in 1760. He began his career at the bar, by holding the office of King's advocate at the Châtelet; and afterwards, by the patronage of the Queen, was appointed advocate-general. Shortly before his arrest he was offered a retreat in Switzerland, and a passport, in a fictitious name, from the agent of Bâle, but his answer was, "I would gladly accept the offer, if I could carry my native country with me." He published "Visite à Buffon," "Théorie de l'Ambition," and "Rapports sur la Constitution," &c., 1793.

[480] Fabre d'Églantine, born at Carcassonne in 1755, was in early life an actor, and performed at Versailles, Brussels, and Lyons, but with moderate success. As an author he discovered considerable talent; the latter part of his name being assumed, in memory of a prize which he had won in his youth. His most successful production was a comedy, entitled, "Le Philinte de Molière, ou La Suite du Misanthrope," in which he has traced the *beau idéal* of an honest man. His "[OE]uvres Mêlées et Posthumes," were published, in two volumes, in 1802. One of the things that seemed most to trouble him after his arrest was, that he had left among his papers an unpublished comedy called "L'Orange de Malte," which he considered better than his "Philinte," and which he feared Billaud-Varennes would get hold of, and publish as his own. Mercier, his colleague, says of him, "I do not know whether Fabre's hands were stained by the lavishing of money not his own, but I know that he was a promoter of assassinations; poor before the 2d of September, 1792, he had afterwards an hotel, and carriages, and servants, and women." "As to Fabre," says Madame Roland, "muffled in a cowl, armed with a poniard, and employed in forging plots to defame the innocent, or to ruin the rich, whose wealth he covets, he is so perfectly in character, that whoever would paint the most abandoned hypocrite, need only draw his portrait in that dress."

distinguished by so many victories and defeats in La Vendée, that he was called, from his activity, the scourge of that district.[481]

Their accusation was, as in all such cases at the period, an olla podrida, if we can be allowed the expression, in which every criminal ingredient was mixed up; but so incoherently mingled and assembled together, so inconsistent with each other, and so obscurely detailed in the charge and in the proof, that it was plain that malignant falsehood had made the gruel thick and slab. Had Danton been condemned for his real crimes, the doom ought, in justice, to have involved judges, jurors, witnesses, and most of the spectators in the court.

Robespierre became much alarmed for the issue of the trial. The Convention showed reviving signs of spirit; and when a revolutionary deputation demanded at the bar, "that death should be the order of the day," and reminded them, that, "had they granted the moderate demand of three hundred thousand heads, when requested by the philanthropic, and now canonized Marat, they would have saved the Republic the wars of La Vendée," they were received with discouraging murmurs. Tallien, the president, informed them, "that not death, but justice, was the order of the day;" and the petitioners, notwithstanding the patriotic turn of their modest request, were driven from the bar with execrations.

DANTON EXECUTED

This looked ill; but the power of Robespierre was still predominant with the Revolutionary Tribunal, and after a gallant and unusually long defence, (of which no notice was permitted to

---

[481] Westermann was born in 1764, at Molsheim, in Alsace. In December, 1792, he was denounced to the Convention, upon proof, as having, in 1786, stolen some silver plate from a coffee-house. "In La Vendée," says Prudhomme, "he ran from massacre to massacre, sparing neither adversaries taken in arms, nor the peaceful inhabitants." M. Beauchamp says that "he delighted in carnage, and would throw off his coat, tuck up his sleeves, and then, with his sabre, rush into the crowd, and hew about him to the right and left. But from the moment that he apprehended death, his dreams were of the horrors which he had perpetrated."

appear in the Moniteur,) Danton[482] and his associates were condemned, and carried to instant execution. They maintained their firmness, or rather hardenedness of character, to the last.[483] The sufferers on this occasion were men whose accomplishments and talents attracted a higher degree of sympathy than that which had been given to the equally eloquent but less successful Girondists. Even honest men looked on the fate of Danton with some regret, as when a furious bull is slain with a slight blow by a crafty Tauridor; and many men of good feelings had hoped, that the cause of order and security might at least have been benefited in some degree, by his obtaining the victory in a struggle with Robespierre. Those, on the other hand, who followed the fortunes of the latter, conceived his power had been rendered permanent by the overthrow of his last and most formidable rival, and exulted in proportion. Both were deceived in their calculations. The predominance of such a man as Danton might possibly have protracted the reign of Jacobinism, even by rendering it somewhat more endurable; but the permanent, at least the ultimate, success of Robespierre, was becoming more impossible, from the repeated decimations to which his jealousy subjected his party. He was like the wild chief, Lope d'Aguirre, whose story is so well told by Southey, who, descending the great river Orellana with a party of Bucaniers, cut off one part of his followers after another, in doubt of their fidelity, until the remainder saw no chance for escaping a similar fate, unless by being beforehand with their leader in murder.

Alluding to Robespierre's having been the instrument of his destruction, Danton had himself exclaimed, "The cowardly poltroon! I am the only person who could have commanded

---

[482] "On the way to execution, Danton cast a calm and contemptuous look around him. Arrived at the steps of the scaffold, he advanced to embrace Hérault Séchelles, who held out his arms to receive him; the executioner interposing, 'What!' said he, with a smile of scorn, 'are you, then, more cruel than death? Begone! you cannot prevent our heads from soon uniting in that basket.' For a moment he was softened, and said, 'Oh! my beloved! oh, my wife, I shall never see thee more!' but instantly checking himself, exclaimed, 'Danton, no weakness!' and ascended the scaffold."—Thiers, tom. vi., p. 169; *Biog. Mod.*, tom. i., p. 332.

[483] It has been said, that when Danton observed Fabre d'Eglantine beginning to look gloomy, he cheered him with a play on words: "Courage, my friend, we are all about to take up your trade—*Nous allons faire des* vers."

influence enough to save him."[484] And the event showed that he spoke with the spirit of prophecy which the approach of fate has been sometimes thought to confer.

In fact, Robespierre was much isolated by the destruction of the party of Hébert, and still more by that of Danton and his followers. He had, so to speak, scarped away the ground which he occupied, until he had scarce left himself standing-room; and, detested by honest men, he had alienated, by his successive cruelties, even the knaves who would otherwise have adhered to him for their own safety. All now looked on him with fear, and none dared hope at the hands of the Dictator a better boon than that which is promised to Outis, that he should be the last devoured.

It was at this period that Robespierre conceived the idea of reversing the profanities of Chaumette, Hébert, and the atheists, by professing a public belief in the existence of a Deity. This, he conceived, would at once be a sacrifice to public opinion, and, as he hoped to manage it, a new and potent spring, to be moved by his own finger. In a word, he seems to have designed to unite, with his power in the state, the character of High Pontiff of the new faith.

As the organ of the Committee of Public Safety, Robespierre, [May 7,] by a speech of great length, and extremely dull, undertook the conversion of the French nation from infidelity. Upon all such occasions he had recourse to that gross flattery, which was his great, rarely-failing, and almost sole receipt for popularity. He began by assuring them, that, in her lights, and the progress of her improvement, France had preceded the rest of Europe by a mark of at least two thousand years; and that, existing among the ordinary nations of the world, she appeared to belong to another race of beings. Still, he thought, some belief in a Deity would do her no harm. Then he was again hurried away by his eloquence, of which we cannot help giving a literal specimen, to show at how little expense of sense, taste or talent, a man may be held an excellent orator, and become dictator of a great nation:—

---

[484] Lacretelle, tom. xi., p. 382.

"Yes, the delicious land which we inhabit, and which Nature caresses with so much predilection, is made to be the domain of liberty and of happiness; and that people, at once so open to feeling and to generous pride, are born for glory and for virtue. O my native country! if fortune had caused my birth in some region remote from thy shores, I would not the less have addressed constant prayers to Heaven in thy behalf, and would have wept over the recital of thy combats and thy virtues. My soul would have followed with restless ardour every change in this eventful Revolution—I would have envied the lot of thy natives—of thy representatives. But I am myself a native of France—I am myself a representative. Intoxicating rapture!—O sublime people, receive the sacrifice of my entire being! Happy is he who is born in the midst of thee! More happy he who can lay down his life for thy welfare!"[485]

FESTIVAL OF THE SUPREME BEING

Such was the language which this great demagogue held to the "sublime people" whose lives he disposed of at the rate of fifty per day, regular task-work;[486] and who were so well protected in person and property, that no man dared call his hat his own, or answer for ten minutes' space for the security of the head that wore it. Much there was, also, about the rashness of the worshippers of Reason, whose steps he accuses of being too premature in her cause—much about England and Mr. Pitt, who, he says, fasted on account of the destruction of the Catholic religion in France, as they wore mourning for Capet and his wife. But the summary of this extraordinary oration was a string of decrees, commencing with a declaration that the Republic of France acknowledged the existence of a Supreme Being, in the precise form in which the grand nation might have recognised the government of a co-ordinate state. The other decrees established the nature of the worship to be rendered to the Great Being whom these frail atoms had restored to his place in their thoughts; and this was to be expressed by dedicating a day in

---

[485] When we read such miserable stuff, and consider the crimes which such oratory occasioned, it reminds us of the opinion of a Mahomedan doctor, who assured Bruce that the Degial, or Antichrist, was to appear in the form of an ass, and that multitudes were to follow him to hell, attracted by the music of his braying.—S.
[486] Thiers, tom. vi., p. 291.

each decade to some peculiar and established Virtue, with hymns and processions in due honour of it, approaching as near to Paganism as could well be accomplished. The last decree appointed a *fête* to be given in honour of the Supreme Being himself, as the nation might have celebrated by public rejoicings a pacification with some neighbouring power.[487]

The speech was received with servile applause by the Convention. Couthon, with affected enthusiasm, demanded that not only the speech should be published in the usual form, by supplying each member with six copies, but that the plan should be translated into all languages, and dispersed through the universe.

The conducting of this heathen mummery, which was substituted for every external sign of rational devotion, was intrusted to the genius of the painter David; and had it not been that the daring blasphemy of the purpose threw a chill upon the sense of ridicule, it was scarcely matched as a masquerade, even by the memorable procession conducted by the notorious Orator of the Human Race.[488] There was a general muster of all Paris, [June 8,] divided into bands of young women and matrons, and old men and youths, with oaken boughs and drawn swords, and all other emblems appertaining to their different ages. They were preceded by the representatives of the people, having their hands full of ears of corn, and spices, and fruits; while Robespierre, their president, clad in a sort of purple garment, moved apart and alone, and played the part of Sovereign Pontiff.[489]

---

[487] Thiers, tom. vi., p. 197.

[488] Poor Anacharsis Clootz! He had been expelled from the Jacobin Club as a Prussian, an ex-noble, and, what perhaps was not previously suspected, a person of fortune enough to be judged an aristocrat. His real offence was being a Hébertist, and he suffered accordingly with the leaders of that party.—This note was rather unnecessary; but Anacharsis Clootz was, in point of absurdity, one of the most inimitable personages in the Revolution.—S.—See *ante*.

[489] "The most indecent irreligion served as a lever for the subversion of the social order. There was a kind of consistency in founding crime upon impiety; it is an homage paid to the intimate union of religious opinions with morality. Robespierre conceived the idea of celebrating a festival in honour of the Supreme Being, flattering himself, doubtless, with being able to rest his political ascendency on a religion arranged according to his own notions; as those have frequently done who have wished to seize the supreme power. But, in the procession of this impious festival, he bethought himself of walking the first, in

After marching up and down through the streets, to the sound of doggrel hymns, the procession drew up in the gardens of the Tuileries, before some fireworks which had been prepared, and Robespierre made a speech, entirely addressed to the bystanders, without a word either of prayer or invocation. His acknowledgment of a Divinity was, it seems, limited to a mere admission in point of fact, and involved no worship of the Great Being, whose existence he at length condescended to own. He had no sooner made his offering, than fire was set to some figures dressed up to resemble Atheism, Ambition, Egotism, and other evil principles. The young men then brandished their weapons, the old patted them on the head, the girls flung about their flowers, and the matrons flourished aloft their children, all as it had been set down in David's programme. And this scene of masking was to pass for the repentance of a great people turning themselves again to the Deity, whose worship they had forsaken, and whose being they had denied![490]

I will appeal—not to a sincere Christian—but to any philosopher forming such idea of the nature of the Deity, as even mere unassisted reason can attain to, whether there does not appear more impiety in Robespierre's mode of acknowledging the Divinity, than in Hébert's horrible avowal of direct Atheism?

The procession did not, in common phrase, *take* with the people: it produced no striking effect—awakened no deep feeling. By Catholics it was regarded with horror, by wise men of every or no principle as ridiculous; and there were politicians, who, under the disguise of this religious ceremony, pretended to detect further and deeper schemes of the dictator Robespierre. Even in the course of the procession, threats and murmurs had reached his ears, which the impatient resentment of the friends of Danton was unable to suppress;[491] and he saw plainly that he must again betake himself to

---

order to mark his pre-eminence; and from that time he was lost."—Mad. de Staël, vol. ii., p. 142.
[490] Thiers, tom. vi., p. 268; Lacretelle, tom. xii., p. 15; Mignet, tom. ii., p. 322; Montgaillard, tom. iv., p. 207.
[491] "Lecointre de Versailles, stepping up to him, said, 'I like your festival, Robespierre, but you I detest mortally.' Bourdon de l'Oise reminded him of Mirabeau's famous saying, 'the Capitol is near the Tarpeian rock;' many among the crowd muttered the word 'Tyrant'

the task of murder, and dispose of Tallien, Collot d'Herbois, and others, as he had done successively of Hébert and Danton himself, or else his former victories would but lead to his final ruin.

Meanwhile the despot, whose looks made even the democrats of The Mountain tremble, when directed upon them, shrunk himself before the apprehended presence of a young female. Cécile Regnault, a girl, and, as it would seem, unarmed, came to his house and demanded to see Robespierre. Her manner exciting some suspicion, she was seized upon by the body-guard of Jacobins, who day and night watched the den of the tyrant, amidst riot and blasphemy, while he endeavoured to sleep under the security of their neighbourhood. When the young woman was brought before the Revolutionary Tribunal, she would return no answer to the questions respecting her purpose, excepting that she wished to see "what a tyrant was like." She was condemned to the guillotine of course; and about sixty persons were executed as associates of a conspiracy, which was never proved, by deed or word, to have existed at all. The victims were drawn at hazard out of the prisons, where most of them had been confined for months previous to the arrest of Cécile Regnault, on whose account they were represented as suffering.[492] Many have thought the crime entirely imaginary, and only invented by Robespierre to represent his person as endangered by the plots of the aristocracy, and attach to himself a part at least of the consequence, which Marat had acquired by the act of Charlotte Corday.[493]

A few weeks brought on a sterner encounter, than that of the supposed female assassin. The Terrorists were divided among themselves. The chosen and ancient bands of the 10th August, 2d September, 31st May, and other remarkable periods of the

---

adding, 'there are still Brutuses;' and when, in the course of his speech, he said, 'It is the Great Eternal who has placed in the bosom of the oppressor the sensation of remorse and terror;' a powerful voice exclaimed, 'True! Robespierre, very true!'"—Lacretelle, tom. xii., p. 18.

[492] This unheard-of iniquity is stated in the report of the committee appointed to examine Robespierre's papers, of which Courtois was the reporter. It is rather a curious circumstance that, about the time of Cécile Regnault's adventure, there appeared, at a masked ball at London, a character dressed like the spectre of Charlotte Corday, come, as she said, to seek Robespierre, and inflict on him the doom of Marat.—S.

[493] Mignet, tom. ii., p. 322; Lacretelle, tom. xii., p. 10; *Biog. Mod.*, tom. iii., p. 149.

Revolution, continued attached to the Jacobins, and the majority of the Jacobin Club adhered to Robespierre; it was there his strength consisted. On the other hand, Tallien, Barras, Legendre, Fouché, and other of the Mountain party, remembered Danton, and feared for a similar fate. The Convention at large were sure to embrace any course which promised to free them from their present thraldom.

CHANGE IN THE PUBLIC MIND

The people themselves were beginning to be less passive. They no longer saw the train of victims pass daily to the guillotine in the Place de la Révolution, with stupid wonder, or overwhelming fear, but, on the contrary, with the sullenness of manifest resentment, that waited but an opportunity to display itself. The citizens in the Rue St. Honoré shut up their shops at the hours when the fatal tumbrils passed to the scene of death, and that whole quarter of the city was covered with gloom.

These ominous feelings were observed, and the fatal engine was removed to a more obscure situation at the Barrièr de la Trône, near the Fauxbourg Saint Antoine, to the inhabitants of which it was thought a daily spectacle of this nature must be an interesting relief from labour. But even the people of that turbulent suburb had lost some of their Republican zeal—the men's feelings were altered. They saw, indeed, blood stream in such quantities, that it was necessary to make an artificial conduit to carry it off; but they did not feel that they, or those belonging to them, received any advantages from the number of victims daily immolated, as they were assured, in their behalf. The constant effusion of blood, without plunder or license to give it zest, disgusted them, as it would have disgusted all but literal cannibals, to whose sustenance, indeed, the Revolutionary Tribunal would have contributed plentifully.[494]

---

[494] Thiers, tom. vi., p. 291; Lacretelle, tom. xii., p. 53.

ROBESPIERRE UNPOPULAR

Robespierre saw all this increasing unpopularity with much anxiety. He plainly perceived that, strong as its impulse was, the stimulus of terror began to lose its effect on the popular mind; and he resolved to give it novelty, not by changing the character of his system, but by varying the mode of its application. Hitherto, men had only been executed for political crimes, although the circle had been so vaguely drawn, and capable of such extension when desired, that the law regarding suspected persons was alone capable of desolating a whole country. But if the penalty of death were to be inflicted for religious and moral delinquencies, as well as for crimes directed against the state, it would at once throw the lives of thousands at his disposal, upon whom he could have no ready hold on political motives, and might support, at the same time, his newly assumed character as a reformer of manners. He would also thus escape the disagreeable and embarrassing necessity, of drawing lines of distinction betwixt his own conduct and that of the old friends whom he found it convenient to sacrifice. He could not say he was less a murderer than the rest of his associates, but he might safely plead more external decency of morals. His own manners had always been reserved and austere; and what a triumph would it have been, had the laws permitted him the benefit of slaying Danton, not under that political character which could hardly be distinguished from his own, but on account of the gross peculation and debauchery, which none could impute to the austere and incorruptible Robespierre.

His subordinate agents began already to point to a reformation of manners. Payan, who succeeded Hébert in the important station of Procureur to the Commune of the metropolis, had already adopted a very different line from his predecessor, whose style derived energy by printing at full length the foulest oaths, and most beastly expressions, used by the refuse of the people. Payan, on the contrary, in direct opposition to Père Duchêsne, is found gravely advising with the Commune of Paris, on a plan of preventing the exposing licentious prints and works to sale, to the evident danger of corrupting the rising generation.

There exists also a curious address from the Convention, which tends to evince a similar purpose in the framer, Robespierre. The guilt of profane swearing, and of introducing the sacred name into ordinary speech, as an unmeaning and blasphemous expletive, is severely censured. The using indecent and vicious expressions in common discourse is also touched upon; but as this unbounded energy of speech had been so very lately one of the most accredited marks of a true Sans-Culotte, the legislators were compelled to qualify their censure by admitting, that, at the commencement of the Revolution, the vulgar mode of speaking had been generally adopted by patriots, in order to destroy the jargon employed by the privileged classes, and to *popularize*, as it was expressed, the general language of society. But these ends being effected, the speech of Republicans ought, it is said, to be simple, manly, and concise, but, at the same time, free from coarseness and violence.[495]

From these indications, and the tenor of a decree to be hereafter quoted, it seems plain, that Robespierre was about to affect a new character, not, perhaps, without the hope of finding a Puritanic party in France, as favourable to his ambitious views as that of the Independents was to Cromwell. He might then have added the word *virtue* to liberty and equality, which formed the national programme, and, doubtless, would have made it the pretext of committing additional crimes. The decree which we allude to was brought forward [June 8] by the philanthropic Couthon, who, with his kindness of manner, rendered more impressive by a silver-toned voice, and an affectation of extreme gentleness, tendered a law, extending the powers of the Revolutionary Tribunal, and the penalty of death, not only to all sorts of persons who should in any manner of way neglect their duty to the Republic, or assist her enemies, but to the following additional classes: All who should have deceived the people or their representatives—all who should have sought to inspire discouragement into good citizens, or to favour the undertakings of tyrants—all who should spread false news—all who should seek to lead astray the public opinion, and to prevent the instruction of the people, or to debauch manners, and corrupt the public conscience; or who should diminish the purity of

---

[495] Lacretelle, tom. xii., p. 22.

revolutionary principles by counter-revolutionary works, &c. &c. &c."[496]

It is evident, that compared with a law couched in terms so vague and general, so obscure and indefinite, the description of crimes concerning suspected persons was broad sunshine, that there was no Frenchman living who might not be brought within the danger of the decree, under one or other of those sweeping clauses; that a loose or careless expression, or the repetition of an inaccurate article of news, might be founded on as corrupting the public conscience, or misleading the public opinion; in short, that the slightest indulgence in the most ordinary functions of speech might be brought under this comprehensive edict, and so cost the speaker his life.

The decree sounded like a death-knell in the ears of the Convention. All were made sensible that another decimation of the legislative body approached; and beheld with terror, that no provision was made in the proposed law for respecting the personal inviolability of the deputies, but that the obnoxious members of the Convention, without costing Robespierre even the formality of asking a decree from their complaisant brethren, might be transferred, like any ordinary individuals, to the butchery of the Revolutionary Tribunal, not only by the medium of either of the committees, but at the instance of the public prosecutor, or even of any of their own brethren of the representative body, who were acting under a commission. Ruamps, one of the deputies, exclaimed, in accents of despair, that "if this decree were resolved upon, the friends of liberty had no other course left than to blow their own brains out."

The law passed for the night, in spite of all opposition; but the terrified deputies returned to the attack next day. The measure was again brought into debate, and the question of privileges was evasively provided for. At a third sitting the theme was renewed; and, after much violence, the fatal decree was carried, without any of

---

[496] See it in Lacretelle, tom. xii., p. 23.

the clogs which had offended Robespierre, and he attained possession of the fatal weapon, such as he had originally forged it.[497]

From this moment there was mortal though secret war betwixt Robespierre and the most distinguished members of the Assembly, particularly those who had sate with him on the celebrated Mountain, and shared all the atrocities of Jacobinism. Collot d'Herbois, the demolisher of Lyons, and regenerator of Ville Affranchie, threw his weight into the scale against his master; and several other members of both committees, which were Robespierre's own organs, began secretly to think on means of screening themselves from a power, which, like the huge Anaconda, enveloped in its coils, and then crushed and swallowed, whatever came in contact with it. The private progress of the schism cannot be traced; but it is said that the dictator found himself in a minority in the Committee of Public Safety, when he demanded the head of Fouché, whom he had accused as a Dantonist in the Convention and the Jacobin Club. It is certain he had not attended the meeting of the Committee for two or three weeks before his fall, leaving his interest there to be managed by Couthon and Saint Just.

Feeling himself thus placed in the lists against his ancient friends the Terrorists, the astucious tyrant endeavoured to acquire allies among the remains of the Girondists, who had been spared in contempt more than clemency, and permitted to hide themselves among the neutral party who occupied The Plain, and who gave generally their votes on the prudential system of adhering to the stronger side.

Finding little countenance from this timid and long-neglected part of the legislative body, Robespierre returned to his more steady supporters in the Jacobin Club. Here he retained his supremacy, and was heard with enthusiastic applause; while he intimated to them the defection of certain members of the legislature from the true revolutionary course; complained of the inactivity and lukewarmness of the Committees of Public Safety and Public Security, and described himself as a persecuted patriot, almost the solitary supporter of the cause of his country, and exposed for that reason

---

[497] Lacretelle, tom. xii., p. 30; Thiers, tom. vi., p. 273.

to the blows of a thousand assassins. "All patriots," exclaimed Couthon, "are brothers and friends! For my part I invoke on myself the poniards destined against Robespierre." "So do we all!" exclaimed the meeting unanimously. Thus encouraged, Robespierre urged a purification of the Society, directing his accusations against Fouché and other members of The Mountain; and he received the encouragement he desired.[498]

He next ascertained his strength among the Judges of the Revolutionary Tribunal, and his willing agents among the reformed Commune of Paris, which, after the fall of Hébert and Chaumette, he had taken care to occupy with his most devoted friends. But still he knew that, in the storm which was about to arise, these out-of-door demagogues were but a sort of tritons of the minnows, compared to Tallien, Fouché, Barras, Collot d'Herbois, Billaud-Varennes, and other deputies of distinguished powers, accustomed to make their voices heard and obeyed amid all the roar of revolutionary tempest. He measured and remeasured his force with theirs; and for more than six weeks avoided the combat, yet without making any overtures for reconciliation, in which, indeed, neither party would probably have trusted the other.

Meantime, the dictator's enemies had also their own ground on which they could engage advantageously in these skirmishes, which were to serve as preludes to the main and fatal conflict. Vadier, on the part of the Committee of Public Safety, laid before the Convention, in a tone of bitter satirical ridicule, the history of the mystical meetings and formation of a religious sect under Catherine Theos, whose pretensions have been already hinted at. No mention was indeed made of Robespierre, or of the countenance he was supposed to have given to these fanatical intriguers. But the fact of his having done so was well known; and the shafts of Vadier were aimed with such malignant dexterity, that while they seemed only directed against the mystics of whom he spoke, they galled to the quick the high pontiff, who had so lately conducted the new and

---

[498] Thiers, tom. vi., p. 307.

singular system of worship which his influence had been employed to ingraft upon the genuine atheism natural to Jacobinism.[499]

Robespierre felt he could not remain long in this situation—that there were no means of securing himself where he stood—that he must climb higher, or fall—and that every moment in which he supported insults and endured menaces without making his vengeance felt, brought with it a diminution of his power. He seems to have hesitated between combat and flight. Among his papers, according to the report of Cortois who examined them, was found an obscure intimation, that he had acquired a competent property, and entertained thoughts of retiring at the close of his horrible career, after the example of the celebrated Sylla. It was a letter from some unknown confidant, unsigned and undated, containing the following singular passage:—"You must employ all your dexterity to escape from the scene on which you are now once more to appear, in order to leave it for ever. Your having attained the president's chair will be but one step to the guillotine, through a rabble who will spit upon you as you pass, as they did upon Egalité. Since you have collected a treasure sufficient to maintain you for a long time, as well as those for whom you have made provision, I will expect you with anxiety, that we may enjoy a hearty laugh together at the expense of a nation as credulous as it is greedy of novelty." If, however, he had really formed such a plan, which would not have been inconsistent with his base spirit, the means of accomplishing it were probably never perfected.[500]

At length his fate urged him on to the encounter. Robespierre descended [July 26] to the Convention, where he had of late but rarely appeared, like the far nobler Dictator of Rome; and in his case also, a band of senators were ready to poniard the tyrant on the spot, had they not been afraid of the popularity he was supposed to enjoy, and which they feared might render them instant victims to the revenge of the Jacobins. The speech which Robespierre addressed to the Convention was as menacing as the first distant

---

[499] Lacretelle, tom. xii., p. 61.
[500] "Robespierre was a fanatic, a monster, but he was incorruptible, and incapable of robbing, or of causing the deaths of others, from a desire of enriching himself. He was an enthusiast, but one who believed that he was acting right, and died not worth a sous."—Napoleon, *Voice from St. Helena*, vol. ii., p. 170.

rustle of the hurricane, and dark and lurid as the eclipse which announces its approach. Anxious murmurs had been heard among the populace who filled the tribunes, or crowded the entrances of the hall of the Convention, indicating that a second 31st of May (being the day on which the Jacobins proscribed the Girondists) was about to witness a similar operation.

The first theme of the gloomy orator was the display of his own virtues and his services as a patriot, distinguishing as enemies to their country all whose opinions were contrary to his own. He then reviewed successively the various departments of the government, and loaded them in turn with censure and contempt. He declaimed against the supineness of the Committees of Public Safety and Public Security, as if the guillotine had never been in exercise; and he accused the committee of finance of having *counter-revolutionized* the revenues of the Republic. He enlarged with no less bitterness on withdrawing the artillerymen (always violent Jacobins) from Paris, and on the mode of management adopted in the conquered countries of Belgium. It seemed as if he wished to collect within the same lists all the functionaries of the state, and in the same breath to utter defiance to them all.[501]

ROBESPIERRE DENOUNCED

The usual honorary motion was made to print the discourse; but then the storm of opposition broke forth, and many speakers vociferously demanded, that before so far adopting the grave inculpations which it contained, the discourse should be referred to the two committees. Robespierre, in his turn, exclaimed, that this was subjecting his speech to the partial criticism and revision of the very parties whom he had accused. Exculpations and defences were heard on all sides against the charges which had been thus sweepingly brought forward; and there were many deputies who complained, in no obscure terms, of individual tyranny, and of a conspiracy on foot to outlaw and murder such part of the Convention as might be disposed to offer resistance. Robespierre was but feebly supported, save by Saint Just, Couthon, and by his

---

[501] Thiers, tom. vi., p. 328; Lacretelle, tom. xii., p. 71.

own brother. After a stormy debate, in which the Convention were alternately swayed by their fear and their hatred of Robespierre, the discourse was finally referred to the committees, instead of being printed; and the haughty and sullen dictator saw, in the open slight thus put on his measures and opinions, the sure mark of his approaching fall.

ROBESPIERRE'S DEFENCE

He carried his complaints to the Jacobin Club, to repose, as he expressed it, his patriotic sorrows in their virtuous bosoms, where alone he hoped to find succour and sympathy. To this partial audience he renewed, in a tone of yet greater audacity, the complaints with which he had loaded every branch of the government, and the representative body itself. He reminded those around him of various heroic eras, when their presence and their pikes had decided the votes of the trembling deputies. He reminded them of their pristine actions of revolutionary vigour—asked them if they had forgot the road to the Convention,[502] and concluded by pathetically assuring them, that if they forsook him, "he stood resigned to his fate; and they should behold with what courage he would drink the fatal hemlock." The artist David caught him by the hand as he closed, exclaiming, in rapture at his elocution, "I will drink it with thee."[503]

The distinguished painter has been reproached, as having, on the subsequent day, declined the pledge which he seemed so eagerly to embrace. But there were many of his original opinion, at the time he expressed it so boldly; and had Robespierre possessed either military talents, or even decided courage, there was nothing to have prevented him from placing himself that very night at the head of a desperate insurrection of the Jacobins and their followers.

---

[502] "I know," said Henriot, "the road to the Convention."—"Go," said Robespierre, "separate the wicked from the weak; deliver the Assembly from the wretches who enthral it. March! you may yet save liberty!"—Thiers, tom. vi., p. 337.
[503] Lacretelle, tom. xii., p. 85.

Payan, the successor of Hébert, actually proposed that the Jacobins should instantly march against the two committees, which Robespierre charged with being the focus of the anti-revolutionary machinations, surprise their handful of guards, and stifle the evil with which the state was menaced, even in the very cradle. This plan was deemed too hazardous to be adopted, although it was one of those sudden and master-strokes of policy which Machiavel would have recommended. The fire of the Jacobins spent itself in tumult and threatening, in expelling from the bosom of their society Collot d'Herbois, Tallien, and about thirty other deputies of the Mountain party, whom they considered as specially leagued to effect the downfall of Robespierre, and whom they drove from their society with execrations and even blows.[504]

Collot d'Herbois, thus outraged, went straight from the meeting of the Jacobins to the place where the Committee of Public Safety was still sitting, in consultation on the report which they had to make to the Convention the next day upon the speech of Robespierre. Saint Just, one of their number, though warmly attached to the dictator, had been intrusted by the committee with the delicate task of drawing up that report. It was a step towards reconciliation; but the entrance of Collot d'Herbois, frantic with the insults he had received, broke off all hope of accommodation betwixt the friends of Danton and those of Robespierre. D'Herbois exhausted himself in threats against Saint Just, Couthon, and their master, Robespierre, and they parted on terms of mortal and avowed enmity. Every exertion now was used by the associated conspirators against the power of Robespierre, to collect and combine against him the whole forces of the Convention, to alarm the deputies of The Plain with fears for themselves, and to awaken the rage of the Mountaineers, against whose throat the dictator now waved the sword, which their shortsighted policy had placed in his hands. Lists of proscribed deputies were handed around, said to have been copied from the tablets of the dictator; genuine or false, they obtained universal credit and currency; and those whose names stood on the fatal scrolls, engaged themselves for protection in the league against their enemy. The opinion that his fall could not be delayed now became general.

---

[504] Lacretelle, tom. xii., p. 86.

THE NINTH THERMIDOR

This sentiment was so commonly entertained in Paris on the 9th Thermidor, or 27th July, that a herd of about eighty victims, who were in the act of being dragged to the guillotine, were nearly saved by means of it. The people, in a generous burst of compassion, began to gather in crowds, and interrupted the melancholy procession, as if the power which presided over these hideous exhibitions had already been deprived of energy. But the hour was not come. The vile Henriot, commandant of the national guards, came up with fresh forces, and on the day destined to be the last of his own life, proved the means of carrying to execution this crowd of unhappy and doubtless innocent persons.

On this eventful day, Robespierre arrived in the Convention, and beheld The Mountain in close array and completely manned, while, as in the case of Cataline, the bench on which he himself was accustomed to sit, seemed purposely deserted. Saint Just, Couthon, Le Bas (his brother-in-law,) and the younger Robespierre, were the only deputies of name who stood prepared to support him. But could he make an effectual struggle, he might depend upon the aid of the servile Barrère, a sort of Belial in the Convention, the meanest, yet not the least able, amongst those fallen spirits, who, with great adroitness and ingenuity, as well as wit and eloquence, caught opportunities as they arose, and was eminently dexterous in being always strong upon the strongest, and safe upon the safest side. There was a tolerably numerous party ready, in times so dangerous, to attach themselves to Barrère, as a leader who professed to guide them to safety, if not to honour; and it was the existence of this vacillating and uncertain body, whose ultimate motions could never be calculated upon, which rendered it impossible to presage with assurance the event of any debate in the Convention during this dangerous period.

Saint Just arose, in the name of the Committee of Public Safety, to make, after his own manner, not theirs, a report on the discourse of Robespierre on the previous evening. He had begun an harangue in the tone of his patron, declaring that, were the tribune which he occupied the Tarpeian rock itself, he would not the less, placed as he stood there, discharge the duties of a patriot.—"I am about," he said, "to lift the veil."—"I tear it asunder," said Tallien, interrupting him: "the public interest is sacrificed by individuals, who come hither to speak exclusively in their own name, and conduct themselves as superior to the whole Convention." He forced Saint Just from the tribune, and a violent debate ensued.

ROBESPIERRE DENOUNCED

Billaud-Varennes called the attention of the Assembly to the sitting of the Jacobin Club on the preceding evening. He declared the military force of Paris was placed under the command of Henriot, a traitor and a parricide, who was ready to march the soldiers whom he commanded against the Convention. He denounced Robespierre himself as a second Cataline, artful as well as ambitious, whose system it had been to nurse jealousies and inflame dissensions in the Convention, so as to disunite parties, and even individuals, from each other, attack them in detail, and thus destroy those antagonists separately, upon whose combined and united strength he dared not have looked.

The Convention echoed with applause every violent expression of the orator, and when Robespierre sprung to the tribune, his voice was drowned by a general shout of "Down with the tyrant!" Tallien moved the denunciation of Robespierre, with the arrest of Henriot, his staff-officers, and of others connected with the meditated violence on the Convention. He had undertaken to lead the attack upon the tyrant, he said, and to poniard him in the Convention itself, if the members did not show courage enough to enforce the law against him. With these words he brandished an unsheathed poniard, as if about to make his purpose good. Robespierre still struggled hard to obtain audience, but the tribune was adjudged to Barrère; and the part taken against the fallen dictator by that versatile and self-interested statesman, was the most absolute sign that his overthrow was irrecoverable. Torrents of invective were now uttered from every quarter of the hall, against him whose single word was wont to hush it into silence.

The scene was dreadful; yet not without its use to those who may be disposed to look at it as an extraordinary crisis, in which human passions were brought so singularly into collision. While the vaults of the hall echoed with exclamations from those who had hitherto been the accomplices, the flatterers, the followers, at least the timid and overawed assentators to the dethroned demagogue—he himself, breathless, foaming, exhausted, like the hunter of classical antiquity when on the point of being overpowered and torn to pieces by his own hounds, tried in vain to raise those screech-owl notes, by which the Convention had formerly been terrified and put to silence. He appealed for a hearing from the president of the assembly, to the various parties of which it was composed. Rejected by the Mountaineers, his former associates, who now headed the clamour against him, he applied to the Girondists, few and feeble as they were, and to the more numerous but equally helpless deputies of The Plain, with whom they sheltered. The former shook him from them with disgust, the last with horror. It was in vain he reminded individuals that he had spared their lives, while at his mercy. This might have been applied to every member in the house; to every man in France; for who was it during two years that had lived on other terms than under Robespierre's permission? and deeply must he internally have regretted the clemency, as he might term it, which had left so many with ungashed throats to bay at him. But his agitated and repeated appeals were repulsed by some with indignation, by others with sullen, or embarrassed and timid silence.

A British historian must say, that even Robespierre ought to have been heard in his defence; and that such calmness would have done honour to the Convention, and dignified their final sentence of condemnation. As it was, they no doubt treated the guilty individual according to his deserts; but they fell short of that regularity and manly staidness of conduct which was due to themselves and to the law, and which would have given to the punishment of the demagogue the effect and weight of a solemn and deliberate sentence, in place of its seeming the result of a hasty and precipitate seizure of a temporary advantage.

Haste was, however, necessary, and must have appeared more so at such a crisis than perhaps it really was. Much must be pardoned to the terrors of the moment, the horrid character of the culprit, and the necessity of hurrying to a decisive conclusion. We have been told that his last audible words, contending against the exclamations of hundreds, and the bell which the president[505] was ringing incessantly, and uttered in the highest tones which despair could give to a voice naturally shrill and discordant, dwelt long on the memory, and haunted the dreams, of many who heard him:—"President of assassins," he screamed, "for the last time I demand privilege of speech!"—After this exertion his breath became short and faint; and while he still uttered broken murmurs and hoarse ejaculations, a member of the Mountain[506] called out, that the blood of Danton choked his voice.

The tumult was closed by a decree of arrest against Robespierre, his brother, Couthon, and Saint Just; Le Bas was included on his own motion, and indeed could scarce have escaped the fate of his brother-in-law, though his conduct then, and subsequently, showed more energy than that of the others. Couthon, hugging in his bosom the spaniel upon which he was wont to exhaust the overflowing of his affected sensibility, appealed to his decrepitude, and asked whether, maimed of proportion and activity as he was, *he* could be suspected of nourishing plans of violence or ambition.—"Wretch," said Legendre, "thou hast the strength of Hercules for the perpetration of crime." Dumas, President of the Revolutionary Tribunal, with Henriot, commandant of the national guards, and other satellites of Robespierre, were included in the doom of arrest.[507]

The officers of the legislative body were ordered to lay hands on Robespierre; but such was the terror of his name, that they hesitated for some time to obey; and the reluctance of their own immediate satellites afforded the Convention an indifferent omen of the respect which was likely to be paid without doors to their decree against this powerful demagogue. Subsequent events seemed for a while to confirm the apprehensions thus excited.

---

[505] Thuriot, whom Robespierre had repeatedly threatened with death.
[506] Garnier de l'Aube.
[507] Thiers, tom. vi., p. 344; Lacretelle, tom. xii., p. 94; Mignet, tom. ii., p. 339; Toulongeon, tom. iv., p. 382; Montgaillard, tom. iv., p. 249.

The Convention had declared their sitting permanent, and had taken all precautions for appealing for protection to the large mass of citizens, who, wearied out by the Reign of Terror, were desirous to close it at all hazards. They quickly had deputations from several of the neighbouring sections, declaring their adherence to the national representatives, in whose defence they were arming, and (many undoubtedly prepared before-hand) were marching in all haste to the protection of the Convention. But they heard also the less pleasing tidings, that Henriot having effected the dispersion of those citizens who had obstructed, as elsewhere mentioned, the execution of the eighty condemned persons, and consummated that final act of murder, was approaching the Tuileries, where they had held their sitting, with a numerous staff, and such of the Jacobinical forces as could hastily be collected.

Happily for the Convention, this commandant of the national guards, on whose presence of mind and courage the fate of France perhaps for the moment depended, was as stupid and cowardly as he was brutally ferocious. He suffered himself, without resistance, to be arrested by a few gendarmes, the immediate guards of the Convention, headed by two of its members, who behaved in the emergency with equal prudence and spirit.

But fortune, or the demon whom he had served, afforded Robespierre another chance for safety, perhaps even for empire; for moments which a man of self-possession might have employed for escape, one of desperate courage might have used for victory, which, considering the divided and extremely unsettled state of the capital, was likely to be gained by the boldest competitor.

TERRORISTS AT THE HOTEL DE VILLE

The arrested deputies had been carried from one prison to another, all the jailors refusing to receive under their official charge Robespierre, and those who had aided him in supplying their dark habitations with such a tide of successive inhabitants. At length the prisoners were secured in the office of the Committee of Public Safety. But by this time all was in alarm amongst the Commune of

Paris, where Fleuriot the mayor, and Payan the successor of Hébert, convoked the civic body, despatched municipal officers to raise the city and the Fauxbourgs in their name, and caused the tocsin to be rung. Payan speedily assembled a force sufficient to liberate Henriot, Robespierre, and the other arrested deputies, and to carry them to the Hôtel de Ville, where about two thousand men were congregated, consisting chiefly of artillerymen, and of insurgents from the suburb of Saint Antoine, who already expressed their resolution of marching against the Convention. But the selfish and cowardly character of Robespierre was unfit for such a crisis. He appeared altogether confounded and overwhelmed with what had passed and was passing around him; and not one of all the victims of the Reign of Terror felt its disabling influence so completely as he, the despot who had so long directed its sway. He had not, even though the means must have been in his power, the presence of mind to disperse money in considerable sums, which of itself would not have failed to ensure the support of the revolutionary rabble.

Meantime, the Convention continued to maintain the bold and commanding front which they had so suddenly and critically assumed. Upon learning the escape of the arrested deputies, and hearing of the insurrection at the Hôtel de Ville, they instantly passed a decree outlawing Robespierre and his associates, inflicting a similar doom upon the Mayor of Paris, the Procureur and other members of the Commune, and charging twelve of their members, the boldest who could be selected, to proceed with the armed force to the execution of the sentence. The drums of the national guards now beat to arms in all the sections under authority of the Convention, while the tocsin continued to summon assistance with its iron voice to Robespierre and the civic magistrates. Every thing appeared to threaten a violent catastrophe, until it was seen clearly that the public voice, and especially amongst the national guards, was declaring itself generally against the Terrorists.

The Hôtel de Ville was surrounded by about fifteen hundred men, and cannon turned upon the doors. The force of the assailants was weakest in point of number, but their leaders were men of spirit, and night concealed their inferiority of force.

The deputies commissioned for the purpose read the decree of the Assembly to those whom they found assembled in front of the city-hall, and they shrunk from the attempt of defending it, some joining the assailants, others laying down their arms and dispersing. Meantime, the deserted group of Terrorists within conducted themselves like scorpions, which, when surrounded by a circle of fire, are said to turn their stings on each other, and on themselves. Mutual and ferocious upbraiding took place among these miserable men. "Wretch, were these the means you promised to furnish?" said Coffinhal to Henriot, whom he found intoxicated and incapable of resolution or exertion; and seizing on him as he spoke, he precipitated the revolutionary general from a window. Henriot survived the fall only to drag himself into a drain, in which he was afterwards discovered and brought out to execution. The younger Robespierre[508] threw himself from the window, but had not the good fortune to perish on the spot. It seemed as if even the melancholy fate of suicide, the last refuge of guilt and despair, was denied to men who had so long refused every species of mercy to their fellow-creatures. Le Bas alone had calmness enough to despatch himself with a pistol-shot. Saint Just, after imploring his comrades to kill him, attempted his own life with an irresolute hand, and failed. Couthon lay beneath the table brandishing a knife, with which he repeatedly wounded his bosom, without daring to add force enough to reach his heart. Their chief, Robespierre, in an unsuccessful attempt to shoot himself,[509] had only inflicted a horrible fracture on his under jaw.[510]

In this situation they were found like wolves in their lair, foul with blood, mutilated, despairing, and yet not able to die. Robespierre lay on a table in an ante-room, his head supported by a

---

[508] "Young Robespierre had but recently returned from the army of Italy, whither he had been sent by the Convention on a mission. He earnestly pressed Buonaparte to accompany him to Paris. 'Had I followed young Robespierre,' said Napoleon, 'how different might have been my career. On what trivial circumstances does human fate depend!'"—Las Cases, vol. i., p. 348.

[509] Baron Méda, then a simple gendarme, states, in his "Précis Historique," that it was the discharge of his pistol that broke Robespierre's jaw.—See *Collection des Mémoires Rév.*, tom. xlii., p. 384.

[510] Toulongeon, tom. iv., p. 390; Montgaillard, tom. iv., p. 257; Thiers, tom. vi., p. 360; Lacretelle, tom. xii., p. 117.

deal-box, and his hideous countenance half hidden by a bloody and dirty cloth bound round the shattered chin.[511]

The captives were carried in triumph to the Convention, who, refusing to admit them to the bar, sent them before the Revolutionary Tribunal, which ordered them, as outlaws, for instant execution. As the fatal cars passed to the guillotine, those who filled them, but especially Robespierre,[512] were overwhelmed with execrations from the friends and relatives of victims whom he had sent on the same melancholy road. The nature of his previous wound, from which the cloth had never been removed till the executioner tore it off, added to the torture of the sufferer. The shattered jaw dropped, and the wretch yelled aloud, to the horror of the spectators.[513] A mask taken from that dreadful head was long exhibited in different nations of Europe, and appalled the spectator by its ugliness, and the mixture of fiendish expression with that of bodily agony. At the same time fell young Robespierre, Couthon,[514] Saint Just, Coffinhal,[515] Henriot, Dumas, President of the Revolutionary Tribunal,[516] the Mayor, and fourteen of their subalterns.

---

[511] It did not escape the minute observers of this scene, that he still held in his hand the bag which had contained the fatal pistol, and which was inscribed with the words *Au grand Monarque*, alluding to the sign, doubtless, of the gunsmith who sold the weapon, but singularly applicable to the high pretensions of the purchaser.—S.—See Montgaillard, tom. iv., p. 257.

[512] The horsemen who escorted him showed him to the spectators with the point of their sabres. The mob stopped him before the house in which he lived; some women danced before the cart, and one of them cried out to him, "Murderer of all my kindred, thy agony fills me with joy; descend to hell, with the curses of all wives, mothers, and children!"— Lacretelle, tom. xii., p. 119; *Biog. Mod.*, vol. i., p. 179.

[513] The fate of no tyrant in story was so hideous at the conclusion, excepting perhaps that of Jugurtha.—S.

[514] "Couthon was born at Orsay in 1756. Before the Revolution he had been distinguished for the gentleness, as well as the integrity of his character. Owing to the malformation of his lower limbs, it was difficult to fasten him to the moving plank of the guillotine; and the executioner was at last obliged to lay him on his side to receive the blow."—*Biog. Mod.*, vol. i., p. 309.

[515] "Coffinhal was born at Aurillac in 1746. He it was who, when Lavoisier requested that his death might be delayed a fortnight, in order that he might finish some important experiments, made answer that the Republic had no need of scholars and chemists."—*Biog. Univ.*

[516] On the very day of his arrest he had signed the warrant for putting sixty persons to death. In the confusion, no person thought of arresting the guillotine. They all suffered.

CHARACTER OF ROBESPIERRE

Thus fell Maximilian Robespierre, after having been the first person in the French Republic for nearly two years, during which time he governed it upon the principles of Nero or Caligula. His elevation to the situation which he held involved more contradictions than perhaps attach to any similar event in history. A low-born and low-minded tyrant was permitted to rule with the rod of the most frightful despotism a people, whose anxiety for liberty had shortly before rendered them unable to endure the rule of a humane and lawful sovereign. A dastardly coward arose to the command of one of the bravest nations in the world; and it was under the auspices of a man who dared scarce fire a pistol, that the greatest generals in France began their careers of conquest. He had neither eloquence nor imagination; but substituted in their stead a miserable, affected, bombastic style, which, until other circumstances gave him consequence, drew on him general ridicule. Yet against so poor an orator, all the eloquence of the philosophical Girondists, all the terrible powers of his associate Danton, employed in a popular assembly, could not enable them to make an effectual resistance. It may seem trifling to mention, that in a nation where a good deal of prepossession is excited by amiable manners and beauty of external appearance, the person who ascended to the highest power was not only ill-looking, but singularly mean in person, awkward and constrained in his address, ignorant how to set about pleasing even when he most desired to give pleasure, and as tiresome nearly as he was odious and heartless.

To compensate all these deficiencies, Robespierre had but an insatiable ambition, founded on a vanity which made him think himself capable of filling the highest situation; and therefore gave him daring, when to dare is frequently to achieve. He mixed a false and overstrained, but rather fluent species of bombastic composition, with the grossest flattery to the lowest classes of the people;[517] in consideration of which, they could not but receive as

---

[517] The following is M. Dumont's report of Robespierre's maiden speech in the National Assembly:—
"I cannot forget the occasion on which a man, who afterwards acquired a fatal celebrity, first brought himself into notice. The clergy were endeavouring, by a subterfuge, to obtain

genuine the praises which he always bestowed on himself. His prudent resolution to be satisfied with possessing the essence of power, without seeming to desire its rank and trappings, formed another art of cajoling the multitude. His watchful envy, his long-protracted but sure revenge, his craft, which to vulgar minds supplies the place of wisdom, were his only means of competing with his distinguished antagonists. And it seems to have been a merited punishment of the extravagances and abuses of the French Revolution, that it engaged the country in a state of anarchy which permitted a wretch such as we have described, to be for a long period master of her destiny. Blood was his element,[518] like that of the other Terrorists, and he never fastened with so much pleasure

---

a conference of the orders; and for this purpose deputed the Archbishop of Aix to the Tiers Etat. This prelate expatiated very pathetically upon the distresses of the people, and the poverty of the country parishes. He produced a piece of black bread, which a dog would have rejected, but which the poor were obliged to eat or starve. He besought the Assembly to appoint some members to confer with those deputed by the nobility and clergy, upon the means of bettering the condition of the indigent classes. The Tiers Etat perceived the snare, but dared not openly reject the proposal, as it would render them unpopular with the lower classes. Then a deputy rose, and after professing sentiments in favour of the poor still stronger than those of the prelate, adroitly threw doubts upon the sincerity of the intentions avowed by the clergy. 'Go,' said he to the archbishop, 'and tell your colleagues, that if they are so impatient to assist the suffering poor, they had better come hither and join the friends of the people. Tell them no longer to embarrass our proceedings with affected delays; tell them no longer to endeavour, by unworthy means, to make us swerve from the resolutions we have taken; but as ministers of religion—as worthy imitators of their master—let them forego that luxury which surrounds them, and that splendour which puts indigence to the blush;—let them resume the modesty of their origin, discharge the proud lackeys by whom they are attended, sell their superb equipages, and convert all their superfluous wealth into food for the indigent.'

"This speech, which coincided so well with the passions of the time, did not elicit loud applause, which would have been a bravado and out of place, but was succeeded by a murmur much more flattering: 'Who is he?' was the general question; but he was unknown; and it was not until some time had elapsed that a name was circulated which, three years later, made France tremble. The speaker was Robespierre. Reybas, who was seated next to me, observed, 'This young man is as yet unpractised; he does not know when to stop, but he has a store of eloquence which will not leave him in the crowd."—*Souvenirs de Mirabeau*, p. 49.

518 "Robespierre had been a studious youth and a respectable man, and his character contributed not a little to the ascendency which he obtained over rivals, some of whom were corrupt, others impudently profligate, and of whom there were few who had any pretensions to morality. He became bloody, because a revolutionist soon learns to consider human lives as the counters with which he plays his perilous game; and he perished after he had cut off every man who was capable of directing the republic, because they who had committed the greatest abominations of the Revolution united against him, that they might secure themselves, and wash their hands in his blood."—*Quarterly Review*, vol. vii., p. 432.

Robespierre wrote, in 1785, an Essay against the Punishment of Death, which gained the prize awarded by the Royal Society of Metz.

on a new victim, as when he was at the same time an ancient associate. In an epitaph,[519] of which the following couplet may serve as a translation, his life was represented as incompatible with the existence of the human race:—

"Here lies Robespierre—let no tear be shed; Reader, if he had lived thou hadst been dead."

When the report of Robespierre's crimes was brought to the Convention, in which he is most justly charged with the intention of possessing himself of the government, the inconsistent accusation is added, that he plotted to restore the Bourbons; in support of which it is alleged that a seal, bearing a fleur-de-lis, was found at the Hôtel de Ville. Not even the crimes of Robespierre were thought sufficiently atrocious, without their being mingled with a tendency to Royalism!

THE THERMIDORIENS

With this celebrated demagogue the Reign of Terror may be said to have terminated, although those by whose agency the tyrant fell were as much Terrorists as himself, being, indeed, the principal members of the very committees of public safety and public security, who had been his colleagues in all the excesses of his revolutionary authority. Among the *Thermidoriens*, as the actors in Robespierre's downfall termed themselves, there were names almost as dreadful as that of the dictator, for whom the ninth Thermidor proved the Ides of March. What could be hoped for from Collot D'Herbois, the butcher of the Lyonnois—what from Billaud-Varennes—what from Barras, who had directed the executions at Marseilles after its ephemeral revolt—what from Tallien, whose arms were afterwards died double red, from finger-nails to elbow, in the blood of the unfortunate emigrant gentlemen who were made prisoners at Quiberon? It seemed that only a new set of Septembrisers had succeeded, and that the same horrible principle would continue to be the moving spring of the government, under

---

[519] Passant! ne pleure point son sort: Car s'il vivait, tu serais mort.

the direction of other chiefs indeed, but men who were scarce less familiar with its horrors, than was the departed tyrant.

Men looked hopelessly towards the Convention, long rather like the corpse of a legislative assembly, actuated, during its apparent activity, like the supposed vampire, by an infernal spirit not its own, which urged it to go forth and drink blood, but which, deserted by the animating demon, must, it was to be expected, sink to the ground in helpless incapacity. What could be expected from Barrère, the ready panegyrist of Robespierre, the tool who was ever ready to show to the weak and the timid the exact point where their safety recommended to them to join the ranks of the wicked and the strong? But, in spite of these discouraging circumstances, the feelings of humanity, and a spirit of self-protection, dictating a determined resistance to the renovation of the horrid system under which the country had so long suffered, began to show itself both in the Convention and without doors. Encouraged by the fall of Robespierre, complaints poured in against his agents on all sides. Lebon was accused before the Convention by a deputation from Cambrai; and as he ascended the tribune to put himself on his defence, he was generally hailed as the hangman of Robespierre. The monster's impudence supported him in a sort of defence; and when it was objected to him, that he had had the common executioner to dine in company with him, he answered, "That delicate people might think that wrong; but Lequinio (another Jacobin proconsul of horrible celebrity) had made the same useful citizen the companion of his leisure, and hours of relaxation."[520] He acknowledged with the

---

[520] Mercier, in his *Nouveau Tableau de Paris*, has devoted a chapter to this personage. "What a man," he says, "is that Samson! Insensible to suffering, he was always identified with the axe of execution. He has beheaded the most powerful monarch in Europe, his Queen, Couthon, Brissot, Robespierre—and all this with a composed countenance. He cuts off the head that is brought to him, no matter whose. What does he say? What does he think? I should like to know what passes in his head, and whether he has considered his terrible functions only as a trade. The more I meditate on this man, the president of the great massacre of the human species, overthrowing crowned heads like that of the purest republican, without moving a muscle, the more my ideas are confounded. How did he sleep, after receiving the last words, the last looks of all these severed heads? I really would give a trifle to be in the soul of this man for a few hours. He sleeps, it is said, and, very likely, his conscience may be at perfect rest. He is sometimes present at the Vaudeville: he laughs, looks at me; my head has escaped him, he knows nothing about it; and as that is very indifferent to him, I never grow weary of contemplating in him the indifference with which he has sent that crowd of men to the other world."

same equanimity, that an aristocrat being condemned to the guillotine, he kept him lying in the usual posture upon his back, with his eyes turned up to the axe, which was suspended above his throat,—in short, in all the agonies which can agitate the human mind, when within a hair's breadth of the distance of the great separation between Time and Eternity,—until he had read to him, at length, the Gazette which had just arrived, giving an account of a victory gained by the Republican armies. This monster, with Heron, Rossignol, and other agents of terror more immediately connected with Robespierre, were ordered for arrest, and shortly after for execution. Tallien and Barras would have here paused in the retrospect; but similar accusations now began to pour in from every quarter, and when once stated, were such as commanded public attention in the most forcible manner. Those who invoked vengeance, backed the solicitations of each other—the general voice of mankind was with them; and leaders who had shared the excesses of the Reign of Terror, Thermidoriens as they were, began to see some danger of being themselves buried in the ruins of the power which they had overthrown.[521]

Tallien, who is supposed to have taken the lead in the extremely difficult navigation which lay before the vessel of the state, seems to have experienced a change in his own sentiments, at least his principles of action, inclining him to the cause of humanity. He was also, it is said, urged to so favourable a modification of feelings by his newly married wife, formerly Madame Fontenai, who, bred a royalist, had herself been a victim to the law of suspicion, and was released from a prison[522] to receive the hand, and influence the activity of the republican statesman. Barras, who, as commanding the armed force, might be termed the hero of the 9th Thermidor, was supposed to be also inclined towards humanity and moderation.

---

[521] Lacretelle, tom. xii., p. 204; Chateaubriand, Etud. Hist., tom. i., p. 102; Prudhomme, Victimes de la Rév., tom. ii., p. 274. On the scaffold, when the red shirt was thrown over him, he exclaimed, "It is not I who should put it on: it should be sent to the Convention, for I have only executed their orders."—*Biog. Mod.*, vol. ii., p. 267.

[522] She was the daughter of Count Cabarus. During her imprisonment, she had formed a close intimacy with Josephine Beauharnais, afterwards the wife of Napoleon. These ladies were the first to proscribe the revolutionary manners, and seized every opportunity of saving those whom the existing government wished to immolate. The marriage of Madame Fontenai with Tallien was not a happy one. On his return from Egypt, a separation took place, and in 1805 she married M. de Caraman, prince of Chemai.

Thus disposed to destroy the monstrous system which had taken root in France, and which, indeed, in the increasing impatience of the country, they would have found it impossible to maintain, Tallien and Barras had to struggle, at the same time to diminish and restrict the general demand for revenge, at a time when, if past tyranny was to be strictly inquired into and punished, the doom, as Carrier himself told them, would have involved every thing in the Convention, not excepting the president's bell and his arm-chair. So powerful were these feelings of resisting a retrospect, that the Thermidoriens declined to support Le Cointre in bringing forward a general charge of inculpation against the two Committees of Public Safety and Public Security, in which accusation, notwithstanding their ultimate quarrel with Robespierre, he showed their intimate connexion with him, and their joint agency in all which had been imputed to him as guilt. But the time was not mature for hazarding such a general accusation, and it was rejected by the Convention with marks of extreme displeasure.[523]

FREEDOM OF THE PRESS

Still, however, the general voice of humanity demanded some farther atonement for two years of outrage, and to satisfy this demand, the Thermidoriens set themselves to seek victims connected more immediately with Robespierre; while they endeavoured gradually to form a party, which, setting out upon a principle of amnesty, and oblivion of the past, should in future pay some regard to that preservation of the lives and property of the governed, which, in every other system saving that which had been just overthrown in France, is regarded as the principal end of civil government. With a view to the consolidation of such a party, the restrictions of the press were removed, and men of talent and literature, silenced during the reign of Robespierre, were once more admitted to exercise their natural influence in favour of civil order and religion. Marmontel, La Harpe, and others, who, in their youth, had been enrolled in the list of Voltaire's disciples, and amongst the infidels of the Encyclopédie, now made amends for their youthful

---

[523] Lacretelle, tom. xii., p. 131.

errors, by exerting themselves in the cause of good morals, and of a regulated government.[524]

At length followed that general and long-desired measure, which gave liberty to so many thousands, by suspending the law denouncing suspected persons, and emptying at once of their inhabitants the prisons, which had hitherto only transmitted them to the guillotine.[525] The tales which these victims of Jacobinism had to repeat, when revealing the secrets of their prison-house, together with the moral influence produced by such a universal gaol-delivery, and the reunion which it effected amongst friends and relations that had been so long separated, tended greatly to strengthen the hands of the Thermidoriens, who still boasted of that name, and to consolidate a rational and moderate party, both in the capital and provinces. It is, however, by no means to be wondered at, that the liberated sufferers showed a disposition to exercise retribution in a degree which their liberators trembled to indulge, lest it might have recoiled upon themselves. Still both parties united against the remains of the Jacobins.

A singular and melancholy species of force supported these movements towards civilisation and order. It was levied among the orphans and youthful friends of those who had fallen under the fatal guillotine, and amounted in number to two or three thousand young men, who acted in concert, were distinguished by black collars, and by their hair being plaited and turned up *à la victime*, as prepared for the guillotine. This costume was adopted in memory of the principle of mourning on which they were associated. These volunteers were not regularly armed or disciplined, but formed a sort of free corps, who opposed themselves readily and effectually to the Jacobins, when they attempted their ordinary revolutionary tactics of exciting partial insurrections, and intimidating the orderly citizens by shouts and violence. Many scuffles took place betwixt the parties, with various success; but ultimately the spirit and courage of the young Avengers seemed to give them daily a more decided superiority. The Jacobins dared not show themselves, that is, to avouch their

---

[524] Lacretelle, tom. xii., p. 138.
[525] "In the space of eight or ten days, out of ten thousand suspected persons, not one remained in the prisons of Paris."—Lacretelle, tom. xii., p. 145.

principles, either at the places of public amusement, or in the Palais Royal, or the Tuileries, all of which had formerly witnessed their victories. Their assemblies now took place under some appearance of secrecy, and were held in remote streets, and with such marks of diminished audacity as augured that the spirit of the party was crest-fallen.[526]

Still, however, the Jacobin party possessed dreadful leaders in Billaud-Varennes and Collot d'Herbois, who repeatedly attempted to awaken its terrific energy. These demagogues had joined, indeed, in the struggle against Robespierre, but it was with the expectation that an Amurath was to succeed an Amurath—a Jacobin a Jacobin—not for the purpose of relaxing the reins of the revolutionary government, far less changing its character. These veteran revolutionists must be considered as separate from those who called themselves Thermidoriens, though they lent their assistance to the revolution on the 9th Thermidor. They viewed as deserters and apostates Legendre, Le Cointre, and others, above all Tallien and Barras, who, in the full height of their career, had paused to take breath, and were now endeavouring to shape a course so different from that which they had hitherto pursued.

JACOBIN CLUB REOPENED

These genuine Sans-Culottes endeavoured to rest their own power and popularity upon the same basis as formerly. They reopened the sittings of the Jacobin Club, shut up on the 9th Thermidor. This ancient revolutionary cavern again heard its roof resound with denunciations, by which Vadier, Billaud-Varennes, and others, devoted to the infernal deities Le Cointre, and those, who, they complained, wished to involve all honest Republicans in the charges brought against Robespierre and his friends. Those threats, however, were no longer rapidly followed by the thunderbolts which used to attend such flashes of Jacobin eloquence. Men's homes were now in comparison safe. A man might be named in a Jacobin club as an Aristocrat, or a Moderate, and yet live. In fact, the demagogues were more anxious to secure immunity for their past crimes, than at

---

[526] Lacretelle, tom. xii., p. 147.

present to incur new censure. The tide of general opinion was flowing strongly against them, and a singular incident increased its power, and rendered it irresistible.

The Parisians had naturally enough imagined, that the provinces could have no instances of Jacobinical cruelty and misrule to describe, more tragic and appalling than the numerous executions which the capital had exhibited every day. But the arrival of eighty prisoners, citizens of Nantes, charged with the usual imputations cast upon suspected persons, undeceived them. These captives had been sent, for the purpose of being tried at Paris, before the Revolutionary Tribunal. Fortunately, they did not arrive till after Robespierre's fall, and consequently when they were looked upon rather as oppressed persons than as criminals, and were listened to more as accusers of those by whom they were persecuted, than as culprits on their defence.

It was then that the metropolis first heard of horrors which we have formerly barely hinted at. It was then they were told of crowds of citizens, most of whom had been favourable to the republican order of things, and had borne arms against the Vendéans in their attack upon Nantes; men accused upon grounds equally slight, and incapable of proof, having been piled together in dungeons, where the air was pestilential from ordure, from the carcasses of the dead, and the infectious diseases of the dying. It was then they heard of Republican baptism and Republican marriages—of men, women, and children sprawling together, like toads and frogs in the season of spring, in the waters of the Loire, too shallow to afford them instant death. It was then they heard of a hundred other abominations—how those uppermost upon the expiring mass prayed to be thrust into the deeper water, that they might have the means of death—and of much more that humanity forbears to detail; but in regard to which, the sharp, sudden, and sure blow of the Parisian guillotine was clemency.[527]

---

[527] Toulongeon, tom. v., p. 119; Thiers, tom. vii., p. 117; Lacretelle, tom. xii., p. 162; Montgaillard, tom. iv., p. 301.

TRIAL OF CARRIER

This tale of horrors could not be endured; and the point of immediate collision between the Thermidoriens, compelled and driven onward by the public voice and feeling, and the remnant of the old Jacobin faction, became the accusation of Carrier, the commissioned deputy under whom these unheard-of horrors had been perpetrated. Vengeance on the head of this wretch was so loudly demanded, that it could not be denied even by those influential persons, who, themselves deeply interested in preventing recrimination, would willingly have drawn a veil over the past. Through the whole impeachment and defence, the Thermidoriens stood on the most delicate and embarrassing ground; for horrid as his actions were, he had in general their own authority to plead for them. For example, a letter was produced with these directions to General Haxo—"It is my plan to carry off from that accursed country all manner of subsistence or provisions for man or beast, all forage—in a word, *every thing*—give all the buildings to the flames, and exterminate the whole inhabitants. Oppose their being relieved by a single grain of corn for their subsistence. I give thee the most positive, most imperious order. Thou art answerable for the execution from this moment. In a word, leave nothing in that proscribed country—let the means of subsistence, provisions, forage, every thing—absolutely every thing, be removed to Nantes." The representatives of the French nation heard with horror such a fiendish commission; but with what sense of shame and abasement must they have listened to Carrier's defence, in which he proved he was only literally executing the decrees of the very Convention which was now inquiring into his conduct! A lunatic, who, in a lucid moment, hears some one recount the crimes and cruelties he committed in his frenzy, might perhaps enter into their feelings. They were not the less obliged to continue the inquiry, fraught as it was with circumstances so disgraceful to themselves; and Carrier's impeachment and conviction proved the point on which the Thermidoriens, and those who continued to entertain the violent popular opinions, were now at issue.

The atrocious Carrier was taken under the avowed protection of the Jacobin Club, before which audience he made out a case which was heard with applause. He acknowledged his enormities, and pleaded his patriotic zeal; ridiculed the delicacy of those who cared whether an aristocrat died by a single blow, or a protracted death; was encouraged throughout by acclamations, and received assurances of protection from the remnant of that once formidable association. But their magic influence was dissolved—their best orators had fallen successively by each other's impeachment—and of their most active ruffians, some had been killed or executed, some had fled, or lay concealed, many were in custody, and the rest had become intimidated. Scarce a man who had signalized himself in the French Revolution, but had enjoyed the applause of these demagogues, as versatile in personal attachments, as steady in their execrable principles—scarce one whom they had not been active in sacrificing.

Nevertheless, those members of the Revolutionary Committees, who had so lately lent their aid to dethrone Robespierre, the last idol of the Society, ventured to invoke them in their own defence, and that of their late agents. Billaud-Varennes, addressing the Jacobins, spoke of the Convention as men spared by their clemency during the reign of Robespierre, who now rewarded the Mountain deputies by terming them Men of Blood, and by seeking the death of those worthy patriots, Joseph Lebon and Carrier, who were about to fall under their counter-revolutionary violence. These excellent citizens, he said, were persecuted, merely because their zeal for the Republic had been somewhat ardent—their forms of proceeding a little rash and severe. He invoked the awaking of the Lion—a new revolutionary rising of the people, to tear the limbs and drink the blood[528]—(these were the very words)—of those who had dared to beard them. The meeting dispersed with shouts, and vows to answer to the halloo of their leaders.

But the opposite party had learned that such menaces were to be met otherwise than by merely awaiting the issue, and then trying the force of remonstrances, or the protection of the law, with those to whom the stronger force is the only satisfying reason.

---

[528] "Briser leurs membres, et boire leur sang."—Thiers, tom. vii., p. 121. "Nager dans leur sang."—Lacretelle, tom. xii., p. 157.

Well organized, and directed by military officers in many instances, large bands of Anti-jacobins, as we may venture to call the volunteer force already mentioned, appeared in the neighbourhood of the suburbs, and kept in check those from whom the Mother Club expected its strongest aid; while the main body of the young Avengers marched down upon the citadel of the enemy, and invested the Jacobin Club itself in the midst of its sitting. These demagogues made but a wretched defence when attacked by that species of popular violence, which they had always considered as their own especial weapon; and the facility with which they were dispersed, amid ridicule and ignominy, served to show how easily, on former occasions, the mutual understanding and spirited exertion of well-disposed men could have at any time prevented criminal violence from obtaining the mastery. Had La Fayette marched against and shut up the Jacobin Club, the world would have been spared many horrors, and in all probability he would have found the task as easy as it proved to those bands of incensed young men.—It must be mentioned, though the recital is almost unworthy of history, that the female Jacobins came to rally and assist their male associates, and that several of them were seized upon and punished in a manner, which might excellently suit their merits, but which shows that the young associates for maintaining order were not sufficiently aristocratic to be under the absolute restraints imposed by the rules of chivalry. It is impossible, however, to grudge the flagellation administered upon this memorable occasion.[529]

When the Jacobins had thus fallen in the popular contest, they could expect little success in the Convention; and the less, that the impulse of general feeling seemed about to recall into that Assembly, by the reversal of their outlawry, the remnant of the unhappy Girondists, and other members, who had been arbitrarily proscribed on the 31st of May. The measure was delayed for some time, as tending to effect a change in the composition of the House, which the ruling party might find inconvenient. At length upwards of sixty deputies were first declared free of the outlawry, and finally re-admitted into the bosom of the Convention, with heads which

---

[529] Lacretelle, tom. xii., p. 154.

had been so long worn in insecurity, that it had greatly cooled their love of political theory.[530]

In the meantime the government, through means of a revolutionary tribunal, acting however with much more of legal formality and caution than that of Robespierre, made a sacrifice to the public desire of vengeance. Lebon, Carrier, already mentioned, Fouquier-Tainville,[531] the public accuser under Robespierre, and one or two others of the same class, selected on account of the peculiar infamy and cruelty of their conduct, were condemned and executed, as an atonement for injured humanity.

Here, probably, the Thermidoriens would have wished the reaction to stop; but this was impossible. Barras and Tallien perceived plainly, that with whatever caution and clemency they might proceed towards their old allies of The Mountain, there was still no hope of any thing like reconciliation; and that their best policy was to get rid of them as speedily and as quietly as they could. The Mountain, like a hydra whose heads bourgeoned, according to the poetic expression, as fast as they were cut off, continued to hiss at and menace the government with unwearied malignity, and to agitate the metropolis by their intrigues, which were the more easily conducted that the winter was severe, bread had become scarce and high-priced, and the common people of course angry and discontented. Scarcity is always the grievance of which the lower classes must be most sensible; and when it is remembered that Robespierre, though at the expense of the grossest injustice to the rest of the kingdom, always kept bread beneath a certain *maximum* or fixed price in the metropolis, it will not be wondered at that the population of Paris should be willing to favour those who followed

---

[530] Lacretelle, tom. xii., p. 177.
[531] Fouquier-Tainville made an able defence, which he concluded with saying, "I was but the axe of the Convention, and would you punish an axe?" Mercier says, "while standing before the Tribunal, from which he had condemned so many victims, he kept constantly writing; but, like Argus, all eyes and ears, he lost nothing that was said or done. He affected to sleep during the public accuser's recapitulation, as if to feign tranquillity, while he had hell in his heart. When led to execution, he answered the hisses of the populace by sinister predictions. At the foot of the scaffold he seemed, for the first time, to feel remorse, and trembled as he ascended it." In early life, Fouquier scribbled poetry for the journals. Some verses of his, in praise of Louis XVI., will be found in the notes to Delille's "*La Pitié.*"

his maxims. The impulse of these feelings, joined to the machinations of the Jacobins, showed itself in many disorders.

JACOBIN CHIEFS BANISHED

At length the Convention, pressed by shame on the one side and fear on the other, saw the necessity of some active measure, and appointed a commission to consider and report upon the conduct of the four most obnoxious Jacobin chiefs, Collot d'Herbois, Billaud-Varennes, Vadier,[532] and Barrère.[533] The report was of course unfavourable; yet, upon the case being considered, the Convention were satisfied to condemn them to transportation to Cayenne. Some resistance was offered to this sentence, so mild in proportion to what those who underwent it had been in the habit of inflicting; but it was borne down, and the sentence was carried into execution. Collot d'Herbois, the demolisher and depopulator of Lyons, is said to have died in the common hospital, in consequence of drinking off at once a whole bottle of ardent spirits.[534] Billaud-Varennes spent his time in teaching the innocent parrots of Guiana the frightful jargon of the Revolutionary Committee; and finally perished in misery.[535]

---

[532] Vadier contrived to conceal himself in Paris, and thereby avoided his sentence. He continued to reside in the capital up to the law of the 12th January, 1816, when he was compelled to quit France. He died at Brussels, in 1828, at the age of ninety-three.

[533] Barrère contrived to be left behind, at the isle of Olèron, when his colleagues sailed for Cayenne; upon which Boursault observed, that "it was the first time he had ever failed to sail with the wind." He also remained in France, till the law of January, 1816, compelled him to leave it.

[534] M. Piton, who, in 1797, was himself transported to Cayenne by the Directory gives, in his "Voyage à Cayenne," the following account of the death of Collot d'Herbois:—"He was lying upon the ground, his face exposed to a burning sun, in a raging fever—the negroes, who were appointed to bear him from Kouron to Cayenne, having thrown him down to perish; a surgeon, who found him in this situation, asked him what ailed him, he replied, 'J'ai la fièvre, et une sueur brulante!'—'Je le crois bien, vous suez le crime,' was the bitter rejoinder. He expired, vomiting froth and blood, calling upon that God whom he had so often renounced!" M. Piton describes Collot as not naturally wicked,—"Il avait d'excellentes qualités du coté du cœur, beaucoup de clinquant du coté de l'esprit; un caractère faible et irascible à l'excès; généreux sans bornes, bon ami, et ennemi implacable. La Révolution a fait sa perte."

[535] "After Billaud-Varennes reached Cayenne, his life was a continued scene of romantic adventures. He escaped to Mexico, and entered, under the name of Polycarpus Varennes, the Dominican convent at Porto Ricco. Obliged to flee the continent for the part he took

These men both belonged to that class of atheists, who, looking up towards heaven, loudly and literally defied the Deity to make his existence known by launching his thunderbolts. Miracles are not wrought on the challenge of a blasphemer more than on the demand of a sceptic; but both these unhappy men had probably before their death reason to confess, that in abandoning the wicked to their own free will, a greater penalty results even in this life, than if Providence had been pleased to inflict the immediate doom which they had impiously defied.

THE FIRST OF PRAIRIAL

The notice of one more desperate attempt at popular insurrection, finishes, in a great measure, the history of Jacobinism and of The Mountain; of those, in short, who professed the most outrageous popular doctrines, considered as a political body. They continued to receive great facilities from the increasing dearth, and to find ready opportunities of agitating the discontented part of a population, disgusted by the diminution not only of comforts, but of the very means of subsistence. The Jacobins, therefore, were easily able to excite an insurrection of the same description as those which had repeatedly influenced the fate of the Revolution, and which, in fact, proceeded to greater extremities than any which had preceded it in the same desperate game. The rallying word of the rabble was "Bread, and the Democratic Constitution of 1793;" a constitution which the Jacobins had projected, but never attempted seriously to put into force. No insurrection had yet appeared more formidable in numbers, or better provided in pikes, muskets, and cannon. On the first of Prairial [20th May] they invested the Convention, without experiencing any effectual opposition; burst into the hall, assassinated one deputy, Ferraud, by a pistol-shot, and paraded his head amongst his trembling brethren, and through the neighbouring streets and environs on a pike. They presented Boissy d'Anglas, the President, with the motions which they demanded

---

in the disputes between the Spanish colonies and the mother country, Pethion, then president of Hayti, not only afforded him an asylum, but made him his secretary. After Pethion's death, Boyer refusing to employ him, he went to the United States, and died at Philadelphia in 1819."—*Biog. Univ.*

should be passed; but were defeated by the firmness with which he preferred his duty to his life.[536]

The steadiness of the Convention gave at length confidence to the friends of good order without. The national guards began to muster strong, and the insurgents to lose spirits. They were at length, notwithstanding their formidable appearance, dispersed with very little effort. The tumult, however, was renewed on the two following days; until at length the necessity of taking sufficient measures to end it at once and for ever, became evident to all.

Pichegru, the conqueror of Holland, who chanced to be in Paris at the time, was placed at the head of the national guards and the volunteers, whose character we have noticed elsewhere. At the head of this force, he marched in military order towards the Fauxbourg Saint Antoine, which had poured forth repeatedly the bands of armed insurgents that were the principal force of the Jacobins.

After a show of defending themselves, the inhabitants of this disorderly suburb were at length obliged to surrender up their arms of every kind. Those pikes, which had so often decided the destinies of France, were now delivered up by cartloads; and the holy right of insurrection was rendered in future a more dangerous and difficult task.[537]

Encouraged by the success of this decisive measure, the government proceeded against some of the Terrorists whom they had hitherto spared, but whose fate was now determined, in order to strike dismay into their party. Six Jacobins, accounted among the most ferocious of the class, were arrested as encouragers of the late insurrection, and delivered up to be tried by a military commission. They were all deputies of The Mountain gang. Certain of their doom, they adopted a desperate resolution. Among the whole party, they possessed but one knife, but they resolved it should serve them

---

[536] "They held up to him the bloody head of Ferraud; he turned aside with horror: they again presented it, and he bowed before the remains of the martyr; nor would he quit the chair till compelled by the efforts of his friends; and the insurgents, awed with respect, allowed him to retire unmolested."—Lacretelle, tom. xii., p. 221.

[537] Mignet, tom. ii., p. 370; Thiers, tom. vii., p. 371; Lacretelle, tom. xii., p. 220.

all for the purpose of suicide. The instant their sentence was pronounced, one stabbed himself with this weapon; another snatched the knife from his companion's dying hand, plunged it in his own bosom, and handed it to the third, who imitated the dreadful example. Such was the consternation of the attendants, that no one arrested the fatal progress of the weapon—all fell either dead or desperately wounded—the last were despatched by the guillotine.[538]

After this decisive victory, and last dreadful catastrophe, Jacobinism, considered as a pure and unmixed party, can scarce be said to have again raised its head in France, although its leaven has gone to qualify and characterise, in some degree, more than one of the different parties which have succeeded them. As a political sect, the Jacobins can be compared to none that ever existed, for none but themselves ever thought of an organized, regular, and continued system of murdering and plundering the rich, that they might debauch the poor by the distribution of their spoils. They bear, however, some resemblance to the frantic followers of John of Leyden and Knipperdoling, who occupied Munster in the seventeenth century and committed, in the name of Religion, the same frantic horrors which the French Jacobins did in that of Freedom. In both cases, the courses adopted by these parties were most foreign to, and inconsistent with, the alleged motives of their conduct. The Anabaptists practised every species of vice and cruelty, by the dictates, they said, of inspiration—the Jacobins imprisoned three hundred thousand of their countrymen in name of liberty, and put to death more than half the number, under the sanction of fraternity.

Now at length, however, society began to resume its ordinary course, and the business and pleasures of life succeeded each other as usual.[539] But even social pleasures brought with them strange and

---

[538] Romme, Bourbotte, Duquesnoy, Duroi, Soubrani, and Goujon. Five out of the six had voted for the death of the King.—See Mignet, tom. ii., p. 373; Montgaillard, tom. iv., p. 335; Lacretelle, tom. xii., p. 230.
[539] At the theatres the favourite air "Le Reveil du Peuple," was called for several times in the course of an evening. The law of the maximum, and the prohibitions against Christian worship were repealed; and this was followed by an act restoring to the families of those

gloomy associations with that Valley of the Shadow of Death, through which the late pilgrimage of France appeared to have lain. An Assembly for dancing, very much frequented by the young of both sexes, and highly fashionable, was called the "Ball of the Victims." The qualification for attendance was the having lost some near and valued relation or friend in the late Reign of Terror. The hair and head-dress were so arranged as to resemble the preparations made for the guillotine, and the motto adopted was, "We dance amidst tombs."[540] In no country but France could the incidents have taken place which gave rise to this association; and certainly in no country but France would they have been used for such a purpose.

But it is time to turn from the consideration of the internal government of France, to its external relations; in regard to which the destinies of the country rose to such a distinguished height, that it is hardly possible to reconcile the two pictures of a nation, triumphant at every point against all Europe coalesced against her, making efforts and obtaining victories, to which history had been yet a stranger; while, at the same time, her affairs at home were directed by ferocious bloodthirsty savages, such as Robespierre. The Republic, regarded in her foreign and domestic relations, might be fancifully compared to the tomb erected over some hero, presenting, without, trophies of arms and the emblems of victory, while, within, there lies only a mangled and corrupted corpse.

---

executed during the Revolution such part of their property as had not been disposed of.— Lacretelle, tom. xii., p. 182.
[540] Mignet, tom. ii., p. 356; Lacretelle, tom. xii., p. 174.

Chapter XVIII

Retrospective View of the External Relations of France—Her great Military Successes—Whence they arose—Effect of the Compulsory Levies—Military Genius and Character of the French—French Generals—New Mode of Training the Troops—Light Troops—Successive Attacks in Column—Attachment of the Soldiers to the Revolution—Also of the Generals—Carnot—Effect of the French principles preached to the Countries invaded by their Arms—Close of the Revolution with the fall of Robespierre—Reflections upon what was to succeed.

EXTERNAL RELATIONS

It may be said of victory, as the English satirist has said of wealth, that it cannot be of much importance in the eye of Heaven, considering in what unworthy association it is sometimes found.[541] While the rulers of France were disowning the very existence of a Deity, her armies appeared to move almost as if protected by the especial favour of Providence. Our former recapitulation presented a slight sketch of the perilous state of France in 1793, surrounded by foes on almost every frontier, and with difficulty maintaining her ground on any point; yet the lapse of two years found her victorious, nay, triumphantly victorious, on all.

On the north-eastern frontier, the English, after a series of hard-fighting, had lost not only Flanders, on which we left them advancing, but Holland itself, and had been finally driven with great loss to abandon the Continent. The King of Prussia had set out on his first campaign as the chief hero of the coalition, and had engaged

---

[541] "Riches, in effect, No grace of Heav'n or token of th' Elect; Giv'n to the fool, the mad, the vain, the evil, To Ward, to Waters, Chartres, and the Devil." Pope.

that the Duke of Brunswick, his general, should put down the revolution in France as easily as he had done that of Holland. But finding the enterprise which he had undertaken was above his strength; that his accumulated treasures were exhausted in an unsuccessful war; and that Austria, not Prussia, was regarded as the head of the coalition, he drew off his forces, after they had been weakened by more than one defeat, and made a separate peace with France, in which he renounced to the new Republic the sovereignty of all those portions of the Prussian territory which lay on the east side of the Rhine. The King, to make up for these losses, sought a more profitable, though less honourable field of warfare, and concurred with Russia and Austria in effecting by conquest a final partition and appropriation of Poland, on the same unprincipled plan on which the first had been conducted.

Spain, victorious at the beginning of the conquest, had been of late so unsuccessful in opposing the French armies, that it was the opinion of many that her character for valour and patriotism was lost for ever. Catalonia was over-run by the Republicans, Rosas taken, and no army intervening betwixt the victors and Madrid, the King of Spain was obliged to clasp hands with the murderers of his kinsman, Louis XVI., acknowledge the French Republic, and withdraw from the coalition.

Austria had well sustained her ancient renown, both by the valour of her troops, the resolution of her cabinet, and the talents of one or two of her generals,—the Archduke Charles in particular, and the veteran Wurmser. Yet she too had succumbed under the Republican superiority. Belgium, as the French called Flanders, was, as already stated, totally lost; and war along the Rhine was continued by Austria, more for defence than with a hope of conquest.

So much and so generally had the fortune of war declared in favour of France upon all points, even while she was herself sustaining the worst of evils from the worst of tyrannies. There must have been unquestionably several reasons for such success as seemed to attend universally on the arms of the Republic, instead of being limited to one peculiarly efficient army, or to one distinguished general.

The first and most powerful cause must be looked for in the extraordinary energy of the Republican government, which, from its very commencement, threw all subordinate considerations aside, and devoted the whole resources of the country to its military defence. It was then that France fully learned the import of the word "Requisition," as meaning that which government needs, and which must at all hazards be supplied. Compulsory levies were universally resorted to; and the undoubted right which a state has to call upon each of its subjects to arise in defence of the community, was extended into the power of sending them upon expeditions of foreign conquest.

In the month of March, 1793, a levy of two hundred thousand men was appointed, and took place; but by a subsequent decree of the 21st August in the same year, a more gigantic mode of recruiting was resorted to.

Every man in France able to bear arms was placed at the orders of the state, and being divided into classes, the youngest, to the amount of five hundred thousand, afterwards augmented to a million, were commanded to march for immediate action. The rest of society were to be so disposed of as might best second the efforts of the actual combatants. The married men were to prepare arms and forward convoys,—the women to make uniforms,—the children to scrape lint,—and the old men to preach Republicanism. All property was in like manner devoted to maintaining the war—all buildings were put to military purposes—all arms appropriated to the public service—and all horses, excepting those which might be necessary for agriculture, seized on for the cavalry, and other military services. Representatives of the people were named to march with the various levies,—those terrible commissioners, who punished no fault with a slighter penalty than death. No excuse was sustained for want of personal compliance with the requisition for personal service—no delay permitted—no substitution allowed—actual and literal compliance was demanded from every one, and of what rank soever. Conscripts who failed to appear, resisted, or fled, were subjected to the penalties which attached to emigration.[542]

---

[542] Jomini, tom. iv., p. 22; Mignet, tom. ii., p. 287.

By successive decrees of this peremptory nature, enforced with the full energy of revolutionary violence, the Government succeeded in bringing into the field, and maintaining, forces to an amount more than double those of their powerful enemies; and the same means of supply—arbitrary requisition, namely—which brought them out, supported and maintained them during the campaign; so that, while there remained food and clothing of any kind in the country, the soldier was sure to be fed, paid, and equipped.

There are countries, however, in which the great numerical superiority thus attained is of little consequence, when a confused levy *en masse* of raw, inexperienced, and disorderly boys, are opposed against the ranks of a much smaller, but a regular and well-disciplined army, such as in every respect is that of Austria. On such occasions the taunting speech of Alaric recurs to recollection,—"The thicker the hay the more easily it is mowed." But this was not found to be the case with the youth of France, who adopted the habits most necessary for a soldier with singular facility and readiness. Military service has been popular amongst them in all ages; and the stories of the grandsire in a French cottage have always tended to excite in his descendants ideas familiar with a military condition. They do not come to it as a violent change of life, which they had never previously contemplated, and where all is new and terrible; but as to a duty which every Frenchman is liable to discharge, and which is as natural to him as to his father or grandfather before him.

MILITARY GENIUS OF THE FRENCH

Besides this propensity, and undoubtedly connected with it, a young Frenchman is possessed of the natural character most desirable in the soldier. He is accustomed to fare hard, to take much exercise, to make many shifts, and to support with patience occasional deprivations. His happy gaiety renders him indifferent to danger, his good-humour patient under hardship. His ingenuity seems to amuse as well as to assist him in the contingencies of a roving life. He can be with ease a cook or an artificer, or what else the occasion may require. His talents for actual war are not less decided. Either in advancing with spirit, or in retreating with order, the Frenchman is one of the finest soldiers in the world; and when requisite, the privates in their army often exhibit a degree of intelligence and knowledge of the profession, which might become individuals of a higher rank in other services. If not absolute water-drinkers, they are less addicted to intoxication than the English soldier, who, perhaps, only brings, to counterbalance the numerous advantages on the part of his opponent, that mastiff-like perseverance and determination in combat, which induces him to repeat, maintain, and prolong his efforts, under every disadvantage of numbers and circumstances.

The spirits of the Frenchman, such as we have described, did not suffer much from the violent summons which tore him from his home. We have unhappily, in our own navy, an example, how little men's courage is broken by their being forced into a dangerous service. But comfortless as the state of France then was, and painful as the sights must have been by which the eyes were daily oppressed—closed up too as were the avenues to every civil walk of life, and cheap as they were held in a nation which had become all one vast camp, a youth of spirit was glad to escape from witnessing the desolation at home, and to take with gaiety the chance of death or promotion, in the only line which might now be accounted comparatively safe, and indubitably honourable. The armies with whom these new levies were incorporated were by degrees admirably supplied with officers. The breaking down the old distinctions of ranks had opened a free career to those desirous of promotion; and in times of hard fighting, men of merit are distinguished and get preferment. The voice of the soldier had often its influence upon the officer's preferment; and that is a vote seldom bestowed, but from ocular proof that it is deserved. The revolutionary rulers, though bloody in their resentment, were liberal, almost extravagant, in their rewards, and spared neither gold nor steel, honours nor denunciations, to incite their generals to victory, or warn them against the consequences of defeat.

Under that stern rule which knew no excuse for ill success, and stimulated by opportunities which seemed to offer every prize to honourable ambition, arose a race of generals whom the world scarce ever saw equalled, and of whom there certainly never at any other period flourished so many, in the same service. Such was Napoleon Buonaparte himself; such were Pichegru and Moreau, doomed to suffer a gloomy fate under his ascendency. Such were those Marshals and Generals who were to share his better fortunes, and cluster around his future throne, as the Paladins around that of Charlemagne, or as the British and Armorican champions begirt the Round Table of Uther's fabled son. In those early wars, and summoned out by the stern conscription, were trained Murat, whose eminence and fall seemed a corollary to that of his brother-in-law—Ney, the bravest of the brave—the calm, sagacious Macdonald—Joubert, who had almost anticipated the part reserved for Buonaparte—Massena, the spoiled Child of Fortune—Augereau—Berthier, Lannes, and many others, whose names began already to stir the French soldier as with the sound of a trumpet.

These adventurers in the race of fame belonged some of them, as Macdonald, to the old military school; some, like Moreau, came from the civil class of society; many arose from origins that were positively mean, and were therefore still more decidedly children of the Revolution. But that great earthquake, by throwing down distinctions of birth and rank, had removed obstacles which would otherwise have impeded the progress of almost all these distinguished men; and they were, therefore, for the greater part, attached to that new order of affairs which afforded full scope to their talents.

NEW MILITARY SYSTEM

The French armies, thus recruited, and thus commanded, were disciplined in a manner suitable to the materials of which they were composed. There was neither leisure nor opportunity to subject the new levies to all that minuteness of training, which was required by the somewhat pedantic formality of the old school of war. Dumouriez, setting the example, began to show that the principle of revolution might be introduced with advantage into the art of war itself; and that the difference betwixt these new conscripts and the veteran troops to whom they were opposed, might be much diminished by resorting to the original and more simple rules of stratagie, and neglecting many formalities which had been once considered as essential to playing the great game of war with success.[543] It is the constant error of ordinary minds to consider matters of mere routine as equally important with those which are essential, and to entertain as much horror at a disordered uniform as at a confused manœuvre. It was to the honour of the French generals, as men of genius, that in the hour of danger they were able to surmount all the prejudices of a profession which has its pedantry as well as others, and to suit the discipline which they retained to the character of their recruits and the urgency of the time.

The foppery of the manual exercise was laid aside, and it was restricted to the few motions necessary for effectual use of the musket and bayonet. Easier and more simple manœuvres were substituted for such as were involved and difficult to execute; and providing the line or column could be formed with activity, and that order was preserved on the march, the mere etiquette of military movements was much relaxed. The quantity of light troops was increased greatly beyond the number which had of late been used by European nations. The Austrians, who used to draw from the Tyrol, and from their wild Croatian frontier, the best light troops in the world, had at this time formed many of them into regiments of the line, and thus limited and diminished their own superiority in a species of force which was becoming of greater importance daily. The French, on the contrary, disciplined immense bodies of their conscripts as irregulars and sharpshooters. Their numbers and galling fire frequently prevented their more systematic and formal adversaries from being able to push forward reconnoitring parties, by which to obtain any exact information as to the numbers and disposition of the French, while the Republican troops of the line, protected by this swarm of wasps, chose their time, place, and manner, of advancing to the attack, or retreating, as the case demanded. It is true, that this service cost an immense number of lives; but the French generals were sensible that human life was the commodity which the Republic set the least value upon; and that when death was served with so wide a feast from one end of France

---

[543] Dumouriez, vol. i., p. 398.

to the other, he was not to be stinted in his own proper banqueting-hall, the field of battle.

The same circumstances dictated another variety or innovation in French tactics, which greatly increased the extent of slaughter. The armies with whom they engaged, disconcerted by the great superiority of numbers which were opposed to them, and baffled in obtaining intelligence by the teazing activity of the French light troops, most frequently assumed the defensive, and taking a strong position, improved perhaps by field-works, waited until the fiery youth of France should come to throw themselves by thousands upon their batteries. It was then that the French generals began first to employ those successive attacks in column, in which one brigade of troops is brought up after another, without interruption, and without regard to the loss of lives, until the arms of the defenders are weary with slaying, and their line being in some point or other carried, through the impossibility of every where resisting an assault so continued and desperate, the battle is lost, and the army is compelled to give way; while the conquerors can, by the multitudes they have brought into action, afford to pay the dreadful price which they have given for the victory.

In this manner the French generals employed whole columns of the young conscripts, termed from that circumstance, "food for the cannon" (*chair à canon,*) before disease had deprived them of bodily activity, or experience had taught them the dangers of the profession on which they entered with the thoughtless vivacity of schoolboys. It also frequently happened, even when the French possessed no numerical superiority upon the whole, that by the celerity of their movements, and the skill with which they at once combined and executed them, they were able suddenly to concentrate such a superiority upon the point which they meant to attack, as ensured them the same advantage.

In enumerating the causes of the general success of the Republican arms, we must not forget the moral motive—the interest which the troops took in the cause of the war. The army, in fact, derived an instant and most flattering advantage from the Revolution, which could scarce be said of any other class of men in

France, excepting the peasant. Their pay was improved, their importance increased. There was not a private soldier against whom the highest ranks of the profession was shut, and many attained to them. Massena was originally a drummer, Ney a common hussar, and there were many others who arose to the command of armies from the lowest condition. Now this was a government for a soldier to live and flourish under, and seemed still more advantageous when contrasted with the old monarchical system, in which the prejudices of birth interfered at every turn with the pretensions of merit, where a *roturier* could not rise above a subaltern rank, and where all offices of distinction were, as matters of inheritance, reserved for the *grande noblesse* alone.

But besides the rewards which it held out to its soldiers, the service of the Republic had this irresistible charm for the soldiery—it was victorious. The conquests which they obtained, and the plunder which attended those conquests, attached the victors to their standards, and drew around them fresh hosts of their countrymen. "*Vive la Republique!*" became a war-cry, as dear to their army as in former times the shout of Dennis Mountjoie, and the Tricoloured flag supplied the place of the Oriflamme. By the confusion, the oppression, the bloodshed of the Revolution, the soldiers were but little affected. They heard of friends imprisoned or guillotined, indeed;[544] but a military man, like a monk, leaves the concerns of the civil world behind him, and while he plays the bloody game for his own life or death with the enemy who faces him, has little time to think of what is happening in the native country which he has abandoned. For any other acquaintance with the politics of the Republic, they were indebted to flowery speeches in the Convention, resounding with the praises of the troops, and to harangues of the representatives accompanying the armies, who never failed by flattery and largesses to retain possession of the affection of the soldiers, whose attachment was so essential to their safety. So well did they accomplish this, that while the Republic flourished, the armies were so much attached to that order of things, as to desert successively some of their most favourite leaders, when they became objects of suspicion to the fierce democracy.

---

[544] Such was the fate of Moreau, who, on the eve of one of his most distinguished victories, had to receive the news that his father had been beheaded.—S.

The generals, indeed, had frequent and practical experience, that the Republic could be as severe with her military as with her civil subjects, and even more so, judging by the ruthlessness with which they were arrested and executed, with scarce the shadow of a pretext. Yet this did not diminish the zeal of the survivors. If the revolutionary government beheaded, they also paid, promised, and promoted; and amid the various risks of a soldier's life, the hazard of the guillotine was only a slight addition to those of the sword and the musket,[545] which, in the sanguine eye of courage and ambition, joined to each individual's confidence in his own good luck, did not seem to render his chance much worse. When such punishment arrived, the generals submitted to it as one of the casualties of war; nor was the Republic worse or more reluctantly served by those who were left.

Such being the admirable quality and talents, the mode of thinking and acting, which the Republican, or rather Revolutionary, armies possessed, it required only the ruling genius of the celebrated Carnot, who, bred in the department of engineers, was probably one of the very best tacticians in the world, to bring them into effectual use. He was a member of the frightful Committee of Public Safety; but it has been said in his defence, that he did not meddle with its atrocities, limiting himself entirely to the war department, for which he showed so much talent, that his colleagues left it to his exclusive management.[546] In his own individual person he constituted the whole *bureau militaire*, or war-office of the Committee of Public Safety, corresponded with and directed the movements of the armies, as if inspired by the Goddess of Victory herself. He first daringly claimed for France her natural boundaries—that is, the boundaries most convenient for her. The Rhine, the Alps, and the Pyrenees, he assigned as the limits of her dominions; and asserted

---

[545] The risk was considered as a matter of course. Madame La Roche-Jacquelein informs us that General Quentineau, a Republican officer who had behaved with great humanity in La Vendée, having fallen into the hands of the insurgents, was pressed by L'Escure, who commanded them, not to return to Paris. "I know the difference of our political opinions," said the Royalist, "but why should you deliver up your life to those men with whom want of success will be a sufficient reason for abridging it?"—"You say truly," replied Quentineau; "but as a man of honour, I must present myself in defence of my conduct wherever it may be impeached." He went, and perished by the guillotine accordingly.—S.—*Mémoires*, p. 130.

[546] Carnot's Mémoires, p. 230.

that all within these belonging to other powers, must have been usurpations on France, and were unhesitatingly to be resumed as such. And he conquered by his genius the countries which his ambition claimed. Belgium became an integral part of the French Republic—Holland was erected into a little dependent democracy, as an outwork for defending the great nation—the Austrians were foiled on the Rhine—the King of Sardinia driven from Savoy—and schemes realized which Louis XIV. never dared to dream of. In return for the complaisance exhibited by the Committee towards himself, he did not express any scruples, if he entertained such, concerning the mode in which they governed the interior of their unhappy country. Yet, notwithstanding his skill and his caution, the blighting eye of Robespierre was fixed on him, as that of the snake which watches its victim. He could not dispense with the talents of Carnot in the career of victory; but it is well known, that if his plans on any occasion had miscarried, the security of his head would have become very precarious.[547]

It must also be allowed, that although the French armies were attached to the Republic, and moved usually under direction of a member of the Committee of Public Security, they did not adopt, in their brutal extent, the orders for exterminating warfare which were transmitted to them by their masters. At one time a decree was passed, refusing quarter to such of the allied troops as might be made prisoners; but the French soldiers could not be prevailed on to take a step which must have aggravated so dreadfully the necessary horrors of war. When we consider how the civil government of France were employed, when the soldiers refused their sanction to this decree, it seems as if Humanity had fled from cities and the peaceful dwellings of men, to seek a home in camps and combats.

One important part of the subject can be here treated but slightly. We allude to the great advantages derived by the French arms from the reception of their political doctrines at this period among the people whom they invaded. They proclaimed aloud that they made war on castles and palaces, but were at peace with cottages; and as on some occasions besieging generals are said to

---

[547] Carnot, p. 255; Thibaudeau, tom. i., p. 37.

have bribed the governor of a place to surrender it, by promising they would leave in his unchallenged possession the military chest of the garrison, so the French in all cases held out to the populace the plunder of their own nobles, as an inducement for them to favour, at least not to oppose, the invasion of their country. Thus their armies were always preceded by their principles. A party favourable to France, and listening with delight to the doctrines of liberty and equality, was formed in the bosom of each neighbouring state, so that the power of the invaded nation was crushed, and its spirit quenched, under a sense of internal discontent and discord. The French were often received at once as conquerors and deliverers by the countries they invaded; and in almost all cases, the governments on which they made war were obliged to trust exclusively to such regular forces as they could bring into the field, being deprived of the inappreciable advantage of general zeal among their subjects in their behalf. It was not long ere the inhabitants of those deceived countries found that the fruits of the misnamed tree of liberty resembled those said to grow by the Dead Sea—fair and goodly to the eye, but to the taste all filth and bitterness.

RETROSPECT

We are now to close our review of the French Revolution, the fall of Robespierre being the era at which its terrors began to ebb and recede, nor did they ever again rise to the same height. If we look back at the whole progress of the change, from the convocation of the States-General to the 9th Thermidor, as the era of that man's overthrow was called, the eye in vain seeks for any point at which even a probability existed of establishing a solid or permanent government. The three successive constitutions of 1791, 1792, and 1795, the successive work of Constitutionalists, Girondists, and Jacobins, possessed no more power to limit or arrest the force of the revolutionary impulse, than a bramble or brier to stop the progress of a rock rushing down from a precipice. Though ratified and sworn to, with every circumstance which could add solemnity to the obligation, each remained, in succession, a dead letter. France, in 1795 and 1796, was therefore a nation without either a regular constitution, or a regular administration; governed by the remnant of an Assembly called a Convention, who continued sitting, merely because the crisis found them in possession of their seats, and who administered the government through the medium of Provisional Committees, with whose dictates they complied implicitly, and who really directed all things, though in the Convention's name.

In the meantime, and since those strange scenes had commenced, France had lost her King and nobles, her church and clergy, her judges, courts, and magistrates, her colonies and commerce. The greater part of her statesmen and men of note had perished by proscription, and her orators' eloquence had been cut short by the guillotine. She had no finances—the bonds of civil society seem to have retained their influence from habit only. The nation possessed only one powerful engine, which France called her own, and one impulsive power to guide it—These were her army and her ambition. She resembled a person in the delirium of a fever, who has stripped himself in his frenzy of all decent and necessary clothing, and retains in his hand only a bloody sword; while those who have endeavoured to check his fury, lie subdued around him. Never had so many great events successively taken place in a nation, without affording something like a fixed or determined result, either already attained, or soon to be expected.

Again and again did reflecting men say to each other,—This unheard-of state of things, in which all seems to be temporary and revolutionary, will not, cannot last;—and especially after the fall of Robespierre, it seemed that some change was approaching. Those who had achieved that work, did not hold on any terms of security the temporary power which it had procured them. They rather retained their influence by means of the jealousy of two extreme parties, than from any confidence reposed in themselves. Those who had suffered so deeply under the rule of the revolutionary government, must have looked with suspicion on the Thermidoriens as regular Jacobins, who had shared all the excesses of the period of Terror, and now employed their power in protecting the perpetrators. On the other hand, those of the Revolutionists who yet continued in the bond of Jacobin fraternity, could not forgive Tallien and Barras the silencing the Jacobin Clubs, the exiling Collot d'Herbois and Billaud-Varennes, putting to death many other patriots, and totally crushing the system of revolutionary government. In fact, if the thoroughbred Revolutionists still endured the domination of Tallien and Barras, it was only because it shielded them from the reaction, or retributive measures threatened by the moderate party. Matters, it was thought, could not remain in this uncertain state, nor was the present temporary pageant of government likely to linger long on the scene. But, by whom was that scene next to be opened? Would a late returning to ancient opinions induce a people, who had suffered so much through innovation, to recall either absolutely, or upon conditions, the banished race of her ancient princes? Or would a new band of Revolutionists be permitted by Heaven, in its continued vengeance, to rush upon the stage? Would the supreme power become the prize of some soldier as daring as Cæsar, or some intriguing statesman as artful as Octavius? Would France succumb beneath a Cromwell or a Monk, or again be ruled by a cabal of hackneyed statesmen, or an Institute of Theoretical Philosophy, or an anarchical Club of Jacobins? These were reflections which occupied almost all bosoms. But the hand of Fate was on the curtain, and about to bring the scene to light.

END OF VOLUME FIRST

www.ingramcontent.com/pod-product-compliance
Lightning Source LLC
Chambersburg PA
CBHW060311230426
43663CB00009B/1667